P9-DFR-473

Beginning Linux® Programming 4th Edition

Beginning
Linux® Programming
4th Edition

Beginning
Linux® Programming
4th Edition

Neil Matthew

Richard Stones

Wiley Publishing, Inc.

Beginning Linux® Programming, 4th Edition

Published by
Wiley Publishing, Inc.
10475 Crosspoint Boulevard
Indianapolis, IN 46256
www.wiley.com

Copyright © 2008 by Wiley Publishing, Inc., Indianapolis, Indiana

Published simultaneously in Canada

ISBN: 978-0-470-14762-7

Manufactured in the United States of America

10 9 8 7 6 5 4 3 2

Library of Congress Cataloging-in-Publication Data is available from the publisher.

For general information on our other products and services please contact our Customer Care Department within the United States at (800) 762-2974, outside the United States at (317) 572-3993 or fax (317) 572-4002.

About the Authors

Neil Matthew has been interested in and has programmed computers since 1974. A mathematics graduate from the University of Nottingham, Neil is just plain keen on programming languages and likes to explore new ways of solving computing problems. He's written systems to program in BCPL, FP (Functional Programming), Lisp, Prolog, and a structured BASIC. He even wrote a 6502 microprocessor emulator to run BBC microcomputer programs on UNIX systems.

In terms of UNIX experience, Neil has used almost every flavor since the late 1970s, including BSD UNIX, AT&T System V, Sun Solaris, IBM AIX, many others, and of course Linux. He can claim to have been using Linux since August 1993 when he acquired a floppy disk distribution of Soft Landing (SLS) from Canada, with kernel version 0.99.11. He's used Linux-based computers for hacking C, C++, Icon, Prolog, Tcl, and Java at home and at work.

All of Neil's "home" projects are developed using Linux. He says Linux is much easier because it supports quite a lot of features from other systems, so that both BSD- and System V-targeted programs will generally compile with little or no change.

Neil is currently working as an Enterprise Architect specializing in IT strategy at Celesio AG. He has a background in technical consultancy, software development techniques, and quality assurance. Neil has also programmed in C and C++ for real-time embedded systems.

Neil is married to Christine and has two children, Alexandra and Adrian. He lives in a converted barn in Northamptonshire, England. His interests include solving puzzles by computer, music, science fiction, squash, mountain biking, and not doing it yourself.

Rick Stones started programming at school (more years ago than he cares to remember) on a 6502-powered BBC micro, which, with the help of a few spare parts, continued to function for the next 15 years. He graduated from Nottingham University with a degree in Electronic Engineering, but decided software was more fun.

Over the years he has worked for a variety of companies, from the very small with just a dozen employees, to the very large, including the IT services giant EDS. Along the way he has worked on a range of projects, from real-time communications to accounting systems, to very large help desk systems. He is currently working as an IT architect, acting as a technical authority on various major projects for a large pan-European company.

A bit of a programming linguist, he has programmed in various assemblers, a rather neat proprietary telecommunications language called SL-1, some FORTRAN, Pascal, Perl, SQL, and smidgeons of Python and C++, as well as C. (Under duress he even admits that he was once reasonably proficient in Visual Basic, but tries not to advertise this aberration.)

Rick lives in a village in Leicestershire, England, with his wife Ann, children Jennifer and Andrew, and a cat. Outside work his main interests are classical music, especially early religious music, and photography, and he does his best to find time for some piano practice.

Credits

Acquisitions Editor
Jenny Watson

Development Editor
Sara Shlaer

Technical Editor
Timothy Boronczyk

Production Editor
William A. Barton

Copy Editor
Kim Cofer

Editorial Manager
Mary Beth Wakefield

Production Manager
Tim Tate

Vice President and Executive Group Publisher
Richard Swadley

Vice President and Executive Publisher
Joseph B. Wikert

Project Coordinator, Cover
Adrienne Martinez

Graphics and Production Specialists
Mike Park, Happenstance-Type-O-Rama
Craig Woods, Happenstance-Type-O-Rama

Proofreader
Amy McCarthy, Word One

Indexer
Johnna VanHoose Dinse

Anniversary Logo Design
Richard Pacifico

Acknowledgments

The authors would like to record their thanks to the many people who helped to make this book possible.

Neil would like to thank his wife, Christine, for her understanding and children Alex and Adrian for not complaining too loudly at Dad spending so long in The Den writing.

Rick would like to thank his wife, Ann, and their children, Jennifer and Andrew, for their very considerable patience during the evenings and weekends while Dad was yet again "doing book work."

As for the publishing team, we'd like to thank the folks at Wiley who helped us get this fourth edition into print. Thanks to Carol Long for getting the process started and sorting out the contracts, and especially to Sara Shlaer for her exceptional editing work and Timothy Boronczyk for his excellent technical reviews. We also wish to thank Jenny Watson for chasing down all those odd bits of extras and generally guiding the book through the administrative layers, Bill Barton for ensuring proper organization and presentation, and Kim Cofer for a thorough copyedit. We are very grateful also to Eric Foster-Johnson for his fantastic work on Chapters 16 and 17. We can say that this is a better book than it would have been without the efforts of all of you.

We would also like to thank our employers, Scientific Generics, Mobicom, and Celesio for their support during the production of all four editions of this book.

Finally we would also like to pay homage to two important motivators who have helped make this book possible. Firstly, Richard Stallman for the excellent GNU tools and the idea of a free software environment, which is now a reality with GNU/Linux, and secondly, Linus Torvalds for starting and continuing to inspire the co-operative development that gives us the ever-improving Linux kernel.

Contents

Contents

Contents

Contents

Contents

Contents

Contents

Foreword

All computer programmers have their own piles of notes and scribbles. They have their code examples saved from the past heroic dive into the manuals or from Usenet, where sometimes even fools fear to follow. (The other body of opinion is that fools all get free Usenet access and use it nonstop.) It is therefore perhaps strange that so few books follow such a style. In the online world there are a lot of short, to-the-point documents about specific areas of programming and administration. The Linux documentation project released a whole pile of documents covering everything from installing Linux and Windows on the same machine to wiring your coffee machine to Linux. Seriously. Take a look at The Linux Documentation Project on `http://www.tldp.org`.

The book world, on the other hand, seems to consist mostly of either learned tomes, detailed and very complete works that you don't have time to read, or books for complete beginners that you buy for friends as a joke. There are very few books that try to cover the basics of a lot of useful areas. This book is one of them, a compendium of those programmers' notes and scribbles, deciphered (try reading a programmer's handwriting), edited, and brought together coherently as a book.

This edition of *Beginning Linux Programming* has been reviewed and updated to reflect today's Linux developments.

—*Alan Cox*

Introduction

Welcome to *Beginning Linux Programming*, 4th Edition, an easy-to-use guide to developing programs for Linux and other UNIX-style operating systems.

In this book we aim to give you an introduction to a wide variety of topics important to you as a developer using Linux. The word *Beginning* in the title refers more to the content than to your skill level. We've structured the book to help you learn more about what Linux has to offer, however much experience you have already. Linux programming is a large field and we aim to cover enough about a wide range of topics to give you a good "beginning" in each subject.

Who's This Book For?

If you're a programmer who wishes to get up to speed with the facilities that Linux (or UNIX) offers software developers, to maximize your programming time and your application's use of the Linux system, you've picked up the right book. Clear explanations and a tried and tested step-by-step approach will help you progress rapidly and pick up all the key techniques.

We assume you have some experience in C and/or C++ programming, perhaps in Windows or some other system, but we try to keep the book's examples simple so that you don't need to be an expert C coder to follow this book. Where direct comparisons exist between Linux programming and C/C++ programming, these are indicated in the text.

> **Watch out if you're totally new to Linux. This isn't a book on installing or configuring Linux. If you want to learn more about administering a Linux system, you may wish to look at some complementary books such as *Linux Bible 2007 Edition*, by Christopher Negus (Wiley, ISBN 978-0470082799).**

Because it aims to be a tutorial guide to the various tools and sets of functions/libraries available to you on most Linux systems as well as a handy reference you can return to, this book is unique in its straightforward approach, comprehensive coverage, and extensive examples.

What's Covered in the Book

The book has a number of aims:

❑ To teach the use of the standard Linux C libraries and other facilities as specified by the various Linux and UNIX standards.

❑ To show how to make the most of the standard Linux development tools.

❑   To give a concise introduction to data storage under Linux using both the DBM and MySQL database systems.

❑   To show how to build graphical user interfaces for the X Window System. We will use both the GTK (the basis of the GNOME environment) and Qt (the basis of the KDE environment) libraries.

❑   To encourage and enable you to develop your own real-world applications.

As we cover these topics, we introduce programming theory and then illustrate it with appropriate examples and a clear explanation. In this way you can learn quickly on a first read and look back over things to brush up on all the essential elements if you need to.

Though the small examples are designed mainly to illustrate a set of functions or some new theory in action, throughout the book lies a larger sample project: a simple database application for recording audio CD details. As your knowledge expands, you can develop, re-implement, and extend the project to your heart's content. That said, however, the CD application doesn't dominate any chapter, so you can skip it if you want to, but we feel that it provides additional useful, in-depth examples of the techniques that we discuss. It certainly provides an ideal way to illustrate each of the more advanced topics as they are introduced. Our first discussion of this application occurs at the end of Chapter 2 and shows how a fairly large shell script is organized, how the shell deals with user input, and how it can construct menus and store and search data.

After recapping the basic concepts of compiling programs, linking to libraries, and accessing the online manuals, you will take a sojourn into shells. You then move into C programming, where we cover working with files, getting information from the Linux environment, dealing with terminal input and output, and the curses library (which makes interactive input and output more tractable). You're then ready to tackle re-implementing the CD application in C. The application design remains the same, but the code uses the curses library for a screen-based user interface.

From there, we cover data management. Meeting the dbm database library is sufficient cause for us to re-implement the application, but this time with a design that will re-emerge in some later chapters. In a later chapter we look at how the data could be stored in a relational database using MySQL, and we also reuse this data storage technique later in the chapter, so you can see how the techniques compare. The size of these recent applications means that we then need to deal with such nuts-and-bolts issues as debugging, source code control, software distribution, and makefiles.

You will also look at how different Linux processes can communicate, using a variety of techniques, and at how Linux programs can use sockets to support TCP/IP networking to different machines, including the issues of talking to machines that use different processor architectures.

After getting the foundations of Linux programming in place, we cover the creation of graphical programs. We do this over two chapters, looking first at the GTK+ toolkit, which underlies the GNOME environment, and then at the Qt toolkit, which underlies the KDE environment.

We finish off with a brief look at the standards that keep Linux systems from different vendors similar enough that we can move between them easily and write programs that will work on different distributions of Linux.

As you'd expect, there's a fair bit more in between, but we hope that this gives you a good idea of the material we'll be discussing.

What You Need to Use This Book

In this book, we'll give you a taste of programming for Linux. To help you get the most from the chapters, you should try out the examples as you read. These also provide a good base for experimentation and will hopefully inspire you to create programs of your own. We hope you will read this book in conjunction with experimenting on your own Linux installation.

Linux is available for many different systems. Its adaptability is such that enterprising souls have persuaded it to run in one form or another on just about anything with a processor in it! Examples include systems based on the Alpha, ARM, IBM Cell, Itanium, PA-RISC, PowerPC, SPARC, SuperH, and 68k CPUs as well as the various $x86$-class processors, in both 32- and 64-bit versions.

We wrote this book and developed the examples on two Linux systems with different specifications, so we're confident that if you can run Linux, you can make good use of this book. Furthermore, we tested the code on other versions of Linux during the book's technical review.

To develop this book we primarily used $x86$-based systems, but very little of what we cover is $x86$ specific. Although it is possible to run Linux on a 486 with 8MB RAM, to run a modern Linux distribution successfully and follow the examples in this book, we recommend that you pick a recent version of one of the more popular Linux distributions such as Fedora, openSUSE, or Ubuntu and check the hardware recommendations they give.

As for software requirements, we suggest that you use a recent version of your preferred Linux distribution and apply the current set of updates, which most vendors make available online by way of automated updates, to keep your system current and up-to-date with the latest bug fixes. Linux and the GNU toolset are released under the GNU General Public License (GPL). Most other components of a typical Linux distribution use either the GPL or one of the many other Open Source licenses, and this means they have certain properties, one of which is freedom. They will always have the source code available, and no one can take that freedom away. See http://www.gnu.org/licenses/ for more details of the GPL, and http://www.opensource.org/ for more details of the definition of Open Source and the different licenses in use. With GNU/Linux, you will always have the option of support — either doing it yourself with the source code, hiring someone else, or going to one of the many vendors offering pay-for support.

Source Code

As you work through the examples in this book, you may choose either to type in all the code manually or to use the source code files that accompany the book. All of the source code used in this book is available for download at http://www.wrox.com. Once at the site, simply locate the book's title (either by using the Search box or by using one of the title lists) and click the Download Code link on the book's detail page to obtain all the source code for the book.

Because many books have similar titles, you may find it easiest to search by ISBN; this book's ISBN is 978-0-470-14762-7.

Once you download the code, just decompress it with your favorite compression tool. Alternatively, you can go to the main Wrox code download page at http://www.wrox.com/dynamic/books/download.aspx to see the code available for this book and all other Wrox books.

A Note on the Code Downloads

We have tried to provide example programs and code snippets that best illustrate the concepts being discussed in the text. Please note that, in order to make the new functionality being introduced as clear as possible, we have taken one or two liberties with coding style.

In particular, we do not always check that the return results from every function we call are what we expect. In production code for real applications we would certainly do this check, and you too should adopt a rigorous approach toward error handling. (We discuss some of the ways that errors can be caught and handled in Chapter 3.)

The GNU General Public License

The source code in the book is made available under the terms of the GNU General Public License version 2, `http://www.gnu.org/licenses/old-licenses/gpl-2.0.html`. The following permission statement applies to all the source code available in this book:

```
This program is free software; you can redistribute it and/or modify
it under the terms of the GNU General Public License as published by
the Free Software Foundation; either version 2 of the License, or
(at your option) any later version.

This program is distributed in the hope that it will be useful,
but WITHOUT ANY WARRANTY; without even the implied warranty of
MERCHANTABILITY or FITNESS FOR A PARTICULAR PURPOSE.  See the
GNU General Public License for more details.

You should have received a copy of the GNU General Public License
along with this program; if not, write to the Free Software
Foundation, Inc., 59 Temple Place, Suite 330, Boston, MA  02111-1307  USA
```

Conventions

To help you get the most from the text and keep track of what's happening, we've used a number of conventions throughout the book:

> **Boxes like this one hold important, not-to-be-forgotten, mission-critical information that is directly relevant to the surrounding text.**

Tips, hints, tricks, and asides to the current discussion are offset and placed in italics like this.

When we introduce them, we highlight *important words* in italics. Characters we want you to **type** are in bold font. We show keyboard strokes like this: Ctrl+A.

We present code and terminal sessions in three different ways:

```
$ who
root      tty1          Sep 10 16:12
rick      tty2          Sep 10 16:10
```

When the command line is shown, it's in the style at the top of the code, whereas output is in the regular style. The $ is the prompt (if the superuser is required for the command, the prompt will be a # instead) and the bold text is what you type in and press Enter (or Return) to execute. Any text following that in the same font but in non-bold is the output of the bolded command. In the preceding example you type in the command who, and you see the output below the command.

Prototypes of Linux-defined functions and structures are shown in bold as follows:

```
#include <stdio.h>

int printf (const char *format, ...);
```

In our code examples, the code foreground style shows new, important material, such as

```
/* This is what new, important, and pertinent code looks like. */
```

whereas code that looks like this (code background style) is less important:

```
/* This is what code that has been seen before looks like. */
```

And often when a program is added to throughout a chapter, code that is added later is in foreground style first and background style later. For example, a new program would look like this:

```
/* Code example */
/* That ends here. */
```

And if we add to that program later in the chapter, it looks like this instead:

```
/* Code example */
/* New code added */
/* on these lines */
/* That ends here. */
```

The last convention we'll mention is that we presage example code with a "Try It Out" heading that aims to split the code up where it's helpful, highlight the component parts, and show the progression of the application. When it's important, we also follow the code with a "How It Works" section to explain any salient points of the code in relation to previous theory. We find these two conventions help break up the more formidable code listings into palatable morsels.

Errata

We make every effort to ensure that there are no errors in the text or in the code. However, no one is perfect, and mistakes do occur. If you find an error in one of our books, like a spelling mistake or faulty piece of code, we would be very grateful for your feedback. By sending in errata you may save another reader hours of frustration and at the same time you will be helping us provide even higher quality information.

To find the errata page for this book, go to http://www.wrox.com and locate the title using the Search box or one of the title lists. Then, on the book details page, click the Book Errata link. On this page you can view all errata that has been submitted for this book and posted by Wrox editors. A complete book list including links to each book's errata is also available at www.wrox.com/misc-pages/ booklist.shtml.

If you don't spot "your" error on the Book Errata page, go to www.wrox.com/contact/techsupport .shtml and complete the form there to send us the error you have found. We'll check the information and, if appropriate, post a message to the book's errata page and fix the problem in subsequent editions of the book.

p2p.wrox.com

For author and peer discussion, join the P2P forums at p2p.wrox.com. The forums are a Web-based system for you to post messages relating to Wrox books and related technologies and interact with other readers and technology users. The forums offer a subscription feature to e-mail you topics of interest of your choosing when new posts are made to the forums. Wrox authors, editors, other industry experts, and your fellow readers are present on these forums.

At http://p2p.wrox.com you will find a number of different forums that will help you not only as you read this book, but also as you develop your own applications. To join the forums, just follow these steps:

1. Go to p2p.wrox.com and click the Register link.
2. Read the terms of use and click Agree.
3. Complete the required information to join as well as any optional information you wish to provide and click Submit.
4. You will receive an e-mail with information describing how to verify your account and complete the joining process.

> *You can read messages in the forums without joining P2P but in order to post your own messages, you must join.*

Once you join, you can post new messages and respond to messages other users post. You can read messages at any time on the Web. If you would like to have new messages from a particular forum e-mailed to you, click the Subscribe to this Forum icon by the forum name in the forum listing.

For more information about how to use the Wrox P2P, be sure to read the P2P FAQs for answers to questions about how the forum software works as well as many common questions specific to P2P and Wrox books. To read the FAQs, click the FAQ link on any P2P page.

Getting Started

In this chapter, you discover what Linux is and how it relates to its inspiration, UNIX. You take a guided tour of the facilities provided by a Linux development system, and write and run your first program. Along the way, you'll be looking at

- ❑ UNIX, Linux, and GNU
- ❑ Programs and programming languages for Linux
- ❑ How to locate development resources
- ❑ Static and shared libraries
- ❑ The UNIX philosophy

An Introduction to UNIX, Linux, and GNU

In recent years Linux has become a phenomenon. Hardly a day goes by without Linux cropping up in the media in some way. We've lost count of the number of applications that have been made available on Linux and the number of organizations that have adopted it, including some government departments and city administrations. Major hardware vendors like IBM and Dell now support Linux, and major software vendors like Oracle support their software running on Linux. Linux truly has become a viable operating system, especially in the server market.

Linux owes its success to systems and applications that preceded it: UNIX and GNU software. This section looks at how Linux came to be and what its roots are.

What Is UNIX?

The UNIX operating system was originally developed at Bell Laboratories, once part of the telecommunications giant AT&T. Designed in the 1970s for Digital Equipment PDP computers, UNIX has become a very popular multiuser, multitasking operating system for a wide variety of hardware platforms, from PC workstations to multiprocessor servers and supercomputers.

A Brief History of UNIX

Strictly, UNIX is a trademark administered by The Open Group, and it refers to a computer operating system that conforms to a particular specification. This specification, known as The Single UNIX Specification, defines the names of, interfaces to, and behaviors of all mandatory UNIX operating system functions. The specification is largely a superset of an earlier series of specifications, the P1003, or POSIX (Portable Operating System Interface) specifications, developed by the IEEE (Institute of Electrical and Electronic Engineers).

Many UNIX-like systems are available commercially, such as IBM's AIX, HP's HP-UX, and Sun's Solaris. Some have been made available for free, such as FreeBSD and Linux. Only a few systems currently conform to The Open Group specification, which allows them to be marketed with the name UNIX.

In the past, compatibility among different UNIX systems has been a real problem, although POSIX was a great help in this respect. These days, by following a few simple rules it is possible to create applications that will run on all UNIX and UNIX-like systems. You can find more details on Linux and UNIX standards in Chapter 18.

UNIX Philosophy

In the following chapters we hope to convey a flavor of Linux (and therefore UNIX) programming. Although programming in C is in many ways the same whatever the platform, UNIX and Linux developers have a special view of program and system development.

The UNIX operating system, and hence Linux, encourages a certain programming style. Following are a few characteristics shared by typical UNIX programs and systems:

❑   **Simplicity:** Many of the most useful UNIX utilities are very simple and, as a result, small and easy to understand. KISS, "Keep It Small and Simple," is a good technique to learn. Larger, more complex systems are guaranteed to contain larger, more complex bugs, and debugging is a chore that we'd all like to avoid!

❑   **Focus:** It's often better to make a program perform one task well than to throw in every feature along with the kitchen sink. A program with "feature bloat" can be difficult to use and difficult to maintain. Programs with a single purpose are easier to improve as better algorithms or interfaces are developed. In UNIX, small utilities are often combined to perform more demanding tasks when the need arises, rather than trying to anticipate a user's needs in one large program.

❑   **Reusable Components:** Make the core of your application available as a library. Well-documented libraries with simple but flexible programming interfaces can help others to develop variations or apply the techniques to new application areas. Examples include the dbm database library, which is a suite of reusable functions rather than a single database management program.

❑   **Filters:** Many UNIX applications can be used as filters. That is, they transform their input and produce output. As you'll see, UNIX provides facilities that allow quite complex applications to be developed from other UNIX programs by combining them in novel ways. Of course, this kind of reuse is enabled by the development methods that we've previously mentioned.

❑   **Open File Formats:** The more successful and popular UNIX programs use configuration files and data files that are plain ASCII text or XML. If either of these is an option for your program development, it's a good choice. It enables users to use standard tools to change and search for configuration items and to develop new tools for performing new functions on the data files. A good example of this is the ctags source code cross-reference system, which records symbol location information as regular expressions suitable for use by searching programs.

❑   **Flexibility:** You can't anticipate exactly how ingeniously users will use your program. Try to be as flexible as possible in your programming. Try to avoid arbitrary limits on field sizes or number of records. If you can, write the program so that it's network-aware and able to run across a network as well as on a local machine. Never assume that you know everything that the user might want to do.

What Is Linux?

As you may already know, Linux is a freely distributed implementation of a UNIX-like kernel, the low-level core of an operating system. Because Linux takes the UNIX system as its inspiration, Linux and UNIX programs are very similar. In fact, almost all programs written for UNIX can be compiled and run on Linux. Also, some commercial applications sold for commercial versions of UNIX can run unchanged in binary form on Linux systems.

Linux was developed by Linus Torvalds at the University of Helsinki, with the help of UNIX programmers from across the Internet. It began as a hobby inspired by Andy Tanenbaum's Minix, a small UNIX-like system, but has grown to become a complete system in its own right. The intention is that the Linux kernel will not incorporate proprietary code but will contain nothing but freely distributable code.

Versions of Linux are now available for a wide variety of computer systems using many different types of CPUs, including PCs based on 32-bit and 64-bit Intel x86 and compatible processors; workstations and servers using Sun SPARC, IBM PowerPC, AMD Opteron, and Intel Itanium; and even some handheld PDAs and Sony's Playstations 2 and 3. If it's got a processor, someone somewhere is trying to get Linux running on it!

The GNU Project and the Free Software Foundation

Linux owes its existence to the cooperative efforts of a large number of people. The operating system kernel itself forms only a small part of a usable development system. Commercial UNIX systems traditionally come bundled with applications that provide system services and tools. For Linux systems, these additional programs have been written by many different programmers and have been freely contributed.

The Linux community (together with others) supports the concept of free software, that is, software that is free from restrictions, subject to the GNU General Public License (the name GNU stands for the recursive *GNU's Not Unix*). Although there may be a cost involved in obtaining the software, it can thereafter be used in any way desired and is usually distributed in source form.

The Free Software Foundation was set up by Richard Stallman, the author of GNU Emacs, one of the best-known text editors for UNIX and other systems. Stallman is a pioneer of the free software concept and started the GNU Project, an attempt to create an operating system and development environment that would be compatible with UNIX, but not suffer the restrictions of the proprietary UNIX name and source code. GNU may one day turn out to be very different from UNIX in the way it handles the hardware and manages running programs, but it will still support UNIX-style applications.

The GNU Project has already provided the software community with many applications that closely mimic those found on UNIX systems. All these programs, so-called GNU software, are distributed under the terms of the GNU General Public License (GPL); you can find a copy of the license at http://www.gnu.org. This license embodies the concept of *copyleft* (a takeoff on "copyright"). Copyleft is intended to prevent others from placing restrictions on the use of free software.

A few major examples of software from the GNU Project distributed under the GPL follow:

- ❑ GCC: The GNU Compiler Collection, containing the GNU C compiler
- ❑ G++: A C++ compiler, included as part of GCC
- ❑ GDB: A source code–level debugger
- ❑ GNU make: A version of UNIX make
- ❑ Bison: A parser generator compatible with UNIX yacc
- ❑ bash: A command shell
- ❑ GNU Emacs: A text editor and environment

Many other packages have been developed and released using free software principles and the GPL, including spreadsheets, source code control tools, compilers and interpreters, Internet tools, graphical image manipulation tools such as the Gimp, and two complete object-based environments: GNOME and KDE. We discuss GNOME and KDE in Chapters 16 and 17.

There is now so much free software available that with the addition of the Linux kernel it could be said that the goal of a creating GNU, a free UNIX-like system, has been achieved with Linux. To recognize the contribution made by GNU software, many people now refer to Linux systems in general as GNU/Linux.

You can learn more about the free software concept at http://www.gnu.org.

Linux Distributions

As we have already mentioned, Linux is actually just a kernel. You can obtain the sources for the kernel to compile and install it on a machine and then obtain and install many other freely distributed software programs to make a complete Linux installation. These installations are usually referred to as *Linux systems*, because they consist of much more than just the kernel. Most of the utilities come from the GNU Project of the Free Software Foundation.

As you can probably appreciate, creating a Linux system from just source code is a major undertaking. Fortunately, many people have put together ready-to-install distributions (often called *flavors*), usually downloadable or on CD-ROMs or DVDs, that contain not just the kernel but also many other programming tools and utilities. These often include an implementation of the X Window System, a graphical environment common on many UNIX systems. The distributions usually come with a setup program and additional documentation (normally all on the CD[s]) to help you install your own Linux system. Some well-known distributions, particularly on the Intel *x*86 family of processors, are Red Hat Enterprise Linux and its community-developed cousin Fedora, Novell SUSE Linux and the free openSUSE variant, Ubuntu Linux, Slackware, Gentoo, and Debian GNU/Linux. Check out the DistroWatch site at http://distrowatch.com for details on many more Linux distributions.

Programming Linux

Many people think that programming Linux means using C. It's true that UNIX was originally written in C and that the majority of UNIX applications are written in C, but C is not the only option available to

Linux programmers, or UNIX programmers for that matter. In the course of the book, we'll mention a couple of the alternatives.

> In fact, the first version of UNIX was written in PDP 7 assembler language in 1969. C was conceived by Dennis Ritchie around that time, and in 1973 he and Ken Thompson rewrote essentially the entire UNIX kernel in C, quite a feat in the days when system software was written in assembly language.

A vast range of programming languages are available for Linux systems, and many of them are free and available on CD-ROM collections or from FTP archive sites on the Internet. Here's a partial list of programming languages available to the Linux programmer:

Ada	C	C++
Eiffel	Forth	Fortran
Icon	Java	JavaScript
Lisp	Modula 2	Modula 3
Oberon	Objective C	Pascal
Perl	PostScript	Prolog
Python	Ruby	Smalltalk
PHP	Tcl/Tk	Bourne Shell

We show how you can use a Linux shell (bash) to develop small- to medium-sized applications in Chapter 2. For the rest of the book, we mainly concentrate on C. We direct our attention mostly toward exploring the Linux programming interfaces from the perspective of the C programmer, and we assume knowledge of the C programming language.

Linux Programs

Linux applications are represented by two special types of files: *executables* and *scripts*. Executable files are programs that can be run directly by the computer; they correspond to Windows .exe files. Scripts are collections of instructions for another program, an interpreter, to follow. These correspond to Windows .bat or .cmd files, or interpreted BASIC programs.

Linux doesn't require executables or scripts to have a specific filename or any extension whatsoever. File system attributes, which we discuss in Chapter 2, are used to indicate that a file is a program that may be run. In Linux, you can replace scripts with compiled programs (and vice versa) without affecting other programs or the people who call them. In fact, at the user level, there is essentially no difference between the two.

When you log in to a Linux system, you interact with a shell program (often bash) that runs programs in the same way that the Windows command prompt does. It finds the programs you ask for by name by searching for a file with the same name in a given set of directories. The directories to search are stored in a shell variable, PATH, in much the same way as with Windows. The search path (to which you can add) is configured by your system administrator and will usually contain some standard places where system programs are stored. These include:

- ❏ /bin: Binaries, programs used in booting the system
- ❏ /usr/bin: User binaries, standard programs available to users
- ❏ /usr/local/bin: Local binaries, programs specific to an installation

An administrator's login, such as root, may use a PATH variable that includes directories where system administration programs are kept, such as /sbin and /usr/sbin.

Optional operating system components and third-party applications may be installed in subdirectories of /opt, and installation programs might add to your PATH variable by way of user install scripts.

> It's not a good idea to delete directories from PATH unless you are sure that you understand what will result if you do.

Note that Linux, like UNIX, uses the colon (:) character to separate entries in the PATH variable, rather than the semicolon (;) that MS-DOS and Windows use. (UNIX chose : first, so ask Microsoft why Windows is different, not why UNIX is different!) Here's a sample PATH variable:

```
/usr/local/bin:/bin:/usr/bin:.:/home/neil/bin:/usr/X11R6/bin
```

Here the PATH variable contains entries for the standard program locations, the current directory (.), a user's home directory, and the X Window System.

> Remember, Linux uses a forward slash (/) to separate directory names in a filename rather than the backslash (\) of Windows. Again, UNIX got there first.

Text Editors

To write and enter the code examples in the book, you'll need to use an editor. There are many to choose from on a typical Linux system. The vi editor is popular with many users.

Both of the authors like Emacs, so we suggest you take the time to learn some of the features of this powerful editor. Almost all Linux distributions have Emacs as an optional package you can install, or you can get it from the GNU website at http://www.gnu.org or a version for graphical environments at the XEmacs site at http://www.xemacs.org.

To learn more about Emacs, you can use its online tutorial. To do this, start the editor by running the emacs command, and then type Ctrl+H followed by t for the tutorial. Emacs also has its entire manual available. When in Emacs, type Ctrl+H and then i for information. Some versions of Emacs may have menus that you can use to access the manual and tutorial.

The C Compiler

On POSIX-compliant systems, the C compiler is called c89. Historically, the C compiler was simply called cc. Over the years, different vendors have sold UNIX-like systems with C compilers with different facilities and options, but often still called cc.

When the POSIX standard was prepared, it was impossible to define a standard cc command with which all these vendors would be compatible. Instead, the committee decided to create a new standard command for the C compiler, c89. When this command is present, it will always take the same options, independent of the machine.

On Linux systems that do try to implement the standards, you might find that any or all of the commands c89, cc, and gcc refer to the system C compiler, usually the GNU C compiler, or gcc. On UNIX systems, the C compiler is almost always called cc.

In this book, we use gcc because it's provided with Linux distributions and because it supports the ANSI standard syntax for C. If you ever find yourself using a UNIX system without gcc, we recommend that you obtain and install it. You can find it at http://www.gnu.org. Wherever we use gcc in the book, simply substitute the relevant command on your system.

Try It Out   Your First Linux C Program

In this example you start developing for Linux using C by writing, compiling, and running your first Linux program. It might as well be that most famous of all starting points, Hello World.

1. Here's the source code for the file hello.c:

```
#include <stdio.h>
#include <stdlib.h>


int main()
{
    printf("Hello World\n");
    exit(0);
}
```

2. Now compile, link, and run your program.

```
$ gcc -o hello hello.c
$ ./hello
Hello World
$
```

How It Works

You invoked the GNU C compiler (on Linux this will most likely be available as cc too) that translated the C source code into an executable file called hello. You ran the program and it printed a greeting. This is just about the simplest example there is, but if you can get this far with your system, you should be able to compile and run the remainder of the examples in the book. If this did not work for you, make sure that the C compiler is installed on your system. For example, many Linux distributions have an install option called Software Development (or something similar) that you should select to make sure the necessary packages are installed.

Because this is the first program you've run, it's a good time to point out some basics. The hello program will probably be in your home directory. If PATH doesn't include a reference to your home directory, the shell won't be able to find hello. Furthermore, if one of the directories in PATH contains another program called hello, that program will be executed instead. This would also happen if such a directory is mentioned in PATH before your home directory. To get around this potential problem, you can prefix program names with ./ (for example, ./hello). This specifically instructs the shell to execute the program in the current directory with the given name. (The dot is an alias for the current directory.)

If you forget the -o name option that tells the compiler where to place the executable, the compiler will place the program in a file called a.out (meaning assembler output). Just remember to look for an a.out if you think you've compiled a program and you can't find it! In the early days of UNIX, people wanting to play games on the system often ran them as a.out to avoid being caught by system administrators, and some UNIX installations routinely delete all files called a.out every evening.

Development System Roadmap

For a Linux developer, it can be important to know a little about where tools and development resources are located. The following sections provide a brief look at some important directories and files.

Applications

Applications are usually kept in directories reserved for them. Applications supplied by the system for general use, including program development, are found in /usr/bin. Applications added by system administrators for a specific host computer or local network are often found in /usr/local/bin or /opt.

Administrators favor /opt and /usr/local, because they keep vendor-supplied files and later additions separate from the applications supplied by the system. Keeping files organized in this way may help when the time comes to upgrade the operating system, because only /opt and /usr/local need be preserved. We recommend that you compile your applications to run and access required files from the /usr/local hierarchy for system-wide applications. For development and personal applications it's best just to use a folder in your home directory.

Additional features and programming systems may have their own directory structures and program directories. Chief among these is the X Window System, which is commonly installed in the /usr/X11 or /usr/bin/X11 directory. Linux distributions typically use the X.Org Foundation version of the X Window System, based on Revision 7 (X11R7). Other UNIX-like systems may choose different versions of the X Window System installed in different locations, such as /usr/openwin for Sun's Open Windows provided with Solaris.

The GNU compiler system's driver program, gcc (which you used in the preceding programming example), is typically located in /usr/bin or /usr/local/bin, but it will run various compiler-support applications from another location. This location is specified when you compile the compiler itself and varies with the host computer type. For Linux systems, this location might be a version-specific subdirectory of /usr/lib/gcc/. On one of the author's machines at the time of writing it is /usr/lib/gcc/i586-suse-linux/4.1.3. The separate passes of the GNU C/C++ compiler, and GNU-specific header files, are stored here.

Header Files

For programming in C and other languages, you need header files to provide definitions of constants and declarations for system and library function calls. For C, these are almost always located in /usr/include and subdirectories thereof. You can normally find header files that depend on the particular incarnation of Linux that you are running in /usr/include/sys and /usr/include/linux.

Other programming systems will also have header files that are stored in directories that get searched automatically by the appropriate compiler. Examples include /usr/include/X11 for the X Window System and /usr/include/c++ for GNU C++.

You can use header files in subdirectories or nonstandard places by specifying the -I flag (for include) to the C compiler. For example,

```
$ gcc -I/usr/openwin/include fred.c
```

will direct the compiler to look in the directory /usr/openwin/include, as well as the standard places, for header files included in the fred.c program. Refer to the manual page for the C compiler (man gcc) for more details.

It's often convenient to use the grep command to search header files for particular definitions and function prototypes. Suppose you need to know the name of the #defines used for returning the exit status from a program. Simply change to the /usr/include directory and grep for a probable part of the name like this:

```
$ grep EXIT_ *.h
...
stdlib.h:#define        EXIT_FAILURE    1       /* Failing exit status.  */
stdlib.h:#define        EXIT_SUCCESS    0       /* Successful exit status.  */
...
$
```

Here grep searches all the files in the directory with a name ending in .h for the string EXIT_. In this example, it has found (among others) the definition you need in the file stdlib.h.

Library Files

Libraries are collections of precompiled functions that have been written to be reusable. Typically, they consist of sets of related functions to perform a common task. Examples include libraries of screen-handling functions (the curses and ncurses libraries) and database access routines (the dbm library). We show you some libraries in later chapters.

Standard system libraries are usually stored in /lib and /usr/lib. The C compiler (or more exactly, the linker) needs to be told which libraries to search, because by default it searches only the standard C library. This is a remnant of the days when computers were slow and CPU cycles were expensive. It's not enough to put a library in the standard directory and hope that the compiler will find it; libraries need to follow a very specific naming convention and need to be mentioned on the command line.

A library filename always starts with lib. Then follows the part indicating what library this is (like c for the C library, or m for the mathematical library). The last part of the name starts with a dot (.), and specifies the type of the library:

❑   .a for traditional, static libraries

❑   .so for shared libraries (see the following)

The libraries usually exist in both static and shared formats, as a quick ls /usr/lib will show. You can instruct the compiler to search a library either by giving it the full path name or by using the -l flag. For example,

```
$ gcc -o fred fred.c /usr/lib/libm.a
```

tells the compiler to compile file fred.c, call the resulting program file fred, and search the mathematical library in addition to the standard C library to resolve references to functions. A similar result is achieved with the following command:

```
$ gcc -o fred fred.c -lm
```

The -lm (no space between the l and the m) is shorthand (shorthand is much valued in UNIX circles) for the library called libm.a in one of the standard library directories (in this case /usr/lib). An additional advantage of the -lm notation is that the compiler will automatically choose the shared library when it exists.

Although libraries are usually found in standard places in the same way as header files, you can add to the search directories by using the -L (uppercase letter) flag to the compiler. For example,

```
$ gcc -o x11fred -L/usr/openwin/lib x11fred.c -lX11
```

will compile and link a program called x11fred using the version of the library libX11 found in the /usr/openwin/lib directory.

Static Libraries

The simplest form of library is just a collection of object files kept together in a ready-to-use form. When a program needs to use a function stored in the library, it includes a header file that declares the function. The compiler and linker take care of combining the program code and the library into a single executable program. You must use the -l option to indicate which libraries other than the standard C runtime library are required.

Static libraries, also known as *archives*, conventionally have names that end with .a. Examples are /usr/lib/libc.a and /usr/lib/libX11.a for the standard C library and the X11 library, respectively.

You can create and maintain your own static libraries very easily by using the ar (for archive) program and compiling functions separately with gcc -c. Try to keep functions in separate source files as much as possible. If functions need access to common data, you can place them in the same source file and use static variables declared in that file.

Try It Out   **Static Libraries**

In this example, you create your own small library containing two functions and then use one of them in an example program. The functions are called fred and bill and just print greetings.

1.   First, create separate source files (imaginatively called fred.c and bill.c) for each function. Here's the first:

```
#include <stdio.h>


void fred(int arg)

{

        printf("fred: we passed %d\n", arg);

}
```

And here's the second:

```
#include <stdio.h>


void bill(char *arg)

{

        printf("bill: we passed %s\n", arg);

}
```

2.   You can compile these functions individually to produce object files ready for inclusion into a library. Do this by invoking the C compiler with the -c option, which prevents the compiler from trying to create a complete program. Trying to create a complete program would fail because you haven't defined a function called main.

```
$ gcc -c bill.c fred.c
$ ls *.o
bill.o  fred.o
```

3.   Now write a program that calls the function bill. First, it's a good idea to create a header file for your library. This will declare the functions in your library and should be included by all applications that want to use your library. It's a good idea to include the header file in the files fred.c and bill.c too. This will help the compiler pick up any errors.

```
/*

    This is lib.h. It declares the functions fred and bill for users
```

```
*/

    void bill(char *);

    void fred(int);
```

4. The calling program (`program.c`) can be very simple. It includes the library header file and calls one of the functions from the library.

```
#include <stdlib.h>

#include "lib.h"


int main()
{
    bill("Hello World");

    exit(0);

}
```

5. You can now compile the program and test it. For now, specify the object files explicitly to the compiler, asking it to compile your file and link it with the previously compiled object module `bill.o`.

```
$ gcc -c program.c
$ gcc -o program program.o bill.o
$ ./program
bill: we passed Hello World
$
```

6. Now you'll create and use a library. Use the `ar` program to create the archive and add your object files to it. The program is called `ar` because it creates archives, or collections, of individual files placed together in one large file. Note that you can also use `ar` to create archives of files of any type. (Like many UNIX utilities, `ar` is a generic tool.)

```
$ ar crv libfoo.a bill.o fred.o
a - bill.o
a - fred.o
```

7. The library is created and the two object files added. To use the library successfully, some systems, notably those derived from Berkeley UNIX, require that a table of contents be created for the library. Do this with the `ranlib` command. In Linux, this step isn't necessary (but it is harmless) when you're using the GNU software development tools.

```
$ ranlib libfoo.a
```

Your library is now ready to use. You can add to the list of files to be used by the compiler to create your program like this:

```
$ gcc -o program program.o libfoo.a
$ ./program
bill: we passed Hello World
$
```

You could also use the -l option to access the library, but because it is not in any of the standard places, you have to tell the compiler where to find it by using the -L option like this:

```
$ gcc -o program program.o -L. -lfoo
```

The -L. option tells the compiler to look in the current directory (.) for libraries. The -lfoo option tells the compiler to use a library called libfoo.a (or a shared library, libfoo.so, if one is present). To see which functions are included in an object file, library, or executable program, you can use the nm command. If you take a look at program and lib.a, you see that the library contains both fred and bill, but that program contains only bill. When the program is created, it includes only functions from the library that it actually needs. Including the header file, which contains declarations for all of the functions in the library, doesn't cause the entire library to be included in the final program.

If you're familiar with Windows software development, there are a number of direct analogies here, illustrated in the following table.

Item	UNIX	Windows
object module	func.o	FUNC.OBJ
static library	lib.a	LIB.LIB
program	program	PROGRAM.EXE

Shared Libraries

One disadvantage of static libraries is that when you run many applications at the same time and they all use functions from the same library, you may end up with many copies of the same functions in memory and indeed many copies in the program files themselves. This can consume a large amount of valuable memory and disk space.

Many UNIX systems and Linux-support shared libraries can overcome this disadvantage. A complete discussion of shared libraries and their implementation on different systems is beyond the scope of this book, so we'll restrict ourselves to the visible implementation under Linux.

Shared libraries are stored in the same places as static libraries, but shared libraries have a different filename suffix. On a typical Linux system, the shared version of the standard math library is /lib/libm.so.

When a program uses a shared library, it is linked in such a way that it doesn't contain function code itself, but references to shared code that will be made available at run time. When the resulting program is loaded into memory to be executed, the function references are resolved and calls are made to the shared library, which will be loaded into memory if needed.

In this way, the system can arrange for a single copy of a shared library to be used by many applications at once and stored just once on the disk. An additional benefit is that the shared library can be updated independently of the applications that rely on it. Symbolic links from the /lib/libm.so file to the actual library revision (/lib/libm.so.N where N represents a major version number — 6 at the time of writing) are used. When Linux starts an application, it can take into account the version of a library required by the application to prevent major new versions of a library from breaking older applications.

> **The following example outputs are taken from a SUSE 10.3 distribution. Your output may differ slightly if you are not using this distribution.**

For Linux systems, the program (the dynamic loader) that takes care of loading shared libraries and resolving client program function references is called ld.so and may be made available as ld-linux.so.2 or ld-lsb.so.2 or ld-lsb.so.3. The additional locations searched for shared libraries are configured in the file /etc/ld.so.conf, which needs to be processed by ldconfig if changed (for example, if X11 shared libraries are added when the X Window System is installed).

You can see which shared libraries are required by a program by running the utility ldd. For example, if you try running it on your example application, you get the following:

```
$ ldd program
        linux-gate.so.1 =>  (0xffffe000)
        libc.so.6 => /lib/libc.so.6 (0xb7db4000)
        /lib/ld-linux.so.2 (0xb7efc000)
```

In this case, you see that the standard C library (libc) is shared (.so). The program requires major Version 6. Other UNIX systems will make similar arrangements for access to shared libraries. Refer to your system documentation for details.

In many ways, shared libraries are similar to dynamic-link libraries used under Windows. The .so libraries correspond to .DLL files and are required at run time, and the .a libraries are similar to .LIB files included in the program executable.

Getting Help

The vast majority of Linux systems are reasonably well documented with respect to the system programming interfaces and standard utilities. This is true because, since the earliest UNIX systems, programmers have been encouraged to supply a manual page with their applications. These manual pages, which are sometimes provided in a printed form, are invariably available electronically.

The man command provides access to the online manual pages. The pages vary considerably in quality and detail. Some may simply refer the reader to other, more thorough documentation, whereas others give a complete list of all options and commands that a utility supports. In either case, the manual page is a good place to start.

The GNU software suite and some other free software use an online documentation system called info. You can browse full documentation online using a special program, info, or via the info command of the emacs editor. The benefit of the info system is that you can navigate the documentation using links and cross-references to jump directly to relevant sections. For the documentation author, the info system has the benefit that its files can be automatically generated from the same source as the printed, typeset documentation.

Try It Out   **Manual Pages and info**

Let's look for documentation of the GNU C compiler (gcc).

1. First take a look at the manual page.

```
$ man gcc
```

```
GCC(1)                          GNU                          GCC(1)



NAME
       gcc - GNU project C and C++ compiler

SYNOPSIS
       gcc [-c|-S|-E] [-std=standard]
           [-g] [-pg] [-Olevel]
           [-Wwarn...] [-pedantic]
           [-Idir...] [-Ldir...]
           [-Dmacro[=defn]...] [-Umacro]
           [-foption...] [-mmachine-option...]
           [-o outfile] infile...

       Only the most useful options are listed here; see below
       for the remainder.  g++ accepts mostly the same options as
       gcc.

DESCRIPTION
       When you invoke GCC, it normally does preprocessing, com
       pilation, assembly and linking.  The ``overall options''
       allow you to stop this process at an intermediate stage.
       For example, the -c option says not to run the linker.
       Then the output consists of object files output by the
       assembler.

       Other options are passed on to one stage of processing.
       Some options control the preprocessor and others the com
       piler itself. Yet other options control the assembler and
       linker; most of these are not documented here, since we
       rarely need to use any of them.
   ...
```

If you want, you can read about the options that the compiler supports. The manual page in this case is quite long, but it forms only a small part of the total documentation for GNU C (and C++).

When reading manual pages, you can use the spacebar to read the next page, Enter (or Return if your keyboard has that key instead) to read the next line, and *q* to quit altogether.

2. To get more information on GNU C, you can try `info`.

```
$ info gcc

File: gcc.info,  Node: Top,  Next: G++ and GCC,  Up: (DIR)
Introduction
************

   This manual documents how to use the GNU compilers, as well as their
features and incompatibilities, and how to report bugs.  It corresponds
to GCC version 4.1.3.  The internals of the GNU compilers, including how
to port them to new targets and some information about how to write
front ends for new languages, are documented in a separate manual.
*Note Introduction: (gccint)Top.

* Menu:

* G++ and GCC::      You can compile C or C++ Applications.
* Standards::        Language standards supported by GCC.
* Invoking GCC::     Command options supported by `gcc'.
* C Implementation:: How GCC implements the ISO C specification.
* C Extensions::     GNU extensions to the C language family.
* C++ Extensions::   GNU extensions to the C++ language.
* Objective-C::      GNU Objective-C runtime features.
* Compatibility::    Binary Compatibility
--zz-Info: (gcc.info.gz)Top, 39 lines --Top-------------------------------
Welcome to Info version 4.8. Type ? for help, m for menu item.
```

You're presented with a long menu of options that you can select to move around a complete text version of the documentation. Menu items and a hierarchy of pages allow you to navigate a very large document. On paper, the GNU C documentation runs to many hundreds of pages.

The `info` system also contains its own help page in `info` form pages, of course. If you type Ctrl+H, you'll be presented with some help that includes a tutorial on using `info`. The `info` program is available with many Linux distributions and can be installed on other UNIX systems.

Summary

In this introductory chapter, we've looked at Linux programming and the things Linux holds in common with proprietary UNIX systems. We've noted the wide variety of programming systems available to UNIX developers. We've also presented a simple program and library to demonstrate the basic C tools, comparing them with their Windows equivalents.

2

Shell Programming

Having started this book on programming Linux using C, we now take a detour into writing shell programs. Why? Well, Linux isn't like systems where the command-line interface is an afterthought to the graphical interface. UNIX, Linux's inspiration, originally had no graphical interface at all; everything was done from the command line. Consequently, the command-line system of UNIX underwent a lot of development and became a very powerful feature. This has been carried into Linux, and some of the most powerful things that you can do are most easily done from the shell. Because the shell is so important to Linux, and is so useful for automating simple tasks, shell programming is covered early.

Throughout this chapter, we'll be showing you the syntax, structures, and commands available to you when you're programming the shell, usually making use of interactive (screen-based) examples. These should serve as a useful synopsis of most of the shell's features and their effects. We will also sneak a look at a couple of particularly useful command-line utilities often called from the shell: grep and find. While looking at grep, we also cover the fundamentals of regular expressions, which crop up in Linux utilities and in programming languages such as Perl, Ruby, and PHP. At the end of the chapter, you'll learn how to program a real-life script, which is reprogrammed and extended in C throughout the book. This chapter covers the following:

- ❑ What a shell is
- ❑ Basic considerations
- ❑ The subtleties of syntax: variables, conditions, and program control
- ❑ Lists
- ❑ Functions
- ❑ Commands and command execution
- ❑ Here documents
- ❑ Debugging
- ❑ grep and regular expressions
- ❑ find

Whether you're faced with a complex shell script in your system administration, or you want to prototype your latest big (but beautifully simple) idea, or just want to speed up some repetitive task, this chapter is for you.

Why Program with a Shell?

One reason to use the shell for programming is that you can program the shell quickly and simply. Moreover, a shell is always available even on the most basic Linux installation, so for simple prototyping you can find out if your idea works. The shell is also ideal for any small utilities that perform some relatively simple task for which efficiency is less important than easy configuration, maintenance, and portability. You can use the shell to organize process control, so that commands run in a predetermined sequence dependent on the successful completion of each stage.

Although the shell has superficial similarities to the Windows command prompt, it's much more powerful, capable of running reasonably complex programs in its own right. Not only can you execute commands and call Linux utilities, you can also write them. The shell executes shell programs, often referred to as *scripts,* which are interpreted at runtime. This generally makes debugging easier because you can easily execute single lines, and there's no recompile time. However, this can make the shell unsuitable for time-critical or processor-intensive tasks.

A Bit of Philosophy

Here we come to a bit of UNIX — and of course Linux — philosophy. UNIX is built on and depends on a high level of code reuse. You build a small and simple utility and people use it as one link in a string of others to form a command. One of the pleasures of Linux is the variety of excellent tools available. A simple example is this command:

```
$ ls -al | more
```

This command uses the ls and more utilities and pipes the output of the file listing to a screen-at-a-time display. Each utility is one more building block. You can often use many small scripts together to create large and complex suites of programs.

For example, if you want to print a reference copy of the bash manual pages, then use

```
$ man bash | col -b | lpr
```

Furthermore, because of Linux's automatic file type handling, the users of these utilities usually don't need to know what language the utilities are written in. If the utility needs to run faster, it's quite common to prototype utilities in the shell and reimplement them later in C or C++, Perl, Python, or some other language that executes more swiftly once an idea has proven its worth. Conversely, if the utility works adequately in the shell, you can leave well enough alone.

Whether or not you ever reimplement the script depends on whether it needs optimizing, whether it needs to be portable, whether it should be easy to change, and whether (as usually happens) it outgrows its original purpose.

Numerous examples of shell scripts are already loaded on your Linux system in case you're curious, including package installers, .xinitrc and startx, and the scripts in /etc/rc.d to configure the system on boot-up.

What Is a Shell?

Before jumping in and discussing how to program using a shell, let's review the shell's function and the different shells available for Linux. A *shell* is a program that acts as the interface between you and the Linux system, enabling you to enter commands for the operating system to execute. In that respect, it resembles the Windows command prompt, but as mentioned earlier, Linux shells are much more powerful. For example, input and output can be redirected using < and >, data piped between simultaneously executing programs using |, and output from a subprocess grabbed by using $(...). On Linux it's quite feasible to have multiple shells installed, with different users able to pick the one they prefer. Figure 2-1 shows how the shell (two shells actually, both bash and csh) and other programs sit around the Linux kernel.

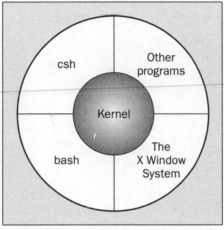

Figure 2-1

Because Linux is so modular, you can slot in one of the many different shells in use, although most of them are derived from the original Bourne shell. On Linux, the standard shell that is always installed as /bin/sh is called *bash* (the GNU Bourne-Again SHell), from the GNU suite of tools. Because this is an excellent shell that is always installed on Linux systems, is open source, and is portable to almost all UNIX variants, bash is the shell we will be using. This chapter uses bash version 3 and mostly uses the features common to all POSIX-compatible shells. We assume that the shell has been installed as /bin/sh and that it is the default shell for your login. On most Linux distributions, the program /bin/sh, the default shell, is actually a link to the program /bin/bash.

You can check the version of bash you have with the following command:

```
$ /bin/bash --version
GNU bash, version 3.2.9(1)-release (i686-pc-linux-gnu)
Copyright (C) 2005 Free Software Foundation, Inc.
```

> To change to a different shell — if bash isn't the default on your system, for example —
> just execute the desired shell's program (e.g., /bin/bash) to run the new shell and
> change the command prompt. If you are using UNIX, and bash isn't installed, you
> can download it free from the GNU Web site at www.gnu.org. The sources are highly
> portable, and chances are good that it will compile on your version of UNIX straight
> out of the box.

When you create Linux users, you can set the shell that they will use, either when the user is created or afterwards by modifying their details. Figure 2-2 shows the selection of the shell for a user using Fedora.

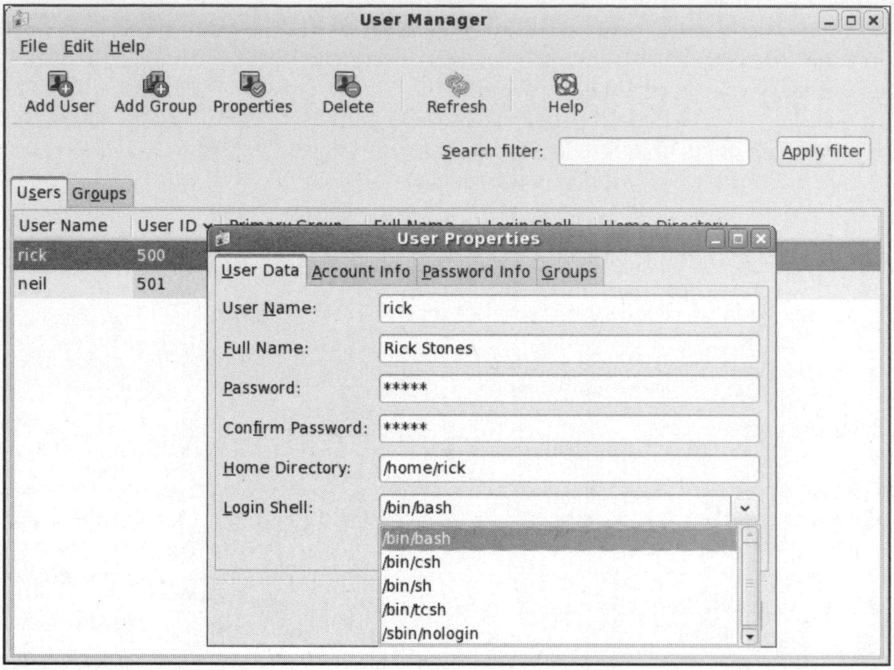

Figure 2-2

Many other shells are available, either free or commercially. The following table offers a brief summary of some of the more common shells available:

Shell Name	A Bit of History
sh (Bourne)	The original shell from early versions of UNIX
csh, tcsh, zsh	The C shell, and its derivatives, originally created by Bill Joy of Berkeley UNIX fame. The C shell is probably the third most popular type of shell after bash and the Korn shell.
ksh, pdksh	The Korn shell and its public domain cousin. Written by David Korn, this is the default shell on many commercial UNIX versions.
bash	The Linux staple shell from the GNU project. bash, or Bourne Again SHell, has the advantage that the source code is freely available, and even if it's not currently running on your UNIX system, it has probably been ported to it. bash has many similarities to the Korn shell.

Except for the C shell and a small number of derivatives, all of these are very similar and are closely aligned with the shell specified in the X/Open 4.2 and POSIX 1003.2 specifications. POSIX 1003.2 provides the minimum specification for a shell, but the extended specification in X/Open provides a more friendly and powerful shell. X/Open is usually the more demanding specification, but it also yields a friendlier system.

Pipes and Redirection

Before we get down to the details of shell programs, we need to say a little about how inputs and outputs of Linux programs (not just shell programs) can be redirected.

Redirecting Output

You may already be familiar with some redirection, such as

```
$ ls -l > lsoutput.txt
```

which saves the output of the ls command into a file called lsoutput.txt.

However, there is much more to redirection than this simple example reveals. You'll learn more about the standard file descriptors in Chapter 3, but for now all you need to know is that file descriptor 0 is the standard input to a program, file descriptor 1 is the standard output, and file descriptor 2 is the standard error output. You can redirect each of these independently. In fact, you can also redirect other file descriptors, but it's unusual to want to redirect any other than the standard ones: 0, 1, and 2.

The preceding example redirects the standard output into a file by using the > operator. By default, if the file already exists, then it will be overwritten. If you want to change the default behavior, you can use the command set -o noclobber (or set -C), which sets the noclobber option to prevent a file from being overwritten using redirection. You can cancel this option using set +o noclobber. You'll see more options for the set command later in the chapter.

To append to the file, use the >> operator. For example,

```
$ ps >> lsoutput.txt
```

will append the output of the ps command to the end of the specified file.

To redirect the standard error output, preface the > operator with the number of the file descriptor you wish to redirect. Because the standard error is on file descriptor 2, use the 2> operator. This is often useful to discard error information and prevent it from appearing on the screen.

Suppose you want to use the kill command to kill a process from a script. There is always a slight risk that the process will die before the kill command is executed. If this happens, kill will write an error message to the standard error output, which, by default, will appear on the screen. By redirecting both the standard output and the error, you can prevent the kill command from writing any text to the screen.

The command

```
$ kill -HUP 1234 >killout.txt 2>killerr.txt
```

will put the output and error information into separate files.

If you prefer to capture both sets of output into a single file, you can use the >& operator to combine the two outputs. Therefore,

```
$ kill -1 1234 >killouterr.txt 2>&1
```

will put both the output and error outputs into the same file. Notice the order of the operators. This reads as "redirect standard output to the file killouterr.txt, and then direct standard error to the same place as the standard output." If you get the order wrong, the redirect won't work as you expect.

Because you can discover the result of the kill command using the return code (discussed in more detail later in this chapter), you don't often want to save either standard output or standard error. You can use the Linux universal "bit bucket" of /dev/null to efficiently discard the entire output, like this:

```
$ kill -1 1234 >/dev/null 2>&1
```

Redirecting Input

Rather like redirecting output, you can also redirect input. For example,

```
$ more < killout.txt
```

Obviously, this is a rather trivial example under Linux; the Linux more command is quite happy to accept filenames as parameters, unlike the Windows command-line equivalent.

Pipes

You can connect processes using the pipe operator (|). In Linux, unlike in MS-DOS, processes connected by pipes can run simultaneously and are automatically rescheduled as data flows between them. As a simple example, you could use the sort command to sort the output from ps.

If you don't use pipes, you must use several steps, like this:

```
$ ps > psout.txt
$ sort psout.txt > pssort.out
```

A much more elegant solution is to connect the processes with a pipe:

```
$ ps | sort > pssort.out
```

Because you probably want to see the output paginated on the screen, you could connect a third process, more, all on the same command line:

```
$ ps | sort | more
```

There's practically no limit to the permissible number of connected processes. Suppose you want to see all the different process names that are running excluding shells. You could use

```
$ ps -xo comm | sort | uniq | grep -v sh | more
```

This takes the output of ps, sorts it into alphabetical order, extracts processes using uniq, uses grep -v sh to remove the process named sh, and finally displays it paginated on the screen.

As you can see, this is a much more elegant solution than a string of separate commands, each with its own temporary file. However, be wary of one thing here: If you have a string of commands, the output file is created or written to immediately when the set of commands is created, so never use the same filename twice in a string of commands. If you try to do something like

```
cat mydata.txt | sort | uniq > mydata.txt
```

you will end up with an empty file, because you will overwrite the mydata.txt file before you read it.

The Shell as a Programming Language

Now that you've seen some basic shell operations, it's time to move on to some actual shell programs. There are two ways of writing shell programs. You can type a sequence of commands and allow the shell to execute them interactively, or you can store those commands in a file that you can then invoke as a program.

Interactive Programs

Just typing the shell script on the command line is a quick and easy way of trying out small code fragments, and is very useful while you are learning or just testing things out.

Suppose you have a large number of C files and wish to examine the files that contain the string POSIX. Rather than search using the grep command for the string in the files and then list the files individually, you could perform the whole operation in an interactive script like this:

```
$ for file in *
> do
> if grep -l POSIX $file
> then
> more $file
> fi
> done
posix
This is a file with POSIX in it - treat it well
$
```

Note how the normal $ shell prompt changes to a > when the shell is expecting further input. You can type away, letting the shell decide when you're finished, and the script will execute immediately.

In this example, the grep command prints the files it finds containing POSIX and then more displays the contents of the file to the screen. Finally, the shell prompt returns. Note also that you called the shell variable that deals with each of the files to self-document the script. You could equally well have used i, but file is more meaningful for humans to read.

The shell also performs wildcard expansion (often referred to as *globbing*). You are almost certainly aware of the use of '*' as a wildcard to match a string of characters. What you may not know is that you can request single-character wildcards using ?, while [set] allows any of a number of single characters to be checked. [^set] negates the set — that is, it includes anything but the set you've specified. Brace expansion using {} (available on some shells, including bash) allows you to group arbitrary strings together in a set that the shell will expand. For example,

```
$ ls my_{finger,toe}s
```

will list the files `my_fingers` and `my_toes`. This command uses the shell to check every file in the current directory. We will come back to these rules for matching patterns near the end of the chapter when we look in more detail at `grep` and the power of regular expressions.

Experienced Linux users would probably perform this simple operation in a much more efficient way, perhaps with a command such as

```
$ more `grep -l POSIX *`
```

or the synonymous construction

```
$ more $(grep -l POSIX *)
```

In addition,

```
$ grep -l POSIX * | more
```

will output the name of the file whose contents contained the string POSIX. In this script, you see the shell making use of other commands, such as `grep` and `more`, to do the hard work. The shell simply enables you to glue several existing commands together in new and powerful ways. You will see wildcard expansion used many times in the following scripts, and we'll look at the whole area of expansion in more detail when we look at regular expressions in the section on the `grep` command.

Going through this long rigmarole every time you want to execute a sequence of commands is a bore. You need to store the commands in a file, conventionally referred to as a *shell script*, so you can execute them whenever you like.

Creating a Script

Using any text editor, you need to create a file containing the commands; create a file called `first` that looks like this:

```
#!/bin/sh

# first
# This file looks through all the files in the current
# directory for the string POSIX, and then prints the names of
# those files to the standard output.

for file in *
do
  if grep -q POSIX $file
  then
    echo $file
  fi
done

exit 0
```

Comments start with a # and continue to the end of a line. Conventionally, though, # is kept in the first column. Having made such a sweeping statement, we next note that the first line, #!/bin/sh, is a special form of comment; the #! characters tell the system that the argument that follows on the line is the program to be used to execute this file. In this case, /bin/sh is the default shell program.

Note the absolute path specified in the comment. It is conventional to keep this shorter than 32 characters for backward compatibility, because some older UNIX versions can only use this limited number of characters when using #!, although Linux generally does not have this limitation.

Since the script is essentially treated as standard input to the shell, it can contain any Linux commands referenced by your PATH environment variable.

The exit command ensures that the script returns a sensible exit code (more on this later in the chapter). This is rarely checked when programs are run interactively, but if you want to invoke this script from another script and check whether it succeeded, returning an appropriate exit code is very important. Even if you never intend to allow your script to be invoked from another, you should still exit with a reasonable code. Have faith in the usefulness of your script: Assume it may need to be reused as part of another script someday.

A zero denotes success in shell programming. Since the script as it stands can't detect any failures, it always returns success. We'll come back to the reasons for using a zero exit code for success later in the chapter, when we look at the exit command in more detail.

Notice that this script does not use any filename extension or suffix; Linux, and UNIX in general, rarely makes use of the filename extension to determine the type of a file. You could have used .sh or added a different extension, but the shell doesn't care. Most preinstalled scripts will not have any filename extension, and the best way to check if they are scripts or not is to use the file command — for example, file first or file /bin/bash. Use whatever convention is applicable where you work, or suits you.

Making a Script Executable

Now that you have your script file, you can run it in two ways. The simpler way is to invoke the shell with the name of the script file as a parameter:

```
$ /bin/sh first
```

This should work, but it would be much better if you could simply invoke the script by typing its name, giving it the respectability of other Linux commands. Do this by changing the file mode to make the file executable for all users using the chmod command:

```
$ chmod +x first
```

> Of course, this isn't the only way to use chmod to make a file executable. Use man chmod to find out more about octal arguments and other options.

You can then execute it using the command

```
$ first
```

You may get an error saying the command wasn't found. This is almost certainly because the shell environment variable PATH isn't set to look in the current directory for commands to execute. To change this, either type PATH=$PATH:. on the command line or edit your .bash_profile file to add this command to the end of the file; then log out and log back in again. Alternatively, type ./first in the directory containing the script, to give the shell the full relative path to the file.

Specifying the path prepended with ./ does have one other advantage: It ensures that you don't accidentally execute another command on the system with the same name as your script file.

> You shouldn't change the PATH variable like this for the superuser, conventionally the user name root. It's a security loophole, because the system administrator logged in as root can be tricked into invoking a fake version of a standard command. One of the authors admits to doing this once — just to prove a point to the system administrator about security, of course! It's only a slight risk on ordinary accounts to include the current directory in the path, so if you are particularly concerned, just get into the habit of prepending ./ to all commands that are in the local directory.

Once you're confident that your script is executing properly, you can move it to a more appropriate location than the current directory. If the command is just for your own use, you could create a bin directory in your home directory and add that to your path. If you want the script to be executable by others, you could use /usr/local/bin or another system directory as a convenient location for adding new programs. If you don't have root permissions on your system, you could ask the system administrator to copy your file for you, although you may have to convince them of its worth first. To prevent other users from changing the script, perhaps accidentally, you should remove write access from it. The sequence of commands for the administrator to set ownership and permissions would be something like this:

```
# cp first /usr/local/bin
# chown root /usr/local/bin/first
# chgrp root /usr/local/bin/first
# chmod 755 /usr/local/bin/first
```

Notice that rather than alter a specific part of the permission flags, you use the absolute form of the chmod here because you know exactly what permissions you require.

If you prefer, you can use the rather longer, but perhaps more obvious, form of the chmod command:

```
# chmod u=rwx,go=rx /usr/local/bin/first
```

Check the manual page of chmod for more details.

> In Linux you can delete a file if you have write permission on the directory that contains it. To be safe, ensure that only the superuser can write to directories containing files that you want to keep safe. This makes sense because a directory is just another file, and having write permission to a directory file allows users to add and remove names.

Shell Syntax

Now that you've seen an example of a simple shell program, it's time to look in greater depth at the programming power of the shell. The shell is quite an easy programming language to learn, not least because it's easy to test small program fragments interactively before combining them into bigger scripts. You can use the bash shell to write quite large, structured programs. The next few sections cover the following:

❑ Variables: strings, numbers, environments, and parameters

❑ Conditions: shell Booleans

❑ Program control: `if`, `elif`, `for`, `while`, `until`, `case`

❑ Lists

❑ Functions

❑ Commands built into the shell

❑ Getting the result of a command

❑ Here documents

Variables

You don't usually declare variables in the shell before using them. Instead, you create them by simply using them (for example, when you assign an initial value to them). By default, all variables are considered and stored as strings, even when they are assigned numeric values. The shell and some utilities will convert numeric strings to their values in order to operate on them as required. Linux is a case-sensitive system, so the shell considers the variable `foo` to be different from `Foo`, and both to be different from `FOO`.

Within the shell you can access the contents of a variable by preceding its name with a $. Whenever you extract the contents of a variable, you must give the variable a preceding $. When you assign a value to a variable, just use the name of the variable, which is created dynamically if necessary. An easy way to check the contents of a variable is to `echo` it to the terminal, preceding its name with a $.

On the command line, you can see this in action when you set and check various values of the variable `salutation`:

```
$ salutation=Hello
$ echo $salutation
Hello
$ salutation="Yes Dear"
$ echo $salutation
Yes Dear
$ salutation=7+5
$ echo $salutation
7+5
```

> **Note how a string must be delimited by quote marks if it contains spaces. In addition, there can't be any spaces on either side of the equals sign.**

You can assign user input to a variable by using the read command. This takes one parameter, the name of the variable to be read into, and then waits for the user to enter some text. The read normally completes when the user presses Enter. When reading a variable from the terminal, you don't usually need the quote marks:

```
$ read salutation
Wie geht's?
$ echo $salutation
Wie geht's?
```

Quoting

Before moving on, you should be clear about one feature of the shell: the use of quotes.

Normally, parameters in scripts are separated by whitespace characters (e.g., a space, a tab, or a newline character). If you want a parameter to contain one or more whitespace characters, you must quote the parameter.

The behavior of variables such as $foo inside quotes depends on the type of quotes you use. If you enclose a $ variable expression in double quotes, then it's replaced with its value when the line is executed. If you enclose it in single quotes, then no substitution takes place. You can also remove the special meaning of the $ symbol by prefacing it with a \.

Usually, strings are enclosed in double quotes, which protects variables from being separated by white space but allows $ expansion to take place.

Try It Out   Playing with Variables

This example shows the effect of quotes on the output of a variable:

```
#!/bin/sh

myvar="Hi there"

echo $myvar
echo "$myvar"
echo '$myvar'
echo \$myvar

echo Enter some text
read myvar

echo '$myvar' now equals $myvar
exit 0
```

This behaves as follows:

```
$ ./variable
Hi there
Hi there
$myvar
$myvar
```

```
Enter some text
Hello World
$myvar now equals Hello World
```

How It Works

The variable `myvar` is created and assigned the string `Hi there`. The contents of the variable are displayed with the `echo` command, showing how prefacing the variable with a $ character expands the contents of the variable. You see that using double quotes doesn't affect the substitution of the variable, while single quotes and the backslash do. You also use the `read` command to get a string from the user.

Environment Variables

When a shell script starts, some variables are initialized from values in the environment. These are normally in all uppercase form to distinguish them from user-defined (shell) variables in scripts, which are conventionally lowercase. The variables created depend on your personal configuration. Many are listed in the manual pages, but the principal ones are listed in the following table:

Environment Variable	Description
$HOME	The home directory of the current user
$PATH	A colon-separated list of directories to search for commands
$PS1	A command prompt, frequently $, but in bash you can use some more complex values; for example, the string [\u@\h \W]$ is a popular default that tells you the user, machine name, and current directory, as well as providing a $ prompt.
$PS2	A secondary prompt, used when prompting for additional input; usually >.
$IFS	An input field separator. This is a list of characters that are used to separate words when the shell is reading input, usually space, tab, and newline characters.
$0	The name of the shell script
$#	The number of parameters passed
$$	The process ID of the shell script, often used inside a script for generating unique temporary filenames; for example /tmp/tmpfile_$$

> If you want to check out how the program works in a different environment by running the `env <command>`, try looking at the `env` manual pages. Later in the chapter you'll see how to set environment variables in subshells using the `export` command.

Parameter Variables

If your script is invoked with parameters, some additional variables are created. If no parameters are passed, the environment variable $# still exists but has a value of 0.

The parameter variables are listed in the following table:

Parameter Variable	Description
$1, $2, …	The parameters given to the script
$*	A list of all the parameters, in a single variable, separated by the first character in the environment variable IFS. If IFS is modified, then the way $* separates the command line into parameters will change.
$@	A subtle variation on $*; it doesn't use the IFS environment variable, so parameters are not run together even if IFS is empty.

It's easy to see the difference between $@ and $* by trying them out:

```
$ IFS=''
$ set foo bar bam
$ echo "$@"
foo bar bam
$ echo "$*"
foobarbam
$ unset IFS
$ echo "$*"
foo bar bam
```

As you can see, within double quotes, $@ expands the positional parameters as separate fields, regardless of the IFS value. In general, if you want access to the parameters, $@ is the sensible choice.

In addition to printing the contents of variables using the echo command, you can also read them by using the read command.

Try It Out   **Manipulating Parameter and Environment Variables**

The following script demonstrates some simple variable manipulation. Once you've typed the script and saved it as try_var, don't forget to make it executable with chmod +x try_var.

```
#!/bin/sh

salutation="Hello"
echo $salutation
echo "The program $0 is now running"
echo "The second parameter was $2"
echo "The first parameter was $1"
echo "The parameter list was $*"
echo "The user's home directory is $HOME"
```

```
echo "Please enter a new greeting"
read salutation

echo $salutation
echo "The script is now complete"
exit 0
```

If you run this script, you get the following output:

```
$ ./try_var foo bar baz
Hello
The program ./try_var is now running
The second parameter was bar
The first parameter was foo
The parameter list was foo bar baz
The user's home directory is /home/rick
Please enter a new greeting
Sire
Sire
The script is now complete
$
```

How It Works

This script creates the variable `salutation`, displays its contents, and then shows how various parameter variables and the environment variable $HOME already exist and have appropriate values.

We'll return to parameter substitution in more detail later in the chapter.

Conditions

Fundamental to all programming languages is the ability to test conditions and perform different actions based on those decisions. Before we talk about that, though, let's look at the conditional constructs that you can use in shell scripts and then examine the control structures that use them.

A shell script can test the exit code of any command that can be invoked from the command line, including the scripts that you have written yourself. That's why it's important to always include an `exit` command with a value at the end of any scripts that you write.

The test or [Command

In practice, most scripts make extensive use of the [or `test` command, the shell's Boolean check. On some systems, the [and `test` commands are synonymous, except that when the [command is used, a trailing] is also used for readability. Having a [command might seem a little odd, but within the code it does make the syntax of commands look simple, neat, and more like other programming languages.

These commands call an external program in some older UNIX shells, but they tend to be built in to more modern ones. We'll come back to this when we look at commands in a later section.

Because the `test` command is infrequently used outside shell scripts, many Linux users who have never written shell scripts try to write simple programs and call them *test*. If such a program doesn't work, it's probably conflicting with the shell's `test` command. To find out whether your system has an external command of a given name, try typing something like `which test`, to check which `test` command is being executed, or use `./test` to ensure that you execute the script in the current directory. When in doubt, just get into the habit of executing your scripts by preceding the script name with `./` when invoking them.

We'll introduce the `test` command using one of the simplest conditions: checking to see whether a file exists. The command for this is `test -f <filename>`, so within a script you can write

```
if test -f fred.c
then
...
fi
```

You can also write it like this:

```
if [ -f fred.c ]
then
...
fi
```

The `test` command's exit code (whether the condition is satisfied) determines whether the conditional code is run.

Note that you must put spaces between the `[` braces and the condition being checked. You can remember this by remembering that `[` is just the same as writing `test`, and you would always leave a space after the `test` command.

If you prefer putting `then` on the same line as `if`, you must add a semicolon to separate the test from the `then`:

```
if [ -f fred.c ]; then
...
fi
```

The condition types that you can use with the `test` command fall into three types: *string comparison, arithmetic comparison,* and *file conditionals.* The following table describes these condition types:

String Comparison	Result
`string1 = string2`	True if the strings are equal
`string1 != string2`	True if the strings are not equal
`-n string`	True if the string is not null
`-z string`	True if the string is null (an empty string)
Arithmetic Comparison	**Result**
`expression1 -eq expression2`	True if the expressions are equal
`expression1 -ne expression2`	True if the expressions are not equal
`expression1 -gt expression2`	True if `expression1` is greater than `expression2`
`expression1 -ge expression2`	True if `expression1` is greater than or equal to `expression2`
`expression1 -lt expression2`	True if `expression1` is less than `expression2`
`expression1 -le expression2`	True if `expression1` is less than or equal to `expression2`
`! expression`	True if the expression is false, and vice versa
File Conditional	**Result**
`-d file`	True if the file is a directory
`-e file`	True if the file exists. Note that historically the `-e` option has not been portable, so `-f` is usually used.
`-f file`	True if the file is a regular file
`-g file`	True if `set-group-id` is set on `file`
`-r file`	True if the file is readable
`-s file`	True if the file has nonzero size
`-u file`	True if `set-user-id` is set on `file`
`-w file`	True if the file is writable
`-x file`	True if the file is executable

> You may be wondering what the set-group-id and set-user-id (also known as set-gid and set-uid) bits are. The set-uid bit gives a program the permissions of its owner, rather than its user, while the set-gid bit gives a program the permissions of its group. The bits are set with chmod, using the s and g options. The set-gid and set-uid flags have no effect on files containing shell scripts, only on executable binary files.

We're getting ahead of ourselves slightly, but following is an example of how you would test the state of the file /bin/bash, just so you can see what these look like in use:

```
#!/bin/sh

if [ -f /bin/bash ]
then
  echo "file /bin/bash exists"
fi

if [ -d /bin/bash ]
then
  echo "/bin/bash is a directory"
else
  echo "/bin/bash is NOT a directory"
fi
```

Before the test can be true, all the file conditional tests require that the file also exists. This list contains just the more commonly used options to the test command, so for a complete list refer to the manual entry. If you're using bash, where test is built in, use the help test command to get more details. We'll use some of these options later in the chapter.

Now that you know about conditions, you can look at the control structures that use them.

Control Structures

The shell has a set of control structures, which are very similar to other programming languages.

> In the following sections, the statements are the series of commands to perform when, while, or until the condition is fulfilled.

if

The if statement is very simple: It tests the result of a command and then conditionally executes a group of statements:

```
if condition
then
  statements
```

```
else
  statements
fi
```

A common use for `if` is to ask a question and then make a decision based on the answer:

```
#!/bin/sh

echo "Is it morning? Please answer yes or no"
read timeofday

if [ $timeofday = "yes" ]; then
  echo "Good morning"
else
  echo "Good afternoon"
fi

exit 0
```

This would give the following output:

```
Is it morning? Please answer yes or no
yes
Good morning
$
```

This script uses the `[` command to test the contents of the variable `timeofday`. The result is evaluated by the `if` command, which then allows different lines of code to be executed.

> Notice that you use extra white space to indent the statements inside the `if`. **This is just a convenience for the human reader; the shell ignores the additional white space.**

elif

Unfortunately, there are several problems with this very simple script. For one thing, it will take any answer except yes as meaning no. You can prevent this by using the `elif` construct, which allows you to add a second condition to be checked when the `else` portion of the `if` is executed.

Try It Out   Doing Checks with an elif

You can modify the previous script so that it reports an error message if the user types in anything other than yes or no. Do this by replacing the `else` with `elif` and then adding another condition:

```
#!/bin/sh

echo "Is it morning? Please answer yes or no"
read timeofday

if [ $timeofday = "yes" ]
then
  echo "Good morning"
```

35

```
elif [ $timeofday = "no" ]; then
  echo "Good afternoon"
else
  echo "Sorry, $timeofday not recognized. Enter yes or no"
  exit 1
fi

exit 0
```

How It Works

This is quite similar to the previous example, but now the `elif` command tests the variable again if the first `if` condition is not true. If neither of the tests is successful, an error message is printed and the script exits with the value 1, which the caller can use in a calling program to check whether the script was successful.

A Problem with Variables

This fixes the most obvious defect, but a more subtle problem is lurking. Try this new script, but just press Enter (or Return on some keyboards), rather than answering the question. You'll get this error message:

```
[: =: unary operator expected
```

What went wrong? The problem is in the first `if` clause. When the variable `timeofday` was tested, it consisted of a blank string. Therefore, the `if` clause looks like

```
if [ = "yes" ]
```

which isn't a valid condition. To avoid this, you must use quotes around the variable:

```
if [ "$timeofday" = "yes" ]
```

An empty variable then gives the valid test:

```
if [ "" = "yes" ]
```

The new script is as follows:

```
#!/bin/sh

echo "Is it morning? Please answer yes or no"
read timeofday

if [ "$timeofday" = "yes" ]
then
  echo "Good morning"
elif [ "$timeofday" = "no" ]; then
  echo "Good afternoon"
else
  echo "Sorry, $timeofday not recognized. Enter yes or no"
```

```
     exit 1
fi

exit 0
```

This is safe should a user just press Enter in answer to the question.

> If you want the echo command to delete the trailing new line, the most portable
> option is to use the printf command (see the printf section later in this chapter),
> rather than the echo command. Some shells use echo -e, but that's not supported on
> all systems. bash allows echo -n to suppress the new line, so if you are confident
> your script needs to work only on bash, we suggest using that syntax.

```
echo -n "Is it morning? Please answer yes or no: "
```

Note that you need to leave an extra space before the closing quotes so that there is a gap before the user-typed response, which looks neater.

for

Use the for construct to loop through a range of values, which can be any set of strings. They could be
simply listed in the program or, more commonly, the result of a shell expansion of filenames.

The syntax is simple:

```
for variable in values
do
   statements
done
```

Try It Out   Using a for Loop with Fixed Strings

The values are normally strings, so you can write the following:

```
#!/bin/sh

for foo in bar fud 43
do
  echo $foo
done
exit 0
```

That results in the following output:

```
bar
fud
43
```

> **What would happen if you changed the first line from** `for foo in bar fud 43`
> **to** `for foo in "bar fud 43"`**? Remember that adding the quotes tells the shell to
> consider everything between them as a single string. This is one way of getting
> spaces to be stored in a variable.**

How It Works

This example creates the variable `foo` and assigns it a different value each time around the `for` loop.
Since the shell considers all variables to contain strings by default, it's just as valid to use the string `43` as
the string `fud`.

Try It Out   Using a for Loop with Wildcard Expansion

As mentioned earlier, it's common to use the `for` loop with a shell expansion for filenames. This means
using a wildcard for the string value and letting the shell fill out all the values at run time.

You've already seen this in the original example, `first`. The script used shell expansion, the `*` expand-
ing to the names of all the files in the current directory. Each of these in turn is used as the variable
`$file` inside the `for` loop.

Let's quickly look at another wildcard expansion. Imagine that you want to print all the script files starting with the letter "f" in the current directory, and you know that all your scripts end in .sh. You could
do it like this:

```
#!/bin/sh

for file in $(ls f*.sh); do
  lpr $file
done
exit 0
```

How It Works

This illustrates the use of the `$(command)` syntax, which is covered in more detail later (in the section on
command execution). Basically, the parameter list for the `for` command is provided by the output of the
command enclosed in the `$()` sequence.

The shell expands `f*.sh` to give the names of all the files matching this pattern.

> **Remember that all expansion of variables in shell scripts is done when the script is
> executed, never when it's written, so syntax errors in variable declarations are found
> only at execution time, as shown earlier when we were quoting empty variables.**

---

while

Because all shell values are considered strings by default, the `for` loop is good for looping through a series of strings, but is not so useful when you don't know in advance how many times you want the loop to be executed.

When you need to repeat a sequence of commands, but don't know in advance how many times they should execute, you will normally use a `while` loop, which has the following syntax:

```
while condition do
   statements
done
```

For example, here is a rather poor password-checking program:

```
#!/bin/sh

echo "Enter password"
read trythis

while [ "$trythis" != "secret" ]; do
  echo "Sorry, try again"
  read trythis
done
exit 0
```

An example of the output from this script is as follows:

```
Enter password
password
Sorry, try again
secret
$
```

Clearly, this isn't a very secure way of asking for a password, but it does serve to illustrate the `while` statement. The statements between `do` and `done` are continuously executed until the condition is no longer true. In this case, you're checking whether the value of `trythis` is equal to `secret`. The loop will continue until `$trythis` equals `secret`. You then continue executing the script at the statement immediately following the `done`.

until

The `until` statement has the following syntax:

```
until condition
do
   statements
done
```

This is very similar to the `while` loop, but with the condition test reversed. In other words, the loop continues until the condition becomes true, not while the condition is true.

> In general, if a loop should always execute at least once, use a `while` loop; if it may
> not need to execute at all, use an `until` loop.

As an example of an `until` loop, you can set up an alarm that is initiated when another user, whose
login name you pass on the command line, logs on:

```
#!/bin/bash

until who | grep "$1" > /dev/null
do
    sleep 60
done

# now ring the bell and announce the expected user.

echo -e '\a'
echo "**** $1 has just logged in ****"

exit 0
```

If the user is already logged on, the loop doesn't need to execute at all, so using `until` is a more natural
choice than `while`.

case

The `case` construct is a little more complex than those you have encountered so far. Its syntax is as follows:

```
case variable in
  pattern [ | pattern] ...) statements;;
  pattern [ | pattern] ...) statements;;
  ...
esac
```

This may look a little intimidating, but the `case` construct enables you to match the contents of a variable
against patterns in quite a sophisticated way and then allows execution of different statements, depending
on which pattern was matched. It is much simpler than the alternative way of checking several conditions,
which would be to use multiple `if`, `elif`, and `else` statements.

*Notice that each pattern line is terminated with double semicolons (; ;). You can put multiple state-
ments between each pattern and the next, so a double semicolon is needed to mark where one statement
ends and the next pattern begins.*

The capability to match multiple patterns and then execute multiple related statements makes the `case`
construct a good way of dealing with user input. The best way to see how `case` works is with an example.
We'll develop it over three Try It Out examples, improving the pattern matching each time.

> Be careful with the `case` construct if you are using wildcards such as '*' in the pat-
> tern. The problem is that the first matching pattern will be taken, even if a later
> pattern matches more exactly.

Try It Out Case I: User Input

You can write a new version of the input-testing script and, using the case construct, make it a little more selective and forgiving of unexpected input:

```
#!/bin/sh

echo "Is it morning? Please answer yes or no"
read timeofday

case "$timeofday" in
    yes)   echo "Good Morning";;
    no )   echo "Good Afternoon";;
    y  )   echo "Good Morning";;
    n  )   echo "Good Afternoon";;
    *  )   echo "Sorry, answer not recognized";;
esac

exit 0
```

How It Works

When the case statement is executing, it takes the contents of timeofday and compares it to each string in turn. As soon as a string matches the input, the case command executes the code following the) and finishes.

The case command performs normal expansion on the strings that it's using for comparison. You can therefore specify part of a string followed by the * wildcard. Using a single * will match all possible strings, so always put one after the other matching strings to ensure that the case statement ends with some default action if no other strings are matched. This is possible because the case statement compares against each string in turn. It doesn't look for a best match, just the first match. The default condition often turns out to be the impossible condition, so using * can help in debugging scripts.

Try It Out Case II: Putting Patterns Together

The preceding case construction is clearly more elegant than the multiple if statement version, but by putting the patterns together, you can make a much cleaner version:

```
#!/bin/sh

echo "Is it morning? Please answer yes or no"
read timeofday

case "$timeofday" in
    yes | y | Yes | YES )    echo "Good Morning";;
    n* | N* )                echo "Good Afternoon";;
    * )                      echo "Sorry, answer not recognized";;
esac

exit 0
```

How It Works

This script uses multiple strings in each entry of the `case` so that `case` tests several different strings for each possible statement. This makes the script both shorter and, with practice, easier to read. This code also shows how the `*` wildcard can be used, although this may match unintended patterns. For example, if the user enters `never`, then this will be matched by `n*` and `Good Afternoon` will be displayed, which isn't the intended behavior. Note also that the `*` wildcard expression doesn't work within quotes.

Try It Out **Case III: Executing Multiple Statements**

Finally, to make the script reusable, you need to have a different exit value when the default pattern is used because the input was not understood:

```
#!/bin/sh

echo "Is it morning? Please answer yes or no"
read timeofday

case "$timeofday" in
    yes | y | Yes | YES )
            echo "Good Morning"
            echo "Up bright and early this morning"
            ;;
    [nN]*)
            echo "Good Afternoon"
            ;;
    *)
            echo "Sorry, answer not recognized"
            echo "Please answer yes or no"
            exit 1
            ;;
esac

exit 0
```

How It Works

To show a different way of pattern matching, this code changes the way in which the no case is matched. You also see how multiple statements can be executed for each pattern in the `case` statement. You must be careful to put the most explicit matches first and the most general match last. This is important because `case` executes the first match it finds, not the best match. If you put the `*)` first, it would always be matched, regardless of what was input.

Note that the `;;` *before* `esac` *is optional. Unlike C programming, where leaving out a break is poor programming practice, leaving out the final* `;;` *is no problem if the last case is the default because no other cases will be considered.*

To make the `case` matching more powerful, you could use something like this:

```
[yY] | [Yy][Ee][Ss] )
```

This restricts the permitted letters while allowing a variety of answers, and offers more control than the * wildcard.

Lists

Sometimes you want to connect commands in a series. For instance, you may want several different conditions to be met before you execute a statement:

```
if [ -f this_file ]; then
    if [ -f that_file ]; then
        if [ -f the_other_file ]; then
            echo "All files present, and correct"
        fi
    fi
fi
```

Or you might want at least one of a series of conditions to be true:

```
if [ -f this_file ]; then
    foo="True"
elif [ -f that_file ]; then
    foo="True"
elif [ -f the_other_file ]; then
    foo="True"
else
    foo="False"
fi
if [ "$foo" = "True" ]; then
    echo "One of the files exists"
fi
```

Although these can be implemented using multiple if statements, you can see that the results are awkward. The shell has a special pair of constructs for dealing with lists of commands: the AND list and the OR list. These are often used together, but we'll review their syntax separately.

The AND List

The AND list construct enables you to execute a series of commands, executing the next command only if all the previous commands have succeeded. The syntax is

```
statement1 && statement2 && statement3 && ...
```

Starting at the left, each statement is executed; if it returns true, the next statement to the right is executed. This continues until a statement returns false, after which no more statements in the list are executed. The && tests the condition of the preceding command.

Each statement is executed independently, enabling you to mix many different commands in a single list, as the following script shows. The AND list as a whole succeeds if all commands are executed successfully, but it fails otherwise.

Try It Out   AND Lists

In the following script, you touch file_one (to check whether it exists and create it if it doesn't) and then remove file_two. Then the AND list tests for the existence of each of the files and echoes some text in between.

```
#!/bin/sh

touch file_one
rm -f file_two

if [ -f file_one ] && echo "hello" && [ -f file_two ] && echo " there"
then
    echo "in if"
else
    echo "in else"
fi

exit 0
```

Try the script and you'll get the following result:

```
hello
in else
```

How It Works

The touch and rm commands ensure that the files in the current directory are in a known state. The && list then executes the [-f file_one] statement, which succeeds because you just made sure that the file existed. Because the previous statement succeeded, the echo command is executed. This also succeeds (echo always returns true). The third test, [-f file_two], is then executed. It fails because the file doesn't exist. Because the last command failed, the final echo statement isn't executed. The result of the && list is false because one of the commands in the list failed, so the if statement executes its else condition.

The OR List

The OR list construct enables us to execute a series of commands until one succeeds, and then not execute any more. The syntax is as follows:

```
statement1 || statement2 || statement3 || ...
```

Starting at the left, each statement is executed. If it returns false, then the next statement to the right is executed. This continues until a statement returns true, at which point no more statements are executed.

The || list is very similar to the && list, except that the rule for executing the next statement is that the previous statement must fail.

Try It Out   OR Lists

Copy the previous example and change the shaded lines in the following listing:

```
#!/bin/sh

rm -f file_one

if [ -f file_one ] || echo "hello" || echo " there"
then
    echo "in if"
else
    echo "in else"
fi

exit 0
```

This results in the following output:

```
hello
in if
```

How It Works

The first two lines simply set up the files for the rest of the script. The first command, `[ -f file_one ]`, fails because the file doesn't exist. The `echo` statement is then executed. Surprise, surprise — this returns `true`, and no more commands in the `||` list are executed. The `if` succeeds because one of the commands in the `||` list (the `echo`) was `true`.

The result of both of these constructs is the result of the last statement to be executed.

These list-type constructs execute in a similar way to those in C when multiple conditions are being tested. Only the minimum number of statements is executed to determine the result. Statements that can't affect the result are not executed. This is commonly referred to as *short circuit evaluation*.

Combining these two constructs is a logician's heaven. Try out the following:

```
[ -f file_one ] && command for true || command for false
```

This will execute the first command if the test succeeds and the second command otherwise. It's always best to experiment with these more unusual lists, and in general you should use braces to force the order of evaluation.

Statement Blocks

If you want to use multiple statements in a place where only one is allowed, such as in an AND or OR list, you can do so by enclosing them in braces {} to make a statement block. For example, in the application presented later in this chapter, you'll see the following code:

```
get_confirm && {
    grep -v "$cdcatnum" $tracks_file > $temp_file
```

```
    cat $temp_file > $tracks_file
    echo
    add_record_tracks
}
```

Functions

You can define functions in the shell; and if you write shell scripts of any size, you'll want to use them to structure your code.

> As an alternative, you could break a large script into lots of smaller scripts, each of which performs a small task. This has some drawbacks: Executing a second script from within a script is much slower than executing a function. It's more difficult to pass back results, and there can be a very large number of small scripts. You should consider the smallest part of your script that sensibly stands alone and use that as your measure of when to break a large script into a collection of smaller ones.

To define a shell function, simply write its name followed by empty parentheses and enclose the statements in braces:

```
function_name () {
    statements
}
```

Try It Out   A Simple Function

Let's start with a really simple function:

```
#!/bin/sh

foo() {
    echo "Function foo is executing"
}

echo "script starting"
foo
echo "script ended"

exit 0
```

Running the script will output the following:

```
script starting
Function foo is executing
script ending
```

How It Works

This script starts executing at the top, so nothing is different there, but when it finds the `foo() {` construct, it knows that a function called `foo` is being defined. It stores the fact that `foo` refers to a function and continues executing after the matching `}`. When the single line `foo` is executed, the shell knows to execute the previously defined function. When this function completes, execution resumes at the line after the call to `foo`.

You must always define a function before you can invoke it, a little like the Pascal style of function definition before invocation, except that there are no forward declarations in the shell. This isn't a problem, because all scripts start executing at the top, so simply putting all the functions before the first call of any function will always cause all functions to be defined before they can be invoked.

When a function is invoked, the positional parameters to the script, `$*`, `$@`, `$#`, `$1`, `$2`, and so on, are replaced by the parameters to the function. That's how you read the parameters passed to the function. When the function finishes, they are restored to their previous values.

> **Some older shells may not restore the value of positional parameters after functions execute. It's wise not to rely on this behavior if you want your scripts to be portable.**

You can make functions return numeric values using the `return` command. The usual way to make functions return strings is for the function to store the string in a variable, which can then be used after the function finishes. Alternatively, you can `echo` a string and catch the result, like this:

```
foo () { echo JAY;}

...

result="$(foo)"
```

Note that you can declare local variables within shell functions by using the `local` keyword. The variable is then only in scope within the function. Otherwise, the function can access the other shell variables that are essentially global in scope. If a local variable has the same name as a global variable, it overlays that variable, but only within the function. For example, you can make the following changes to the preceding script to see this in action:

```
#!/bin/sh

sample_text="global variable"

foo() {

    local sample_text="local variable"
    echo "Function foo is executing"
    echo $sample_text
}

echo "script starting"
echo $sample_text
```

```
    foo

    echo "script ended"
    echo $sample_text

    exit 0
```

In the absence of a `return` command specifying a return value, a function returns the exit status of the last command executed.

Returning a Value

The next script, `my_name`, shows how parameters to a function are passed and how functions can return a `true` or `false` result. You call this script with a parameter of the name you want to use in the question.

1. After the shell header, define the function `yes_or_no`:

```
#!/bin/sh

yes_or_no() {
    echo "Is your name $* ?"
    while true
    do
      echo -n "Enter yes or no: "
      read x
      case "$x" in
        y | yes ) return 0;;
        n | no )  return 1;;
        * )       echo "Answer yes or no"
      esac
    done
}
```

2. Then the main part of the program begins:

```
echo "Original parameters are $*"

if yes_or_no "$1"
then
  echo "Hi $1, nice name"
else
  echo "Never mind"
fi
exit 0
```

Typical output from this script might be as follows:

```
$ ./my_name Rick Neil
Original parameters are Rick Neil
Is your name Rick ?
```

```
Enter yes or no: yes
Hi Rick, nice name
$
```

How It Works

As the script executes, the function yes_or_no is defined but not yet executed. In the if statement, the script executes the function yes_or_no, passing the rest of the line as parameters to the function after substituting the $1 with the first parameter to the original script, Rick. The function uses these parameters, which are now stored in the positional parameters $1, $2, and so on, and returns a value to the caller. Depending on the return value, the if construct executes the appropriate statement.

As you've seen, the shell has a rich set of control structures and conditional statements. You need to learn some of the commands that are built into the shell; then you'll be ready to tackle a real programming problem with no compiler in sight!

Commands

You can execute two types of commands from inside a shell script. There are "normal" commands that you could also execute from the command prompt (called *external commands*), and there are "built-in" commands (called *internal commands*), as mentioned earlier. Built-in commands are implemented internally to the shell and can't be invoked as external programs. However, most internal commands are also provided as standalone programs — this requirement is part of the POSIX specification. It generally doesn't matter if the command is internal or external, except that internal commands execute more efficiently.

Here we'll cover only the main commands, both internal and external, that we use when we're programming scripts. As a Linux user, you probably know many other commands that are valid at the command prompt. Always remember that you can use any of these in a script in addition to the built-in commands presented here.

break

Use break for escaping from an enclosing for, while, or until loop before the controlling condition has been met. You can give break an additional numeric parameter, which is the number of loops to break out of, but this can make scripts very hard to read, so we don't suggest you use it. By default, break escapes a single level.

```
#!/bin/sh

rm -rf fred*
echo > fred1
echo > fred2
mkdir fred3
echo > fred4

for file in fred*
do
    if [ -d "$file" ]; then
        break;
```

```
      fi
done

echo first directory starting fred was $file

rm -rf fred*
exit 0
```

The : Command

The colon command is a null command. It's occasionally useful to simplify the logic of conditions, being an alias for true. Since it's built-in, : runs faster than true, though its output is also much less readable.

You may see it used as a condition for while loops; while : implements an infinite loop in place of the more common while true.

The : construct is also useful in the conditional setting of variables. For example,

```
: ${var:=value}
```

Without the :, the shell would try to evaluate $var as a command.

> In some, mostly older, shell scripts, you may see the colon used at the start of a line to introduce a comment, but modern scripts should always use # to start a comment line because this executes more efficiently.

```
#!/bin/sh

rm -f fred
if [ -f fred ]; then
    :
else
    echo file fred did not exist
fi

exit 0
```

continue

Rather like the C statement of the same name, this command makes the enclosing for, while, or until loop continue at the next iteration, with the loop variable taking the next value in the list:

```
#!/bin/sh

rm -rf fred*
echo > fred1
echo > fred2
mkdir fred3
echo > fred4
```

```
for file in fred*
do
    if [ -d "$file" ]; then
        echo "skipping directory $file"
      continue
    fi
    echo file is $file
done

rm -rf fred*
exit 0
```

continue can take the enclosing loop number at which to resume as an optional parameter so that you can partially jump out of nested loops. This parameter is rarely used, as it often makes scripts much harder to understand. For example,

```
for x in 1 2 3
do
  echo before $x
  continue 1
  echo after $x
done
```

The output for the preceding will be

```
before 1
before 2
before 3
```

The . Command

The dot (.) command executes the command in the current shell:

```
. ./shell_script
```

Normally, when a script executes an external command or script, a new environment (a subshell) is created, the command is executed in the new environment, and the environment is then discarded apart from the exit code that is returned to the parent shell. However, the external source and the dot command (two more synonyms) run the commands listed in a script in the same shell that called the script.

Because, by default, a new environment is created when a shell script is executed, any changes to environment variables that the script makes are lost. The dot command, on the other hand, allows the executed script to change the current environment. This is often useful when you use a script as a wrapper to set up your environment for the later execution of some other command. For example, when you're working on several different projects at the same time, you may find you need to invoke commands with different parameters, perhaps to invoke an older version of the compiler for maintaining an old program.

In shell scripts, the dot command works a little like the #include directive in C or C++. Though it doesn't literally include the script, it does execute the command in the current context, so you can use it to incorporate variable and function definitions into a script.

The Dot Command

The following example uses the dot command on the command line, but you can just as well use it within a script:

1. Suppose you have two files containing the environment settings for two different development environments. To set the environment for the old, classic commands, classic_set, you could use the following:

```
#!/bin/sh

version=classic
PATH=/usr/local/old_bin:/usr/bin:/bin:.
PS1="classic> "
```

2. For the new commands, use latest_set:

```
#!/bin/sh

version=latest
PATH=/usr/local/new_bin:/usr/bin:/bin:.
PS1=" latest version> "
```

You can set the environment by using these scripts in conjunction with the dot command, as in the following sample session:

```
$ . ./classic_set
classic> echo $version
classic
classic> . /latest_set
latest version> echo $version
latest
latest version>
```

How It Works

The scripts are executed using the dot command, so each script is executed in the current shell. This enables the script to change environment settings in the current shell, which remains changed even when the script finishes executing.

---

echo

Despite the X/Open exhortation to use the printf command in modern shells, we've been following common practice by using the echo command to output a string followed by a newline character.

A common problem is how to suppress the newline character. Unfortunately, different versions of UNIX have implemented different solutions. The common method in Linux is to use

```
echo -n "string to output"
```

but you'll often come across

```
echo -e "string to output\c"
```

The second option, echo -e, ensures that the interpretation of backslashed escape characters, such as \c for suppressing a newline, \t for outputting a tab and \n for outputting carriage returns, is enabled. In older versions of bash this was often set by default, but more recent versions often default to not interpreting backslashed escape characters. See the manual pages for details of the behavior on your distribution.

> If you need a portable way to remove the trailing newline, you can use the external tr command to get rid of it, but it will execute somewhat more slowly. If you need portability to UNIX systems, it's generally better to stick to printf if you need to lose the newline. If your scripts need to work only on Linux and bash, echo -n should be fine, though you may need to start the file with #!/bin/bash, to make it explicit that you desire bash-style behavior.

eval

The eval command enables you to evaluate arguments. It's built into the shell and doesn't normally exist as a separate command. It's probably best demonstrated with a short example borrowed from the X/Open specification itself:

```
foo=10
x=foo
y='$'$x
echo $y
```

This gives the output $foo. However,

```
foo=10
x=foo
eval y='$'$x
echo $y
```

gives the output 10. Thus, eval is a bit like an extra $: It gives you the value of the value of a variable.

The eval command is very useful, enabling code to be generated and run on-the-fly. It does complicate script debugging, but it enables you to do things that are otherwise difficult or even impossible.

exec

The exec command has two different uses. Its typical use is to replace the current shell with a different program. For example,

```
exec wall "Thanks for all the fish"
```

in a script will replace the current shell with the wall command. No lines in the script after the exec will be processed, because the shell that was executing the script no longer exists.

The second use of exec is to modify the current file descriptors:

```
exec 3< afile
```

This causes file descriptor three to be opened for reading from file afile. It's rarely used.

exit n

The exit command causes the script to exit with exit code n. If you use it at the command prompt of any interactive shell, it will log you out. If you allow your script to exit without specifying an exit status, then the status of the last command executed in the script is used as the return value. It's always good practice to supply an exit code.

In shell script programming, exit code 0 is success, and codes 1 through 125, inclusive, are error codes that can be used by scripts. The remaining values have reserved meanings, as shown in the following table:

Exit Code	Description
126	The file was not executable
127	A command was not found
128 and above	A signal occurred

Using zero as success may seem a little unusual to many C or C++ programmers. The big advantage in scripts is that they enable you to use 125 user-defined error codes without the need for a global error code variable.

Here's a simple example that returns success if a file called .profile exists in the current directory:

```
#!/bin/sh

if [ -f .profile ]; then
    exit 0
fi

exit 1
```

If you're a glutton for punishment, or at least for terse scripts, you can rewrite this script using the combined AND and OR list shown earlier, all on one line:

```
[ -f .profile ] && exit 0 || exit 1
```

export

The export command makes the variable named as its parameter available in subshells. By default, variables created in a shell are not available in further (sub)shells invoked from that shell. The export command creates an environment variable from its parameter that can be seen by other scripts and programs invoked from the current program. More technically, the exported variables form the environment variables in any child processes derived from the shell. This is best illustrated with an example of two scripts, export1 and export2.

Try It Out   **Exporting Variables**

1. First, list `export2`:

```
#!/bin/sh

echo "$foo"
echo "$bar"
```

2. Now for `export1`. At the end of this script, invoke `export2`:

```
#!/bin/sh

foo="The first meta-syntactic variable"
export bar="The second meta-syntactic variable"

export2
```

If you run these, you get the following:

```
$ ./export1

The second meta-syntactic variable
$
```

How It Works

The `export2` script simply echoes the values of the two variables. The `export1` script sets both the variables, but only marks `bar` as exported, so when it subsequently invokes `export1`, the value of `foo` has been lost, but the value of `bar` has been exported to the second script. The blank line occurs because `$foo` evaluated to nothing, and echoing a `null` variable gives a newline.

Once a variable has been exported from a shell, it's exported to any scripts invoked from that shell and to any shell they invoke in turn, and so on. If the script `export2` called another script, it would also have the value of `bar` available to it.

> The commands `set -a` or `set -allexport` **will export all variables thereafter.**

---

expr

The `expr` command evaluates its arguments as an expression. It's most commonly used for simple arithmetic in the following form:

```
x=`expr $x + 1`
```

The `` (backtick) characters make x take the result of executing the command `expr $x + 1`. You could also write it using the syntax `$( )` rather than backticks, like this:

```
x=$(expr $x + 1)
```

The `expr` command is powerful and can perform many expression evaluations. The principal ones are shown in the following table:

Expression Evaluation	Description
expr1 | expr2	expr1 if expr1 is nonzero, otherwise expr2
expr1 & expr2	Zero if either expression is zero, otherwise expr1
expr1 = expr2	Equal
expr1 > expr2	Greater than
expr1 >= expr2	Greater than or equal to
expr1 < expr2	Less than
expr1 <= expr2	Less than or equal to
expr1 != expr2	Not equal
expr1 + expr2	Addition
expr1 - expr2	Subtraction
expr1 * expr2	Multiplication
expr1 / expr2	Integer division
expr1 % expr2	Integer modulo

In newer scripts, the use of `expr` is normally replaced with the more efficient `$((...))` syntax, which is covered later in the chapter.

printf

The `printf` command is available only in more recent shells. X/Open suggests that it should be used in preference to `echo` for generating formatted output, though few people seem to follow this advice.

The syntax is

```
printf "format string" parameter1 parameter2 ...
```

The format string is very similar to that used in C or C++, with some restrictions. Principally, floating point isn't supported, because all arithmetic in the shell is performed as integers. The format string consists of any combination of literal characters, escape sequences, and conversion specifiers. All characters in the format string other than % and \ appear literally in the output.

The following escape sequences are supported:

Escape Sequence	Description
\"	Double quote
\\	Backslash character
\a	Alert (ring the bell or beep)
\b	Backspace character
\c	Suppress further output
\f	Form feed character
\n	Newline character
\r	Carriage return
\t	Tab character
\v	Vertical tab character
\ooo	The single character with octal value ooo
\xHH	The single character with the hexadecimal value HH

The conversion specifier is quite complex, so we list only the common usage here. More details can be found in the bash online manual or in the `printf` pages from section 1 of the online manual (`man 1 printf`). (If you can't find it in section 1 of the manual, try section 3 as an alternative). The conversion specifier consists of a % character, followed by a conversion character. The principal conversions are shown in the following table:

Conversion Specifier	Description
D	Output a decimal number.
C	Output a character.
S	Output a string.
%	Output the % character.

The format string is then used to interpret the remaining parameters and output the result, as shown in the following example,

```
$ printf "%s\n" hello
hello
$ printf "%s %d\t%s" "Hi There" 15 people
Hi There 15    people
```

Notice you must use " " to protect the Hi There string and make it a single parameter.

return

The return command causes functions to return, as mentioned when we looked at functions earlier. return takes a single numeric parameter that is available to the script calling the function. If no parameter is specified, then return defaults to the exit code of the last command.

set

The set command sets the parameter variables for the shell. It can be a useful way of using fields in commands that output space-separated values.

Suppose you want to use the name of the current month in a shell script. The system provides a date command, which contains the month as a string, but you need to separate it from the other fields. You can do this using a combination of the set command and the $(...) construct to execute the date command and return the result (described in more detail very soon). The date command output has the month string as its second parameter:

```
#!/bin/sh

echo the date is $(date)
set $(date)
echo The month is $2

exit 0
```

This program sets the parameter list to the date command's output and then uses the positional parameter $2 to get at the month.

Notice that we used the date command as a simple example to show how to extract positional parameters. Since the date command is sensitive to the language locale, in reality you would have extracted the name of the month using date +%B. The date command has many other formatting options; see the manual page for more details.

You can also use the set command to control the way the shell executes by passing it parameters. The most commonly used form of the command is set -x, which makes a script display a trace of its currently executing command. We discuss set and more of its options when we look at debugging, later in the chapter.

shift

The shift command moves all the parameter variables down by one, so that $2 becomes $1, $3 becomes $2, and so on. The previous value of $1 is discarded, while $0 remains unchanged. If a numerical parameter is specified in the call to shift, the parameters move that many spaces. The other variables, $*, $@, and $#, are also modified in line with the new arrangement of parameter variables.

shift is often useful for scanning through parameters passed into a script, and if your script requires 10 or more parameters, you'll need shift to access the tenth and beyond.

For example, you can scan through all the positional parameters like this:

```
#!/bin/sh

while [ "$1" != "" ]; do
    echo "$1"
    shift
done

exit 0
```

trap

The `trap` command is used to specify the actions to take on receipt of signals, which you'll meet in more detail later in the book. A common use is to tidy up a script when it is interrupted. Historically, shells always used numbers for the signals, but new scripts should use names taken from the `#include` file `signal.h`, with the `SIG` prefix omitted. To see the signal numbers and associated names, you can just type `trap -l` at a command prompt.

> **For those not familiar with signals, they are events sent asynchronously to a program. By default, they normally cause the program to terminate.**

The `trap` command is passed the action to take, followed by the signal name (or names) to trap on:

trap command signal

Remember that the scripts are normally interpreted from top to bottom, so you must specify the `trap` command before the part of the script you wish to protect.

To reset a trap condition to the default, simply specify the command as -. To ignore a signal, set the command to the empty string ' '. A `trap` command with no parameters prints out the current list of traps and actions.

The following table lists the more important signals covered by the X/Open standard that can be caught (with the conventional signal number in parentheses). More details can be found in the `signal` manual pages in section 7 of the online manual (`man 7 signal`).

Signal	Description
HUP (1)	Hang up; usually sent when a terminal goes offline, or a user logs out
INT (2)	Interrupt; usually sent by pressing Ctrl+C
QUIT (3)	Quit; usually sent by pressing Ctrl+\
ABRT (6)	Abort; usually sent on some serious execution error
ALRM (14)	Alarm; usually used for handling timeouts
TERM (15)	Terminate; usually sent by the system when it's shutting down

Try It Out   **Trapping Signals**

The following script demonstrates some simple signal handling:

```
#!/bin/sh

trap 'rm -f /tmp/my_tmp_file_$$' INT
echo creating file /tmp/my_tmp_file_$$
date > /tmp/my_tmp_file_$$

echo "press interrupt (CTRL-C) to interrupt ...."
while [ -f /tmp/my_tmp_file_$$ ]; do
    echo File exists
    sleep 1
done
echo The file no longer exists

trap INT
echo creating file /tmp/my_tmp_file_$$
date >  /tmp/my_tmp_file_$$

echo "press interrupt (control-C) to interrupt ...."
while [ -f /tmp/my_tmp_file_$$ ]; do
    echo File exists
    sleep 1
done

echo we never get here
exit 0
```

If you run this script, holding down Ctrl and then pressing C (or whatever your interrupt key combination is) in each of the loops, you get the following output:

```
creating file /tmp/my_tmp_file_141
press interrupt (CTRL-C) to interrupt ....
File exists
File exists
File exists
File exists
The file no longer exists
creating file /tmp/my_tmp_file_141
press interrupt (CTRL-C) to interrupt ....
File exists
File exists
File exists
File exists
```

How It Works

This script uses the `trap` command to arrange for the command `rm -f /tmp/my_tmp_file_$$` to be executed when an `INT` (interrupt) signal occurs. The script then enters a `while` loop that continues while the file exists. When the user presses Ctrl+C, the statement `rm -f /tmp/my_tmp_file_$$` is executed, and then the `while` loop resumes. Since the file has now been deleted, the first `while` loop terminates normally.

The script then uses the `trap` command again, this time to specify that no command be executed when an `INT` signal occurs. It then re-creates the file and loops inside the second `while` statement. When the user presses Ctrl+C this time, no statement is configured to execute, so the default behavior occurs, which is to immediately terminate the script. Because the script terminates immediately, the final `echo` and `exit` statements are never executed.

---

unset

The `unset` command removes variables or functions from the environment. It can't do this to read-only variables defined by the shell itself, such as IFS. It's not often used.

The following script writes `Hello World` once and a newline the second time:

```sh
#!/bin/sh

foo="Hello World"
echo $foo

unset foo
echo $foo
```

> Writing `foo=` would have a very similar, but not identical, effect to `unset` in the preceding program. Writing `foo=` has the effect of setting `foo` to null, but `foo` still exists. Using `unset foo` has the effect of removing the variable `foo` from the environment.

Two More Useful Commands and Regular Expressions

Before you see how to put this new knowledge of shell programming to use, let's look at a couple of other very useful commands, which, although not part of the shell, are often useful when writing shell programs. Along the way we will also be looking at regular expressions, a pattern-matching feature that crops up all over Linux and its associated programs.

The find Command

The first command you will look at is `find`. This command, which you use to search for files, is extremely useful, but newcomers to Linux often find it a little tricky to use, not least because it takes options, tests, and action-type arguments, and the results of one argument can affect the processing of subsequent arguments.

Before delving into the options, tests, and arguments, let's look at a very simple example for the file `test` on your local machine. Do this as root to ensure that you have permissions to search the whole machine:

```
# find / -name test -print
/usr/bin/test
#
```

Depending on your installation, you may well find several other files also called `test`. As you can probably guess, this says "search starting at / for a file named *test* and then print out the name of the file." Easy, wasn't it? Of course.

However, it did take quite a while to run on our machine, and the disk on our Windows machine on the network rattled away as well. This is because our Linux machine mounts (using SAMBA) a chunk of the Windows machine's file system. It seems like that might have been searched as well, even though we knew the file we were looking for would be on the Linux machine.

This is where the first of the options comes in. If you specify -mount, you can tell `find` not to search mounted directories:

```
# find / -mount -name test -print
/usr/bin/test
#
```

We still find the file on our machine, but faster this time, and without searching other mounted file systems.

The full syntax for the `find` command is as follows:

```
find [path] [options] [tests] [actions]
```

The `path` part is nice and easy: You can use either an absolute path, such as /bin, or a relative path, such as .. If you need to, you can also specify multiple paths — for example, `find /var /home`.

There are several options; the main ones are shown in the following table:

Option	Meaning
-depth	Search the contents of a directory before looking at the directory itself.
-follow	Follow symbolic links.
-maxdepths N	Search at most N levels of the directory when searching.
-mount (or -xdev)	Don't search directories on other file systems.

Now for the tests. A large number of tests can be given to `find`, and each test returns either `true` or `false`. When `find` is working, it considers each file it finds in turn and applies each test, in the order they were defined, on that file. If a test returns `false`, then `find` stops considering the file it is currently looking at and moves on; if the test returns `true`, then `find` processes the next test or action on the current file. The tests listed in the following table are just the most common; consult the manual pages for the extensive list of possible tests you can apply using `find`.

Test	Meaning
-atime N	The file was last accessed N days ago.
-mtime N	The file was last modified N days ago.
-name pattern	The name of the file, excluding any path, matches the pattern provided. To ensure that the pattern is passed to find, and not evaluated by the shell immediately, the pattern must always be in quotes.
-newer otherfile	The file is newer than the file otherfile.
-type C	The file is of type C, where C can be of a particular type; the most common are "d" for a directory and "f" for a regular file. For other types consult the manual pages.
-user username	The file is owned by the user with the given name.

You can also combine tests using operators. Most have two forms: a short form and a longer form, as shown in the following table:

Operator, Short Form	Operator, Long Form	Meaning
!	-not	Invert the test.
-a	-and	Both tests must be true.
-o	-or	Either test must be true.

You can force the precedence of tests and operators by using parentheses. Since these have a special meaning to the shell, you also have to quote the braces using a backslash. In addition, if you use a pattern for the filename, then you must use quotes so that the name is not expanded by the shell but passed directly to the find command. For example, if you wanted to write the test "newer than file X or called a name that starts with an underscore," you could write the following test:

```
\(-newer X -o -name "_*" \)
```

We present an example just after the next "How it Works" section.

Try It Out   Using find with Tests

Try searching in the current directory for files modified more recently than the file while2:

```
$ find . -newer while2 -print
.
./elif3
./words.txt
./words2.txt
./_trap
$
```

That looks good, except that you also find the current directory, which you didn't want. You were interested only in regular files, so you add an additional test, -type f:

```
$ find . -newer while2 -type f -print
./elif3
./words.txt
./words2.txt
./_trap
$
```

How It Works

How did it work? You specified that find should search in the current directory (.), for files newer than the file while2 (-newer while2) and that, if that test passed, then to also test that the file was a regular file (-type f). Finally, you used the action you already met, -print, just to confirm which files were found.

Now find files that either start with an underscore or are newer than the file while2, but must in either case be regular files. This will show you how to combine tests using parentheses:

```
$ find . \( -name "_*" -or -newer while2 \) -type f -print
./elif3
./words.txt
./words2.txt
./_break
./_if
./_set
./_shift
./_trap
./_unset
./_until
$
```

That wasn't so hard, was it? You had to escape the parentheses so that they were not processed by the shell, and quote the * so that it was passed directly into find as well.

Now that you can reliably search for files, look at the actions you can perform when you find a file matching your specification. Again, this is just a list of the most common actions; the manual page has the full set.

Action	Meaning
-exec command	Execute a command. This is one of the most common actions. See the explanation following this table for how parameters may be passed to the command. This action must be terminated with a \; character pair.
-ok command	Like -exec, except that it prompts for user confirmation of each file on which it will carry out the command before executing the command. This action must be terminated with a \; character pair.
-print	Print out the name of the file.
-ls	Use the command ls -dils on the current file.

The -exec and -ok commands take subsequent parameters on the line as part of their parameters, until terminated with a \; sequence. Effectively, the -exec and -ok commands are executing an embedded command, so that embedded command has to be terminated with an escaped semicolon so that the find command can determine when it should resume looking for command-line options that are intended for itself. The magic string "{}" is a special type of parameter to an -exec or -ok command and is replaced with the full path to the current file.

That explanation is perhaps not so easy to understand, but an example should make things clearer. Take a look at a simple example, using a nice safe command like ls:

```
$ find . -newer while2 -type f -exec ls -l {} \;
-rwxr-xr-x    1 rick     rick          275 Feb  8 17:07 ./elif3
-rwxr-xr-x    1 rick     rick          336 Feb  8 16:52 ./words.txt
-rwxr-xr-x    1 rick     rick         1274 Feb  8 16:52 ./words2.txt
-rwxr-xr-x    1 rick     rick          504 Feb  8 18:43 ./_trap
$
```

As you can see, the find command is extremely useful; it just takes a little practice to use it well. However, that practice will pay dividends, so do experiment with the find command.

The grep Command

The second very useful command to look at is grep, an unusual name that stands for *general regular expression parser*. You use find to search your system for files, but you use grep to search files for strings. Indeed, it's quite common to have grep as a command passed after -exec when using find.

The grep command takes options, a pattern to match, and files to search in:

```
grep [options] PATTERN [FILES]
```

If no filenames are given, it searches standard input.

Let's start by looking at the principal options to grep. Again we list only the principal options here; see the manual pages for the full list.

Option	Meaning
-c	Rather than print matching lines, print a count of the number of lines that match.
-E	Turn on extended expressions.
-h	Suppress the normal prefixing of each output line with the name of the file it was found in.
-i	Ignore case.
-l	List the names of the files with matching lines; don't output the actual matched line.
-v	Invert the matching pattern to select nonmatching lines, rather than matching lines.

Try It Out   Basic grep Usage

Take a look at grep in action with some simple matches:

```
$ grep in words.txt
When shall we three meet again.  In thunder, lightning, or in rain?
I come, Graymalkin!
$ grep -c in words.txt words2.txt
words.txt:2
words2.txt:14
$ grep -c -v in words.txt words2.txt
words.txt:9
words2.txt:16
$
```

How It Works

The first example uses no options; it simply searches for the string "in" in the file words.txt and prints out any lines that match. The filename isn't printed because you are searching on just a single file.

The second example counts the number of matching lines in two different files. In this case, the filenames are printed out.

Finally, use the -v option to invert the search and count lines in the two files that don't match.

Regular Expressions

As you have seen, the basic usage of grep is very easy to master. Now it's time to look at the basics of regular expressions, which enable you to do more sophisticated matching. As mentioned earlier in the chapter, regular expressions are used in Linux and many other open-source languages. You can use them in the vi editor and in writing Perl scripts, with the basic principles common wherever they appear.

During the use of regular expressions, certain characters are processed in a special way. The most frequently used are shown in the following table:

Character	Meaning
^	Anchor to the beginning of a line
$	Anchor to the end of a line
.	Any single character
[ ]	The square braces contain a range of characters, any one of which may be matched, such as a range of characters like a–e or an inverted range by preceding the range with a ^ symbol.

If you want to use any of these characters as "normal" characters, precede them with a \. For example, if you wanted to look for a literal "$" character, you would simply use \$.

There are also some useful special match patterns that can be used in square braces, as described in the following table:

Match Pattern	Meaning
[:alnum:]	Alphanumeric characters
[:alpha:]	Letters
[:ascii:]	ASCII characters
[:blank:]	Space or tab
[:cntrl:]	ASCII control characters
[:digit:]	Digits
[:graph:]	Noncontrol, nonspace characters
[:lower:]	Lowercase letters
[:print:]	Printable characters
[:punct:]	Punctuation characters
[:space:]	Whitespace characters, including vertical tab
[:upper:]	Uppercase letters
[:xdigit:]	Hexadecimal digits

In addition, if the -E for extended matching is also specified, other characters that control the completion of matching may follow the regular expression (see the following table). With grep it is also necessary to precede these characters with a \.

Option	Meaning
?	Match is optional but may be matched at most once
*	Must be matched zero or more times
+	Must be matched one or more times
{n}	Must be matched n times
{n,}	Must be matched n or more times
{n,m}	Must be matched between n or m times, inclusive

That all looks a little complex, but if you take it in stages, you will see it's not as complex as it perhaps looks at first sight. The easiest way to get the hang of regular expressions is simply to try a few:

1. Start by looking for lines that end with the letter *e*. You can probably guess you need to use the special character $:

```
$ grep  e$ words2.txt
Art thou not, fatal vision, sensible
I see thee yet, in form as palpable
Nature seems dead, and wicked dreams abuse
$
```

As you can see, this finds lines that end in the letter *e*.

2. Now suppose you want to find words that end with the letter *a*. To do this, you need to use the special match characters in braces. In this case, you use [[:blank:]], which tests for a space or a tab:

```
$ grep a[[:blank:]] words2.txt
Is this a dagger which I see before me,
A dagger of the mind, a false creation,
Moves like a ghost. Thou sure and firm-set earth,
$
```

3. Now look for three-letter words that start with *Th*. In this case, you need both [[:space:]] to delimit the end of the word and . to match a single additional character:

```
$ grep Th.[[:space:]] words2.txt
The handle toward my hand? Come, let me clutch thee.
The curtain'd sleep; witchcraft celebrates
Thy very stones prate of my whereabout,
$
```

4. Finally, use the extended grep mode to search for lowercase words that are exactly 10 characters long. Do this by specifying a range of characters to match *a* to *z*, and a repetition of 10 matches:

```
$ grep -E [a-z]\{10\} words2.txt
Proceeding from the heat-oppressed brain?
And such an instrument I was to use.
The curtain'd sleep; witchcraft celebrates
Thy very stones prate of my whereabout,
$
```

This only touches on the more important parts of regular expressions. As with most things in Linux, there is a lot more documentation out there to help you discover more details, but the best way of learning about regular expressions is to experiment.

Command Execution

When you're writing scripts, you often need to capture the result of a command's execution for use in the shell script; that is, you want to execute a command and put the output of the command into a variable.

You can do this by using the $(command) syntax introduced in the earlier set command example. There is also an older form, `command`, that is still in common usage.

> **Note that with the older form of the command execution, the backtick, or backquote, (`), is used, not the single quote (') that we used in earlier shell quoting (to protect against variable expansion). Use this form for shell scripts only when you need them to be very portable.**

All new scripts should use the $(...) form, which was introduced to avoid some rather complex rules covering the use of the characters $, ` , and \ inside the backquoted command. If a backtick is used within the `...` construct, it must be escaped with a \ character. These relatively obscure characters often confuse programmers, and sometimes even experienced shell programmers are forced to experiment to get the quoting correct in backticked commands.

The result of the $(command) is simply the output from the command. Note that this isn't the return status of the command but the string output, as shown here:

```
#!/bin/sh

echo The current directory is $PWD
echo The current users are $(who)

exit 0
```

Since the current directory is a shell environment variable, the first line doesn't need to use this command execution construct. The result of who, however, does need this construct if it is to be available to the script.

If you want to get the result into a variable, you can just assign it in the usual way:

```
whoisthere=$(who)
echo $whoisthere
```

The capability to put the result of a command into a script variable is very powerful, as it makes it easy to use existing commands in scripts and capture their output. If you ever find yourself trying to convert a set of parameters that are the output of a command on standard output and capture them as arguments for a program, you may well find the command xargs can do it for you. Look in the manual pages for further details.

A problem sometimes arises when the command you want to invoke outputs some white space before the text you want, or more output than you require. In such a case, you can use the set command as shown earlier.

Arithmetic Expansion

We've already used the expr command, which enables simple arithmetic commands to be processed, but this is quite slow to execute because a new shell is invoked to process the expr command.

A newer and better alternative is $((...))$ expansion. By enclosing the expression you wish to evaluate in $((...))$, you can perform simple arithmetic much more efficiently:

```
#!/bin/sh

x=0
while [ "$x" -ne 10 ]; do
    echo $x
    x=$(($x+1))
done

exit 0
```

> Notice that this is subtly different from the x=$(...) command. The double paren-
> theses are used for arithmetic substitution. The single parentheses form shown ear-
> lier is used for executing commands and grabbing the output.

Parameter Expansion

You've seen the simplest form of parameter assignment and expansion:

```
foo=fred
echo $foo
```

A problem occurs when you want to append extra characters to the end of a variable. Suppose you want to write a short script to process files called 1_tmp and 2_tmp. You could try this:

```
#!/bin/sh

for i in 1 2
do
    my_secret_process $i_tmp
done
```

But on each loop, you'll get the following:

```
my_secret_process: too few arguments
```

What went wrong?

The problem is that the shell tried to substitute the value of the variable $i_tmp, which doesn't exist. The shell doesn't consider this an error; it just substitutes nothing, so no parameters at all were passed to my_secret_process. To protect the expansion of the $i part of the variable, you need to enclose the i in braces like this:

```
#!/bin/sh

for i in 1 2
do
    my_secret_process ${i}_tmp
done
```

On each loop, the value of i is substituted for ${i} to give the actual filenames. You substitute the value of the parameter into a string.

You can perform many parameter substitutions in the shell. Often, these provide an elegant solution to many parameter-processing problems. The common ones are shown in the following table:

Parameter Expansion	Description
${param:-default}	If param is null, then set it to the value of default.
${#param}	Gives the length of param
${param%word}	From the end, removes the smallest part of param that matches word and returns the rest
${param%%word}	From the end, removes the longest part of param that matches word and returns the rest
${param#word}	From the beginning, removes the smallest part of param that matches word and returns the rest
${param##word}	From the beginning, removes the longest part of param that matches word and returns the rest

These substitutions are often useful when you're working with strings. The last four, which remove parts of strings, are especially useful for processing filenames and paths, as the following example shows.

Try It Out   Parameter Processing

Each portion of the following script illustrates the parameter-matching operators:

```
#!/bin/sh

unset foo
echo ${foo:-bar}

foo=fud
echo ${foo:-bar}

foo=/usr/bin/X11/startx
echo ${foo#*/}
echo ${foo##*/}

bar=/usr/local/etc/local/networks
echo ${bar%local*}
echo ${bar%%local*}

exit 0
```

This gives the following output:

```
bar
fud
usr/bin/X11/startx
startx
/usr/local/etc
/usr
```

How It Works

The first statement, `${foo:-bar}`, gives the value `bar`, because `foo` had no value when the statement was executed. The variable `foo` is unchanged, as it remains unset.

> `${foo:=bar}`, however, would set the variable to `$foo`. This string operator checks that `foo` exists and isn't `null`. If it isn't `null`, then it returns its value, but otherwise it sets `foo` to `bar` and returns that instead.
>
> `${foo:?bar}` will print `foo: bar` and abort the command if `foo` doesn't exist or is set to null. Lastly, `${foo:+bar}` returns `bar` if `foo` exists and isn't `null`. What a set of choices!

The `{foo#*/}` statement matches and removes only the left / (remember * matches zero or more characters). The `{foo##*/}` matches and removes as much as possible, so it removes the rightmost / and all the characters before it.

The `{bar%local*}` statement matches characters from the right until the first occurrence of `local` (followed by any number of characters) is matched, but the `{bar%%local*}` matches as many characters as possible from the right until it finds the leftmost `local`.

Since both UNIX and Linux are based heavily around the idea of filters, the result of one operation must often be redirected manually. Let's say you want to convert a GIF file into a JPEG file using the `cjpeg` program:

```
$ cjpeg image.gif > image.jpg
```

Sometimes you may want to perform this type of operation on a large number of files. How do you automate the redirection? It's as easy as this:

```
#!/bin/sh

for image in  *.gif
do
  cjpeg $image > ${image%%gif}jpg
done
```

This script, `giftojpeg`, creates a JPEG file for each GIF file in the current directory.

Here Documents

One special way of passing input to a command from a shell script is to use a *here document*. This document allows a command to execute as though it were reading from a file or the keyboard, whereas in fact it's getting input from the script.

A here document starts with the leader <<, followed by a special sequence of characters that is repeated at the end of the document. << is the shell's label redirector, which in this case forces the command input to be the here document. This special sequence acts as a marker to tell the shell where the here document ends. The marker sequence must not appear in the lines to be passed to the command, so it's best to make them memorable and fairly unusual.

Try It Out   **Using Here Documents**

The simplest example is simply to feed input to the `cat` command:

```
#!/bin/sh

cat <<!FUNKY!
hello
this is a here
document
!FUNKY!
```

This gives the following output:

```
hello
this is a here
document
```

Here documents might seem a rather curious feature, but they're very powerful because they enable you to invoke an interactive program such as an editor and feed it some predefined input. However, they're more commonly used for outputting large amounts of text from inside a script, as you saw previously, and avoiding having to use `echo` statements for each line. You can use exclamation marks (!) on each side of the identifier to ensure that there's no confusion.

If you wish to process several lines in a file in a predetermined way, you could use the `ed` line editor and feed it commands from a here document in a shell script.

Try It Out   **Another Use for a Here Document**

1.   Start with a file called `a_text_file` that contains the following lines:

```
That is line 1
That is line 2
That is line 3
That is line 4
```

2.   You can edit this file using a combination of a here document and the `ed` editor:

```
#!/bin/sh
```

```
ed a_text_file <<!FunkyStuff!
3
d
.,\$s/is/was/
w
q
!FunkyStuff!

exit 0
```

If you run this script, the file now contains the following:

```
That is line 1
That is line 2
That was line 4
```

How It Works

The shell script simply invokes the ed editor and passes to it the commands that it needs to move to the third line, delete the line, and then replace it with what was in the current line (because line 3 was deleted, the current line is now what was the last line). These ed commands are taken from the lines in the script that form the here document — the lines between the markers !FunkyStuff!.

> **Notice the \ inside the here document to protect the $ from shell expansion. The \ escapes the $, so the shell knows not to try to expand $s/is/was/ to its value, which of course it doesn't have. Instead, the shell passes the text \$ as $, which can then be interpreted by the ed editor.**

Debugging Scripts

Debugging shell scripts is usually quite easy, but there are no specific tools to help. In this section we'll quickly summarize the common methods.

When an error occurs, the shell will normally print out the line number of the line containing the error. If the error isn't immediately apparent, you can add some extra echo statements to display the contents of variables and test code fragments by simply typing them into the shell interactively.

Since scripts are interpreted, there's no compilation overhead in modifying and retrying a script. The main way to trace more complicated errors is to set various shell options. To do this, you can either use command-line options after invoking the shell or use the set command. The following table summarizes the options:

Command Line Option	set Option	Description
sh -n <script>	set -o noexec set -n	Checks for syntax errors only; doesn't execute commands
sh -v <script>	set -o verbose set -v	Echoes commands before running them
sh -x <script>	set -o xtrace set -x	Echoes commands after processing on the command line
sh -u <script>	set -o nounset set -u	Gives an error message when an undefined variable is used

You can set the set option flags on, using -o, and off, using +o, and likewise for the abbreviated versions. You can achieve a simple execution trace by using the xtrace option. For an initial check, you can use the command-line option, but for finer debugging, you can put the xtrace flags (setting an execution trace on and off) inside the script around the problem code. The execution trace causes the shell to print each line in the script, with variables expanded, before executing the line.

Use the following command to turn xtrace on:

```
set -o xtrace
```

Use this command to turn xtrace off again:

```
set +o xtrace
```

The level of expansion is denoted (by default) by the number of + signs at the start of each line. You can change the + to something more meaningful by setting the PS4 shell variable in your shell configuration file.

In the shell, you can also find out the program state wherever it exits by trapping the EXIT signal with a line something like the following placed at the start of the script:

```
trap 'echo Exiting: critical variable = $critical_variable' EXIT
```

Going Graphical — The dialog Utility

Before we finish discussing shell scripts, there is one more feature that, although not strictly part of the shell, is generally useful only from shell programs, so we cover it here.

If you know that your script will only ever need to run on the Linux console, there is a rather neat way to brighten up your scripts using a utility command called dialog. This command uses text mode graphics and color, but it still looks pleasantly graphical.

On some distributions `dialog` is not installed by default; for example, on Ubuntu you may have to add the publicly maintained repositories to find a ready-built version. On other distributions you may find already installed an alternative, `gdialog`. This is very similar, but relies on the GNOME user interface to display its dialog. However, in return you get a true graphical interface. In general, you can take any program that uses `dialog` and replace all calls to `gdialog`, and you will get a graphical version of your program. We show an example of a program using `gdialog` at the end of this section.

The whole idea of `dialog` is beautifully simple — a single program with a variety of parameters and options that allows you to display various types of graphical boxes, ranging from simple Yes/No boxes to input boxes and even menu selections. The utility generally returns when the user has made some sort of input, and the result can be found either from the exit status or if text was entered by retrieving the standard error stream.

Before we move on to more detail, let's look at a very simple use of `dialog` in operation. You can use `dialog` directly from the command line, which is great for prototyping, so let's create a simple message box to display the traditional first program:

```
dialog --msgbox "Hello World" 9 18
```

On the screen appears a graphical information box, complete with OK dialog (see Figure 2-3).

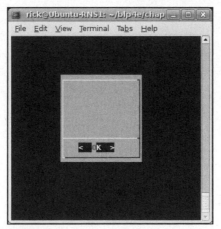

Figure 2-3

Now that you have seen how easy `dialog` is, let's look at the possibilities in more detail. The principal types of dialogs you can create are described in the following table:

Type	Option Used to Create Type	Meaning
Check boxes	`--checklist`	Allows you to display a list of items, each of which may be individually selected
Info boxes	`--infobox`	A simple display in a box that returns immediately, without clearing the screen
Input boxes	`--inputbox`	Allows the user to type in text
Menu boxes	`--menu`	Allow the user to pick a single item from a list
Message boxes	`--msgbox`	Displays a message to users, with an OK button when they wish to continue
Radio selection boxes	`--radiolist`	Allows the user to select an option from a list
Text boxes	`--textbox`	Allows you to display a file in a scrolling box
Yes/No boxes	`--yesno`	Allows you to ask a question, to which the user can select either *yes* or *no*

Some additional `dialog` box types are available (for example, a gauge and a password-entry box). If you want to know more about the more unusual `dialog` types, details can be found, as always, in the online manual pages.

To get the output of any type of box that allows textual input, or selections, you have to capture the standard error stream, usually by directing it to a temporary file, which you can then process afterward. To get the result of yes/no type questions, just look at the exit code, which, like all well-behaved programs, returns 0 for success (i.e., a "yes" selection) or 1 for failure.

All `dialog` types have various additional parameters to control, such as the size and shape of the dialog presented. We list the different parameters required for each type in the following table, and then demonstrate some of them on the command line. Finally, you'll see a simple program to combine several dialogs into a single program.

Dialog Type	Parameters
`--checklist`	text height width list-height [tag text status] ...
`--infobox`	text height width
`--inputbox`	text height width [initial string]

Continued on next page

Dialog Type	Parameters
--menu	text height width menu-height [tag item] ...
--msgbox	text height width
--radiolist	text height width list-height [tag text status] ...
--textbox	filename height width
--yesno	text height width

In addition, all the dialog types take several options. We won't list them all here, except to mention two: --title, which allows you to specify a title for the box, and --clear, which is used on its own for clearing the screen. Check the manual page for the full list of options.

Try It Out   **Using the dialog Utility**

Let's leap straight in with a nice complex example. Once you understand this example, all the others will be easy! In this example, you create a checklist-type box, with a title Check me and the instructions Pick Numbers. The checklist box will be 15 characters high by 25 characters wide, and each option will occupy 3 characters of height. Last, but not least, you list the options to be displayed, along with a default on/off selection.

```
dialog --title "Check me" --checklist "Pick Numbers" 15 25 3 1 "one" "off" 2 "two"
"on" 3 "three" "off"
```

Figure 2-4 shows the result onscreen.

How It Works

In this example, the --checklist parameter specifies that you are to create a checklist-type dialog. You use the --title option to set the title to Check me, and the next parameter is the prompt message of Pick Numbers.

You then move on to set the size of the dialog. It will be 15 lines high by 25 characters wide, and 3 lines will be used for the menu. It's not a perfect sizing, but it does enable you to see how things are laid out.

The options look a little tricky, but all you have to remember is that each menu item has three values:

❑   Bullet number

❑   Text

❑   Status

The first item has a number of 1, and text display of "one" and is set to "off". You then start on the next menu item, which is 2, "two" and selected. This continues until you run out of menu items.

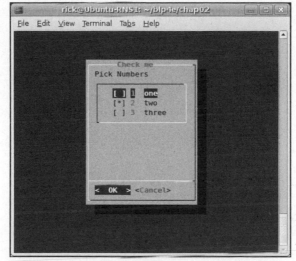

Figure 2-4

Easy, wasn't it? Just try some out on the command line and see how easy it is to use. In order to put this together in a program, you need to be able to access the results of the user input. This is quite easy; simply redirect the standard error stream for text input, or check the environment variable $?, which you will recall is the exit status of the previous command.

Try It Out   **A More Complex Program Using dialog**

Let's look at a simple program called questions, which takes note of user responses:

1. Start off by displaying a simple dialog box to tell the user what is happening. You don't need to get the result or obtain any user input, so this is nice and simple:

```
#!/bin/sh

# Ask some questions and collect the answer

dialog --title "Questionnaire" --msgbox "Welcome to my simple survey" 9 18
```

2. Ask the user if he wants to proceed, using a simple yes/no dialog box. Use the environment variable $? to check if the user selected yes (result code 0) or not. If he didn't want to proceed, use a simple infobox that requires no user input before exiting:

```
dialog --title "Confirm" --yesno "Are you willing to take part?"  9 18
if [ $? != 0 ]; then
  dialog --infobox "Thank you anyway" 5 20
  sleep 2
  dialog --clear
  exit 0
fi
```

3. Ask the user his name, using an input box. Redirect the standard error stream, 2, into a temporary file, _1.txt, which you can then process into the variable QNAME:

```
dialog --title "Questionnaire" --inputbox "Please enter your name" 9 30 2>_1.txt
Q_NAME=$(cat _1.txt)
```

4. Here you have the menu item with four different options. Again you redirect the standard error stream and load it into a variable:

```
dialog --menu "$Q_NAME, what music do you like best?" 15 30 4 1 "Classical" 2
"Jazz" 3 "Country" 4 "Other" 2>_1.txt
Q_MUSIC=$(cat _1.txt)
```

5. The number the user selects will be stored in the temporary file _1.txt, which is grabbed in to the variable Q_MUSIC so that you can test the result:

```
if [ "$Q_MUSIC" = "1" ]; then
  dialog --title "Likes Classical" --msgbox "Good choice!" 12 25
else
  dialog --title "Doesn't like Classical" --msgbox "Shame" 12 25
fi
```

6. Finally, clear the last dialog box and exit the program:

```
sleep 2
dialog --clear
exit 0
```

Figure 2-5 shows the onscreen result.

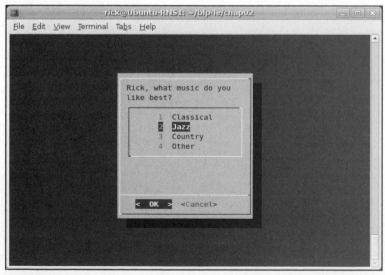

Figure 2-5

How It Works

In this example you combine the `dialog` command with some simple shell programming to show how you can build simple GUI programs using only shell script. You start with a simple welcome screen, before asking the user if he will take part using the simple `--yesno` option of `dialog`. You use the `$?` variable to check the reply. If he agreed, you then get his name, store it in a variable `Q_NAME`, and ask what sort of music he likes, using the `--menu` option of `dialog`. By storing the numerical output in the variable `Q_MUSIC`, you can see what he answered, and give an appropriate response.

If you are running a GNOME-based GUI, and are just using a terminal session within in it, you can use the command `gdialog` in place of `dialog`. The two commands have the same parameters, so you can use exactly the same code apart from changing the name of the command you invoke from `dialog` to `gdialog`. Figure 2-6 shows what this script looks like when modified to use `gdialog` under Ubuntu.

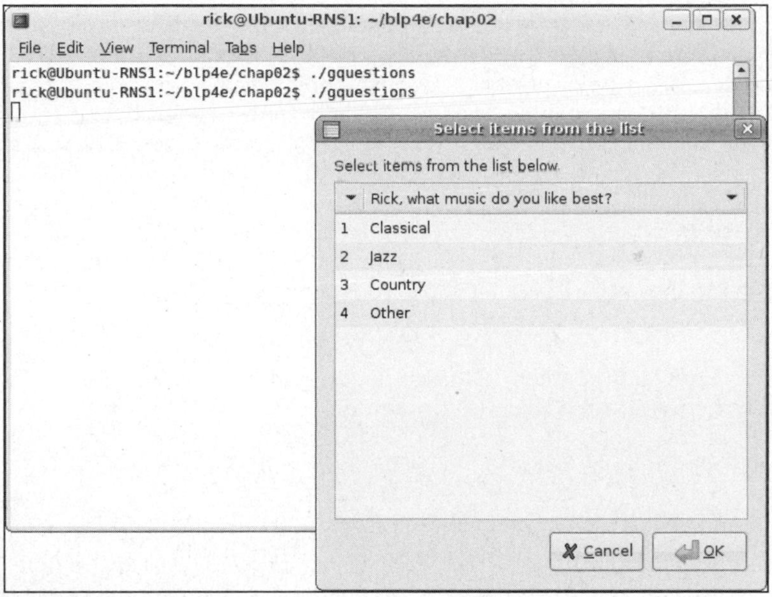

Figure 2-6

This is a very easy way of generating a usable GUI interface from a script.

Putting It All Together

Now that you've seen the main features of the shell as a programming language, it's time to write an example program to put some of what you have learned to use.

Throughout this book, you're going to be building a CD database application to show the techniques you've been learning. You start with a shell script, but pretty soon you'll do it again in C, add a database, and so on.

Requirements

Suppose you have an extensive CD collection. To make your life easier, you're going to design and implement a program for managing CDs. An electronic catalogue seems an ideal project to implement as you learn about programming Linux.

You want, at least initially, to store some basic information about each CD, such as the label, type of music, and artist or composer. You would also like to store some simple track information. You want to be able to search on any of the "per CD" items, but not on any of the track details. To make the mini-application complete, you would also like to be able to enter, update, and delete any of the information from within the application.

Design

The three requirements — updating, searching, and displaying the data — suggest that a simple menu will be adequate. All the data you need to store is textual; and assuming your CD collection isn't too big, you have no need for a complex database, so some simple text files will do. Storing information in text files will keep the application simple, and if your requirements change, then it's almost always easier to manipulate a text file than any other sort of file. As a last resort, you could even use an editor to manually enter and delete data, rather than write a program to do it.

You need to make an important design decision about data storage: Will a single file suffice? If so, what format should it have? Most of the information you expect to store occurs only once per CD (we'll skip lightly over the fact that some CDs contain the work of many composers or artists), except track information. Just about all CDs have more than one track.

Should you fix a limit on the number of tracks you can store per CD? That seems rather an arbitrary and unnecessary restriction, so reject that idea right away!

If you allow a flexible number of tracks, you have three options:

❑ Use a single file, with one line for the "title" type information and then *n* lines for the track information for that CD.

❑ Put all the information for each CD on a single line, allowing the line to continue until no more track information needs to be stored.

❑ Separate the title information from the track information and use a different file for each.

Only the third option enables you to easily fix the format of the files, which you'll need to do if you ever wish to convert your database into a relational form (more on this in Chapter 7), so that's the option to choose.

The next decision is what to put in the files.

Initially, for each CD title, you choose to store the following:

❑ The CD catalog number

❑ The title

- ❑   The type (classical, rock, pop, jazz, etc.)
- ❑   The composer or artist

For the tracks, you'll store simply two items:

- ❑   Track number
- ❑   Track name

In order to join the two files, you must relate the track information to the rest of the CD information. To do this, you'll use the CD catalog number. Since this is unique for each CD, it will appear only once in the titles file and once per track in the tracks file.

Take a look at an example titles file:

Catalog	Title	Type	Composer
CD123	Cool sax	Jazz	Bix
CD234	Classic violin	Classical	Bach
CD345	Hits99	Pop	Various

Its corresponding tracks file will look like this:

Catalog	Track No.	Title
CD123	1	Some jazz
CD123	2	More jazz
CD234	1	Sonata in D minor
CD345	1	Dizzy

The two files join using the Catalog field. Remember that there are normally multiple rows in the tracks file for a single entry in the titles file.

The last thing you need to decide is how to separate the entries. Fixed-width fields are normal in a relational database, but are not always the most convenient. Another common method, used for this example, is a comma (i.e., a comma-separated variable, or CSV, file).

In the following "Try It Out" section, just so you don't get totally lost, you'll be using the following functions:

```
get_return()
get_confirm()
set_menu_choice()
```

```
insert_title()
insert_track()
add_record_tracks()
add_records()
find_cd()
update_cd()
count_cds()
remove_records()
list_tracks()
```

Try It Out   **A CD Application**

1. First in the sample script is, as always, a line ensuring that it's executed as a shell script, followed by some copyright information:

```
#!/bin/bash

# Very simple example shell script for managing a CD collection.
# Copyright (C) 1996-2007 Wiley Publishing Inc.

# This program is free software; you can redistribute it and/or modify it
# under the terms of the GNU General Public License as published by the
# Free Software Foundation; either version 2 of the License, or (at your
# option) any later version.

# This program is distributed in the hopes that it will be useful, but
# WITHOUT ANY WARRANTY; without even the implied warranty of
# MERCHANTABILITY or FITNESS FOR A PARTICULAR PURPOSE. See the GNU General
# Public License for more details.

# You should have received a copy of the GNU General Public License along
# with this program; if not, write to the Free Software Foundation, Inc.
# 675 Mass Ave, Cambridge, MA 02139, USA.
```

2. Now ensure that some global variables that you'll be using throughout the script are set up. Set the title and track files and a temporary file, and trap Ctrl+C, so that your temporary file will be removed if the user interrupts the script:

```
menu_choice=""
current_cd=""
title_file="title.cdb"
tracks_file="tracks.cdb"
temp_file=/tmp/cdb.$$
trap 'rm -f $temp_file' EXIT
```

3. Define your functions, so that the script, executing from the top line, can find all the function definitions before you attempt to call any of them for the first time. To avoid rewriting the same code in several places, the first two functions are simple utilities:

```
get_return() {
  echo -e "Press return \c"
  read x
  return 0
}
```

```
get_confirm() {
  echo -e "Are you sure? \c"
  while true
  do
    read x
    case "$x" in
      y | yes | Y | Yes | YES )
        return 0;;
      n | no  | N | No  | NO )
        echo
        echo "Cancelled"
        return 1;;
      *) echo "Please enter yes or no" ;;
    esac
  done
}
```

4. Here you come to the main menu function, `set_menu_choice`. The contents of the menu vary dynamically, with extra options being added if a CD entry has been selected:

> Note that `echo -e` **may not be portable to some shells.**

```
set_menu_choice() {
  clear
  echo "Options :-"
  echo
  echo "    a) Add new CD"
  echo "    f) Find CD"
  echo "    c) Count the CDs and tracks in the catalog"
  if [ "$cdcatnum" != "" ]; then
    echo "    l) List tracks on $cdtitle"
    echo "    r) Remove $cdtitle"
    echo "    u) Update track information for $cdtitle"
  fi
  echo "    q) Quit"
  echo
  echo -e "Please enter choice then press return \c"
  read menu_choice
  return
}
```

5. Here are two more very short functions, `insert_title` and `insert_track`, for adding to the database files. Though some people hate one-liners like these, they help make other functions clearer.

They are followed by the larger `add_record_track` function that uses them. This function uses pattern matching to ensure that no commas are entered (since we're using commas as a field separator) and arithmetic operations to increment the current track number as tracks are entered:

```
insert_title() {
  echo $* >> $title_file
```

```
    return
}

insert_track() {
  echo $* >> $tracks_file
  return
}

add_record_tracks() {
  echo "Enter track information for this CD"
  echo "When no more tracks enter q"
  cdtrack=1
  cdttitle=""
  while [ "$cdttitle" != "q" ]
  do
      echo -e "Track $cdtrack, track title? \c"
      read tmp
      cdttitle=${tmp%%,*}
      if [ "$tmp" != "$cdttitle" ]; then
        echo "Sorry, no commas allowed"
        continue
      fi
      if [ -n "$cdttitle" ] ; then
        if [ "$cdttitle" != "q" ]; then
           insert_track $cdcatnum,$cdtrack,$cdttitle
        fi
      else
        cdtrack=$((cdtrack-1))
      fi
    cdtrack=$((cdtrack+1))
  done
}
```

6. The `add_records` function allows entry of the main CD information for a new CD:

```
add_records() {
  # Prompt for the initial information

  echo -e "Enter catalog name \c"
  read tmp
  cdcatnum=${tmp%%,*}

  echo -e "Enter title \c"
  read tmp
  cdtitle=${tmp%%,*}

  echo -e "Enter type \c"
  read tmp
  cdtype=${tmp%%,*}

  echo -e "Enter artist/composer \c"
  read tmp
  cdac=${tmp%%,*}
```

```
# Check that they want to enter the information

echo About to add new entry
echo "$cdcatnum $cdtitle $cdtype $cdac"

# If confirmed then append it to the titles file

if get_confirm ; then
  insert_title $cdcatnum,$cdtitle,$cdtype,$cdac
  add_record_tracks
else
  remove_records
fi

return
}
```

7. The `find_cd` function searches for the catalog name text in the CD title file, using the `grep` command. You need to know how many times the string was found, but `grep` returns a value indicating only if it matched zero times or many. To get around this, store the output in a file, which will have one line per match, and then count the lines in the file.

The word count command, `wc`, has white space in its output, separating the number of lines, words, and characters in the file. Use the `$(wc -l $temp_file)` notation to extract the first parameter from the output in order to set the `linesfound` variable. If you wanted another, later parameter, you would use the `set` command to set the shell's parameter variables to the command output.

Change the `IFS` (Internal Field Separator) to a comma so you can separate the comma-delimited fields. An alternative command is `cut`.

```
find_cd() {
  if [ "$1" = "n" ]; then
    asklist=n
  else
    asklist=y
  fi
  cdcatnum=""
  echo -e "Enter a string to search for in the CD titles \c"
  read searchstr
  if [ "$searchstr" = "" ]; then
    return 0
  fi

  grep "$searchstr" $title_file > $temp_file

  set $(wc -l $temp_file)
  linesfound=$1

  case "$linesfound" in
  0)    echo "Sorry, nothing found"
        get_return
        return 0
        ;;
```

```
1)     ;;
2)     echo "Sorry, not unique."
       echo "Found the following"
       cat $temp_file
       get_return
       return 0
esac

IFS=","
read cdcatnum cdtitle cdtype cdac < $temp_file
IFS=" "

if [ -z "$cdcatnum" ]; then
  echo "Sorry, could not extract catalog field from $temp_file"
  get_return
  return 0
fi

echo
echo Catalog number: $cdcatnum
echo Title: $cdtitle
echo Type: $cdtype
echo Artist/Composer: $cdac
echo
get_return

if [ "$asklist" = "y" ]; then
  echo -e "View tracks for this CD? \c"
    read x
  if [ "$x" = "y" ]; then
    echo
    list_tracks
    echo
  fi
fi
return 1
}
```

8.   update_cd allows you to re-enter information for a CD. Notice that you search (using grep) for lines that start (^) with the $cdcatnum followed by a , and that you need to wrap the expansion of $cdcatnum in {} so you can search for a , with no white space between it and the catalog number. This function also uses {} to enclose multiple statements to be executed if get_confirm returns true.

```
update_cd() {
  if [ -z "$cdcatnum" ]; then
    echo "You must select a CD first"
    find_cd n
  fi
  if [ -n "$cdcatnum" ]; then
    echo "Current tracks are :-"
    list_tracks
    echo
```

```
    echo "This will re-enter the tracks for $cdtitle"
    get_confirm && {
      grep -v "^${cdcatnum}," $tracks_file > $temp_file
      mv $temp_file $tracks_file
      echo
      add_record_tracks
    }
  fi
  return
}
```

9. `count_cds` gives a quick count of the contents of the database:

```
count_cds() {
  set $(wc -l $title_file)
  num_titles=$1
  set $(wc -l $tracks_file)
  num_tracks=$1
  echo found $num_titles CDs, with a total of $num_tracks tracks
  get_return
  return
}
```

10. `remove_records` strips entries from the database files, using `grep -v` to remove all matching strings. Notice you must use a temporary file.

If you tried to use

```
grep -v "^$cdcatnum" > $title_file
```

the `$title_file` would be set to empty by the `>` output redirection before `grep` had the chance to execute, so `grep` would read from an empty file.

```
remove_records() {
  if [ -z "$cdcatnum" ]; then
    echo You must select a CD first
    find_cd n
  fi
  if [ -n "$cdcatnum" ]; then
    echo "You are about to delete $cdtitle"
    get_confirm && {
      grep -v "^${cdcatnum}," $title_file > $temp_file
      mv $temp_file $title_file
      grep -v "^${cdcatnum}," $tracks_file > $temp_file
      mv $temp_file $tracks_file
      cdcatnum=""
      echo Entry removed
    }
    get_return
  fi
  return
}
```

11. `list_tracks` again uses `grep` to extract the lines you want, `cut` to access the fields you want, and then `more` to provide a paginated output. If you consider how many lines of C code it would take to reimplement these 20-odd lines of code, you'll appreciate how powerful a tool the shell can be.

```
list_tracks() {
  if [ "$cdcatnum" = "" ]; then
    echo no CD selected yet
    return
  else
    grep "^${cdcatnum}," $tracks_file > $temp_file
    num_tracks=$(wc -l $temp_file)
    if [ "$num_tracks" = "0" ]; then
      echo no tracks found for $cdtitle
    else {
      echo
      echo "$cdtitle :-"
      echo
      cut -f 2- -d , $temp_file
      echo
    } | ${PAGER:-more}
    fi
  fi
  get_return
  return
}
```

12. Now that all the functions have been defined, you can enter the main routine. The first few lines simply get the files into a known state; then you call the menu function, `set_menu_choice`, and act on the output.

When `quit` is selected, you delete the temporary file, write a message, and exit with a successful completion condition:

```
rm -f $temp_file
if [ ! -f $title_file ]; then
  touch $title_file
fi
if [ ! -f $tracks_file ]; then
  touch $tracks_file
fi

# Now the application proper

clear
echo
echo
echo "Mini CD manager"
sleep 1

quit=n
while [ "$quit" != "y" ];
do
  set_menu_choice
  case "$menu_choice" in
    a) add_records;;
```

```
   r)  remove_records;;
   f)  find_cd y;;
   u)  update_cd;;
   c)  count_cds;;
   l)  list_tracks;;
   b)
      echo
      more $title_file
      echo
      get_return;;
   q | Q ) quit=y;;
   *) echo "Sorry, choice not recognized";;
 esac
done

#Tidy up and leave

rm -f $temp_file
echo "Finished"
exit 0
```

Notes on the Application

The `trap` command at the start of the script is intended to trap the user's pressing of Ctrl+C. This may be either the `EXIT` or the `INT` signal, depending on the terminal setup.

There are other ways of implementing the menu selection, notably the `select` construct in `bash` and `ksh` (which isn't, however, specified in X/Open). This construct is a dedicated menu choice selector. Check it out if your script can afford to be slightly less portable. Multiline information given to users could also make use of here documents.

You might have noticed that there's no validation of the primary key when a new record is started; the new code just ignores the subsequent titles with the same code, but incorporates their tracks into the first title's listing:

```
1 First CD Track 1
2 First CD Track 2
1 Another CD
2 With the same CD key
```

We'll leave this and other improvements to your imagination and creativity, as you can modify the code under the terms of the GPL.

Summary

In this chapter, you've seen that the shell is a powerful programming language in its own right. Its ability to call other programs easily and then process their output makes the shell an ideal tool for tasks involving the processing of text and files.

Next time you need a small utility program, consider whether you can solve your problem by combining some of the many Linux commands with a shell script. You'll be surprised just how many utility programs you can write without a compiler.

Working with Files

In this chapter, you look at Linux files and directories and how to manipulate them. You learn how to create files, open them, read, write, and close them. You also learn how programs can manipulate directories (to create, scan, and delete them, for example). After the preceding chapter's diversion into shells, you now start programming in C.

Before proceeding to the way Linux handles file I/O, we review the concepts associated with files, directories, and devices. To manipulate files and directories, you need to make system calls (the UNIX and Linux parallel of the Windows API), but there also exists a whole range of library functions, the standard I/O library (stdio), to make file handling more efficient.

We spend the majority of the chapter detailing the various calls to handle files and directories. So this chapter covers various file-related topics:

- ❏ Files and devices
- ❏ System calls
- ❏ Library functions
- ❏ Low-level file access
- ❏ Managing files
- ❏ The standard I/O library
- ❏ Formatted input and output
- ❏ File and directory maintenance
- ❏ Scanning directories
- ❏ Errors
- ❏ The /proc file system
- ❏ Advanced topics: fcntl and mmap

Linux File Structure

"Why," you may be asking, "are we covering file structure? I know about that already." Well, as with UNIX, files in the Linux environment are particularly important, because they provide a simple and consistent interface to the operating system services and devices. In Linux, *everything is a file*. Well, almost!

This means that, in general, programs can use disk files, serial ports, printers, and other devices in exactly the same way they would use a file. We cover some exceptions, such as network connections, in Chapter 15, but mainly you need to use only five basic functions: open, close, read, write, and ioctl.

Directories, too, are special sorts of files. In modern UNIX versions, including Linux, even the superuser may not write to them directly. All users ordinarily use the high-level opendir/readdir interface to read directories without needing to know the system-specific details of directory implementation. We'll return to special directory functions later in this chapter.

Really, almost everything is represented as a file under Linux, or can be made available via special files. Even though there are, by necessity, subtle differences from the conventional files you know and love, the general principle still holds. Let's look at the special cases we've mentioned so far.

Directories

As well as its contents, a file has a name and some properties, or "administrative information"; that is, the file's creation/modification date and its permissions. The properties are stored in the file's *inode*, a special block of data in the file system that also contains the length of the file and where on the disk it's stored. The system uses the number of the file's inode; the directory structure just names the file for our benefit.

A directory is a file that holds the inode numbers and names of other files. Each directory entry is a link to a file's inode; remove the filename and you remove the link. (You can see the inode number for a file by using ln -i.) Using the ln command, you can make links to the same file in different directories.

When you delete a file all that happens is that the directory entry for the file is removed and the number of links to the file goes down by one. The data for the file is possibly still available through other links to the same file. When the number of links to a file (the number after the permissions in ls -l) reaches zero, the inode and the data blocks it references are then no longer in use and are marked as free.

Files are arranged in directories, which may also contain subdirectories. These form the familiar file system hierarchy. A user, say neil, usually has his files stored in a "home" directory, perhaps /home/neil, with subdirectories for e-mail, business letters, utility programs, and so on. Note that many command shells for UNIX and Linux have an excellent notation for getting straight to your home directory: the tilde (~). For another user, type ~**user**. As you know, home directories for each user are usually subdirectories of a higher-level directory created specifically for this purpose, in this case /home.

> *Note that the standard library functions unfortunately do not understand the shell's tilde shorthand notation in filename parameters, so you must always use the real name of the file in your programs.*

The /home directory is itself a subdirectory of the root directory, /, which sits at the top of the hierarchy and contains all of the system's files in subdirectories. The root directory normally includes /bin for system programs ("binaries"), /etc for system configuration files, and /lib for system libraries. Files that represent physical devices and provide the interface to those devices are conventionally found in a directory called /dev. See Figure 3-1 for an example of part of a typical Linux hierarchy. We cover the Linux file system layout in more detail in Chapter 18, when we look at Linux File System Standard.

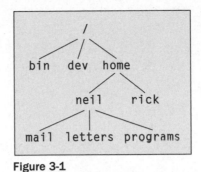

Figure 3-1

Files and Devices

Even hardware devices are very often represented (mapped) by files. For example, as the superuser, you can mount an IDE CD-ROM drive as a file:

```
# mount -t iso9660 /dev/hdc /mnt/cdrom
# cd /mnt/cdrom
```

which takes the CD-ROM device (in this case the secondary master IDE device loaded as /dev/hdc during boot-up; other types of device will have different /dev entries) and mounts its current contents as the file structure beneath /mnt/cdrom. You then move around within the CD-ROM's directories just as normal, except, of course, that the contents are read-only.

Three important device files found in both UNIX and Linux are /dev/console, /dev/tty, and /dev/null.

/dev/console

This device represents the system console. Error messages and diagnostics are often sent to this device. Each UNIX system has a designated terminal or screen to receive console messages. At one time, it might have been a dedicated printing terminal. On modern workstations, and on Linux, it's usually the "active" virtual console, and under X, it will be a special console window on the screen.

/dev/tty

The special file /dev/tty is an alias (logical device) for the controlling terminal (keyboard and screen, or window) of a process, if it has one. (For instance, processes and scripts run automatically by the system won't have a controlling terminal, and therefore won't be able to open /dev/tty.)

Where it can be used, /dev/tty allows a program to write directly to the user, without regard to which pseudo-terminal or hardware terminal the user is using. It is useful when the standard output has been redirected. One example is displaying a long directory listing as a group of pages with the command ls -R | more, where the program more has to prompt the user for each new page of output. You'll see more of /dev/tty in Chapter 5.

Note that whereas there's only one /dev/console device, there are effectively many different physical devices accessed through /dev/tty.

/dev/null

The /dev/null file is the null device. All output written to this device is discarded. An immediate end of file is returned when the device is read, and it can be used as a source of empty files by using the cp command. Unwanted output is often redirected to /dev/null.

Another way of creating empty files is to use the touch <filename> *command, which changes the modification time of a file or creates a new file if none exists with the given name. It won't empty it of its contents, though.*

```
$ echo do not want to see this >/dev/null
$ cp /dev/null empty_file
```

Other devices found in /dev include hard and floppy disks, communications ports, tape drives, CD-ROMs, sound cards, and some devices representing the system's internal state. There's even a /dev/zero, which acts as a source of null bytes to create files full of zeros. You need superuser permissions to access some of these devices; normal users can't write programs to directly access low-level devices like hard disks. The names of the device files may vary from system to system. Linux distributions usually have applications that run as superuser to manage the devices that would otherwise be inaccessible, for example, mount for user-mountable file systems.

Devices are classified as either *character devices* or *block devices*. The difference refers to the fact that some devices need to be accessed a block at a time. Typically, the only block devices are those that support some type of file system, like hard disks.

In this chapter, we concentrate on disk files and directories. We cover another device, the user's terminal, in Chapter 5.

System Calls and Device Drivers

You can access and control files and devices using a small number of functions. These functions, known as *system calls*, are provided by UNIX (and Linux) directly, and are the interface to the operating system itself.

At the heart of the operating system, the kernel, are a number of *device drivers*. These are a collection of low-level interfaces for controlling system hardware. For example, there will be a device driver for a tape drive, which knows how to start the tape, wind it forward and backward, read and write to it, and so on. It will also know that tapes have to be written to in blocks of a certain size. Because tapes are sequential in nature, the driver can't access tape blocks directly, but must wind the tape to the right place. Similarly, a low-level hard disk device driver will only write whole numbers of disk sectors at a time, but will be able to access any desired disk block directly, because the disk is a random access device.

To provide a similar interface, device drivers encapsulate all of the hardware-dependent features. Idiosyncratic features of the hardware are usually available through the ioctl (for I/O control) system call.

Device files in /dev are used in the same way; they can be opened, read, written, and closed. For example, the same open call used to access a regular file is used to access a user terminal, a printer, or a tape drive.

The low-level functions used to access the device drivers, the system calls, include:

- ❑   open: Open a file or device
- ❑   read: Read from an open file or device
- ❑   write: Write to a file or device
- ❑   close: Close the file or device
- ❑   ioctl: Pass control information to a device driver

The ioctl system call is used to provide some necessary hardware-specific control (as opposed to regular input and output), so its use varies from device to device. For example, a call to ioctl can be used to rewind a tape drive or set the flow control characteristics of a serial port. For this reason, ioctl isn't necessarily portable from machine to machine. In addition, each driver defines its own set of ioctl commands.

These and other system calls are usually documented in section 2 of the manual pages. Prototypes providing the parameter lists and function return types for system calls, and associated #defines of constants, are provided in include files. The particular ones required for each system call will be included with the descriptions of individual calls.

Library Functions

One problem with using low-level system calls directly for input and output is that they can be very inefficient. Why? Well:

- ❑   There's a performance penalty in making a system call. System calls are therefore expensive compared to function calls because Linux has to switch from running your program code to executing its own kernel code and back again. It's a good idea to keep the number of system calls used in a program to a minimum and get each call to do as much work as possible, for example, by reading and writing large amounts of data rather than a single character at a time.

- ❑   The hardware has limitations that can impose restrictions on the size of data blocks that can be read or written by the low-level system call at any one time. For example, tape drives often have a block size, say 10k, to which they can write. So, if you attempt to write an amount that is not an exact multiple of 10k, the drive will still advance the tape to the next 10k block, leaving gaps on the tape.

To provide a higher-level interface to devices and disk files, a Linux distribution (and UNIX) provides a number of standard libraries. These are collections of functions that you can include in your own programs to handle these problems. A good example is the standard I/O library that provides buffered output. You can effectively write data blocks of varying sizes, and the library functions arrange for the low-level system calls to be provided with full blocks as the data is made available. This dramatically reduces the system call overhead.

Library functions are usually documented in section 3 of the manual pages and often have a standard include file associated with them, such as stdio.h for the standard I/O library.

To summarize the discussion of the last few sections, Figure 3-2 illustrates the Linux system, showing where the various file functions exist relative to the user, the device drivers, the kernel, and the hardware.

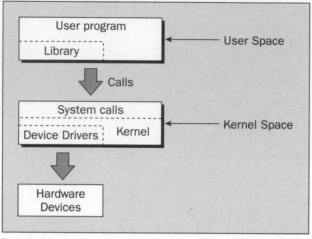

Figure 3-2

Low-Level File Access

Each running program, called a *process*, has a number of file descriptors associated with it. These are small integers that you can use to access open files or devices. How many of these are available will vary depending on how the system has been configured. When a program starts, it usually has three of these descriptors already opened. These are:

- ❑   0: Standard input
- ❑   1: Standard output
- ❑   2: Standard error

You can associate other file descriptors with files and devices by using the open system call, which we discuss shortly. The file descriptors that are automatically opened, however, already allow you to create some simple programs using write.

write

The write system call arranges for the first nbytes bytes from buf to be written to the file associated with the file descriptor fildes. It returns the number of bytes actually written. This may be less than nbytes if there has been an error in the file descriptor or if the underlying device driver is sensitive to block size. If the function returns 0, it means no data was written; if it returns –1, there has been an error in the write call, and the error will be specified in the errno global variable.

Here's the syntax:

```
#include <unistd.h>

size_t write(int fildes, const void *buf, size_t nbytes);
```

With this knowledge, you can write your first program, `simple_write.c`:

```
#include <unistd.h>
#include <stdlib.h>

int main()
{
    if ((write(1, "Here is some data\n", 18)) != 18)
        write(2, "A write error has occurred on file descriptor 1\n",46);

    exit(0);
}
```

This program simply prints a message to the standard output. When a program exits, all open file descriptors are automatically closed, so you don't need to close them explicitly. This won't be the case, however, when you're dealing with buffered output.

```
$ ./simple_write
Here is some data
$
```

A point worth noting again is that `write` might report that it wrote fewer bytes than you asked it to. This is not necessarily an error. In your programs, you will need to check `errno` to detect errors and call `write` to write any remaining data.

read

The `read` system call reads up to `nbytes` bytes of data from the file associated with the file descriptor `fildes` and places them in the data area `buf`. It returns the number of data bytes actually read, which may be less than the number requested. If a `read` call returns 0, it had nothing to read; it reached the end of the file. Again, an error on the call will cause it to return –1.

```
#include <unistd.h>

size_t read(int fildes, void *buf, size_t nbytes);
```

This program, `simple_read.c`, copies the first 128 bytes of the standard input to the standard output. It copies all of the input if there are fewer than 128 bytes.

```
#include <unistd.h>
#include <stdlib.h>

int main()
{
    char buffer[128];
    int nread;

    nread = read(0, buffer, 128);
    if (nread == -1)
        write(2, "A read error has occurred\n", 26);

    if ((write(1,buffer,nread)) != nread)
        write(2, "A write error has occurred\n",27);
```

```
        exit(0);
}
```

If you run the program, you should see the following:

```
$ echo hello there | ./simple_read
hello there
$ ./simple_read < draft1.txt
Files
In this chapter we will be looking at files and directories and how to manipulate
them. We will learn how to create files,$
```

In the first execution, you create some input for the program using echo, which is piped to your program. In the second execution, you redirect input from a file. In this case, you see the first part of the file draft1.txt appearing on the standard output.

Note how the next shell prompt appears at the end of the last line of output because, in this example, the 128 bytes don't form a whole number of lines.

open

To create a new file descriptor, you need to use the open system call.

```
#include <fcntl.h>
#include <sys/types.h>
#include <sys/stat.h>

int open(const char *path, int oflags);
int open(const char *path, int oflags, mode_t mode);
```

Strictly speaking, you don't need to include sys/types.h and sys/stat.h to use open on systems that comply with POSIX standards, but they may be necessary on some UNIX systems.

In simple terms, open establishes an access path to a file or device. If successful, it returns a file descriptor that can be used in read, write, and other system calls. The file descriptor is unique and isn't shared by any other processes that may be running. If two programs have a file open at the same time, they maintain distinct file descriptors. If they both write to the file, they will continue to write where they left off. Their data isn't interleaved, but one will overwrite the other. Each keeps its own idea of how far into the file (the offset) it has read or written. You can prevent unwanted clashes of this sort by using file locking, which you'll see in Chapter 7.

The name of the file or device to be opened is passed as a parameter, path; the oflags parameter is used to specify actions to be taken on opening the file.

The oflags are specified as a combination of a mandatory file access mode and other optional modes. The open call must specify one of the file access modes shown in the following table:

Mode	Description
O_RDONLY	Open for read-only
O_WRONLY	Open for write-only
O_RDWR	Open for reading and writing

The call may also include a combination (using a bitwise OR) of the following optional modes in the oflags parameter:

- ❑   O_APPEND: Place written data at the end of the file.
- ❑   O_TRUNC: Set the length of the file to zero, discarding existing contents.
- ❑   O_CREAT: Creates the file, if necessary, with permissions given in mode.
- ❑   O_EXCL: Used with O_CREAT, ensures that the caller creates the file. The open is atomic; that is, it's performed with just one function call. This protects against two programs creating the file at the same time. If the file already exists, open will fail.

Other possible values for oflags are documented in the open manual page, which you can find in section 2 of the manual pages (use man 2 open).

open returns the new file descriptor (always a nonnegative integer) if successful, or –1 if it fails, at which time open also sets the global variable errno to indicate the reason for the failure. We look at errno more closely in a later section. The new file descriptor is always the lowest-numbered unused descriptor, a feature that can be quite useful in some circumstances. For example, if a program closes its standard output and then calls open again, the file descriptor 1 will be reused and the standard output will have been effectively redirected to a different file or device.

There is also a creat call standardized by POSIX, but it is not often used. creat doesn't only create the file, as one might expect, but also opens it. It is the equivalent of calling open with oflags equal to O_CREAT|O_WRONLY|O_TRUNC.

The number of files that any one running program may have open at once is limited. The limit, usually defined by the constant OPEN_MAX in limits.h, varies from system to system, but POSIX requires that it be at least 16. This limit may itself be subject to local system-wide limits so that a program may not always be able to open this many files. On Linux, the limit may be changed at runtime so OPEN_MAX is not a constant. It typically starts out at 256.

Initial Permissions

When you create a file using the O_CREAT flag with open, you must use the three-parameter form. mode, the third parameter, is made from a bitwise OR of the flags defined in the header file sys/stat.h. These are:

- ❑   S_IRUSR: Read permission, owner
- ❑   S_IWUSR: Write permission, owner

- ❑   S_IXUSR: Execute permission, owner
- ❑   S_IRGRP: Read permission, group
- ❑   S_IWGRP: Write permission, group
- ❑   S_IXGRP: Execute permission, group
- ❑   S_IROTH: Read permission, others
- ❑   S_IWOTH: Write permission, others
- ❑   S_IXOTH: Execute permission, others

For example,

```
open ("myfile", O_CREAT, S_IRUSR|S_IXOTH);
```

has the effect of creating a file called myfile, with read permission for the owner and execute permission for others, and only those permissions.

```
$ ls -ls myfile
0 -r-------x   1 neil     software        0 Sep 22 08:11 myfile*
```

There are a couple of factors that may affect the file permissions. First, the permissions specified are used only if the file is being created. Second, the user mask (specified by the shell's umask command) affects the created file's permissions. The mode value given in the open call is ANDed with the inverse of the user mask value at runtime. For example, if the user mask is set to 001 and the S_IXOTH mode flag is specified, the file won't be created with "other" execute permission because the user mask specifies that "other" execute permission isn't to be provided. The flags in the open and creat calls are, in fact, requests to set permissions. Whether or not the requested permissions are set depends on the runtime value of umask.

umask

The umask is a system variable that encodes a mask for file permissions to be used when a file is created. You can change the variable by executing the umask command to supply a new value. The value is a three-digit octal value. Each digit is the result of ORing values from 1, 2, or 4; the meanings are shown in the following table. The separate digits refer to "user," "group," and "other" permissions, respectively.

Digit	Value	Meaning
1	0	No user permissions are to be disallowed.
	4	User read permission is disallowed.
	2	User write permission is disallowed.
	1	User execute permission is disallowed.
2	0	No group permissions are to be disallowed.
	4	Group read permission is disallowed.

Digit	Value	Meaning
	2	Group write permission is disallowed.
	1	Group execute permission is disallowed.
3	0	No other permissions are to be disallowed.
	4	Other read permission is disallowed.
	2	Other write permission is disallowed.
	1	Other execute permission is disallowed.

For example, to block "group" write and execute, and "other" write, the umask would be

Digit	Value
1	0
2	2
	1
3	2

Values for each digit are ORed together; so the second digit will need to be 2 | 1, giving 3. The resulting umask is 032.

When you create a file via an open or creat call, the mode parameter is compared with the current umask. Any bit setting in the mode parameter that is also set in the umask is removed. The end result is that users can set up their environment to say things like "Don't create any files with write permission for others, even if the program creating the file requests that permission." This doesn't prevent a program or user from subsequently using the chmod command (or chmod system call in a program) to add other write permissions, but it does help protect users by saving them from having to check and set permissions on all new files.

close

You use close to terminate the association between a file descriptor, fildes, and its file. The file descriptor becomes available for reuse. It returns 0 if successful and −1 on error.

```
#include <unistd.h>

int close(int fildes);
```

Note that it can be important to check the return result from close. Some file systems, particularly networked ones, may not report an error writing to a file until the file is closed, because data may not have been confirmed as written when writes are performed.

ioctl

`ioctl` is a bit of a ragbag of things. It provides an interface for controlling the behavior of devices and their descriptors and configuring underlying services. Terminals, file descriptors, sockets, and even tape drives may have `ioctl` calls defined for them and you need to refer to the specific device's man page for details. POSIX defines only `ioctl` for streams, which are beyond the scope of this book. Here's the syntax:

```
#include <unistd.h>

int ioctl(int fildes, int cmd, ...);
```

`ioctl` performs the function indicated by `cmd` on the object referenced by the descriptor `fildes`. It may take an optional third argument, depending on the functions supported by a particular device.

For example, the following call to `ioctl` on Linux turns on the keyboard LEDs:

```
ioctl(tty_fd, KDSETLED, LED_NUM|LED_CAP|LED_SCR);
```

Try It Out   A File Copy Program

You now know enough about the `open`, `read`, and `write` system calls to write a low-level program, `copy_system.c`, to copy one file to another, character by character.

We'll do this in a number of ways during this chapter to compare the efficiency of each method. For brevity, we'll assume that the input file exists and the output file does not, and that all reads and writes succeed. Of course, in real-life programs, we would check that these assumptions are valid!

1. First you will need to make a test input file, say 1Mb in size, and name it `file.in`.

2. Then compile `copy_system.c`:

```c
#include <unistd.h>
#include <sys/stat.h>
#include <fcntl.h>
#include <stdlib.h>

int main()
{
    char c;
    int in, out;

    in = open("file.in", O_RDONLY);
    out = open("file.out", O_WRONLY|O_CREAT, S_IRUSR|S_IWUSR);
    while(read(in,&c,1) == 1)
        write(out,&c,1);

    exit(0);
}
```

Note that the `#include <unistd.h>` *line must come first, because it defines flags regarding POSIX compliance that may affect other* `include` *files.*

3. Running the program will give something like the following:

```
$ TIMEFORMAT="" time ./copy_system
4.67user 146.90system 2:32.57elapsed 99%CPU

...
$ ls -ls file.in file.out
1029 -rw-r---r-   1 neil     users      1048576 Sep 17 10:46 file.in
1029 -rw-------   1 neil     users      1048576 Sep 17 10:51 file.out
```

How It Works

Here you use the time facility to measure how long the program takes to run. The TIMEFORMAT variable is used on Linux to override the default POSIX output format of time, which does not include the CPU usage. You can see that for this fairly old system, the 1Mb input file, file.in, was successfully copied to file.out, which was created with read/write permissions for owner only. However, the copy took two-and-a-half minutes and consumed virtually all the CPU time. It was this slow because it had to make more than two million system calls.

In recent years, Linux has seen great strides in its system call and file system performance. By comparison, a similar test using a 2.6 kernel completed in a little under 14 seconds.

```
$ TIMEFORMAT="" time ./copy_system
2.08user 10.59system 0:13.74elapsed 92%CPU

...
```

Try It Out   A Second File Copy Program

You can improve matters by copying in larger blocks. Take a look at this modified program, copy_block.c, which copies the files in 1K blocks, again using system calls:

```c
#include <unistd.h>
#include <sys/stat.h>
#include <fcntl.h>
#include <stdlib.h>

int main()
{
    char block[1024];
    int in, out;
    int nread;

    in = open("file.in", O_RDONLY);
    out = open("file.out", O_WRONLY|O_CREAT, S_IRUSR|S_IWUSR);
    while((nread = read(in,block,sizeof(block))) > 0)
        write(out,block,nread);

    exit(0);
}
```

Now try the program, first removing the old output file:

```
$ rm file.out
$ TIMEFORMAT="" time ./copy_block
0.00user 0.02system 0:00.04elapsed 78%CPU
...
```

How It Works

Now the program takes just hundredths of a second, because it requires only around 2,000 system calls. Of course, these times are very system-dependent, but they do show that system calls have a measurable overhead, so it's worth optimizing their use.

Other System Calls for Managing Files

There are a number of other system calls that operate on these low-level file descriptors. These allow a program to control how a file is used and to return status information.

lseek

The lseek system call sets the read/write pointer of a file descriptor, fildes; that is, you can use it to set where in the file the next read or write will occur. You can set the pointer to an absolute location in the file or to a position relative to the current position or the end of file.

```
#include <unistd.h>
#include <sys/types.h>

off_t lseek(int fildes, off_t offset, int whence);
```

The offset parameter is used to specify the position, and the whence parameter specifies how the offset is used. whence can be one of the following:

- ❑ SEEK_SET: offset is an absolute position
- ❑ SEEK_CUR: offset is relative to the current position
- ❑ SEEK_END: offset is relative to the end of the file

lseek returns the offset measured in bytes from the beginning of the file that the file pointer is set to, or –1 on failure. The type off_t, used for the offset in seek operations, is an implementation-dependent integer type defined in sys/types.h.

fstat, stat, and lstat

The fstat system call returns status information about the file associated with an open file descriptor. The information is written to a structure, buf, the address of which is passed as a parameter.

Here's the syntax:

```
#include <unistd.h>
#include <sys/stat.h>
#include <sys/types.h>

int fstat(int fildes, struct stat *buf);
int stat(const char *path, struct stat *buf);
int lstat(const char *path, struct stat *buf);
```

Note that the inclusion of sys/types.h *is optional, but we recommend it when using system calls, because some of their definitions use aliases for standard types that may change one day.*

The related functions stat and lstat return status information for a named file. They produce the same results, except when the file is a symbolic link. lstat returns information about the link itself, and stat returns information about the file to which the link refers.

The members of the structure, stat, may vary between UNIX-like systems, but will include those in the following table:

stat Member	Description
st_mode	File permissions and file-type information
st_ino	The inode associated with the file
st_dev	The device the file resides on
st_uid	The user identity of the file owner
st_gid	The group identity of the file owner
st_atime	The time of last access
st_ctime	The time of last change to permissions, owner, group, or content
st_mtime	The time of last modification to contents
st_nlink	The number of hard links to the file

The st_mode flags returned in the stat structure also have a number of associated macros defined in the header file sys/stat.h. These macros include names for permission and file-type flags and some masks to help with testing for specific types and permissions.

The permissions flags are the same as for the open system call described earlier. File-type flags include

❑   S_IFBLK: Entry is a block special device

❑   S_IFDIR: Entry is a directory

❑   S_IFCHR: Entry is a character special device

❑   S_IFIFO: Entry is a FIFO (named pipe)

107

❑   S_IFREG: Entry is a regular file

❑   S_IFLNK: Entry is a symbolic link

Other mode flags include

❑   S_ISUID: Entry has setUID on execution

❑   S_ISGID: Entry has setGID on execution

Masks to interpret the st_mode flags include

❑   S_IFMT: File type

❑   S_IRWXU: User read/write/execute permissions

❑   S_IRWXG: Group read/write/execute permissions

❑   S_IRWXO: Others' read/write/execute permissions

There are some macros defined to help with determining file types. These just compare suitably masked mode flags with a suitable device-type flag. These include

❑   S_ISBLK: Test for block special file

❑   S_ISCHR: Test for character special file

❑   S_ISDIR: Test for directory

❑   S_ISFIFO: Test for FIFO

❑   S_ISREG: Test for regular file

❑   S_ISLNK: Test for symbolic link

For example, to test that a file doesn't represent a directory and has execute permission set for the owner but no other permissions, you can use the following test:

```
struct stat statbuf;
mode_t modes;

stat("filename",&statbuf);
modes = statbuf.st_mode;

if(!S_ISDIR(modes) && (modes & S_IRWXU) == S_IXUSR)
    ...
```

dup and dup2

The dup system calls provide a way of duplicating a file descriptor, giving two or more different descriptors that access the same file. These might be used for reading and writing to different locations in the file. The dup system call duplicates a file descriptor, fildes, returning a new descriptor. The dup2 system call effectively copies one file descriptor to another by specifying the descriptor to use for the copy.

Here's the syntax:

```
#include <unistd.h>

int dup(int fildes);
int dup2(int fildes, int fildes2);
```

These calls can also be useful when you're using multiple processes communicating via pipes. We discuss the dup system in more depth in Chapter 13.

The Standard I/O Library

The standard I/O library (stdio) and its header file, stdio.h, provide a versatile interface to low-level I/O system calls. The library, now part of ANSI standard C, whereas the system calls you met earlier are not, provides many sophisticated functions for formatting output and scanning input. It also takes care of the buffering requirements for devices.

In many ways, you use this library in the same way that you use low-level file descriptors. You need to open a file to establish an access path. This returns a value that is used as a parameter to other I/O library functions. The equivalent of the low-level file descriptor is called a *stream* and is implemented as a pointer to a structure, a FILE *.

> Don't confuse these file streams with either C++ iostreams or with the STREAMS paradigm of inter-process communication introduced in AT&T UNIX System V Release 3, which is beyond the scope of this book. For more information on STREAMS, check out the X/Open spec (at http://www.opengroup.org) and the AT&T STREAMS Programming Guide that accompanies System V.

Three file streams are automatically opened when a program is started. They are stdin, stdout, and stderr. These are declared in stdio.h and represent the standard input, output, and error output, respectively, which correspond to the low-level file descriptors 0, 1, and 2.

In this section, we look at the following functions:

- ❑   fopen, fclose
- ❑   fread, fwrite
- ❑   fflush-
- ❑   fseek-
- ❑   fgetc, getc, getchar
- ❑   fputc, putc, putchar
- ❑   fgets, gets
- ❑   printf, fprintf, and sprintf
- ❑   scanf, fscanf, and sscanf

fopen

The `fopen` library function is the analog of the low-level `open` system call. You use it mainly for files and terminal input and output. Where you need explicit control over devices, you're better off with the low-level system calls, because they eliminate potentially undesirable side effects from libraries, like input/output buffering.

Here's the syntax:

```
#include <stdio.h>

FILE *fopen(const char *filename, const char *mode);
```

`fopen` opens the file named by the `filename` parameter and associates a stream with it. The `mode` parameter specifies how the file is to be opened. It's one of the following strings:

❑ `"r"` or `"rb"`: Open for reading only

❑ `"w"` or `"wb"`: Open for writing, truncate to zero length

❑ `"a"` or `"ab"`: Open for writing, append to end of file

❑ `"r+"` or `"rb+"` or `"r+b"`: Open for update (reading and writing)

❑ `"w+"` or `"wb+"` or `"w+b"`: Open for update, truncate to zero length

❑ `"a+"` or `"ab+"` or `"a+b"`: Open for update, append to end of file

The `b` indicates that the file is a binary file rather than a text file.

> Note that, unlike MS-DOS, UNIX and Linux do not make a distinction between text and binary files. UNIX and Linux treat all files exactly the same, effectively as binary files. It's also important to note that the mode parameter must be a string, and not a character. Always use double quotes and not single quotes.

If successful, `fopen` returns a non-null `FILE *` pointer. If it fails, it returns the value `NULL`, defined in `stdio.h`.

The number of available streams is limited, in the same way that file descriptors are limited. The actual limit is `FOPEN_MAX`, which is defined through `stdio.h`, and is always at least eight and typically 16 on Linux.

fread

The `fread` library function is used to read data from a file stream. Data is read into a data buffer given by `ptr` from the stream, `stream`. Both `fread` and `fwrite` deal with data records. These are specified by a record size, `size`, and a count, `nitems`, of records to transfer. The function returns the number of items (rather than the number of bytes) successfully read into the data buffer. At the end of a file, fewer than `nitems` may be returned, including zero.

Here's the syntax:

```
#include <stdio.h>

size_t fread(void *ptr, size_t size, size_t nitems, FILE *stream);
```

As with all of the standard I/O functions that write to a buffer, it's the programmer's responsibility to allocate the space for the data and check for errors. See also `ferror` and `feof` later in this chapter.

fwrite

The `fwrite` library call has a similar interface to `fread`. It takes data records from the specified data buffer and writes them to the output stream. It returns the number of records successfully written.

Here's the syntax:

```
#include <stdio.h>

size_t fwrite (const void *ptr, size_t size, size_t nitems, FILE *stream);
```

Note that `fread` and `fwrite` are not recommended for use with structured data. Part of the problem is that files written with `fwrite` are potentially not portable between different machine architectures.

fclose

The `fclose` library function closes the specified `stream`, causing any unwritten data to be written. It's important to use `fclose` because the `stdio` library will buffer data. If the program needs to be sure that data has been completely written, it should call `fclose`. Note, however, that `fclose` is called automatically on all file streams that are still open when a program ends normally, but then, of course, you do not get a chance to check for errors reported by `fclose`.

Here's the syntax:

```
#include <stdio.h>

int fclose(FILE *stream);
```

fflush

The `fflush` library function causes all outstanding data on a file stream to be written immediately. You can use this to ensure that, for example, an interactive prompt has been sent to a terminal before any attempt to read a response. It's also useful for ensuring that important data has been committed to disk before continuing. You can sometimes use it when you're debugging a program to make sure that the program is writing data and not hanging. Note that an implicit flush operation is carried out when `fclose` is called, so you don't need to call `fflush` before `fclose`.

Here's the syntax:

```
#include <stdio.h>

int fflush(FILE *stream);
```

fseek

The fseek function is the file stream equivalent of the lseek system call. It sets the position in the stream for the next read or write on that stream. The meaning and values of the offset and whence parameters are the same as those we gave previously for lseek. However, where lseek returns an off_t, fseek returns an integer: 0 if it succeeds, –1 if it fails, with errno set to indicate the error. So much for standardization!

Here's the syntax:

```
#include <stdio.h>

int fseek(FILE *stream, long int offset, int whence);
```

fgetc, getc, and getchar

The fgetc function returns the next byte, as a character, from a file stream. When it reaches the end of the file or there is an error, it returns EOF. You must use ferror or feof to distinguish the two cases.

Here's the syntax:

```
#include <stdio.h>

int fgetc(FILE *stream);
int getc(FILE *stream);
int getchar();
```

The getc function is equivalent to fgetc, except that it may be implemented as a macro. In that case the stream argument may be evaluated more than once so it does not have side effects (for example, it shouldn't affect variables). Also, you can't guarantee to be able use the address of getc as a function pointer.

The getchar function is equivalent to getc(stdin) and reads the next character from the standard input.

fputc, putc, and putchar

The fputc function writes a character to an output file stream. It returns the value it has written, or EOF on failure.

```
#include <stdio.h>

int fputc(int c, FILE *stream);
int putc(int c, FILE *stream);
int putchar(int c);
```

As with fgetc/getc, the function putc is equivalent to fputc, but it may be implemented as a macro.

The putchar function is equivalent to putc(c, stdout), writing a single character to the standard output. Note that putchar takes and getchar returns characters as ints, not char. This allows the end-of-file (EOF) indicator to take the value –1, outside the range of character codes.

fgets and gets

The `fgets` function reads a string from an input file `stream`.

```
#include <stdio.h>

char *fgets(char *s, int n, FILE *stream);
char *gets(char *s);
```

`fgets` writes characters to the string pointed to by s until a newline is encountered, n-1 characters have been transferred, or the end of file is reached, whichever occurs first. Any newline encountered is transferred to the receiving string and a terminating null byte, \0, is added. Only a maximum of n-1 characters are transferred in any one call because the null byte must be added to mark the end of the string and bring the total up to n bytes.

When it successfully completes, `fgets` returns a pointer to the string s. If the stream is at the end of a file, it sets the EOF indicator for the stream and `fgets` returns a null pointer. If a read error occurs, `fgets` returns a null pointer and sets errno to indicate the type of error.

The `gets` function is similar to `fgets`, except that it reads from the standard input and discards any newline encountered. It adds a trailing null byte to the receiving string.

Note that gets *doesn't limit the number of characters that can be transferred so it could overrun its transfer buffer. Consequently, you should avoid using it and use* fgets *instead. Many security issues can be traced back to functions in programs that are made to overflow a buffer of some sort or another. This is one such function, so be careful!*

Formatted Input and Output

There are a number of library functions for producing output in a controlled fashion that you may be familiar with if you've programmed in C. These functions include `printf` and friends for printing values to a file stream, and `scanf` and others for reading values from a file stream.

printf, fprintf, and sprintf

The `printf` family of functions format and output a variable number of arguments of different types. The way each is represented in the output stream is controlled by the `format` parameter, which is a string that contains ordinary characters to be printed and codes called *conversion specifiers*, which indicate how and where the remaining arguments are to be printed.

```
#include <stdio.h>

int printf(const char *format, ...);
int sprintf(char *s, const char *format, ...);
int fprintf(FILE *stream, const char *format, ...);
```

The `printf` function produces its output on the standard output. The `fprintf` function produces its output on a specified `stream`. The `sprintf` function writes its output and a terminating null character into the string s passed as a parameter. This string must be large enough to contain all of the output.

113

There are other members of the printf family that deal with their arguments in different ways. See the printf manual page for more details.

Ordinary characters are passed unchanged into the output. Conversion specifiers cause printf to fetch and format additional arguments passed as parameters. They always start with a % character. Here's a simple example:

```
printf("Some numbers: %d, %d, and %d\n", 1, 2, 3);
```

This produces, on the standard output:

```
Some numbers: 1, 2, and 3
```

To print a % character, you need to use %%, so that it doesn't get confused with a conversion specifier.

Here are some of the most commonly used conversion specifiers:

- ❑ %d, %i: Print an integer in decimal
- ❑ %o, %x: Print an integer in octal, hexadecimal
- ❑ %c: Print a character
- ❑ %s: Print a string
- ❑ %f: Print a floating-point (single precision) number
- ❑ %e: Print a double precision number, in fixed format
- ❑ %g: Print a double in a general format

It's very important that the number and type of the arguments passed to printf match the conversion specifiers in the format string. An optional size specifier is used to indicate the type of integer arguments. This is either h, for example %hd, to indicate a short int, or l, for example %ld, to indicate a long int. Some compilers can check these printf statements, but they aren't infallible. If you are using the GNU compiler gcc, you can add the -Wformat option to your compilation command to do this.

Here's another example:

```
char initial = 'A';
char *surname = "Matthew";
double age = 13.5;

printf("Hello Mr %c %s, aged %g\n", initial, surname, age);
```

This produces

```
Hello Mr A Matthew, aged 13.5
```

You can gain greater control over the way items are printed by using field specifiers. These extend the conversion specifiers to include control over the spacing of the output. A common use is to set the number of decimal places for a floating-point number or to set the amount of space around a string.

Field specifiers are given as numbers immediately after the % character in a conversion specifier. The following table contains some more examples of conversion specifiers and resulting output. To make things a little clearer, we'll use vertical bars to show the limits of the output.

Format	Argument	|Output|
%10s	"Hello"	| Hello|
%-10s	"Hello"	|Hello |
%10d	1234	| 1234|
%-10d	1234	|1234 |
%010d	1234	|0000001234|
%10.4f	12.34	| 12.3400|
%*s	10, "Hello"	| Hello|

All of these examples have been printed in a field width of 10 characters. Note that a negative field width means that the item is written left-justified within the field. A variable field width is indicated by using an asterisk (*). In this case, the next argument is used for the width. A leading zero indicates the item is written with leading zeros. According to the POSIX specification, printf doesn't truncate fields; rather, it expands the field to fit. So, for example, if you try to print a string longer than the field, the field grows:

Format	Argument	|Output|
%10s	"HelloTherePeeps"	|HelloTherePeeps|

The printf functions return an integer, the number of characters written. This doesn't include the terminating null in the case of sprintf. On error, these functions return a negative value and set errno.

scanf, fscanf, and sscanf

The scanf family of functions works in a way similar to the printf group, except that these functions read items from a stream and place values into variables at the addresses they're passed as pointer parameters. They use a format string to control the input conversion in the same way, and many of the conversion specifiers are the same.

```
#include <stdio.h>

int scanf(const char *format, ...);
int fscanf(FILE *stream, const char *format, ...);
int sscanf(const char *s, const char *format, ...);
```

It's very important that the variables used to hold the values scanned in by the scanf functions are of the correct type and that they match the format string precisely. If they don't, your memory could be corrupted and your program could crash. There won't be any compiler errors, but if you're lucky, you might get a warning!

115

The format string for scanf and friends contains both ordinary characters and conversion specifiers, as for printf. However, the ordinary characters are used to specify characters that must be present in the input.

Here is a simple example:

```
int num;
scanf("Hello %d", &num);
```

This call to scanf will succeed only if the next five characters on the standard input are Hello. Then, if the next characters form a recognizable decimal number, the number will be read and the value assigned to the variable num. A space in the format string is used to ignore all whitespace (spaces, tabs, form feeds, and newlines) in the input between conversion specifiers. This means that the call to scanf will succeed and place 1234 into the variable num given either of the following inputs:

```
Hello      1234
Hello1234
```

Whitespace is also usually ignored in the input when a conversion begins. This means that a format string of %d will keep reading the input, skipping over spaces and newlines until a sequence of digits is found. If the expected characters are not present, the conversion fails and scanf returns.

This can lead to problems if you are not careful. An infinite loop can occur in your program if you leave a non-digit character in the input while scanning for integers.

Other conversion specifiers are

❏   %d: Scan a decimal integer

❏   %o, %x: Scan an octal, hexadecimal integer

❏   %f, %e, %g: Scan a floating-point number

❏   %c: Scan a character (whitespace not skipped)

❏   %s: Scan a string

❏   %[]: Scan a set of characters (see the following discussion)

❏   %%: Scan a % character

Like printf, scanf conversion specifiers may also have a field width to limit the amount of input consumed. A size specifier (either h for short or l for long) indicates whether the receiving argument is shorter or longer than the default. This means that %hd indicates a short int, %ld a long int, and %lg a double precision floating-point number.

A specifier beginning with an asterisk indicates that the item is to be ignored. This means that the information is not stored and therefore does not need a variable to receive it.

Use the %c specifier to read a single character in the input. This doesn't skip initial whitespace characters.

Use the %s specifier to scan strings, but take care. It skips leading whitespace, but stops at the first whitespace character in the string; so, you're better off using it for reading words rather than general strings. Also, without a field-width specifier, there's no limit to the length of string it might read, so the receiving string must be sufficient to hold the longest string in the input stream. It's better to use a field specifier, or a combination of `fgets` and `sscanf`, to read in a line of input and then scan it. This will prevent possible buffer overflows that could be exploited by a malicious user.

Use the `%[]` specifier to read a string composed of characters from a set. The format `%[A-Z]` will read a string of capital letters. If the first character in the set is a caret, `^`, the specifier reads a string that consists of characters not in the set. So, to read a string with spaces in it, but stopping at the first comma, you can use `%[^,]`.

Given the input line,

```
Hello, 1234, 5.678, X, string to the end of the line
```

this call to `scanf` will correctly scan four items:

```
char s[256];
int n;
float f;
char c;

scanf("Hello,%d,%g, %c, %[^\n]", &n,&f,&c,s);
```

The `scanf` functions return the number of items successfully read, which will be zero if the first item fails. If the end of the input is reached before the first item is matched, `EOF` is returned. If a read error occurs on the file stream, the stream error flag will be set and the error variable, `errno`, will be set to indicate the type of error. See the "Stream Errors" section later in this chapter for more details.

In general, `scanf` and friends are not highly regarded; this is for three reasons:

❏ Traditionally, the implementations have been buggy.

❏ They're inflexible to use.

❏ They can lead to code where it's difficult to work out what is being parsed.

As an alternative, try using other functions, like `fread` or `fgets`, to read input lines and then use the string functions to break the input into the items you need.

Other Stream Functions

There are a number of other `stdio` library functions that use either stream parameters or the standard streams `stdin`, `stdout`, `stderr`:

❏ `fgetpos`: Get the current position in a file stream.

❏ `fsetpos`: Set the current position in a file stream.

❏ `ftell`: Return the current file offset in a stream.

❏ `rewind`: Reset the file position in a stream.

❏ `freopen`: Reuse a file stream.

❑   `setvbuf`: Set the buffering scheme for a stream.

❑   `remove`: Equivalent to `unlink` unless the `path` parameter is a directory, in which case it's equivalent to `rmdir`.

These are all library functions documented in section 3 of the manual pages.

You can use the file stream functions to re-implement the file copy program, using library functions instead. Take a look at `copy_stdio.c` in the following Try It Out exercise.

Try It Out   A Third File Copy Program

This program is very similar to earlier versions, but the character-by-character copy is accomplished using calls to the functions referenced in `stdio.h`:

```
#include <stdio.h>
#include <stdlib.h>

int main()
{
    int c;
    FILE *in, *out;

    in = fopen("file.in","r");
    out = fopen("file.out","w");

    while((c = fgetc(in)) != EOF)
        fputc(c,out);

    exit(0);
}
```

Running this program as before, you get

```
$ TIMEFORMAT="" time ./copy_stdio
0.06user 0.02system 0:00.11elapsed 81%CPU
...
```

How It Works

This time, the program runs in 0.11 seconds, not as fast as the low-level block version, but a great deal better than the other single-character-at-a-time version. This is because the stdio library maintains an internal buffer within the `FILE` structure and the low-level system calls are made only when the buffer fills. Feel free to experiment with testing line-by-line and block stdio copying code to see how they perform relative to the three examples we've tested.

Stream Errors

To indicate an error, many stdio library functions return out-of-range values, such as null pointers or the constant EOF. In these cases, the error is indicated in the external variable errno:

```
#include <errno.h>

extern int errno;
```

Note that many functions may change the value of errno. *Its value is valid only when a function has failed. You should inspect it immediately after a function has indicated failure. You should always copy it into another variable before using it, because printing functions, such as* fprintf, *might alter* errno *themselves.*

You can also interrogate the state of a file stream to determine whether an error has occurred, or the end of file has been reached.

```
#include <stdio.h>

int ferror(FILE *stream);
int feof(FILE *stream);
void clearerr(FILE *stream);
```

The ferror function tests the error indicator for a stream and returns nonzero if it's set, but zero otherwise.

The feof function tests the end-of-file indicator within a stream and returns nonzero if it is set, zero otherwise. Use it like this:

```
if(feof(some_stream))
    /* We're at the end */
```

The clearerr function clears the end-of-file and error indicators for the stream to which stream points. It has no return value and no errors are defined. You can use it to recover from error conditions on streams. One example might be to resume writing to a stream after a "disk full" error has been resolved.

Streams and File Descriptors

Each file stream is associated with a low-level file descriptor. You can mix low-level input and output operations with higher-level stream operations, but this is generally unwise, because the effects of buffering can be difficult to predict.

```
#include <stdio.h>

int fileno(FILE *stream);
FILE *fdopen(int fildes, const char *mode);
```

You can determine which low-level file descriptor is being used for a file stream by calling the fileno function. It returns the file descriptor for a given stream, or –1 on failure. This function can be useful if you need low-level access to an open stream, for example, to call fstat on it.

You can create a new file stream based on an already-opened file descriptor by calling the fdopen function. Essentially, this function provides stdio buffers around an already-open file descriptor, which might be an easier way to explain it.

The fdopen function operates in the same way as the fopen function, but instead of a filename it takes a low-level file descriptor. This can be useful if you have used open to create a file, perhaps to get fine control over the permissions, but want to use a stream for writing to it. The mode parameter is the same as for the fopen function and must be compatible with the file access modes established when the file was originally opened. fdopen returns the new file stream or NULL on failure.

File and Directory Maintenance

The standard libraries and system calls provide complete control over the creation and maintenance of files and directories.

chmod

You can change the permissions on a file or directory using the chmod system call. This forms the basis of the chmod shell program.

Here's the syntax:

```
#include <sys/stat.h>

int chmod(const char *path, mode_t mode);
```

The file specified by path is changed to have the permissions given by mode. The modes are specified as in the open system call, a bitwise OR of required permissions. Unless the program has been given appropriate privileges, only the owner of the file or a superuser can change its permissions.

chown

A superuser can change the owner of a file using the chown system call.

```
#include <sys/types.h>
#include <unistd.h>

int chown(const char *path, uid_t owner, gid_t group);
```

The call uses the numeric values of the desired new user and group IDs (culled from getuid and get-gid calls) and a system value that is used to restrict who can change file ownership. The owner and group of a file are changed if the appropriate privileges are set.

POSIX actually allows systems where non-superusers can change file ownerships. All "proper" POSIX systems won't allow this, but, strictly speaking, it's an extension (for FIPS 151-2). The kinds of systems we deal with in this book conform to the XSI (X/Open System Interface) specification and do enforce ownership rules.

unlink, link, and symlink

You can remove a file using unlink.

The unlink system call removes the directory entry for a file and decrements the link count for it. It returns 0 if the unlinking was successful, –1 on an error. You must have write and execute permissions in the directory where the file has its directory entry for this call to function.

```
#include <unistd.h>

int unlink(const char *path);
int link(const char *path1, const char *path2);
int symlink(const char *path1, const char *path2);
```

If the count reaches zero and no process has the file open, the file is deleted. In fact, the directory entry is always removed immediately, but the file's space will not be recovered until the last process (if any) closes it. The rm program uses this call. Additional links represent alternative names for a file, normally created by the ln program. You can create new links to a file programmatically by using the link system call.

Creating a file with open and then calling unlink on it is a trick some programmers use to create transient files. These files are available to the program only while they are open; they will effectively be automatically deleted when the program exits and the file is closed.

The link system call creates a new link to an existing file, path1. The new directory entry is specified by path2. You can create symbolic links using the symlink system call in a similar fashion. Note that symbolic links to a file do not increment a file's reference count and so do not prevent the file from being effectively deleted as normal (hard) links do.

mkdir and rmdir

You can create and remove directories using the mkdir and rmdir system calls.

```
#include <sys/types.h>
#include <sys/stat.h>

int mkdir(const char *path, mode_t mode);
```

The mkdir system call is used for creating directories and is the equivalent of the mkdir program. mkdir makes a new directory with path as its name. The directory permissions are passed in the parameter mode and are given as in the O_CREAT option of the open system call and, again, subject to umask.

```
#include <unistd.h>

int rmdir(const char *path);
```

The rmdir system call removes directories, but only if they are empty. The rmdir program uses this system call to do its job.

chdir and getcwd

A program can navigate directories in much the same way as a user moves around the file system. As you use the cd command in the shell to change directory, so a program can use the chdir system call.

```
#include <unistd.h>

int chdir(const char *path);
```

A program can determine its current working directory by calling the getcwd function.

```
#include <unistd.h>

char *getcwd(char *buf, size_t size);
```

The getcwd function writes the name of the current directory into the given buffer, buf. It returns NULL if the directory name would exceed the size of the buffer (an ERANGE error), given as the parameter size. It returns buf on success.

getcwd may also return NULL if the directory is removed (EINVAL) or permissions changed (EACCESS) while the program is running.

Scanning Directories

A common problem on Linux systems is scanning directories, that is, determining the files that reside in a particular directory. In shell programs, it's easy — just let the shell expand a wildcard expression. In the past, different UNIX variants have allowed programmatic access to the low-level file system structure. You can still open a directory as a regular file and directly read the directory entries, but different file system structures and implementations have made this approach nonportable. A standard suite of library functions has now been developed that makes directory scanning much simpler.

The directory functions are declared in a header file dirent.h. They use a structure, DIR, as a basis for directory manipulation. A pointer to this structure, called a *directory stream* (a DIR *), acts in much the same way as a file steam (FILE *) does for regular file manipulation. Directory entries themselves are returned in dirent structures, also declared in dirent.h, because one should never alter the fields in the DIR structure directly.

We'll review these functions:

- ❑ opendir, closedir
- ❑ readdir
- ❑ telldir
- ❑ seekdir
- ❑ closedir

opendir

The opendir function opens a directory and establishes a directory stream. If successful, it returns a pointer to a DIR structure to be used for reading directory entries.

```
#include <sys/types.h>
#include <dirent.h>

DIR *opendir(const char *name);
```

opendir returns a null pointer on failure. Note that a directory stream uses a low-level file descriptor to access the directory itself, so opendir could fail with too many open files.

readdir

The readdir function returns a pointer to a structure detailing the next directory entry in the directory stream dirp. Successive calls to readdir return further directory entries. On error, and at the end of the directory, readdir returns NULL. POSIX-compliant systems leave errno unchanged when returning NULL at end of directory and set it when an error occurs.

```
#include <sys/types.h>
#include <dirent.h>

struct dirent *readdir(DIR *dirp);
```

Note that readdir scanning isn't guaranteed to list all the files (and subdirectories) in a directory if there are other processes creating and deleting files in the directory at the same time.

The dirent structure containing directory entry details includes the following entries:

❑ ino_t d_ino: The inode of the file

❑ char d_name[]: The name of the file

To determine further details of a file in a directory, you need to make a call to stat, which we covered earlier in this chapter.

telldir

The telldir function returns a value that records the current position in a directory stream. You can use this in subsequent calls to seekdir to reset a directory scan to the current position.

```
#include <sys/types.h>
#include <dirent.h>

long int telldir(DIR *dirp);
```

seekdir

The seekdir function sets the directory entry pointer in the directory stream given by dirp. The value of loc, used to set the position, should have been obtained from a prior call to telldir.

```
#include <sys/types.h>
#include <dirent.h>

void seekdir(DIR *dirp, long int loc);
```

closedir

The closedir function closes a directory stream and frees up the resources associated with it. It returns 0 on success and –1 if there is an error.

```
#include <sys/types.h>
#include <dirent.h>

int closedir(DIR *dirp);
```

In the next program, printdir.c, you will put together a lot of the file manipulation functions to create a simple directory listing. Each file in a directory is listed on a line by itself. Each subdirectory has its name followed by a slash and the files listed in it are indented by four spaces.

The program changes a directory into the subdirectories so that the files it finds have usable names, that is, they can be passed directly to opendir. The program will fail on very deeply nested directory structures because there's a limit on the allowed number of open directory streams.

We could, of course, make it more general by taking a command-line argument to specify the start point. Check out the Linux source code of such utilities as ls and find for ideas on a more general implementation.

Try It Out   A Directory-Scanning Program

1. Start with the appropriate headers and then a function, printdir, which prints out the current directory. It will recurse for subdirectories using the depth parameter for indentation.

```
#include <unistd.h>
#include <stdio.h>
#include <dirent.h>
#include <string.h>
#include <sys/stat.h>
#include <stdlib.h>

void printdir(char *dir, int depth)
{
    DIR *dp;
    struct dirent *entry;
    struct stat statbuf;

    if((dp = opendir(dir)) == NULL) {
        fprintf(stderr,"cannot open directory: %s\n", dir);
```

```
        return;
    }
    chdir(dir);
    while((entry = readdir(dp)) != NULL) {
        lstat(entry->d_name,&statbuf);
        if(S_ISDIR(statbuf.st_mode)) {
            /* Found a directory, but ignore . and .. */
            if(strcmp(".",entry->d_name) == 0 ||
                strcmp("..",entry->d_name) == 0)
                continue;
            printf("%*s%s/\n",depth,"",entry->d_name);
            /* Recurse at a new indent level */
            printdir(entry->d_name,depth+4);
        }
        else printf("%*s%s\n",depth,"",entry->d_name);
    }
    chdir("..");
    closedir(dp);
}
```

2. Now move onto the `main` function:

```
int main()
{
    printf("Directory scan of /home:\n");
    printdir("/home",0);
    printf("done.\n");

    exit(0);
}
```

The program scans the home directories and produces output like that following (edited for brevity). To see into other users' directories you may need superuser permissions.

```
$ ./printdir
Directory scan of /home:
neil/
    .Xdefaults
    .Xmodmap
    .Xresources
    .bash_history
    .bashrc
    .kde/
        share/
            apps/
                konqueror/
                    dirtree/
                        public_html.desktop
                    toolbar/
                    bookmarks.xml
                    konq_history
                kdisplay/
                    color-schemes/
```

125

```
BLP4e/
    Gnu_Public_License
    chapter04/
        argopt.c
        args.c
    chapter03/
        file.out
        mmap.c
        printdir
done.
```

How It Works

Most of the action is within the `printdir` function. After some initial error checking using `opendir` to see that the directory exists, `printdir` makes a call to `chdir` to the directory specified. While the entries returned by `readdir` aren't null, the program checks to see whether the entry is a directory. If it isn't, it prints the file entry with indentation `depth`.

If the entry *is* a directory, you meet a little bit of recursion. After the `.` and `..` entries (the current and parent directories) have been ignored, the `printdir` function calls itself and goes through the same process again. How does it get out of these loops? Once the `while` loop has finished, the call `chdir("..")` takes it back up the directory tree and the previous listing can continue. Calling `closedir(dp)` makes sure that the number of open directory streams isn't higher than it needs to be.

For a brief taste of the discussion of the Linux environment in Chapter 4, let's look at one way you can make the program more general. The program is limited because it's specific to the directory `/home`. With the following changes to `main`, you could turn it into a more useful directory browser:

```c
int main(int argc, char* argv[])
{
    char *topdir = ".";
    if (argc >= 2)
      topdir=argv[1];

    printf("Directory scan of %s\n",topdir);
    printdir(topdir,0);
    printf("done.\n");

    exit(0);
}
```

Three lines were changed and five added, but now it's a general-purpose utility with an optional parameter of the directory name, which defaults to the current directory. You can run it using the following command:

```
$ ./printdir2 /usr/local | more
```

The output will be paged so that the user can page through the output. Hence, the user has quite a convenient little general-purpose directory tree browser. With very little effort, you could add space usage statistics, limit depth of display, and so on.

Errors

As you've seen, many of the system calls and functions described in this chapter can fail for a number of reasons. When they do, they indicate the reason for their failure by setting the value of the external variable errno. Many different libraries use this variable as a standard way to report problems. It bears repeating that the program must inspect the errno variable immediately after the function giving problems because it may be overwritten by the next function called, even if that function itself doesn't fail.

The values and meanings of the errors are listed in the header file errno.h. They include

❏ EPERM: Operation not permitted

❏ ENOENT: No such file or directory

❏ EINTR: Interrupted system call

❏ EIO: I/O Error

❏ EBUSY: Device or resource busy

❏ EEXIST: File exists

❏ EINVAL: Invalid argument

❏ EMFILE: Too many open files

❏ ENODEV: No such device

❏ EISDIR: Is a directory

❏ ENOTDIR: Isn't a directory

There are a couple of useful functions for reporting errors when they occur: strerror and perror.

strerror

The strerror function maps an error number into a string describing the type of error that has occurred. This can be useful for logging error conditions.

Here's the syntax:

```
#include <string.h>

char *strerror(int errnum);
```

perror

The perror function also maps the current error, as reported in errno, into a string and prints it on the standard error stream. It's preceded by the message given in the string s (if not NULL), followed by a colon and a space.

Here's the syntax:

```
#include <stdio.h>

void perror(const char *s);
```

For example,

```
perror("program");
```

might give the following on the standard error output:

```
program: Too many open files
```

The /proc File System

Earlier in the chapter we mentioned that Linux treats most things as files and that there are entries in the file system for hardware devices. These /dev files are used to access hardware in a specific way using low-level system calls.

The software drivers that control hardware can often be configured in certain ways, or are capable of reporting information. For example, a hard disk controller may be configured to use a particular DMA mode. A network card might be able to report whether it has negotiated a high-speed, duplex connection.

Utilities for communicating with device drivers have been common in the past. For example, hdparm is used to configure some disk parameters and ifconfig can report network statistics. In recent years, there has been a trend toward providing a more consistent way of accessing driver information, and, in fact, to extend this to include communication with various elements of the Linux kernel.

Linux provides a special file system, procfs, that is usually made available as the directory /proc. It contains many special files that allow higher-level access to driver and kernel information. Applications can read and write these files to get information and set parameters as long as they are running with the correct access permissions.

The files that appear in /proc will vary from system to system, and more are included with each Linux release as more drivers and facilities support the procfs file system. Here, we look at some of the more common files and briefly consider their use.

A directory listing of /proc on the computer being used to write this chapter shows the following entries:

```
1/        10514/   20254/   6/      9057/   9623/        ide/          mtrr
10359/    10524/   29/      698/    9089/   9638/        interrupts    net/
10360/    10530/   2983/    699/    9118/   acpi/        iomem         partitions
10381/    10539/   3/       710/    9119/   asound/      ioports       scsi/
10438/    10541/   30/      711/    9120/   buddyinfo    irq/          self@
10441/    10555/   3069/    742/    9138/   bus/         kallsyms      slabinfo
10442/    10688/   3098/    7808/   9151/   cmdline      kcore         splash
10478/    10689/   3099/    7813/   92/     config.gz    keys          stat
10479/    10784/   31/      8357/   9288/   cpuinfo      key-users     swaps
10482/    113/     3170/    8371/   93/     crypto       kmsg          sys/
10484/    115/     3171/    840/    9355/   devices      loadavg       sysrq-trigger
10486/    116/     3177/    8505/   9407/   diskstats    locks         sysvipc/
10495/    1167/    32288/   8543/   9457/   dma          mdstat        tty/
10497/    1168/    3241/    8547/   9479/   driver/      meminfo       uptime
```

```
10498/   1791/   352/    8561/  9618/  execdomains  misc      version
10500/   19557/  4/      8677/  9619/  fb           modules   vmstat
10502/   19564/  4010/   888/   9621/  filesystems  mounts@   zoneinfo
10510/   2/      5/      8910/  9622/  fs/          mpt/
```

In many cases, the files can just be read and will give status information. For example, /proc/cpuinfo gives details of the processors available:

```
$ cat /proc/cpuinfo
processor       : 0
vendor_id       : GenuineIntel
cpu family      : 15
model           : 2
model name      : Intel(R) Pentium(R) 4 CPU 2.66GHz
stepping        : 8
cpu MHz         : 2665.923
cache size      : 512 KB
fdiv_bug        : no
hlt_bug         : no
f00f_bug        : no
coma_bug        : no
fpu             : yes
fpu_exception   : yes
cpuid level     : 2
wp              : yes
flags           : fpu vme de pse tsc msr pae mce cx8 apic sep mtrr pge mca cmov pat
pse36 clflush dts acpi mmx fxsr sse sse2 ss up
bogomips        : 5413.47
clflush size    : 64
```

Similarly, /proc/meminfo and /proc/version give information about memory usage and kernel version, respectively:

```
$ cat /proc/meminfo
MemTotal:        776156 kB
MemFree:          28528 kB
Buffers:         191764 kB
Cached:          369520 kB
SwapCached:          20 kB
Active:          406912 kB
Inactive:        274320 kB
HighTotal:            0 kB
HighFree:             0 kB
LowTotal:        776156 kB
LowFree:          28528 kB
SwapTotal:      1164672 kB
SwapFree:       1164652 kB
Dirty:               68 kB
Writeback:            0 kB
AnonPages:        95348 kB
Mapped:           49044 kB
Slab:             57848 kB
SReclaimable:     48008 kB
SUnreclaim:        9840 kB
PageTables:        1500 kB
```

129

```
NFS_Unstable:          0 kB
Bounce:                0 kB
CommitLimit:     1552748 kB
Committed_AS:     189680 kB
VmallocTotal:     245752 kB
VmallocUsed:       10572 kB
VmallocChunk:     234556 kB
HugePages_Total:       0
HugePages_Free:        0
HugePages_Rsvd:        0
Hugepagesize:       4096 kB
$ cat /proc/version
Linux version 2.6.20.2-2-default (geeko@buildhost) (gcc version 4.1.3 20070218
(prerelease) (SUSE Linux)) #1 SMP Fri Mar 9 21:54:10 UTC 2007
```

The information given by these files is generated each time the file is read. So rereading the meminfo file at a later time will give up-to-the-second results.

You can find more information from specific kernel functions in subdirectories of /proc. For example, you can get network socket usage statistics from /proc/net/sockstat:

```
$ cat /proc/net/sockstat
sockets: used 285
TCP: inuse 4 orphan 0 tw 0 alloc 7 mem 1
UDP: inuse 3
UDPLITE: inuse 0
RAW: inuse 0
FRAG: inuse 0 memory 0
```

Some of the /proc entries can be written to as well as read. For example, the total number of files that all running programs can open at the same time is a Linux kernel parameter. The current value can be read at /proc/sys/fs/file-max:

```
$ cat /proc/sys/fs/file-max
76593
```

Here the value is set to 76,593. If you need to increase this value, you can do so by writing to the same file. You may need to do this if you are running a specialist application suite — such as a database system that uses many tables — that needs to open many files at once.

Writing /proc files requires superuser access. You must take great care when writing /proc files; it's possible to cause severe problems including system crashes and loss of data by writing inappropriate values.

To increase the system-wide file handle limit to 80,000, you can simply write the new limit to the file-max file:

```
# echo 80000 >/proc/sys/fs/file-max
```

Now, when you reread the file, you see the new value:

```
$ cat /proc/sys/fs/file-max
80000
```

The subdirectories of /proc that have numeric names are used to provide access to information about running programs. You learn more about how programs are executed as processes in Chapter 11.

For now, just notice that each process has a unique identifier: a number between 1 and about 32,000. The ps command provides a list of currently running processes. For example, as this chapter is being written:

```
neil@suse103:~/BLP4e/chapter03> ps -a
  PID TTY          TIME CMD
 9118 pts/1     00:00:00 ftp
 9230 pts/1     00:00:00 ps
10689 pts/1     00:00:01 bash
neil@suse103:~/BLP4e/chapter03>
```

Here, you can see several terminal sessions running the bash shell and a file transfer session running the ftp program. You can get more details about the ftp session by looking in /proc.

The process identifier for ftp here is given as 9118, so you need to look in /proc/9118 for details about it:

```
$ ls -l /proc/9118
total 0
0 dr-xr-xr-x 2 neil users 0 2007-05-20 07:43 attr
0 -r-------- 1 neil users 0 2007-05-20 07:43 auxv
0 -r--r--r-- 1 neil users 0 2007-05-20 07:35 cmdline
0 -r--r--r-- 1 neil users 0 2007-05-20 07:43 cpuset
0 lrwxrwxrwx 1 neil users 0 2007-05-20 07:43 cwd -> /home/neil/BLP4e/chapter03
0 -r-------- 1 neil users 0 2007-05-20 07:43 environ
0 lrwxrwxrwx 1 neil users 0 2007-05-20 07:43 exe -> /usr/bin/pftp
0 dr-x------ 2 neil users 0 2007-05-20 07:19 fd
0 -rw-r--r-- 1 neil users 0 2007-05-20 07:43 loginuid
0 -r--r--r-- 1 neil users 0 2007-05-20 07:43 maps
0 -rw------- 1 neil users 0 2007-05-20 07:43 mem
0 -r--r--r-- 1 neil users 0 2007-05-20 07:43 mounts
0 -r-------- 1 neil users 0 2007-05-20 07:43 mountstats
0 -rw-r--r-- 1 neil users 0 2007-05-20 07:43 oom_adj
0 -r--r--r-- 1 neil users 0 2007-05-20 07:43 oom_score
0 lrwxrwxrwx 1 neil users 0 2007-05-20 07:43 root -> /
0 -rw------- 1 neil users 0 2007-05-20 07:43 seccomp
0 -r--r--r-- 1 neil users 0 2007-05-20 07:43 smaps
0 -r--r--r-- 1 neil users 0 2007-05-20 07:33 stat
0 -r--r--r-- 1 neil users 0 2007-05-20 07:43 statm
0 -r--r--r-- 1 neil users 0 2007-05-20 07:33 status
0 dr-xr-xr-x 3 neil users 0 2007-05-20 07:43 task
0 -r--r--r-- 1 neil users 0 2007-05-20 07:43 wchan
```

Here, you can see various special files that can tell us what is happening with this process.

You can tell that the program /usr/bin/pftp is running and that its current working directory is /home/neil/BLP4e/chapter03. It is possible to read the other files in this directory to see the command line used to start it as well as the shell environment it has. The cmdline and environ files provide this information as a series of null-terminated strings, so you need to take care when viewing them. We discuss the Linux environment in depth in Chapter 4.

```
$ od -c /proc/9118/cmdline
0000000   f   t   p  \0   1   9   2   .   1   6   8   .   0   .   1   2
```

```
0000020  \0
0000021
```

Here, you can see that `ftp` was started with the command line `ftp 192.168.0.12`.

The `fd` subdirectory provides information about the open file descriptors in use by the process. This information can be useful in determining how many files a program has open at one time. There is one entry per open descriptor; the name matches the number of the descriptor. In this case, you can see that `ftp` has open descriptors 0, 1, 2, and 3, as we might expect. These are the standard input, output, and error descriptors plus a connection to the remote server.

```
$ ls /proc/9118/fd
0  1  2  3
```

Advanced Topics: fcntl and mmap

Here, we cover a couple of topics that you might like to skip because they're seldom used. Having said that, we've put them here for your reference because they can provide simple solutions to some tricky problems.

fcntl

The `fcntl` system call provides further ways to manipulate low-level file descriptors.

```
#include <fcntl.h>

int fcntl(int fildes, int cmd);
int fcntl(int fildes, int cmd, long arg);
```

You can perform several miscellaneous operations on open file descriptors with the `fcntl` system call, including duplicating them, getting and setting file descriptor flags, getting and setting file status flags, and managing advisory file locking.

The various operations are selected by different values of the command parameter `cmd`, as defined in `fcntl.h`. Depending on the command chosen, the system call will require a third parameter, `arg`:

❑   `fcntl(fildes, F_DUPFD, newfd)`: This call returns a new file descriptor with a numerical value equal to or greater than the integer `newfd`. The new descriptor is a copy of the descriptor `fildes`. Depending on the number of open files and the value of `newfd`, this can be effectively the same as `dup(fildes)`.

❑   `fcntl(fildes, F_GETFD)`: This call returns the file descriptor flags as defined in `fcntl.h`. These include `FD_CLOEXEC`, which determines whether the file descriptor is closed after a successful call to one of the `exec` family of system calls.

❑   `fcntl(fildes, F_SETFD, flags)`: This call is used to set the file descriptor flags, usually just `FD_CLOEXEC`.

❑   `fcntl(fildes, F_GETFL)` and `fcntl(fildes, F_SETFL, flags)`: These calls are used, respectively, to get and set the file status flags and access modes. You can extract the file access modes by using the mask `O_ACCMODE` defined in `fcntl.h`. Other flags include those passed in a third argument to `open` when used with `O_CREAT`. Note that you can't set all flags. In particular, you can't set file permissions using `fcntl`.

You can also implement advisory file locking via `fcntl`. Refer to section 2 of the manual pages for more information, or see Chapter 7, where we discuss file locking.

mmap

UNIX provides a useful facility that allows programs to share memory, and the good news is that it's been included in versions 2.0 and later of the Linux kernel. The `mmap` (for memory map) function sets up a segment of memory that can be read or written by two or more programs. Changes made by one program are seen by the others.

You can use the same facility to manipulate files. You can make the entire contents of a disk file look like an array in memory. If the file consists of records that can be described by C structures, you can update the file using structure array accesses.

This is made possible by the use of virtual memory segments that have special permissions set. Reading from and writing to the segment causes the operating system to read and write the appropriate part of the disk file.

The `mmap` function creates a pointer to a region of memory associated with the contents of the file accessed through an open file descriptor.

```
#include <sys/mman.h>

void *mmap(void *addr, size_t len, int prot, int flags, int fildes, off_t off);
```

You can alter the start of the file data that is accessed by the shared segment by passing the `off` parameter. The open file descriptor is passed as `fildes`. The amount of data that can be accessed (that is, the length of the memory segment) is set via the `len` parameter.

You can use the `addr` parameter to request a particular memory address. If it's zero, the resulting pointer is allocated automatically. This is the recommended usage, because it is difficult to be portable otherwise; systems vary as to the available address ranges.

The `prot` parameter is used to set access permissions for the memory segment. This is a bitwise OR of the following constant values:

❑   PROT_READ: The segment can be read

❑   PROT_WRITE: The segment can be written

❑   PROT_EXEC: The segment can be executed

❑   PROT_NONE: The segment can't be accessed

The `flags` parameter controls how changes made to the segment by the program are reflected elsewhere; these options are displayed in the following table.

MAP_PRIVATE	The segment is private, changes are local
MAP_SHARED	The segment changes are made in the file
MAP_FIXED	The segment must be at the given address, addr

The `msync` function causes the changes in part or all of the memory segment to be written back to (or read from) the mapped file.

```
#include <sys/mman.h>

int msync(void *addr, size_t len, int flags);
```

The part of the segment to be updated is given by the passed start address, `addr`, and length, `len`. The `flags` parameter controls how the update should be performed using the options shown in the following table.

MS_ASYNC	Perform asynchronous writes
MS_SYNC	Perform synchronous writes
MS_INVALIDATE	Read data back in from the file

The `munmap` function releases the memory segment.

```
#include <sys/mman.h>

int munmap(void *addr, size_t len);
```

The following program, `mmap.c`, shows a file of structures being updated using `mmap` and array-style accesses. Linux kernels before 2.0 don't fully support this use of `mmap`. The program does work correctly on Sun Solaris and other systems.

Try It Out   Using mmap

1. Start by defining a RECORD structure and then creating NRECORDS versions, each recording their number. These are appended to the file `records.dat`.

```
#include <unistd.h>
#include <stdio.h>
#include <sys/mman.h>
#include <fcntl.h>
#include <stdlib.h>

typedef struct {
    int integer;
    char string[24];
} RECORD;

#define NRECORDS (100)

int main()
{
    RECORD record, *mapped;
    int i, f;
    FILE *fp;

    fp = fopen("records.dat","w+");
```

```
    for(i=0; i<NRECORDS; i++) {
        record.integer = i;
        sprintf(record.string,"RECORD-%d",i);
        fwrite(&record,sizeof(record),1,fp);
    }
    fclose(fp);
```

2. Next, change the integer value of record 43 to 143 and write this to the 43rd record's string:

```
    fp = fopen("records.dat","r+");
    fseek(fp,43*sizeof(record),SEEK_SET);
    fread(&record,sizeof(record),1,fp);

    record.integer = 143;
    sprintf(record.string,"RECORD-%d",record.integer);

    fseek(fp,43*sizeof(record),SEEK_SET);
    fwrite(&record,sizeof(record),1,fp);
    fclose(fp);
```

3. Now map the records into memory and access the 43rd record in order to change the integer to 243 (and update the record string), again using memory mapping:

```
    f = open("records.dat",O_RDWR);
    mapped = (RECORD *)mmap(0, NRECORDS*sizeof(record),
                        PROT_READ|PROT_WRITE, MAP_SHARED, f, 0);

    mapped[43].integer = 243;
    sprintf(mapped[43].string,"RECORD-%d",mapped[43].integer);

    msync((void *)mapped, NRECORDS*sizeof(record), MS_ASYNC);
    munmap((void *)mapped, NRECORDS*sizeof(record));
    close(f);

    exit(0);
}
```

In Chapter 13, you meet another shared memory facility: System V shared memory.

Summary

In this chapter, you've seen how Linux provides direct access to files and devices. You've seen how library functions build upon these low-level functions to provide flexible solutions to programming problems. As a result, you can write a fairly powerful directory-scanning routine in just a few lines of code.

You've also learned enough about file and directory handling to convert the fledgling CD application created at the end of Chapter 2 to a C program using a more structured file-based solution. At this stage, however, you can add no new functionality to the program, so we'll postpone the next rewrite until you've learned how to handle the screen and keyboard, which are the subjects of the next two chapters.

4

The Linux Environment

When you write a program for Linux (or UNIX and UNIX-like systems), you have to take into account that the program will run in a *multitasking environment*. This means that there will be multiple programs running at the same time and sharing machine resources such as memory, disk space, and CPU cycles. There may even be several instances of the same program running at the same time. It's important that these programs don't interfere with one another, are aware of their surroundings, and can act appropriately to avoid conflicts such as trying to write the same file at the same time as another program.

This chapter considers the environment in which programs operate, how they can use that environment to gain information about operating conditions, and how users of the programs can alter their behavior. In particular, this chapter looks at

❏ Passing arguments to programs

❏ Environment variables

❏ Finding out what the time is

❏ Temporary files

❏ Getting information about the user and the host computer

❏ Causing and configuring log messages

❏ Discovering the limits imposed by the system

Program Arguments

When a Linux or UNIX program written in C runs, it starts at the function main. For these programs, main is declared as

```
int main(int argc, char *argv[])
```

where argc is a count of the program arguments and argv is an array of character strings representing the arguments themselves.

You might also see C programs for Linux simply declaring `main` as

```
main()
```

This will still work, because the return type will default to `int` and formal parameters that are not used in a function need not be declared. `argc` and `argv` are still there, but if you don't declare them, you can't use them.

Whenever the operating system starts a new program, the parameters `argc` and `argv` are set up and passed to `main`. These parameters are usually supplied by another program, very often the shell that has requested that the operating system start the new program. The shell takes the command line that it's given, breaks it up into individual words, and uses these for the `argv` array. Remember that a Linux shell normally performs wild card expansion of filename arguments before `argc` and `argv` are set, whereas the MS-DOS shell expects programs to accept arguments with wild cards and perform their own wild card expansion.

For example, if we give the shell the following command,

```
$ myprog left right 'and center'
```

the program `myprog` will start at `main` with parameters:

```
argc: 4
argv: {"myprog", "left", "right", "and center"}
```

Note that the argument count includes the name of the program itself and the `argv` array contains the program name as its first element, `argv[0]`. Because we used quotes in the shell command, the fourth argument consists of a string containing spaces.

You'll be familiar with all of this if you've programmed in ISO/ANSI C. The arguments to `main` correspond to the positional parameters in shell scripts, `$0`, `$1`, and so on. Whereas ISO/ANSI C states that `main` must return `int`, the X/Open specification contains the explicit declaration given earlier.

Command-line arguments are useful for passing information to programs. For example, you could use them in a database application to pass the name of the database you want to use, which would allow you to use the same program on more than one database. Many utility programs also use command-line arguments to change their behavior or to set options. You would usually set these so-called *flags*, or *switches*, using command-line arguments that begin with a dash. For example, the `sort` program takes a switch to reverse the normal sort order:

```
$ sort -r file
```

Command-line options are very common and using them consistently will be a real help to those who use your program. In the past, each utility program adopted its own approach to command-line options, which led to some confusion. For example, take a look at the way these commands take parameters:

```
$ tar cvfB /tmp/file.tar 1024
$ dd if=/dev/fd0 of=/tmp/file.dd bs=18k
$ ps ax
$ gcc --help
$ ls -lstr
$ ls -l -s -t -r
```

We recommend that in your applications all command line switches start with a dash and consist of a single letter or number. If required, options that take no further arguments can be grouped together behind one dash. So, the two ls examples shown here do follow our guidelines. Each option should be followed by any value it requires as a separate argument. The dd example breaks our rule by using multi-character options that do not start with dashes (if=/dev/fd0); and the tar example separates options and their values completely! It is advisable to add longer, more meaningful switch names as alternatives to the single character versions and to use a double dash to distinguish them. So we might have -h and --help as options to get help.

Another little foible of some programs is to make the option +x (for example) perform the opposite function to -x. For example, in Chapter 2 we used set -o xtrace to set shell execution tracing on, and set +o xtrace to turn it off again.

As you can probably tell, remembering the order and meaning of all these program options is difficult enough without having to cope with idiosyncratic formats. Often, the only recourse is to use an -h (help) option or a man page if the programmer has provided one. As we show you a bit later in this chapter, getopt provides a neat solution to these problems. For the moment, though, let's just look at dealing with program arguments as they are passed.

Try It Out   Program Arguments

Here's a program, args.c, that examines its own arguments:

```c
#include <stdio.h>
#include <stdlib.h>

int main(int argc, char *argv[])
{
    int arg;

    for(arg = 0; arg < argc; arg++) {
        if(argv[arg][0] == '-')
            printf("option: %s\n", argv[arg]+1);
        else
            printf("argument %d: %s\n", arg, argv[arg]);
    }
    exit(0);
}
```

When you run this program, it just prints out its arguments and detects options. The intention is that the program takes a string argument and an optional filename argument introduced by an -f option. Other options might also be defined.

```
$ ./args -i -lr 'hi there' -f fred.c
argument 0: ./args
option: i
option: lr
argument 3: hi there
option: f
argument 5: fred.c
```

How It Works

The program simply uses the argument count, `argc`, to set up a loop to examine all of the program arguments. It detects options by looking for an initial dash.

In this example, if we intended the options -1 and -r to be available, we've missed the fact that the -1r perhaps ought to be treated the same as -1 -r.

The X/Open specification (available at http://opengroup.org/) defines a standard usage for command-line options (the Utility Syntax Guidelines) as well as a standard programming interface for providing command-line switches in C programs: the `getopt` function.

getopt

To help us adhere to these guidelines, Linux provides the `getopt` facility, which supports the use of options with and without values and is simple to use.

```
#include <unistd.h>

int getopt(int argc, char *const argv[], const char *optstring);
extern char *optarg;
extern int optind, opterr, optopt;
```

The `getopt` function takes the `argc` and `argv` parameters as passed to the program's `main` function and an options specifier string that tells `getopt` what options are defined for the program and whether they have associated values. The `optstring` is simply a list of characters, each representing a single character option. If a character is followed by a colon, it indicates that the option has an associated value that will be taken as the next argument. The `getopts` command in `bash` performs a very similar function.

For example, the following call would be used to handle the preceding example:

```
getopt(argc, argv, "if:lr");
```

It allows for simple options -i, -l, -r, and -f, followed by a filename argument. Calling the command with the same parameters but in a different order will alter the behavior. You can try this out when you get to the sample code in the next Try It Out section.

The return result for `getopt` is the next option character found in the `argv` array (if there is one). Call `getopt` repeatedly to get each option in turn. It has the following behavior:

❑   If the option takes a value, that value is pointed to by the external variable `optarg`.

❑   `getopt` returns -1 when there are no more options to process. A special argument, --, will cause `getopt` to stop scanning for options.

❑   `getopt` returns ? if there is an unrecognized option, which it stores in the external variable `optopt`.

❑   If an option requires a value (such as -f in our example) and no value is given, `getopt` normally returns ?. By placing a colon as the first character of the options string, `getopt` returns : instead of ? when no value is given.

The external variable, optind, is set to the index of the next argument to process. getopt uses it to remember how far it's got. Programs would rarely need to set this variable. When all the option arguments have been processed, optind indicates where the remaining arguments can be found at the end of the argv array.

Some versions of getopt will stop at the first non-option argument, returning –1 and setting optind. Others, such as those provided with Linux, can process options wherever they occur in the program arguments. Note that, in this case, getopt effectively rewrites the argv array so that all of the non-option arguments are presented together, starting at argv[optind]. For the GNU version of getopt, this behavior is controlled by the POSIXLY_CORRECT environment variable. If set, getopt will stop at the first non-option argument. Additionally, some getopt implementations print error messages for unknown options. Note that the POSIX specification says that if the opterr variable is non-zero, getopt will print an error message to stderr.

Try It Out   getopt

In this Try It Out, you use getopt for your example; call the new program argopt.c:

```c
#include <stdio.h>
#include <unistd.h>
#include <stdlib.h>

int main(int argc, char *argv[])
{
    int opt;

    while((opt = getopt(argc, argv, ":if:lr")) != -1) {
        switch(opt) {
        case 'i':
        case 'l':
        case 'r':
            printf("option: %c\n", opt);
            break;
        case 'f':
            printf("filename: %s\n", optarg);
            break;
        case ':':
            printf("option needs a value\n");
            break;
        case '?':
            printf("unknown option: %c\n", optopt);
            break;
        }
    }
    for(; optind < argc; optind++)
        printf("argument: %s\n", argv[optind]);
    exit(0);
}
```

Now when you run the program, you see that all the command-line arguments are handled automatically:

```
$ ./argopt -i -lr 'hi there' -f fred.c -q
option: i
option: l
option: r
```

```
filename: fred.c
unknown option: q
argument: hi there
```

How It Works

The program repeatedly calls `getopt` to process option arguments until none remain, at which point `getopt` returns -1. The appropriate action is taken for each option, including dealing with unknown options and missing values. Depending on your version of `getopt`, you might see slightly different output from that shown here — especially error messages — but the meaning will be clear.

Once all options have been processed, the program simply prints out the remaining arguments as before, but starting from `optind`.

---

getopt_long

Many Linux applications also accept arguments that are more meaningful than the single character options used in the previous example. The GNU C library contains a version of `getopt` called `getopt_long` that accepts so-called *long arguments* that are introduced with a double dash.

Try It Out   getopt_long

You can use `getopt_long` to create a new version of the example program that can be invoked using long equivalents of options like this:

```
$ ./longopt --initialize --list 'hi there'  --file fred.c -q
option: i
option: l
filename: fred.c
./longopt: invalid option -- q
unknown option: q
argument: hi there
```

In fact, both the new long options and the original single character options can be mixed. As long as they remain distinguishable, long options also can be abbreviated. Long options that take an argument can be given as a single argument in the form *--option=value*, as follows

```
$ ./longopt --init -l --file=fred.c 'hi there'
option: i
option: l
filename: fred.c
argument: hi there
```

The new program, `longopt.c`, is shown here with changes required from `argopt.c` to support the long options highlighted:

```
#include <stdio.h>
#include <unistd.h>
```

```
#include <stdlib.h>

#define _GNU_SOURCE
#include <getopt.h>

int main(int argc, char *argv[])
{
    int opt;
    struct option longopts[] = {
        {"initialize", 0, NULL, 'i'},
        {"file", 1, NULL, 'f'},
        {"list", 0, NULL, 'l'},
        {"restart", 0, NULL, 'r'},
        {0,0,0,0}};

    while((opt = getopt_long(argc, argv, ":if:lr", longopts, NULL)) != -1) {
        switch(opt) {
        case 'i':
        case 'l':
        case 'r':
            printf("option: %c\n", opt);
            break;
        case 'f':
            printf("filename: %s\n", optarg);
            break;
        case ':':
            printf("option needs a value\n");
            break;
        case '?':
            printf("unknown option: %c\n", optopt);
            break;
        }
    }
    for(; optind < argc; optind++)
        printf("argument: %s\n", argv[optind]);
    exit(0);
}
```

How It Works

The getopt_long function takes two additional parameters over getopt. The first of these is an array of structures that describes the long options and tells getopt_long how to handle them. The second additional parameter is the address of a variable that can be used like a long option version of optind; for each long option recognized, its index in the long options array can be written into this variable. In this example, you do not need this information, so you use NULL as the second additional parameter.

The long options array consists of a number of structures of type struct option, each of which describes the desired behavior of a long option. The array must end with a structure containing all zeros.

The long option structure is defined in getopt.h and must be included with the constant _GNU_SOURCE, defined to enable the getopt_long functionality.

```
struct option {
    const char *name;
```

```
            int has_arg;
            int *flag;
            int val;
        };
```

The members of the structure are shown in the following table.

Option Member	Description
name	The name of the long option. Abbreviations will be accepted as long as they cannot be confused with other options.
has_arg	Whether this option takes an argument. Set to 0 for options that do not take an argument, 1 for options that must have a value, and 2 for those that have an optional argument.
flag	Set to NULL to have getopt_long return the value given in val when this option is found. Otherwise, getopt_long returns 0 and writes the value of val into the variable pointed to by flag.
val	The value getopt_long is to return for this option.

For other options associated with the GNU extensions to getopt and related functions, refer to the getopt manual page.

Environment Variables

We discussed environment variables in Chapter 2. These are variables that can be used to control the behavior of shell scripts and other programs. You can also use them to configure the user's environment. For example, each user has an environment variable, HOME, that defines his home directory, the default starting place for his or her session. As you've seen, you can examine environment variables from the shell prompt:

```
$ echo $HOME
/home/neil
```

You can also use the shell's set command to list all of the environment variables.

The UNIX specification defines many standard environment variables used for a variety of purposes, including terminal type, default editors, time zones, and so on. A C program may gain access to environment variables using the putenv and getenv functions.

```
#include <stdlib.h>

char *getenv(const char *name);
int putenv(const char *string);
```

The environment consists of strings of the form name=value. The getenv function searches the environment for a string with the given name and returns the value associated with that name. It will return null if the requested variable doesn't exist. If the variable exists but has no value, getenv succeeds and returns an empty string, one in which the first byte is null. The string returned by getenv is held in static storage owned by getenv, so to use it further you must copy it to another string because it will be overwritten by subsequent calls to getenv.

The putenv function takes a string of the form name=value and adds it to the current environment. It will fail and return -1 if it can't extend the environment due to lack of available memory. When this happens, the error variable errno will be set to ENOMEM.

In the following example, you write a program to print out the value of any environment variable you choose. You also arrange to set the value if you give the program a second argument.

Try It Out   getenv and putenv

1. The first few lines after the declaration of main ensure that the program, environ.c, has been called correctly with just one or two arguments:

```
#include <stdlib.h>
#include <stdio.h>
#include <string.h>

int main(int argc, char *argv[])
{
    char *var, *value;

    if(argc == 1 || argc > 3) {
        fprintf(stderr,"usage: environ var [value]\n");
        exit(1);
    }
```

2. That done, you fetch the value of the variable from the environment, using getenv:

```
var = argv[1];
value = getenv(var);
if(value)
    printf("Variable %s has value %s\n", var, value);
else
    printf("Variable %s has no value\n", var);
```

3. Next, check whether the program was called with a second argument. If it was, you set the variable to the value of that argument by constructing a string of the form name=value and then calling putenv:

```
if(argc == 3) {
    char *string;
    value = argv[2];
    string = malloc(strlen(var)+strlen(value)+2);
    if(!string) {
        fprintf(stderr,"out of memory\n");
        exit(1);
    }
```

145

```
        strcpy(string,var);
        strcat(string,"=");
        strcat(string,value);
        printf("Calling putenv with: %s\n",string);
        if(putenv(string) != 0) {
            fprintf(stderr,"putenv failed\n");
            free(string);
            exit(1);
        }
```

4. Finally, you discover the new value of the variable by calling `getenv` once again:

```
        value = getenv(var);
        if(value)
            printf("New value of %s is %s\n", var, value);
        else
            printf("New value of %s is null??\n", var);
    }
    exit(0);
}
```

When you run this program, you can see and set environment variables:

```
$ ./environ HOME
Variable HOME has value /home/neil
$ ./environ FRED
Variable FRED has no value
$ ./environ FRED hello
Variable FRED has no value
Calling putenv with: FRED=hello
New value of FRED is hello
$ ./environ FRED
Variable FRED has no value
```

Notice that the environment is local only to the program. Changes that you make within the program are not reflected outside it because variable values are not propagated from the child process (your program) to the parent (the shell).

Use of Environment Variables

Programs often use environment variables to alter the way they work. Users can set the values of these environment variables either in their default environment, via a `.profile` file read by their login shell, using a shell-specific startup (`rc`) file, or by specifying variables on the shell command line. For example:

```
$ ./environ FRED
Variable FRED has no value
$ FRED=hello ./environ FRED
Variable FRED has value hello
```

The shell takes initial variable assignments as temporary changes to environment variables. In the second part of the preceding example, the program `environ` runs in an environment where the variable FRED has a value.

For instance, in a future version of the CD database application, you could change an environment variable, say CDDB, to indicate the database to use. Each user could then specify his or her own default value or use a shell command to set it on a run-by-run basis:

```
$ CDDB=mycds; export CDDB
$ cdapp
```

or

```
$ CDDB=mycds cdapp
```

Environment variables are a mixed blessing and you should use them with care. They are more "hidden" to the user than command-line options and, as such, this can make debugging harder. In a sense, environment variables are like global variables in that they may alter the behavior of a program, giving unexpected results.

The environ Variable

As you've seen, the program environment is made up of strings of the form name=value. This array of strings is made available to programs directly via the environ variable, which is declared as

```
#include <stdlib.h>

extern char **environ;
```

Try It Out   environ

Here's a program, showenv.c, that uses the environ variable to print out the environment variables:

```c
#include <stdlib.h>
#include <stdio.h>

extern char **environ;

int main()
{
    char **env = environ;

    while(*env) {
        printf("%s\n",*env);
        env++;
    }
    exit(0);
}
```

When you run this program on a Linux system, you get something like the following output, which has been abbreviated somewhat. The number, order of appearance, and values of these variables depend on the operating system version, the command shell being used, and the user settings in force at the time the program is run.

```
$ ./showenv
HOSTNAME=tilde.provider.com
```

```
LOGNAME=neil
MAIL=/var/spool/mail/neil
TERM=xterm
HOSTTYPE=i386
PATH=/usr/local/bin:/bin:/usr/bin:
HOME=/usr/neil
LS_OPTIONS=-N --color=tty -T 0
SHELL=/bin/bash
OSTYPE=Linux
...
```

How It Works

This program iterates through the environ variable, a null-terminated array of strings, to print out the whole environment.

Time and Date

Often it can be useful for a program to be able to determine the time and date. It may want to log the length of time it is run, or it may need to change the way it behaves at certain times. For example, a game might refuse to run during working hours, or a backup scheduling program might want to wait until the early hours before starting an automatic backup.

UNIX systems all use the same starting point for times and dates: midnight GMT on January 1, 1970. This is the "start of the UNIX epoch" and Linux is no exception. All times in a Linux system are measured as seconds since then. This is similar to the way MS-DOS handles times, except that the MS-DOS epoch started in 1980. Other systems use other epoch start times.

Times are handled using a defined type, a time_t. This is an integer type intended to be large enough to contain dates and times in seconds. On Linux systems, it's a long integer and is defined, together with functions for manipulating time values, in the header file time.h.

Never assume that times are 32 bits. On UNIX and Linux systems using a 32-bit time_t type, the time will "roll over" in the year 2038. By that time, we expect systems will have moved to using a time_t type that is larger than 32 bits. With the recent introduction of 64-bit processors into the mainstream, this is pretty much inevitable.

#include <time.h>

time_t time(time_t *tloc);

You can find the low-level time value by calling the time function, which returns the number of seconds since the start of the epoch. It will also write the returned value to a location pointed to by tloc, if this isn't a null pointer.

Try It Out   **time**

Here's a simple program, envtime.c, to demonstrate the time function:

```
#include <time.h>
#include <stdio.h>
#include <unistd.h>
#include <stdlib.h>

int main()
{
    int i;
    time_t the_time;

    for(i = 1; i <= 10; i++) {
        the_time = time((time_t *)0);
        printf("The time is %ld\n", the_time);
        sleep(2);
    }
    exit(0);
}
```

When you run this program, it prints the low-level time value every two seconds for 20 seconds.

```
$ ./envtime
The time is 1179643852
The time is 1179643854
The time is 1179643856
The time is 1179643858
The time is 1179643860
The time is 1179643862
The time is 1179643864
The time is 1179643866
The time is 1179643868
The time is 1179643870
```

How It Works

The program calls time with a null pointer argument, which returns the time and date as a number of seconds. The program sleeps for two seconds and repeats the call to time for a total of ten times.

Using the time and date as a number of seconds since the start of 1970 can be useful for measuring how long something takes to happen. You could consider simply subtracting the values you get from two calls to time. However, in its deliberations, the ISO/ANSI C standard committee didn't specify that the time_t type be used to measure arbitrary time intervals in seconds, so they invented a function, difftime, which will calculate the difference in seconds between two time_t values and return it as a double:

```
#include <time.h>

double difftime(time_t time1, time_t time2);
```

The difftime function calculates the difference between two time values and returns a value equivalent to time1-time2 as a floating-point number. For Linux, the return value from time is a number of seconds and can be manipulated, but for the ultimate in portability you should use difftime.

To present the time and date in a more meaningful way (to humans), you need to convert the time value into a recognizable time and date. There are standard functions to help with this.

The function gmtime breaks down a low-level time value into a structure containing more usual fields:

```
#include <time.h>

struct tm *gmtime(const time_t timeval);
```

The structure tm is defined to contain at least the following members:

tm Member	Description
int tm_sec	Seconds, 0-61
int tm_min	Minutes, 0-59
int tm_hour	Hours, 0-23
int tm_mday	Day in the month, 1-31
int tm_mon	Month in the year, 0-11 (January = 0)
int tm_year	Years since 1900
int tm_wday	Day in the week, 0-6 (Sunday = 0)
int tm_yday	Day in the year, 0-365
int tm_isdst	Daylight savings in effect

The range for tm_sec allows for the occasional leap second or double leap second.

Try It Out   gmtime

Here's a program, gmtime.c, which prints out the current time and date using the tm structure and gmtime:

```c
#include <time.h>
#include <stdio.h>
#include <stdlib.h>

int main()
{
    struct tm *tm_ptr;
    time_t the_time;
```

```
    (void) time(&the_time);
    tm_ptr = gmtime(&the_time);

    printf("Raw time is %ld\n", the_time);
    printf("gmtime gives:\n");
    printf("date: %02d/%02d/%02d\n",
        tm_ptr->tm_year, tm_ptr->tm_mon+1, tm_ptr->tm_mday);
    printf("time: %02d:%02d:%02d\n",
        tm_ptr->tm_hour, tm_ptr->tm_min, tm_ptr->tm_sec);
    exit(0);
}
```

When you run this program, you get a good approximation of the time and date:

```
$ ./gmtime; date
Raw time is 1179644196
gmtime gives:
date: 107/05/20
time: 06:56:36
Sun May 20 07:56:37 BST 2007
```

How It Works

The program calls time to get the low-level time value and then calls gmtime to convert this into a structure with useful time and date values. It prints these out using printf. Strictly speaking, you shouldn't print the raw time value in this way because it isn't guaranteed to be a long type on all systems. Running the date command immediately after gmtime allows you to compare its output.

However, you have a little problem here. If you're running this program in a time zone other than Greenwich Mean Time, or if your local daylight savings time is in effect as here, you'll notice that the time (and possibly date) is incorrect. This is because gmtime returns the time as GMT (now known as Coordinated Universal Time, or UTC). Linux and UNIX do this so that all programs and systems across the world are synchronized. Files created at the same moment in different time zones will appear to have the same creation time. To see the local time, you need to use the function localtime instead:

```
#include <time.h>

struct tm *localtime(const time_t *timeval);
```

The localtime function is identical to gmtime, except that it returns a structure containing values adjusted for local time zone and daylight savings. If you try the gmtime program again, but use localtime in place of gmtime, you should see a correct time and date reported.

To convert a broken-down tm structure into a raw time_t value, you can use the function mktime:

```
#include <time.h>

time_t mktime(struct tm *timeptr);
```

mktime will return -1 if the structure can't be represented as a time_t value.

For "friendly" (as opposed to machine) time, and date output provided by the date program, you can use the functions asctime and ctime:

```
#include <time.h>

char *asctime(const struct tm *timeptr);
char *ctime(const time_t *timeval);
```

The asctime function returns a string that represents the time and date given by the tm structure timeptr. The string returned has a format similar to the following:

```
Sun Jun  9 12:34:56 2007\n\0
```

It's always a fixed format, 26 characters long. The function ctime is equivalent to calling

```
asctime(localtime(timeval))
```

It takes a raw time value and converts it to a more readable local time.

Try It Out   ctime

In this example, you see ctime in action, using the following code:

```
#include <time.h>
#include <stdio.h>
#include <stdlib.h>

int main()
{
    time_t timeval;

    (void)time(&timeval);
    printf("The date is: %s", ctime(&timeval));
    exit(0);
}
```

Compile and then run ctime.c and you should see something like this:

```
$ ./ctime
The date is: Sat Jun  9 08:02:08 2007
```

How It Works

The ctime.c program calls time to get the low-level time value and lets ctime do all the hard work, converting it to a readable string, which it then prints.

To gain more control of the exact formatting of time and date strings, Linux and modern UNIX-like systems provide the `strftime` function. This is rather like a `sprintf` for dates and times and works in a similar way:

```
#include <time.h>

size_t strftime(char *s, size_t maxsize, const char *format, struct tm *timeptr);
```

The `strftime` function formats the time and date represented by the `tm` structure pointed to by `timeptr` and places the result in the string `s`. This string is specified as (at least) `maxsize` characters long. The `format` string is used to control the characters written to the string. Like `printf`, it contains ordinary characters that will be transferred to the string and conversion specifiers for formatting time and date elements. The conversion specifiers include the following:

Conversion Specifier	Description
%a	Abbreviated weekday name
%A	Full weekday name
%b	Abbreviated month name
%B	Full month name
%c	Date and time
%d	Day of the month, 01-31
%H	Hour, 00-23
%I	Hour in 12-hour clock, 01-12
%j	Day of the year, 001-366
%m	Month of the year, 01-12
%M	Minutes, 00-59
%p	a.m. or p.m.
%S	Seconds, 00-61
%u	Day in the week, 1-7 (1 = Monday)
%U	Week in the year, 01-53 (Sunday is the first day of the week.)
%V	Week in the year, 01-53 (Monday is the first day of the week.)
%w	Day in the week, 0-6 (0 = Sunday)
%x	Date in local format

Continued on next page

Conversion Specifier	Description
%X	Time in local format
%y	Year number less 1900
%Y	Year
%Z	Time zone name
%%	A % character

So, the usual date as given by the `date` program corresponds to a `strftime` format string of

```
"%a %b %d %H:%M:%S %Y"
```

To help with reading dates, you can use the `strptime` function, which takes a string representing a date and time and creates a `tm` structure representing the same date and time:

```
#include <time.h>

char *strptime(const char *buf, const char *format, struct tm *timeptr);
```

The `format` string is constructed in exactly the same way as the `format` string for `strftime`. `strptime` acts in a similar way to `sscanf` in that it scans a string, looking for identifiable fields, and writes them into variables. Here it's the members of a `tm` structure that are filled in according to the `format` string. However, the conversion specifiers for `strptime` are a little more relaxed than those for `strftime` because `strptime` will allow both abbreviated and full names for days and months. Either representation will match a `%a` specifier in `strptime`. Also, where `strftime` always uses leading zeros on numbers less than 10, `strptime` regards them as optional.

`strptime` returns a pointer to the character following the last one consumed in the conversion process. If it encounters characters that can't be converted, the conversion simply stops at that point. The calling program needs to check that enough of the passed string has been consumed to ensure that meaningful values have been written to the `tm` structure.

Try It Out   strftime and strptime

Have a look at the selection of conversion specifiers used in the following program:

```
#include <time.h>
#include <stdio.h>
#include <stdlib.h>

int main()
{
    struct tm *tm_ptr, timestruct;
    time_t the_time;
    char buf[256];
```

```
    char *result;

    (void) time(&the_time);
    tm_ptr = localtime(&the_time);
    strftime(buf, 256, "%A %d %B, %I:%S %p", tm_ptr);

    printf("strftime gives: %s\n", buf);

    strcpy(buf,"Thu 26 July 2007, 17:53 will do fine");

    printf("calling strptime with: %s\n", buf);
    tm_ptr = &timestruct;

    result = strptime(buf,"%a %d %b %Y, %R", tm_ptr);
    printf("strptime consumed up to: %s\n", result);

    printf("strptime gives:\n");
    printf("date: %02d/%02d/%02d\n",
        tm_ptr->tm_year % 100, tm_ptr->tm_mon+1, tm_ptr->tm_mday);
    printf("time: %02d:%02d\n",
        tm_ptr->tm_hour, tm_ptr->tm_min);
    exit(0);
}
```

When you compile and run this program, `strftime.c`, you get

```
$ ./strftime
strftime gives: Saturday 09 June, 08:16 AM
calling strptime with: Thu 26 July 2007, 17:53 will do fine
strptime consumed up to:  will do fine
strptime gives:
date: 07/07/26
time: 17:53
```

How It Works

The `strftime` program obtains the current local time by calling `time` and `localtime`. It then converts it to a readable form by calling `strftime` with an appropriate formatting argument. To demonstrate the use of `strptime`, the program sets up a string containing a date and time, then calls `strptime` to extract the raw time and date values, and prints them. The conversion specifier `%R` is a shortcut for `%H:%M` in `strptime`.

It's important to note that `strptime` needs an accurate format string to successfully scan a date. Typically, it won't accurately scan dates read from strings entered by users unless the format is very much restricted.

It is possible that you will find the compiler issuing a warning when you compile `strftime.c`. This is because the GNU library does not by default declare `strptime`. The fix for this is to explicitly request X/Open standard features by adding the following line before including `time.h`:

```
#define _XOPEN_SOURCE
```

Temporary Files

Often, programs will need to make use of temporary storage in the form of files. These might hold intermediate results of a computation or represent backup copies of files made before critical operations. For example, a database application could use a temporary file when deleting records. The file collects the database entries that need to be retained, and then, at the end of the process, the temporary file becomes the new database and the original is deleted.

This popular use of temporary files has a hidden disadvantage. You must take care to ensure that the applications choose a unique filename to use for the temporary file. If they don't there may be a problem. Because Linux is a multitasking system, another program could choose the same name and the two will interfere with each other.

A unique filename can be generated by the tmpnam function:

```
#include <stdio.h>

char *tmpnam(char *s);
```

The tmpnam function returns a valid filename that isn't the same as any existing file. If the string s isn't null, the filename will also be written to it. Further calls to tmpnam will overwrite the static storage used for return values, so it's essential to use a string parameter if tmpnam is to be called many times. The string is assumed to be at least L_tmpnam (usually around 20) characters long. tmpnam can be called up to TMP_MAX times (several thousand at least) in a single program, and it will generate a different filename each time.

If the temporary file is to be used immediately, you can name it and open it at the same time using the tmpfile function. This is important because another program could create a file with the same name as that returned by tmpnam. The tmpfile function avoids this problem altogether:

```
#include <stdio.h>

FILE *tmpfile(void);
```

The tmpfile function returns a stream pointer that refers to a unique temporary file. The file is opened for reading and writing (via fopen with w+), and it will be automatically deleted when all references to the file are closed.

tmpfile returns a null pointer and sets errno on error.

Try It Out   **tmpnam and tmpfile**

Let's see these two functions in action:

```
#include <stdio.h>
#include <stdlib.h>

int main()
{
    char tmpname[L_tmpnam];
    char *filename;
```

```
        FILE *tmpfp;

        filename = tmpnam(tmpname);

        printf("Temporary file name is: %s\n", filename);
        tmpfp = tmpfile();
        if(tmpfp)
            printf("Opened a temporary file OK\n");
        else
            perror("tmpfile");
        exit(0);
}
```

When you compile and run this program, tmpnam.c, you can see the unique filename generated by tmpnam:

```
$ ./tmpnam
Temporary file name is: /tmp/file2S64zc
Opened a temporary file OK
```

How It Works

The program calls tmpnam to generate a unique filename for a temporary file. If you wanted to use it, you would have to open it quickly to minimize the risk that another program would open a file with the same name. The tmpfile call creates and opens a temporary file at the same time, thus avoiding this risk. In fact, the GNU C compiler may give a warning about the use of tmpnam when compiling a program that uses it.

Versions of UNIX introduced another way to generate temporary filenames using the functions mktemp and mkstemp. These are supported by Linux and are similar to tmpnam, except that you can specify a template for the temporary filename, which gives you a little more control over their location and name:

```
#include <stdlib.h>

char *mktemp(char *template);
int mkstemp(char *template);
```

The mktemp function creates a unique filename from the given template. The template argument must be a string with six trailing X characters. The mktemp function replaces these X characters with a unique combination of valid filename characters. It returns a pointer to the generated string or a null pointer if it couldn't generate a unique name.

The mkstemp function is similar to tmpfile in that it creates and opens a temporary file. The filename is generated in the same way as mktemp, but the returned result is an open, low-level file descriptor.

You should always use the "create and open" functions tmpfile *and* mkstemp *in your own programs rather than* tmpnam *and* mktemp.

User Information

All Linux programs, with the notable exception of init, are started by other programs or users. You learn more about how running programs, or processes, interact in Chapter 11. Users most often start programs from a shell that responds to their commands. You've seen that a program can determine a great deal about its environment by examining environment variables and reading the system clock. A program can also find out information about the person using it.

When a user logs in to a Linux system, he or she has a username and password. Once these have been validated, the user is presented with a shell. Internally, the user also has a unique user identifier known as a *UID*. Each program that Linux runs is run on behalf of a user and has an associated UID.

You can set up programs to run as if a different user had started them. When a program has its UID permission set, it will run as if started by the owner of the executable file. When the su command is executed, the program runs as if it had been started by the superuser. It then validates the user's access, changes the UID to that of the target account, and executes that account's login shell. This also allows a program to be run as if a different user had started it and is often used by system administrators to perform maintenance tasks.

Because the UID is key to the user's identity, let's start with that.

The UID has its own type — uid_t — defined in sys/types.h. It's normally a small integer. Some are predefined by the system; others are created by the system administrator when new users are made known to the system. Normally, users usually have UID values larger than 100.

```
#include <sys/types.h>
#include <unistd.h>

uid_t getuid(void);
char *getlogin(void);
```

The getuid function returns the UID with which the program is associated. This is usually the UID of the user who started the program.

The getlogin function returns the login name associated with the current user.

The system file /etc/passwd contains a database dealing with user accounts. It consists of lines, one per user, that contain the username, encrypted password, user identifier (UID), group identifier (GID), full name, home directory, and default shell. Here's an example line:

```
neil:zBqxfqedfpk:500:100:Neil Matthew:/home/neil:/bin/bash
```

If you write a program that determines the UID of the user who started it, you could extend it to look in the password file to find out the user's login name and full name. We don't recommend this because modern UNIX-like systems have moved away from using simple password files to improve system security. Many systems, including Linux, have the option to use *shadow password* files that don't contain any useful encrypted password information at all (this is often held in /etc/shadow, a file that ordinary users cannot read). For this reason, a number of functions have been defined to provide a standard and effective programming interface to this user information:

```
#include <sys/types.h>
#include <pwd.h>
```

```
struct passwd *getpwuid(uid_t uid);
struct passwd *getpwnam(const char *name);
```

The password database structure, passwd, defined in pwd.h includes the following members:

passwd Member	Description
char *pw_name	The user's login name
uid_t pw_uid	The UID number
gid_t pw_gid	The GID number
char *pw_dir	The user's home directory
char *pw_gecos	The user's full name
char *pw_shell	The user's default shell

Some UNIX systems may use a different name for the field for the user's full name: on some systems, it's pw_gecos, as on Linux, and on others, it's pw_comment. This means that we can't recommend its use.

The getpwuid and getpwnam functions both return a pointer to a passwd structure corresponding to a user. The user is identified by UID for getpwuid and by login name for getpwnam. They both return a null pointer and set errno on error.

Try It Out   User Information

Here's a program, user.c, which extracts some user information from the password database:

```
#include <sys/types.h>
#include <pwd.h>
#include <stdio.h>
#include <unistd.h>
#include <stdlib.h>

int main()
{
    uid_t uid;
    gid_t gid;

    struct passwd *pw;
    uid = getuid();
    gid = getgid();

    printf("User is %s\n", getlogin());

    printf("User IDs: uid=%d, gid=%d\n", uid, gid);
```

```
    pw = getpwuid(uid);
    printf("UID passwd entry:\n name=%s, uid=%d, gid=%d, home=%s, shell=%s\n",
        pw->pw_name, pw->pw_uid, pw->pw_gid, pw->pw_dir, pw->pw_shell);

    pw = getpwnam("root");
    printf("root passwd entry:\n");
    printf("name=%s, uid=%d, gid=%d, home=%s, shell=%s\n",
        pw->pw_name, pw->pw_uid, pw->pw_gid, pw->pw_dir, pw->pw_shell);
    exit(0);
}
```

It gives the following output, which may differ in minor respects between versions of Linux and UNIX:

```
$ ./user
User is neil
User IDs: uid=1000, gid=100
UID passwd entry:
 name=neil, uid=1000, gid=100, home=/home/neil, shell=/bin/bash
root passwd entry:
name=root, uid=0, gid=0, home=/root, shell=/bin/bash
```

How It Works

This program calls getuid to obtain the UID of the current user. This UID is used in getpwuid to obtain detailed password file information. As an alternative, we show how the username root can be given to getpwnam to obtain user information.

If you take a look at the Linux source code, you can see another example of using getuid *in the* id *command.*

To scan all the password file information, you can use the getpwent function. This fetches successive file entries:

```
#include <pwd.h>
#include <sys/types.h>

void endpwent(void);
struct passwd *getpwent(void);
void setpwent(void);
```

The getpwent function returns each user information entry in turn. When none remain, it returns a null pointer. You can use the endpwent function to terminate processing once sufficient entries have been scanned. The setpwent function resets the position in the password file to the start so that a new scan can be started with the next call to getpwent. These functions operate in a similar way to the directory scanning functions opendir, readdir, and closedir that were discussed in Chapter 3.

User and group identifiers (effective and actual) can be obtained by other, less commonly used functions:

```
#include <sys/types.h>
#include <unistd.h>

uid_t geteuid(void);
```

```
gid_t getgid(void);
gid_t getegid(void);
int setuid(uid_t uid);
int setgid(gid_t gid);
```

You should refer to the system manual pages for details on group identifiers and effective user identifiers, although you'll probably find that you won't need to manipulate these at all.

Only the superuser can call setuid *and* setgid.

Host Information

Just as it can determine information about the user, a program can also establish some details about the computer on which it's running. The uname command provides such information. uname also exists as a system call to provide the same information within a C program — check it out in the system calls section of the manual pages (section 2) using man 2 uname.

Host information can be useful in a number of situations. You might want to customize a program's behavior, depending on the name of the machine it's running on in a network, say, a student's machine or an administrator's. For licensing purposes, you might want to restrict a program to running on one machine only. All this means that you need a way to establish which machine the program is running on.

If the system has networking components installed, you can obtain its network name very easily with the gethostname function:

```
#include <unistd.h>

int gethostname(char *name, size_t namelen);
```

The gethostname function writes the machine's network name into the string name. This string is assumed to be at least namelen characters long. gethostname returns 0 if successful and –1 otherwise.

You can obtain more detailed information about the host computer from the uname system call:

```
#include <sys/utsname.h>

int uname(struct utsname *name);
```

The uname function writes host information into the structure pointed to by the name parameter. The utsname structure, defined in sys/utsname.h, must contain at least these members:

utsname Member	Description
char sysname[]	The operating system name
char nodename[]	The host name

Continued on next page

utsname Member	Description
char release[]	The release level of the system
char version[]	The version number of the system
char machine[]	The hardware type

uname returns a nonnegative integer on success, –1 otherwise, with errno set to indicate any error.

Try It Out   Host Information

Here's a program, hostget.c, which extracts some host computer information:

```c
#include <sys/utsname.h>
#include <unistd.h>
#include <stdio.h>
#include <stdlib.h>

int main()
{
    char computer[256];
    struct utsname uts;

    if(gethostname(computer, 255) != 0 || uname(&uts) < 0) {
        fprintf(stderr, "Could not get host information\n");
        exit(1);
    }

    printf("Computer host name is %s\n", computer);
    printf("System is %s on %s hardware\n", uts.sysname, uts.machine);
    printf("Nodename is %s\n", uts.nodename);
    printf("Version is %s, %s\n", uts.release, uts.version);
    exit(0);
}
```

It gives the following Linux-specific output. If your machine is networked, you may see an extended host name that includes the network:

```
$ ./hostget
Computer host name is suse103
System is Linux on i686 hardware
Nodename is suse103
Version is 2.6.20.2-2-default, #1 SMP Fri Mar 9 21:54:10 UTC 2007
```

How It Works

This program calls gethostname to obtain the network name of the host computer. In the preceding example, it gets the name suse103. More detailed information about this Intel Pentium-4-based Linux computer is returned by the call to uname. Note that the format of the strings returned by uname is implementation-dependent; in the example, the version string contains the date that the kernel was compiled.

> *For another example of the use of the* uname *function, have a look at the Linux source code for the* uname *command, which uses it.*

A unique identifier for each host computer may be available from the gethostid function:

```
#include <unistd.h>

long gethostid(void);
```

The gethostid function is intended to return a unique value for the host computer. License managers use this to ensure that software programs can run only on machines that hold valid licenses. On Sun workstations, it returns a number that is set in non-volatile memory when the computer is built, and so is unique to the system hardware. Other systems, such as Linux, return a value based on the Internet address of the machine, which isn't usually secure enough to be used for licensing.

Logging

Many applications need to record their activities. System programs very often will write messages to the console, or a log file. These messages might indicate errors, warnings, or more general information about the state of the system. For example, the su program might record the fact that a user has tried and failed to gain superuser privileges.

Very often, these log messages are recorded in system files in a directory made available for that purpose. This might be /usr/adm or /var/log. On a typical Linux installation, the file /var/log/messages contains all system messages, /var/log/mail contains other log messages from the mail system, and /var/log/debug may contain debug messages. You can check your system's configuration in the /etc/syslog.conf or /etc/syslog-ng/syslog-ng.conf files, depending on your Linux version.

Here are some sample log messages:

```
Mar 26 18:25:51 suse103 ifstatus:      eth0       device: Advanced Micro Devices
 [AMD] 79c970 [PCnet32 LANCE] (rev 10)
Mar 26 18:25:51 suse103 ifstatus:      eth0       configuration: eth-id-
00:0c:29:0e:91:72
...
May 20 06:56:56 suse103 SuSEfirewall2: Setting up rules from
 /etc/sysconfig/SuSEfirewall2 ...
May 20 06:56:57 suse103 SuSEfirewall2: batch committing...
May 20 06:56:57 suse103 SuSEfirewall2: Firewall rules successfully set
...
Jun  9 09:11:14 suse103 su: (to root) neil on /dev/pts/18 09:50:35
```

Here, you can see the sort of messages that are logged. The first few are reported by the Linux kernel itself as it boots and detects installed hardware. The firewall reports that it's reconfiguring. Finally, the su program reports a superuser account access by user neil.

You may require superuser privilege to view log messages.

Some UNIX systems don't provide a readable messages file in this way, but do provide the administrator with tools to read a database of system events. Refer to your system documentation for details.

Even though the format and storage of system messages may vary, the method of producing the messages is standard. The UNIX specification provides an interface for all programs to produce logging messages using the syslog function:

```
#include <syslog.h>

void syslog(int priority, const char *message, arguments...);
```

The syslog function sends a logging message to the logging facility. Each message has a priority argument that is a bitwise OR of a severity level and a facility value. The severity level controls how the log message is acted upon and the facility value records the originator of the message.

Facility values (from syslog.h) include LOG_USER, used to indicate that the message has come from a user application (the default), and LOG_LOCAL0, LOG_LOCAL1, up to LOG_LOCAL7, which can be assigned meanings by the local administrator.

The severity levels in descending order of priority are shown in the following table.

Priority Level	Description
LOG_EMERG	An emergency situation
LOG_ALERT	High-priority problem, such as database corruption
LOG_CRIT	Critical error, such as hardware failure
LOG_ERR	Errors
LOG_WARNING	Warning
LOG_NOTICE	Special conditions requiring attention
LOG_INFO	Informational messages
LOG_DEBUG	Debug messages

Depending on system configuration, LOG_EMERG messages might be broadcast to all users, LOG_ALERT messages might be mailed to the administrator, LOG_DEBUG messages might be ignored, and the others written to a messages file. You can write a program that uses the logging facility simply by calling syslog when you want to create a log message.

The log message created by `syslog` consists of a message header and a message body. The header is created from the facility indicator and the date and time. The message body is created from the `message` parameter to `syslog`, which acts like a `printf` format string. Further arguments to `syslog` are used according to `printf` style conversion specifiers in the `message` string. Additionally, the specifier `%m` may be used to insert the error message string associated with the current value of the error variable, `errno`. This can be useful for logging error messages.

Try It Out   syslog

In this program, you try to open a nonexistent file:

```
#include <syslog.h>
#include <stdio.h>
#include <stdlib.h>

int main()
{
    FILE *f;

    f = fopen("not_here","r");
    if(!f)
        syslog(LOC_ERR|LOG_USER,"oops - %m\n");
    exit(0);
}
```

When you compile and run this program, `syslog.c`, you see no output, but the file `/var/log/messages` now contains the following line at the end:

```
Jun  9 09:24:50 suse103 syslog: oops - No such file or directory
```

How It Works

In this program, you try to open a file that doesn't exist. When this fails, you call `syslog` to record the fact in the system logs.

Notice that the log message doesn't indicate which program called the log facility; it just records the fact that `syslog` was called with a message. The `%m` conversion specifier has been replaced by a description of the error, in this case, that the file couldn't be found. This is more useful than just reporting the raw error number.

Other functions used to alter the behavior of logging facilities are also defined in `syslog.h`. These are:

```
#include <syslog.h>

void closelog(void);
void openlog(const char *ident, int logopt, int facility);
int setlogmask(int maskpri);
```

You can alter the way that your log messages are presented by calling the openlog function. This allows you to set up a string, ident, which will be pre-pended to your log messages. You can use this to indicate which program is creating the message. The facility parameter records a default facility value to be used for future calls to syslog. The default is LOG_USER. The logopt parameter configures the behavior of future calls to syslog. It's a bitwise OR of zero or more of the parameters in the following table.

logopt Parameter	Description
LOG_PID	Includes the process identifier, a unique number allocated to each process by the system, in the messages.
LOG_CONS	Sends messages to the console if they can't be logged.
LOG_ODELAY	Opens the log facility at first call to syslog.
LOG_NDELAY	Opens the log facility immediately, rather than at first log.

The openlog function will allocate and open a file descriptor that will be used for writing to the logging facility. You can close this by calling the closelog function. Note that you don't need to call openlog before calling syslog because syslog will open the logging facility itself if required.

You can control the priority level of your log messages by setting a log mask using setlogmask. All future calls to syslog with priority levels not set in the log mask will be rejected, so you could, for example, use this to turn off LOG_DEBUG messages without having to alter the body of the program.

You can create the mask for log messages using LOG_MASK(priority), which creates a mask consisting of just one priority level, or LOG_UPTO(priority), which creates a mask consisting of all priorities up to and including the specified priority.

Try It Out   logmask

In this example, you see logmask in action:

```c
#include <syslog.h>
#include <stdio.h>
#include <unistd.h>
#include <stdlib.h>

int main()
{
    int logmask;

    openlog("logmask", LOG_PID|LOG_CONS, LOG_USER);
    syslog(LOG_INFO,"informative message, pid = %d", getpid());
    syslog(LOG_DEBUG,"debug message, should appear");
    logmask = setlogmask(LOG_UPTO(LOG_NOTICE));
```

```
        syslog(LOG_DEBUG,"debug message, should not appear");
        exit(0);
}
```

This `logmask.c` program produces no output, but on a typical Linux system, toward the end of `/var/log/messages`, you should see the following line:

```
Jun  9 09:28:52 suse103 logmask[19339]: informative message, pid = 19339
```

The file that is configured to receive debug log entries (depending on logging configuration, this is often the file `/var/log/debug` or sometimes `/var/log/messages`) should contain the following line:

```
Jun  9 09:28:52 suse103 logmask[19339]: debug message, should appear
```

How It Works

The program initializes the logging facility with its name, `logmask`, and requests that log messages contain the process identifier. The informative message is logged to `/var/log/messages`, and the debug message to `/var/log/debug`. The second debug message doesn't appear because you call `setlogmask` to ignore all messages with a priority below `LOG_NOTICE`. (Note that this may not work on early Linux kernels.)

If your installation does not have debug message logging enabled, or it is configured differently, you may not see the debug messages appear. To enable all debug messages, check your system documentation for `syslog` or `syslog-ng` for the exact configuration details.

`logmask.c` also uses the `getpid` function, which is defined along with the closely related `getppid` as follows:

```
#include <sys/types.h>
#include <unistd.h>

pid_t getpid(void);
pid_t getppid(void);
```

The functions return the process and parent process identifiers of the calling process. For more information on PIDs, see Chapter 11.

Resources and Limits

Programs running on a Linux system are subject to resource limitations. These might be physical limits imposed by hardware (such as memory), limits imposed by system policies (for example, allowed CPU time), or implementation limits (such as the size of an integer or the maximum number of characters allowed in a filename). The UNIX specification defines some of these limits that can be determined by an application. See Chapter 7 for a further discussion of limits and the consequences of breaking them.

The header file `limits.h` defines many manifest constants that represent the constraints imposed by the operating system. These include the constraints shown in the following table.

Limit Constant	Purpose
NAME_MAX	The maximum number of characters in a filename
CHAR_BIT	The number of bits in a `char` value
CHAR_MAX	The maximum `char` value
INT_MAX	The maximum `int` value

There will be many other limits that may be of use to an application, so you should refer to your installation's header files.

> Note that NAME_MAX *is file-system specific. For more portable code, you should use the* `pathconf`
> *function. Refer to the manual page on* `pathconf` *for more information.*

The header file `sys/resource.h` provides definitions for resource operations. These include functions for determining and setting limits on a program's allowed size, execution priority, and file resources:

```
#include <sys/resource.h>

int getpriority(int which, id_t who);
int setpriority(int which, id_t who, int priority);
int getrlimit(int resource, struct rlimit *r_limit);
int setrlimit(int resource, const struct rlimit *r_limit);
int getrusage(int who, struct rusage *r_usage);
```

`id_t` is an integral type used for user and group identifiers. The `rusage` structure, defined in `sys/resource.h`, is used to determine how much CPU time has been used by the current program. It must contain at least the following two members:

rusage Member	Description
struct timeval ru_utime	The user time used
struct timeval ru_stime	The system time used

The `timeval` structure is defined in `sys/time.h` and contains fields `tv_sec` and `tv_usec`, representing seconds and microseconds, respectively.

CPU time consumed by a program is separated into *user time* (the time that the program itself has consumed executing its own instructions) and *system time* (the CPU time consumed by the operating system on the program's behalf; that is, the time spent in system calls performing input and output or other system functions).

The getrusage function writes CPU time information to the rusage structure pointed to by the parameter r_usage. The who parameter can be one of the following constants:

who Constant	Description
RUSAGE_SELF	Returns usage information about current program only.
RUSAGE_CHILDREN	Includes usage information of child processes as well.

We discuss child processes and task priorities in Chapter 11, but for completeness, we cover their implications for system resources here. For now, it's enough to say that each program that's running has a priority associated with it, and that higher priority programs are allocated more of the available CPU time.

Ordinary users are only able to reduce the priorities of their programs, not increase them.

Applications can determine and alter their (and others') priority with the getpriority and setpriority functions. The process to be examined or changed by the priority functions can be identified either by process identifier, group identifier, or user. The which parameter specifies how the who parameter is to be treated.

which Parameter	Description
PRIO_PROCESS	who is a process identifier.
PRIO_PGRP	who is a process group.
PRIO_USER	who is a user identifier.

So, to determine the priority of the current process, you might call

```
priority = getpriority(PRIO_PROCESS, getpid());
```

The setpriority function allows a new priority to be set, if possible.

The default priority is 0. Positive priorities are used for background tasks that run when no other higher priority task is ready to run. Negative priorities cause a program to run more frequently, taking a larger share of the available CPU time. The range of valid priorities is -20 to +20. This is often confusing because the higher the numerical value, the lower the execution precedence.

getpriority returns a valid priority if successful or a −1 with errno set on error. Because −1 is itself a valid priority, errno should be set to zero before calling getpriority and checked that it's still zero on return. setpriority returns 0 if successful, −1 otherwise.

Limits on system resources can be read and set by `getrlimit` and `setrlimit`. Both of these functions make use of a general-purpose structure, `rlimit`, to describe resource limits. It's defined in `sys/resource.h` and has the following members:

rlimit Member	Description
`rlim_t rlim_cur`	The current, soft limit
`rlim_t rlim_max`	The hard limit

The defined type `rlim_t` is an integral type used to describe resource levels. Typically, the soft limit is an advisory limit that shouldn't be exceeded; doing so may cause library functions to return errors. The hard limit, if exceeded, may cause the system to attempt to terminate the program by sending a signal to it. Examples would be the signal `SIGXCPU` on exceeding the CPU time limit and the signal `SIGSEGV` on exceeding a data size limit. A program may set its own soft limits to any value less than the hard limit. It may reduce its hard limit. Only a program running with superuser privileges may increase a hard limit.

A number of system resources can be limited. These are specified by the `resource` parameter of the `rlimit` functions and are defined in `sys/resource.h` as indicated in the following table.

resource Parameter	Description
`RLIMIT_CORE`	The core dump file size limit, in bytes
`RLIMIT_CPU`	The CPU time limit, in seconds
`RLIMIT_DATA`	The `data ()` segment limit, in bytes
`RLIMIT_FSIZE`	The file size limit, in bytes
`RLIMIT_NOFILE`	The limit on the number of open files
`RLIMIT_STACK`	The limit on stack size, in bytes
`RLIMIT_AS`	The limit on address space (stack and data), in bytes

The following Try It Out shows a program, `limits.c`, that simulates a typical application. It also sets and breaks a resource limit.

Try It Out Resource Limits

1. Include the header files for all the functions you're going to be using in this program:

```
#include <sys/types.h>
#include <sys/resource.h>
#include <sys/time.h>
#include <unistd.h>
#include <stdio.h>
#include <stdlib.h>
#include <math.h>
```

2. The `void` function writes a string to a temporary file 10,000 times and then performs some arithmetic to generate load on the CPU:

```c
void work()
{
    FILE *f;
    int i;
    double x = 4.5;

    f = tmpfile();
    for(i = 0; i < 10000; i++) {
        fprintf(f,"Do some output\n");
        if(ferror(f)) {
            fprintf(stderr,"Error writing to temporary file\n");
            exit(1);
        }
    }
    for(i = 0; i < 1000000; i++)
        x = log(x*x + 3.21);
}
```

3. The `main` function calls `work` and then uses the `getrusage` function to discover how much CPU time it has used. It displays this information onscreen:

```c
int main()
{
    struct rusage r_usage;
    struct rlimit r_limit;
    int priority;

    work();
    getrusage(RUSAGE_SELF, &r_usage);

    printf("CPU usage: User = %ld.%06ld, System = %ld.%06ld\n",
        r_usage.ru_utime.tv_sec, r_usage.ru_utime.tv_usec,
        r_usage.ru_stime.tv_sec, r_usage.ru_stime.tv_usec);
```

4. Next, it calls `getpriority` and `getrlimit` to find out its current priority and file size limits, respectively:

```c
    priority = getpriority(PRIO_PROCESS, getpid());
    printf("Current priority = %d\n", priority);

    getrlimit(RLIMIT_FSIZE, &r_limit);
    printf("Current FSIZE limit: soft = %ld, hard = %ld\n",
        r_limit.rlim_cur, r_limit.rlim_max);
```

5. Finally, set a file size limit using `setrlimit` and call `work` again, which fails because it attempts to create too large a file:

```c
    r_limit.rlim_cur = 2048;
    r_limit.rlim_max = 4096;
    printf("Setting a 2K file size limit\n");
```

```
        setrlimit(RLIMIT_FSIZE, &r_limit);

    work();
    exit(0);
}
```

When you run this program, you can see how much CPU resource is being consumed and the default priority at which the program is running. Once a file size limit has been set, the program can't write more than 2,048 bytes to a temporary file.

```
$ cc -o limits limits.c -lm
$ ./limits
CPU usage: User = 0.140008, System = 0.020001
Current priority = 0
Current FSIZE limit: soft = -1, hard = -1
Setting a 2K file size limit
File size limit exceeded
```

You can change the program priority by starting it with the `nice` command. Here, you see the priority changes to +10 and, as a result, it takes slightly longer to execute the program:

```
$ nice ./limits
CPU usage: User = 0.152009, System = 0.020001
Current priority = 10
Current FSIZE limit: soft = -1, hard = -1
Setting a 2K file size limit
File size limit exceeded
```

How It Works

The `limits` program calls the `work` function to simulate the actions of a typical program. It performs some calculations and produces some output, in this case, about 150K to a temporary file. It calls the resource functions to discover its priority and file size limits. In this case, the file size limits are unset, allowing you to create as large a file as you like (disk space permitting). The program then sets its file size limit to just 2K and again tries to perform some work. This time, the `work` function fails because it can't create such a large temporary file.

> *Limits may also be placed on a program running under a particular shell with the bash* `ulimit` *command.*

In this example, the error message `'Error writing to temporary file'` is not printed as you might expect. This is because some systems (such as Linux 2.2 and later) terminate the program when the resource limit is exceeded. It does this by sending a signal, `SIGXFSZ`. You learn more about signals and how to use them in Chapter 11. Other POSIX-compliant systems may simply cause the function that exceeds the limit to return an error.

Summary

In this chapter, you've looked at the Linux environment and examined the conditions under which programs run. You learned about command-line arguments and environment variables, both of which can be used to alter a program's default behavior and provide useful program options.

You've seen how a program can make use of library functions to manipulate date and time values and obtain information about itself and the user and the computer on which it's running.

Linux programs typically have to share precious resources, so the chapter also looked at how those resources can be determined and managed.

Terminals

In this chapter, you take a look at some improvements you might like to make to your basic application from Chapter 2. Perhaps the most obvious failing is the user interface; it's functional, but not very elegant. Here, you look at how to take more control of the user's terminal; that is, both keyboard input and screen output. More than this though, you learn how to "guarantee" that the programs you write can get input from the user, even in the presence of input redirection, and ensure that the output goes to the right place on the screen.

Though the reimplemented CD database application won't see the light of day until the end of Chapter 7, you'll do much of the groundwork for that chapter here. Chapter 6 is on curses, which is not some ancient malediction, but rather a library of functions that provide a higher level of code to control the terminal screen display. Along the way, you'll examine a little more of the thinking of the early UNIX meisters by introducing you to some philosophy of Linux and UNIX and the concept of terminal input and output. The low-level access presented here might be just what you're looking for. Most of what we cover applies equally well to programs running in a console window, such as KDE's Konsole, GNOME's gnome-terminal, or the standard X11 xterm.

Specifically, in this chapter, you learn about

- ❑ Reading and writing to the terminal
- ❑ Terminal drivers and the General Terminal Interface
- ❑ termios
- ❑ Terminal output and terminfo
- ❑ Detecting keystrokes

Reading from and Writing to the Terminal

In Chapter 3, you learned that when a program is invoked from the command prompt, the shell arranges for the standard input and output streams to be connected to your program. You should be able to interact with the user simply by using the getchar and printf routines to read and write these default streams.

In the following Try It Out, you try to rewrite the menu routines in C, using just those two routines, in a program called menu1.c.

Try It Out   Menu Routines in C

1. Start with the following lines, which define the array to be used as a menu, and prototype the getchoice function:

```
#include <stdio.h>
#include <stdlib.h>

char *menu[] = {
    "a - add new record",
    "d - delete record",
    "q - quit",
    NULL,

};

int getchoice(char *greet, char *choices[]);
```

2. The main function calls getchoice with the sample menu, menu:

```
int main()
{
    int choice = 0;

    do
    {
        choice = getchoice("Please select an action", menu);
        printf("You have chosen: %c\n", choice);
    } while(choice != 'q');
    exit(0);
}
```

3. Now for the important code — the function that both prints the menu and reads the user's input:

```
int getchoice(char *greet, char *choices[])
{
    int chosen = 0;
    int selected;
    char **option;

    do {
        printf("Choice: %s\n",greet);
        option = choices;
        while(*option) {
            printf("%s\n",*option);
            option++;
        }
        selected = getchar();
        option = choices;
```

```
        while(*option) {
            if(selected == *option[0]) {
                chosen = 1;
                break;
            }
            option++;
        }
        if(!chosen) {
            printf("Incorrect choice, select again\n");
        }
    } while(!chosen);
    return selected;
}
```

How It Works

getchoice prints the program introduction greet and the sample menu choices and asks the user to choose the initial character. The program then loops until getchar returns a character that matches the first letter of one of the option array's entries.

When you compile and run this program, you discover that it doesn't behave as you expected. Here's some terminal dialogue to demonstrate the problem:

```
$ ./menu1
Choice: Please select an action
a - add new record
d - delete record
q - quit
a
You have chosen: a
Choice: Please select an action
a - add new record
d - delete record
q - quit
Incorrect choice, select again
Choice: Please select an action
a - add new record
d - delete record
q - quit
q
You have chosen: q
$
```

Here, the user has to press A/Enter/Q/Enter and so on to make selections. There seem to be at least two problems: The most serious problem is that you are getting Incorrect choice after every correct choice. Plus, you still have to press Enter (or the Return key) before your program reads the input.

Canonical versus Non-Canonical Modes

The two problems are closely related. By default, terminal input is not made available to a program until the user presses Enter or Return. In most cases, this is a benefit because it allows the user to correct typing mistakes using Backspace or Delete. Only when they're happy with what they see on the screen do they press Enter to make the input available to the program.

This behavior is called *canonical*, or *standard*, mode. All the input is processed in terms of lines. Until a line of input is complete (usually when the user presses Enter), the terminal interface manages all the key presses, including Backspace, and no characters may be read by the application.

The opposite of this is *non-canonical* mode, where the application has much greater control over the processing of input characters. We'll come back to these two modes again a little later.

Among other things, the Linux terminal handler helps by translating interrupt characters to signals (for example, stopping your program when you press Ctrl+C) and it can automatically perform Backspace and Delete processing for you, so you don't have to reimplement it in each program you write. You find out more about signals in Chapter 11.

So, what's happening in this program? Well, Linux is saving the input until the user presses Enter, and then passing both the choice character and the subsequent Enter to the program. So, each time you enter a menu choice, the program calls getchar, processes the character, then calls getchar again, which immediately returns with the Enter character.

The character the program actually sees isn't an ASCII carriage return, CR (decimal 13, hex 0D), but a line feed, LF (decimal 10, hex 0A). This is because, internally, Linux (like UNIX) always uses a line feed to end lines of text; that is, UNIX uses a line feed alone to mean a newline, where other systems, such as MS-DOS, use a carriage return and a line feed together as a pair. If the input or output device also sends or requires a carriage return, the Linux terminal processing takes care of it. This might seem a little strange if you're used to MS-DOS or other environments, but one of the very considerable benefits is that there is no real difference between text and binary files on Linux. Only when you input or output to a terminal or some printers and plotters are carriage returns processed.

You can correct the major deficiency in your menu routine simply by ignoring the additional line feed character with some code such as this:

```
do {
        selected = getchar();
} while(selected == '\n');
```

This solves the immediate problem and you would then see output like this

```
$ ./menu1
Choice: Please select an action
a - add new record
d - delete record
q - quit
a
You have chosen: a
Choice: Please select an action
a - add new record
```

```
d - delete record
q - quit
q
You have chosen: q
$
```

We return to the second problem of needing to press Enter, and a more elegant solution to the line feed handling later.

Handling Redirected Output

It's very common for Linux programs, even interactive ones, to have their input or output redirected, either to files or other programs. Let's see how your program behaves when you redirect its output to a file:

```
$ ./menu1 > file
a
q
$
```

You could regard this as successful because the output has been redirected to a file rather than the terminal. However, there are cases where you want to prevent this from happening, or where you want to separate prompts that you want the user to see from other output that can be redirected safely.

You can tell whether the standard output has been redirected by finding out if the low-level file descriptor is associated with a terminal. The isatty system call does this. You simply pass it a valid file descriptor and it tests to see if that is currently connected to a terminal.

```
#include <unistd.h>

int isatty(int fd);
```

The isatty system call returns 1 if the open file descriptor, fd, is connected to a terminal and 0 otherwise.

In this program, you are using file streams, but isatty operates only on file descriptors. To provide the necessary conversion, you need to combine the isatty call with the fileno routine discussed in Chapter 3.

What are you going to do if stdout has been redirected? Just quitting isn't good enough because the user has no way of knowing why the program failed to run. Printing a message on stdout won't help either because it must have been redirected away from the terminal. One solution is to write to the standard error stream, stderr, which isn't redirected by the shell > file command.

Try It Out   Checking for Output Redirection

Using the program menu1.c you created in the previous Try It Out, make the following changes to the header file inclusions and the main function. Call the new file menu2.c.

```
#include <unistd.h>
...
int main()
{
    int choice = 0;
```

```
        if(!isatty(fileno(stdout))) {
            fprintf(stderr,"You are not a terminal!\n");
            exit(1);
        }
        do {
            choice = getchoice("Please select an action", menu);
            printf("You have chosen: %c\n", choice);
        } while(choice != 'q');
        exit(0);
    }
```

Now look at the following sample output:

```
$ ./menu2
Choice: Please select an action
a - add new record
d - delete record
q - quit
q
You have chosen: q
$ menu2 > file
You are not a terminal!
$
```

How It Works

The new section of code uses the `isatty` function to test whether the standard output is connected to a terminal and halts execution if it isn't. This is the same test the shell uses to decide whether to offer prompts. It's possible, and quite common, to redirect both `stdout` and `stderr` away from the terminal. You can direct the error stream to a different file like this:

```
$ ./menu2 >file 2>file.error
$
```

Or combine the two output streams into a single file like this:

```
$ ./menu2 >file 2>&1
$
```

(If you're not familiar with output redirection, take another look at Chapter 2, where we explain this syntax in more detail.) In this case, you'll need to send a message directly to the user's terminal.

Talking to the Terminal

If you need to prevent the parts of your program that interact with the user from being redirected, but still allow it to happen to other input or output, you need to separate the interaction from `stdout` and `stderr`. You can do this by reading and writing directly to the terminal. Because Linux is inherently a multiuser system, usually with many terminals either directly connected or connected across a network, how can you discover the correct terminal to use?

Fortunately, Linux and UNIX make things easy by providing a special device, /dev/tty, which is always the current terminal, or login session. Because Linux treats everything as a file, you can use normal file operations to read and write to /dev/tty.

In this Try It Out, you modify the choice program so that you can pass parameters to the getchoice routine, to provide better control over the output. This is menu3.c.

Try It Out   Using /dev/tty

Load up menu2.c and change the code to the following, so that input and output come from and are directed to /dev/tty:

```c
#include <stdio.h>
#include <unistd.h>
#include <stdlib.h>

char *menu[] = {
    "a - add new record",
    "d - delete record",
    "q - quit",
    NULL,
};

int getchoice(char *greet, char *choices[], FILE *in, FILE *out);

int main()
{
    int choice = 0;
    FILE *input;
    FILE *output;

    if(!isatty(fileno(stdout))) {
        fprintf(stderr,"You are not a terminal, OK.\n");
    }

    input = fopen("/dev/tty", "r");
    output = fopen("/dev/tty", "w");
    if(!input || !output) {
        fprintf(stderr,"Unable to open /dev/tty\n");
        exit(1);
    }
    do {
        choice = getchoice("Please select an action", menu, input, output);
        printf("You have chosen: %c\n", choice);
    } while(choice != 'q');
    exit(0);
}

int getchoice(char *greet, char *choices[], FILE *in, FILE *out)
{
    int chosen = 0;
    int selected;
    char **option;

    do {
```

```
            fprintf(out,"Choice: %s\n",greet);
        option = choices;
        while(*option) {
            fprintf(out,"%s\n",*option);
            option++;
        }
        do {
            selected = fgetc(in);
        } while(selected == '\n');
        option = choices;
        while(*option) {
            if(selected == *option[0]) {
                chosen = 1;
                break;
            }
            option++;
        }
        if(!chosen) {
            fprintf(out,"Incorrect choice, select again\n");
        }
    } while(!chosen);
    return selected;
}
```

Now, when you run the program with the output redirected, you can still see the prompts and the normal program output (indicating the options that have been chosen) is redirected to a file that you can look at later.

```
$ ./menu3 > file
You are not a terminal, OK.
Choice: Please select an action
a - add new record
d - delete record
q - quit
d
Choice: Please select an action
a - add new record
d - delete record
q - quit
q
$ cat file
You have chosen: d
You have chosen: q
```

The Terminal Driver and the General Terminal Interface

Sometimes a program needs much finer control over the terminal than can be achieved using simple file operations. Linux provides a set of interfaces that allow you to control the behavior of the terminal driver, giving you much greater control of the processing of terminal input and output.

Overview

As Figure 5-1 shows, you can control the terminal through a set of function calls (the General Terminal Interface, or GTI) separate from those used for reading and writing. This keeps the data (read/write) interface very clean while still allowing detailed control over the terminal behavior. That's not to say that the terminal I/O interface is clean — it has to deal with a wide variety of different hardware.

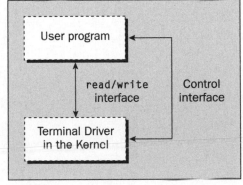

Figure 5-1

In UNIX terminology, the control interface sets a "line discipline" that allows a program considerable flexibility in specifying the behavior of the terminal driver.

The main features that you can control are

❑ **Line editing:** Choose whether to allow *Backspace* for editing.

❑ **Buffering:** Choose whether to read characters immediately, or read them after a configurable delay.

❑ **Echo:** Allows you to control echoing, such as when reading passwords.

❑ **CR/LF:** Determine mapping for input and output: what happens when you print a line feed character ($\backslash$n).

❑ **Line speeds:** Rarely used on a PC console, these speeds are very important for modems and terminals on serial lines.

Hardware Model

Before you look at the General Terminal Interface in detail, it's very important that you understand the hardware model that it's intended to drive.

The conceptual arrangement shown in Figure 5-2 (for some ancient UNIX sites, it was physically like this) is to have a UNIX machine connected via a serial port to a modem and then via a telephone line and another modem to a remote terminal. In fact, this is just the kind of setup used by some small Internet service providers when the Internet was young. It's a distant relative of the client/server paradigm, used when the program ran on a mainframe and users worked at dumb terminals.

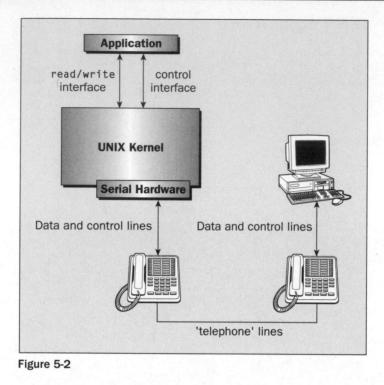

Figure 5-2

If you're working on a PC running Linux, this may seem like an overly complex model. However, because both of the authors have modems, we can, if we choose, use a terminal emulation program like minicom to run a remote logon session on each other's machines just like this, using a pair of modems and a telephone line. Of course, today fast broadband access has rendered this kind of working obsolete, but this hardware model still has its benefits.

The advantage of using such a hardware model is that most real-world situations will form a subset of this, the most complex case. Supporting them will be much easier than if the model had omitted such functionality.

The termios Structure

termios is the standard interface specified by POSIX and is similar to the System V interface termio. The terminal interface is controlled by setting values in a structure of type termios and using a small set of function calls. Both are defined in the header file termios.h.

Programs that use the function calls defined in termios.h *will need to be linked with an appropriate function library. This may be simply the standard C library or it may be the* curses *library, depending on your installation. If necessary, when compiling the examples in this chapter, add* -lcurses *to the end of the compiler command line. On some older Linux systems, the* curses *library is provided by a version known as "new curses." In these cases, the library name and link argument become* ncurses *and* -lncurses, *respectively.*

The values that can be manipulated to affect the terminal are grouped into various modes:

- ❏ Input
- ❏ Output
- ❏ Control
- ❏ Local
- ❏ Special control characters

A minimum termios structure is typically declared as follows (although the X/Open specification allows additional fields to be included):

```
#include <termios.h>
struct termios {
    tcflag_t c_iflag;
    tcflag_t c_oflag;
    tcflag_t c_cflag;
    tcflag_t c_lflag;
    cc_t     c_cc[NCCS];
};
```

The member names correspond with the five parameter types in the previous list.

You can initialize a termios structure for the terminal by calling the function tcgetattr, which has the following prototype:

```
#include <termios.h>

int tcgetattr(int fd, struct termios *termios_p);
```

This call writes the current values of the terminal interface variables into the structure pointed to by termios_p. If these values are then altered, you can reconfigure the terminal interface with the tcsetattr function as follows:

```
#include <termios.h>

int tcsetattr(int fd, int actions, const struct termios *termios_p);
```

The actions field for tcsetattr controls how any changes are applied. The three possibilities are

- ❏ TCSANOW: Changes values immediately.
- ❏ TCSADRAIN: Changes values when current output is complete.
- ❏ TCSAFLUSH: Changes values when current output is complete, but discards any input currently available and not yet returned in a read call.

Note that it's very important for programs to restore terminal settings to the values they had before the program started. It's always the responsibility of a program to initially save and then restore these settings when it finishes.

We'll now look more closely at the modes and related function calls. Some of the detail of the modes is rather specialized and rarely used, so we cover only the main features here. If you need to know more, you should consult your local man pages or a copy of the POSIX or X/Open specification.

The most important mode to take in on your first read is the local mode. The canonical and non-canonical modes are the solution to the second of the problems in the first application — the user must press Enter or Return for the program to read the input. You can instruct the program to wait for a line of input or pounce on input as soon as it is typed.

Input Modes

The input modes control how input (characters received by the terminal driver at a serial port or keyboard) is processed before being passed on to the program. You control them by setting flags in the c_iflag member of the termios structure. All the flags are defined as macros and can be combined with a bitwise OR. This is the case for all the terminal modes.

The macros that can be used for c_iflag are

- ❑ BRKINT: Generate an interrupt when a break condition (loss of connection) is detected on the line
- ❑ IGNBRK: Ignore break conditions on the line
- ❑ ICRNL: Convert a received carriage return to a newline
- ❑ IGNCR: Ignore received carriage returns
- ❑ INLCR: Convert received newlines to carriage returns
- ❑ IGNPAR: Ignore characters with parity errors
- ❑ INPCK: Perform parity checking on received characters
- ❑ PARMRK: Mark parity errors
- ❑ ISTRIP: Strip (set to seven bits) all incoming characters
- ❑ IXOFF: Enable software flow control on input
- ❑ IXON: Enable software flow control on output

If neither BRKINT nor IGNBRK is set, a break condition on the line is read as a NULL (0x00) character.

You won't need to change the input modes very often, because the default values are usually the most suitable, so we won't discuss them further here.

Output Modes

These modes control how output characters are processed; that is, how characters sent from a program are processed before being transmitted to the serial port or screen. As you might expect, many of these are counterparts of the input modes. Several additional flags exist, which are mainly concerned with allowing for slow terminals that require time to process characters such as carriage returns. Almost all of these are either redundant (as terminals get faster) or better handled using the terminfo database of terminal capabilities, which you use later in this chapter.

You control output modes by setting flags in the c_oflag member of the termios structure. The macros that you can use in c_oflag are

- ❏ OPOST: Turn on output processing
- ❏ ONLCR: Convert any output newline to a carriage return/line feed pair
- ❏ OCRNL: Convert any output carriage return to a newline
- ❏ ONOCR: No carriage return output in column 0
- ❏ ONLRET: A newline also does a carriage return
- ❏ OFILL: Send fill characters to provide delays
- ❏ OFDEL: Use DEL as a fill character, rather than NULL
- ❏ NLDLY: Newline delay selection
- ❏ CRDLY: Carriage return delay selection
- ❏ TABDLY: Tab delay selection
- ❏ BSDLY: Backspace delay selection
- ❏ VTDLY: Vertical tab delay selection
- ❏ FFDLY: Form feed delay selection

If OPOST is not set, all the other flags are ignored.

The output modes are also not commonly used, so we won't consider them further here.

Control Modes

These modes control the hardware characteristics of the terminal. You specify control modes by setting flags in the c_cflag member of the termios structure, which has the following macros:

- ❏ CLOCAL: Ignore any modem status lines.
- ❏ CREAD: Enable the receipt of characters.
- ❏ CS5: Use five bits in sent or received characters.
- ❏ CS6: Use six bits in sent or received characters.
- ❏ CS7: Use seven bits in sent or received characters.
- ❏ CS8: Use eight bits in sent or received characters.
- ❏ CSTOPB: Use two stop bits per character, rather than one.
- ❏ HUPCL: Hang up modem on close.
- ❏ PARENB: Enable parity generation and detection.
- ❏ PARODD: Use odd parity rather than even parity.

If HUPCL is set, when the terminal driver detects that the last file descriptor referring to the terminal has been closed, it will set the modem control lines to "hang-up" the line.

187

The control modes are used mainly when the serial line is connected to a modem, although they may be used when talking to a terminal. Normally, it's easier to change your terminal's configuration than to change the default line behavior by using the control modes of termios.

Local Modes

These modes control various characteristics of the terminal. You specify local modes by setting flags in the c_lflag member of the termios structure, with the following macros:

❑ ECHO: Enable local echoing of input characters

❑ ECHOE: Perform a Backspace, Space, Backspace combination on receiving ERASE

❑ ECHOK: Perform erase line on the KILL character

❑ ECHONL: Echo newline characters

❑ ICANON: Enable canonical input processing (see the text following this list)

❑ IEXTEN: Enable implementation-specific functions

❑ ISIG: Enable signals

❑ NOFLSH: Disable flush on queue

❑ TOSTOP: Send background processes a signal on write attempts

The two most important flags here are ECHO, which allows you to suppress the echoing of typed characters, and ICANON, which switches the terminal between two very distinct modes of processing received characters. If the ICANON flag is set, the line is said to be in canonical mode; if not, the line is in noncanonical mode.

Special Control Characters

Special control characters are a collection of characters, like Ctrl+C, acted upon in particular ways when the user types them. The c_cc array member of the termios structure contains the characters mapped to each of the supported functions. The position of each character (its index into the array) is defined by a macro, but there's no limitation that they must be control characters.

The c_cc array is used in two very different ways, depending on whether the terminal is set to canonical mode (that is, the setting of the ICANON flag in the c_lflag member of termios).

It's important to realize that there is some overlap in the way the array index values are used for the two different modes. Because of this, you should never mix values from these two modes.

For canonical mode, the array indices are

❑ VEOF: EOF character

❑ VEOL: EOL character

❑ VERASE: ERASE character

❑ VINTR: INTR character

❑ VKILL: KILL character

❑   VQUIT: QUIT character

❑   VSUSP: SUSP character

❑   VSTART: START character

❑   VSTOP: STOP character

For non-canonical mode, the array indices are

❑   VINTR: INTR character

❑   VMIN: MIN value

❑   VQUIT: QUIT character

❑   VSUSP: SUSP character

❑   VTIME: TIME value

❑   VSTART: START character

❑   VSTOP: STOP character

Characters

Because the special characters and non-canonical values are so important for more advanced input character processing, we explain them in some detail in the following table.

Character	Description
INTR	Causes the terminal driver to send a SIGINT signal to processes connected to the terminal. We discuss signals in more detail in Chapter 11.
QUIT	Causes the terminal driver to send a SIGQUIT signal to processes connected to the terminal.
ERASE	Causes the terminal driver to delete the last character on the line.
KILL	Causes the terminal driver to delete the entire line.
EOF	Causes the terminal driver to pass all characters on the line to the application reading input. If the line is empty, a read call will return zero characters as though a read had been attempted at the end of a file.
EOL	Acts as a line terminator in addition to the more usual newline character.
SUSP	Causes the terminal driver to send a SIGSUSP signal to processes connected to the terminal. If your UNIX supports job control, the current application will be suspended.
STOP	Acts to "flow off"; that is, prevent further output to the terminal. It's used to support XON/XOFF flow control and is usually set to the ASCII XOFF character, Ctrl+S.
START	Restarts output after a STOP character, often the ASCII XON character.

The TIME and MIN Values

The values of TIME and MIN are used only in non-canonical mode and act together to control the reading of input. Together, they control what happens when a program attempts to read a file descriptor associated with a terminal.

There are four cases:

❑ MIN = 0 and TIME = 0: In this case, a read will always return immediately. If some characters are available, they will be returned; if none are available, read will return zero and no characters will have been read.

❑ MIN = 0 and TIME > 0: In this case, the read will return when any character is available to be read or when TIME tenths of a second have elapsed. If no character was read because the timer expired, read will return zero. Otherwise, it will return the number of characters read.

❑ MIN > 0 and TIME = 0: In this case, the read will wait until MIN characters can be read and then return that number of characters. Zero is returned on end of file.

❑ MIN > 0 and TIME > 0: This is the most complex case. When read is called, it waits for a character to be received. When the first character is received, and every subsequent time a character is received, an inter-character timer is started (or restarted if it was already running). The read will return when either MIN characters can be read or the inter-character time of TIME tenths of a second expires. This can be useful for telling the difference between a single press of the Escape key and the start of a function key escape sequence. Be aware, though, that network communications or high processor loads neatly erase such fine timing information.

By setting non-canonical mode and using the MIN and TIME values, programs can perform character-by-character processing of input.

Accessing Terminal Modes from the Shell

If you want to see the termios settings that are being used while you're using the shell, you can get a list using the command:

```
$ stty -a
```

On the authors' Linux systems, which have some extensions to the standard termios, the output is

```
speed 38400 baud; rows 24; columns 80; line = 0;
intr = ^C; quit = ^\; erase = ^?; kill = ^U; eof = ^D; eol = <undef>;
eol2 = <undef>; swtch = <undef>; start = ^Q; stop = ^S; susp = ^Z; rprnt = ^R;
werase = ^W; lnext = ^V; flush = ^O; min = 1; time = 0;
-parenb -parodd cs8 -hupcl -cstopb cread -clocal -crtscts
-ignbrk -brkint -ignpar -parmrk -inpck -istrip -inlcr -igncr icrnl -ixon -ixoff
-iuclc -ixany -imaxbel iutf8
opost -olcuc -ocrnl onlcr -onocr -onlret -ofill -ofdel nl0 cr0 tab0 bs0 vt0 ff0
isig icanon iexten echo echoe echok -echonl -noflsh -xcase -tostop -echoprt
echoctl echoke
```

Among other things, you can see that the EOF character is Ctrl+D and that echoing is enabled. When you're experimenting with terminal control, it's very easy to get the terminal left in a non-standard state, which makes using it very difficult. There are several ways out of this difficulty:

❑   The first method, if your version of stty supports it, is to use the command

```
$ stty sane
```

❑   If you have lost the mapping of the carriage return key to the newline character (which terminates the line), you may need to enter stty sane, but rather than press Enter, press Ctrl+J (which is the newline character).

❑   The second method is to use the stty -g command to write the current stty setting in a form ready to reread. On the command line, you can use

```
$ stty -g > save_stty
..
<experiment with settings>
..
$ stty $(cat save_stty)
```

❑   You still may need to use Ctrl+J rather than Enter for the final stty command. You can use the same technique in a shell script:

```
save_stty="$(stty -g)"
<alter stty settings>
stty $save_stty
```

❑   If you're really stuck, the third method is to go to a different terminal, use the ps command to find the shell you have made unusable, and then use kill HUP <process id> to force the shell to terminate. Because stty parameters are always reset before a logon prompt is issued, you should be able to log in again normally.

Setting Terminal Modes from the Command Prompt

You can also use the stty command to set the terminal modes directly from the command prompt.

To set a mode in which your shell script could perform single character reads, you need to turn off canonical mode and set it to 1 and to 0. The command is as follows:

```
$ stty -icanon min 1 time 0
```

Now that the terminal is set to read characters immediately, you can try to run the first program, menu1, again. You should find it works as originally intended.

You also could improve your attempt to check for a password (Chapter 2) by turning echoing off before you prompt for the password. The command to do this is

```
$ stty -echo
```

Remember to use stty echo *to turn echoing back on after you try this!*

Terminal Speed

The final function served by the `termios` structure is manipulating the line speed. No members are defined for terminal speed; instead, it's set by function calls. Input and output speeds are handled separately.

The four call prototypes are

```
#include <termios.h>

speed_t cfgetispeed(const struct termios *);
speed_t cfgetospeed(const struct termios *);
int cfsetispeed(struct termios *, speed_t speed);
int cfsetospeed(struct termios *, speed_t speed);
```

Notice that these act on a `termios` structure, not directly on a port. This means that to set a new speed, you must read the current settings with `tcgetattr`, set the speed using one of the preceding calls, and then write the `termios` structure back using `tcsetattr`. Only after the call to `tcsetattr` will the line speed be changed.

Various values are allowed for `speed` in the preceding function calls, but the most important are

❑   `B0`: Hang up the terminal

❑   `B1200`: 1200 baud

❑   `B2400`: 2400 baud

❑   `B9600`: 9600 baud

❑   `B19200`: 19200 baud

❑   `B38400`: 38400 baud

There are no speeds greater than 38400 defined by the standard and no standard method of supporting serial ports at speeds greater than this.

> *Some systems, including Linux, define `B57600`, `B115200`, and `B230400` for selecting faster speeds. If you're using an earlier version of Linux and these constants are unavailable, you can use the command `setserial` to obtain nonstandard speeds of 57600 and 115200. In this case, these speeds will be used when `B38400` is selected. Both of these methods are nonportable, so be careful when you're using them.*

Additional Functions

There are a small number of additional functions for the control of terminals. These work directly on file descriptors, without needing to get and set `termios` structures. Their definitions are

```
#include <termios.h>

int tcdrain(int fd);
int tcflow(int fd, int flowtype);
int tcflush(int fd, int in_out_selector);
```

The functions have the following purposes:

- ❏ tcdrain causes the calling program to wait until all queued output has been sent.
- ❏ tcflow is used to suspend or restart output.
- ❏ tcflush can be used to flush input, output, or both.

Now that we've covered the rather large subject of the termios structure, let's look at a few practical examples. Possibly the simplest is the disabling of echo to read a password. Do this by turning off the ECHO flag.

Try It Out   A Password Program with termios

1. Begin your password program, password.c, with the following definitions:

```c
#include <termios.h>
#include <stdio.h>
#include <stdlib.h>

#define PASSWORD_LEN 8

int main()
{
    struct termios initialrsettings, newrsettings;
    char password[PASSWORD_LEN + 1];
```

2. Next, add a line to get the current settings from the standard input and copy them into the termios structure that you created previously:

```c
tcgetattr(fileno(stdin), &initialrsettings);
```

3. Make a copy of the original settings to replace them at the end. Turn off the ECHO flag on the newrsettings and ask the user for his password:

```c
newrsettings = initialrsettings;
newrsettings.c_lflag &= ~ECHO;

printf("Enter password: ");
```

4. Next, set the terminal attributes to newrsettings and read in the password. Lastly, reset the terminal attributes to their original setting and print the password to render all the previous security effort useless.

```c
    if(tcsetattr(fileno(stdin), TCSAFLUSH, &newrsettings) != 0) {
        fprintf(stderr,"Could not set attributes\n");
    }
    else {
        fgets(password, PASSWORD_LEN, stdin);
        tcsetattr(fileno(stdin), TCSANOW, &initialrsettings);
        fprintf(stdout, "\nYou entered %s\n", password);
    }
    exit(0);
}
```

When you run the program, you should see the following:

```
$ ./password
Enter password:
You entered hello

$
```

How It Works

In this example, the word `hello` is typed but not echoed at the `Enter password:` prompt. No output is produced until the user presses Enter.

Be careful to change only the flags you need to change, using the construct `X &= ~FLAG` (which clears the bit defined by `FLAG` in the variable `X`). If needed, you could use `X |= FLAG` to set a single bit defined by `FLAG`, although this wasn't necessary in the preceding example.

When you're setting the attributes, you use `TCSAFLUSH` to discard any typeahead, characters users enter before the program is ready to read them. This is a good way of encouraging users not to start typing their password until echo has been turned off. You also restore the previous setting before your program terminates.

Another common use of the `termios` structure is to put the terminal into a state where you can read each character as it is typed. Do this by turning off canonical mode and using the `MIN` and `TIME` settings.

Try It Out   Reading Each Character

Using your new knowledge, you can make changes to the `menu` program. The following program, `menu4.c`, is based on `menu3.c` and has much of the code from `password.c` inserted into it. Changes are highlighted and explained in the following steps.

1.   For a start, you must include a new header file at the top of the program:

```
#include <stdio.h>
#include <unistd.h>
#include <stdlib.h>
#include <termios.h>

char *menu[] = {
    "a - add new record",
    "d - delete record",
    "q - quit",
    NULL,
};
```

2.   Then you need to declare a couple of new variables in the main function:

```
int getchoice(char *greet, char *choices[], FILE *in, FILE *out);
```

```
int main()
{
    int choice = 0;
    FILE *input;
    FILE *output;
    struct termios initial_settings, new_settings;
```

3. You need to change the terminal's characteristics before you call the getchoice function, so that's where you place these lines:

```
    if (!isatty(fileno(stdout))) {
        fprintf(stderr,"You are not a terminal, OK.\n");
    }

    input = fopen("/dev/tty", "r");
    output = fopen("/dev/tty", "w");
    if(!input || !output) {
        fprintf(stderr, "Unable to open /dev/tty\n");
        exit(1);
    }
    tcgetattr(fileno(input),&initial_settings);
    new_settings = initial_settings;
    new_settings.c_lflag &= ~ICANON;
    new_settings.c_lflag &= ~ECHO;
    new_settings.c_cc[VMIN] = 1;
    new_settings.c_cc[VTIME] = 0;
    new_settings.c_lflag &= ~ISIG;
    if(tcsetattr(fileno(input), TCSANOW, &new_settings) != 0) {
        fprintf(stderr,"could not set attributes\n");
    }
```

4. You should also return the settings to their original values before exiting:

```
    do {
        choice = getchoice("Please select an action", menu, input, output);
        printf("You have chosen: %c\n", choice);
    } while (choice != 'q');
    tcsetattr(fileno(input),TCSANOW,&initial_settings);
    exit(0);
}
```

5. You need to check against carriage returns now that you're in non-canonical mode, because the default mapping of CR to LF is no longer being performed.

```
int getchoice(char *greet, char *choices[], FILE *in, FILE *out)
{
    int chosen = 0;
    int selected;
    char **option;

    do {
        fprintf(out, "Choice: %s\n",greet);
        option = choices;
        while (*option) {
            fprintf(out, "%s\n",*option);
```

```
                option++;
        }
        do {
            selected = fgetc(in);
        } while (selected == '\n' || selected == '\r');
        option = choices;
        while(*option) {
            if(selected == *option[0]) {
                chosen = 1;
                break;
            }
            option++;
        }
        if(!chosen) {
            fprintf(out, "Incorrect choice, select again\n");
        }
    } while(!chosen);
    return selected;
}
```

Unless you arrange otherwise, if the user now types Ctrl+C at your program, the program will terminate. You can disable processing of these special characters by clearing the ISIG flag in the local modes. To do this, the following line is included in main, as shown in the preceding step.

```
        new_settings.c_lflag &= ~ISIG;
```

If you put these changes into your menu program, you now get an immediate response and the character you type isn't echoed.

```
$ ./menu4
Choice: Please select an action
a - add new record
d - delete record
q - quit
You have chosen: a
Choice: Please select an action
a - add new record
d - delete record
q - quit
You have chosen: q
$
```

If you type Ctrl+C, it's passed directly to the program and treated as an incorrect choice.

Terminal Output

Using the termios structure, you have control over keyboard input, but it would be good to have the same level of control over the way a program's output is presented on the screen. You used printf at the beginning of the chapter to output characters to the screen, but with no way of placing the output at a particular position on the screen.

Terminal Type

Many UNIX systems are used with terminals, although in many cases today, the "terminal" may actually be a PC running a terminal emulation program or a terminal application in a windowing environment such as xterm in X11.

Historically, there have been a very large number of hardware terminals from different manufacturers. Although they nearly all use escape sequences (a string of characters starting with the escape character) to provide control over the position of the cursor and other attributes, such as bold and blinking, they are generally not very well standardized in the way they do this. Some older terminals also have different scrolling capabilities that may or may not erase when backspace is sent, and so on.

There is an ANSI standard set of escape sequences (mostly based on the sequences used in the Digital Equipment Corporation VT series terminals, but not identical). Many software terminal programs provide an emulation of a standard hardware terminal, often VT100, VT220, or ANSI, and sometimes others as well.

This variety of hardware terminals would be a major problem for programmers wanting to write software that controls the screen and runs on many terminal types. For example, an ANSI terminal uses the sequence Escape,[,A to move the cursor up one line. An ADM-3a terminal (very common some years ago) uses the single control character Ctrl+K.

Writing a program that can deal with the many different types of terminals that might be connected to a UNIX system would seem to be an extremely daunting task. The program would need different source code for each type of terminal.

Not surprisingly, there is a solution in a package known as terminfo. Instead of each program having to cater for every sort of terminal, the program looks up a database of terminal types to get the correct information. In most modern UNIX systems, including Linux, this has been integrated with another package called curses, which you learn about in the next chapter.

To use terminfo functions you normally have include the curses header file, curses.h, and terminfo's own header file, term.h. On some Linux systems, you may have to use the implementation of curses known as ncurses, and include ncurses.h to provide prototypes for your terminfo functions.

Identify Your Terminal Type

The Linux environment contains a variable, TERM, which is set to the type of terminal being used. It's usually set automatically by the system at logon time. The system administrator may set a default terminal type for each of the directly connected terminals and may arrange for remote, networked users to be prompted for a terminal type. The value of TERM can be negotiated via telnet and is passed by rlogin.

A user can query the shell to discover the system's idea of the terminal he or she is using.

```
$ echo $TERM
xterm
$
```

In this case, the shell is being run from a program called xterm, a terminal emulator for the X Window System, or a program that provides similar functionality such as KDE's Konsole or GNOME's gnome-terminal.

The `terminfo` package contains a database of capabilities and escape sequences for a large number of terminals and provides a uniform programming interface for using them. A single program can then be written that will take advantage of future terminals as the database is extended, rather than each application having to provide support for the many different terminals.

The `terminfo` capabilities are described by attributes. These are stored in a set of compiled `terminfo` files, which are conventionally found in `/usr/lib/terminfo` or `/usr/share/terminfo`. For each terminal (and many printers, which can also be specified in `terminfo`) there's a file that defines its capabilities and how its features can be accessed. To avoid creating a very large directory, the actual files are stored in subdirectories, where the subdirectory name is simply the first letter of the terminal type. Thus, the VT100 definition is found in . . . `terminfo/v/vt100`.

`terminfo` files are written one per terminal type in a source format that is (just about!) readable, then compiled using the `tic` command into a more compact and efficient format for use by application programs. Curiously, the X/Open specification refers to source and compiled format definitions, but fails to mention the `tic` command for actually getting from source to compiled formats. You can use the `infocmp` program to print a readable version of a compiled `terminfo` entry.

Here's an example `terminfo` file for the VT100 terminal:

```
$ infocmp vt100
vt100|vt100-am|dec vt100 (w/advanced video),
 am, mir, msgr, xenl, xon,
 cols#80, it#8, lines#24, vt#3,
 acsc=``aaffggjjkkllmmnnooppqqrrssttuuvvwwxxyyzz{{||}}~~,
 bel=^G, blink=\E[5m$<2>, bold=\E[1m$<2>,
 clear=\E[H\E[J$<50>, cr=\r, csr=\E[%i%p1%d;%p2%dr,
 cub=\E[%p1%dD, cub1=\b, cud=\E[%p1%dB, cud1=\n,
 cuf=\E[%p1%dC, cuf1=\E[C$<2>,
 cup=\E[%i%p1%d;%p2%dH$<5>, cuu=\E[%p1%dA,
 cuu1=\E[A$<2>, ed=\E[J$<50>, el=\E[K$<3>,
 el1=\E[1K$<3>, enacs=\E(B\E)0, home=\E[H, ht=\t,
 hts=\EH, ind=\n, ka1=\EOq, ka3=\EOs, kb2=\EOr, kbs=\b,
 kc1=\EOp, kc3=\EOn, kcub1=\EOD, kcud1=\EOB,
 kcuf1=\EOC, kcuu1=\EOA, kent=\EOM, kf0=\EOy, kf1=\EOP,
 kf10=\EOx, kf2=\EOQ, kf3=\EOR, kf4=\EOS, kf5=\EOt,
 kf6=\EOu, kf7=\EOv, kf8=\EOl, kf9=\EOw, rc=\E8,
 rev=\E[7m$<2>, ri=\EM$<5>, rmacs=^O, rmkx=\E[?1l\E>,
 rmso=\E[m$<2>, rmul=\E[m$<2>,
 rs2=\E>\E[?3l\E[?4l\E[?5l\E[?7h\E[?8h, sc=\E7,
 sgr=\E[0%?%p1%p6%|%t;1%;%?%p2%t;4%;%?%p1%p3%|%t;7%;%?%p4%t;5%;m%?%p9%t^N%e^O%;,
 sgr0=\E[m^O$<2>, smacs=^N, smkx=\E[?1h\E=,
 smso=\E[1;7m$<2>, smul=\E[4m$<2>, tbc=\E[3g,
```

Each `terminfo` definition consists of three types of entry. Each entry is called a *capname* and defines a terminal capability.

Boolean capabilities simply indicate whether a terminal supports a particular feature. For example, the Boolean capability `xon` is present if the terminal supports XON/XOFF flow control.

Numeric capabilities define sizes, such as lines, the number of lines on the screen, and cols, the number of columns on the screen. The actual number is separated from the capability name by a # character. To define a terminal as having 80 columns and 24 lines, you would write cols#80, lines#24.

String capabilities are slightly more complex. They are used for two distinct types of capability: defining output strings needed to access terminal features and defining the input strings that will be received when the user presses certain keys, normally function keys or special keys on the numeric keypad. Some string capabilities are quite simple, such as el, which is "erase to end of line." On a VT100 terminal, the escape sequence needed to do this is Esc,[,K. This is written el=\E[K in terminfo source format.

Special keys are defined in a similar way. For example, the F1 function key on a VT100 sends the sequence Esc,O,P. This is defined as kf1=\EOP.

Things get slightly more complicated where the escape sequence needs some parameters. Most terminals can move the cursor to a specified row and column location. It's clearly impractical to have a different capability for each possible cursor location, so a generic capability string is used, with parameters defining the values to be inserted when the stings are used. For example, a VT100 terminal uses the sequence Esc,[,<row>,;,<col>,H to move the cursor to a specified location. In terminfo source format, this is written with the rather intimidating cup=\E[%i%p1%d;%p2%dH$<5>.

This means

- ❏   \E: Send Escape
- ❏   [: Send the [character
- ❏   %i: Increment the arguments
- ❏   %p1: Put the first argument on the stack
- ❏   %d: Output the number on the stack as a decimal number
- ❏   ;: Send the ; character
- ❏   %p2: Put the second argument on the stack
- ❏   %d: Output the number on the stack as a decimal number
- ❏   H: Send the H character

This seems complex, but allows for the parameters to be in a fixed order, independent of which order the terminal expects them to appear in the final escape sequence. The %i to increment the arguments is required because standard cursor addressing is specified as starting from (0,0) at the top left of the screen, but the VT100 addresses this location as (1,1). The final $<5> indicates that a delay equivalent to five character output times is required to allow the terminal to process the cursor movement.

> We could define many, many capabilities, but, fortunately, most UNIX and Linux systems come with most terminals predefined. If you need to add a new terminal, you'll find the complete capability list in the terminfo manual page. A good starting point is usually to locate a terminal that is similar to your new terminal and define the new terminal as a variation on the existing terminal or to work through the capabilities one at a time, updating them where required.

> The standard reference outside of the man pages is the Termcap and Terminfo by John Strang, Linda Mui, and Tim O'Reilly (O'Reilly).

Using terminfo Capabilities

Now that you know how to define terminal capabilities, you need to learn how to access them. When you're using `terminfo`, the first thing you need to do is set up the terminal type by calling `setupterm`. This will initialize a TERMINAL structure for the current terminal type. You'll then be able to ask for capabilities for the terminal and use its facilities. You do this with the `setupterm` call like this:

```
#include <term.h>

int setupterm(char *term, int fd, int *errret);
```

The `setupterm` library function sets the current terminal type to that specified by the parameter `term`. If `term` is a null pointer, the TERM environment variable will be used. An open file descriptor to be used for writing to the terminal must be passed as `fd`. The function outcome is stored in the integer variable pointed to by `errret`, if this isn't a null pointer. The value written will be

❑   –1: No `terminfo` database

❑   0: No matching entry in `terminfo` database

❑   1: Success

The `setupterm` function returns the constant OK if it succeeds and ERR if it fails. If `errret` is set to a null pointer, `setupterm` will print a diagnostic message and exit the program if it fails, as in this example:

```
#include <stdio.h>
#include <term.h>
#include <curses.h>
#include <stdlib.h>

int main()
{
    setupterm("unlisted",fileno(stdout),(int *)0);
    printf("Done.\n");
    exit(0);
}
```

The output from running this program on your system may not be exactly that given here, but the meaning should be clear enough. `Done.` isn't printed, because `setupterm` caused the program to exit when it failed.

```
$ cc -o badterm badterm.c -lncurses
$ ./badterm
'unlisted': unknown terminal type.
$
```

Notice the compilation line in the example: On this Linux system, we are using the `ncurses` implementation of the `curses` library with a standard header file, which is available in the standard locations. On such systems, you can simply include `curses.h`, and specify `-lncurses` for the library.

For the menu choice function, you would like to be able to clear the screen, move the cursor around the screen, and write at different locations on the screen. Once you've called setupterm, you can access the terminfo capabilities with three function calls, one for each of the capability types:

```
#include <term.h>

int tigetflag(char *capname);
int tigetnum(char *capname);
char *tigetstr(char *capname);
```

The functions tigetflag, tigetnum, and tigetstr return the value of Boolean, numeric, and string terminfo capabilities, respectively. On failure (for example, if the capability isn't present), tigetflag returns -1, tigetnum returns -2, and tigetstr returns (char *)-1.

You can use the terminfo database to find out the size of the terminal by retrieving the cols and lines capabilities with this program, sizeterm.c:

```
#include <stdio.h>
#include <term.h>
#include <curses.h>
#include <stdlib.h>

int main()
{
    int nrows, ncolumns;

    setupterm(NULL, fileno(stdout), (int *)0);
    nrows = tigetnum("lines");
    ncolumns = tigetnum("cols");
    printf("This terminal has %d columns and %d rows\n", ncolumns, nrows);
    exit(0);
}
```

```
$ echo $TERM
vt100
$ ./sizeterm
This terminal has 80 columns and 24 rows
$
```

If you run the program inside a window on a workstation, you'll get answers that reflect the current window's size:

```
$ echo $TERM
xterm
$ ./sizeterm
This terminal has 88 columns and 40 rows
$
```

If you use tigetstr to retrieve the cursor motion capability (cup) of the xterm terminal type, you get a parameterized answer: \E[%p1%d;%p2%dH.

This capability requires two parameters: a row and column to move the cursor to. Both coordinates are measured starting at zero from the top-left corner of the screen.

You can substitute the parameters in a capability with actual values using the tparm function. Up to nine parameters can be substituted and a usable escape sequence is returned.

```
#include <term.h>

char *tparm(char *cap, long p1, long p2, ..., long p9);
```

Once you've constructed the terminal escape sequence with tparm, you must send it to the terminal. To process this properly, you shouldn't send the string to the terminal with printf. Instead, use one of the special functions provided that correctly process any required delays while the terminal completes an operation. These functions are

```
#include <term.h>

int putp(char *const str);
int tputs(char *const str, int affcnt, int (*putfunc)(int));
```

On success, putp returns OK; on failure, it returns ERR. The putp function takes the terminal control string and sends it to stdout.

So, to move to row 5, column 30 of the screen, you can use a block of code like this:

```
char *cursor;
char *esc_sequence;
cursor = tigetstr("cup");
esc_sequence = tparm(cursor,5,30);
putp(esc_sequence);
```

The tputs function is provided for those situations when the terminal isn't accessed via stdout and allows you to specify the function to be used for outputting the characters. It returns the result of the user-specified function putfunc. The affcnt parameter is intended to indicate the number of lines affected by the change. It's normally set to 1. The function used to output the string must have the same parameters and return type as the putchar function. Indeed, putp(string) is equivalent to the call tputs(string, 1, putchar). You'll see tputs used with a user-specified output function in the next example.

Be aware that some older Linux distributions define the final parameter of the tputs function as int (*putfunc)(char), which would oblige you to alter the definition of the char_to_terminal function in the next Try It Out section.

If you consult the manual pages for information on tparm and terminal capabilities, you may come across the tgoto function. The reason we haven't used this function, when it apparently offers an easier solution to moving the cursor, is that the X/Open specification (Single UNIX Specification Version 2) does not include it as of the 1997 edition. We therefore recommend that you don't use any of these functions in new programs.

You're almost ready to add screen handling to your menu choice function. The only thing left to do is to clear the screen simply by using clear. Some terminals don't support the clear capability, which leaves the cursor at the top-left corner of the screen. In this case, you can position the cursor at the top-left corner and use the "delete to end of display" command, ed.

Putting all this information together, you'll write the final version of your sample menu program, screenmenu.c, where you "paint" the options on the screen for the user to pick a valid one.

Try It Out   **Total Terminal Control**

You can rewrite the getchoice function from menu4.c to give you total terminal control. In this listing, the main function has been omitted because it isn't changed. Other differences from menu4.c are highlighted.

```c
#include <stdio.h>
#include <unistd.h>
#include <stdlib.h>
#include <termios.h>
#include <term.h>
#include <curses.h>

static FILE *output_stream = (FILE *)0;

char *menu[] = {
    "a - add new record",
    "d - delete record",
    "q - quit",
    NULL,
};

int getchoice(char *greet, char *choices[], FILE *in, FILE *out);
int char_to_terminal(int char_to_write);

int main()
{
...
}


int getchoice(char *greet, char *choices[], FILE *in, FILE *out)
{
    int chosen = 0;
    int selected;
    int screenrow, screencol = 10;

    char **option;
    char *cursor, *clear;

    output_stream = out;

    setupterm(NULL, fileno(out), (int *)0);
    cursor = tigetstr("cup");
    clear = tigetstr("clear");

    screenrow = 4;
    tputs(clear, 1, (int *) char_to_terminal);
    tputs(tparm(cursor, screenrow, screencol), 1, char_to_terminal);
    fprintf(out, "Choice: %s, greet);
    screenrow += 2;
    option = choices;
    while(*option) {
        tputs(tparm(cursor, screenrow, screencol), 1, char_to_terminal);
        fprintf(out,"%s", *option);
        screenrow++;
        option++;
```

```
        }
        fprintf(out, "\n");

        do {
            fflush(out);
            selected = fgetc(in);
            option = choices;
            while(*option) {
                if(selected == *option[0]) {
                    chosen = 1;
                    break;
                }
                option++;
            }
            if(!chosen) {
                tputs(tparm(cursor, screenrow, screencol), 1, char_to_terminal);
                fprintf(out,"Incorrect choice, select again\n");
            }
        } while(!chosen);
        tputs(clear, 1, char_to_terminal);
        return selected;
}

int char_to_terminal(int char_to_write)
{
        if (output_stream) putc(char_to_write, output_stream);
        return 0;
}
```

Save this program as menu5.c.

How It Works

The rewritten getchoice function implements the same menu as in previous examples, but the output routines are modified to make use of the terminfo capabilities. If you want to see the You have chosen: message for more than a moment before the screen is cleared, ready for the next selection, add a call to sleep in the main function:

```
do {
        choice = getchoice("Please select an action", menu, input, output);
        printf("\nYou have chosen: %c\n", choice);
        sleep(1);
} while (choice != 'q');
```

The last function in this program, char_to_terminal, includes a call to the putc function, which we mentioned in Chapter 3.

To round off this chapter, let's look at a quick example of how to detect keystrokes.

Detecting Keystrokes

People who have programmed MS-DOS often look for the Linux equivalent of the kbhit function, which detects whether a key has been pressed without actually reading it. Unfortunately, they fail to find it, because there's no direct equivalent. UNIX programmers don't notice the omission because UNIX is normally programmed in such a way that programs should rarely, if ever, busy-wait on an event. Because this is the normal use for kbhit, it's rarely missed on UNIX and Linux.

However, when you're porting programs from MS-DOS, it's often convenient to emulate kbhit, which you can do using the non-canonical input mode.

Try It Out   **Your Very Own kbhit**

1. You begin with the standard headings and declare a couple of structures for the terminal settings. peek_character is used in the test of whether a key has been pressed. Then you prototype the functions you'll be using later.

```
#include <stdio.h>
#include <stdlib.h>
#include <termios.h>
#include <term.h>
#include <curses.h>
#include <unistd.h>
static struct termios initial_settings, new_settings;
static int peek_character = -1;
void init_keyboard();
void close_keyboard();
int kbhit();
int readch();
```

2. The main function calls init_keyboard to configure the terminal, then loops once a second, calling kbhit each time it does. If the key hit is *q*, close_keyboard returns the behavior to normal and the program exits.

```
int main()
{
    int ch = 0;

    init_keyboard();
    while(ch != 'q') {
        printf("looping\n");
        sleep(1);
        if(kbhit()) {
            ch = readch();
            printf("you hit %c\n",ch);
        }
    }

    close_keyboard();
    exit(0);
}
```

3. `init_keyboard` and `close_keyboard` configure the terminal at the start and end of the program.

```
void init_keyboard()
{
    tcgetattr(0,&initial_settings);
    new_settings = initial_settings;
    new_settings.c_lflag &= ~ICANON;
    new_settings.c_lflag &= ~ECHO;
    new_settings.c_lflag &= ~ISIG;
    new_settings.c_cc[VMIN] = 1;
    new_settings.c_cc[VTIME] = 0;
    tcsetattr(0, TCSANOW, &new_settings);
}
void close_keyboard()
{
    tcsetattr(0, TCSANOW, &initial_settings);
}
```

4. Now for the function that checks for the keyboard hit:

```
int kbhit()
{
    char ch;
    int nread;

    if(peek_character != -1)
        return 1;
    new_settings.c_cc[VMIN]=0;
    tcsetattr(0, TCSANOW, &new_settings);
    nread = read(0,&ch,1);
    new_settings.c_cc[VMIN]=1;
    tcsetattr(0, TCSANOW, &new_settings);

    if(nread == 1) {
        peek_character = ch;
        return 1;
    }
    return 0;
}
```

5. The character pressed is read by the next function, `readch`, which then resets `peek_character` to –1 for the next loop.

```
int readch()
{
    char ch;

    if(peek_character != -1) {
        ch = peek_character;
        peek_character = -1;
        return ch;
    }
    read(0,&ch,1);
    return ch;
}
```

When you run the program (`kbhit.c`), you get

```
$ ./kbhit
looping
looping
looping
you hit h
looping
looping
looping
you hit d
looping
you hit q
$
```

How It Works

The terminal is configured in `init_keyboard` to read one character before returning (`MIN=1,TIME=0`). `kbhit` changes this behavior to check for input and return immediately (`MIN=0,TIME=0`) and then restores the original settings before exiting.

Notice that you have to read the character that has been pressed but that you store it locally, ready for returning when it's required.

Virtual Consoles

Linux provides a feature called virtual consoles. A number of terminal devices are available, all of which share the PC's screen, keyboard, and mouse. Typically, a Linux installation will be configured for 8 or 12 of these virtual consoles. The virtual consoles are made available through the character devices `/dev/ttyN` where `N` is a number, starting at 1.

If you use a text login for your Linux system, you will be presented with a login prompt once Linux is up and running. You then log in using a username and password. The device that you are using at this point is the first virtual console, the terminal device `/dev/tty1`.

Using `who` and `ps`, you can see who is logged in and the shell and programs being executed on this virtual console:

```
$ who
neil      tty1      Mar  8 18:27
$ ps -e
  PID TTY          TIME CMD
 1092 tty1     00:00:00 login
 1414 tty1     00:00:00 bash
 1431 tty1     00:00:00 emacs
```

Here, you can see in this cut-down output that user `neil` is logged in and running Emacs on the PC console device `/dev/tty1`.

Linux will normally start a `getty` process running on the first six virtual consoles so that it is possible to log in six times using the same screen, keyboard, and mouse. You can see these processes with `ps`:

```
$ ps -e
  PID TTY          TIME CMD
 1092 tty1     00:00:00 login
 1093 tty2     00:00:00 mingetty
 1094 tty3     00:00:00 mingetty
 1095 tty4     00:00:00 mingetty
 1096 tty5     00:00:00 mingetty
 1097 tty6     00:00:00 mingetty
```

Here, you can see the SUSE default getty program, `mingetty`, running on five further virtual consoles, waiting for a user to log in.

You can switch between virtual consoles using a special key combination: Ctrl+Alt+F<N> where N is the number of the virtual console you want to switch to. So, to switch to the second virtual console, you would press Alt+Ctrl+F2, and Ctrl+Alt+F1 to return to the first console. (When switching from text logins rather than graphical logins, the combination Ctrl+F<N> also works.)

If Linux starts a graphical login, either by `startx` or via a display manager such as `xdm`, the X Window System will start up using the first free virtual console, normally `/dev/tty7`. When using the X Window System, you can switch out to a text console with Ctrl+Alt+F<N> and back with Ctrl+Alt+F7.

It is possible to run more than one X session on Linux. If you do this, for example, with

```
$ startx -- :1
```

Linux will start the X server on the next free virtual console, in this case, `/dev/tty8`, and it is then possible to switch between them with Ctrl+Alt+F8 and Ctrl+Alt+F7.

In all other respects, the virtual consoles behave as a terminal, as described in this chapter. If a process has the correct permissions, the virtual consoles can be opened, read from, and written to in the same way as a normal terminal.

Pseudo-Terminals

Many UNIX-like systems, including Linux, have a feature called pseudo-terminals. These are devices that behave much like the terminals we have been using in this chapter, except that they have no associated hardware. They can be used to provide a terminal-like interface to other programs.

For example, using pseudo-terminals, it is possible to make two chess programs play each other, despite the fact that the programs themselves were designed to interact with a human player at a terminal. An application acting as an intermediary passes one program's moves to the other and vice versa. It uses pseudo-terminals to fool the programs into behaving normally without a terminal being present.

Pseudo-terminals were at one time implemented in a system-specific manner, if at all. They have now been incorporated into the Single UNIX Specification as UNIX98 Pseudo-Terminals or PTYs.

Summary

In this chapter, you've learned about three different aspects of controlling the terminal. In the first part of the chapter, you learned about detecting redirection and how to talk directly to a terminal even when the standard file descriptors have been redirected. You saw the hardware model for terminals and a little of their history. You then learned about the General Terminal Interface and the `termios` structure that provides detailed control over Linux terminal handling. You also saw how to use the `terminfo` database and related functions to manage screen output in a terminal-independent fashion, and you looked at immediately detecting keystrokes. Finally, you learned about Linux virtual consoles and pseudo-terminals.

Managing Text-Based Screens with curses

In Chapter 5, you learned how to obtain much finer control over the input of characters and how to provide character output in a terminal-independent way. The problem with using the general terminal interface (GTI, or termios) and manipulating escape sequences with tparm and its related functions is that it requires a lot of lower-level code. For many programs, a higher-level interface is more desirable. We would like to be able to simply draw on the screen and use a library of functions to take care of terminal dependencies automatically.

In this chapter, you'll learn about just such a library, the curses library. The curses standard is important as a halfway house between simple "line-based" programs and the fully graphical (and generally harder to program) X Window System programs, such as GTK+/GNOME and Qt/KDE. Linux does have the svgalib (Super VGA Library, a low-level graphics library), but that is not a UNIX standard library, so is not generally available in other UNIX-like operating systems. The curses library is used in many full-screen applications as a reasonably easy and terminal-independent way to write full-screen, albeit character-based, programs. It's almost always easier to write such programs with curses than to use escape sequences directly. curses can also manage the keyboard, providing an easy-to-use, nonblocking character input mode.

You may find that a few of the examples in this chapter don't always display on the plain Linux console exactly as you expect. There are occasions when the combination of the curses library and the terminal definition of the console get slightly out of step and the effect is usually some slightly odd layouts when using curses. However, if you use the X Window System and use an xterm window to display the output, then things should display as you expect.

This chapter covers the following:

❑   Using the curses library
❑   The concepts of curses
❑   Basic input and output control

❑ Using multiple windows

❑ Using keypad mode

❑ Adding color

We finish the chapter by reimplementing the CD Collection program in C, summarizing what you've learned so far.

Compiling with curses

The curses library takes its name from its ability to optimize the movement of the cursor and minimize the updates needed on a screen, and hence, reduce the number of characters that need to be sent to a text-based terminal. Although the number of characters output is much less important than it was in the days of dumb terminals and low-speed modems, the curses library survives as a useful addition to the programmer's toolkit.

Because curses is a library, to use it you must include a header file, function declarations, and macros from an appropriate system library. There have been several different implementations of curses. The original version appeared in BSD UNIX and was then incorporated into the System V flavors of UNIX, before being standardized by X/Open. Linux uses ncurses ("new curses"), a freeware emulation of System V Release 4.0 curses that was developed on Linux. This implementation is highly portable to other UNIX versions, although a few nonportable additional features are included. There are even versions of curses for MS-DOS and Windows. If you find that the curses library bundled with your flavor of UNIX doesn't support some features, try to obtain a copy of ncurses as an alternative. Linux users will usually find they have ncurses already installed, or at least the components required for running curses-based programs. If the development libraries for it are not pre-installed in your distribution (there is no curses.h file or no curses library file to link against), they are generally available for most major distributions as a standard package, probably named something like libncurses5-dev.

> The X/Open specification defines two levels of curses: base and extended. Extended curses contains a somewhat motley crew of additional routines, including a range of functions for handling multicolumn characters and color manipulation routines. Apart from showing how to use color later in this chapter, we will be sticking mostly to the base functions.

When you're compiling curses programs, you must include the header file curses.h, and link against the curses library with -lcurses. On many Linux systems you can simply use curses but will find you are actually using the superior, and newer, ncurses implementation.

You can check how your curses is set up by executing the command

```
ls -l /usr/include/*curses.h
```

to look at the header files, and

```
ls -l /usr/lib/lib*curses*
```

to check the library files. If you find that curses.h and ncurses.h are just linked files, and an ncurses library file is present, you should be able to compile the files in this chapter using a command such as the following:

```
$ gcc program.c -o program -lcurses
```

If, however, your curses setup is not automatically using ncurses, then you may have to explicitly force the use of ncurses by including ncurses.h, rather than curses.h, and by executing a compile command such as this:

```
$ gcc -I/usr/include/ncurses program.c -o program -lncurses
```

where the -I option specifies the directory in which to search for the header file.

> *The* Makefile *in the downloadable code assumes your setup uses* curses *by default, so you must change it or compile it by hand if this is not the case on your system.*

If you're unsure how curses is set up on your system, refer to the manual pages for ncurses, or look for other online documentation; a common location is under /usr/share/doc/, where you may find a curses or ncurses directory, often with a version number appended.

Curses Terminology and Concepts

The curses routines work on screens, windows, and subwindows. A *screen* is the device (usually a terminal screen, but it could also be an xterm screen) to which you are writing. It occupies all the available display on that device. Of course, if it's a terminal window inside an X window, the screen is simply all the character positions available inside the terminal window. There is always at least one curses window, stdscr, that is the same size as the physical screen. You can create additional windows that are smaller than the screen. Windows can overlap each other and have many subwindows, but each subwindow must always be contained inside its parent window.

The curses library maintains two data structures that act like a map of the terminal screen: stdscr, and curscr. stdscr, the more important of the two data structures, is updated when curses functions produce output. The stdscr data structure is the "standard screen." It acts in much the same way as stdout, the standard output, does for the stdio library. It's the default output window in curses programs. The curscr structure is similar, but holds what the displayed screen actually looks like at the current moment. Output written to stdscr doesn't appear on the screen until the program calls refresh, when the curses library compares the contents of stdscr (what the screen should look like) with the second structure curscr (what the screen currently looks like). curses then uses the differences between these two structures to update the screen.

Some curses programs need to know that curses maintains a stdscr structure, which is required as a parameter to a few curses functions. However, the actual stdscr structure is implementation-dependent and should never be accessed directly. curses programs should never need to use the curscr structure.

Thus, the process for the output of characters in a curses program is as follows:

1. Use curses functions to update a logical screen.

2. Ask curses to update the physical screen with refresh.

The advantage of a two-level approach, in addition to being much easier to program, is that curses screen updates are very efficient. In addition, although this isn't so important on a console screen, it can make a considerable difference if you're running your program over a slow network link.

A curses program will make many calls to logical screen output functions, possibly moving the cursor all over the screen to get to the right position for writing text and drawing lines and boxes. At some stage, the user needs to see all of this output. When this happens, typically during a call to refresh, curses will calculate the optimum way of making the physical screen correspond to the logical screen. By using appropriate terminal capabilities and by optimizing cursor motions, curses can often update the screen with far fewer characters being output than if all the screen writes had happened immediately.

The layout of the logical screen is a character array, arranged by lines and columns, with the screen position (0,0) at the top left-hand corner, as shown in Figure 6-1.

Figure 6-1

All the curses functions use coordinates with the y value (lines) before the x (columns) value. Each position holds not only the character for that screen location, but also its attributes. The attributes that can be displayed depend on the physical terminal's capabilities, but usually at least bold and underline are available. On Linux consoles, you usually also have reverse video and color, which are covered later in the chapter.

Because the curses library needs to create and destroy some temporary data structures, all curses programs must initialize the library before use and then allow curses to restore settings after use. This is done with a pair of function calls: initscr and endwin.

Try It Out   **A Hello World curses Program**

In this example, you write a very simple curses program, screen1.c, to show these and other basic function calls in action. You then describe the function prototypes:

1.   Add the curses.h header file, and in the main function make calls to initialize and reset the curses library:

```
#include <unistd.h>
#include <stdlib.h>
#include <curses.h>

int main() {
    initscr();

...

    endwin();
    exit(EXIT_SUCCESS);
}
```

2.   In between, add code to move the cursor to the point (5,15) on the logical screen, print "Hello World," and refresh the actual screen. Lastly, use the call sleep(2) to suspend the program for two seconds so that you can see the output before the program ends:

```
    move(5, 15);
    printw("%s", "Hello World");
    refresh();

    sleep(2);
```

While the program is running, you see "Hello World" in the top-left quadrant of an otherwise blank screen, as shown in Figure 6-2.

How It Works

This program initialized the curses library, moved the cursor to a point on the screen, and displayed some text. After a brief pause it then closed down the library and exited.

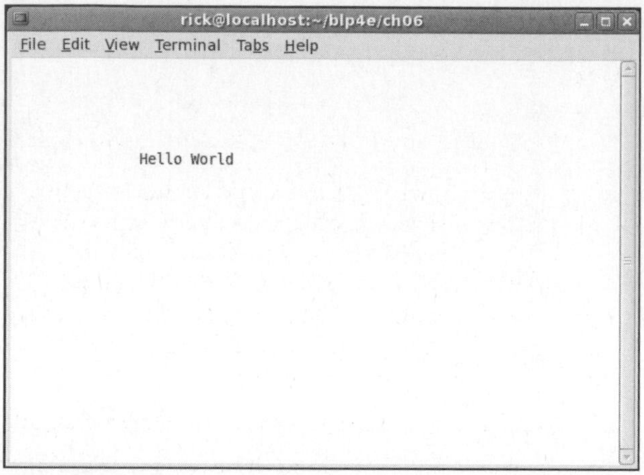

Figure 6-2

The Screen

As you've already seen, all curses programs must start with initscr and end with endwin. Here are their header file definitions:

```
#include <curses.h>

WINDOW *initscr(void);
int endwin(void);
```

The initscr function must only be called once in each program. The initscr function returns a pointer to the stdscr structure if it succeeds. If it fails, it simply prints a diagnostic error message and causes the program to exit.

The endwin function returns OK on success and ERR on failure. You can call endwin to leave curses and then later resume curses operation by calling clearok(stdscr, 1) and refresh. This effectively makes curses forget what the physical screen looks like and forces it to perform a complete redisplay.

Output to the Screen

Several basic functions are provided for updating the screen:

```
#include <curses.h>

int addch(const chtype char_to_add);
int addchstr(chtype *const string_to_add);
int printw(char *format, ...);
int refresh(void);
int box(WINDOW *win_ptr, chtype vertical_char, chtype horizontal_char);
int insch(chtype char_to_insert);
```

```
int insertln(void);
int delch(void);
int deleteln(void);
int beep(void);
int flash(void);
```

curses has its own character type, chtype, which may have more bits than a standard char. In the standard Linux version of ncurses, chtype is actually a typedef for unsigned long.

The add... functions add the character or string specified at the current location. The printw function formats a string in the same way as printf and adds it to the current location. The refresh function causes the physical screen to be updated, returning OK on success and ERR if an error occurred. The box function allows you to draw a box around a window.

> In standard curses, you may only use "normal" characters for the vertical and horizontal line characters. In extended curses, though, you can use the two defines ACS_VLINE and ACS_HLINE to provide vertical and horizontal line characters, respectively, which enable you to draw a better-looking box. For this, your terminal needs to support line-drawing characters. Generally, these will work better in an xterm window than on the standard console, but support tends to be patchy, so we suggest you avoid them if portability is important.

The insch function inserts a character, moving existing characters right, though what will happen at the end of a line isn't specified and depends on the terminal you're using. insertln inserts a blank line, moving existing lines down by one. The two delete functions are analogous to the two insert functions.

To make a sound, you can call beep. A very small number of terminals are unable to make any sound, so some curses setups will cause the screen to flash when beep is called. If you work in a busy office, where beeps can come from any number of machines, you might find you prefer this. As you might expect, flash causes the screen to flash, but if this isn't possible, it tries to make a sound on the terminal instead.

Reading from the Screen

You can read characters from the screen, although this facility isn't commonly used because normally it's easier to keep track of what was written. If you need it, it's done with the following functions:

```
#include <curses.h>

chtype inch(void);
int instr(char *string);
int innstr(char *string, int number_of_characters);
```

The inch function should always be available, but the instr and innstr functions are not always supported. The inch function returns a character and its attribute information from the current screen location of the cursor. Notice that inch doesn't return a character, but a chtype, while instr and innstr write to arrays of chars.

Clearing the Screen

There are four principal ways of clearing an area of the screen:

```
#include <curses.h>

int erase(void);
int clear(void);
int clrtobot(void);
int clrtoeol(void);
```

The erase function writes blanks to every screen location. The clear function, like erase, clears the screen, but forces a screen redisplay by internally calling a lower-level function, clearok, which enforces a clear screen sequence and redisplay when the next refresh is called.

The clear function usually uses a terminal command that erases the entire screen, rather than simply attempting to erase any currently nonblank screen locations. This makes the clear function a reliable way of completely erasing the screen. The combination of clear followed by refresh can provide a useful redraw command if the screen display has become confused or corrupted in some way.

clrtobot clears the screen from the cursor position onward to the end of the screen, and clrtoeol clears from the cursor position to the end of the line the cursor is on.

Moving the Cursor

A single function is provided for moving the cursor, with an additional command for controlling where curses leaves the cursor after screen updates:

```
#include <curses.h>

int move(int new_y, int new_x);
int leaveok(WINDOW *window_ptr, bool leave_flag);
```

The move function simply moves the logical cursor position to the specified location. Remember that the screen coordinates are specified with (0,0) as the top left-hand corner of the screen. In most versions of curses, the two extern integers LINES and COLUMNS contain the physical screen size and can be used to determine the maximum allowed values for new_y and new_x. Calling move won't, in itself, cause the physical cursor to move. It only changes the location on the logical screen at which the next output will appear. If you want the screen cursor to move immediately after calling move, follow it with a call to refresh.

The leaveok function sets a flag that controls where curses leaves the physical cursor after a screen update. By default, the flag is false, and after a refresh the hardware cursor is left in the same position on the screen as the logical cursor. If the flag is set to true, the hardware cursor may be left randomly, anywhere on the screen. Generally, the default option is preferred to ensure that the cursor is left in a sensible location.

Character Attributes

Each curses character can have certain attributes that control how it's displayed on the screen, assuming that the display hardware can support the requested attribute. The defined attributes are A_BLINK, A_BOLD,

A_DIM, A_REVERSE, A_STANDOUT, and A_UNDERLINE. You can use these functions to set attributes singly or collectively:

```
#include <curses.h>

int attron(chtype attribute);
int attroff(chtype attribute);
int attrset(chtype attribute);
int standout(void);
int standend(void);
```

The attrset function sets the curses attributes, attron and attroff turn on and off specified attributes without disturbing others, while standout and standend provide a more generic emphasized, or "stand out" mode. This is commonly mapped to reverse video on most terminals.

Try It Out   Moving, Inserting, and Attributes

Now that you know more about managing the screen, you can try out a more complex example, moveadd.c. For the purposes of this example, you'll include several calls to refresh and sleep, to enable you to see what the screen looks like at each stage. Normally, curses programs would refresh the screen as little as possible because it's not a very efficient operation. The code is slightly contrived for the purposes of illustration.

1. To begin, include some header files, define some character arrays and a pointer to those arrays, and then initialize the curses structures:

```
#include <stdio.h>
#include <unistd.h>
#include <stdlib.h>
#include <string.h>
#include <curses.h>


int main()
{
    const char witch_one[] = " First Witch  ";
    const char witch_two[] = " Second Witch ";
    const char *scan_ptr;

    initscr();
```

2. Now for the three initial sets of text that appear at intervals on the screen — note the on and off flagging of text attributes:

```
    move(5, 15);
    attron(A_BOLD);
    printw("%s", "Macbeth");
    attroff(A_BOLD);
    refresh();
    sleep(1);

    move(8, 15);
```

```
attron(A_STANDOUT);
printw("%s", "Thunder and Lightning");
attroff(A_STANDOUT);
refresh();
sleep(1);

move(10, 10);
printw("%s", "When shall we three meet again");
move(11, 23);
printw("%s", "In thunder, lightning, or in rain ?");
move(13, 10);
printw("%s", "When the hurlyburly's done,");
move(14,23);
printw("%s", "When the battle's lost and won.");
refresh();
sleep(1);
```

3. The actors are identified and their names are inserted one character at a time:

```
attron(A_DIM);
scan_ptr = witch_one + strlen(witch_one) - 1;
while(scan_ptr != witch_one) {
    move(10,10);
    insch(*scan_ptr--);
}
scan_ptr = witch_two + strlen(witch_two) - 1;
while (scan_ptr != witch_two) {
    move(13, 10);
    insch(*scan_ptr--);
}
attroff(A_DIM);
refresh();
sleep(1);
```

4. Finally, move the cursor to the bottom-right corner of the screen and then tidy up an exit:

```
move(LINES - 1, COLS - 1);

refresh();
sleep(1);

endwin();
exit(EXIT_SUCCESS);
}
```

When you run this program, the final screen looks like the one shown in Figure 6-3.

Unfortunately, the screenshot doesn't convey the full effect very well, nor does it show the cursor, which is parked at the bottom right-hand corner.

You may find that xterm is a more reliable medium for accurately displaying programs than the raw console.

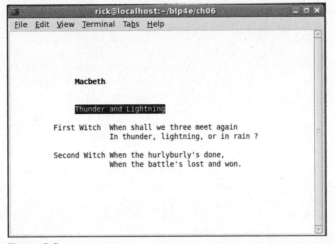

Figure 6-3

How It Works

After initializing some variables and the curses screen, you used the move functions to move the cursor about the screen. By using the attron and attroff functions, you controlled the attributes of the text written out at each location. The program then demonstrated how characters can be inserted with insch, before closing the curses library and terminating.

The Keyboard

As well as providing an easier interface for controlling the screen, curses also provides an easier method for controlling the keyboard.

Keyboard Modes

The keyboard reading routines are controlled by modes. The functions that set the modes are as follows:

```
#include <curses.h>

int echo(void);
int noecho(void);
int cbreak(void);
int nocbreak(void);
int raw(void);
int noraw(void);
```

The two echo functions simply turn the echoing of typed characters on and off. The remaining four function calls control how characters typed on the terminal are made available to the curses program.

To explain cbreak, you need to understand the default input mode. When a curses program starts by calling initscr, the input mode is set to what is termed *cooked mode*. This means that all processing is done on a line-by-line basis; that is, input is only available after the user has pressed Enter (or the Return key on some keyboards). Keyboard special characters are enabled, so typing the appropriate key sequences can generate a signal in the program. Flow control, if the terminal is running from a terminal, is also enabled. By calling cbreak, a program may set the input mode to *cbreak mode* whereby characters are available to the program immediately after they are typed, rather than being buffered up and only made available to the program when Enter is pressed. As in cooked mode, keyboard special characters are enabled, but simple keys, such as Backspace, are passed directly to the program to be processed, so if you want the Backspace key to function as expected, you have to program it yourself.

A call to raw turns off special character processing, so it becomes impossible to generate signals or flow control by typing special character sequences. Calling nocbreak sets the input mode back to cooked mode, but leaves special character processing unchanged; calling noraw restores both cooked mode and special character handling.

Keyboard Input

Reading the keyboard is very simple. The principal functions are as follows:

```
#include <curses.h>

int getch(void);
int getstr(char *string);
int getnstr(char *string, int number_of_characters);
int scanw(char *format, ...);
```

These act in a very similar way to their non-curses equivalents getchar, gets, and scanf. Note that getstr provides no way of limiting the string length returned, so you should use it only with great caution. If your version of curses supports getnstr, which allows you to limit the number of characters read, always use it in preference to getstr. This is very similar to the behavior of gets and fgets that you saw in Chapter 3.

Here's a short example program, ipmode.c, to show how to handle the keyboard.

Try It Out   Keyboard Modes and Input

1.   Set up the program and the initial curses calls:

```
#include <unistd.h>
#include <stdlib.h>
#include <curses.h>
#include <string.h>

#define PW_LEN 256
#define NAME_LEN 256

int main() {
    char name[NAME_LEN];
    char password[PW_LEN];
    const char *real_password = "xyzzy";
```

```
int i = 0;

initscr();

move(5, 10);
printw("%s", "Please login:");

move(7, 10);
printw("%s", "User name: ");
getstr(name);

move(8, 10);
printw("%s", "Password: ");
refresh();
```

2. When the user enters his or her password, you need to stop the password being echoed to the screen. Then check the password against xyzzy:

```
cbreak();
noecho();

memset(password, '\0', sizeof(password));
while (i < PW_LEN) {
    password[i] = getch();
    if (password[i] == '\n') break;
    move(8, 20 + i);
    addch('*');
    refresh();
    i++;
}
```

3. Finally, re-enable the keyboard echo and print out success or failure:

```
echo();
nocbreak();

move(11, 10);
if (strncmp(real_password, password, strlen(real_password)) == 0)
    printw("%s", "Correct");
else printw("%s", "Wrong");
printw("%s", " password");
refresh();
sleep(2);

endwin();
exit(EXIT_SUCCESS);
}
```

How It Works

Having stopped the echoing of keyboard input and set the input mode to cbreak, you set up a region of memory ready for the password. Each character of the password entered is processed immediately and a

* is shown at the next position on the screen. You need to refresh the screen each time, and compare the two strings, entered and real passwords, using strcmp.

If you're using a very old version of the curses *library, you may need to make an additional* refresh *call before the* getstr *call. In* ncurses, *calling* getstr *will refresh the screen automatically.*

Windows

Until now, you have used the terminal as a full-screen output medium. This is often sufficient for small and simple programs, but the curses library goes a long way beyond that. You can display multiple windows of different sizes concurrently on the physical screen. Many of the functions in this section are only supported by what X/Open terms "extended" curses. However, since they are supported by ncurses, there should be little problem in them being made available on most platforms. Now it's time to move on and use multiple windows. You'll also see how the commands used so far are generalized to the multiple window scenario.

The WINDOW Structure

Although we have mentioned stdscr, the standard screen, you have so far had little need to use it, as almost all of the functions that we've discussed so far assume that they're working on stdscr and it does not need to be passed as a parameter.

The stdscr is just a special case of the WINDOW structure, like stdout is a special case of a file stream. The WINDOW structure is normally declared in curses.h, and while it can be instructive to examine it, programs should never access it directly, as the structure can and does change between implementations.

You can create and destroy windows using the newwin and delwin calls:

```
#include <curses.h>

WINDOW *newwin(int num_of_lines, int num_of_cols, int start_y, int start_x);
int delwin(WINDOW *window_to_delete);
```

The newwin function creates a new window, with a screen location of (start_y, start_x) and with the specified number of lines and columns. It returns a pointer to the new window, or null if the creation failed. If you want the new window to have its bottom right-hand corner in the bottom right-hand corner of the screen, you can provide the number of lines or columns as zero. All windows must fit within the current screen, so newwin will fail if any part of the new window would fall outside the screen area. The new window created by newwin is completely independent of all existing windows. By default, it is placed on top of any existing windows, hiding (but not changing) their contents.

The delwin function deletes a window previously created by newwin. Since memory was probably allocated when newwin was called, you should always delete windows when they are no longer required.

Take care never to try to delete curses' **own windows,** stdscr **and** curscr!

Having created a new window, how do you write to it? The answer is that almost all the functions that you've seen so far have generalized versions that operate on specified windows, and for convenience these also include cursor motion.

Generalized Functions

You've already used the addch and printw functions for adding characters to the screen. Along with many other functions, these can be prefixed, either with a w for window, mv for move, or mvw for move and window. If you look in the curses header file for most implementations of curses, you'll find that many of the functions used so far are simply macros (#defines) that call these more general functions.

When the w prefix is added, an additional WINDOW pointer must be pre-pended to the argument list. When the mv prefix is added, two additional parameters, a y and an x location, must be pre-pended. These specify the location where the operation will be performed. The y and x are relative to the window, rather than the screen, (0,0) being the top left of the window.

When the mvw prefix is added, three additional parameters, a WINDOW pointer and both y and x values, must be passed. Confusingly, the WINDOW pointer always comes before the screen coordinates, even though the prefix might suggest the y and x come first.

As an example, here is the full set of prototypes for just the addch and printw sets of functions:

```
#include <curses.h>

int addch(const chtype char);
int waddch(WINDOW *window_pointer, const chtype char)
int mvaddch(int y, int x, const chtype char);
int mvwaddch(WINDOW *window_pointer, int y, int x, const chtype char);
int printw(char *format, ...);
int wprintw(WINDOW *window_pointer, char *format, ...);
int mvprintw(int y, int x, char *format, ...);
int mvwprintw(WINDOW *window_pointer, int y, int x, char *format, ...);
```

Many other functions, such as inch, also have move and window variants available.

Moving and Updating a Window

These commands enable you to move and redraw windows:

```
#include <curses.h>

int mvwin(WINDOW *window_to_move, int new_y, int new_x);
int wrefresh(WINDOW *window_ptr);
int wclear(WINDOW *window_ptr);
int werase(WINDOW *window_ptr);
int touchwin(WINDOW *window_ptr);
int scrollok(WINDOW *window_ptr, bool scroll_flag);
int scroll(WINDOW *window_ptr);
```

The mvwin function moves a window on the screen. Since all parts of a window must fit within the screen area, mvwin will fail if you attempt to move a window so that any part of it falls outside the screen area.

225

The `wrefresh`, `wclear`, and `werase` functions are simply generalizations of the functions you met earlier; they just take a `WINDOW` pointer so that they can refer to a specific window, rather than `stdscr`.

The `touchwin` function is rather special. It informs the `curses` library that the contents of the window pointed to by its parameter have been changed. This means that `curses` will always redraw that window the next time `wrefresh` is called, even if you haven't actually changed the contents of the window. This function is often useful for arranging which window to display when you have several overlapping windows stacked on the screen.

The two scroll functions control scrolling of a window. The `scrollok` function, when passed a Boolean `true` (usually nonzero) allows a window to scroll. By default, windows can't scroll. The `scroll` function simply scrolls the window up one line. Some `curses` implementations also have a `wsctl` function that also takes a number of lines to scroll, which may be a negative number. We'll return to scrolling a little later in the chapter.

Try It Out — Managing Multiple Windows

Now that you know how to manage more than a single window, you can put these new functions to work in a program, `multiw1.c`. For the sake of brevity, error checking is omitted:

1. As usual, let's get the definitions sorted first:

```
#include <unistd.h>
#include <stdlib.h>
#include <curses.h>

int main()
{
    WINDOW *new_window_ptr;
    WINDOW *popup_window_ptr;
    int x_loop;
    int y_loop;
    char a_letter = 'a';

    initscr();
```

2. Fill the base window with characters, refreshing the actual screen once the logical screen has been filled:

```
move(5, 5);
    printw("%s", "Testing multiple windows");
    refresh();

    for (y_loop = 0; y_loop < LINES - 1; y_loop++) {
        for (x_loop = 0; x_loop < COLS - 1; x_loop++) {
            mvwaddch(stdscr, y_loop, x_loop, a_letter);
            a_letter++;
            if (a_letter > 'z') a_letter = 'a';
        }
    }
```

```
/* Update the screen */
refresh();
sleep(2);
```

3. Now create a new 10 x 20 window and add some text to it before drawing it on the screen:

```
new_window_ptr = newwin(10, 20, 5, 5);
mvwprintw(new_window_ptr, 2, 2, "%s", "Hello World");
mvwprintw(new_window_ptr, 5, 2, "%s",
          "Notice how very long lines wrap inside the window");
wrefresh(new_window_ptr);
sleep(2);
```

4. Change the contents of the background window. When you refresh the screen, the window pointed to by new_window_ptr is obscured:

```
a_letter = '0';
for (y_loop = 0; y_loop < LINES -1; y_loop++) {
  for (x_loop = 0; x_loop < COLS - 1; x_loop++) {
      mvwaddch(stdscr, y_loop, x_loop, a_letter);
      a_letter++;
      if (a_letter > '9')
          a_letter = '0';
  }
}

refresh();
sleep(2);
```

5. If you make a call to refresh the new window, nothing will change, because you haven't changed the new window:

```
wrefresh(new_window_ptr);
sleep(2);
```

6. But if you touch the window first and trick curses into thinking that the window has been changed, the next call to wrefresh will bring the new window to the front again:

```
touchwin(new_window_ptr);
wrefresh(new_window_ptr);
sleep(2);
```

7. Add another overlapping window with a box around it:

```
popup_window_ptr = newwin(10, 20, 8, 8);
box(popup_window_ptr, '|', '-');
mvwprintw(popup_window_ptr, 5, 2, "%s", "Pop Up Window!");
wrefresh(popup_window_ptr);
sleep(2);
```

8. Fiddle with the new and pop-up windows before clearing and deleting them:

```
touchwin(new_window_ptr);
wrefresh(new_window_ptr);
sleep(2);
wclear(new_window_ptr);
wrefresh(new_window_ptr);
sleep(2);
delwin(new_window_ptr);
touchwin(popup_window_ptr);
wrefresh(popup_window_ptr);
sleep(2);
delwin(popup_window_ptr);
touchwin(stdscr);
refresh();
sleep(2);
endwin();
exit(EXIT_SUCCESS);
}
```

Unfortunately, it's not practical to show this running in the book, but Figure 6-4 shows a screenshot after the first pop-up window has been drawn.

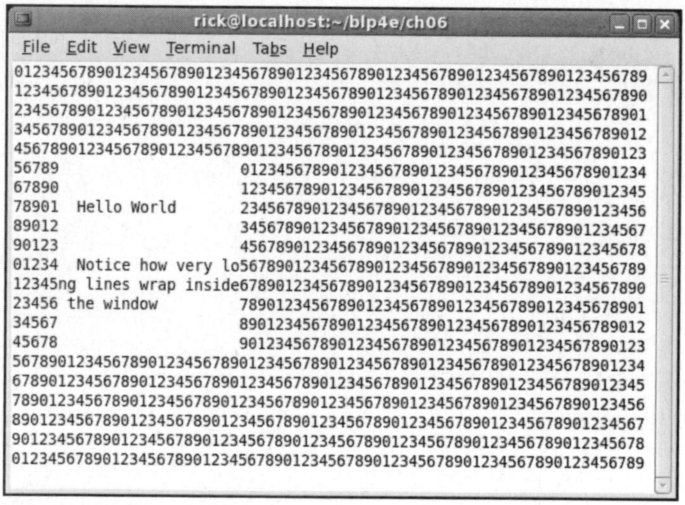

Figure 6-4

After the background has been changed and a new pop-up window has been drawn, you see the display shown in Figure 6-5.

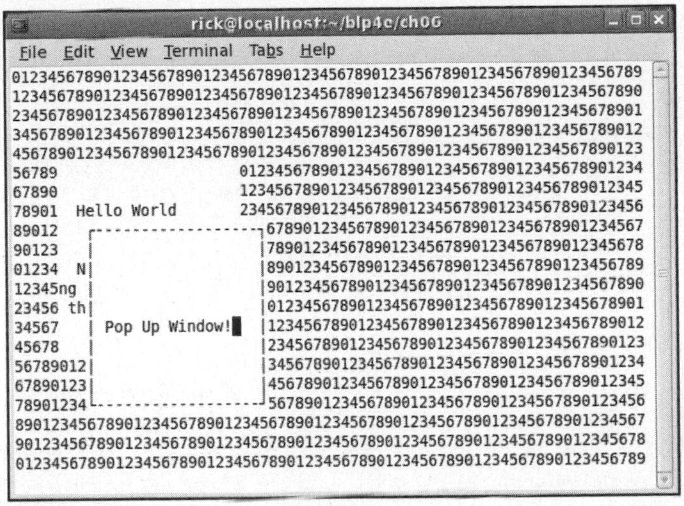

Figure 6-5

How It Works

After the usual initialization, the program fills the standard screen with numbers, to make it easier to see the new curses windows being added on top. It then demonstrates how a new window can be added over the background, with text inside the new window wrapping. You then saw how to use touchwin to force curses to redraw the window, even if nothing has been changed.

A second window was then added which overlapped the first window, to demonstrate how curses can mange overlapping windows, before the program closes the curses library and exits.

As you can see from the example code, you need to be quite careful about refreshing windows to ensure that they appear on the screen in the correct order. The curses library doesn't store any information about the hierarchy of windows, so if you ask curses to refresh several windows, you must manage any window hierarchy.

> To ensure that curses draws the windows in the correct order, you must refresh them in the correct order. One way of doing this is to store all the pointers to your windows in an array or list, which you maintain in the order they should appear on the screen.

Optimizing Screen Refreshes

As you saw in the example in the previous section, refreshing multiple windows can be a little tricky, but not overly onerous. However, a potentially more serious problem arises when the terminal to be updated is on a slow network. Fortunately, this is now a very rare problem, but handling it is so easy that we will show you just for the sake of completeness.

The aim is to minimize the number of characters drawn on the screen, because on slow links screen draws can be uncomfortably slow. curses provides a special way of doing this, with a pair of functions: wnoutrefresh and doupdate:

```
#include <curses.h>

int wnoutrefresh(WINDOW *window_ptr);
int doupdate(void);
```

The wnoutrefresh function determines which characters would need sending to the screen, but doesn't actually send them. The doupdate function actually sends the changes to the terminal. If you simply call wnoutrefresh, followed immediately by doupdate, the effect is the same as calling wrefresh. However, if you wish to redraw a stack of windows, you can call wnoutrefresh on each window (in the correct order, of course) and then call doupdate only after the last wnoutrefresh. This allows curses to perform its screen update calculations on each window in turn and only then output the updated screen. This almost always enables curses to minimize the number of characters that needs to be sent.

Subwindows

Now that we've looked at multiple windows, we can look at a special case of multiple windows, called *subwindows*. You create and destroy subwindows with these calls:

```
#include <curses.h>

WINDOW *subwin(WINDOW *parent, int num_of_lines, int num_of_cols,
               int start_y, int start_x);
int delwin(WINDOW *window_to_delete);
```

The subwin function has almost the same parameter list as newwin, and subwindows are deleted in just the same way as other windows, with a delwin call. Just like new windows, you can use the range of mvw functions to write to subwindows. Indeed, most of the time, subwindows behave in a very similar fashion to new windows, with one very important exception: Subwindows don't themselves store a separate set of screen characters; they share the same character storage space as the parent window specified when the subwindow is created. This means that any changes made in a subwindow are also made in the underlying parent window, so when a subwindow is deleted, the screen doesn't change.

At first sight, subwindows seem like a pointless exercise. Why not just make the changes to the parent window? The main use for subwindows is to provide a clean way of scrolling parts of another window. The need to scroll a small subsection of the screen is surprisingly common when writing a curses program. By making this a subwindow and then scrolling the subwindow, you achieve the desired result.

One restriction imposed by using subwindows is that the application should call touchwin *on the parent window before refreshing the screen.*

Try It Out **Subwindows**

Now that you have met the new functions, this short example shows you how they work, and how they differ from the windows functions used earlier:

1. The initial code section of subscl.c initializes the base window display with some text:

```
#include <unistd.h>
#include <stdlib.h>
#include <curses.h>

int main()

{
    WINDOW *sub_window_ptr;
    int x_loop;
    int y_loop;
    int counter;
    char a_letter = '1';

    initscr();

    for (y_loop = 0; y_loop < LINES - 1; y_loop++) {
        for (x_loop = 0; x_loop < COLS - 1; x_loop++) {
            mvwaddch(stdscr, y_loop, x_loop, a_letter);
            a_letter++;
            if (a_letter > '9') a_letter = '1';
        }
    }
```

2. Now create the new scrolling subwindow. As advised, you must "touch" the parent window before refreshing the screen:

```
sub_window_ptr = subwin(stdscr, 10, 20, 10, 10);
scrollok(sub_window_ptr, 1);

touchwin(stdscr);
refresh();
sleep(1);
```

3. Erase the contents of the subwindow, print text to it, and refresh it. The scrolling text is achieved by a loop:

```
werase(sub_window_ptr);
mvwprintw(sub_window_ptr, 2, 0, "%s", "This window will now scroll");
wrefresh(sub_window_ptr);
sleep(1);

for (counter = 1; counter < 10; counter++) {
    wprintw(sub_window_ptr, "%s", "This text is both wrapping and \
                scrolling.");
    wrefresh(sub_window_ptr);
    sleep(1);
}
```

4.   Having finished this loop, delete the subwindow, and then refresh the base screen:

```
delwin(sub_window_ptr);

touchwin(stdscr);
refresh();
sleep(1);

endwin();
exit(EXIT_SUCCESS);
}
```

Toward the end of the program, you see the output shown in Figure 6-6.

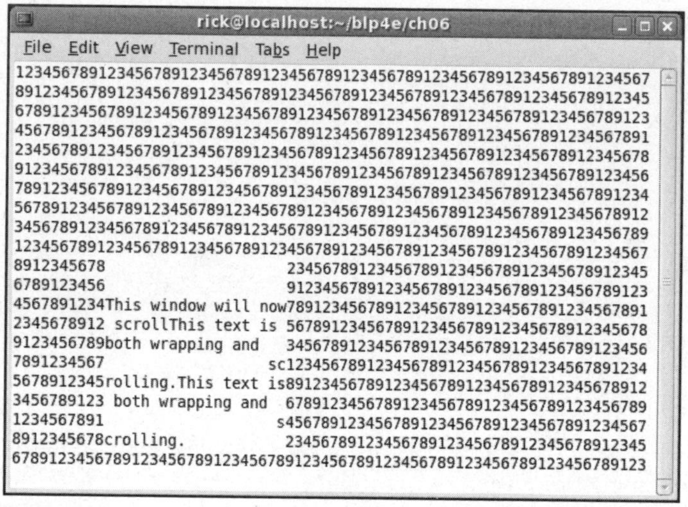

Figure 6-6

How It Works

After arranging for the `sub_window_ptr` to point to the result of the `subwin` call, you make the sub-window scrollable. Even after the subwindow has been deleted and the base window (`strdcr`) is refreshed, the text on the screen remains the same because the subwindow was actually updating the character data for `stdscr`.

The Keypad

You've already seen some of the facilities that `curses` provides for handling the keyboard. Many keyboards have, at the very least, cursor keys and function keys. Many also have a keypad and other keys, such as Insert and Home.

Decoding these keys is a difficult problem on most terminals because they normally send a string of characters, starting with the escape character. Not only does the application have the problem of distinguishing between a single press of the Esc key and a string of characters caused by pressing a function key, it must also cope with different terminals using different sequences for the same logical key.

Fortunately, curses provides an elegant facility for managing function keys. For each terminal, the sequence sent by each of its function keys is stored, normally in a terminfo structure, and the include file curses.h has a set of defines prefixed by KEY_ that define the logical keys.

The translation between the sequences and logical keys is disabled when curses starts and has to be turned on by the keypad function. If the call succeeds, then it returns OK; otherwise it returns ERR:

```
#include <curses.h>

int keypad(WINDOW *window_ptr, bool keypad_on);
```

Once *keypad mode* has been enabled by calling keypad with keypad_on set to true, curses takes over the processing of key sequences so that reading the keyboard may now not only return the key that was pressed, but also one of the KEY_ defines for logical keys.

Note three slight restrictions when using keypad mode:

❑　The recognition of escape sequences is timing-dependent, and many network protocols will group characters into packets (leading to improper recognition of escape sequences), or separate them (leading to function key sequences being recognized as escape and individual characters). This behavior is worst over WANs and other slower links. The only workaround is to try to program terminals to send single, unique characters for each function key that you want to use, although this limits the number of control characters.

❑　In order for curses to separate a press of the Esc key from a keyboard sequence starting with Esc, it must wait for a brief period of time. Sometimes, a very slight delay on processing of the Esc key can be noticed once keypad mode has been enabled.

❑　curses can't process non-unique escape sequences. If your terminal has two different keys that can send the same sequence, curses will simply not process that sequence, as it can't tell which logical key it should return.

Try It Out　Using the Keypad

Here's a short program, keypad.c, showing how the keypad mode can be used. When you run this program, try pressing the Esc key and notice the slight delay while the program waits to see whether the Esc is simply the start of an escape sequence or a single key press:

1.　Having initialized the program and the curses library, set the keypad mode to TRUE:

```
#include <unistd.h>
#include <stdlib.h>
#include <curses.h>

#define LOCAL_ESCAPE_KEY    27
```

```
int main()
{
    int key;

    initscr();
    crmode();
    keypad(stdscr, TRUE);
```

2. Turn echo off to prevent the cursor from being moved when some cursor keys are pressed. The screen is cleared and some text displayed. The program waits for each keystroke and, unless it's Q or produces an error, the key is printed. If the keystrokes match one of the terminal's keypad sequences, this is printed instead:

```
    noecho();
    clear();
    mvprintw(5, 5, "Key pad demonstration. Press 'q' to quit");
    move(7, 5);
    refresh();
    key = getch();

    while(key != ERR && key != 'q') {
        move(7, 5);
        clrtoeol();

        if ((key >= 'A' && key <= 'Z') ||
            (key >= 'a' && key <= 'z')) {
            printw("Key was %c", (char)key);
        }
        else {
            switch(key) {
            case LOCAL_ESCAPE_KEY: printw("%s", "Escape key"); break;
            case KEY_END: printw("%s", "END key"); break;
            case KEY_BEG: printw("%s", "BEGINNING key"); break;
            case KEY_RIGHT: printw("%s", "RIGHT key"); break;
            case KEY_LEFT: printw("%s", "LEFT key"); break;
            case KEY_UP: printw("%s", "UP key"); break;
            case KEY_DOWN: printw("%s", "DOWN key"); break;
            default: printw("Unmatched - %d", key); break;
            } /* switch */
        } /* else */

        refresh();
        key = getch();
    } /* while */

    endwin();
    exit(EXIT_SUCCESS);
}
```

How It Works

Having turned on keypad mode, you saw how it's possible to recognize the various additional keys on the keypad, which generate escape sequences. You will probably also be able to notice how detection of the Esc key is slightly slower than the others.

Using Color

Originally, very few "dumb" terminals supported color, so most very early versions of curses had no support for it. Color is supported in ncurses and most other modern curses implementations. Unfortunately the "dumb screen" origins of curses has influenced the API, and curses uses color in a very restricted way, reflecting the poor capabilities of early color terminals.

Each character cell on the screen can be written in one of a number of different colors, against one of a number of different colored backgrounds. For example, you can write text in green on a red background.

Color support in curses is slightly unusual in that the color for a character isn't defined independently of its background. You must define the foreground and background colors of a character as a pair, called, not surprisingly, a *color pair*.

Before you can use color capability in curses, you must check that the current terminal supports color and then initialize the curses color routines. For this, use a pair of routines: has_colors and start_color:

```
#include <curses.h>

bool has_colors(void);
int start_color(void);
```

The has_colors routine returns true if color is supported. You should then call start_color, which returns OK if color has been initialized successfully. Once start_color has been called and the colors initialized, the variable COLOR_PAIRS is set to the maximum number of color pairs that the terminal can support. A limit of 64 color pairs is common. The variable COLORS defines the maximum number of colors available, which is often as few as eight. Internally, numbers from 0 to 63 act as a unique ID for each of the colors available.

Before you can use colors as attributes, you must initialize the color pairs that you wish to use. You do this with the init_pair function. Color attributes are accessed with the COLOR_PAIR function:

```
#include <curses.h>

int init_pair(short pair_number, short foreground, short background);
int COLOR_PAIR(int pair_number);
int pair_content(short pair_number, short *foreground, short *background);
```

curses.h usually defines some basic colors, starting with COLOR_. An additional function, pair_content, allows previously defined color-pair information to be retrieved.

To define color pair number 1 to be red on green, you would use

```
init_pair(1, COLOR_RED, COLOR_GREEN);
```

You can then access this color pair as an attribute, using COLOR_PAIR like this:

```
wattron(window_ptr, COLOR_PAIR(1));
```

This would set future additions to the screen to be red on a green background.

Since a COLOR_PAIR is an attribute, you can combine it with other attributes. On a PC, you can often access screen high-intensity colors by combining the COLOR_PAIR attribute with the additional attribute A_BOLD, by using a bitwise OR of the attributes:

```
wattron(window_ptr, COLOR_PAIR(1) | A_BOLD);
```

Let's check these functions in an example, color.c.

Try It Out   Colors

1. First, check whether the program's display terminal supports color. If it does, start the color display:

```
#include <unistd.h>
#include <stdlib.h>
#include <stdio.h>
#include <curses.h>

int main()
{
    int i;

    initscr();

    if (!has_colors()) {
        endwin();
        fprintf(stderr, "Error - no color support on this terminal\n");
        exit(1);
    }

    if (start_color() != OK) {
        endwin();
        fprintf(stderr, "Error - could not initialize colors\n");
        exit(2);
    }
```

2. You can now print out the allowed number of colors and color pairs. Create seven color pairs and display them one at a time:

```
    clear();
    mvprintw(5, 5, "There are %d COLORS, and %d COLOR_PAIRS available",
             COLORS, COLOR_PAIRS);
    refresh();
```

```
        init_pair(1, COLOR_RED, COLOR_BLACK);
        init_pair(2, COLOR_RED, COLOR_GREEN);
        init_pair(3, COLOR_GREEN, COLOR_RED);
        init_pair(4, COLOR_YELLOW, COLOR_BLUE);
        init_pair(5, COLOR_BLACK, COLOR_WHITE);
        init_pair(6, COLOR_MAGENTA, COLOR_BLUE);
        init_pair(7, COLOR_CYAN, COLOR_WHITE);

        for (i = 1; i <= 7; i++) {
            attroff(A_BOLD);
            attrset(COLOR_PAIR(i));
            mvprintw(5 + i, 5, "Color pair %d", i);
            attrset(COLOR_PAIR(i) | A_BOLD);
            mvprintw(5 + i, 25, "Bold color pair %d", i);
            refresh();
            sleep(1);
        }

        endwin();
        exit(EXIT_SUCCESS);
    }
```

This example results in the output shown in Figure 6-7, minus the actual colors, of course, which don't show up in the black-and-white screenshot.

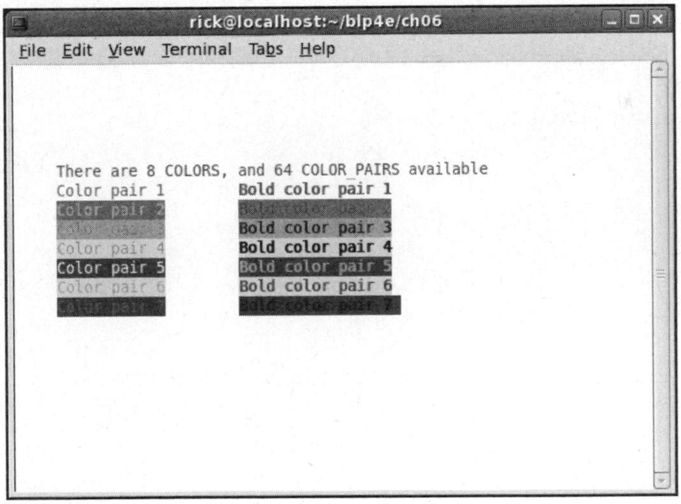

Figure 6-7

How It Works

After checking that the screen supports color, the program initializes color handling and defines some color pairs. Some text is then written to the screen using the color pairs, to show different color combinations on the screen.

Redefining Colors

As a leftover from early dumb terminals that could display very few colors at any one time, but allowed the active color set to be configured, curses allows color redefinition with the init_color function:

```
#include <curses.h>

int init_color(short color_number, short red, short green, short blue);
```

This allows an existing color (in the range 0 to COLORS) to be redefined with new intensity values in the range 0 to 1,000. This is a little like defining color values for GIF format image files.

Pads

When you're writing more advanced curses programs, it's sometimes easier to build a logical screen and then output all or part of it to the physical screen later. Occasionally, it's also better to have a logical screen that is actually bigger than the physical screen and to display only part of the logical screen at any one time.

It's not easy to do this with the curses functions that you've met so far, as all windows must be no larger than the physical screen. curses does provide a special data structure, a *pad*, for manipulating logical screen information that doesn't fit within a normal window.

A pad structure is very similar to a WINDOW structure, and all the curses routines that write to windows can also be used on pads. However, pads do have their own routines for creation and refreshing.

You create pads in much the same way that you create normal windows:

```
#include <curses.h>

WINDOW *newpad(int number_of_lines, int number_of_columns);
```

Note that the return value is a pointer to a WINDOW structure, the same as newwin. Pads are deleted with delwin, just like windows.

Pads do have different routines for refreshing. Since a pad isn't confined to a particular screen location, you must specify the region of the pad you wish to put on the screen, and the location it should occupy on the screen. Do this with the prefresh function:

```
#include <curses.h>

int prefresh(WINDOW *pad_ptr, int pad_row, int pad_column,
             int screen_row_min, int screen_col_min,
             int screen_row_max, int screen_col_max);
```

This causes an area of the pad, starting at (pad_row, pad_column) to be written to the screen in the region defined by (screen_row_min, screen_col_min) to (screen_row_max, screen_col_max).

An additional routine, pnoutrefresh, is also provided. It acts in the same way as wnoutrefresh, for more efficient screen updates.

Let's check these out with a quick program, pad.c.

Try It Out   Using a Pad

1. At the start of this program, you initialize the pad structure and then create a pad, which returns a pointer to that pad. Add characters to fill the pad structure (which is 50 characters wider and longer than the terminal display):

```c
#include <unistd.h>
#include <stdlib.h>
#include <curses.h>

int main()
{
    WINDOW *pad_ptr;
    int x, y;
    int pad_lines;
    int pad_cols;
    char disp_char;

    initscr();
    pad_lines = LINES + 50;
    pad_cols = COLS + 50;
    pad_ptr = newpad(pad_lines, pad_cols);
    disp_char = 'a';

    for (x = 0; x < pad_lines; x++) {
        for (y = 0; y < pad_cols; y++) {
            mvwaddch(pad_ptr, x, y, disp_char);
            if (disp_char == 'z') disp_char = 'a';
            else disp_char++;
        }
    }
```

2. Now draw different areas of the pad on the screen at different locations before quitting:

```c
    prefresh(pad_ptr, 5, 7, 2, 2, 9, 9);
    sleep(1);
    prefresh(pad_ptr, LINES + 5, COLS + 7, 5, 5, 21, 19);
    sleep(1);
    delwin(pad_ptr);
    endwin();
    exit(EXIT_SUCCESS);
}
```

Running the program, you should see something like what is shown in Figure 6-8.

```
rick@localhost:~/blp4e/ch06

File  Edit  View  Terminal  Tabs  Help

opqrstuv
fghijklm
wxyzabcd
noprstuvwxyzabcdef
efgijklmnopqrstuvw
vwxzabcdefghijklmn
mnoqrstuvwxyzabcde
defhijklmnopqrstuv
    yzabcdefghijklm
    pqrstuvwxyzabcd
    ghijklmnopqrstu
    xyzabcdefghijkl
    opqrstuvwxyzabc
    fghijklmnopqrst
    wxyzabcdefghijk
    nopqrstuvwxyzab
    efghijklmnopqrs
    vwxyzabcdefghij
    mnopqrstuvwxyza
    defghijklmnopqr
```

Figure 6-8

The CD Collection Application

Now that you've learned about the facilities that curses has to offer, you can develop the sample application. Here's a version written in C using the curses library. It offers some advantages in that the information is more clearly displayed on the screen and a scrolling window is used for track listings.

The whole application is eight pages long, so we've split it up into sections and functions within each section. You can get the source code, curses_app.c, from the Wrox Web site. As with all the programs in this book, it's under the GNU Public License.

> We've written this version of the CD database application using the information presented in earlier chapters. It's derived from the original shell script presented in Chapter 2. It hasn't been redesigned for the C implementation, so you can still see many features of the shell in this version. Note that there are some significant limitations with this implementation that we will resolve in later revisions.

We have broken the code for this application into several distinct portions as indicated by the following headings. The code conventions used here are slightly different from most of the rest of the book; here, highlighted code is used only to show where other application functions are called.

Starting a New CD Collection Application

This first section of code is just concerned with declaring the variables and functions you will use later, and initializing some data structures:

1. Include all those header files and then some global constants:

```
#include <unistd.h>
#include <stdlib.h>
```

```
#include <stdio.h>
#include <string.h>
#include <curses.h>

#define MAX_STRING 80          /* Longest allowed response      */
#define MAX_ENTRY 1024         /* Longest allowed database entry */

#define MESSAGE_LINE 6          /* Misc. messages on this line   */
#define ERROR_LINE   22         /* Line to use for errors        */
#define Q_LINE       20         /* Line for questions            */
#define PROMPT_LINE  18         /* Line for prompting on         */
```

2. Now you need some global variables. The variable `current_cd` is used to store the current CD title with which you are working. It's initialized so that the first character is null, to indicate that no CD selected. The \0 is not strictly necessary, but it ensures that the variable is initialized, which is generally a good thing. The variable `current_cat` is used to record the catalog number of the current CD.

```
static char current_cd[MAX_STRING] = "\0";
static char current_cat[MAX_STRING];
```

3. Now declare some filenames. To keep things simple, the files are fixed in this version, as is the temporary filename.

> This could cause a problem if the program is run by two users in the same directory. A better way to obtain database filenames would be either by program arguments or from environment variables. We also need an improved method of generating a unique temporary filename, for which we could use the POSIX `tmpnam` function. We'll address many of these issues in Chapter 8, when we use MySQL to store the data.

```
const char *title_file = "title.cdb";
const char *tracks_file = "tracks.cdb";
const char *temp_file = "cdb.tmp";
```

4. Finally, the function prototypes:

```
void clear_all_screen(void);
void get_return(void);
int get_confirm(void);
int getchoice(char *greet, char *choices[]);
void draw_menu(char *options[], int highlight,
               int start_row, int start_col);
void insert_title(char *cdtitle);
void get_string(char *string);
void add_record(void);
void count_cds(void);
void find_cd(void);
void list_tracks(void);
void remove_tracks(void);
void remove_cd(void);
void update_cd(void);
```

5. Before you look at their implementation, you need some structures (actually, an array of menu options) for the menus. The first character of each menu text is returned when the option is selected. Fox example, if the menu item is Add New CD, then the first letter, a, will be returned when this menu item is selected. The extended menu is displayed when a CD is currently selected:

```c
char *main_menu[] =
{
    "add new CD",
    "find CD",
    "count CDs and tracks in the catalog",
    "quit",
    0,
};

char *extended_menu[] =
{
    "add new CD",
    "find CD",
    "count CDs and tracks in the catalog",
    "list tracks on current CD",
    "remove current CD",
    "update track information",
    "quit",
    0,
};
```

That finishes the initialization. Now you can move on to the program functions, but first you need to summarize the interrelations of these functions, all 16 of them. They are divided into three program subsections:

❑ Drawing the menu

❑ Adding CDs to the database

❑ Retrieving and displaying CD data

See Figure 6-9 for a visual representation.

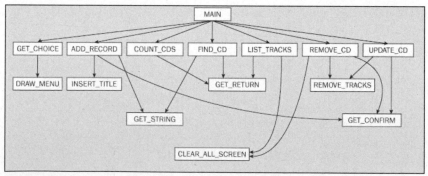

Figure 6-9

Looking at main

main enables you to make selections from the menu until you select quit. Here's the code:

```
int main()
{
    int choice;
    initscr();
    do {
        choice = getchoice("Options:",
                            current_cd[0] ? extended_menu : main_menu);
        switch (choice) {
        case 'q':
            break;
        case 'a':
            add_record();
            break;
        case 'c':
            count_cds();
            break;
        case 'f':
            find_cd();
            break;
        case 'l':
            list_tracks();
            break;
        case 'r':
            remove_cd();
            break;
        case 'u':
            update_cd();
            break;
        }
    } while (choice != 'q');
    endwin();
    exit(EXIT_SUCCESS);
}
```

Let's now look at the detail of the functions associated with the three program subsections.

Building the Menu

This section looks at the three functions that relate to the program's user interface:

1. The getchoice function called by main is the principal function in this section. getchoice is passed greet, an introduction, and choices, which points either to the main or to the extended menu (depending on whether a CD has been selected). You can see how either main_menu or extended_menu is passed as a parameter in the preceding main function:

```
int getchoice(char *greet, char *choices[])
{
    static int selected_row = 0;
```

```
        int max_row = 0;
        int start_screenrow = MESSAGE_LINE, start_screencol = 10;
        char **option;
        int selected;
        int key = 0;

        option = choices;
        while (*option) {
            max_row++;
            option++;
        }
    /* protect against menu getting shorter when CD deleted */
        if (selected_row >= max_row)
            selected_row = 0;
        clear_all_screen();
        mvprintw(start_screenrow - 2, start_screencol, greet);
        keypad(stdscr, TRUE);
        cbreak();
        noecho();
        key = 0;
        while (key != 'q' && key != KEY_ENTER && key != '\n') {
            if (key == KEY_UP) {
                if (selected_row == 0)
                    selected_row = max_row - 1;
                else
                    selected_row--;
            }
            if (key == KEY_DOWN) {
                if (selected_row == (max_row - 1))
                    selected_row = 0;
                else
                    selected_row++;
            }
            selected = *choices[selected_row];
            draw_menu(choices, selected_row, start_screenrow,
                            start_screencol);
            key = getch();
        }
        keypad(stdscr, FALSE);
        nocbreak();
        echo();

        if (key == 'q')
            selected = 'q';

        return (selected);
    }
```

2. Note how two more local functions are called from within getchoice: clear_all_screen and draw_menu. Let's look at draw_menu first:

```
void draw_menu(char *options[], int current_highlight,
                int start_row, int start_col)
{
```

```
        int current_row = 0;
        char **option_ptr;
        char *txt_ptr;
        option_ptr = options;
        while (*option_ptr) {
            if (current_row == current_highlight) attron(A_STANDOUT);
            txt_ptr = options[current_row];
            txt_ptr++;
            mvprintw(start_row + current_row, start_col, "%s", txt_ptr);
            if (current_row == current_highlight) attroff(A_STANDOUT);
            current_row++;
            option_ptr++;
        }

        mvprintw(start_row + current_row + 3, start_col,
                "Move highlight then press Return ");
        refresh();
    }
```

3. Next look at `clear_all_screen`, which, surprisingly enough, clears the screen and rewrites the title. If a CD is selected, then its information is displayed:

```
void clear_all_screen()
{
    clear();
    mvprintw(2, 20, "%s", "CD Database Application");
    if (current_cd[0]) {
        mvprintw(ERROR_LINE, 0, "Current CD: %s: %s\n",
                current_cat, current_cd);
    }
    refresh();
}
```

Database File Manipulation

This section covers the functions that add to or update the CD database. The functions called from `main` are `add_record`, `update_cd`, and `remove_cd`.

Adding Records

1. Add a new CD record to the database:

```
void add_record()
{
    char catalog_number[MAX_STRING];
    char cd_title[MAX_STRING];
    char cd_type[MAX_STRING];
    char cd_artist[MAX_STRING];
    char cd_entry[MAX_STRING];

    int screenrow = MESSAGE_LINE;
    int screencol = 10;
```

```
    clear_all_screen();
    mvprintw(screenrow, screencol, "Enter new CD details");
    screenrow += 2;

    mvprintw(screenrow, screencol, "Catalog Number: ");
    get_string(catalog_number);
    screenrow++;

    mvprintw(screenrow, screencol, "      CD Title: ");
    get_string(cd_title);
    screenrow++;

    mvprintw(screenrow, screencol, "       CD Type: ");
    get_string(cd_type);
    screenrow++;

    mvprintw(screenrow, screencol, "        Artist: ");
    get_string(cd_artist);
    screenrow++;

    mvprintw(PROMPT_LINE-2, 5, "About to add this new entry:");
    sprintf(cd_entry, "%s,%s,%s,%s",
            catalog_number, cd_title, cd_type, cd_artist);
    mvprintw(PROMPT_LINE, 5, "%s", cd_entry);
    refresh();
    move(PROMPT_LINE, 0);
    if (get_confirm()) {
        insert_title(cd_entry);
        strcpy(current_cd, cd_title);
        strcpy(current_cat, catalog_number);
    }
}
```

2.   get_string prompts for and reads in a string at the current screen position. It also deletes any trailing newline:

```
void get_string(char *string)
{
    int len;

    wgetnstr(stdscr, string, MAX_STRING);
    len = strlen(string);
    if (len > 0 && string[len - 1] == '\n')
        string[len - 1] = '\0';
}
```

3.   get_confirm prompts and reads user confirmation. It reads the user's input string and checks the first character for Y or y. If it finds any other character, it gives no confirmation:

```
int get_confirm()
{
    int confirmed = 0;
    char first_char;
```

```
        mvprintw(Q_LINE, 5, "Are you sure? ");
        clrtoeol();
        refresh();

        cbreak();
        first_char = getch();
        if (first_char == 'Y' || first_char == 'y') {
            confirmed = 1;
        }
        nocbreak();

        if (!confirmed) {
            mvprintw(Q_LINE, 1, "    Cancelled");
            clrtoeol();
            refresh();
            sleep(1);
        }
        return confirmed;
    }
```

4.   Lastly, look at `insert_title`. This adds a title to the CD database by appending the title string to the end of the titles file:

```
void insert_title(char *cdtitle)
{
    FILE *fp = fopen(title_file, "a");
    if (!fp) {
        mvprintw(ERROR_LINE, 0, "cannot open CD titles database");
    } else {
        fprintf(fp, "%s\n", cdtitle);
        fclose(fp);
    }
}
```

Updating Records

1.   On to the other file manipulation functions called by `main`. Next is `update_cd`. This function uses a scrolling, boxed subwindow and needs some constants, which you define globally because they will be needed later for the `list_tracks` function.

```
#define BOXED_LINES     11
#define BOXED_ROWS      60
#define BOX_LINE_POS    8
#define BOX_ROW_POS     2
```

2.   `update_cd` enables the user to reenter the tracks for the current CD. Having deleted the previous tracks record, it prompts for new information:

```
void update_cd()
{
    FILE *tracks_fp;
```

```
char track_name[MAX_STRING];
int len;
int track = 1;
int screen_line = 1;
WINDOW *box_window_ptr;
WINDOW *sub_window_ptr;

clear_all_screen();
mvprintw(PROMPT_LINE, 0, "Re-entering tracks for CD. ");
if (!get_confirm())
    return;
move(PROMPT_LINE, 0);
clrtoeol();

remove_tracks();

mvprintw(MESSAGE_LINE, 0, "Enter a blank line to finish");

tracks_fp = fopen(tracks_file, "a");
```

We'll continue the listing in just a moment; here, we want to take a brief intermission to highlight how you enter the information in a scrolling, boxed window. The trick is to set up a subwindow, draw a box around the edge, and then add a new scrolling subwindow just inside the boxed subwindow.

```
box_window_ptr = subwin(stdscr, BOXED_LINES + 2, BOXED_ROWS + 2,
                        BOX_LINE_POS - 1, BOX_ROW_POS - 1);
if (!box_window_ptr)
    return;
box(box_window_ptr, ACS_VLINE, ACS_HLINE);

sub_window_ptr = subwin(stdscr, BOXED_LINES, BOXED_ROWS,
                        BOX_LINE_POS, BOX_ROW_POS);
if (!sub_window_ptr)
    return;
scrollok(sub_window_ptr, TRUE);
werase(sub_window_ptr);
touchwin(stdscr);

do {
    mvwprintw(sub_window_ptr, screen_line++, BOX_ROW_POS + 2,
            "Track %d: ", track);
    clrtoeol();
    refresh();
    wgetnstr(sub_window_ptr, track_name, MAX_STRING);
    len = strlen(track_name);
    if (len > 0 && track_name[len - 1] == '\n')
        track_name[len - 1] = '\0';
if (*track_name)
fprintf(tracks_fp, "%s,%d,%s\n", current_cat, track, track_name);
    track++;
    if (screen_line > BOXED_LINES - 1) {
```

```
                    /* time to start scrolling */
                    scroll(sub_window_ptr);
                    screen_line - ;
            }
        } while (*track_name);
        delwin(sub_window_ptr);

        fclose(tracks_fp);
}
```

Removing Records

1. The last function called from main is remove_cd:

```
void remove_cd()
{
    FILE *titles_fp, *temp_fp;
    char entry[MAX_ENTRY];
    int cat_length;

    if (current_cd[0] == '\0')
        return;

    clear_all_screen();
    mvprintw(PROMPT_LINE, 0, "About to remove CD %s: %s. ",
            current_cat, current_cd);
    if (!get_confirm())
        return;

    cat_length = strlen(current_cat);

    /* Copy the titles file to a temporary, ignoring this CD */
    titles_fp = fopen(title_file, "r");
    temp_fp = fopen(temp_file, "w");

    while (fgets(entry, MAX_ENTRY, titles_fp)) {
        /* Compare catalog number and copy entry if no match */
        if (strncmp(current_cat, entry, cat_length) != 0)
            fputs(entry, temp_fp);
    }
    fclose(titles_fp);
    fclose(temp_fp);

    /* Delete the titles file, and rename the temporary file */
    unlink(title_file);
    rename(temp_file, title_file);

    /* Now do the same for the tracks file */
    remove_tracks();

    /* Reset current CD to 'None' */
    current_cd[0] = '\0';
}
```

2. You now need to only list `remove_tracks`, the function that deletes the tracks from the current CD. It's called by both `update_cd` and `remove_cd`:

```
void remove_tracks()
{
    FILE *tracks_fp, *temp_fp;
    char entry[MAX_ENTRY];
    int cat_length;

    if (current_cd[0] == '\0')
        return;

    cat_length = strlen(current_cat);

    tracks_fp = fopen(tracks_file, "r");
    if (tracks_fp == (FILE *)NULL) return;
    temp_fp = fopen(temp_file, "w");

    while (fgets(entry, MAX_ENTRY, tracks_fp)) {
        /* Compare catalog number and copy entry if no match */
        if (strncmp(current_cat, entry, cat_length) != 0)
            fputs(entry, temp_fp);
    }
    fclose(tracks_fp);
    fclose(temp_fp);

    /* Delete the tracks file, and rename the temporary file */
    unlink(tracks_file);
    rename(temp_file, tracks_file);
}
```

Querying the CD Database

Now look at the functions for accessing the data, which is simply stored in a pair of flat files as comma-separated fields, for easy access:

1. Essential to all acquisitive hobbies is the knowledge of how many you own of whatever you collect. The next function performs this task admirably; it scans the database, counting titles and tracks:

```
void count_cds()
{
    FILE *titles_fp, *tracks_fp;
    char entry[MAX_ENTRY];
    int titles = 0;
    int tracks = 0;

    titles_fp = fopen(title_file, "r");
    if (titles_fp) {
        while (fgets(entry, MAX_ENTRY, titles_fp))
            titles++;
        fclose(titles_fp);
    }
```

```
    tracks_fp = fopen(tracks_file, "r");
    if (tracks_fp) {
        while (fgets(entry, MAX_ENTRY, tracks_fp))
            tracks++;
        fclose(tracks_fp);
    }
    mvprintw(ERROR_LINE, 0,
            "Database contains %d titles, with a total of %d tracks.",
            titles, tracks);
    get_return();
}
```

2.   You've lost the sleeve notes from your favorite CD, but don't worry! Having carefully entered the
     details into the database, you can now find the track listing using find_cd. It prompts for a sub-
     string to match in the database and sets the global variable current_cd to the CD title found:

```
void find_cd()
{
    char match[MAX_STRING], entry[MAX_ENTRY];
    FILE *titles_fp;
    int count = 0;
    char *found, *title, *catalog;

    mvprintw(Q_LINE, 0, "Enter a string to search for in CD titles: ");
    get_string(match);

    titles_fp = fopen(title_file, "r");
    if (titles_fp) {
        while (fgets(entry, MAX_ENTRY, titles_fp)) {

            /* Skip past catalog number */
            catalog = entry;
            if (found == strstr(catalog, ",")) {
                *found = '\0';
                title = found + 1;

                /* Zap the next comma in the entry to reduce it to
                   title only */
                if (found == strstr(title, ",")) {
                    *found = '\0';

                    /* Now see if the match substring is present */
                    if (found == strstr(title, match)) {
                        count++;
                        strcpy(current_cd, title);
                        strcpy(current_cat, catalog);
                    }
                }
            }
        }
        fclose(titles_fp);
    }
    if (count != 1) {
        if (count == 0) {
```

251

```
                    mvprintw(ERROR_LINE, 0, "Sorry, no matching CD found. ");
            }
            if (count > 1) {
                mvprintw(ERROR_LINE, 0,
                            "Sorry, match is ambiguous: %d CDs found. ", count);
            }
            current_cd[0] = '\0';
            get_return();
        }
    }
```

Though `catalog` points at a larger array than `current_cat` and could conceivably overwrite memory, the check in `fgets` prevents this.

3. You also need to be able to list the selected CD's tracks on the screen. You can make use of the `#defines` for the subwindows used in `update_cd` in the last section:

```
void list_tracks()
{
    FILE *tracks_fp;
    char entry[MAX_ENTRY];
    int cat_length;
    int lines_op = 0;
    WINDOW *track_pad_ptr;
    int tracks = 0;
    int key;
    int first_line = 0;

    if (current_cd[0] == '\0') {
        mvprintw(ERROR_LINE, 0, "You must select a CD first. ");
        get_return();
        return;
    }
    clear_all_screen();
    cat_length = strlen(current_cat);

    /* First count the number of tracks for the current CD */
    tracks_fp = fopen(tracks_file, "r");
    if (!tracks_fp)
        return;
    while (fgets(entry, MAX_ENTRY, tracks_fp)) {
        if (strncmp(current_cat, entry, cat_length) == 0)
            tracks++;
    }
    fclose(tracks_fp);

     /* Make a new pad, ensure that even if there is only a single
        track the PAD is large enough so the later prefresh() is always
        valid. */
    track_pad_ptr = newpad(tracks + 1 + BOXED_LINES, BOXED_ROWS + 1);
    if (!track_pad_ptr)
        return;

    tracks_fp = fopen(tracks_file, "r");
    if (!tracks_fp)
```

```
        return;

    mvprintw(4, 0, "CD Track Listing\n");

    /* write the track information into the pad */
    while (fgets(entry, MAX_ENTRY, tracks_fp)) {

        /* Compare catalog number and output rest of entry */
        if (strncmp(current_cat, entry, cat_length) == 0) {
            mvwprintw(track_pad_ptr, lines_op++, 0, "%s",
                        entry + cat_length + 1);
        }
    }
    fclose(tracks_fp);

    if (lines_op > BOXED_LINES) {
        mvprintw(MESSAGE_LINE, 0,
                    "Cursor keys to scroll, RETURN or q to exit");
    } else {
        mvprintw(MESSAGE_LINE, 0, "RETURN or q to exit");
    }
    wrefresh(stdscr);
    keypad(stdscr, TRUE);
    cbreak();
    noecho();
    key = 0;
    while (key != 'q' && key != KEY_ENTER && key != '\n') {
        if (key == KEY_UP) {
            if (first_line > 0)
                first_line--;
        }
        if (key == KEY_DOWN) {
            if (first_line + BOXED_LINES + 1 < tracks)
                first_line++;
        }

        /* now draw the appropriate part of the pad on the screen */
        prefresh(track_pad_ptr, first_line, 0,
                    BOX_LINE_POS, BOX_ROW_POS,
                    BOX_LINE_POS + BOXED_LINES, BOX_ROW_POS + BOXED_ROWS);
        key = getch();
    }

    delwin(track_pad_ptr);
    keypad(stdscr, FALSE);
    nocbreak();
    echo();
}
```

4. The last two functions call get_return, which prompts for and reads a carriage return, ignoring other characters:

```
void get_return()
{
```

```
        int ch;
        mvprintw(23, 0, "%s", " Press return ");
        refresh();
        while ((ch = getchar()) != '\n' && ch != EOF);
}
```

If you run this program, you should see something like what is shown in Figure 6-10.

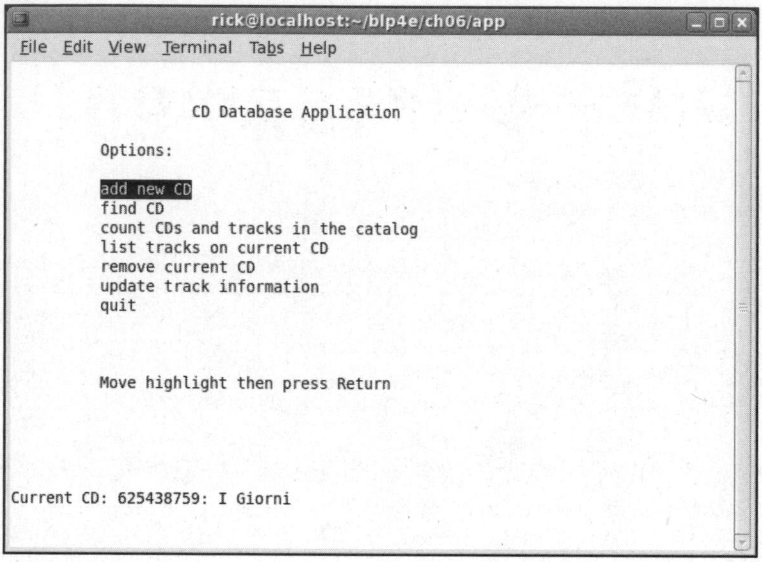

Figure 6-10

Summary

In this chapter, we have explored the curses library. curses provides a good way for text-based programs to control the screen and read the keyboard. Although curses doesn't offer as much control as the general terminal interface (GTI) and direct terminfo access, it's considerably easier to use. If you're writing a full-screen, text-based application, you should consider using the curses library to manage the screen and keyboard for you.

7

Data Management

In earlier chapters, we touched on the subject of resource limits. In this chapter, we're going to look first at ways of managing your resource allocation, then at ways of dealing with files that are accessed by many users more or less simultaneously, and lastly at one tool provided in Linux systems for overcoming the limitations of flat files as a data storage medium.

We can summarize these topics as three ways of managing data:

- ❑ **Dynamic memory management:** what to do and what Linux won't let you do
- ❑ **File locking:** cooperative locking, locking regions of shared files, and avoiding deadlocks
- ❑ **The dbm database:** a basic, non-SQL-based database library featured in most Linux systems

Managing Memory

On all computer systems memory is a scarce resource. No matter how much memory is available, it never seems to be enough. It doesn't seem so long ago that 256MB of RAM was considered sufficient, but now 2GB of RAM is commonplace as a sensible minimum requirement even for desktop systems, with servers usefully having significantly more.

From the earliest versions of the operating system, UNIX-style operating systems have had a very clean approach to managing memory, which Linux, because it implements the X/Open specification, has inherited. Linux applications, except for a few specialized embedded applications, are never permitted to access physical memory directly. It might appear so to the application, but what the application is seeing is a carefully controlled illusion.

Linux provides applications with a clean view of a huge directly addressable memory space. Additionally, it provides protection so that different applications are protected from each other, and it allows applications to apparently access more memory than is physically present in the machine, provided the machine is at least well configured and has sufficient swap space.

Simple Memory Allocation

You allocate memory using the `malloc` call in the standard C library:

```
#include <stdlib.h>
void *malloc(size_t size);
```

Notice that Linux (following the X/Open specification) differs from some UNIX implementations by not requiring a special `malloc.h` include file. Note also that the `size` parameter that specifies the number of bytes to allocate isn't a simple `int`, although it's usually an unsigned integer type.

You can allocate a great deal of memory on most Linux systems. Let's start with a very simple program, but one that would defeat old MS-DOS-based programs, because they cannot access memory outside the base 640K memory map of PCs.

Try It Out   Simple Memory Allocation

Type the following program, `memory1.c`:

```c
#include <unistd.h>
#include <stdlib.h>
#include <stdio.h>

#define A_MEGABYTE (1024 * 1024)

int main()
{
    char *some_memory;
    int  megabyte = A_MEGABYTE;
    int exit_code = EXIT_FAILURE;

    some_memory = (char *)malloc(megabyte);
    if (some_memory != NULL) {
        sprintf(some_memory, "Hello World\n");
        printf("%s", some_memory);
        exit_code = EXIT_SUCCESS;
    }
    exit(exit_code);
}
```

When you run this program, it gives the following output:

```
$ ./memory1
Hello World
```

How It Works

This program asks the `malloc` library to give it a pointer to a megabyte of memory. You check to ensure that `malloc` was successful and then use some of the memory to show that it exists. When you run the program, you should see `Hello World` printed out, showing that `malloc` did indeed return the megabyte of usable memory. We don't check that all of the megabyte is present; we have to put some trust in the `malloc` code!

Notice that because `malloc` returns a `void *` pointer, you cast the result to the `char *` that you need. The `malloc` function is guaranteed to return memory that is aligned so that it can be cast to a pointer of any type.

The simple reason is that most current Linux systems use 32-bit integers and 32-bit pointers for pointing to memory, which allows you to specify up to 4 gigabytes. This ability to address directly with a 32-bit pointer, without needing segment registers or other tricks, is termed a *flat 32-bit memory model*. This model is also used in 32-bit versions of Windows XP and Vista. You should never rely on integers being 32-bit however, as an ever-increasing number of 64-bit versions of Linux are in use.

Allocating Lots of Memory

Now that you've seen Linux exceed the limitations of the MS-DOS memory model, let's give it a more difficult problem. The next program asks to allocate somewhat more memory than is physically present in the machine, so you might expect `malloc` to start failing somewhere a little short of the actual amount of memory present, because the kernel and all the other running processes are using some memory.

Try It Out   Asking for All Physical Memory

With `memory2.c`, we're going to ask for more than the machine's physical memory. You should adjust the define `PHY_MEM_MEGS` depending on your physical machine:

```
#include <unistd.h>
#include <stdlib.h>
#include <stdio.h>

#define A_MEGABYTE (1024 * 1024)
#define PHY_MEM_MEGS   1024 /* Adjust this number as required */

int main()
{
    char *some_memory;
    size_t  size_to_allocate = A_MEGABYTE;
    int  megs_obtained = 0;

    while (megs_obtained < (PHY_MEM_MEGS * 2)) {
        some_memory = (char *)malloc(size_to_allocate);
        if (some_memory != NULL) {
            megs_obtained++;
            sprintf(some_memory, "Hello World");
            printf("%s - now allocated %d Megabytes\n", some_memory, megs_obtained);
        }
        else {
            exit(EXIT_FAILURE);
        }
    }
    exit(EXIT_SUCCESS);
}
```

The output, somewhat abbreviated, is as follows:

```
$ ./memory2
Hello World - now allocated 1 Megabytes
Hello World - now allocated 2 Megabytes
...
Hello World - now allocated 2047 Megabytes
Hello World - now allocated 2048 Megabytes
```

How It Works

The program is very similar to the previous example. It simply loops, asking for more and more memory, until it has allocated twice the amount of memory you said your machine had when you adjusted the define PHY_MEM_MEGS. The surprise is that it works at all, because we appear to have created a program that uses every single byte of physical memory on the author's machine. Notice that we use the size_t type for our call to malloc.

The other interesting feature is that, at least on this machine, it ran the program in the blink of an eye. So not only have we apparently used up all the memory, but we've done it very quickly indeed.

Let's investigate further and see just how much memory we can allocate on this machine with memory3.c. Since it's now clear that Linux can do some very clever things with requests for memory, we'll allocate memory just 1K at a time and write to each block that we obtain.

Try It Out   Available Memory

This is memory3.c. By its very nature, it's extremely system-unfriendly and could affect a multiuser machine quite seriously. If you're at all concerned about the risk, it's better not to run it at all; it won't harm your understanding if you don't:

```c
#include <unistd.h>
#include <stdlib.h>
#include <stdio.h>

#define ONE_K (1024)

int main()
{
    char *some_memory;
    int  size_to_allocate = ONE_K;
    int  megs_obtained = 0;
    int  ks_obtained = 0;

    while (1) {
        for (ks_obtained = 0; ks_obtained < 1024; ks_obtained++) {
            some_memory = (char *)malloc(size_to_allocate);
            if (some_memory == NULL) exit(EXIT_FAILURE);
            sprintf(some_memory, "Hello World");
        }
        megs_obtained++;
```

```
        printf("Now allocated %d Megabytes\n", megs_obtained);
    }
    exit(EXIT_SUCCESS);
}
```

This time, the output, again abbreviated, is

```
$ ./memory3
Now allocated 1 Megabytes
...
Now allocated 1535 Megabytes
Now allocated 1536 Megabytes
Out of Memory: Killed process 2365
Killed
```

and then the program ends. It also takes quite a few seconds to run, and slows down significantly around the same number as the physical memory in the machine, and exercises the hard disk quite noticeably. However, the program has allocated, and accessed, more memory than this author physically has in his machine at the time of writing. Finally, the system protects itself from this rather aggressive program and kills it. On some systems it may simply exit quietly when `malloc` fails.

How It Works

The application's allocated memory is managed by the Linux kernel. Each time the program asks for memory or tries to read or write to memory that it has allocated, the Linux kernel takes charge and decides how to handle the request.

Initially, the kernel was simply able to use free physical memory to satisfy the application's request for memory, but once physical memory was full, it started using what's called *swap space*. On Linux, this is a separate disk area allocated when the system was installed. If you're familiar with Windows, the Linux swap space acts a little like the hidden Windows swap file. However, unlike Windows, there are no local heap, global heap, or discardable memory segments to worry about in code — the Linux kernel does all the management for you.

The kernel moves data and program code between physical memory and the swap space so that each time you read or write memory, the data always appears to have been in physical memory, wherever it was actually located before you attempted to access it.

In more technical terms, Linux implements a demand paged virtual memory system. All memory seen by user programs is *virtual*; that is, it doesn't actually exist at the physical address the program uses. Linux divides all memory into pages, commonly 4,096 bytes per page. When a program tries to access memory, a virtual-to-physical translation is made, although how this is implemented and the time it takes depend on the particular hardware you're using. When the access is to memory that isn't physically resident, a *page fault* results and control is passed to the kernel.

The Linux kernel checks the address being accessed and, if it's a legal address for that program, determines which page of physical memory to make available. It then either allocates it, if it has never been written before, or, if it has been stored on the disk in the swap space, reads the memory page containing the data into physical memory (possibly moving an existing page out to disk). Then, after mapping the virtual memory address to match the physical address, it allows the user program to continue. Linux applications don't need to worry about this activity because the implementation is all hidden in the kernel.

Eventually, when the application exhausts both the physical memory and the swap space, or when the maximum stack size is exceeded, the kernel finally refuses the request for further memory and may preemptively terminate the program.

> This "killing the process" behavior is different from early versions of Linux and many other flavors of UNIX, where `malloc` simply fails. It's termed the "out of memory (OOM) killer," and although it may seem rather drastic, it is in fact a good compromise between letting processes allocate memory rapidly and efficiently and having the Linux kernel protect itself from a total lack of resources, which is a serious issue.

So what does this mean to the application programmer? Basically, it's all good news. Linux is very good at managing memory and will allow applications to use very large amounts of memory and even very large single blocks of memory. However, you must remember that allocating two blocks of memory won't result in a single continuously addressable block of memory. What you get is what you ask for: two separate blocks of memory.

Does this apparently limitless supply of memory, followed by preemptive killing of the process, mean that there's no point in checking the return from `malloc`? Definitely not. One of the most common problems in C programs using dynamically allocated memory is writing beyond the end of an allocated block. When this happens, the program may not terminate immediately, but you have probably overwritten some data used internally by the `malloc` library routines.

Usually, the result is that future calls to `malloc` may fail, not because there's no memory to allocate, but because the memory structures have been corrupted. These problems can be quite difficult to track down, and in programs the sooner the error is detected, the better the chances of tracking down the cause. In Chapter 10, on debugging and optimizing, we'll discuss some tools that can help you track down memory problems.

Abusing Memory

Suppose you try to do "bad" things with memory. In this exercise, you allocate some memory and then attempt to write past the end, in memory4.c.

Try It Out   **Abusing Your Memory**

```
#include <stdlib.h>

#define ONE_K (1024)

int main()
{
    char *some_memory;
    char *scan_ptr;
```

```
some_memory = (char *)malloc(ONE_K);
if (some_memory == NULL) exit(EXIT_FAILURE);

scan_ptr = some_memory;
while(1) {
    *scan_ptr = '\0';
    scan_ptr++;
}
exit(EXIT_SUCCESS);
}
```

The output is simply

```
$ /memory4
Segmentation fault
```

How It Works

The Linux memory management system has protected the rest of the system from this abuse of memory. To ensure that one badly behaved program (this one) can't damage any other programs, Linux has terminated it.

Each running program on a Linux system sees its own memory map, which is different from every other program's. Only the operating system knows how physical memory is arranged, and not only manages it for user programs, but also protects user programs from each other.

The Null Pointer

Unlike MS-DOS, but more like newer flavors of Windows, modern Linux systems are very protective about writing or reading from the address referred to by a null pointer, although the actual behavior is implementation-specific.

Try It Out   Accessing a Null Pointer

Let's find out what happens when you access a null pointer in memory5a.c:

```
#include <unistd.h>
#include <stdlib.h>
#include <stdio.h>

int main()
{

    char *some_memory = (char *)0;

    printf("A read from null %s\n", some_memory);
    sprintf(some_memory, "A write to null\n");
    exit(EXIT_SUCCESS);
}
```

The output is

```
$ ./memory5a
A read from null (null)
Segmentation fault
```

How It Works

The first printf attempts to print out a string obtained from a null pointer; then the sprintf attempts to write to a null pointer. In this case, Linux (in the guise of the GNU "C" library) has been forgiving about the read and has simply provided a "magic" string containing the characters (n u l l) \0. It hasn't been so forgiving about the write and has terminated the program. This can sometimes be helpful in tracking down program bugs.

If you try this again but this time don't use the GNU "C" library, you'll discover that reading from location zero is not permitted. Here is memory5b.c:

```
#include <unistd.h>
#include <stdlib.h>
#include <stdio.h>

int main()
{
    char z = *(const char *)0;
     printf("I read from location zero\n");

    exit(EXIT_SUCCESS);
}
```

The output is

```
$ ./memory5b
Segmentation fault
```

This time you attempt to read directly from location zero. There is no GNU libc library between you and the kernel now, and the program is terminated. Note that some versions of UNIX do permit reading from location zero, but Linux doesn't.

Freeing Memory

Up to now, we've been simply allocating memory and then hoping that when the program ends, the memory we've used hasn't been lost. Fortunately, the Linux memory management system is quite capable of reliably ensuring that memory is returned to the system when a program ends. However, most programs don't simply want to allocate some memory, use it for a short period, and then exit. A much more common use is dynamically using memory as required.

Programs that use memory on a dynamic basis should always release unused memory back to the malloc memory manager using the free call. This enables separate blocks to be remerged and enables the malloc library to look after memory, rather than have the application manage it. If a running program (process) uses and then frees memory, that free memory remains allocated to the process. Behind the scenes, Linux is managing the blocks of memory the programmer is using as a set of physical "pages," usually 4K bytes each, in memory. However, if a page of memory is not being used, then the Linux memory manager will be able to move it from physical memory to swap space (termed paging), where it has little impact on the use of resources. If the program tries to access data inside the memory page that has be moved to swap space, then Linux will very briefly suspend the program, move the memory page back from swap space into physical memory again, and then allow the program to continue, just as though the data had been in memory all along.

```
#include <stdlib.h>

void free(void *ptr_to memory);
```

A call to free should be made only with a pointer to memory allocated by a call to malloc, calloc, or realloc. You'll meet calloc and realloc very shortly.

Try It Out   Freeing Memory

This program is called memory6.c:

```
#include <stdlib.h>
#include <stdio.h>


#define ONE_K (1024)

int main()
{
    char *some_memory;
    int exit_code = EXIT_FAILURE;

    some_memory = (char *)malloc(ONE_K);
    if (some_memory != NULL) {
        free(some_memory);
        printf("Memory allocated and freed again\n");
        exit_code = EXIT_SUCCESS;
    }
    exit(exit_code);
}
```

The output is

```
$ ./memory6
Memory allocated and freed again
```

How It Works

This program simply shows how to call free with a pointer to some previously allocated memory.

> Remember that once you've called `free` on a block of memory, it no longer belongs to the process. It's not being managed by the `malloc` library. Never try to read or write memory after calling `free` on it.

Other Memory Allocation Functions

Two other memory allocation functions are not used as often as `malloc` and `free`: `calloc` and `realloc`. The prototypes are

```
#include <stdlib.h>

void *calloc(size_t number_of_elements, size_t element_size);
void *realloc(void *existing_memory, size_t new_size);
```

Although `calloc` allocates memory that can be freed with `free`, it has somewhat different parameters from `malloc`: It allocates memory for an array of structures and requires the number of elements and the size of each element as its parameters. The allocated memory is filled with zeros; and if `calloc` is successful, a pointer to the first element is returned. Like `malloc`, subsequent calls are not guaranteed to return contiguous space, so you can't enlarge an array created by `calloc` by simply calling `calloc` again and expecting the second call to return memory appended to that returned by the first call.

The `realloc` function changes the size of a block of memory that has been previously allocated. It's passed a pointer to some memory previously allocated by `malloc`, `calloc`, or `realloc` and resizes it up or down as requested. The `realloc` function may have to move data around to achieve this, so it's important to ensure that once memory has been `realloced`, you always use the new pointer and never try to access the memory using pointers set up before `realloc` was called.

Another problem to watch out for is that `realloc` returns a null pointer if it has been unable to resize the memory. This means that in some applications you should avoid writing code like this:

```
my_ptr = malloc(BLOCK_SIZE);
....
my_ptr = realloc(my_ptr, BLOCK_SIZE * 10);
```

If `realloc` fails, then it returns a null pointer; `my_ptr` will point to null; and the original memory allocated with `malloc` can no longer be accessed via `my_ptr`. It may therefore be to your advantage to request the new memory first with `malloc` and then copy data from the old block to the new block using `memcpy` before `freeing` the old block. On error, this would allow the application to retain access to the data stored in the original block of memory, perhaps while arranging a clean termination of the program.

File Locking

File locking is a very important part of multiuser, multitasking operating systems. Programs frequently need to share data, usually through files, and it's very important that those programs have some way of establishing control of a file. The file can then be updated in a safe fashion, or a second program can stop itself from trying to read a file that is in a transient state while another program is writing to it.

Linux has several features that you can use for file locking. The simplest method is a technique to create *lock files* in an atomic way, so that nothing else can happen while the lock is being created. This gives a program a method of creating files that are guaranteed to be unique and could not have been simultaneously created by a different program.

The second method is more advanced; it enables programs to lock parts of a file for exclusive access. There are two different ways of achieving this second form of locking. We'll look at only one in detail, as the second is very similar — it just has a slightly different programming interface.

Creating Lock Files

Many applications just need to be able to create a lock file for a resource. Other programs can then check the file to see whether they are permitted to access the resource.

Usually, these lock files are in a special place with a name that relates to the resource being controlled. For example, when a modem is in use, Linux creates a lock file, often using a directory in the /var/spool directory.

Remember that lock files act only as indicators; programs need to cooperate to use them. They are termed *advisory locks* as opposed to mandatory locks, where the system will enforce the lock behavior.

To create a file to use as a lock indicator, you can use the open system call defined in fcntl.h (which you met in an earlier chapter) with the O_CREAT and O_EXCL flags set. This enables you to check that the file doesn't already exist and then create it in a single, atomic operation.

Try It Out   **Creating a Lock File**

You can see this in action with lock1.c:

```
#include <unistd.h>
#include <stdlib.h>
#include <stdio.h>
#include <fcntl.h>
#include <errno.h>

int main()
{
    int file_desc;
    int save_errno;

    file_desc = open("/tmp/LCK.test", O_RDWR | O_CREAT | O_EXCL, 0444);
    if (file_desc == -1) {
        save_errno = errno;
        printf("Open failed with error %d\n", save_errno);
    }
    else {
        printf("Open succeeded\n");
    }
    exit(EXIT_SUCCESS);
}
```

The first time you run the program, the output is

```
$ ./lock1
Open succeeded
```

but the next time you try, you get

```
$ ./lock1
Open failed with error 17
```

How It Works

The program calls open to create a file called /tmp/LCK.test, using the O_CREAT and O_EXCL flags. The first time you run the program, the file doesn't exist, so the open call is successful. Subsequent invocations of the program fail because the file already exists. To get the program to succeed again, you have to manually remove the lock file.

On Linux systems at least, error 17 refers to EEXIST, an error used to indicate that a file already exists. Error numbers are defined in the header file errno.h or, more commonly, by files included by it. In this case, the definition, actually in /usr/include/asm-generic/errno-base.h, reads

```
#define EEXIST           17      /* File exists */
```

This is an appropriate error for an open(O_CREAT | O_EXCL) failure.

If a program simply needs a resource exclusively for a short period of its execution, often termed a *critical section*, it should create the lock file using the open system call before entering the critical section, and use the unlink system call to delete it afterward, when the program exits the critical section.

You can demonstrate how programs can cooperate with this locking mechanism by writing a sample program and running two copies of it at the same time. You'll use the getpid call, which you saw in Chapter 4; it returns the process identifier, a unique number for each currently executing program.

Try It Out   Cooperative Lock Files

1. Here's the source of the test program, lock2.c:

```c
#include <unistd.h>
#include <stdlib.h>
#include <stdio.h>
#include <fcntl.h>
#include <errno.h>

const char *lock_file = "/tmp/LCK.test2";

int main()
{
    int file_desc;
    int tries = 10;
```

```
    while (tries--) {
        file_desc = open(lock_file, O_RDWR | O_CREAT | O_EXCL, 0444);
        if (file_desc == -1) {
            printf("%d - Lock already present\n", getpid());
            sleep(3);
        }
        else {
```

2. The critical section starts here:

```
            printf("%d - I have exclusive access\n", getpid());
            sleep(1);
            (void)close(file_desc);
            (void)unlink(lock_file);
```

3. It ends here:

```
            sleep(2);
        }
    }
    exit(EXIT_SUCCESS);
}
```

To run the program, you should first use this command to ensure that the lock file doesn't exist:

```
$ rm -f /tmp/LCK.test2
```

Then run two copies of the program by using this command:

```
$ ./lock2 & ./lock2
```

This starts a copy of lock2 in the background and a second copy running in the foreground. This is the output:

```
1284 - I have exclusive access
1283 - Lock already present
1283 - I have exclusive access
1284 - Lock already present
1284 - I have exclusive access
1283 - Lock already present
1283 - I have exclusive access
1284 - Lock already present
1284 - I have exclusive access
1283 - Lock already present
1283 - I have exclusive access
1284 - Lock already present
1284 - I have exclusive access
1283 - Lock already present
1283 - I have exclusive access
1284 - Lock already present
1284 - I have exclusive access
1283 - Lock already present
1283 - I have exclusive access
1284 - Lock already present
```

The preceding example shows how the two invocations of the same program are cooperating. If you try this, you'll almost certainly see different process identifiers in the output, but the program behavior will be the same.

How It Works

For the purposes of demonstration, you make the program loop 10 times using the `while` loop. The program then tries to access the critical resource by creating a unique lock file, `/tmp/LCK.test2`. If this fails because the file already exists, then the program waits for a short time and tries again. If it succeeds, then it can access the resource and, in the part marked "critical section," carry out whatever processing is required with exclusive access.

Since this is just a demonstration, you wait for only a short period. When the program has finished with the resource, it releases the lock by deleting the lock file. It can then carry out some other processing (just the `sleep` function in this case) before trying to reacquire the lock. The lock file acts as a binary semaphore, giving each program a yes or no answer to the question, "Can I use the resource?" You will learn more about semaphores in Chapter 14.

> It's important to realize that this is a cooperative arrangement and that you must write the programs correctly for it to work. A program failing to create the lock file can't simply delete the file and try again. It might then be able to create the lock file, but the other program that created the lock file has no way of knowing that it no longer has exclusive access to the resource.

Locking Regions

Creating lock files is fine for controlling exclusive access to resources such as serial ports or infrequently accessed files, but it isn't so good for access to large shared files. Suppose you have a large file that is written by one program but updated by many different programs simultaneously. This might occur if a program is logging some data that is obtained continuously over a long period and is being processed by several other programs. The processing programs can't wait for the logging program to finish — it runs continuously — so they need some way of cooperating to provide simultaneous access to the same file.

You can accommodate this situation by locking regions of the file so that a particular section of the file is locked, but other programs may access other parts of the file. This is called *file-segment*, or *file-region, locking*. Linux has (at least) two ways to do this: using the `fcntl` system call and using the `lockf` call. We'll look primarily at the `fcntl` interface because that is the most commonly used interface. `lockf` is reasonably similar, and, on Linux, is normally just an alternative interface to `fcntl`. However, the `fcntl` and `lockf` locking mechanisms do not work together: They use different underlying implementations, so you should never mix the two types of call; stick to one or the other.

You met the `fcntl` call in Chapter 3. Its definition is

```
#include <fcntl.h>

int fcntl(int fildes, int command, ...);
```

fcntl operates on open file descriptors and, depending on the command parameter, can perform different tasks. The three command options of interest for file locking are as follows:

- ❏ F_GETLK

- ❏ F_SETLK

- ❏ F_SETLKW

When you use these the third argument must be a pointer to a struct flock, so the prototype is effectively this:

```
int fcntl(int fildes, int command, struct flock *flock_structure);
```

The flock (file lock) structure is implementation dependent, but it will contain at least the following members:

- ❏ short l_type;

- ❏ short l_whence;

- ❏ off_t l_start;

- ❏ off_t l_len;

- ❏ pid_t l_pid;

The l_type member takes one of several values, also defined in fcntl.h. These are shown in the following table:

Value	Description
F_RDLCK	A shared (or "read") lock. Many different processes can have a shared lock on the same (or overlapping) regions of the file. If any process has a shared lock, then no process will be able to get an exclusive lock on that region. In order to obtain a shared lock, the file must have been opened with read or read/write access.
F_UNLCK	Unlock; used for clearing locks
F_WRLCK	An exclusive (or "write") lock. Only a single process may have an exclusive lock on any particular region of a file. Once a process has such a lock, no other process will be able to get any sort of lock on the region. To obtain an exclusive lock, the file must have been opened with write or read/write access.

The l_whence, l_start, and l_len members define a region — a contiguous set of bytes — in a file.. The l_whence must be one of SEEK_SET, SEEK_CUR, SEEK_END (from unistd.h). These correspond to the start, current position, and end of a file, respectively. l_whence defines the offset to which l_start, the first byte in the region, is relative. Normally, this would be SEEK_SET, so l_start is counted from the beginning of the file. The l_len parameter defines the number of bytes in the region.

The l_pid parameter is used for reporting the process holding a lock; see the F_GETLK description that follows.

Each byte in a file can have only a single type of lock on it at any one time, and may be locked for shared access, locked for exclusive access, or unlocked. There are quite a few combinations of commands and options to the fcntl call, so let's look at each of them in turn.

The F_GETLK Command

The first command is F_GETLK. It gets locking information about the file that fildes (the first parameter) has open. It doesn't attempt to lock the file. The calling process passes information about the type of lock it might wish to create, and fcntl used with the F_GETLK command returns any information that would prevent the lock from occurring.

The values used in the flock structure are described in the following table:

Value	Description
l_type	Either F_RDLCK for a shared (read-only) lock or F_WRLCK for an exclusive (write) lock
l_whence	One of SEEK_SET, SEEK_CUR, or SEEK_END LCK
l_start	The start byte of the file region of interest
l_len	The number of bytes in the file region of interest
l_pid	The identifier of the process with the lock

A process may use the F_GETLK call to determine the current state of locks on a region of a file. It should set up the flock structure to indicate the type of lock it may require and define the region it's interested in. The fcntl call returns a value other than -1 if it's successful. If the file already has locks that would prevent a lock request from succeeding, it overwrites the flock structure with the relevant information. If the lock will succeed, the flock structure is unchanged. If the F_GETLK call is unable to obtain the information, it returns –1 to indicate failure.

If the F_GETLK call is successful (i.e., it returns a value other than -1), the calling application must check the contents of the flock structure to determine whether it was modified. Since the l_pid value is set to the locking process (if one was found), this is a convenient field to check to determine whether the flock structure has been changed.

The F_SETLK Command

This command attempts to lock or unlock part of the file referenced by fildes. The values used in the flock structure (and different from those used by F_GETLK) are as follows:

Value	Description
l_type	One of the following: F_RDLCK for a read-only, or shared, lock F_WRLCK for an exclusive or write lock F_UNLCK to unlock a region
l_pid	Unused

As with F_GETLK, the region to be locked is defined by the values of the l_start, l_whence, and l_len fields of the flock structure. If the lock is successful, fcntl returns a value other than -1; on failure, -1 is returned. The function always returns immediately.

The F_SETLKW Command

The F_SETLKW command is the same as the F_SETLK command above except that if it can't obtain the lock, the call will wait until it can. Once this call has started waiting, it will return only when the lock can be obtained or a signal occurs. We cover signals in Chapter 11.

All locks held by a program on a file are automatically cleared when the relevant file descriptor is closed. This also happens automatically when the program finishes.

Use of read and write with Locking

When you're using locking on regions of a file, it's very important to use the lower-level read and write calls to access the data in the file, rather than the higher-level fread and fwrite. This is necessary because fread and fwrite perform buffering of data read or written inside the library, so executing an fread call to read the first 100 bytes of a file may (in fact almost certainly will) read more than 100 bytes and buffer the additional data inside the library. If the program then uses fread to read the next 100 bytes, it will actually read data already buffered inside the library and not allow a low-level read to pull more data from the file.

To see why this is a problem, consider two programs that wish to update the same file. Suppose the file consists of 200 bytes of data, all zeros. The first program starts first and obtains a write lock on the first 100 bytes of the file. It then uses fread to read in those 100 bytes. However, as shown in an earlier chapter, fread will read ahead by up to BUFSIZ bytes at a time, so it actually reads the entire file into memory, but only passes the first 100 bytes back to the program.

The second program then starts. It obtains a write lock on the second 100 bytes of the program. This is successful because the first program locked only the first 100 bytes. The second program writes twos to bytes 100 to 199, closes the file, unlocks it, and exits. The first program then locks the second 100 bytes of the file and calls fread to read them in. As that data was already buffered in memory by the library, what the program actually sees is 100 bytes of zeros, not the 100 twos that actually exist in the file on the hard disk. This problem doesn't occur when you're using read and write.

That description of file locking may seem a bit complex, but it's actually more difficult to describe than it is to use.

Try It Out   **Locking a File with fcntl**

Let's look at an example of how file locking works: lock3.c. To try out locking, you need two programs: one to do the locking and one to test. The first program does the locking.

1. Start with the includes and variable declarations:

```
#include <unistd.h>
#include <stdlib.h>
#include <stdio.h>
#include <fcntl.h>
```

```
const char *test_file = "/tmp/test_lock";

int main()
{
    int file_desc;
    int byte_count;
    char *byte_to_write = "A";
    struct flock region_1;
    struct flock region_2;
    int res;
```

2.   Open a file descriptor:

```
file_desc = open(test_file, O_RDWR | O_CREAT, 0666);
if (!file_desc) {
    fprintf(stderr, "Unable to open %s for read/write\n", test_file);
    exit(EXIT_FAILURE);
}
```

3.   Put some data in the file:

```
for(byte_count = 0; byte_count < 100; byte_count++) {
    (void)write(file_desc, byte_to_write, 1);
}
```

4.   Set up region 1 with a shared lock, from bytes 10 to 30:

```
region_1.l_type = F_RDLCK;
region_1.l_whence = SEEK_SET;
region_1.l_start = 10;
region_1.l_len = 20;
```

5.   Set up region 2 with an exclusive lock, from bytes 40 to 50:

```
region_2.l_type = F_WRLCK;
region_2.l_whence = SEEK_SET;
region_2.l_start = 40;
region_2.l_len = 10;
```

6.   Now lock the file:

```
printf("Process %d locking file\n", getpid());
res = fcntl(file_desc, F_SETLK, &region_1);
if (res == -1) fprintf(stderr, "Failed to lock region 1\n");
res = fcntl(file_desc, F_SETLK, &region_2);
if (res == -1) fprintf(stderr, "Failed to lock region 2\n");
```

7.   Wait for a while:

```
sleep(60);

printf("Process %d closing file\n", getpid());
```

```
        close(file_desc);
        exit(EXIT_SUCCESS);
    }
```

How It Works

The program first creates a file, opens it for both reading and writing, and then fills the file with data. It then sets up two regions: the first from bytes 10 to 30, for a shared (read) lock, and the second from bytes 40 to 50, for an exclusive (write) lock. It then calls fcntl to lock the two regions and waits for a minute before closing the file and exiting.

Figure 7-1 shows this scenario with locks when the program starts to wait.

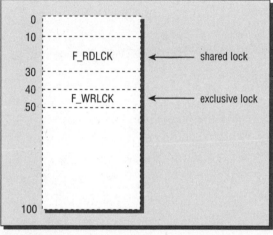

Figure 7-1

On its own, this program isn't very useful. You need a second program to test the locks, lock4.c.

Testing Locks on a File

In this example, you'll write a program that tests the different sorts of locks that you might need on different regions of a file:

1. As usual, begin with the includes and declarations:

```
#include <unistd.h>
#include <stdlib.h>
#include <stdio.h>
#include <fcntl.h>

const char *test_file = "/tmp/test_lock";
#define SIZE_TO_TRY 5
```

```
void show_lock_info(struct flock *to_show);

int main()
{
    int file_desc;
    int res;
    struct flock region_to_test;
    int start_byte;
```

2. Open a file descriptor:

```
file_desc = open(test_file, O_RDWR | O_CREAT, 0666);
if (!file_desc) {
    fprintf(stderr, "Unable to open %s for read/write", test_file);
    exit(EXIT_FAILURE);
}

for (start_byte = 0; start_byte < 99; start_byte += SIZE_TO_TRY) {
```

3. Set up the region you wish to test:

```
region_to_test.l_type = F_WRLCK;
region_to_test.l_whence = SEEK_SET;
region_to_test.l_start = start_byte;
region_to_test.l_len = SIZE_TO_TRY;
region_to_test.l_pid = -1;

printf("Testing F_WRLCK on region from %d to %d\n",
        start_byte, start_byte + SIZE_TO_TRY);
```

4. Now test the lock on the file:

```
res = fcntl(file_desc, F_GETLK, &region_to_test);
if (res == -1) {
    fprintf(stderr, "F_GETLK failed\n");
    exit(EXIT_FAILURE);
}
if (region_to_test.l_pid != -1) {
    printf("Lock would fail. F_GETLK returned:\n");
    show_lock_info(&region_to_test);
}
else {

    printf("F_WRLCK - Lock would succeed\n");
}
```

5. Now repeat the test with a shared (read) lock. Set up the region you wish to test again:

```
region_to_test.l_type = F_RDLCK;
region_to_test.l_whence = SEEK_SET;
region_to_test.l_start = start_byte;
region_to_test.l_len = SIZE_TO_TRY;
region_to_test.l_pid = -1;
printf("Testing F_RDLCK on region from %d to %d\n",
        start_byte, start_byte + SIZE_TO_TRY);
```

6. Test the lock on the file again:

```
        res = fcntl(file_desc, F_GETLK, &region_to_test);
        if (res == -1) {
            fprintf(stderr, "F_GETLK failed\n");
            exit(EXIT_FAILURE);
        }
        if (region_to_test.l_pid != -1) {
            printf("Lock would fail. F_GETLK returned:\n");
            show_lock_info(&region_to_test);
        }
        else {
            printf("F_RDLCK - Lock would succeed\n");
        }
    }
    close(file_desc);
    exit(EXIT_SUCCESS);
}

void show_lock_info(struct flock *to_show) {
    printf("\tl_type %d, ", to_show->l_type);
    printf("l_whence %d, ", to_show->l_whence);
    printf("l_start %d, ", (int)to_show->l_start);
    printf("l_len %d, ", (int)to_show->l_len);
    printf("l_pid %d\n", to_show->l_pid);
}
```

To test locking, you first need to run the lock3 program; then run the lock4 program to test the locked file. You do this by executing the lock3 program in the background, with the following command:

```
$ ./lock3 &
$ process 1534 locking file
```

The command prompt returns because lock3 is running in the background, and you then immediately run the lock4 program with the following command:

```
$ ./lock4
```

The output you get, with some omissions for brevity, is as follows:

```
Testing F_WRLOCK on region from 0 to 5
F_WRLCK - Lock would succeed
Testing F_RDLOCK on region from 0 to 5
F_RDLCK - Lock would succeed
...
Testing F_WRLOCK on region from 10 to 15
Lock would fail. F_GETLK returned:
l_type 0, l_whence 0, l_start 10, l_len 20, l_pid 1534
Testing F_RDLOCK on region from 10 to 15
F_RDLCK - Lock would succeed
Testing F_WRLOCK on region from 15 to 20
Lock would fail. F_GETLK returned:
l_type 0, l_whence 0, l_start 10, l_len 20, l_pid 1534
```

275

```
Testing F_RDLOCK on region from 15 to 20
F_RDLCK - Lock would succeed
...
Testing F_WRLOCK on region from 25 to 30
Lock would fail. F_GETLK returned:
l_type 0, l_whence 0, l_start 10, l_len 20, l_pid 1534
Testing F_RDLOCK on region from 25 to 30
F_RDLCK - Lock would succeed
...
Testing F_WRLOCK on region from 40 to 45
Lock would fail. F_GETLK returned:
l_type 1, l_whence 0, l_start 40, l_len 10, l_pid 1534
Testing F_RDLOCK on region from 40 to 45
Lock would fail. F_GETLK returned:
l_type 1, l_whence 0, l_start 40, l_len 10, l_pid 1534
...
Testing F_RDLOCK on region from 95 to 100
F_RDLCK - Lock would succeed
```

How It Works

For each group of five bytes in the file, lock4 sets up a region structure to test for locks on the file, which it then uses to determine whether the region can be either write or read locked. The returned information shows the region bytes, offset from byte zero, that would cause the lock request to fail. Since the l_pid part of the returned structure contains the process identifier of the program that currently has the file locked, the program sets it to -1 (an invalid value) and then checks whether it has been changed when the fcntl call returns. If the region isn't currently locked, l_pid will be unchanged.

To understand the output, you need to look in the include file fcntl.h (normally /usr/include/ fcntl.h) to find that an l_type of 1 is from the definition of F_WRLCK as 1, and an l_type of 0 is from the definition of F_RDLCK as 0. Thus, an l_type of 1 tells you that the lock would fail because of an existing write lock, and an l_type of 0 is caused by an existing read lock. On the regions of the file that lock3 has not locked, both shared and exclusive locks will succeed.

From bytes 10 to 30, you can see that it would be possible to have a shared lock, because the existing lock from the lock3 program is a shared, not an exclusive, lock. On the region from bytes 40 to 50, both types of lock will fail because lock3 has an exclusive (F_WRLCK) lock on this region.

Once the program lock4 has completed, you need to wait for a short period for lock3 to complete its sleep call and exit.

Competing Locks

Now that you've seen how to test for existing locks on a file, let's see what happens when two programs compete for locks on the same section of the file. You'll use the lock3 program again for locking the file, and a new program, lock5, to try to lock it again. To complete the example you'll also add some calls for unlocking into lock5.

Try It Out   **Competing Locks**

Here's a program, `lock5.c`, that tries to lock regions of a file that are already locked, rather than test the lock status of different parts of the file:

1.   After the `#includes` and declarations, open a file descriptor:

```
#include <unistd.h>
#include <stdlib.h>
#include <stdio.h>
#include <fcntl.h>

const char *test_file = "/tmp/test_lock";

int main()
{
    int file_desc;
    struct flock region_to_lock;
    int res;

    file_desc = open(test_file, O_RDWR | O_CREAT, 0666);
    if (!file_desc) {
        fprintf(stderr, "Unable to open %s for read/write\n", test_file);
        exit(EXIT_FAILURE);
    }
```

2.   The remainder of the program specifies different regions of the file and tries different locking operations on them:

```
    region_to_lock.l_type = F_RDLCK;
    region_to_lock.l_whence = SEEK_SET;
    region_to_lock.l_start = 10;
    region_to_lock.l_len = 5;
    printf("Process %d, trying F_RDLCK, region %d to %d\n", getpid(),
            (int)region_to_lock.l_start, (int)(region_to_lock.l_start +
region_to_lock.l_len));
    res = fcntl(file_desc, F_SETLK, &region_to_lock);
    if (res == -1) {
        printf("Process %d - failed to lock region\n", getpid());
    } else {
        printf("Process %d - obtained lock region\n", getpid());
    }

    region_to_lock.l_type = F_UNLCK;
    region_to_lock.l_whence = SEEK_SET;
    region_to_lock.l_start = 10;
    region_to_lock.l_len = 5;
    printf("Process %d, trying F_UNLCK, region %d to %d\n", getpid(),
                    (int)region_to_lock.l_start,
(int)(region_to_lock.l_start +
        region_to_lock.l_len));
    res = fcntl(file_desc, F_SETLK, &region_to_lock);
    if (res == -1) {
```

```
               printf("Process %d - failed to unlock region\n", getpid());
    } else {
        printf("Process %d - unlocked region\n", getpid());
    }


    region_to_lock.l_type = F_UNLCK;
    region_to_lock.l_whence = SEEK_SET;
    region_to_lock.l_start = 0;
    region_to_lock.l_len = 50;
    printf("Process %d, trying F_UNLCK, region %d to %d\n", getpid(),
                    (int)region_to_lock.l_start,
(int)(region_to_lock.l_start +
        region_to_lock.l_len));
    res = fcntl(file_desc, F_SETLK, &region_to_lock);
    if (res == -1) {
        printf("Process %d - failed to unlock region\n", getpid());
    } else {
        printf("Process %d - unlocked region\n", getpid());
    }


    region_to_lock.l_type = F_WRLCK;
    region_to_lock.l_whence = SEEK_SET;
    region_to_lock.l_start = 16;
    region_to_lock.l_len = 5;
    printf("Process %d, trying F_WRLCK, region %d to %d\n", getpid(),
                    (int)region_to_lock.l_start,
(int)(region_to_lock.l_start +
        region_to_lock.l_len));
    res = fcntl(file_desc, F_SETLK, &region_to_lock);
    if (res == -1) {
        printf("Process %d - failed to lock region\n", getpid());
    } else {
        printf("Process %d - obtained lock on region\n", getpid());
    }


    region_to_lock.l_type = F_RDLCK;
    region_to_lock.l_whence = SEEK_SET;
    region_to_lock.l_start = 40;
    region_to_lock.l_len = 10;
    printf("Process %d, trying F_RDLCK, region %d to %d\n", getpid(),
                    (int)region_to_lock.l_start,
(int)(region_to_lock.l_start +
        region_to_lock.l_len));
    res = fcntl(file_desc, F_SETLK, &region_to_lock);
    if (res == -1) {
        printf("Process %d - failed to lock region\n", getpid());
    } else {
        printf("Process %d - obtained lock on region\n", getpid());
    }


    region_to_lock.l_type = F_WRLCK;
    region_to_lock.l_whence = SEEK_SET;
    region_to_lock.l_start = 16;
    region_to_lock.l_len = 5;
```

```
        printf("Process %d, trying F_WRLCK with wait, region %d to %d\n", getpid(),
                       (int)region_to_lock.l_start,
(int)(region_to_lock.l_start +
        region_to_lock.l_len));
    res = fcntl(file_desc, F_SETLKW, &region_to_lock);
     if (res == -1) {
        printf("Process %d - failed to lock region\n", getpid());
    } else {
        printf("Process %d - obtained lock on region\n", getpid());
    }

    printf("Process %d ending\n", getpid());
    close(file_desc);
    exit(EXIT_SUCCESS);
}
```

If you first run the lock3 program in the background, then immediately run this new program:

```
$ ./lock3 &
$ process 227 locking file
$ ./lock5
```

The output you get is as follows:

```
Process 227 locking file
Process 228, trying F_RDLCK, region 10 to 15
Process 228 - obtained lock on region
Process 228, trying F_UNLCK, region 10 to 15
Process 228 - unlocked region
Process 228, trying F_UNLCK, region 0 to 50
Process 228 - unlocked region
Process 228, trying F_WRLCK, region 16 to 21
Process 228 - failed to lock on region
Process 228, trying F_RDLCK, region 40 to 50
Process 228 - failed to lock on region
Process 228, trying F_WRLCK with wait, region 16 to 21
Process 227 closing file
Process 228 - obtained lock on region
Process 228 ending
```

How It Works

First, the program attempts to lock a region from bytes 10 to 15 with a shared lock. This region is already locked with a shared lock, but simultaneous shared locks are allowed and the lock is successful.

It then unlocks its own shared lock on the region, which is also successful. The program then attempts to unlock the first 50 bytes of the file, even though it doesn't have any locks set. This is also successful because, even though this program had no locks in the first place, the final result of the unlock request is that no locks are held by this program in the first 50 bytes.

Next, the program attempts to lock the region from bytes 16 to 21 with an exclusive lock. This region is also already locked with a shared lock, so this time the new lock fails, because an exclusive lock could not be created.

After that, the program attempts a shared lock on the region from bytes 40 to 50. This region is already locked with an exclusive lock, so again the lock fails.

Finally, the program again attempts to obtain an exclusive lock on the region from bytes 16 to 21, but this time it uses the F_SETLCKW command to wait until it can obtain a lock. There is then a long pause in the output until the lock3 program, which has already locked the region, completes its sleep and closes the file, thus releasing all the locks it had acquired. The lock5 program resumes execution, successfully locking the region, before it also exits.

Other Lock Commands

There is a second method of locking files: the lockf function. This also operates using file descriptors. It has the prototype

```
#include <unistd.h>

int lockf(int fildes, int function, off_t size_to_lock);
```

It can take the following function values:

- ❑   F_ULOCK: Unlock
- ❑   F_LOCK: Lock exclusively
- ❑   F_TLOCK: Test and lock exclusively
- ❑   F_TEST: Test for locks by other processes

The size_to_lock parameter is the number of bytes to operate on, from the current offset in the file.

lockf has a simpler interface than the fcntl interface, principally because it has rather less functionality and flexibility. To use the function, you must seek the start of the region you wish to lock and then call it with the number of bytes to lock.

Like the fcntl method of file locking, all locks are only advisory; they won't actually prevent reading from or writing to the file. It's the responsibility of programs to check for locks. The effect of mixing fcntl locks and lockf locks is undefined, so you must decide which type of locking you wish to use and stick to it.

Deadlocks

No discussion of locking would be complete without a mention of the dangers of *deadlocks*. Suppose two programs wish to update the same file. They both need to update byte 1 and byte 2 at the same time. Program A chooses to update byte 2 first, then byte 1. Program B tries to update byte 1 first, then byte 2.

Both programs start at the same time. Program A locks byte 2 and program B locks byte 1. Program A tries for a lock on byte 1. Since this is already locked by program B, program A waits. Program B tries for a lock on byte 2. Since this is locked by program A, program B too waits.

This situation, when neither program is able to proceed, is called a *deadlock*, or *deadly embrace*. It is a common problem with database applications in which many users are frequently trying to access the same data. Most commercial relational databases detect deadlocks and break them automatically; the Linux kernel doesn't. Some external intervention, perhaps forcibly terminating one of the programs, is required to sort out the resulting mess.

Programmers must be wary of this situation. When you have multiple programs waiting for locks, you need to be very careful to consider whether a deadlock could occur. In this example it's quite easy to avoid: Both programs should simply lock the bytes they require in the same order, or use a larger region to lock.

We don't have the space to consider the difficulties of concurrent programs here. If you're interested in reading further, you might like to consider obtaining a copy of Principles of Concurrent and Distributed Programming *by M. Ben-Ari (Prentice Hall, 1990).*

Databases

You've seen how to use files for storing data, so why should you want to use a database? Quite simply, there are some circumstances where the features of a database provide a better way to solve the problem. Using a database is better than storing files for two reasons:

❑   You can store data records that vary in size, which can be a little difficult to implement using flat, unstructured files.

❑   Databases store and retrieve data efficiently using an index. The big advantage is that this index need not be a simple record number, which would be quite easy to implement in a flat file, but can be an arbitrary string.

The dbm Database

All versions of Linux, and most flavors of UNIX, come with a basic, but very efficient, data storage set of routines called the dbm database. The dbm database is excellent for storing indexed data that is relatively static. Some database purists might argue that dbm isn't a database at all, simply an indexed file storage system. The X/Open specification, however, refers to dbm as a database, so we'll continue to refer to it as such in this book.

Introduction to dbm

In spite of the rise of free relational databases, such as MySQL and PostgreSQL, the dbm database continues to play an important role in Linux. Distributions that use RPM, such as Red Hat and SUSE, use dbm as the underlying storage for installed package information. The open-source implementation of LDAP, Open LDAP, can also use dbm as a storage mechanism. The advantage of dbm over a more complete database product such as MySQL is that it is very lightweight, and much easier to build into a distributed binary because no separate database server installation is required. At the time of this writing, both Sendmail and Apache use dbm.

The dbm database enables you store data structures of variable size, using an index, and then retrieve the structure either using the index or simply by sequentially scanning the database. The dbm database is best used for data that is accessed frequently but updated rarely, because it tends to be rather slow to create entries but quick to retrieve them.

At this point, we come to a minor problem: Over the years, there have been several variations of the dbm database with slightly different APIs and features. There is the original dbm set, the "new" dbm set, called ndbm, and the GNU implementation, gdbm. The GNU implementation can also emulate the older dbm and ndbm interfaces, but natively has a significantly different interface than the other implementations. Different Linux distributions ship with different versions of the dbm libraries, although the most common choice is to ship with the gdbm library, but installed such that it can emulate the other two interface types.

Here we are going to concentrate on the ndbm interface because that is the one standardized by X/OPEN and because it is somewhat simpler to use than the raw gdbm implementation.

Getting dbm

Most mainstream Linux distributions come with a version of gdbm already installed, although on a few distributions you may need to use the relevant package manager to install the appropriate development libraries. For example, on Ubuntu you may need to use the Synaptic package manager to install the libgdbm-dev package, as it is not generally installed by default.

If you want to look at the source code, or are using a distribution for which no pre-built development package is available, the GNU implementation can be found at www.gnu.org/software/gdbm/gdbm.html.

Troubleshooting and Reinstalling dbm

This chapter was written with the assumption that you have the GNU implementation of gdbm installed, complete with the ndbm compatibility libraries. This is generally the case for Linux distributions; however, as noted earlier, you may have to explicitly install the development library package in order to compile files using the ndbm routines.

Unfortunately, the include and link libraries required do vary slightly among distributions, so although installed, you may have to experiment slightly to discover how to compile source files using ndbm. The most common case is that gdbm is installed and by default supports the ndbm compatibility mode. Red Hat distributions, for example, commonly do this. In this case you need to do the following:

1. Include the file ndbm.h in your C file.
2. Include the header file directory /usr/include/gdbm using -I/usr/include/gdbm.
3. Link against the gdbm library using -lgdbm.

If this doesn't work, a common alternative, as used by recent Ubuntu and SUSE distributions, for example, is that gdbm is installed, but you must explicitly request ndbm compatibility if you require it, and you may have to link against the compatability library before the main library. In this case you need to do the following:

1. Include the file gdbm-ndbm.h in your C file instead of ndbm.h.
2. Include the header file directory /usr/include/gdbm using -I/usr/include/gdbm.
3. Link against the additional gdbm compatibility library using -lgdbm_compat -lgdbm.

The downloadable Makefile and dbm C files are set to the first option by default, but contain comments about how they need to be edited to easily select the second option. For the rest of this chapter we assume your system comes with ndbm compatibility as the default behavior.

The dbm Routines

Like curses, which we discussed in Chapter 6, the dbm facility consists of a header file and a library that must be linked when the program is compiled. The library is called simply dbm, but because we are normally using the GNU implementation on Linux, we need to link against this implementation using -lgdbm on the compilation line. The header file is ndbm.h.

Before we can attempt to explain each of these functions, it's important to understand what the dbm database is trying to achieve. Once you understand this, you'll be in a much better position to understand how to use the dbm functions.

The dbm database's basic element is a block of data to store, coupled with a companion block of data that acts as a key for retrieving that data. Each dbm database must have a unique key for each block of data to be stored. The key value acts as an index into the data stored. There's no restriction on either the keys or the data, nor are any errors defined for using data or keys that are too large. The specification allows an implementation to limit the size of the key/data pair to be 1,023 bytes, but generally there is no limit, because implementations have been more flexible than they were required to be.

To manipulate these blocks as data, the ndbm.h include file defines a new type called datum. The exact content of this type is implementation dependent, but it must have at least the following members:

```
void *dptr;
size_t dsize
```

datum will be a type defined by a typedef. Also declared in the ndbm.h file is a type definition for dbm, which is a structure used for accessing the database, much like a FILE is used for accessing files. The internals of the dbm typedef are implementation dependent and should never be used.

To reference a block of data when you're using the dbm library, you must declare a datum, set dptr to point to the start of the data, and set dsize to contain its size. Both the data to store and the index used to access it are always referenced by a datum type.

The dbm type is best thought of as analogous to a FILE type. When you open a dbm database, two physical files are normally created: one with a .pag extension and one with a .dir extension. A single dbm pointer is returned, which is used to access these two files as a pair. The files should never be read or written to directly; they are intended to be accessed only via the dbm routines.

In some implementations the two files have been merged and only a single new file is created.

If you're familiar with SQL databases, you'll notice that there are no table or column structures associated with a dbm database. These structures are unnecessary because dbm neither imposes a fixed size on each item of data to be stored nor requires internal structure to the data. The dbm library works on blocks of unstructured binary data.

dbm Access Functions

Now that we've introduced the basis on which the dbm library works, we can take a look at the functions in detail. The prototypes for the main dbm functions are as follows:

```
#include <ndbm.h>
```

```
DBM *dbm_open(const char *filename, int file_open_flags, mode_t file_mode);
int dbm_store(DBM *database_descriptor, datum key, datum content, int store_mode);
datum dbm_fetch(DBM *database_descriptor, datum key);
void dbm_close(DBM *database_descriptor);
```

dbm_open

This function is used to open existing databases and can be used to create new databases. The `filename` argument is a base filename, without a .dir or .pag extension.

The remaining parameters are the same as the second and third parameters to the `open` function, which you met in Chapter 3. You can use the same #defines. The second argument controls whether the database can be read from, written to, or both. If you are creating a new database, the flags must be binary O_RED with O_CREAT to allow the files to be created. The third argument specifies the initial permissions of the files that will be created.

`dbm_open` returns a pointer to a DBM type. This is used in all subsequent accesses of the database. On failure, a (DBM *)0 is returned.

dbm_store

You use this function for entering data into the database. As mentioned earlier, all data must be stored with a unique index. To define the data you wish to store and the index used to refer to it, you must set up two datum types: one to refer to the index and one for the actual data. The final parameter, store_mode, controls what happens if an attempt is made to store some data using a key that already exists. If it's set to dbm_insert, the store fails and dbm_store returns 1. If it's set to dbm_replace, the new data overwrites the existing data and dbm_store returns 0. dbm_store will return negative numbers on other errors.

dbm_fetch

The dbm_fetch routine is used for retrieving data from the database. It takes a dbm pointer, as returned from a previous call to dbm_open, and a datum type, which must be set up to point to a key. A datum type is returned. If the data relating to the key used was found in the database, the returned datum structure will have dptr and dsize values set up to refer to the returned data. If the key was not found, the dptr will be set to null.

> It's important to remember that dbm_fetch is returning only a datum containing a pointer to the data. The actual data may still be held in local storage space inside the dbm library and must be copied into program variables before any further dbm functions are called.

dbm_close

This routine closes a database opened with dbm_open and must be passed a dbm pointer returned from a previous call to dbm_open.

Try It Out   A Simple dbm Database

Now that you've learned the basic functions of the dbm database, you know enough to write your first dbm program: dbm1.c. In this program, you'll use a structure called test_data.

1. First, here are its `#include` files, `#defines`, the `main` function, and the declaration of the `test_data` structure:

```
#include <unistd.h>
#include <stdlib.h>
#include <stdio.h>
#include <fcntl.h>

#include <ndbm.h>
/* On some systems you need to replace the above with
#include <gdbm-ndbm.h>
*/

#include <string.h>

#define TEST_DB_FILE "/tmp/dbm1_test"
#define ITEMS_USED 3

struct test_data {
    char misc_chars[15];
    int  any_integer;
    char more_chars[21];
};

int main()
{
```

2. Within `main`, set up the `items_to_store` and `items_received` structures, the `key` string, and the `datum` types:

```
    struct test_data items_to_store[ITEMS_USED];
    struct test_data item_retrieved;

    char key_to_use[20];
    int i, result;

    datum key_datum;
    datum data_datum;

    DBM *dbm_ptr;
```

3. Having declared a pointer to a `dbm` type structure, now open your test database for reading and writing, creating it if necessary:

```
    dbm_ptr = dbm_open(TEST_DB_FILE, O_RDWR | O_CREAT, 0666);
    if (!dbm_ptr) {
        fprintf(stderr, "Failed to open database\n");
        exit(EXIT_FAILURE);
    }
```

4. Now add some data to the `items_to_store` structure:

```
    memset(items_to_store, '\0', sizeof(items_to_store));
    strcpy(items_to_store[0].misc_chars, "First!");
```

```
items_to_store[0].any_integer = 47;
strcpy(items_to_store[0].more_chars, "foo");

strcpy(items_to_store[1].misc_chars, "bar");
items_to_store[1].any_integer = 13;
strcpy(items_to_store[1].more_chars, "unlucky?");

strcpy(items_to_store[2].misc_chars, "Third");
items_to_store[2].any_integer = 3;
strcpy(items_to_store[2].more_chars, "baz");
```

5. For each entry, you need to build a key for future referencing. This is the first letter of each string and the integer. This key is then identified with the key_datum, while the data_datum refers to the items_to_store entry. Then you store the data in the database:

```
for (i = 0; i < ITEMS_USED; i++) {
    sprintf(key_to_use, "%c%c%d",
            items_to_store[i].misc_chars[0],
            items_to_store[i].more_chars[0],
            items_to_store[i].any_integer);

    key_datum.dptr = (void *)key_to_use;
    key_datum.dsize = strlen(key_to_use);
    data_datum.dptr = (void *)&items_to_store[i];
    data_datum.dsize = sizeof(struct test_data);

    result = dbm_store(dbm_ptr, key_datum, data_datum, DBM_REPLACE);
    if (result != 0) {
        fprintf(stderr, "dbm_store failed on key %s\n", key_to_use);
        exit(2);
    }
}
```

6. Next, see if you can retrieve this new data, and then, finally, you must close the database:

```
sprintf(key_to_use, "bu%d", 13);
key_datum.dptr = key_to_use;
key_datum.dsize = strlen(key_to_use);

data_datum = dbm_fetch(dbm_ptr, key_datum);
if (data_datum.dptr) {
    printf("Data retrieved\n");
    memcpy(&item_retrieved, data_datum.dptr, data_datum.dsize);
    printf("Retrieved item - %s %d %s\n",
            item_retrieved.misc_chars,
            item_retrieved.any_integer,
            item_retrieved.more_chars);
}
else {
    printf("No data found for key %s\n", key_to_use);
}
dbm_close(dbm_ptr);
exit(EXIT_SUCCESS);
}
```

When you compile and run the program, the output is simply

```
$ gcc -o dbm1 -I/usr/include/gdbm dbm1.c -lgdbm
$ ./dbm1
Data retrieved
Retrieved item - bar 13 unlucky?
```

This is the output you'll get if you have gdbm installed in compatible mode. If this fails to compile, you may need to change the include directive as shown in the file to use the gdbm-ndbm.h file in place of ndbm.h, and specify the compatibility library before the main library when you compile, as shown here:

```
$ gcc -o dbm1 -I/usr/include/gdbm dbm1.c -lgdbm_compat -lgdbm
```

How It Works

First, you open the database, creating it if necessary. You then fill in three members of items_to_store to use as test data. For each of these three members you create an index key. To keep it simple, use the first characters of each of the two strings, plus the integer stored.

You then set up two datum structures, one for the key and one for the data to store. Having stored the three items in the database, you construct a new key and set up a datum structure to point at it. You then use this key to retrieve data from the database. Check for success by making sure that the dptr in the returned datum isn't null. Provided it isn't, you can then copy the retrieved data (which may be stored internally within the dbm library) into your own structure, being careful to use the size dbm_fetch has returned (if you didn't do this and were using variable-sized data, you might attempt to copy nonexistent data). Finally, you print out the retrieved data to show it was retrieved correctly.

Additional dbm Functions

Now that you've seen the principal dbm functions, we can cover the few remaining functions that are used with dbm:

```
int dbm_delete(DBM *database_descriptor, datum key);
int dbm_error(DBM *database_descriptor);
int dbm_clearerr(DBM *database_descriptor);
datum dbm_firstkey(DBM *database_descriptor);
datum dbm_nextkey(DBM *database_descriptor);
```

dbm_delete

The dbm_delete function is used to delete entries from the database. It takes a key datum just like dbm_fetch but rather than retrieve the data, it deletes the data. It returns 0 on success.

dbm_error

The dbm_error function simply tests whether an error has occurred in the database, returning 0 if there is none.

dbm_clearerr

The dbm_clearerr clears any error condition flag that may be set in the database.

dbm_firstkey and dbm_nextkey

These routines are normally used as a pair to scan through all the keys of all the items in a database. The loop structure required is as follows:

```
DBM *db_ptr;
datum key;

for(key = dbm_firstkey(db_ptr); key.dptr; key = dbm_nextkey(db_ptr));
```

Try It Out   **Retrieving and Deleting**

In this example, you amend dbm1.c with some of these new functions to create a new file, dbm2.c:

1. Make a copy of dbm1.c and open it for editing. Edit the #define TEST_DB_FILE line:

```
#include <unistd.h>
#include <stdlib.h>
#include <stdio.h>
#include <fcntl.h>
#include <ndbm.h>
#include <string.h>

#define TEST_DB_FILE "/tmp/dbm2_test"
#define ITEMS_USED 3
```

2. Now the only change you need to make is in the retrieval section:

```
        /* now try to delete some data */
    sprintf(key_to_use, "bu%d", 13);
    key_datum.dptr = key_to_use;
    key_datum.dsize = strlen(key_to_use);

    if (dbm_delete(dbm_ptr, key_datum) == 0) {
        printf("Data with key %s deleted\n", key_to_use);
    }
    else {
        printf("Nothing deleted for key %s\n", key_to_use);
    }
    for (key_datum = dbm_firstkey(dbm_ptr);
         key_datum.dptr;
         key_datum = dbm_nextkey(dbm_ptr)) {
        data_datum = dbm_fetch(dbm_ptr, key_datum);
        if (data_datum.dptr) {
            printf("Data retrieved\n");
            memcpy(&item_retrieved, data_datum.dptr, data_datum.dsize);
            printf("Retrieved item - %s %d %s\n",
                    item_retrieved.misc_chars,
                    item_retrieved.any_integer,
                    item_retrieved.more_chars);
        }
        else {
```

```
        printf("No data found for key %s\n", key_to_use);
    }
}
```

The output is

```
$ ./dbm2
Data with key bu13 deleted
Data retrieved
Retrieved item - Third 3 baz
Data retrieved
Retrieved item - First! 47 foo
```

How It Works

The first part of this program is identical to the previous example, simply storing some data in the database. You then build a key to match the second item and delete it from the database.

The program then uses dbm_firstkey and dbm_nextkey to access each key in the database in turn, retrieving the data. Notice that the data isn't retrieved in order: No retrieval order is implied in the key order; it's simply a way of scanning all the entries.

The CD Application

Now that you've learned about the environment and about managing data, it's time to update the application. The dbm database seems well suited to storing CD information, so you'll use that as the basis for your new implementation.

Updating the Design

Because this update involves a significant rewrite, now would be a good time to look at your design decisions to see if they need revising. Using comma-separated variable files to store the information, although it gave an easy implementation in the shell, has turned out to be very restrictive. A lot of CD titles and tracks turn out to have commas in them. You can discard this method of separation entirely using dbm, so that's one element of the design that we will change.

The split of the information between title and tracks, using a separate file for each, seems to have been a good decision, so you'll stick to the same logical arrangement.

Both the previous implementations have, to some extent, mixed the data access parts of the application with the user interface parts, not least because it was all implemented in a single file. In this implementation, you'll use a header file to describe the data and the routines to access it, and split the user interface and data manipulation into separate files.

Although you could keep the curses implementation of the user interface, you'll return to a simple line-based system. This will keep the user interface part of the application small and simple and allow you to concentrate on the other implementation aspects.

You can't use SQL with dbm code, but you can express your new database in more formal terms using SQL terminology. Don't worry if you're not familiar with SQL; we will explain the definitions, and you'll see more SQL in Chapter 8. In code, the table can be described as follows:

```
CREATE TABLE cdc_entry (
    catalog CHAR(30) PRIMARY KEY REFERENCES cdt_entry(catalog),
    title    CHAR(70),
    type     CHAR(30),
    artist   CHAR(70)
);

CREATE TABLE cdt_entry (
    catalog CHAR(30) REFERENCES cdc_entry(catalog),
    track_no  INTEGER,
    track_txt CHAR(70),
    PRIMARY KEY(catalog, track_no)
);
```

This very succinct description tells you the names and sizes of the fields. For the cdc_entry table, it says that there's a unique catalog column for every entry. For the cdt_entry table, it says that the track number can't be zero and that the combination of catalog and track_no columns is unique. You will see these being defined as typedef struct structures in the next section of code.

The CD Database Application Using dbm

You're now going to reimplement the application using the dbm database to store the information you need, with the files cd_data.h, app_ui.c, and cd_access.c.

You'll also rewrite the user interface as a command-line program. Later in the book, you'll be reusing the database interface and parts of the user interface as you explore implementing your application using different client/server mechanisms and, finally, as an application that can be accessed across a network using a Web browser. Converting the interface to a simpler line-driven interface makes it easier to focus on the important parts of the application, rather than on the interface.

You'll see the database header file cd_data.h and functions from the file cd_access.c reused several times in later chapters.

> Remember that some Linux distributions require slightly different build options, such as using the include file gdbm-ndbm.h in your C file instead of ndbm.h, and using -lgdbm_compat -lgdbm instead of simply -lgdbm. If this is the case with your Linux distribution, you will need to make the appropriate changes to the files access.c and Makefile.

Try It Out   **cd_data.h**

Start here with the header file, to define the structure of your data and the routines that you'll use to access it:

1. This is the data structure definition for the CD database. It defines structures and sizes for the two tables that make up the database. Start by defining some sizes for the fields that you'll use and two structures: one for the catalog entry and one for the track entry:

```
/* The catalog table */
#define CAT_CAT_LEN        30
#define CAT_TITLE_LEN      70
#define CAT_TYPE_LEN       30
#define CAT_ARTIST_LEN     70

typedef struct {
    char catalog[CAT_CAT_LEN + 1];
    char title[CAT_TITLE_LEN + 1];
    char type[CAT_TYPE_LEN + 1];
    char artist[CAT_ARTIST_LEN + 1];
} cdc_entry;

/* The tracks table, one entry per track */
#define TRACK_CAT_LEN      CAT_CAT_LEN
#define TRACK_TTEXT_LEN    70

typedef struct {
    char catalog[TRACK_CAT_LEN + 1];
    int  track_no;
    char track_txt[TRACK_TTEXT_LEN + 1];
} cdt_entry;
```

2. Now that you have some data structures, you can define some access routines that you'll need. Functions with cdc_ are for catalog entries; functions with cdt_ are for track entries:

> Notice that some of the functions return data structures. You can indicate the failure of these functions by forcing the contents of the structure to be empty.

```
/* Initialization and termination functions */
int database_initialize(const int new_database);
void database_close(void);

/* two for simple data retrieval */
cdc_entry get_cdc_entry(const char *cd_catalog_ptr);
cdt_entry get_cdt_entry(const char *cd_catalog_ptr, const int track_no);

/* two for data addition */
int add_cdc_entry(const cdc_entry entry_to_add);
int add_cdt_entry(const cdt_entry entry_to_add);

/* two for data deletion */
```

```
int del_cdc_entry(const char *cd_catalog_ptr);
int del_cdt_entry(const char *cd_catalog_ptr, const int track_no);

/* one search function */
cdc_entry search_cdc_entry(const char *cd_catalog_ptr, int *first_call_ptr);
```

Try It Out   **app_ui.c**

Now move on to the user interface. This gives you a (relatively) simple program with which to access your database functions. You'll implement the interface in a separate file.

1. As usual, start with some header files:

```
#define _XOPEN_SOURCE

#include <stdlib.h>
#include <unistd.h>
#include <stdio.h>
#include <string.h>

#include "cd_data.h"

#define TMP_STRING_LEN 125 /* this number must be larger than the biggest
                              single string in any database structure */
```

2. Make your menu options typedefs. This is in preference to using #defined constants, as it allows the compiler to check the types of the menu option variables:

```
typedef enum {
    mo_invalid,
    mo_add_cat,
    mo_add_tracks,
    mo_del_cat,
    mo_find_cat,
    mo_list_cat_tracks,
    mo_del_tracks,
    mo_count_entries,
    mo_exit
} menu_options;
```

3. Now write the prototypes for the local functions. Remember that the prototypes for actually accessing the database were included in cd_data.h:

```
static int command_mode(int argc, char *argv[]);
static void announce(void);
static menu_options show_menu(const cdc_entry *current_cdc);
static int get_confirm(const char *question);
static int enter_new_cat_entry(cdc_entry *entry_to_update);
static void enter_new_track_entries(const cdc_entry *entry_to_add_to);
static void del_cat_entry(const cdc_entry *entry_to_delete);
static void del_track_entries(const cdc_entry *entry_to_delete);
```

```
static cdc_entry find_cat(void);
static void list_tracks(const cdc_entry *entry_to_use);
static void count_all_entries(void);
static void display_cdc(const cdc_entry *cdc_to_show);
static void display_cdt(const cdt_entry *cdt_to_show);
static void strip_return(char *string_to_strip);
```

4. Finally, you get to main. This starts by ensuring that the current_cdc_entry, which you use to keep track of the currently selected CD catalog entry, is initialized. You also parse the command line, announce what program is being run, and initialize the database:

```
void main(int argc, char *argv[])
{
    menu_options current_option;
    cdc_entry current_cdc_entry;
    int command_result;

    memset(&current_cdc_entry, '\0', sizeof(current_cdc_entry));

    if (argc > 1) {
        command_result = command_mode(argc, argv);
        exit(command_result);
    }

    announce();

    if (!database_initialize(0)) {
        fprintf(stderr, "Sorry, unable to initialize database\n");
        fprintf(stderr, "To create a new database use %s -i\n", argv[0]);
        exit(EXIT_FAILURE);
    }
```

5. You're now ready to process user input. You sit in a loop, asking for a menu choice and processing it, until the user selects the exit option. Notice that you pass the current_cdc_entry structure to the show_menu function to allow the menu options to change if a catalog entry is currently selected:

```
while(current_option != mo_exit) {
        current_option = show_menu(&current_cdc_entry);

        switch(current_option) {
            case mo_add_cat:
                if (enter_new_cat_entry(&current_cdc_entry)) {
                    if (!add_cdc_entry(current_cdc_entry)) {
                        fprintf(stderr, "Failed to add new entry\n");
                        memset(&current_cdc_entry, '\0',
                                sizeof(current_cdc_entry));
                    }
                }
                break;
            case mo_add_tracks:
                enter_new_track_entries(&current_cdc_entry);
                break;
```

```
                    case mo_del_cat:
                        del_cat_entry(&current_cdc_entry);
                        break;
                    case mo_find_cat:
                        current_cdc_entry = find_cat();
                        break;
                    case mo_list_cat_tracks:
                        list_tracks(&current_cdc_entry);
                        break;
                    case mo_del_tracks:
                        del_track_entries(&current_cdc_entry);
                        break;
                    case mo_count_entries:
                        count_all_entries();
                        break;
                    case mo_exit:
                        break;
                    case mo_invalid:
                        break;
                    default:
                        break;
                } /* switch */
            } /* while */
```

6.   When the `main` loop exits, close the database and exit back to the environment. The welcoming sentence is printed by the `announce` function:

```
        database_close();
        exit(EXIT_SUCCESS);
    } /* main */

    static void announce(void)
    {
        printf("\n\nWelcome to the demonstration CD catalog database \
                program\n");
    }
```

7.   Here you implement the `show_menu` function. This function checks whether a current catalog entry is selected, using the first character of the catalog name. More options are available if a catalog entry is selected:

Note that numbers are now used to select menu items, rather than the initial letters used in the previous two examples.

```
static menu_options show_menu(const cdc_entry *cdc_selected)
{
    char tmp_str[TMP_STRING_LEN + 1];
    menu_options option_chosen = mo_invalid;

    while (option_chosen == mo_invalid) {
        if (cdc_selected->catalog[0]) {
```

```
            printf("\n\nCurrent entry: ");
            printf("%s, %s, %s, %s\n", cdc_selected->catalog,
                    cdc_selected->title,
                    cdc_selected->type,
                    cdc_selected->artist);

            printf("\n");
            printf("1 - add new CD\n");
            printf("2 - search for a CD\n");
            printf("3 - count the CDs and tracks in the database\n");
            printf("4 - re-enter tracks for current CD\n");
            printf("5 - delete this CD, and all its tracks\n");
            printf("6 - list tracks for this CD\n");
            printf("q - quit\n");
            printf("\nOption: ");
            fgets(tmp_str, TMP_STRING_LEN, stdin);

            switch(tmp_str[0]) {
                case '1': option_chosen = mo_add_cat; break;
                case '2': option_chosen = mo_find_cat; break;
                case '3': option_chosen = mo_count_entries; break;
                case '4': option_chosen = mo_add_tracks; break;
                case '5': option_chosen = mo_del_cat; break;
                case '6': option_chosen = mo_list_cat_tracks; break;
                case 'q': option_chosen = mo_exit; break;
            }
        }
        else {
            printf("\n\n");
            printf("1 - add new CD\n");
            printf("2 - search for a CD\n");
            printf("3 - count the CDs and tracks in the database\n");
            printf("q - quit\n");
            printf("\nOption: ");
            fgets(tmp_str, TMP_STRING_LEN, stdin);
            switch(tmp_str[0]) {
                case '1': option_chosen = mo_add_cat; break;
                case '2': option_chosen = mo_find_cat; break;
                case '3': option_chosen = mo_count_entries; break;
                case 'q': option_chosen = mo_exit; break;
            }
        }
    } /* while */
    return(option_chosen);
}
```

8. There are several places where you wish to ask the user if he is sure about what he requested. Rather than have several places in the code asking the question, extract the code as a separate function, get_confirm:

```
static int get_confirm(const char *question)
{
    char tmp_str[TMP_STRING_LEN + 1];
```

```
    printf("%s", question);
    fgets(tmp_str, TMP_STRING_LEN, stdin);
    if (tmp_str[0] == 'Y' || tmp_str[0] == 'y') {
        return(1);
    }
    return(0);
}
```

9. The function `enter_new_cat_entry` allows the user to enter a new catalog entry. You don't want to store the linefeed that `fgets` returns, so strip it off:

> Notice that you don't use the `gets` function, because you have no way of checking for an overflow of the buffer. Always avoid the `gets` function!

```
static int enter_new_cat_entry(cdc_entry *entry_to_update)
{
    cdc_entry new_entry;
    char tmp_str[TMP_STRING_LEN + 1];

    memset(&new_entry, '\0', sizeof(new_entry));

    printf("Enter catalog entry: ");
    (void)fgets(tmp_str, TMP_STRING_LEN, stdin);
    strip_return(tmp_str);
    strncpy(new_entry.catalog, tmp_str, CAT_CAT_LEN - 1);

    printf("Enter title: ");
    (void)fgets(tmp_str, TMP_STRING_LEN, stdin);
    strip_return(tmp_str);
    strncpy(new_entry.title, tmp_str, CAT_TITLE_LEN - 1);

    printf("Enter type: ");
    (void)fgets(tmp_str, TMP_STRING_LEN, stdin);
    strip_return(tmp_str);
    strncpy(new_entry.type, tmp_str, CAT_TYPE_LEN - 1);

    printf("Enter artist: ");
    (void)fgets(tmp_str, TMP_STRING_LEN, stdin);
    strip_return(tmp_str);
    strncpy(new_entry.artist, tmp_str, CAT_ARTIST_LEN - 1);

    printf("\nNew catalog entry entry is :-\n");
    display_cdc(&new_entry);
    if (get_confirm("Add this entry ?")) {
        memcpy(entry_to_update, &new_entry, sizeof(new_entry));
        return(1);
    }
    return(0);
}
```

10. Now you come to the function for entering the track information: `enter_new_track_entries`. This is slightly more complex than the catalog entry function because you allow an existing track entry to be left alone:

```c
static void enter_new_track_entries(const cdc_entry *entry_to_add_to)
{
    cdt_entry new_track, existing_track;
    char tmp_str[TMP_STRING_LEN + 1];
    int track_no = 1;
    if (entry_to_add_to->catalog[0] == '\0') return;

    printf("\nUpdating tracks for %s\n", entry_to_add_to->catalog);
    printf("Press return to leave existing description unchanged,\n");
    printf(" a single d to delete this and remaining tracks,\n");
    printf(" or new track description\n");

    while(1) {
```

11. First, you must check whether a track already exists with the current track number. Depending on what you find, you change the prompt:

```c
        memset(&new_track, '\0', sizeof(new_track));
        existing_track = get_cdt_entry(entry_to_add_to->catalog,
                                        track_no);
        if (existing_track.catalog[0]) {
            printf("\tTrack %d: %s\n", track_no,
                        existing_track.track_txt);
            printf("\tNew text: ");
        }
        else {
            printf("\tTrack %d description: ", track_no);
        }
        fgets(tmp_str, TMP_STRING_LEN, stdin);
        strip_return(tmp_str);
```

12. If there was no existing entry for this track and the user hasn't added one, assume that there are no more tracks to be added:

```c
        if (strlen(tmp_str) == 0) {
            if (existing_track.catalog[0] == '\0') {
                    /* no existing entry, so finished adding */
                break;
            }
            else {
                /* leave existing entry, jump to next track */
                track_no++;
                continue;
            }
        }
```

13. If the user enters a single d character, this deletes the current and any higher-numbered tracks. The del_cdt_entry function will return false if it can't find a track to delete:

```
if ((strlen(tmp_str) == 1) && tmp_str[0] == 'd') {
        /* delete this and remaining tracks */
    while (del_cdt_entry(entry_to_add_to->catalog, track_no)) {
        track_no++;
    }
    break;
}
```

14. Here you get to the code for adding a new track or updating an existing one. You construct the cdt_entry structure new_track, and then call the database function add_cdt_entry to add it to the database:

```
strncpy(new_track.track_txt, tmp_str, TRACK_TTEXT_LEN - 1);
strcpy(new_track.catalog, entry_to_add_to->catalog);
new_track.track_no = track_no;
if (!add_cdt_entry(new_track)) {
    fprintf(stderr, "Failed to add new track\n");
    break;
}
track_no++;
} /* while */
}
```

15. The function del_cat_entry deletes a catalog entry. Never allow tracks for a nonexistent catalog entry to exist:

```
static void del_cat_entry(const cdc_entry *entry_to_delete)
{
    int track_no = 1;
    int delete_ok;

    display_cdc(entry_to_delete);
    if (get_confirm("Delete this entry and all it's tracks? ")) {
        do {
            delete_ok = del_cdt_entry(entry_to_delete->catalog,
                                      track_no);
            track_no++;
        } while(delete_ok);

        if (!del_cdc_entry(entry_to_delete->catalog)) {
            fprintf(stderr, "Failed to delete entry\n");
        }
    }
}
```

16. The next function is a utility for deleting all the tracks for a catalog:

```
static void del_track_entries(const cdc_entry *entry_to_delete)
{
    int track_no = 1;
```

```
        int delete_ok;

    display_cdc(entry_to_delete);
    if (get_confirm("Delete tracks for this entry? ")) {
        do {
            delete_ok = del_cdt_entry(entry_to_delete->catalog, track_no);
            track_no++;
        } while(delete_ok);
    }
}
```

17. Create a very simple catalog search facility. You allow the user to enter a string, and then check for catalog entries that contain the string. Because there could be multiple entries that match, you simply offer the user each match in turn:

```
static cdc_entry find_cat(void)
{
    cdc_entry item_found;
    char tmp_str[TMP_STRING_LEN + 1];
    int first_call = 1;
    int any_entry_found = 0;
    int string_ok;
    int entry_selected = 0;

    do {
        string_ok = 1;
        printf("Enter string to search for in catalog entry: ");
        fgets(tmp_str, TMP_STRING_LEN, stdin);
        strip_return(tmp_str);
        if (strlen(tmp_str) > CAT_CAT_LEN) {
            fprintf(stderr, "Sorry, string too long, maximum %d \
                            characters\n", CAT_CAT_LEN);
            string_ok = 0;
        }
    } while (!string_ok);

    while (!entry_selected) {
        item_found = search_cdc_entry(tmp_str, &first_call);
        if (item_found.catalog[0] != '\0') {
            any_entry_found = 1;
            printf("\n");
            display_cdc(&item_found);
            if (get_confirm("This entry? ")) {
                entry_selected = 1;
            }
        }
        else {
            if (any_entry_found) printf("Sorry, no more matches found\n");
            else printf("Sorry, nothing found\n");
            break;
        }
    }
    return(item_found);
}
```

18. `list_tracks` is a utility function that prints out all the tracks for a given catalog entry:

```
static void list_tracks(const cdc_entry *entry_to_use)
{
    int track_no = 1;
    cdt_entry entry_found;

    display_cdc(entry_to_use);
    printf("\nTracks\n");
    do {
            entry_found = get_cdt_entry(entry_to_use->catalog,
                                        track_no);
            if (entry_found.catalog[0]) {
                display_cdt(&entry_found);
                track_no++;
            }
    } while(entry_found.catalog[0]);
    (void)get_confirm("Press return");
} /* list_tracks */
```

19. The `count_all_entries` function counts all the tracks:

```
static void count_all_entries(void)
{
    int cd_entries_found = 0;
    int track_entries_found = 0;
    cdc_entry cdc_found;
    cdt_entry cdt_found;
    int track_no = 1;
    int first_time = 1;
    char *search_string = "";

    do {
        cdc_found = search_cdc_entry(search_string, &first_time);
        if (cdc_found.catalog[0]) {
            cd_entries_found++;
            track_no = 1;
            do {
                cdt_found = get_cdt_entry(cdc_found.catalog, track_no);
                if (cdt_found.catalog[0]) {
                    track_entries_found++;
                    track_no++;
                }
            } while (cdt_found.catalog[0]);
        }
    } while (cdc_found.catalog[0]);

    printf("Found %d CDs, with a total of %d tracks\n", cd_entries_found,
                track_entries_found);
    (void)get_confirm("Press return");
}
```

20. Now you have `display_cdc`, a utility for displaying a catalog entry:

```
static void display_cdc(const cdc_entry *cdc_to_show)
{
    printf("Catalog: %s\n", cdc_to_show->catalog);
    printf("\ttitle: %s\n", cdc_to_show->title);
    printf("\ttype: %s\n", cdc_to_show->type);
    printf("\tartist: %s\n", cdc_to_show->artist);
}
```

and `display_cdt`, for displaying a single track entry:

```
static void display_cdt(const cdt_entry *cdt_to_show)
{
    printf("%d: %s\n", cdt_to_show->track_no, cdt_to_show->track_txt);
}
```

21. The utility function `strip_return` removes a trailing linefeed character from a string. Remember that Linux, like UNIX, uses a single linefeed to indicate end of line:

```
static void strip_return(char *string_to_strip)
{
    int len;

    len = strlen(string_to_strip);
    if (string_to_strip[len - 1] == '\n') string_to_strip[len - 1] = '\0';
}
```

22. `command_mode` is a function for parsing the command-line arguments. The `getopt` function is a good way of ensuring that your program accepts arguments conforming to the standard Linux conventions:

```
static int command_mode(int argc, char *argv[])
{
    int c;
    int result = EXIT_SUCCESS;
    char *prog_name = argv[0];

    /* these externals used by getopt */
    extern char *optarg;
    extern optind, opterr, optopt;

    while ((c = getopt(argc, argv, ":i")) != -1) {
        switch(c) {
            case 'i':
                if (!database_initialize(1)) {
                    result = EXIT_FAILURE;
                    fprintf(stderr, "Failed to initialize database\n");
                }
                break;
            case ':':
            case '?':
            default:
```

```
                        fprintf(stderr, "Usage: %s [-i]\n", prog_name);
                        result = EXIT_FAILURE;
                        break;
            } /* switch */
      } /* while */
      return(result);
}
```

Try It Out   cd_access.c

Now you come to the functions that access the dbm database:

1. As usual, you start with some #include files. You then use some #defines for specifying the files that you'll use for storing the data:

```c
#define _XOPEN_SOURCE

#include <unistd.h>
#include <stdlib.h>
#include <stdio.h>
#include <fcntl.h>
#include <string.h>

#include <ndbm.h>
/* The above may need to be changed to gdbm-ndbm.h on some distributions */

#include "cd_data.h"

#define CDC_FILE_BASE "cdc_data"
#define CDT_FILE_BASE "cdt_data"
#define CDC_FILE_DIR  "cdc_data.dir"
#define CDC_FILE_PAG  "cdc_data.pag"
#define CDT_FILE_DIR "cdt_data.dir"
#define CDT_FILE_PAG "cdt_data.pag"
```

2. Use these two file scope variables to keep track of the current database:

```c
static DBM *cdc_dbm_ptr = NULL;
static DBM *cdt_dbm_ptr = NULL;
```

3. By default, the database_initialize function opens an existing database, but by passing a nonzero (i.e., true) parameter, new_database, you can force it to create a new (empty) database, effectively removing any existing database. If the database is successfully initialized, the two database pointers are also initialized, indicating that a database is open:

```c
int database_initialize(const int new_database)
{
    int open_mode = O_CREAT | O_RDWR;

    /* If any existing database is open then close it */
    if (cdc_dbm_ptr) dbm_close(cdc_dbm_ptr);
```

```
        if (cdt_dbm_ptr) dbm_close(cdt_dbm_ptr);

        if (new_database) {
            /* delete the old files */
            (void) unlink(CDC_FILE_PAG);
            (void) unlink(CDC_FILE_DIR);
            (void) unlink(CDT_FILE_PAG);
            (void) unlink(CDT_FILE_DIR);
        }

        /* Open some new files, creating them if required */
        cdc_dbm_ptr = dbm_open(CDC_FILE_BASE, open_mode, 0644);
        cdt_dbm_ptr = dbm_open(CDT_FILE_BASE, open_mode, 0644);
        if (!cdc_dbm_ptr || !cdt_dbm_ptr) {
            fprintf(stderr, "Unable to create database\n");
            cdc_dbm_ptr = cdt_dbm_ptr = NULL;
            return (0);
        }
        return (1);
}
```

4.   database_close simply closes the database if it was open and sets the two database pointers
to null to indicate that no database is currently open:

```
void database_close(void)
{
    if (cdc_dbm_ptr) dbm_close(cdc_dbm_ptr);
    if (cdt_dbm_ptr) dbm_close(cdt_dbm_ptr);

    cdc_dbm_ptr = cdt_dbm_ptr = NULL;
}
```

5.   Next, you have a function that retrieves a single catalog entry when passed a pointer pointing to
a catalog text string. If the entry isn't found, the returned data has an empty catalog field:

```
cdc_entry get_cdc_entry(const char *cd_catalog_ptr)
{
    cdc_entry entry_to_return;
    char entry_to_find[CAT_CAT_LEN + 1];
    datum local_data_datum;
    datum local_key_datum;

    memset(&entry_to_return, '\0', sizeof(entry_to_return));
```

6.   Start with some sanity checks, to ensure that a database is open and that you were passed
reasonable parameters — that is, the search key contains only the valid string and nulls:

```
        if (!cdc_dbm_ptr || !cdt_dbm_ptr) return (entry_to_return);
        if (!cd_catalog_ptr) return (entry_to_return);
        if (strlen(cd_catalog_ptr) >= CAT_CAT_LEN) return (entry_to_return);

        memset(&entry_to_find, '\0', sizeof(entry_to_find));
        strcpy(entry_to_find, cd_catalog_ptr);
```

7. Set up the `datum` structure the `dbm` functions require, and then use `dbm_fetch` to retrieve the data. If no data was retrieved, you return the empty `entry_to_return` structure that you initialized earlier:

```
    local_key_datum.dptr = (void *) entry_to_find;
    local_key_datum.dsize = sizeof(entry_to_find);

    memset(&local_data_datum, '\0', sizeof(local_data_datum));
    local_data_datum = dbm_fetch(cdc_dbm_ptr, local_key_datum);
    if (local_data_datum.dptr) {
        memcpy(&entry_to_return, (char *)local_data_datum.dptr,
                local_data_datum.dsize);
    }
    return (entry_to_return);
} /* get_cdc_entry */
```

8. You'd better be able to get a single track entry as well, which is what the next function does, in the same fashion as `get_cdc_entry`, but with a pointer pointing to a catalog string and a track number as parameters:

```
cdt_entry get_cdt_entry(const char *cd_catalog_ptr, const int track_no)
{
    cdt_entry entry_to_return;
    char entry_to_find[CAT_CAT_LEN + 10];
    datum local_data_datum;
    datum local_key_datum;

    memset(&entry_to_return, '\0', sizeof(entry_to_return));

    if (!cdc_dbm_ptr || !cdt_dbm_ptr) return (entry_to_return);
    if (!cd_catalog_ptr) return (entry_to_return);
    if (strlen(cd_catalog_ptr) >= CAT_CAT_LEN) return (entry_to_return);
    /* set up the search key, which is a composite key of catalog entry
       and track number */
    memset(&entry_to_find, '\0', sizeof(entry_to_find));
    sprintf(entry_to_find, "%s %d", cd_catalog_ptr, track_no);

    local_key_datum.dptr = (void *) entry_to_find;
    local_key_datum.dsize = sizeof(entry_to_find);

    memset(&local_data_datum, '\0', sizeof(local_data_datum));
    local_data_datum = dbm_fetch(cdt_dbm_ptr, local_key_datum);
    if (local_data_datum.dptr) {
        memcpy(&entry_to_return, (char *) local_data_datum.dptr,
                local_data_datum.dsize);
    }
    return (entry_to_return);
}
```

9. The next function, `add_cdc_entry`, adds a new catalog entry:

```
int add_cdc_entry(const cdc_entry entry_to_add)
{
    char key_to_add[CAT_CAT_LEN + 1];
```

```
        datum local_data_datum;
        datum local_key_datum;
        int result;

        /* check database initialized and parameters valid */
        if (!cdc_dbm_ptr || !cdt_dbm_ptr) return (0);
        if (strlen(entry_to_add.catalog) >= CAT_CAT_LEN) return (0);

        /* ensure the search key contains only the valid string and nulls */
        memset(&key_to_add, '\0', sizeof(key_to_add));
        strcpy(key_to_add, entry_to_add.catalog);

        local_key_datum.dptr = (void *) key_to_add;
        local_key_datum.dsize = sizeof(key_to_add);
        local_data_datum.dptr = (void *) &entry_to_add;
        local_data_datum.dsize = sizeof(entry_to_add);

        result = dbm_store(cdc_dbm_ptr, local_key_datum, local_data_datum,
                           DBM_REPLACE);

        /* dbm_store() uses 0 for success */
        if (result == 0) return (1);
        return (0);
}
```

10. add_cdt_entry adds a new track entry. The access key is the catalog string and track number acting as a composite:

```
int add_cdt_entry(const cdt_entry entry_to_add)
{
    char key_to_add[CAT_CAT_LEN + 10];
    datum local_data_datum;
    datum local_key_datum;
    int result;

    if (!cdc_dbm_ptr || !cdt_dbm_ptr) return (0);
    if (strlen(entry_to_add.catalog) >= CAT_CAT_LEN) return (0);

    memset(&key_to_add, '\0', sizeof(key_to_add));
    sprintf(key_to_add, "%s %d", entry_to_add.catalog,
                entry_to_add.track_no);

    local_key_datum.dptr = (void *) key_to_add;
    local_key_datum.dsize = sizeof(key_to_add);
    local_data_datum.dptr = (void *) &entry_to_add;
    local_data_datum.dsize = sizeof(entry_to_add);

    result = dbm_store(cdt_dbm_ptr, local_key_datum, local_data_datum,
                       DBM_REPLACE);

    /* dbm_store() uses 0 for success and -ve numbers for errors */
    if (result == 0)
        return (1);
    return (0);
}
```

11. If you can add things, you'd better be able to delete them, too. This function deletes catalog entries:

```
int del_cdc_entry(const char *cd_catalog_ptr)
{
    char key_to_del[CAT_CAT_LEN + 1];
    datum local_key_datum;
    int result;

    if (!cdc_dbm_ptr || !cdt_dbm_ptr) return (0);
    if (strlen(cd_catalog_ptr) >= CAT_CAT_LEN) return (0);

    memset(&key_to_del, '\0', sizeof(key_to_del));
    strcpy(key_to_del, cd_catalog_ptr);

    local_key_datum.dptr = (void *) key_to_del;
    local_key_datum.dsize = sizeof(key_to_del);

    result = dbm_delete(cdc_dbm_ptr, local_key_datum);

    /* dbm_delete() uses 0 for success */
    if (result == 0) return (1);
    return (0);
}
```

12. Here's the equivalent function for deleting a track. Remember that the track key is a composite index of both the catalog entry string and the track number:

```
int del_cdt_entry(const char *cd_catalog_ptr, const int track_no)
{
    char key_to_del[CAT_CAT_LEN + 10];
    datum local_key_datum;
    int result;

    if (!cdc_dbm_ptr || !cdt_dbm_ptr) return (0);
    if (strlen(cd_catalog_ptr) >= CAT_CAT_LEN) return (0);

    memset(&key_to_del, '\0', sizeof(key_to_del));
    sprintf(key_to_del, "%s %d", cd_catalog_ptr, track_no);

    local_key_datum.dptr = (void *) key_to_del;
    local_key_datum.dsize = sizeof(key_to_del);

    result = dbm_delete(cdt_dbm_ptr, local_key_datum);

    /* dbm_delete() uses 0 for success */
    if (result == 0) return (1);
    return (0);
}
```

13. Last but not least, you have a simple search function. It's not very sophisticated, but it does demonstrate how you can scan through dbm entries without knowing the keys in advance.

Since you don't know in advance how many entries there might be, you implement this function to return a single entry on each call. If nothing is found, the entry will be empty. To scan the whole database, start by calling this function with a pointer to an integer, `*first_call_ptr`, which should be 1 the first time the function is called. This function then knows it should start searching at the start of the database. On subsequent calls, the variable is 0 and the function resumes searching after the last entry it found.

When you wish to restart your search, probably with a different catalog entry, you must again call this function with `*first_call_ptr` set to true, which reinitializes the search.

Between calls, the function maintains some internal state information. This hides the complexity of continuing a search from the client and preserves the "secrecy" of how the search function is implemented.

If the search text points to a `null` character, then all entries are considered to match.

```
cdc_entry search_cdc_entry(const char *cd_catalog_ptr, int *first_call_ptr)
{
    static int local_first_call = 1;
    cdc_entry entry_to_return;
    datum local_data_datum;
    static datum local_key_datum;     /* notice this must be static */

    memset(&entry_to_return, '\0', sizeof(entry_to_return));
```

14. As usual, start with sanity checks:

```
    if (!cdc_dbm_ptr || !cdt_dbm_ptr) return (entry_to_return);
    if (!cd_catalog_ptr || !first_call_ptr) return (entry_to_return);
    if (strlen(cd_catalog_ptr) >= CAT_CAT_LEN) return (entry_to_return);

    /* protect against never passing *first_call_ptr true */
    if (local_first_call) {
        local_first_call = 0;
        *first_call_ptr = 1;
    }
```

15. If this function has been called with `*first_call_ptr` set to true, you need to start (or restart) searching from the beginning of the database. If `*first_call_ptr` isn't true, then simply move on to the next key in the database:

```
    if (*first_call_ptr) {
        *first_call_ptr = 0;
        local_key_datum = dbm_firstkey(cdc_dbm_ptr);
    }
    else {
        local_key_datum = dbm_nextkey(cdc_dbm_ptr);
    }

    do {
        if (local_key_datum.dptr != NULL) {
            /* an entry was found */
            local_data_datum = dbm_fetch(cdc_dbm_ptr, local_key_datum);
            if (local_data_datum.dptr) {
                memcpy(&entry_to_return, (char *) local_data_datum.dptr,
                        local_data_datum.dsize);
```

16. The search facility is a very simple check to see whether the search string occurs in the current catalog entry:

```
                /* check if search string occurs in the entry */
                if (!strstr(entry_to_return.catalog, cd_catalog_ptr))
                    {
                    memset(&entry_to_return, '\0',
                                    sizeof(entry_to_return));
                    local_key_datum = dbm_nextkey(cdc_dbm_ptr);
                    }
                }
            }
        } while (local_key_datum.dptr &&
            local_data_datum.dptr &&
            (entry_to_return.catalog[0] == '\0'));
    return (entry_to_return);
} /* search_cdc_entry */
```

You're now in a position to be able to put everything together with this makefile. Don't worry about it too much right now, because you'll be looking at how it works in the next chapter. For the time being, type it and save it as Makefile:

```
all:    application


INCLUDE=/usr/include/gdbm
LIBS=gdbm
# On some distributions you may need to change the above line to include
# the compatability library, as shown below.
# LIBS= -lgdbm_compat -lgdbm
CFLAGS=

app_ui.o: app_ui.c cd_data.h
    gcc $(CFLAGS) -c app_ui.c

access.o: access.c cd_data.h
    gcc $(CFLAGS) -I$(INCLUDE) -c access.c

application:    app_ui.o access.o
    gcc $(CFLAGS) -o application app_ui.o access.o -l$(LIBS)


clean:
    rm -f application *.o

nodbmfiles:
    rm -f *.dir *.pag
```

To compile your new CD application, type this at the prompt:

$ **make**

If all has gone well, the application executable will be compiled and placed in the current directory.

Summary

In this chapter, you learned about three aspects of data management. First, you learned about the Linux memory system and how simple it is to use, even though the internal implementation of demand paged virtual memory is quite involved. You also saw how it protects both the operating system and other programs from attempts at illegal memory access.

We then moved on to look at how file locking enables multiple programs to cooperate in their access to data. You looked first at a simple binary semaphore scheme and then at a more complex situation in which you lock different parts of a file for either shared or exclusive access. Next you looked at the dbm library and its ability to store and efficiently retrieve arbitrary blocks of data using a very flexible indexing arrangement.

Finally, we redesigned and reimplemented the example CD database application to use the dbm library as its data storage technique.

MySQL

Now that you've explored some basic data management using flat files and then the simple but very quick dbm, you're ready to move on to a more full-featured data tool: the RDBMS, or Relational Database Management System.

The two best-known Open Source RDBMS applications are probably PostgreSQL and MySQL, although there are many others. There are also many commercial RDBMS products, such as Oracle, Sybase, and DB2, all of which are highly capable and run on multiple platforms. The Windows-only Microsoft SQL Server is another popular choice in the commercial marketplace. All these packages have their particular strengths; but for reasons of space, and a commitment to Open Source software, this book focuses exclusively on MySQL.

MySQL has origins going back to about 1984, but it has been commercially developed and managed under the auspices of MySQL AB for several years now. Because MySQL is Open Source, its terms of use are often confused with those of other Open Source projects. It's worth pointing out that although MySQL can be used under the GNU General Public License (GPL) in many circumstances, there are circumstances where you must buy a commercial license to use the product. You should check the license requirements on the MySQL website (www.mysql.com) carefully, and determine which edition of MySQL is applicable to your requirements.

If you need an Open Source database and the terms for using MySQL under the GPL are not acceptable, and if you don't want to purchase a commercial license, then the licensing terms for using PostgreSQL are, at the time of writing, much less restrictive, so you may want to consider the highly capable PostgreSQL database as an alternative. You can find details at www.postgresql.org.

> *To learn more about PostgreSQL, check out our book,* Beginning Databases with PostgreSQL: From Novice to Professional, Second Edition *(Apress, 2005, ISBN 1590594789).*

This chapter covers the following MySQL topics:

- ❑ Installing MySQL
- ❑ The administrative commands necessary to work with MySQL
- ❑ Basic MySQL features

❑   The API for interfacing your C programs with MySQL databases

❑   Creating a relational database that you can use for your CD database application using C

Installation

Whatever your preferred flavor of Linux, it's likely that a version of MySQL is available pre-built and ready to install. For example, Red Hat, SUSE, and Ubuntu all have pre-built packages available in their current distributions. In general we recommend you use one of the pre-built versions because this will provide the easiest way to get up and running with MySQL quickly. If your distribution does not provide a MySQL package, or if you want to get the most current release, you can download binary and source packages from the MySQL website.

In this chapter we address installing only pre-built versions of MySQL.

MySQL Packages

If for any reason you need to download MySQL rather than using a bundled version, for the purposes of this book you should be able to use the community edition Standard build. You will see some Max and Debug packages are also available. The Max package contains additional features, such as support for more unusual storage file types and advanced features such as clustering. The Debug packages have been compiled with additional debugging code and information; hopefully you will not need such low-level debugging.

> *Don't use the Debug versions for production use; the performance is degraded by the additional debug support.*

For developing MySQL applications you need to install not only the server, but also the development libraries. Generally you should find your package manager has a MySQL option; you just need to ensure that the development libraries are also installed. In Figure 8-1, you can see Fedora's package manager ready to install MySQL, with the additional development package selected ready for install.

On other distributions the arrangement of packages is slightly different. For example, Figure 8-2 shows Ubuntu's synaptic package manager ready to install MySQL.

The MySQL installation also creates the user "mysql", which by default is the user name that the MySQL server demon runs as.

After you have the packages installed, you need to check if MySQL has been automatically started for you. At the time of writing some distributions such as Ubuntu do this, whereas others, such as Fedora, do not. Fortunately it's very easy to check if the MySQL server is running:

```
$ ps -el | grep mysqld
```

If you see one or more `mysqld` processes running, the server has been started. On many systems you will also see `safe_mysqld`, which is a utility used to start the actual `mysqld` process under the correct user id.

If you need to start (or restart or stop) the MySQL server, you can use the GUI services control panel. Fedora's Service Configuration panel is shown in Figure 8-3.

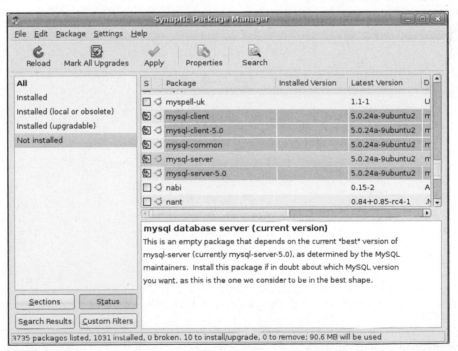

Figure 8-1

Figure 8-2

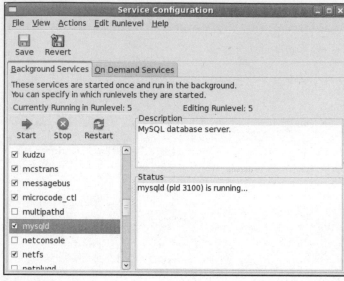

Figure 8-3

You should also use the service configuration editor to determine if you want the MySQL server to auto-matically start each time Linux starts.

Post-Install Configuration

Assuming everything went correctly, MySQL is now installed and started with a common default set of options. You can test that assumption:

```
$ mysql -u root mysql
```

If you get a "Welcome to the MySQL monitor" message and then a mysql> prompt, the server is running. Of course, at the moment anyone can connect to the server and have administrator privileges, but we address that shortly. Try typing \s to get some additional information on your server. When you've seen enough, type quit, or \q, to exit the monitor.

You can get more information by using the mysql -? command, which prints even more details about the server. In the output there is one important thing to check for. After the list of arguments, you will usually see something like Default options are read from the following files in the given order:. This tells you where to find the configuration file that you will use if you need to config-ure your MySQL server. The usual configuration file is /etc/my.cnf, though some distributions, like Ubuntu, use /etc/mysql/my.cnf.

You can also check the status of a running server with the mysqladmin command:

```
$ mysqladmin -u root version
```

The output will serve not only to confirm that the server is running but also to give you the version number of the server you are using.

Another very useful thing you can do with mysqladmin is to check all the configuration options in the running server, using the variables option:

```
$ mysqladmin variables
```

This will print a long list of variable settings. A couple of particularly useful ones are datadir, which tells you where MySQL is storing its data, and have_innodb, which is usually YES, indicating that the InnoDB storage engine is supported. MySQL supports a number of *storage engines*, that is, underlying implementation handlers for data storage. The most common (and most useful) two are InnoDB and MyISAM, but there are others, such as a memory engine, which doesn't use permenant storage at all, and the CSV engine, which uses comma-separated variable files. The different engines have different features and performance. InnoDB is the storage engine we would currently recommend for general-purpose database usage, because it has a good compromise between performance and support for enforcing relationships between different data elements. If you don't have InnoDB support enabled, check the configuration file /etc/my.cnf, and comment out the line skip-innodb by putting a hash mark at the start of the line, and use the service editor to restart MySQL. If this doesn't work you may have a version of MySQL that was compiled without InnoDB support. Check the MySQL website for a version supporting InnoDB if this is important to you. For the purposes of this chapter it shouldn't matter if you use the alternative MyISAM storage engine, which is the default engine in many distributions.

Once you know that InnoDB support is included in your server binary, to make it the default storage engine you must configure it as such in the /etc/my.cnf file, or by default the MyISAM engine will be used. The edit is very simple; in the mysqld section add an additional line reading default-storage-engine=INNODB. For example, the start of the file would now look something like this:

```
[mysqld]
default-storage-engine=INNOD
datadir=/var/lib/mysql
...
```

For the rest of this chapter we assume that the default storage engine has been set to InnoDB.

In a production environment you will also normally want to change the default storage location, specified by the datadir variable setting. This is also done by editing the mysqld section of the /etc/my.cnf configuration file. For example, if you are using the InnoDB storage engine, to put the data files on /vol02 and the log files on /vol03, plus give the data file an initial size of 10M but allow it to extend, you could use configuration lines such as:

```
innodb_data_home_dir = /vol02/mysql/data
innodb_data_file_path = ibdata1:10M:autoextend
innodb_log_group_home_dir = /vol03/mysql/logs
```

You can find more details and other configuration options in the online manuals on the www.mysql.com website.

> *If the server won't start or you can't connect to the database once it does start, see the next section to troubleshoot your installation.*

OK, remember that gaping security hole a few paragraphs back that allowed anyone to connect as root with no password? Now is a good time to make things more secure. Don't let yourself be confused by the name of the root user in a MySQL installation. There is no relationship between the MySQL root user and the system root user; MySQL simply defaults to having a user called "root" as the administration user, like Linux does. The users of a MySQL database and Linux user IDs are not related; MySQL has its own built-in user and permission management. By default, any user with an account on your Linux installation can log in to your MySQL server as the MySQL administrator. Once you've tightened down the MySQL root user permissions, such as allowing only a local user to log in as root and to set a password for this access, you can add only the users and permissions that are absolutely necessary to the functioning of your application.

Any number of ways will suffice to set a root password, most easily using the command

```
$ mysqladmin -u root password newpassword
```

This will set an initial password of *newpassword*.

This method poses a problem, however, in that the clear text password will be left behind in your shell history and could have been seen by someone using the ps command while your command was executing, or may possibly be recovered from your command history. A better method is to use the MySQL monitor again, this time to send some SQL that will change your password.

```
$ mysql -u root
Welcome to the MySQL monitor.  Commands end with ; or \g.
Your MySQL connection id is 4

Type 'help;' or '\h' for help. Type '\c' to clear the buffer.

mysql> SET password=PASSWORD('secretpassword');
Query OK, 0 rows affected (0.00 sec)
```

Pick, of course, a password known only to yourself, not the example "secretpassword" that we used here to show you where your own password needs to be entered. If you ever want to remove the password again, you can simply give an empty string in place of "secretpassword", and the password will be deleted.

Notice that we terminate SQL commands with a semicolon (;). This is not, strictly speaking, part of the actual SQL command; it is used to tell the MySQL client program that we are ready for our SQL statement to be executed. We also use uppercase for SQL keywords, such as SET. This is not necessary, because the actual syntax of MySQL allows keywords in either upper- or lowercase, but we use it as a convention in this book, as well as in our day jobs, because we find it makes the SQL easier to read.

Now have a look at the permissions table to verify that a password has been set. First switch to the mysql database, with the use command, and then query the internal tables:

```
mysql> use mysql
mysql> SELECT user, host, password FROM user;
+------+-----------+------------------+
| user | host      | password         |
+------+-----------+------------------+
| root | localhost | 2dxf8e9c23age6ed |
| root | fc7blp4e  |                  |
|      | localhost |                  |
|      | fc7blp4e  |                  |
+------+-----------+------------------+
```

```
4 rows in set (0.01 sec)

mysql>
```

Observe that you have created a password for root only when connecting from the `localhost`. MySQL can store distinct privileges not only for users, but also for connection classes based on host name. The next step in securing your installation will be to get rid of those unnecessary users that MySQL installed by default. The following command will remove all nonroot users from the permissions table:

```
mysql> DELETE FROM user WHERE user != 'root';
Query OK, 2 rows affected (0.01 sec)
```

The next command deletes any login from a host other than `localhost`:

```
mysql> DELETE FROM user WHERE host != 'localhost';
Query OK, 1 row affected (0.01 sec)
```

Last, use the following command to check that there are no stray logins:

```
mysql> SELECT user, host, password FROM user;
+------+-----------+------------------+
| user | host      | password         |
+------+-----------+------------------+
| root | localhost | 2dxf8e9c23age6ed |
+------+-----------+------------------+
1 row in set (0.00 sec)

mysql>exit
```

As you can see from the preceding output, you now have a single login that can connect from only `localhost`.

Now for the moment of truth: Can you still log in using the password you set? This time you give the -p parameter, which tells MySQL that it must prompt for a password:

```
$ mysql -u root -p
Enter password:
Welcome to the MySQL monitor.  Commands end with ; or \g.
Your MySQL connection id is 7

Type 'help;' or '\h' for help. Type '\c' to clear the buffer.

mysql>
```

You now have a running version of MySQL that is locked down so that only the root user, with a password you have set, can connect to the database server, and that the root user can connect from only the local machine. It is possible to connect to MySQL and provide the password on the command line. You do this by using the parameter --password, for example --password=secretpassword, or by -psecretpassword, but obviously this is less secure, because the password might be seen by a ps command, or retrieved from command history. However, providing the password on the command line can sometimes be necessary if you are writing scripts that need to connect to MySQL.

The next step is to add back in the user, or users, you require. As with a Linux system, it's a bad idea to use the root account to log in to MySQL unless it's absolutely necessary, so you should create an every-day user for normal use.

As we hinted earlier, you can create users with different connect permissions from different machines; in the example, the root user is allowed to connect from only the local machine as a security measure. For the purposes of this chapter, you are going to create a new user, rick, with fairly wide-ranging permissions. rick will be able to connect in three different ways:

❑ He can connect from the local host.

❑ He can connect from any machine with IP addresses in the range 192.168.0.0 through to 192.168.0.255.

❑ He can connect from any machine in the wiley.com domain.

The easiest way of doing this in a secure manner is to create three different users with three different connection origins. They could, if you wanted, even have three different passwords, depending on which network address they are connecting from.

You create users and assign them privileges by using the grant command. Here you create the user with the three connection origins just listed. The IDENTIFIED BY is slightly odd syntax for setting an initial password. Notice the way quotes are used; it's important to use the single quote characters exactly as shown or you will not create the users exactly as intended.

Connect to MySQL as the root user and then perform the following sequence:

1. Create a local login for rick:

```
mysql> GRANT ALL ON *.* TO rick@localhost IDENTIFIED BY 'secretpassword';
Query OK, 0 rows affected (0.03 sec)
```

2. Then create a login from anywhere on the class C subnet of 192.168.0. Notice that you must use single quotes to protect the IP range, and use a mask /255.255.255.0 to identify the range of IP addresses that are allowed:

```
mysql> GRANT ALL ON *.* TO rick@'192.168.0.0/255.255.255.0' IDENTIFIED BY
'secretpassword';
Query OK, 0 rows affected (0.00 sec)
```

3. Finally, create a login so that rick can log on from any machine in the wiley.com domain (again notice the single quotes):

```
mysql> GRANT ALL ON *.* TO rick@'%.wiley.com' IDENTIFIED BY 'secretpassword';
Query OK, 0 rows affected (0.00 sec)
```

4.   Now look again at the user table to double-check the entries:

```
mysql> SELECT user, host, password FROM mysql.user;
+------+-------------------------+------------------+
| user | host                    | password         |
+------+-------------------------+------------------+
| root | localhost               | 2dxf8e8c17ade6ed |
| rick | localhost               | 3742g6348q8378d9 |
| rick | %.wiley.com             | 3742g6348q8378d9 |
| rick | 192.168.0.0/255.255.255.0 | 3742g6348q8378d9 |
+------+-------------------------+------------------+
4 rows in set (0.00 sec)

mysql>
```

Naturally, you need to adjust the preceding commands and passwords to suit your local configuration. You will notice the GRANT ALL ON *.* command, which as you probably surmised gave user rick pretty widespread permissions. That's fine for a power user but won't work for creating more restricted users. We discuss the grant command in more detail in the "Creating Users and Giving Them Permissions" section in this chapter, where, among other things, we show you how to create a more restricted user.

Now that you have MySQL up and running (if not, see the next section), have made the installation more secure, and have a non-root user created ready to do some work with, we briefly discuss troubleshooting after installation and then go back briefly and take a lightning tour through the essentials of MySQL database administration.

Post-Installation Troubleshooting

If the connection failed when you used mysql, check that the server process is running using the system ps command. If you can't find it in the list, try launching mysql_safed -log. This should write a file to MySQL's log directory with some additional information. You can also try starting the mysqld process directly; use mysqld --verbose --help for a full list of command-line options.

It's also possible that the server is running, but simply refusing your connection. If so, the next item to check will be the presence of a database, in particular the default MySQL permissions database. The location /var/lib/mysql is commonly used by default for Red Hat distributions, but other distributions use varying locations. Check the MySQL startup script (for example, in /etc/init.d) and the configuration file /etc/my.cnf. Alternatively, invoke the program directly, using mysqld --verbose -help, and look for the variable datadir. Once you find the database directory, verify that it contains at least a default permissions database (called mysql) and that the server demon is using this location as specified in my.cnf.

If you're still not connecting, use the service editor to stop the server, check that no mysqld process is running, and then restart it and try connecting again. In the unlikely event you are still not getting anywhere, you could try totally uninstalling MySQL and re-installing from scratch. Also very helpful is the MySQL documentation on the MySQL website (which is always more current than the local manual pages, plus it has some user-edited hints and suggestions, as well as a forum) to explore some of the more esoteric possibilities.

MySQL Administration

A handful of the utility programs included with the MySQL distribution facilitate administration. The most commonly used of these is the `mysqladmin` program. We cover this utility and the others in the following section.

Commands

All of the MySQL commands except `mysqlshow` take at least three standard parameters:

Command Option	Parameter	Description
-u	username	By default `mysql utilities` will attempt to use the same MySQL `username` as your current Linux user name. Use the -u parameter to specify a different user name.
-p	[password]	If -p is given but the password is omitted, the password is prompted for. If the -p parameter is not present, MySQL commands assume no password is needed.
-h	host	Used to connect to a server on a different host (can always be omitted for local servers).

> **Again, we recommend you avoid putting a password on the command line, because it can be seen by the `ps` command.**

myisamchk

The `myisamchk` utility is designed to check and repair any data tables using the default MYISAM table format natively supported by MySQL. Normally, `myisamchk` should be run as the `mysql` user created at installation from the directory in which the tables reside. In order to check a database, do `su mysql`, change into the directory name corresponding to the name of the database; and run `myisamchk` with one or more of the options suggested by the following table. For example,

```
myisamchk -e -r *.MYI
```

The most common command options for `myisamchk` are shown in the following table:

Command option	Description
-c	Check the table for errors.
-e	Perform an extended check.
-r	Recover (correct) errors found.

Again, for more information, you can invoke `myisamchk` with no parameters and look through the extensive help messages. This utility has no effect on InnoDB type tables.

mysql

This is the principal, and very powerful, MySQL command-line tool. Almost every administrative or user-level task can be performed here in one way or another. You can start `mysql` from the command line; by adding a final additional parameter, a database name, you can bypass the `use <database>` command from within the monitor. For example, to start the monitor as user `rick`, prompt for a password (notice the space after -p) and using database `foo` as the default:

```
$ mysql -u rick -p foo
```

Use `mysql --help | less` to page through a list of other command-line options for the `mysql` monitor.

If you start MySQL without specifying a database, you can use the `use <databasename>` option from within MySQL to select one, as you can see from the list of commands in the next table.

Alternatively, you can run `mysql` in a non-interactive mode by bundling commands into an input file and reading it in from the command line. In this case you have to specify the password on the command line:

```
$ mysql -u rick --password=secretpassword foo < sqlcommands.sql
```

Once `mysql` has read and processed your commands, it will return to the command prompt.

While the `mysql` client is connected to the server, a number of specific commands in addition to the standard SQL92 set are supported, as shown in the following table:

Command	Alternative Short Form	Description
help or ?	\h or \?	Displays a list of commands.
edit	\e	Edit the command. The editor used is determined by the environment variable $EDITOR.
exit or quit	\q	Exit the MySQL client.
go	\g	Execute the command.
source <filename>	\.	Execute SQL from the given file.
status	\s	Display server status information.
system <command>	\!	Execute a system command.
tee <filename>	\T	Append a copy of all output to the given filename.
use <database>	\u	Use the given database.

A very important command in this set is use. The mysqld server supports the idea of having many different databases, all served and managed by the same server process. Many other database servers, such as Oracle and Sybase, use the terminology *schema*, whereas MySQL more frequently uses *database*. (The MySQL Query Browser uses *schema*, for example). Each database (in MySQL terminology) is a mostly independent set of tables. This enables you to set up different databases for different purposes, and assign different users to different databases, all while using the same database server to efficiently manage them. Using the use command, you can, if you have appropriate permissions, switch between different databases.

The special database *mysql*, which is automatically created with every MySQL installation, is used as a master repository for data like users and permissions.

> SQL92 is the most widely used version of the ANSI SQL standard. Its purpose is to create uniformity for how SQL databases work, facilitating interoperability and communication among different database products.

mysqladmin

This utility is the principal tool for quick MySQL database administration. In addition to the usual parameters, the principal commands it supports are:

Command	Description
create <database_name>	Create a new database.
drop <database_name>	Delete a database.
password <new_password>	Change a password (as you saw earlier).
ping	Check that the server is running.
reload	Reload the grant tables that control permissions.
status	Provide the status of the server.
shutdown	Shut down the server.
variables	Show the variables that control MySQL operation and their current values.
version	Provide the version number of the server and how long it has been running.

Invoke mysqladmin without any parameters to see the full list of options from the command prompt. You'll want to use | less.

mysqlbug

With a little luck, you'll never have the opportunity to use this. As the name implies, this tool creates a bug report for mailing to the maintainers of MySQL. Before sending it off, you may want to edit the generated file to provide additional information that may be useful to the developers.

mysqldump

This is an extremely useful utility that allows you to dump a partial or an entire database to a single file as a set of SQL commands that can be read back into MySQL or even another SQL RDBMS. It takes as a parameter the standard user and password info as well as database and table names. The additional options in the following table greatly extend its utility:

Command	Description
--add-drop-table	Add SQL commands to the output file to drop (delete) any tables before the commands to create them.
-e	Use extended insert syntax. This is nonstandard SQL, but if you are dumping a large amount of data, this will help your database dump to reload much more quickly when you try to reload it into MySQL.
-t	Dump only the data from tables, not the information to create tables.
-d	Dump only the table structure, not the actual data.

By default, mysqldump sends its data to standard output, so you'll want to redirect this to a file.

This utility is handy for migrating data or quick backups, and thanks to the client server implementation of MySQL it can even be used for a nice remote backup implementation, by using a mysqldump client installed on a different machine. As an example here is a command to connect as rick, and dump the database myplaydb:

```
$ mysqldump -u rick -p myplaydb > myplaydb.dump
```

The resulting file, which on our system has only a single table in the database, looks like this:

```
-- MySQL dump 10.11
--
-- Host: localhost    Database: myplaydb
-- -------------------------------------------------------
-- Server version       5.0.37

/*!40101 SET @OLD_CHARACTER_SET_CLIENT=@@CHARACTER_SET_CLIENT */;
/*!40101 SET @OLD_CHARACTER_SET_RESULTS=@@CHARACTER_SET_RESULTS */;
/*!40101 SET @OLD_COLLATION_CONNECTION=@@COLLATION_CONNECTION */;
/*!40101 SET NAMES utf8 */;
/*!40103 SET @OLD_TIME_ZONE=@@TIME_ZONE */;
/*!40103 SET TIME_ZONE='+00:00' */;
/*!40014 SET @OLD_UNIQUE_CHECKS=@@UNIQUE_CHECKS, UNIQUE_CHECKS=0 */;
/*!40014 SET @OLD_FOREIGN_KEY_CHECKS=@@FOREIGN_KEY_CHECKS, FOREIGN_KEY_CHECKS=0 */;
/*!40101 SET @OLD_SQL_MODE=@@SQL_MODE, SQL_MODE='NO_AUTO_VALUE_ON_ZERO' */;
/*!40111 SET @OLD_SQL_NOTES=@@SQL_NOTES, SQL_NOTES=0 */;


--
-- Table structure for table 'children'
--
```

```
DROP TABLE IF EXISTS 'children';
CREATE TABLE 'children' (
  'childno' int(11) NOT NULL auto_increment,
  'fname' varchar(30) default NULL,
  'age' int(11) default NULL,
  PRIMARY KEY  ('childno')
) ENGINE=InnoDB DEFAULT CHARSET=latin1;


--
-- Dumping data for table 'children'
--

LOCK TABLES 'children' WRITE;
/*!40000 ALTER TABLE 'children' DISABLE KEYS */;
INSERT INTO 'children' VALUES
(1,'Jenny',21),(2,'Andrew',17),(3,'Gavin',8),(4,'Duncan',6),(5,'Emma',4),
(6,'Alex',15),(7,'Adrian',9);
/*!40000 ALTER TABLE 'children' ENABLE KEYS */;
UNLOCK TABLES;
/*!40103 SET TIME_ZONE=@OLD_TIME_ZONE */;

/*!40101 SET SQL_MODE=@OLD_SQL_MODE */;
/*!40014 SET FOREIGN_KEY_CHECKS=@OLD_FOREIGN_KEY_CHECKS */;
/*!40014 SET UNIQUE_CHECKS=@OLD_UNIQUE_CHECKS */;
/*!40101 SET CHARACTER_SET_CLIENT=@OLD_CHARACTER_SET_CLIENT */;
/*!40101 SET CHARACTER_SET_RESULTS=@OLD_CHARACTER_SET_RESULTS */;
/*!40101 SET COLLATION_CONNECTION=@OLD_COLLATION_CONNECTION */;
/*!40111 SET SQL_NOTES=@OLD_SQL_NOTES */;

-- Dump completed on 2007-06-22 20:11:48
```

mysqlimport

The `mysqlimport` command is used for bulk loading data into a table. Using `mysqlimport`, you can read in large quantities of text data from an input file. The only command-specific parameters required are a filename and a database; `mysqlimport` will load the data into a table with the same name as the filename (excluding any filename extension) into the database. You must ensure that the text file has the same number of columns of data as there are columns in the table to be populated with data, and that the data types are compatible. By default, data should be separated with a tab delimiter.

It's also possible to perform SQL commands from a text file by simply running `mysql` with input redirected from a file, as we mentioned earlier.

mysqlshow

This little utility can provide quick information about your MySQL installation and its component databases:

❑ With no parameters, it lists all available databases.

❑ With a database as a parameter, it lists the tables in that database.

❑ With both a database and a table name, it lists the columns in that table.

❑ With a database, table, and column, it lists the details of the specified column.

Creating Users and Giving Them Permissions

As a MySQL administrator, one of your most common tasks will be user maintenance — adding and removing users from MySQL and managing their privileges. Since MySQL 3.22, user permissions are managed with the `grant` and `revoke` commands from within the MySQL monitor — a task considerably less daunting than editing the privilege tables directly as was necessary in early versions of MySQL.

grant

The MySQL `grant` command closely, though not exactly, follows SQL92 syntax. The general format is

```
grant <privilege> on <object> to <user> [identified by user-password] [with
grant option];
```

There are several privilege values that can be granted, shown in the following table:

Value	Description
alter	Alter tables and indexes.
create	Create databases and tables.
delete	Delete data from the database.
drop	Remove databases and tables.
index	Manage indexes.
insert	Add data to the database.
lock tables	Allow locking of tables.
select	Retrieve data.
update	Modify data.
all	All the above.

Some the commands have further options. For example, `create view` gives the user permission to create views. For a definitive list of permissions consult the MySQL documentation for your version of MySQL, because this is an area that is being expanded with each new version of MySQL. There are also several special administration privileges, but these do not concern us here.

The object on which you grant these privileges is identified as

databasename.tablename

and in the best Linux tradition, * is the anything-goes operator, so that *.* means every object in the every database, and `foo.*` means every table in the `foo` database.

325

If the specified user already exists, privileges are edited to reflect your changes. If no such user exists, the user is created with the specified privileges. As you saw earlier, users can be specified as being on particular host machines. You should specify user and host in the same command to get the full flexibility of the MySQL permission scheme.

In SQL syntax, the special character % is a wildcard character, much the same as * in a shell environment. You can, of course, issue separate commands for each desired privilege set; but if, for example, you want to grant access to user `rick` from any host in the `wiley.com` domain, you could describe `rick` as

> *rick@'%.wiley.com'*

Any use of the % wildcard character must be enclosed in quotes to set it off from any literal text.

You can also use IP/Netmask notation (N.N.N.N/M.M.M.M) to set a network address for access control.

Just as you earlier used `rick@'192.168.0.0/255.255.255.0'` to grant access to `rick` from any local network computer, you can specify `rick@'192.168.0.1'` to limit `rick`'s access to a single workstation or specify `rick@'192.0.0.0/255.0.0.0'` to broaden the scope to include any machine in the 192 class A network.

As one more example, the command

```
mysql> GRANT ALL ON foo.* TO rick@'%' IDENTIFIED BY 'bar';
```

will create a user `rick`, with full permissions on the database `foo`, to connect from any machine with an initial password of `bar`.

If the database `foo` does not yet exist, then the user `rick` will now have permissions to create it using the `create database` SQL command.

The `IDENTIFIED BY` clause is optional; but it's a good idea to be certain that all users have passwords as soon as they are created.

You need to be extra careful in the unfortunate circumstance where you have user names, host names, or database names that contain an underscore, because the _ character in SQL is a pattern that matches any single character in much the same way that % matches a string of characters. Whenever possible, avoid user names and database names containing an underscore.

Typically, the `with grant option` is used only to create a secondary administrative user; however, it can be used to allow a newly created user to confer the privileges granted to her on other users. Always use the `with grant option` judiciously.

revoke

Naturally the administrator can not only give, but also take away, privileges. This is done with the with the `revoke` command:

```
revoke <a_privilege> on <an_object> from <a_user>
```

using much the same format as the grant command. For example:

```
mysql> REVOKE INSERT ON foo.* FROM rick@'%';
```

The revoke command, however, does not delete users. If you want to completely remove a user, don't simply modify his privileges, but use revoke to remove his privileges. Then you can completely remove him from the user table by switching to the internal mysql database, and deleting the appropriate rows from the user table:

```
mysql> use mysql
mysql> DELETE FROM user WHERE user = "rick"
mysql> FLUSH PRIVILEGES;
```

In declining to specify a host, you ensure that you get rid of every instance of the MySQL user, in this case rick, that you want removed. After doing this, be sure to return to your own database (using the use command) or you may accidentally continuing working in MySQL's own internal database.

> *Understand that* delete *is not part of the same concept as* grant *and* revoke. *It's SQL syntax that happens to be necessary as a result of the way MySQL handles permissions. You are directly updating MySQL permission tables (hence the* use mysql *command first) to efficiently achieve the changes you need.*
>
> *After updating the tables, you must use the* FLUSH PRIVILEGES *command to tell the MySQL server it needs to reload its permissions tables, as shown in the examples.*

Passwords

If you want to specify passwords for existing users who do not already have them, or you want to change your own or somebody else's password, you'll need to connect to the MySQL server as the root user and directly update the user information. For example:

```
mysql> use mysql
mysql> SELECT host, user, password FROM user;
```

You should get a list like this:

```
+-----------+----------+------------------+
| host      | user     | password         |
+-----------+----------+------------------+
| localhost | root     | 67457e226a1a15bd |
| localhost | foo      |                  |
+-----------+----------+------------------+
2 rows in set (0.00 sec)
```

If you want to assign the password bar to user foo, you can do so like this:

```
mysql> UPDATE user SET password = password('bar') WHERE user = 'foo';
```

Display the relevant columns in the `user` table again, to check:

```
mysql> SELECT host, user, password FROM user;
+-----------+----------+------------------+
| host      | user     | password         |
+-----------+----------+------------------+
| localhost | root     | 65457e236g1a1wbq |
| localhost | foo      | 7c9e0a41222752fa |
+-----------+----------+------------------+
2 rows in set (0.00 sec)
mysql>
```

Sure enough, the user foo now has a password. Remember to return to your original database.

Since MySQL 4.1, the password scheme has been updated from earlier versions. However, you can still set a password using the old algorithm for backward compatibility with the function `OLD_PASSWORD('password to set')` if you need to.

Creating a Database

Your next step is to create a database. Let's assume you want one called `rick`. Recall that you've already created a user with the same name. First you'll give the user rick wide-ranging permissions, so that he can create new databases. On a development system this is particularly useful, because it allows people more flexibility.

```
mysql> GRANT ALL ON *.* TO rick@localhost IDENTIFIED BY 'secretpassword';
```

Now test that privilege set by logging in as `rick` and creating the database:

```
$ mysql -u rick -p
Enter password:
...
mysql> CREATE DATABASE rick;
Query OK, 1 row affected (0.01 sec)
mysql>
```

Now tell MySQL you want to switch to your new database:

```
mysql> use rick
```

Now you can populate this database with the tables and information you want. On future logins, you can specify the database on the end of the command line, bypassing the need for the `use` command:

```
$ mysql -u rick -p rick
```

After entering the password when prompted, you will then automatically change to use the database `rick` by default as part of the connection process.

Data Types

So now you have a running MySQL server, a secure login for your user, and a database ready to use. What's next? Well, now you need to create some tables with columns to store your data. Before you can do that, however, you need to know about the data types that MySQL supports.

MySQL data types are fairly standard, so we will just run briefly though the main types here. As always, the MySQL manual on the MySQL website discusses this in more detail.

Boolean

A Boolean column can be defined using the keyword BOOL. As you would expect, it can hold TRUE and FALSE values. It may also hold the special database "unknown" value NULL.

Character

A variety of character types are available and are shown in the following table. The first three are standard and the remaining three specific to MySQL. We suggest you stick to the standard types if practical.

Definition	Description
CHAR	A single character.
CHAR(N)	A character string on exactly N characters, which will be padded with space characters if necessary. Limited to 255 characters.
VARCHAR(N)	A variable-length array of N characters. Limited to 255 characters.
TINYTEXT	Similar to VARCHAR(N).
MEDIUMTEXT	A text string of up to 65,535 characters.
LONGTEXT	A text string of up to $2^{32} - 1$ characters.

Number

The number types are broken down into integer and floating-point number types, as shown in the following table:

Definition	Type	Description
TINYINT	Integer	An 8-bit data type.
SMALLINT	Integer	A 16-bit data type.
MEDIUMINT	Integer	A 24-bit data type.
INT	Integer	A 32-bit data type. This is a standard type, and a good general-purpose choice.

Continued on next page

Definition	Type	Description
BIGINT	Integer	A 64-bit signed data type.
FLOAT(P)	Floating	A floating-point number with at least *P* digits of precision.
DOUBLE(D, N)	Floating	A signed double-precision floating-point number, with *D* digits and *N* decimal places.
NUMERIC(P, S)	Floating	A real number with a total of *P* digits, with *S* of the digits after the decimal place. Unlike DOUBLE, this is an exact number, so it is better for storing currency, but less efficiently processed.
DECIMAL(P, S)	Floating	A synonym for NUMERIC.

In general, we suggest you stick to INT, DOUBLE, and NUMERIC types, because these are closest to the standard SQL types. The other types are nonstandard and may not be available in other database systems if you find you need to move your data at some point in the future.

Temporal

Five temporal data types are available, shown in the following table:

Definition	Description
DATE	Stores dates between January 1, 1000, and December 31, 9999.
TIME	Stores times between –838:59:59 and 838:59:59.
TIMESTAMP	Stores a timestamp between January 1, 1970, and the year 2037.
DATETIME	Stores dates between January 1, 1000, and the last second of December 31, 9999.
YEAR	Stores year values. Be careful with two-digit year values because they are ambiguous and are automatically converted to four-digit years.

Note that you need to be careful when comparing DATE and DATETIME values as to how the time portion is handled; you may see unexpected results. Check the MySQL manual for details, because the behavior varies slightly with different versions of MySQL.

Creating a Table

Now that you have your database server running, know how to assign user permissions, and know how to create a database and some basic database types, you can move on to creating tables.

A database table is simply a sequence of rows, each of which consists of a fixed set of columns. It's rather like a spreadsheet, except that each row must have exactly the same number and type of columns, and each row must, in some way, be different from all other rows in the table.

A database can, within reason, contain pretty much an unlimited number of tables. However, few databases need more than 100 tables, and for most small systems 25 or so tables usually suffice.

The full SQL syntax for creating database objects, known as DDL (data definition language), is too complex to go into fully in one chapter; the full details can be found in the documentation section of the MySQL website.

The basic syntax for creating a table is

```
CREATE TABLE <table_name> (
column type [NULL | NOT NULL] [AUTO_INCREMENT] [PRIMARY KEY]
[, ... ]
[, PRIMARY KEY ( column [, ... ] ) ]
)
```

You can discard tables using the DROP TABLE syntax, which is very simple:

```
DROP TABLE <table_name>
```

For now, there are just a small number of additional keywords, shown in the following table, you need to know to get up to speed with creating tables.

Keyword	Description
AUTO_INCREMENT	This special keyword tells MySQL that, whenever you write a NULL into this column, it should automatically fill in the column data using an automatically allocated incrementing number. This is an immensely useful feature; it allows you to use MySQL to automatically assign unique numbers to rows in your tables, although it can only be used on columns that are also a primary key. In other databases this functionality is often provided by a serial type, or is managed more explicitly with a sequence.
NULL	A special database value that is normally used to mean "not known," but can also be used to mean "not relevant." For example, if you are filling in a table with employee details, you might have a column for personal e-mail address, but perhaps some employees don't have a personal e-mail address. In this case, you would store a NULL against the e-mail address for that employee to show that the information was not relevant to that particular person. The syntax NOT NULL means that this column cannot store a NULL value, and it can be useful to prevent columns from holding NULL values if, for example, the value must always be known, such as an employee's last name.
PRIMARY KEY	Indicates that the data for this column will be unique and different in every row in this table. Each table can have just a single primary key.

Try It Out   Creating a Table and Adding Data

It's much easier to see table creation in practice than to look at the base syntax, so you'll do that now by creating a table called `children` that will store a unique number for each child, a first name, and an age. You'll make the child number a primary key.

1.   The SQL command you need is:

```
CREATE TABLE children (
        childno INTEGER AUTO_INCREMENT NOT NULL PRIMARY KEY,
        fname VARCHAR(30),
        age INTEGER
);
```

*Notice that, unlike most programming languages, the column name (**childno**) comes before the column type (**INTEGER**).*

2.   You can also use a syntax that defines the primary key separately from the column; here's an interactive session that shows the alternative syntax:

```
mysql> use rick
Database changed
mysql> CREATE table children (
    -> childno INTEGER AUTO_INCREMENT NOT NULL,
    -> fname varchar(30),
    -> age INTEGER,
    -> PRIMARY KEY(childno)
    -> );
Query OK, 0 rows affected (0.04 sec)
mysql>
```

Notice how you can write the SQL across several lines, and mysql uses the `->` prompt to show you are on a continuation line. Also notice, as mentioned earlier, you terminate the SQL command with a semicolon to indicate you have finished and are ready for the database server to process the request.

If you make a mistake, MySQL should allow you to scroll backward through previous commands, edit them, and re-enter them by simply pressing Enter.

3.   Now you have a table to which you can add some data. You add data with the `INSERT` SQL command. Because you defined the `childno` column as an `AUTO_INCREMENT` column, you don't give any data from that column; you simply allow MySQL to allocate a unique number.

```
mysql> INSERT INTO children(fname, age) VALUES("Jenny", 21);
Query OK, 1 row affected (0.00 sec)

mysql> INSERT INTO children(fname, age) VALUES("Andrew", 17);
Query OK, 1 row affected (0.00 sec)
```

To check that the data was added correctly, you can retrieve the data again. Do this by SELECTing the data from the table:

```
mysql> SELECT childno, fname, age FROM children;
+---------+--------+------+
| childno | fname  | age  |
+---------+--------+------+
|       1 | Jenny  |   21 |
|       2 | Andrew |   17 |
+---------+--------+------+
2 rows in set (0.00 sec)

mysql>
```

Rather than explicitly list the columns you wanted to select, you could just have used an asterisk (*) for the columns, which will list all columns in the named table. This is fine for interactive use, but in production code you should always explicitly name the column or columns you want to select.

How It Works

You started an interactive session to the database server, and switched to the rick database. You then typed in the SQL to create your table, using as many lines as needed for the command. As soon as you terminated the SQL command with a ;, MySQL created your table. You then used the INSERT statement to add data to your new table, allowing the childno column to automatically be allocated numbers. Finally, you used SELECT to display the data in your table.

We don't have space in this chapter to go into full details of SQL, much less database design. For more information see www.mysql.com.

Graphical Tools

Manipulating tables and data on the command line is all well and good, but these days many people prefer graphical tools.

MySQL has two main graphical tools, the MySQL Administrator and the MySQL Query Browser. The exact package name for these tools varies depending on the distribution you are using; for example, in Red Hat distributions look for mysql-gui-tools and mysql-administrator. For Ubuntu you may need to turn on the "Universe" repository first, and then look for mysql-admin.

MySQL Query Browser

The query browser is a reasonably simple, but effective tool. After installation it can be invoked from the GUI menu. When it starts you get an initial screen asking for connection details, as shown in Figure 8-4.

If you are running it on the same machine as the server, just use localhost as the server host name.

Once you have connected you get a simple GUI, shown in Figure 8-5, that allows you to run queries in a GUI shell, giving you all the advantages of graphical editing as well as a graphical way to edit data in the table, and some help screens with SQL syntax.

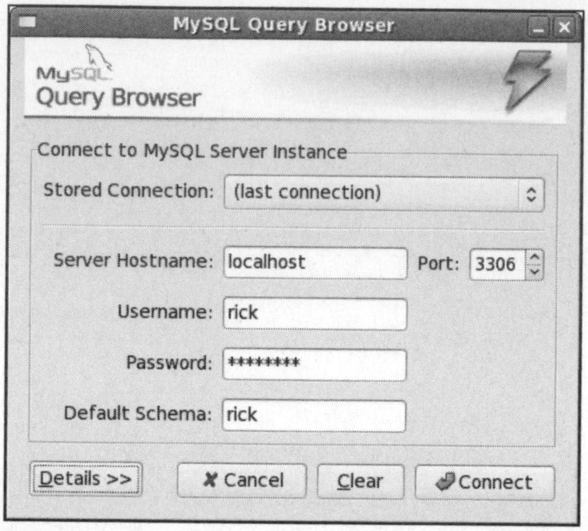

Figure 8-4

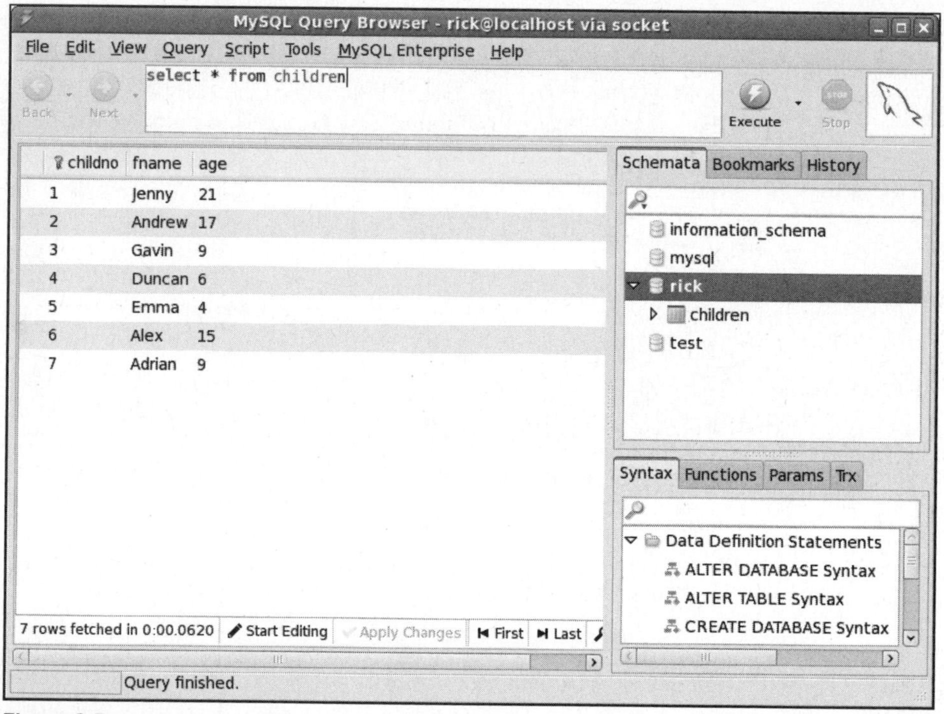

Figure 8-5

MySQL Administrator

We strongly suggest you look at MySQL Administrator; it's a powerful, stable, and easy-to-use graphical interface for MySQL that is available precompiled for both Linux and Windows (even the source code is available if you want it). It allows you to both administer a MySQL server and execute SQL through a GUI interface.

When you start MySQL Administrator you get a connection screen very similar to the MySQL Query Browser connection screen. After entering the details you get the main control page, shown in Figure 8-6.

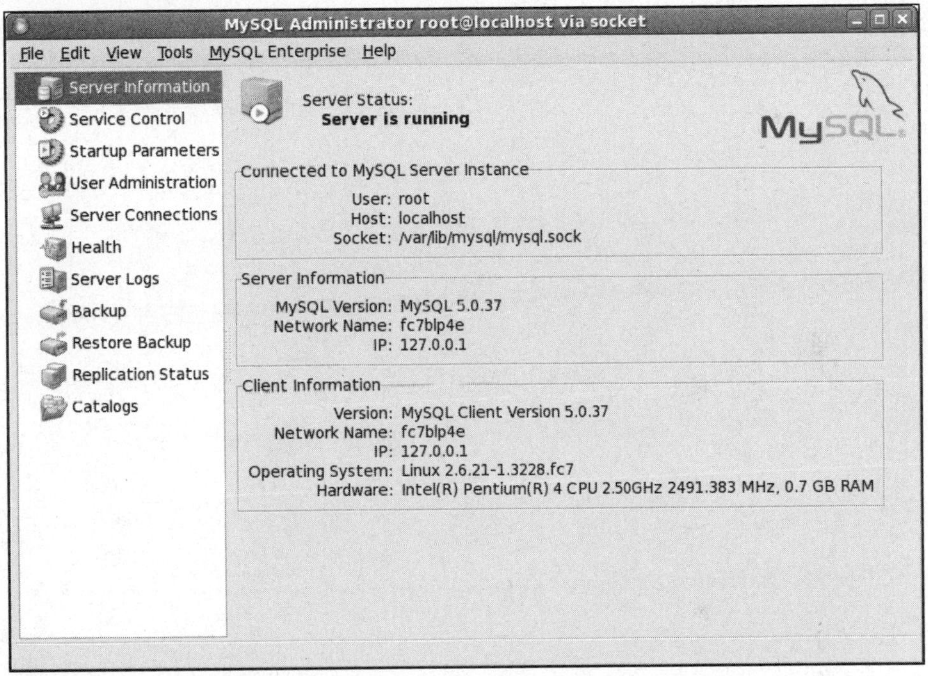

Figure 8-6

If you want to administer your MySQL server from a Windows client, you can download a Windows version of MySQL Administrator from the GUI tools section of the MySQL website. At the time of writing the download contains the administrator, the query browser, and a database migration utility. The status screen is shown in Figure 8-7; as you can see it's almost identical to the Linux version.

Do remember that if you have followed the instructions so far you have secured your MySQL server so that root can only connect from the localhost, not from any other machines on the network.

Once you have MySQL Administrator running you can look around at the different configuration and monitoring options. It's a very easy-to-use tool, but we don't have the space to go into details in this single chapter.

Accessing MySQL Data from C

Now that we have the rudiments of MySQL out of the way, let's explore how to access it from your application, rather than using the GUI tools or the basic mysql client.

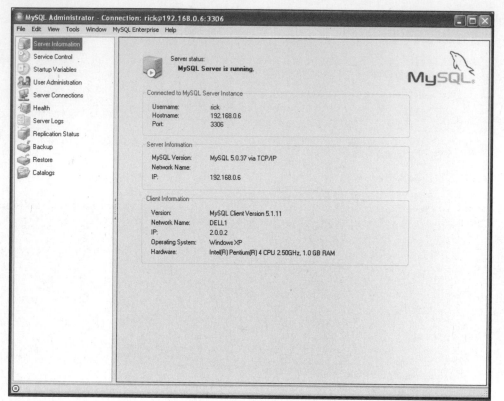

Figure 8-7

MySQL can be accessed from many different languages, including

- C
- C++
- Java
- Perl
- Python
- Eiffel
- Tcl
- Ruby
- PHP

An ODBC driver is also available for accessing MySQL from Windows native applications such as Access; and there is even an ODBC driver for Linux, although little reason exists to use it.

In this chapter, we limit ourselves to the C interface because that is the primary focus of this book and because the same libraries facilitate connection by a number of other languages.

Connection Routines

The two steps involved in connecting to a MySQL database from C are:

❏ Initializing a connection handle structure

❏ Physically making the connection

First, use `mysql_init` to initialize your connection handle:

```
#include <mysql.h>

MYSQL *mysql_init(MYSQL *);
```

Normally you pass NULL to the routine, and a pointer to a newly allocated connection handle structure is returned. If you pass an existing structure, it will be reinitialized. On error, NULL is returned.

So far, you've simply allocated and initialized a structure. You still need to offer the parameters for a connection using `mysql_real_connect`:

```
MYSQL *mysql_real_connect(MYSQL *connection,
         const char *server_host,
         const char *sql_user_name,
         const char *sql_password,
         const char *db_name,
         unsigned int port_number,
         const char *unix_socket_name,
         unsigned int flags);
```

The connection pointer has to identify a structure already initialized using `mysql_init`. The parameters are fairly self-explanatory; however, it should be noted that the `server_host` can take a host name or an IP address. If connecting only to the local machine, you can optimize the connection type by specifying simply `localhost` here.

`sql_user_name` and `sql_password` are exactly what they sound like. If the login name is NULL, the login ID of the current Linux user is assumed. If the password is NULL, you will be able to access data only on the server that's accessible without a password. The password is encrypted before being sent across the network.

The `port_number` and `unix_socket_name` should be 0 and NULL, respectively, unless you have changed the defaults in your MySQL installation. They will default to appropriate values.

Finally, the `flags` parameter allows you to OR together some bit-pattern `defines`, allowing you to alter certain features of the protocol being used. None of these flag options are relevant to this introductory chapter; all are fully documented in the manual.

If you are unable to connect, NULL is returned. Using `mysql_error` can provide helpful information.

When you are finished with the connection, normally at program termination, call `mysql_close` like this:

```
void mysql_close(MYSQL *connection);
```

This will shut down the connection. If the connection was set up by `mysql_init`, the structure will be freed. The pointer will become invalid and cannot be used again. It is wasteful of resources to leave an unneeded connection open; but there's additional overhead associated with reopening a connection, so use your judgment about when to use these options.

The `mysql_options` routine (which can be called only between `mysql_init` and `mysql_real_connect`) allows you to set some options:

```
int mysql_options(MYSQL *connection, enum option_to_set,
                                  const char *argument);
```

Because `mysql_options` is capable of setting only one option at a time, it must be called once for each option you would like to set. You can use it as many times as necessary so long as all uses appear between `mysql_init` and `mysql_real_connect`. Not all of the options are of the `char` type, which must be cast as `const char *`. The three most common options are shown in the following table. As always, the extensive online manual lists them all.

enum Option	Actual Argument Type	Description
MYSQL_OPT_ CONNECT_TIMEOUT	const unsigned int *	The number of seconds to wait before timing out a connection.
MYSQL_OPT_COMPRESS	None, use NULL	Use compression on the network connection.
MYSQL_INIT_COMMAND	const char *	Command to send each time a connection is established.

A successful call returns zero. Because this is just for setting flags, failure always means that an invalid option has been used.

To set the connection timeout to seven seconds, use a fragment of code such as this:

```
unsigned int timeout = 7;
...
connection = mysql_init(NULL);
ret = mysql_options(connection, MYSQL_OPT_CONNECT_TIMEOUT, (const char *)&timeout);

if (ret) {
     /* Handle error */
     ...
}

connection = mysql_real_connect(connection ...
```

Now that you've learned how to set up and close your connection, let's try a short program just to test things.

Start by setting a new password for the user (rick on localhost, in the following code) and then creating a database called foo to connect to. This should all be familiar by now, so we will just show the sequence as it is executed:

```
$ mysql -u root -p
Enter password:
Welcome to the MySQL monitor.  Commands end with ; or \g.

mysql>  GRANT ALL ON *.* TO rick@localhost IDENTIFIED BY 'secret';
Query OK, 0 rows affected (0.01 sec)

mysql> \q
Bye
$ mysql -u rick -p
Enter password:
Welcome to the MySQL monitor.  Commands end with ; or \g.

mysql> CREATE DATABASE foo;
Query OK, 1 row affected (0.01 sec)

mysql> \q
```

You have now created your new database. Rather than type a lot of table creation and population commands directly into the mysql command line, which is somewhat prone to error and not very productive if you ever need to type it again, you will create a file with the commands you need in it.

This file is create_children.sql:

```
--
-- Create the table children
--

CREATE TABLE children (
    childno int(11) NOT NULL auto_increment,
    fname varchar(30),
    age int(11),
    PRIMARY KEY (childno)
);

--
--  Populate the table 'children'
--

INSERT INTO children(childno, fname, age) VALUES (1,'Jenny',21);
INSERT INTO children(childno, fname, age) VALUES (2,'Andrew',17);
INSERT INTO children(childno, fname, age)  VALUES (3,'Gavin',8);
INSERT INTO children(childno, fname, age)  VALUES (4,'Duncan',6);
INSERT INTO children(childno, fname, age)  VALUES (5,'Emma',4);
INSERT INTO children(childno, fname, age)  VALUES (6,'Alex',15);
INSERT INTO children(childno, fname, age)  VALUES (7,'Adrian',9);
```

You can now sign back on to MySQL, selecting the database foo, and execute this file. For the sake of brevity, and as an example in case you want to put this in a script, we will put the password on the command line:

```
$ mysql -u rick --password=secret foo
Welcome to the MySQL monitor.  Commands end with ; or \g.

mysql> \. create_children.sql
Query OK, 0 rows affected (0.01 sec)

Query OK, 1 row affected (0.00 sec)
```

We have removed the many duplicate lines of output as the rows are created in the database. Now that you have a user, a database, and a table with some data stored in it, it's time to see how you can access the data from code.

This is connect1.c, which connects to a server on the local machine, as user rick with password secret, to the database called foo:

```c
#include <stdlib.h>
#include <stdio.h>

#include "mysql.h"

int main(int argc, char *argv[]) {
    MYSQL *conn_ptr;

    conn_ptr = mysql_init(NULL);
    if (!conn_ptr) {
        fprintf(stderr, "mysql_init failed\n");
        return EXIT_FAILURE;
    }

    conn_ptr = mysql_real_connect(conn_ptr, "localhost", "rick", "secret",
                                            "foo", 0, NULL, 0);

    if (conn_ptr) {
        printf("Connection success\n");
    } else {
        printf("Connection failed\n");
    }

    mysql_close(conn_ptr);

    return EXIT_SUCCESS;
}
```

Now compile the program and see how you did. You may need to add both the include path and a library path, as well as specifying that the file needs linking with the library module mysqlclient. On some systems you may also need -lz, to link the compression library. On the author's system, the required compile line is

```
$ gcc -I/usr/include/mysql connect1.c -L/usr/lib/mysql -lmysqlclient -o connect1
```

You may need to check that you have the client packages installed, and the locations they have been installed, depending on your distribution, and adjust the preceding compile line accordingly.

When you run it, you should get a message saying the connection succeeded:

```
$ ./connect1
Connection success
$
```

In Chapter 9, we show you how to build a makefile to automate this connection.

As you can see, getting a connection to a MySQL database is very easy.

Error Handling

Before we move on to more sophisticated programs, it's useful to have a look at how MySQL handles errors. MySQL uses a number of return codes reported by the connection handle structure. The two must-have routines are

```
unsigned int mysql_errno(MYSQL *connection);
```

and

```
char *mysql_error(MYSQL *connection);
```

You can retrieve the error code, generally any nonzero value, by calling `mysql_errno` and passing the connection structure. Zero is returned if the error code has not been set. Because the code is updated each time a call is made to the library, you can retrieve the error code only for the last command executed, with the exception of these two error routines, which do not cause the error code to be updated.

The return value actually is the error code, and these values are defined in either the `errmsg.h` include file or `mysqld_error.h`. Both of these can be found in the MySQL `include` directory. The first reports on client-side errors, and the second focuses on server-specific errors.

If you prefer a textual error message, you can call `mysql_error`, which provides a meaningful text message instead. The message text is written to some internal static memory space, so you need to copy it elsewhere if you want to save the error text.

You can add some rudimentary error handling to your code in order to see this all in action. You probably have already noticed, however, that you are likely to experience a problem because `mysql_real_connect` returns a NULL pointer on failure, depriving you of an error code. If you make the connection handle a variable, you can still get at it should `mysql_real_connect` fail.

Here is `connect2.c`, which illustrates how to use the connection structure when it isn't dynamically allocated, and also how you might write some basic error-handling code. The changes are highlighted:

```
#include <stdlib.h>
#include <stdio.h>

#include "mysql.h"
```

```
int main(int argc, char *argv[]) {
    MYSQL my_connection;

    mysql_init(&my_connection);
    if (mysql_real_connect(&my_connection, "localhost", "rick",
                                    "I do not know", "foo", 0, NULL, 0)) {
        printf("Connection success\n");
        mysql_close(&my_connection);
    } else {
        fprintf(stderr, "Connection failed\n");
        if (mysql_errno(&my_connection)) {
        fprintf(stderr, "Connection error %d: %s\n",
mysql_errno(&my_connection), mysql_error(&my_connection));
        }
    }

    return EXIT_SUCCESS;
}
```

You could have solved your problem quite simply by avoiding overwriting your connection pointer with the return result if mysql_real_connect failed. Still, this is a nice example of the other way of using connection structures. You can force an error by choosing an incorrect user or password, and you will still get an error code similar to that offered by the mysql tool.

```
$ ./connect2
Connection failed
Connection error 1045: Access denied for user: 'rick@localhost' (Using
password: YES)
$
```

Executing SQL Statements

Now that you can connect to your database and correctly handle errors, it's time to put your program to some real work. The primary API function for executing SQL statements is aptly named:

```
int mysql_query(MYSQL *connection, const char *query)
```

Not too difficult, is it? This routine takes the connection structure pointer and hopefully some valid SQL as a text string (with no terminating semicolon as in the mysql tool). A zero is returned if you are successful. A second routine, mysql_real_query, can be used if binary data is called for; but in this chapter we use only mysql_query.

SQL Statements That Return No Data

For the sake of simplicity, let's start by looking at some SQL statements that do not return any data: UPDATE, DELETE, and INSERT.

Another important function that we will introduce at this point checks the number of rows affected by the query:

```
my_ulonglong mysql_affected_rows(MYSQL *connection);
```

The first thing you are likely to notice about this function is the very unusual data type returned. An unsigned type is used for reasons of portability. When you are using printf, it's recommended that this be cast as unsigned long with a format of %lu. This function returns the number of rows affected by the previously issued UPDATE, INSERT, or DELETE query. The return value that MySQL uses may catch you unprepared if you have worked with other SQL databases. MySQL returns the number of rows modified by an update, whereas many other databases would consider a record updated simply because it matches any WHERE clause.

In general for the mysql_ functions, a return of 0 indicates no rows affected and a positive number is the actual result, typically the number of rows affected by the statement.

First you need to create your children table in the foo database, if you haven't already. Delete (using the drop command) any existing table to ensure you have a clean table definition, and to resend any IDs used in the AUTO_INCREMENT column:

```
$ mysql -u rick -p foo
Enter password:
Welcome to the MySQL monitor.  Commands end with ; or \g.

mysql> DROP TABLE children;
Query OK, 0 rows affected (0.58 sec)

mysql> CREATE TABLE children (
    ->     childno int(11) AUTO_INCREMENT NOT NULL PRIMARY KEY,
    ->     fname varchar(30),
    ->     age int
    -> );
Query OK, 0 rows affected (0.09 sec)
mysql>
```

So now add some code to connect2.c in order to insert a new row into your table; call this new program insert1.c. Observe that the wrapping shown is a physical page limitation; you would not normally use a line break in your actual SQL statement unless it was a very long statement, when you can use a \ at the end of the line to allow the SQL to continue onto the next line.

```
#include <stdlib.h>
#include <stdio.h>

#include "mysql.h"

int main(int argc, char *argv[]) {
    MYSQL my_connection;
    int res;

    mysql_init(&my_connection);
    if (mysql_real_connect(&my_connection, "localhost",
                           "rick", "secret", "foo", 0, NULL, 0)) {
        printf("Connection success\n");

        res = mysql_query(&my_connection, "INSERT INTO children(fname, age)
                                                        VALUES('Ann', 3)");
        if (!res) {
```

```
            printf("Inserted %lu rows\n",
                       (unsigned long)mysql_affected_rows(&my_connection));
        } else {
            fprintf(stderr, "Insert error %d: %s\n", mysql_errno(&my_connection),
                                        mysql_error(&my_connection));
        }
```

```
        mysql_close(&my_connection);
    } else {
        fprintf(stderr, "Connection failed\n");
        if (mysql_errno(&my_connection)) {
        fprintf(stderr, "Connection error %d: %s\n",
                    mysql_errno(&my_connection), mysql_error(&my_connection));
        }
    }

    return EXIT_SUCCESS;
}
```

Not surprisingly, one row is inserted.

Now change the code to include an UPDATE, rather than INSERT, and see how affected rows are reported.

```
            mysql_errno(&my_connection), mysql_error(&my_connection));
        }
    }
```

```
    res = mysql_query(&my_connection, "UPDATE children SET AGE = 4
                                            WHERE fname = 'Ann'");
    if (!res) {
        printf("Updated %lu rows\n",
                        (unsigned long)mysql_affected_rows(&my_connection));
    } else {
        fprintf(stderr, "Update error %d: %s\n", mysql_errno(&my_connection),
                                    mysql_error(&my_connection));
    }
```

Call this program update1.c. It attempts to set the age of all children called Ann to 4.

Now suppose your children table has data in it, like this:

```
mysql> SELECT * from CHILDREN;
+---------+--------+------+
| childno | fname  | age  |
+---------+--------+------+
|       1 | Jenny  |   21 |
|       2 | Andrew |   17 |
|       3 | Gavin  |    9 |
|       4 | Duncan |    6 |
|       5 | Emma   |    4 |
|       6 | Alex   |   15 |
|       7 | Adrian |    9 |
|       8 | Ann    |    3 |
```

```
|        9 | Ann    |    4 |
|       10 | Ann    |    3 |
|       11 | Ann    |    4 |
+----------+--------+------+
11 rows in set (0.00 sec)
```

Notice that there are four children matching the name Ann. If you execute update1, you might reasonably expect the number of affected rows to be four, the number of rows mandated by the WHERE clause. However, if you execute update1 you will see that the program reports a change of only two rows because those were the only rows that actually required a change to the data. You can opt for more traditional reporting by using the CLIENT_FOUND_ROWS flag to mysql_real_connect.

```
    if (mysql_real_connect(&my_connection, "localhost",
                      "rick", "secret", "foo", 0, NULL, CLIENT_FOUND_ROWS)) {
```

If you reset the data in your database, and then run the program with this modification, it reports the number of affected rows as four.

The function mysql_affected_rows has one last oddity, which appears when you delete data from the database. If you delete data with a WHERE clause, the mysql_affected_rows returns the number of rows deleted, as you would expect. However, if there is no WHERE clause on a DELETE statement, all rows in the table will be deleted, but the number of rows affected is reported by the program as zero. This is because MySQL optimizes the deletion of all rows, rather than performing many single-row deletions. This behavior is not affected by the CLIENT_FOUND_ROWS option flag.

Discovering What You Inserted

There is a small but crucial aspect of inserting data. Remember we mentioned the AUTO_INCREMENT type of column, where MySQL automatically assigned IDs for you? This feature is extremely useful, particularly when you have several users.

Take a look at that table definition again:

```
CREATE TABLE children (
        childno INTEGER AUTO_INCREMENT NOT NULL PRIMARY KEY,
        fname VARCHAR(30),
        age INTEGER
);
```

As you can see, the childno column is an AUTO_INCREMENT field. That's all very well, but once you have inserted a row, how do you know which number was allocated for the child whose name you just inserted?

You could execute a SELECT statement to retrieve the data, searching on the child's name, but this is very inefficient, and not guaranteed to be unique — suppose you had two children with the same name? Or perhaps multiple users inserting data rapidly, so there might be other rows inserted between your update and SELECT statement? Because discovering the value of an AUTO_INCREMENT column is such a common problem, MySQL provides a special solution in the form of the LAST_INSERT_ID() function.

Whenever MySQL inserts a data value into an AUTO_INCREMENT column, it keeps track, on a per-user basis, of the last value it assigned. User programs can recover this value by simply SELECTing the rather special function LAST_INSERT_ID(), which acts a little like a pseudo column.

Try It Out   **Retrieving the ID Generated by AUTO_INCREMENT**

You can see how this works by inserting some values into your table, and then using the
LAST_INSERT_ID() function.

```
mysql> INSERT INTO children(fname, age) VALUES('Tom', 13);
Query OK, 1 row affected (0.06 sec)
mysql> SELECT LAST_INSERT_ID();
+------------------+
| last_insert_id() |
+------------------+
|               14 |
+------------------+
1 row in set (0.01 sec)
mysql> INSERT INTO children(fname, age) VALUES('Harry', 17);
Query OK, 1 row affected (0.02 sec)
mysql> SELECT LAST_INSERT_ID();
+------------------+
| last_insert_id() |
+------------------+
|               15 |
+------------------+
1 row in set (0.00 sec)
mysql>
```

How It Works

Each time you inserted a row, MySQL allocated a new id column value and kept track of it so you could
retrieve it using LAST_INSERT_ID().

If you want to experiment to see that the number returned is indeed unique to your session, open a different session and insert another row. In the original session re-execute the SELECT LAST_INSERT_ID();
statement. You will see the number hasn't changed because the number returned is the last number
inserted by the current session. However, if you do SELECT * FROM children, you should see that the
other session has indeed inserted data.

Try It Out   **Using Automatic IDs from a C Program**

In this example, you will modify your insert1.c program to see how this works in C. The key changes
are highlighted. Call this modified program insert2.c.

```
#include <stdlib.h>
#include <stdio.h>

#include "mysql.h"

int main(int argc, char *argv[]) {
    MYSQL my_connection;
    MYSQL_RES *res_ptr;
    MYSQL_ROW sqlrow;
    int res;
```

```
    mysql_init(&my_connection);
    if (mysql_real_connect(&my_connection, "localhost",
                           "rick", "bar", "rick", 0, NULL, 0)) {
        printf("Connection success\n");

        res = mysql_query(&my_connection, "INSERT INTO children(fname, age)
VALUES('Robert', 7)");
        if (!res) {
            printf("Inserted %lu rows\n", (unsigned
long)mysql_affected_rows(&my_connection));
        } else {
            fprintf(stderr, "Insert error %d: %s\n", mysql_errno(&my_connection),
                                                mysql_error(&my_connection));

        }

        res = mysql_query(&my_connection, "SELECT LAST_INSERT_ID()");

        if (res) {
            printf("SELECT error: %s\n", mysql_error(&my_connection));
        } else {
            res_ptr = mysql_use_result(&my_connection);
            if (res_ptr) {
                while ((sqlrow = mysql_fetch_row(res_ptr))) {
                    printf("We inserted childno %s\n", sqlrow[0]);
                }
                mysql_free_result(res_ptr);
            }
        }

        mysql_close(&my_connection);
    } else {
        fprintf(stderr, "Connection failed\n");
        if (mysql_errno(&my_connection)) {
            fprintf(stderr, "Connection error %d: %s\n",
                    mysql_errno(&my_connection), mysql_error(&my_connection));
        }
    }

    return EXIT_SUCCESS;
}
```

Here is the output:

```
$ gcc -I/usr/include/mysql insert2.c -L/usr/lib/mysql -lmysqlclient -o insert2
$ ./insert2
Connection success
Inserted 1 rows
We inserted childno 6
$ ./insert2
Connection success
Inserted 1 rows
We inserted childno 7
```

How It Works

After you inserted a row, you retrieved the allocated ID using the LAST_INSERT_ID() function just like a normal SELECT statement. You then used mysql_use_result(), which we explain shortly, to retrieve the data from the SELECT statement you executed and print it out. Don't worry too much about the mechanics of retrieving the value just now; all is explained in the next few pages.

Statements That Return Data

The most common use of SQL, of course, is retrieving rather than inserting or updating data. Data is retrieved with the SELECT statement.

> *MySQL also supports* SHOW, DESCRIBE, *and* EXPLAIN *SQL statements for returning results, but we're not going to be considering these here. As usual, the manual contains explanations of these statements.*

Retrieving data into your C application will typically involve four steps:

❑   Issue the query.

❑   Retrieve the data.

❑   Process the data.

❑   Tidy up if necessary.

Just as you did with the INSERT and DELETE statements, you'll use mysql_query to send the SQL. Next you'll retrieve the data using either mysql_store_result or mysql_use_result, depending on how you want the data retrieved. Next you'll use a sequence of mysql_fetch_row calls to process the data. Finally, you'll use mysql_free_result to clear the memory you used for your query.

The difference between mysql_use_result and mysql_store_result basically amounts to whether you want to get your data back a row at a time, or get the whole result set in one go. The latter is more appropriate in circumstances where you anticipate a smaller result set.

Functions for All-At-Once Data Retrieval

You can retrieve all the data from a SELECT (or other statement that returns data), in a single call, using mysql_store_result:

```
MYSQL_RES *mysql_store_result(MYSQL *connection);
```

Clearly, you want to use this function after a successful call to mysql_query. The function will store all the data returned in the client immediately. It returns a pointer to a new structure called a result set structure, or NULL if the statement failed.

Upon success, you'll next call mysql_num_rows to get the number of records returned, which we hope will be a positive number but may be 0 if no rows were returned.

```
my_ulonglong mysql_num_rows(MYSQL_RES *result);
```

This takes the result structure returned from mysql_store_result and returns the number of rows in that result set. Providing mysql_store_result succeeded, mysql_num_rows will always succeed.

This combination of functions is an easy way to retrieve the data you need. At this point, all data is local to the client and you no longer have to be concerned with the possibility of network or database errors. By getting the number of rows returned, you'll facilitate the coding that is to come.

If you happen to be working with a particularly large dataset, it will be better to retrieve smaller, more manageable chunks of information. This will return control to the application more quickly and is an unselfish way to use network resources. We explore this idea in more depth later, when we cover `mysql_use_result`.

Now that you have the data, you can process it using `mysql_fetch_row` and move around in the dataset using `mysql_data_seek`, `mysql_row_seek`, and `mysql_row_tell`. Let's take a look at these functions:

❑   The `mysql_fetch_row` function pulls a single row out of the result structure you got using `mysql_store_result` and puts it in a row structure. NULL is returned when the data runs out or if an error occurs. We come back to processing the data in this row structure in the next section.

   MYSQL_ROW mysql_fetch_row(MYSQL_RES *result);

❑   The `mysql_data_seek` function allows you to jump about in the result set, setting the row that will be returned by the next `mysql_fetch row` operation. The offset value is a row number, and it must be in the range from zero to one less than the number of rows in the result set. Passing zero will cause the first row to be returned on the next call to `mysql_fetch_row`.

   void mysql_data_seek(MYSQL_RES *result, my_ulonglong offset);

❑   The function `mysql_row_tell` returns an offset value, indicating the current position in the result set. It is not a row number, and you can't use it with `mysql_data_seek`.

   MYSQL_ROW_OFFSET mysql_row_tell(MYSQL_RES *result);

❑   However, you can use it with

   MYSQL_ROW_OFFSET mysql_row_seek(MYSQL_RES *result, MYSQL_ROW_OFFSET offset);

   which moves the current position in the result set and returns the previous position.

   This pair of functions is most useful for moving between known points in the result set. Be careful not to confuse the offset value used by `row_tell` *and* `row_seek` *with the* `row_number` *used by* `data_seek`. *Your results will be unpredictable.*

❑   When you've done everything you need to do with your data, you must explicitly use `mysql_free_result`, which allows the MySQL library to clean up after itself.

   void mysql_free_result(MYSQL_RES *result);

❑   When you've finished with a result set you must always call this function to allow the MySQL library to tidy up the objects it has allocated.

Retrieving the Data

Now you can write your first data-retrieval application. You want to select all records where age is greater than 5. You don't how to process this data yet, so you'll start by simply retrieving it. The important section, where you retrieve a result set and loop through the retrieved data, is highlighted. This is select1.c:

```c
#include <stdlib.h>
#include <stdio.h>

#include "mysql.h"

MYSQL my_connection;
MYSQL_RES *res_ptr;
MYSQL_ROW sqlrow;

int main(int argc, char *argv[]) {
    int res;

    mysql_init(&my_connection);
    if (mysql_real_connect(&my_connection, "localhost", "rick",
                                        "secret", "foo", 0, NULL, 0)) {
        printf("Connection success\n");

        res = mysql_query(&my_connection, "SELECT childno, fname,
                                        age FROM children WHERE age > 5");

        if (res) {
            printf("SELECT error: %s\n", mysql_error(&my_connection));
        } else {
            res_ptr = mysql_store_result(&my_connection);
            if (res_ptr) {
                printf("Retrieved %lu rows\n", (unsigned long)mysql_num_rows(res_ptr));
                while ((sqlrow = mysql_fetch_row(res_ptr))) {
                    printf("Fetched data...\n");
                }
                if (mysql_errno(&my_connection)) {
                    fprintf(stderr, "Retrive error: %s\n", mysql_error(&my_connection));
                }
                mysql_free_result(res_ptr);        }

        }
        mysql_close(&my_connection);

    } else {
        fprintf(stderr, "Connection failed\n");
        if (mysql_errno(&my_connection)) {
            fprintf(stderr, "Connection error %d: %s\n",
                    mysql_errno(&my_connection), mysql_error(&my_connection));
        }
    }

    return EXIT_SUCCESS;
}
```

Retrieving the Data One Row at a Time

To retrieve the data row by row, which is what you really want to do, you'll rely on `mysql_use_result` rather than `mysql_store_result`.

```
MYSQL_RES *mysql_use_result(MYSQL *connection);
```

Like the `mysql_store_result` function, `mysql_use_result` returns NULL on error; if successful, it returns a pointer to a result set object. However, it differs in that hasn't retrieved any data into the result set that it initialized.

> *You must use* `mysql_fetch_row` *repeatedly until all the data has been retrieved in order to actually get at the data. If you don't get all the data from* `mysql_use_result`, *subsequent operations by your program to retrieve data may return corrupt information.*

So what's the impact of calling `mysql_use_result` versus `mysql_store_result`? There are substantial resource management benefits to the former; but it can't be used with `mysql_data_seek`, `mysql_row_seek`, or `mysql_row_tell`, and the utility of `mysql_num_rows` is limited by the fact that it won't actually fire until all the data has been retrieved.

You've also increased your latency, because each row request has to go across the network and the results sent back the same way. Another possibility is that the network connection could fail in mid-operation, leaving you with incomplete data.

None of this diminishes in any way, however, the benefits alluded to earlier: a better-balanced network load and less storage overhead for possibly very large data sets.

Changing `select1.c` into `select2.c`, which will use the `mysql_use_result` method, is easy, so we just show the changed section here with shaded lines:

```
if (res) {
    printf("SELECT error: %s\n", mysql_error(&my_connection));
} else {
    res_ptr = mysql_use_result(&my_connection);
    if (res_ptr) {
        while ((sqlrow = mysql_fetch_row(res_ptr))) {
            printf("Fetched data...\n");
        }
        if (mysql_errno(&my_connection)) {
            printf("Retrive error: %s\n", mysql_error(&my_connection));
        }
        mysql_free_result(res_ptr);
    }

}
```

Observe that you still can't get a row count until your last result is retrieved. However, by checking for errors early and often, you've made the move to `mysql_use_result` much easier to apply. Coding in this way can save a lot of headache on subsequent modifications to the application.

Processing Returned Data

Now that you know how to retrieve the rows, you can look at processing the actual data returned.

MySQL, like most SQL databases, gives back two sorts of data:

❑ The retrieved information from the table, namely the column data

❑ Data about the data, so-called *metadata*, **such as column names and types**

Let's first focus on getting the data itself into a usable form.

The `mysql_field_count` function provides some basic information about a query result. It takes your connection object and returns the number of fields (columns) in the result set:

```
unsigned int mysql_field_count(MYSQL *connection);
```

In a more generic way, you can use `mysql_field_count` for other things, such as determining why a call to `mysql_store_result` failed. For example, if `mysql_store_result` returns NULL, but `mysql_field_count` returns a positive number, you can hint at a retrieval error. However, if `mysql_field_count` returns a 0, there were no columns to retrieve, which would explain the failure to store the result. It's reasonable to expect that you will know how many columns are supposed to be returned by a particular query. This function is most useful, therefore, in generic query-processing components or any situation where queries are constructed on the fly.

In code written for older versions of MySQL, you may see `mysql_num_fields` *being used. This could take either a connection structure or a result structure pointer and return the number of columns.*

If you lay aside concerns about formatting, then you already know how to print out the data right away. You'll add the simple `display_row` function to your `select2.c` program.

Notice that you have made the connection, result, and row information returned from `mysql_fetch_row` *all global to simplify the example. In production code we would not recommend this.*

1. Here is a very simple routine for printing out the data:

```
void display_row() {
   unsigned int field_count;

   field_count = 0;
   while (field_count < mysql_field_count(&my_connection)) {
      printf("%s ", sqlrow[field_count]);
      field_count++;
   }
   printf("\n");
}
```

2. Append it to `select2.c` and add a declaration and a function call:

```
void display_row();
```

```
int main(int argc, char *argv[]) {
   int res;
```

```
mysql_init(&my_connection);
if (mysql_real_connect(&my_connection, "localhost", "rick",
                                        "bar", "rick", 0, NULL, 0)) {

    printf("Connection success\n");

    res = mysql_query(&my_connection, "SELECT childno, fname,
                                    age FROM children WHERE age > 5");

    if (res) {
        printf("SELECT error: %s\n", mysql_error(&my_connection));
    } else {
        res_ptr = mysql_use_result(&my_connection);
        if (res_ptr) {
            while ((sqlrow = mysql_fetch_row(res_ptr))) {
                printf("Fetched data...\n");
                display_row();
            }
        }
    }
}
```

3. Now save the finished product as `select3.c`. Finally, compile and run `select3` as follows:

```
$ gcc -I/usr/include/mysql select3.c -L/usr/lib/mysql -lmysqlclient -o select3
$ ./select3
Connection success
Fetched data...
1 Jenny 21
Fetched data...
2 Andrew 17
$
```

So the program is working, even if its output is not aesthetically pleasing. But you've failed to account for possible NULL values in the result. If you want to print out more neatly formatted (perhaps tabular) data, you'll need both the data and the metadata returned by MySQL. You can simultaneously retrieve both the metadata and the data into a new structure using `mysql_fetch_field`:

`MYSQL_FIELD *mysql_fetch_field(MYSQL_RES *result);`

You need to call this function repeatedly until a NULL is returned, which will signal the end of the data. Then you can use the pointer to the field structure data to get information about the column. The structure of MYSQL_FIELD is defined in `mysql.h`, as shown in the following table.

Field in **MYSQL_FIELD** Structure	Description
`char *name;`	The name of the column, as a string.
`char *table;`	The name of the table from which the column came. This tends to be more useful where a query uses multiple tables. Beware that a calculated value in the result, such as MAX, will have an empty string for the table name.

Continued on next page

Field in **MYSQL_FIELD** Structure	Description
`char *def;`	If you call the `mysql_list_fields` (which we are not covering here), this will contain the default value of the column.
`enum enum_field_types type;`	Type of the column. See the explanation immediately following this table.
`unsigned int length;`	The width of the column, as specified when the table was defined.
`unsigned int max_length;`	If you used `mysql_store_result`, this contains the length in bytes of the longest column value retrieved. It is not set if you used `mysql_use_result`.
`unsigned int flags;`	Flags tell you about the definition of the column, not about the data found. The common flags have obvious meanings and are NOT_NULL_FLAG, PRI_KEY_FLAG, UNSIGNED_FLAG, AUTO_INCREMENT_FLAG, and BINARY_FLAG. You can find the full list in the MySQL documentation.
`unsigned int decimals;`	The number of digits after the decimal place. Valid only for numeric fields.

Column types are quite extensive. You can find the full list in `mysql_com.h` and in the documentation. The common ones are

```
FIELD_TYPE_DECIMAL
FIELD_TYPE_LONG
FIELD_TYPE_STRING
FIELD_TYPE_VAR_STRING
```

One particularly useful defined macro is IS_NUM, which returns `true` if the type of the field is numeric, like this:

```
if (IS_NUM(myslq_field_ptr->type)) printf("Numeric type field\n");
```

Before you update your program, we should mention one extra function:

```
MYSQL_FIELD_OFFSET mysql_field_seek(MYSQL_RES *result,
                        MYSQL_FIELD_OFFSET offset);
```

You can use this to override the current field number that is internally incremented for each call to `mysql_fetch_field`. If you pass an offset of zero, you'll jump back to the first column.

Now that you have the information, you need to make your `select` program show all the additional data available concerning a given column.

This is `select4.c`; we reproduce the entire program here so that you can get a complete example to look at. Notice that it does not attempt an extensive analysis of the column types; it just demonstrates the principles required.

```c
#include <stdlib.h>
#include <stdio.h>

#include "mysql.h"

MYSQL my_connection;
MYSQL_RES *res_ptr;
MYSQL_ROW sqlrow;

void display_header();
void display_row();


int main(int argc, char *argv[]) {
    int res;
    int first_row = 1; /* Used to ensure we display the row header exactly once
when data is successfully retrieved */

    mysql_init(&my_connection);
    if (mysql_real_connect(&my_connection, "localhost", "rick",
                                           "secret", "foo", 0, NULL, 0)) {
        printf("Connection success\n");

        res = mysql_query(&my_connection, "SELECT childno, fname,
                                           age FROM children WHERE age > 5");

        if (res) {
            fprintf(stderr, "SELECT error: %s\n", mysql_error(&my_connection));
        } else {
            res_ptr = mysql_use_result(&my_connection);
            if (res_ptr) {
                while ((sqlrow = mysql_fetch_row(res_ptr))) {
                    if (first_row) {
                        display_header();
                        first_row = 0;
                    }
                    display_row();
                }
                if (mysql_errno(&my_connection)) {
                    fprintf(stderr, "Retrive error: %s\n",
                                    mysql_error(&my_connection));
                }
                mysql_free_result(res_ptr);
            }

        }
        mysql_close(&my_connection);
    } else {
        fprintf(stderr, "Connection failed\n");
```

```
        if (mysql_errno(&my_connection)) {
          fprintf(stderr, "Connection error %d: %s\n",
                              mysql_errno(&my_connection),
                              mysql_error(&my_connection));
        }
    }

    return EXIT_SUCCESS;
}


void display_header() {
    MYSQL_FIELD *field_ptr;

    printf("Column details:\n");
    while ((field_ptr = mysql_fetch_field(res_ptr)) != NULL) {
        printf("\t Name: %s\n", field_ptr->name);
        printf("\t Type: ");
        if (IS_NUM(field_ptr->type)) {
            printf("Numeric field\n");
        } else {
            switch(field_ptr->type) {
                case FIELD_TYPE_VAR_STRING:
                    printf("VARCHAR\n");
                break;
                case FIELD_TYPE_LONG:
                    printf("LONG\n");
                break;
                default:
                    printf("Type is %d, check in mysql_com.h\n", field_ptr->type);
            } /* switch */
        } /* else */

        printf("\t Max width %ld\n", field_ptr->length);
        if (field_ptr->flags & AUTO_INCREMENT_FLAG)
            printf("\t Auto increments\n");
        printf("\n");
    } /* while */
}


void display_row() {
    unsigned int field_count;

    field_count = 0;
    while (field_count < mysql_field_count(&my_connection)) {
        if (sqlrow[field_count]) printf("%s ", sqlrow[field_count]);
        else printf("NULL");
        field_count++;
    }
    printf("\n");
}
```

When you compile and run this program, the output you get is

```
$ ./select4
Connection success
Column details:
        Name: childno
        Type: Numeric field
        Max width 11
        Auto increments

        Name: fname
        Type: VARCHAR
        Max width 30

        Name: age
        Type: Numeric field
        Max width 11
Column details:
1 Jenny 21
2 Andrew 17
$
```

It's still not very pretty; but it illustrates nicely how you can process both raw data and the metadata that allows you to work more efficiently with your data.

There are other functions that allow you to retrieve arrays of fields and jump between columns. Generally all you need are the routines shown here; the interested reader can find more information in the MySQL manual.

Miscellaneous Functions

There are some additional API functions, shown in the following table, that we recommend you investigate. Generally, what's been discussed so far is enough for a functional program; however, you should find this partial listing useful.

Example API Call	Description
`char *mysql_get_client_info(void);`	Returns version information about the library that the client is using.
`char *mysql_get_host_info(MYSQL *connection);`	Returns server connection information.
`char *mysql_get_server_info(MYSQL *connection);`	Returns information about the server that you are currently connected to.
`char *mysql_info(MYSQL *connection);.`	Returns information about the most recently executed query, but works for only a few query types — generally INSERT and UPDATE statements. Otherwise returns NULL.

Continued on next page

Example API Call	...ption
`int mysql_select_db(MYSQL *connection, const char *dbname);`	Changes the default database to the one given as a parameter, provided that the user has appropriate permissions. On success, zero is returned.
`int mysql_shutdown(MYSQL *connection, enum mysql_enum_shutdown_level);`	If you have appropriate permissions, shuts down the database server you are connected to. Currently the shutdown level must be set to `SHUTDOWN_DEFAULT`. On success, zero is returned.

The CD Database Application

You are now going to see how you might create a simple database to store information about your CDs and then write some code to access that data. To keep things very simple, you will stick to just three database tables with a very simple relationship among them.

Start by creating a new database to use and then make it the current database:

```
mysql> create database blpcd;
Query OK, 1 row affected (0.00 sec)

mysql> use blpcd
Connection id:    10
Current database: blpcd

mysql>
```

Now you're ready to design and create the tables you need.

This example is slightly more sophisticated than before, in that you'll separate three distinct elements of a CD: the artist (or group), the main catalog entry, and the tracks. If you think about a CD collection and the elements it is comprised of, you realize that each CD is composed of a number of different tracks, but different CDs are related to each other in many ways: by the performer or group, by the company that produced it, by the music style portrayed, and so on.

You could make your database quite complex, attempting to store all these different elements in a flexible way; however, in this example you will restrict yourself to just the two most important relationships.

First, each CD is composed of a variable number of tracks, so you will store the track data in a table separate from the other CD data. Second, each artist (or band) will often have more than one album, so it would be useful to store the details of the artist once and then separately retrieve all the CDs the artist has made. You will not attempt to break down bands into different artists who may themselves have made solo albums, or deal with compilation CDs — you are trying to keep this simple!

Keep the relationships quite simple as well — each artist (which might be the name of a band) will have produced one or more CDs and each CD will be composed of one or more tracks. The relationships are illustrated in Figure 8-8.

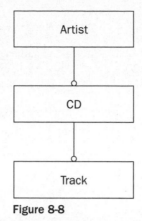

Figure 8-8

Creating the Tables

Now you need to determine the actual structure of the tables. Start with the main table — the CD table — which stores most of the information. You will need to store a CD ID, a catalog number, a title, and perhaps some of your own notes. You will also need an ID number from the artist table to tell you which artist made the album.

The artist table is quite simple; just store an artist name and a unique artist ID number. The track table is also very simple; you just need a CD ID to tell you which CD the track relates to, a track number, and the title of the track.

The CD table first:

```
CREATE TABLE cd (
    id INTEGER AUTO_INCREMENT NOT NULL PRIMARY KEY,
    title VARCHAR(70) NOT NULL,
    artist_id INTEGER NOT NULL,
    catalogue VARCHAR(30) NOT NULL,
    notes VARCHAR(100)
);
```

This creates a table called `cd` with the following columns:

❑   An `id` column, containing an integer that autoincrements and is the primary key for the table

❑   A `title` up to 70 characters long

❑   `artist_id`, an integer that you will use in your artist table

❑   A `catalogue` number of up to 30 characters

❑   Up to 100 characters of `notes`

Notice that only the `notes` column may be NULL; all the others must have values.

Now the artist table:

```
CREATE TABLE artist (
    id INTEGER AUTO_INCREMENT NOT NULL PRIMARY KEY,
    name VARCHAR(100) NOT NULL
);
```

Again you have an id column and one other column for the artist name.

Finally, the track table:

```
CREATE TABLE track (
    cd_id INTEGER NOT NULL,
    track_id INTEGER NOT NULL,
    title VARCHAR(70),
    PRIMARY KEY(cd_id, track_id)
);
```

Notice that this time you declare the primary key rather differently. The track table is unusual in that the ID for each CD will appear several times, and the ID for any given track, say track one, will also appear several times for different CDs. However, the combination of the two will always be unique, so declare your primary key to be a combination of the two columns. This is called a composite key, because it comprises more than one column taken in combination.

Store this SQL in a file called create_tables.sql, save it in the current directory, and then go ahead and create a database and then these tables in it. The sample script provided contains additional lines, commented out by default, to drop these tables if they already exist.

```
$ mysql -u rick -p
Enter password:
Welcome to the MySQL monitor.  Commands end with ; or \g.

mysql> use blpcd;
Database changed
mysql> \. create_tables.sql
Query OK, 0 rows affected (0.04 sec)

Query OK, 0 rows affected (0.10 sec)

Query OK, 0 rows affected (0.00 sec)

mysql>
```

Notice the use of the \. command to take input from the create_tables.sql file as input.

You could just as well have created the tables by executing the SQL, or simply typing in the data, using the MySQL Query Browser.

Once you have created your tables you can look at them using MySQL Administrator, as shown in Figure 8-9, where you are examining the indices tab of the blpcd database (or schema, depending on your preferred terminology).

By choosing to edit the table (right-click, or double-click the table name from the Tables tab), you can see more details about the columns. This is shown in Figure 8-10.

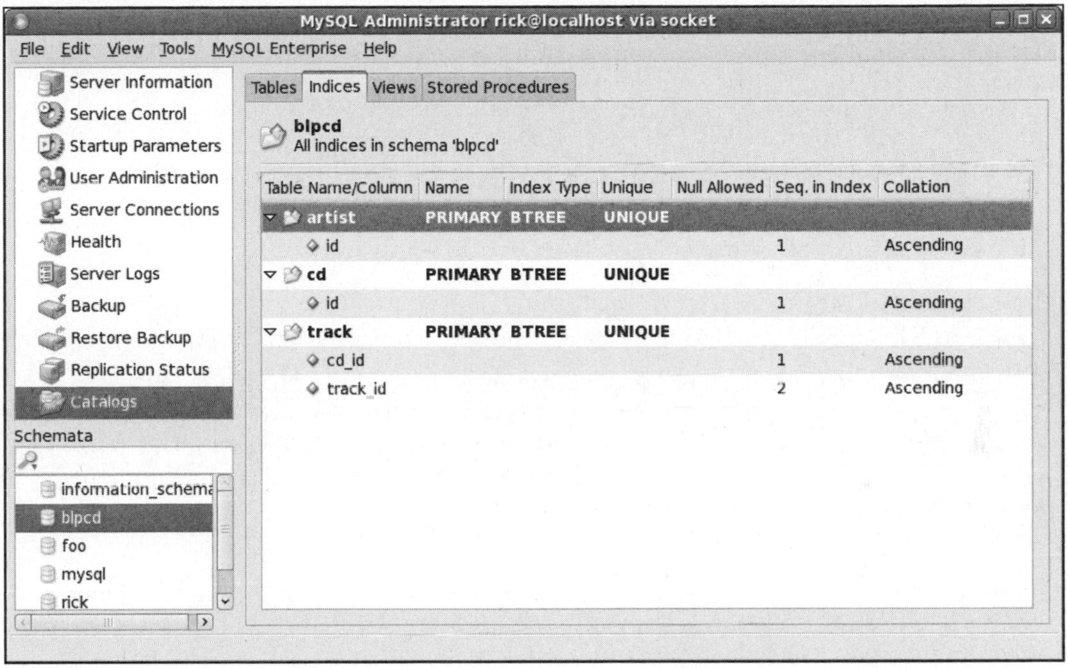

Figure 8-9

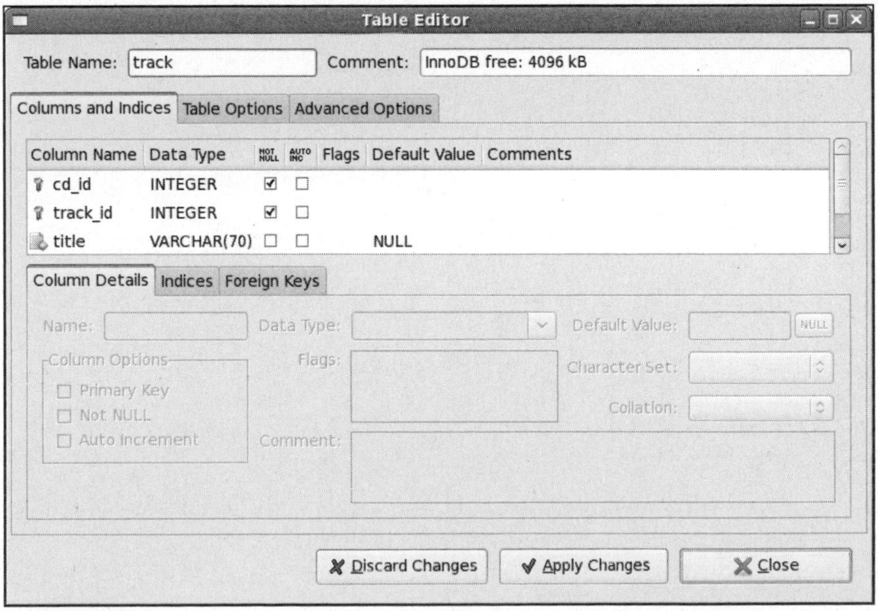

Figure 8-10

Do you notice the two key symbols against the `cd_id` and `track_id` columns in Figure 8-10? This shows that they are both contributing to the composite primary key. Allowing the track title to be NULL (notice that NOT NULL is not checked) allows for the uncommon but not unseen occurrence of a CD track that has no title.

Adding Some Data

Now you need to add some data. The best way of checking any database design is to add some sample data and check that it all works.

We will just show a sample of the test import data here, as it's not critical to understanding what is happening because all the imports are basically similar — they just load different tables. There are two important points to note here:

❏ The script deletes any existing data to ensure the script starts from a clean position.

❏ Insert values into the ID fields rather than allowing the AUTO_INCREMENT to take place. It's safer to do this here because the different inserts need to know which values have been used to ensure that the data relationships are all correct, so it's better to force the values, rather than allow the AUTO_INCREMENT function to automatically allocate values.

This file is called `insert_data.sql` and can be executed using the \. command you saw before.

```
--- Delete existing data
delete from track;
delete from cd;
delete from artist;


-- Now the data inserts

--- First the artist (or group) tables
insert into artist(id, name) values(1, 'Pink Floyd');
insert into artist(id, name) values(2, 'Genesis');
insert into artist(id, name) values(3, 'Einaudi');
insert into artist(id, name) values(4, 'Melanie C');

--- Then the cd table
insert into cd(id, title, artist_id, catalogue) values(1, 'Dark Side of the Moon',
1, 'B000024D4P');
insert into cd(id, title, artist_id, catalogue) values(2, 'Wish You Were Here', 1,
'B000024D4S');
insert into cd(id, title, artist_id, catalogue) values(3, 'A Trick of the Tail', 2,
'B000024EXM');
insert into cd(id, title, artist_id, catalogue) values(4, 'Selling England By the
Pound', 2, 'B000024E9M');
insert into cd(id, title, artist_id, catalogue) values(5, 'I Giorni', 3,
'B000071WEV');
insert into cd(id, title, artist_id, catalogue) values(6, 'Northern Star', 4,
'B00004YMST');

--- populate the tracks
insert into track(cd_id, track_id, title) values(1, 1, 'Speak to me');
insert into track(cd_id, track_id, title) values(1, 2, 'Breathe');
```

and the rest of the tracks for this album, and then the next album:

```
insert into track(cd_id, track_id, title) values(2, 1, 'Shine on you crazy
diamond');
insert into track(cd_id, track_id, title) values(2, 2, 'Welcome to the machine');
insert into track(cd_id, track_id, title) values(2, 3, 'Have a cigar');
insert into track(cd_id, track_id, title) values(2, 4, 'Wish you were here');
insert into track(cd_id, track_id, title) values(2, 5, 'Shine on you crazy diamond
pt.2');
```

and so on . . .

```
insert into track(cd_id, track_id, title) values(5, 1, 'Melodia Africana (part
1)');
insert into track(cd_id, track_id, title) values(5, 2, 'I due fiumi');
insert into track(cd_id, track_id, title) values(5, 3, 'In un\'altra vita');
```

. . . until the final tracks:

```
insert into track(cd_id, track_id, title) values(6, 11, 'Closer');
insert into track(cd_id, track_id, title) values(6, 12, 'Feel The Sun');
```

Next save this in pop_tables.sql and execute it from the mysql prompt using the \. command, as before.

> *Notice that in cd 5 (I Giorni) track 3, the track is In un'altra vita with an apostrophe. To insert this into the database you must use a backslash (\) to quote the apostrophe.*

Now would be a good time to check that your data is looking reasonable. You can use the mysql command-line client and some SQL to check for this. Start by selecting the first two tracks from every album in your database:

```
SELECT artist.name, cd.title AS "CD Title", track.track_id, track.title AS
"Track" FROM artist, cd, track WHERE artist.id = cd.artist_id AND track.cd_id
= cd.id AND track.track_id < 3
```

If you try this in MySQL Query Browser, you can see that the data looks fine, as shown in Figure 8-11.

The SQL looks complex, but it's not so bad if you take it a piece at a time.

Ignoring the AS parts of the SELECT command for a moment, the first part is simply this:

```
SELECT artist.name, cd.title, track.track_id, track.title
```

This simply tells which columns you want displayed, using the notation tablename.column name.

The AS parts of the SELECT statement, SELECT artist.name, cd.title AS "CD Title", track.track_id, and track.title AS "Track", simply rename the columns in the displayed output. Hence the header column for title from the cd table (cd.title) is named "CD Title," and the track.track.id column is titled "Track." This use of AS gives more user-friendly output. You would almost never use these names when calling SQL from another language, but AS is a useful clause for working with SQL on the command line.

363

Figure 8-11

The next section is also straightforward; it tells the server the name of the tables you are using:

```
FROM artist, cd, track
```

The WHERE clause is the slightly tricky part:

```
WHERE artist.id = cd.artist_id AND track.cd_id = cd.id AND track.track_id < 3
```

The first part tells the server that the ID in the artist's table is the same number as the artist_id in the cd column. Remember that you store the artist's name only once and use an ID to refer to it in the CD table. The next section, track.cd_id = cd.id, does the same for the tables track and cd, telling the server that the track table's cd_id column is the same as the id column in the cd table. The third section, track.track_id < 3, cuts down the amount of data returned so that you get only tracks 1 and 2 from each CD. Last, but not least, you join these three conditions together using AND because you want all three conditions to be true.

Accessing the Application Data from C

You are not going to write a complete application with a GUI in this chapter; rather, you are going to concentrate on writing an interface file to allow you to access your data from C in reasonably simple fashion. A common problem in writing code like this is the unknown number of results that can be returned and how to pass them between the client code and the code that accesses the database. In this application, to keep it simple and focus on the database interface — which is the important part of the code — you will use fixed-size structures. In a real application this may not be acceptable. A common solution, which also helps the network traffic, is to always retrieve the data one row at a time, as you saw earlier in the chapter with the functions mysql_use_result and mysql_fetch_row.

Interface Definition

Start with a header file that defines your structures and functions, named app_mysql.h.

First, some structures:

```
/* A simplistic structure to represent the current CD, excluding the track
information */
struct current_cd_st {
  int artist_id;
  int cd_id;
  char artist_name[100];
  char title[100];
  char catalogue[100];
};

/* A simplistic track details structure */
struct current_tracks_st {
  int cd_id;
  char track[20][100];
};

#define MAX_CD_RESULT 10
struct cd_search_st {
  int cd_id[MAX_CD_RESULT];
};
```

Now a pair of functions for connecting and disconnecting from the database:

```
/* Database backend functions */
int  database_start(char *name, char *password);
void database_end();
```

Now turn to the functions for manipulating the data. Notice that there are no functions for creating or deleting artists. You will implement this behind the scenes, creating artist entries as required and then deleting them when they are no longer in use by any album.

```
/* Functions for adding a CD */
int add_cd(char *artist, char *title, char *catalogue, int *cd_id);
int add_tracks(struct current_tracks_st *tracks);
/* Functions for finding and retrieving a CD */
int find_cds(char *search_str, struct cd_search_st *results);
int get_cd(int cd_id, struct current_cd_st *dest);
int get_cd_tracks(int cd_id, struct current_tracks_st *dest);
/* Function for deleting items */
int delete_cd(int cd_id);
```

The search function is fairly general: You pass a string and it searches for that string in the artist, title, or catalogue entries.

Test Application Interface

Before you implement your interface, you're going to write some code to use it. This might seem a little odd, but often it is a good way of understanding how the interface should behave in detail, before you settle down to implement it.

This is `app_test.c`. First some `includes` and `structs`:

```c
#include <stdlib.h>
#include <stdio.h>
#include <string.h>

#include "app_mysql.h"

int main() {
    struct current_cd_st cd;
    struct cd_search_st cd_res;
    struct current_tracks_st ct;
    int cd_id;
    int res, i;
```

The first thing your application must always do is initialize a database connection, providing a valid user name and password (be sure to substitute your own):

```c
database_start("rick", "secret");
```

Then you test adding a CD:

```c
res = add_cd("Mahler", "Symphony No 1", "4596102", &cd_id);
printf("Result of adding a cd was %d, cd_id is %d\n", res, cd_id);

memset(&ct, 0, sizeof(ct));
ct.cd_id = cd_id;
strcpy(ct.track[0], "Langsam Schleppend");
strcpy(ct.track[1], "Kraftig bewegt");
strcpy(ct.track[2], "Feierlich und gemessen");
strcpy(ct.track[3], "Sturmisch bewegt");
add_tracks(&ct);
```

Now search for the CD and retrieve information from the first CD found:

```c
res = find_cds("Symphony", &cd_res);
printf("Found %d cds, first has ID %d\n", res, cd_res.cd_id[0]);

res = get_cd(cd_res.cd_id[0], &cd);
printf("get_cd returned %d\n", res);

memset(&ct, 0, sizeof(ct));
res = get_cd_tracks(cd_res.cd_id[0], &ct);
printf("get_cd_tracks returned %d\n", res);
printf("Title: %s\n", cd.title);
i = 0;
while (i < res) {
```

```
        printf("\ttrack %d is %s\n", i, ct.track[i]);
        i++;
    }
```

Finally, delete the CD:

```
    res = delete_cd(cd_res.cd_id[0]);
    printf("Delete_cd returned %d\n", res);
```

Then disconnect and exit:

```
    database_end();

    return EXIT_SUCCESS;

}
```

Implementing the Interface

Now comes the harder part: implementing the interface you specified. This is all in the file app_mysql.c.

Start with some basic includes, the global connection structure you will need, and a flag, dbconnected, that you will use to ensure applications don't try to access data unless they have a connection. You also use an internal function, get_artist_id, to improve the structure of your code.

```
    #include <stdlib.h>
    #include <stdio.h>
    #include <string.h>

    #include "mysql.h"
    #include "app_mysql.h"

    static MYSQL my_connection;
    static int dbconnected = 0;

    static int get_artist_id(char *artist);
```

Getting a connection to the database is very simple, as you saw earlier in the chapter, and disconnecting again even easier:

```
    int database_start(char *name, char *pwd) {

        if (dbconnected) return 1;

        mysql_init(&my_connection);
        if (!mysql_real_connect(&my_connection, "localhost", name, pwd, "blpcd", 0,
    NULL, 0)) {
            fprintf(stderr, "Database connection failure: %d, %s\n",
    mysql_errno(&my_connection), mysql_error(&my_connection));
            return 0;
        }
        dbconnected = 1;
        return 1;
```

```
} /* database start */

void database_end() {
    if (dbconnected) mysql_close(&my_connection);
    dbconnected = 0;
} /* database_end */
```

Now the real work begins, with the function add_cd. You need some declarations first as well as a sanity check to ensure that you're connected to the database. You will see this in all the externally accessible functions you write.

Remember we said that the code would take care of artist names automatically:

```
int add_cd(char *artist, char *title, char *catalogue, int *cd_id) {

    MYSQL_RES *res_ptr;
    MYSQL_ROW mysqlrow;

    int res;
    char is[250];
    char es[250];
    int artist_id = -1;
    int new_cd_id = -1;

    if (!dbconnected) return 0;
```

The next thing is to check if the artist already exists; if not, you create one. This is all taken care of in the function get_artist_id, which you will see shortly.

```
    artist_id = get_artist_id(artist);
```

Now having got an artist_id, you can insert the main CD record. Notice the use of mysql_escape_string to protect any special characters in the title of the CD.

```
    mysql_escape_string(es, title, strlen(title));
    sprintf(is, "INSERT INTO cd(title, artist_id, catalogue)
VALUES('%s', %d, '%s')", es, artist_id, catalogue);
    res = mysql_query(&my_connection, is);
    if (res) {
       fprintf(stderr, "Insert error %d: %s\n",
mysql_errno(&my_connection), mysql_error(&my_connection));
       return 0;
    }
```

When you come to add the tracks for this CD, you will need to know the ID that was used when the CD record was inserted. You made the field an auto-increment field, so the database has automatically assigned an ID, but you need to explicitly retrieve the value. You can do this with the special function LAST_INSERT_ID, as you saw earlier in the chapter:

```
    res = mysql_query(&my_connection, "SELECT LAST_INSERT_ID()");
    if (res) {
      printf("SELECT error: %s\n", mysql_error(&my_connection));
```

```
        return 0;
    } else {
      res_ptr = mysql_use_result(&my_connection);
      if (res_ptr) {
        if ((mysqlrow = mysql_fetch_row(res_ptr))) {
        sscanf(mysqlrow[0], "%d", &new_cd_id);
        }
        mysql_free_result(res_ptr);
      }
```

You don't need to worry about other clients inserting CDs at the same time and the IDs becoming messed up; MySQL keeps track of the ID assigned on a per-client connection basis, so even if another application inserted a CD before you retrieved the ID, you would still get the ID corresponding to your row, not the row inserted by the other application.

Last, but not least, set the ID of the newly added row and return success or failure:

```
      *cd_id = new_cd_id;
      if (new_cd_id != -1) return 1;
      return 0;
    }
  } /* add_cd */
```

Now take a look at the implementation of get_artist_id; the process is very similar to inserting a CD record:

```
  /* Find or create an artist_id for the given string */
  static int get_artist_id(char *artist) {
    MYSQL_RES *res_ptr;
    MYSQL_ROW mysqlrow;

    int res;
    char qs[250];
    char is[250];
    char es[250];
    int artist_id = -1;

    /* Does it already exist? */
    mysql_escape_string(es, artist, strlen(artist));
    sprintf(qs, "SELECT id FROM artist WHERE name = '%s'", es);

    res = mysql_query(&my_connection, qs);
    if (res) {
      fprintf(stderr, "SELECT error: %s\n", mysql_error(&my_connection));
    } else {
      res_ptr = mysql_store_result(&my_connection);
      if (res_ptr) {
        if (mysql_num_rows(res_ptr) > 0) {
      if (mysqlrow = mysql_fetch_row(res_ptr)) {
        sscanf(mysqlrow[0], "%d", &artist_id);
      }
        }
        mysql_free_result(res_ptr);
```

```
        }
      }
      if (artist_id != -1) return artist_id;

      sprintf(is, "INSERT INTO artist(name) VALUES('%s')", es);
      res = mysql_query(&my_connection, is);
      if (res) {
        fprintf(stderr, "Insert error %d: %s\n",
  mysql_errno(&my_connection), mysql_error(&my_connection));
        return 0;
      }
      res = mysql_query(&my_connection, "SELECT LAST_INSERT_ID()");
      if (res) {
        printf("SELECT error: %s\n", mysql_error(&my_connection));
        return 0;
      } else {
        res_ptr = mysql_use_result(&my_connection);
        if (res_ptr) {
          if ((mysqlrow = mysql_fetch_row(res_ptr))) {
        sscanf(mysqlrow[0], "%d", &artist_id);
          }
          mysql_free_result(res_ptr);
        }
      }
      return artist_id;
    } /* get_artist_id */
```

Now move on to adding the track information for your CD. Again you protect against special characters in the track titles:

```
    int add_tracks(struct current_tracks_st *tracks) {

      int res;
      char is[250];
      char es[250];
      int i;

      if (!dbconnected) return 0;

      i = 0;
      while (tracks->track[i][0]) {
        mysql_escape_string(es, tracks->track[i], strlen(tracks->track[i]));
        sprintf(is, "INSERT INTO track(cd_id, track_id, title)
  VALUES(%d, %d, '%s')", tracks->cd_id, i + 1, es);
        res = mysql_query(&my_connection, is);
        if (res) {
          fprintf(stderr, "Insert error %d: %s\n",
  mysql_errno(&my_connection), mysql_error(&my_connection));
          return 0;
        }
        i++;
      }
      return 1;
    } /* add_tracks */
```

Now move on to retrieving information about a CD, given a CD ID value. You will use a database join to retrieve the artist ID at the same time you retrieve the CD information. This is generally good practice: Databases are good at knowing how to perform complex queries efficiently, so never write application code to do work that you could simply have asked the database to do by passing it SQL. Chances are that you can save yourself effort by not writing extra code, and have your application execute more efficiently by allowing the database to do as much of the hard work as possible.

```
int get_cd(int cd_id, struct current_cd_st *dest) {
  MYSQL_RES *res_ptr;
  MYSQL_ROW mysqlrow;

  int res;
  char qs[250];

  if (!dbconnected) return 0;
  memset(dest, 0, sizeof(*dest));
  dest->artist_id = -1;

  sprintf(qs, "SELECT artist.id, cd.id, artist.name, cd.title, cd.catalogue \
FROM artist, cd WHERE artist.id = cd.artist_id and cd.id = %d", cd_id);

  res = mysql_query(&my_connection, qs);
  if (res) {
    fprintf(stderr, "SELECT error: %s\n", mysql_error(&my_connection));
  } else {
    res_ptr = mysql_store_result(&my_connection);
    if (res_ptr) {
      if (mysql_num_rows(res_ptr) > 0) {
      if (mysqlrow = mysql_fetch_row(res_ptr)) {
        sscanf(mysqlrow[0], "%d", &dest->artist_id);
        sscanf(mysqlrow[1], "%d", &dest->cd_id);
        strcpy(dest->artist_name, mysqlrow[2]);
        strcpy(dest->title, mysqlrow[3]);
        strcpy(dest->catalogue, mysqlrow[4]);
      }
      }
      mysql_free_result(res_ptr);
    }
  }
  if (dest->artist_id != -1) return 1;
  return 0;
} /* get_cd */
```

Next you implement the retrieval of track information. Notice that you specify an ORDER BY clause in your SQL to ensure that tracks are returned in a sensible order. Again, this allows the database to do the work, which it will do much more efficiently than if you retrieved the rows in any order and then wrote your own code to sort them.

```
int get_cd_tracks(int cd_id, struct current_tracks_st *dest) {
  MYSQL_RES *res_ptr;
  MYSQL_ROW mysqlrow;

  int res;
  char qs[250];
  int i = 0, num_tracks = 0;
```

```
    .   if (!dbconnected) return 0;
        memset(dest, 0, sizeof(*dest));
        dest->cd_id = -1;

        sprintf(qs, "SELECT track_id, title FROM track WHERE track.cd_id = %d \
    ORDER BY track_id", cd_id);

        res = mysql_query(&my_connection, qs);
        if (res) {
          fprintf(stderr, "SELECT error: %s\n", mysql_error(&my_connection));
        } else {
          res_ptr = mysql_store_result(&my_connection);
          if (res_ptr) {
            if ((num_tracks = mysql_num_rows(res_ptr)) > 0) {
          while (mysqlrow = mysql_fetch_row(res_ptr)) {
            strcpy(dest->track[i], mysqlrow[1]);
            i++;
          }
          dest->cd_id = cd_id;
            }
            mysql_free_result(res_ptr);
          }
        }
        return num_tracks;
    } /* get_cd_tracks */
```

So far, you have added and retrieved information about CDs; now it's time to search for CDs. You kept the interface simple by limiting the number of results that could be returned, but you still want your function to tell you how many rows there were, even if that's more results than you can retrieve.

```
    int find_cds(char *search_str, struct cd_search_st *dest) {
      MYSQL_RES *res_ptr;
      MYSQL_ROW mysqlrow;

      int res;
      char qs[500];
      int i = 0;
      char ss[250];
      int num_rows = 0;

      if (!dbconnected) return 0;
```

Now clear the result structure and protect against special characters in the query string:

```
      memset(dest, -1, sizeof(*dest));
      mysql_escape_string(ss, search_str, strlen(search_str));
```

Next you build a query string. Notice the need to use rather a lot of % characters; this is because % is both the character you need to insert in the SQL to match any string and also a special character to sprintf.

```
      sprintf(qs, "SELECT DISTINCT artist.id, cd.id FROM artist, cd WHERE artist.id =
    cd.artist_id and (artist.name LIKE '%%%s%%' OR cd.title LIKE '%%%s%%' OR
    cd.catalogue LIKE '%%%s%%')", ss, ss, ss);
```

Now you can execute the query:

```
res = mysql_query(&my_connection, qs);
if (res) {
  fprintf(stderr, "SELECT error: %s\n", mysql_error(&my_connection));
} else {
  res_ptr = mysql_store_result(&my_connection);
  if (res_ptr) {
    num_rows = mysql_num_rows(res_ptr);
    if ( num_rows > 0) {
  while ((mysqlrow = mysql_fetch_row(res_ptr)) && i < MAX_CD_RESULT) {
    sscanf(mysqlrow[1], "%d", &dest->cd_id[i]);
    i++;
  }
    }
    mysql_free_result(res_ptr);
  }
}
return num_rows;
} /* find_cds */
```

Last, but not least, you implement a way of deleting CDs. In line with the policy of managing artist entries silently, you will delete the artist for this CD if no other CDs exist that have the same artist string. Curiously, SQL has no way of expressing deletes from multiple tables, so you must delete from each table in turn.

```
int delete_cd(int cd_id) {

  int res;
  char qs[250];
  int artist_id, num_rows;
  MYSQL_RES *res_ptr;
  MYSQL_ROW mysqlrow;

  if (!dbconnected) return 0;

  artist_id = -1;
  sprintf(qs, "SELECT artist_id FROM cd WHERE artist_id =
               (SELECT artist_id FROM cd WHERE id = '%d')", cd_id);
  res = mysql_query(&my_connection, qs);
  if (res) {
    fprintf(stderr, "SELECT error: %s\n", mysql_error(&my_connection));
  } else {
    res_ptr = mysql_store_result(&my_connection);
    if (res_ptr) {
      num_rows = mysql_num_rows(res_ptr);
      if (num_rows == 1) {
        /* Artist not used by any other CDs */
        mysqlrow = mysql_fetch_row(res_ptr);
        sscanf(mysqlrow[0], "%d", &artist_id);
      }
      mysql_free_result(res_ptr);
    }
  }
```

```
      sprintf(qs, "DELETE FROM track WHERE cd_id = '%d'", cd_id);
      res = mysql_query(&my_connection, qs);
      if (res) {
         fprintf(stderr, "Delete error (track) %d: %s\n",
mysql_errno(&my_connection), mysql_error(&my_connection));
         return 0;
      }

      sprintf(qs, "DELETE FROM cd WHERE id = '%d'", cd_id);
      res = mysql_query(&my_connection, qs);
      if (res) {
         fprintf(stderr, "Delete error (cd) %d: %s\n",
mysql_errno(&my_connection), mysql_error(&my_connection));
         return 0;
      }

      if (artist_id != -1) {
         /* artist entry is now unrelated to any CDs, delete it */
         sprintf(qs, "DELETE FROM artist WHERE id = '%d'", artist_id);
         res = mysql_query(&my_connection, qs);
         if (res) {
            fprintf(stderr, "Delete error (artist) %d: %s\n",
mysql_errno(&my_connection), mysql_error(&my_connection));
         }
      }

      return 1;

   } /* delete_cd */
```

That completes the code.

For the sake of completeness, add a Makefile to make your life easier. You may need to adjust the `include` path depending on how MySQL is installed on your system.

```
all:  app

app: app_mysql.c app_test.c app_mysql.h
     gcc -o app -I/usr/include/mysql app_mysql.c app_test.c
                               -lmysqlclient -L/usr/lib/mysql
```

In later chapters, you will see this interface being used with a real GUI. For now, if you want to watch the database changing as the code executes, we suggest you step through the code in the `gdb` debugger in one window while watching the database data change in another. If you use the MySQL Query Browser, remember that you will need to refresh the data displays to see the data change.

Summary

In this chapter, we've looked briefly at MySQL. More experienced users will discover many advanced features we have not had time to discuss in this chapter, such as foreign key constraints and triggers.

You've learned the basics of installing MySQL and looked at the basic administration of a MySQL database using the client utilities. We examined its C API, one of several languages that can be used with MySQL. You've also learned some SQL in the process.

We hope this chapter has encouraged you to try using a SQL-based database for your data, and also to find out more about these powerful database management tools.

As a reminder, the main resource for MySQL is the MySQL home page at `www.mysql.com`.

Development Tools

This chapter looks at some of the tools available for developing programs on Linux systems, some of which are also available for UNIX. In addition to the obvious necessities of compilers and debuggers, Linux provides a set of tools, each of which does a single job, and allows the developer to combine these tools in new and innovative ways. This is part of the UNIX philosophy Linux has inherited. Here, you look at a few of the more important tools and see some examples of their being used to solve problems. These tools include:

❑   The make command and makefiles

❑   Source code control using RCS and CVS

❑   Writing a manual page

❑   Distributing software using patch and tar

❑   Development environments

Problems of Multiple Source Files

When they're writing small programs, many people simply rebuild their application after edits by recompiling all the files. However, with larger programs, some problems with this simple approach become apparent. The time for the edit-compile-test cycle will grow. Even the most patient programmer will want to avoid recompiling all the files when only one file has been changed.

A potentially much more difficult problem arises when multiple header files are created and included in different source files. Suppose you have header files a.h, b.h, and c.h, and C source files main.c, 2.c, and 3.c. (We hope that you choose better names than these for real projects!) You could have the following situation:

```
/* main.c */
#include "a.h"
...
/* 2.c */
```

```
#include "a.h"
#include "b.h"
...
/* 3.c */
#include "b.h"
#include "c.h"
...
```

If the programmer changes c.h, the files main.c and 2.c don't need to be recompiled, because they don't *depend* on this header file. The file 3.c does depend on c.h and should therefore be recompiled if c.h is changed. However, if b.h was changed and the programmer forgot to recompile 2.c, the resulting program might no longer function correctly.

The make utility can solve both of these problems by ensuring that all the files affected by changes are recompiled when necessary.

> *The* make *command is not used only to compile programs. It can be used whenever you produce output files from several input files. Other uses include document processing (such as with troff or TeX).*

The make Command and Makefiles

Although, as you will see, the make command has a lot of built-in knowledge, it can't know how to build your application all by itself. You must provide a file that tells make how your application is constructed. This file is called the *makefile*.

The makefile most often resides in the same directory as the other source files for the project. You can have many different makefiles on your machine at any one time. Indeed, if you have a large project, you may choose to manage it using separate makefiles for different parts of the project.

The combination of the make command and a makefile provides a very powerful tool for managing projects. It's often used not only to control the compilation of source code, but also to prepare manual pages and to install the application into a target directory.

The Syntax of Makefiles

A makefile consists of a set of dependencies and rules. A *dependency* has a target (a file to be created) and a set of source files upon which it is dependent. The *rules* describe how to create the target from the dependent files. Typically, the *target* is a single executable file.

The makefile is read by the make command, which determines the target file or files that are to be made and then compares the dates and times of the source files to decide which rules need to be invoked to construct the target. Often, other intermediate targets have to be created before the final target can be made. The make command uses the makefile to determine the order in which the targets have to be made and the correct sequence of rules to invoke.

Options and Parameters to make

The make program itself has several options. The three most commonly used are

❑ -k, which tells make to keep going when an error is found, rather than stopping as soon as the first problem is detected. You can use this, for example, to find out in one go which source files fail to compile.

❑ -n, which tells make to print out what it would have done without actually doing it.

❑ -f <filename>, which allows you to tell make which file to use as its makefile. If you don't use this option, the standard version of make looks first for a file called makefile in the current directory. If that doesn't exist, it looks for a file called Makefile. However if you are using GNU Make, which you probably are on Linux, that version of make looks for GNUmakefile first, before searching for makefile and then Makefile. By convention, many Linux programmers use Makefile; this allows the makefile to appear first in a directory listing of a directory filled with lowercase-named files. We suggest you don't use the name GNUmakefile, because it is specific to the GNU implementation of make.

To tell make to build a particular target, which is usually an executable file, you can pass the target name to make as a parameter. If you don't, make will try to make the first target listed in the makefile. Many programmers specify all as the first target in their makefile and then list the other targets as being dependencies for all. This convention makes it clear which target the makefile should attempt to build by default when no target is specified. We suggest you stick to this convention.

Dependencies

The dependencies specify how each file in the final application relates to the source files. In the programming example shown earlier in the chapter, you might specify dependencies that say your final application requires (depends on) main.o, 2.o, and 3.o; and likewise for main.o (main.c and a.h); 2.o (2.c, a.h, and b.h); and 3.o (3.c, b.h, and c.h). Thus main.o is affected by changes to main.c and a.h, and it needs to be re-created by recompiling main.c if either of these two files changes.

In a makefile, you write these rules by writing the name of the target, a colon, spaces or tabs, and then a space- or tab-separated list of files that are used to create the target file. The dependency list for the earlier example is

```
myapp: main.o 2.o 3.o
main.o: main.c a.h
2.o: 2.c a.h b.h
3.o: 3.c b.h c.h
```

This says that myapp depends on main.o, 2.o, and 3.o, main.o depends on main.c and a.h, and so on.

This set of dependencies gives a hierarchy showing how the source files relate to one other. You can see quite easily that, if b.h changes, you need to revise both 2.o and 3.o, and because 2.o and 3.o will have changed, you also need to rebuild myapp.

If you want to make several files, you can use the phony target `all`. Suppose your application consisted of both the binary file `myapp` and a manual page, `myapp.1`. You could specify this with the line

```
all: myapp myapp.1
```

Again, if you don't specify an `all` target, `make` simply creates the first target it finds in the makefile.

Rules

The second part of the makefile specifies the rules that describe how to create a target. In the example in the previous section, what command should be used after the `make` command has determined that `2.o` needs rebuilding? It may be that simply using `gcc -c 2.c` is sufficient (and, as you'll see later, `make` does indeed know many default rules), but what if you needed to specify an `include` directory, or set the symbolic information option for later debugging? You can do this by specifying explicit rules in the makefile.

At this point, we have to clue you in to a very strange and unfortunate syntax of makefiles: the difference between a space and a tab. All rules must be on lines that start with a tab; a space won't do. Because several spaces and a tab look much the same and because almost everywhere else in Linux programming there's little distinction between spaces and tabs, this can cause problems. Also, a space at the end of a line in the makefile may cause a make *command to fail. However, it's an accident of history and there are far too many makefiles in existence to contemplate changing it now, so take care! Fortunately, it's usually reasonably obvious when the* make *command isn't working because a tab is missing.*

Try It Out   A Simple Makefile

Most rules consist of a simple command that could have been typed on the command line. For the example, you create your first makefile, `Makefile1`:

```
myapp: main.o 2.o 3.o
    gcc -o myapp main.o 2.o 3.o

main.o: main.c a.h
    gcc -c main.c

2.o: 2.c a.h b.h
    gcc -c 2.c

3.o: 3.c b.h c.h
    gcc -c 3.c
```

You invoke the `make` command with the `-f` option because your makefile doesn't have either of the usual default names of `makefile` or `Makefile`. If you invoke this code in a directory containing no source code, you get this message:

```
$ make -f Makefile1
make: *** No rule to make target 'main.c', needed by 'main.o'.  Stop.
$
```

The `make` command has assumed that the first target in the makefile, `myapp`, is the file that you want to create. It has then looked at the other dependencies and, in particular, determined that a file called `main.c` is needed. Because you haven't created this file yet and the makefile does not say how it might be created, make has reported an error. So now create the source files and try again. Because you're not interested in the result, these files can be very simple. The header files are actually empty, so you can create them with touch:

```
$ touch a.h
$ touch b.h
$ touch c.h
```

main.c contains main, which calls function_two and function_three. The other two files define function_two and function_three. The source files have #include lines for the appropriate headers, so they appear to be dependent on the contents of the included headers. It's not much of an application, but here are the listings:

```
/* main.c */
#include <stdlib.h>
#include "a.h"

extern void function_two();
extern void function_three();

int main()
{
    function_two();
    function_three();
    exit (EXIT_SUCCESS);
}
```

```
/* 2.c */
#include "a.h"
#include "b.h"

void function_two() {
}
```

```
/* 3.c */
#include "b.h"
#include "c.h"

void function_three() {
}
```

Now try make again:

```
$ make -f Makefile1
gcc -c main.c
gcc -c 2.c
gcc -c 3.c
gcc -o myapp main.o 2.o 3.o
$
```

This is a successful make.

How It Works

The `make` command has processed the dependencies section of the makefile and determined the files that need to be created and in which order. Even though you listed how to create `myapp` first, `make` has determined the correct order for creating the files. It has then invoked the appropriate commands you gave it in the rules section for creating those files. The `make` command displays the commands as it executes them. You can now test your makefile to see whether it handles changes to the file `b.h` correctly:

```
$ touch b.h
$ make -f Makefile1
gcc -c 2.c
gcc -c 3.c
gcc -o myapp main.o 2.o 3.o
$
```

The `make` command has read your makefile, determined the minimum number of commands required to rebuild `myapp`, and carried them out in the correct order. Now see what happens if you delete an object file:

```
$ rm 2.o
$ make -f Makefile1
gcc -c 2.c
gcc -o myapp main.o 2.o 3.o
$
```

Again, `make` correctly determines the actions required.

Comments in a Makefile

A comment in a makefile starts with # and continues to the end of the line. As in C source files, comments in a makefile can help both the author and others to understand what was intended when the file was written.

Macros in a Makefile

Even if this was all there was to `make` and makefiles, they would be powerful tools for managing multiple source file projects. However, they would also tend to be large and inflexible for projects consisting of a very large number of files. Makefiles therefore allow you to use macros so that you can write them in a more generalized form.

You define a macro in a makefile by writing `MACRONAME=value`, then accessing the value of `MACRONAME` by writing either `$(MACRONAME)` or `${MACRONAME}`. Some versions of `make` may also accept `$MACRONAME`. You can set the value of a macro to blank (which expands to nothing) by leaving the rest of the line after the = blank.

Macros are often used in makefiles for options to the compiler. Often, while an application is being developed, it will be compiled with no optimization, but with debugging information included. For a release version the opposite is usually needed: a small binary with no debugging information that runs as fast as possible.

Another problem with `Makefile1` is that it assumes the compiler is called `gcc`. On other UNIX systems, you might be using `cc` or `c89`. If you ever wanted to take your makefile to a different version of UNIX, or even if you obtained a different compiler to use on your existing system, you would have to change several lines of your makefile to make it work. Macros are a good way of collecting all these system-dependent parts, making it easy to change them.

Macros are normally defined inside the makefile itself, but they can be specified by calling `make` with the macro definition, for example, `make CC=c89`. Command-line definitions like this override `defines` in the makefile. When used outside makefiles, macro definitions must be passed as a single argument, so either avoid spaces or use quotes like this: `make "CC = c89"`.

Try It Out   **A Makefile with Macros**

Here's a revised version of the makefile, `Makefile2`, using some macros:

```
all: myapp

# Which compiler
CC = gcc

# Where are include files kept
INCLUDE = .

# Options for development
CFLAGS = -g -Wall -ansi

# Options for release
# CFLAGS = -O -Wall -ansi

myapp: main.o 2.o 3.o
    $(CC) -o myapp main.o 2.o 3.o

main.o: main.c a.h
    $(CC) -I$(INCLUDE) $(CFLAGS) -c main.c

2.o: 2.c a.h b.h
    $(CC) -I$(INCLUDE) $(CFLAGS) -c 2.c

3.o: 3.c b.h c.h
    $(CC) -I$(INCLUDE) $(CFLAGS) -c 3.c
```

If you delete your old installation and create a new one with this new makefile, you get

```
$ rm *.o myapp
$ make -f Makefile2
gcc -I. -g -Wall -ansi -c main.c
gcc -I. -g -Wall -ansi -c 2.c
gcc -I. -g -Wall -ansi -c 3.c
gcc -o myapp main.o 2.o 3.o
$
```

383

How It Works

The `make` program replaces macro references `$(CC)`, `$(CFLAGS)`, and `$(INCLUDE)` with the appropriate definitions, rather like the C compiler does with `#define`. Now if you want to change the compile command, you need to change only a single line of the makefile.

In fact, `make` has several special internal macros that you can use to make makefiles even more succinct. We list the more common ones in the following table; you will see them in use in later examples. Each of these macros is only expanded just before it's used, so the meaning of the macro may vary as the makefile progresses. In fact, these macros would be of very little use if they didn't work this way.

Macro	Definition
`$?`	List of prerequisites (files the target depends on) changed more recently than the current target
`$@`	Name of the current target
`$<`	Name of the current prerequisite
`$*`	Name of the current prerequisite, without any suffix

There are two other useful special characters you may see in a makefile, preceding a command:

❑ `-` tells `make` to ignore any errors. For example, if you wanted to make a directory but wished to ignore any errors, perhaps because the directory might already exist, you just precede `mkdir` with a minus sign. You will see `-` in use a bit later in this chapter.

❑ `@` tells `make` not to print the command to standard output before executing it. This character is handy if you want to use `echo` to display some instructions.

Multiple Targets

It's often useful to make more than a single target file, or to collect several groups of commands into a single place. You can extend your makefile to do this. In the following example, you add a `clean` option that removes unwanted objects and an `install` option that moves the finished application to a different directory.

Try It Out   Multiple Targets

Here's the next version of the makefile, `Makefile3`:

```
all: myapp

# Which compiler
CC = gcc

# Where to install
INSTDIR = /usr/local/bin
```

```
# Where are include files kept
INCLUDE = .

# Options for development
CFLAGS = -g -Wall -ansi

# Options for release
# CFLAGS = -O -Wall -ansi

myapp: main.o 2.o 3.o
    $(CC) -o myapp main.o 2.o 3.o

main.o: main.c a.h
    $(CC) -I$(INCLUDE) $(CFLAGS) -c main.c

2.o: 2.c a.h b.h
    $(CC) -I$(INCLUDE) $(CFLAGS) -c 2.c

3.o: 3.c b.h c.h
    $(CC) -I$(INCLUDE) $(CFLAGS) -c 3.c
```

```
clean:
    -rm main.o 2.o 3.o

install: myapp
    @if [ -d $(INSTDIR) ]; \
        then \
        cp myapp $(INSTDIR);\
        chmod a+x $(INSTDIR)/myapp;\
        chmod og-w $(INSTDIR)/myapp;\
        echo "Installed in $(INSTDIR)";\
    else \
        echo "Sorry, $(INSTDIR) does not exist";\
    fi
```

There are several things to notice in this makefile. First, the special target all still specifies only myapp as a target. Thus, when you execute make without specifying a target, the default behavior is to build the target myapp.

The next important point concerns the two additional targets, clean and install. The clean target uses the rm command to remove the objects. The command starts with -, which tells make to ignore the result of the command, so make clean will succeed even if there are no objects and the rm command returns an error. The rules for making the target "clean" don't specify clean as depending on anything; the rest of the line after clean: is blank. Thus the target is always considered out of date, and its rule is always executed if clean is specified as a target.

The install target is dependent on myapp, so make knows that it must create myapp before carrying out other commands for making install. The rules for making install consist of some shell script commands. Because make invokes a shell for executing rules and uses a new shell for each rule, you must add backslashes so that all the script commands are on one logical line and are all passed together to a single invocation of the shell for execution. This command starts with an @ sign, which tells make not to print the command on standard output before executing the rule.

The `install` target executes several commands one after the other to install the application in its final resting place. It does not check that each command succeeds before executing the next. If it was very important that subsequent commands executed only if the previous one had succeeded, you could have written the commands joined by `&&`, like this:

```
@if [ -d $(INSTDIR) ]; \
    then \
    cp myapp $(INSTDIR) &&\
    chmod a+x $(INSTDIR)/myapp && \
    chmod og-w $(INSTDIR/myapp && \
    echo "Installed in $(INSTDIR)" ;\
else \
    echo "Sorry, $(INSTDIR) does not exist" ; false ; \
fi
```

As you may remember from Chapter 2, this is an "and" command to the shell and has the effect that each subsequent command gets executed only if the previous one succeeded. Here you don't care too much about whether ensuring previous commands succeeded, so you can stick to the simpler form.

You may not have permission as an ordinary user to install new commands in `/usr/local/bin`. You can either change the makefile to use a different install directory, change permissions on this directory, or change user (with the `su` command) to root before invoking `make install`.

```
$ rm *.o myapp
$ make -f Makefile3
gcc -I. -g -Wall -ansi -c main.c
gcc -I. -g -Wall -ansi -c 2.c
gcc -I. -g -Wall -ansi -c 3.c
gcc -o myapp main.o 2.o 3.o
$ make -f Makefile3
make: Nothing to be done for 'all'.
$ rm myapp
$ make -f Makefile3 install
gcc -o myapp main.o 2.o 3.o
Installed in /usr/local/bin
$ make -f Makefile3 clean
rm main.o 2.o 3.o
$
```

How It Works

First you delete `myapp` and all the objects. The `make` command on its own uses the target `all`, which causes `myapp` to be built. Next you run `make` again, but because `myapp` is up to date, `make` does nothing. You then delete the file `myapp` and do a `make install`. This re-creates the binary and copies it to the install directory. Finally, you run `make clean`, which deletes the objects.

Built-in Rules

So far, you've specified in the makefile exactly how to perform each step of the process. In fact, make has a large number of built-in rules that can significantly simplify makefiles, particularly if you have many source files. To check this, create foo.c, a traditional Hello World program:

```
#include <stdlib.h>
#include <stdio.h>

int main()
{
    printf("Hello World\n");
    exit(EXIT_SUCCESS);
}
```

Without specifying a makefile, try to compile it using make:

```
$ make foo
cc      foo.c   -o foo
$
```

As you can see, make knows how to invoke the compiler, although, in this case, it chose cc rather than gcc (on Linux this is okay, because cc is usually a link to gcc). Sometimes, these built-in rules are referred to as *inference rules*. The default rules use macros, so by specifying some new values for the macros you can change the default behavior.

```
$ rm foo
$ make CC=gcc CFLAGS="-Wall -g" foo
gcc -Wall -g     foo.c   -o foo
$
```

You can ask make to print its built-in rules with the -p option. There are far too many built-in rules to list them all here, but here's a short extract from the output of make -p for the GNU version of make, showing part of the rules:

```
OUTPUT_OPTION = -o $@
COMPILE.c = $(CC) $(CFLAGS) $(CPPFLAGS) $(TARGET_ARCH) -c
%.o: %.c
#   commands to execute (built-in):
        $(COMPILE.c) $(OUTPUT_OPTION) $<
```

You can now simplify your makefile to take account of these built-in rules by taking out the rules for making objects and just specifying the dependencies, so the relevant section of the makefile reads simply

```
main.o: main.c a.h
2.o: 2.c a.h b.h
3.o: 3.c b.h c.h
```

You can find this version in the downloadable code as Makefile4.

Suffix and Pattern Rules

The built-in rules that you've seen work by using suffixes (similar to Windows and MS-DOS filename extensions), so that when it's given a file with one ending, make knows which rule can be used to create a file with a different ending. The most common rule here is the one used to create a file ending in .o from a file ending in .c. The rule is to use the compiler to compile but not to link the source file.

Sometimes you need to be able to create new rules. The authors used to work on source files that needed to be compiled by several different compilers: two under MS-DOS and gcc under Linux. To keep one of the MS-DOS compilers happy, the source files, which were C++ rather than C, needed to be named with a suffix of .cpp. Unfortunately, the version of make being used with Linux at the time didn't have a built-in rule for compiling .cpp files. (It did have a rule for .cc, a more common C++ file extension under UNIX.)

Thus either a rule had to be specified for each individual source file, or we needed to teach make a new rule for creating objects from files with the extension .cpp. Given that there were rather a large number of source files in this project, specifying a new rule saved a lot of typing and also made adding new source files to the project much easier.

To add a new suffix rule, you first add a line to the makefile telling make about the new suffix; you can then write a rule using this new suffix. make uses the special syntax

```
.<old_suffix>.<new_suffix>:
```

to define a general rule for creating files with the new suffix from files with the same base name but the old suffix.

Here's a fragment of the makefile with a new general rule for compiling .cpp files to .o files:

```
.SUFFIXES:          .cpp
.cpp.o:
    $(CC) -xc++ $(CFLAGS) -I$(INCLUDE) -c $<
```

The special dependency .cpp.o: tells make that the rules that follow are for translating from a file with a suffix of .cpp to a file with a suffix of .o. You use special macro names when writing this dependency because you don't yet know the actual names of the files that you'll be translating. To understand this rule, you simply need to remember that $< is expanded to the starting filename (with the old suffix). Notice that you tell make how to get only from a .cpp to a .o file; make already knows how to get from an object file to a binary executable file.

When you invoke make, it uses your new rule to get from bar.cpp to bar.o, then uses its built-in rules to get from the .o to an executable file. The extra -xc++ flag is to tell gcc that this is a C++ source file.

These days make knows how to deal with C++ source files with .cpp extensions, but the technique is a useful one when transforming from one kind of file to another.

More recent versions of make include an alternative syntax for achieving the same effect, and more besides. For example, pattern rules use % as a wildcard syntax for matching filenames rather than relying on file-name extensions alone.

The pattern rule equivalent for the preceding .cpp rule example would be

```
%.cpp: %o
    $(CC) -xc++ $(CFLAGS) -I$(INCLUDE) -c $<
```

Managing Libraries with make

When you're working on larger projects, it's often convenient to manage several compilation products using a *library*. Libraries are files, conventionally with the extension .a (for *archive*), that contain a collection of object files. The make command has a special syntax for dealing with libraries that makes them very easy to manage.

The syntax is lib(file.o), which means the object file file.o, as stored in the library lib.a. The make command has a built-in rule for managing libraries that is usually equivalent to something like this:

```
.c.a:
    $(CC) -c $(CFLAGS) $<
    $(AR) $(ARFLAGS) $@ $*.o
```

The macros $(AR) and $(ARFLAGS) normally default to the command ar and the options rv, respectively. The rather terse syntax tells make that to get from a .c file to an .a library it must apply two rules:

❑   The first rule says that it must compile the source file and generate an object.

❑   The second rule says to use the ar command to revise the library, adding the new object file.

So, if you have a library fud, containing the file bas.o, in the first rule $< is replaced by bas.c. In the second rule $@ is replaced by the library fud.a and $* is replaced by the name bas.

Try It Out   Managing a Library

In practice, the rules for managing libraries are quite simple to use. Here you change your application so that the files 2.o and 3.o are kept in a library called mylib.a. The makefile needs very few changes, and Makefile5 looks like this:

```
all: myapp

# Which compiler
CC = gcc

# Where to install
INSTDIR = /usr/local/bin

# Where are include files kept
INCLUDE = .

# Options for development
CFLAGS = -g -Wall -ansi

# Options for release
# CFLAGS = -O -Wall -ansi
```

```
# Local Libraries
MYLIB = mylib.a

myapp: main.o $(MYLIB)
    $(CC) -o myapp main.o $(MYLIB)

$(MYLIB): $(MYLIB)(2.o) $(MYLIB)(3.o)
main.o: main.c a.h
2.o: 2.c a.h b.h
3.o: 3.c b.h c.h

clean:
    -rm main.o 2.o 3.o $(MYLIB)
```

```
install: myapp
    @if [ -d $(INSTDIR) ]; \
    then \
        cp myapp $(INSTDIR);\
        chmod a+x $(INSTDIR)/myapp;\
        chmod og-w $(INSTDIR)/myapp;\
        echo "Installed in $(INSTDIR)";\
    else \
        echo "Sorry, $(INSTDIR) does not exist";\
    fi
```

Notice how we allow the default rules to do most of the work. Now test your new version of the makefile:

```
$ rm -f myapp *.o mylib.a
$ make -f Makefile5
gcc -g -Wall -ansi    -c -o main.o main.c
gcc -g -Wall -ansi    -c -o 2.o 2.c
ar rv mylib.a 2.o
a - 2.o
gcc -g -Wall -ansi    -c -o 3.o 3.c
ar rv mylib.a 3.o
a - 3.o
gcc -o myapp main.o mylib.a
$ touch c.h
$ make -f Makefile5
gcc -g -Wall -ansi    -c -o 3.o 3.c
ar rv mylib.a 3.o
r - 3.o
gcc -o myapp main.o mylib.a
$
```

How It Works

You first delete all the objects and the library and allow make to build myapp, which it does by compiling and creating the library before linking main.o with the library to create myapp. You then test the dependency rule for 3.o, which tells make that, if c.h changes, then 3.c must be recompiled. It does this correctly, compiling 3.c and updating the library before re-linking to create a new myapp executable file.

Advanced Topic: Makefiles and Subdirectories

If you're working on a large project, it's sometimes convenient to split some files that compose a library away from the main files and store them in a subdirectory. There are two ways of doing this with make.

First, you can have a second makefile in the subdirectory to compile the files, store them in a library, and then copy the library up a level into the main directory. The main makefile in the higher-level directory then has a rule for making the library, which invokes the second makefile like this:

```
mylib.a:
    (cd mylibdirectory;$(MAKE))
```

This says that you must always try to make mylib.a. When make invokes the rule for building the library, it changes into the subdirectory mylibdirectory and then invokes a new make command to manage the library. Because a new shell is invoked for this, the program using the makefile doesn't execute the cd. However, the shell invoked to carry out the rule to build the library is in a different directory. The brackets ensure that it's all processed by a single shell.

The second way is to use some additional macros in a single makefile. The extra macros are generated by appending a D for directory or an F for filename to those macros we've already discussed. You could then override the built-in .c.o suffix rule with

```
.c.o:
      $(CC) $(CFLAGS) -c $(@D)/$(<F) -o $(@D)/$(@F)
```

for compiling files in a subdirectory and leaving the objects in the subdirectory. You then update the library in the current directory with a dependency and rule something like this:

```
mylib.a:    mydir/2.o mydir/3.o
      ar -rv mylib.a $?
```

You need to decide which approach you prefer for your own project. Many projects simply avoid having subdirectories, but this can lead to a source directory with a ridiculous number of files in it. As you can see from the preceding brief overview, you can use make with subdirectories with only slightly increased complexity.

GNU make and gcc

If you're using GNU make and the GNU gcc compiler, there are two interesting extra options:

❑ The first is the -jN ("jobs") option to make. This allows make to execute N commands at the same time. Where several different parts of the project can be compiled independently, make will invoke several rules simultaneously. Depending on your system configuration, this can give a significant improvement in the time to recompile. If you have many source files, it may be worth trying this option. In general, smaller numbers such as -j3 are a good starting point. If you share your computer with other users, use this option with care. Other users may not appreciate your starting large numbers of processes every time you compile!

❑ The other useful addition is the -MM option to gcc. This produces a dependency list in a form suitable for make. On a project with a significant number of source files, each including different combinations of header files, it can be quite difficult (but very important) to get the dependencies correct. If you make every source file depend on every header file, sometimes you'll compile files unnecessarily. If, on the other hand, you omit some dependencies, the problem is even worse because you're now failing to compile files that need recompiling.

Try It Out   gcc -MM

In this Try It Out, you use the -MM option to gcc to generate a dependency list for your example project:

```
$ gcc -MM main.c 2.c 3.c
main.o: main.c a.h
2.o: 2.c a.h b.h
3.o: 3.c b.h c.h
$
```

How It Works

The gcc compiler simply scans the source files looking for includes and outputs the required dependency lines in a format ready for insertion into a makefile. All you have to do is save the output into a temporary file and then insert it into the makefile for a perfect set of dependency rules. There are no excuses for getting your dependencies wrong if you have a copy of gcc!

If you really feel confident about makefiles, you might try using the makedepend tool, which performs a function similar to the -MM option but actually appends the dependencies at the end of the specified makefile.

Before we leave the topic of makefiles, it's perhaps worth pointing out that you don't have to confine yourself to using makefiles to compile code or create libraries. You can use them to automate any task where there is a sequence of commands that get you from some sort of input file to an output file. A typical "non compiler" use might be for calling awk or sed to process some files, or even generating manual pages. You can automate just about any file manipulation, just as long as make can work out, from the date and time information on the files, which ones have changed.

Another possibility for controlling your builds, or indeed other automation of tasks, is ANT. This is a Java-based tool that uses XML-based configuration files. This tool isn't commonly used for automating the build of C files on Linux, so we will not discuss it further here. You can find more details of ANT at http://ant.apache.org/.

Source Code Control

If you move beyond simple projects, particularly if more than one person is working on the project, it becomes important to manage changes to source files properly to avoid conflicting changes and to track changes that have been made.

There are several widely used UNIX systems for managing source files:

❑   SCCS (Source Code Control System)

❑   RCS (Revision Control System)

❑   CVS (Concurrent Version System)

❑   Subversion

SCCS was the original source code control system introduced by AT&T in the System V versions of UNIX, and is now part of the X/Open standard. RCS was developed later as a free replacement for SCCS, and is distributed by the Free Software foundation. RCS is functionally very similar to SCCS, but has a more intuitive interface and some additional options, so SCCS has mostly been superceded by RCS.

The RCS utilities are a common option in Linux distributions or you can download them, along with their sources, from the Free Software Foundation at `http://directory.fsf.org/rcs.html`.

CVS, which is more advanced than SCCS or RCS, is the tool of choice for collaborative, Internet-based developments. You can find it on most Linux distributions, or at `http://www.nongnu.org/cvs/`. It has two significant advantages over RCS: it can be used over a network, and also allows concurrent development.

Subversion is the new kid on the block, designed to one day replace CVS. Its homepage is `http://www.subversion.org`.

In this chapter, we focus on RCS and CVS; RCS because it is easy to use for a one-person project and integrates well with `make`, and CVS because it is the commonest form of source code control used for collaborative projects. We also briefly compare the RCS commands with the SCCS commands because of SCCS's status as a POSIX standard and compare some CVS user commands with those in Subversion.

RCS

The Revision Control System (RCS) comprises a number of commands for managing source files. It works by tracking a source file as it's changed by maintaining a single file with a list of changes in sufficient detail to re-create any previous version. It also allows you to store comments associated with every change, which can be very useful if you're looking back through the history of changes to a file.

As a project progresses, you can log each major change or bug fix you make to a source file separately and store comments against each change. This can be very useful for reviewing the changes made to a file, checking where bugs were fixed and occasionally, perhaps, where bugs were introduced!

Because the RCS saves only the changes between versions, it's also very space efficient. The system also allows you to retrieve previous revisions in case of an accidental deletion.

The rcs Command

To illustrate, start with an initial version of the file you want to manage. In this case, let's use `important.c`, which starts life as a copy of `foo.c` with the following comment at the beginning:

```
/*
   This is an important file for managing this project.
   It implements the canonical "Hello World" program.
*/
```

The first task is to initialize RCS control over the file, using the rcs command. The command rcs -i initializes the RCS control file.

```
$ rcs -i important.c
RCS file: important.c,v
enter description, terminated with single '.' or end of file:
NOTE: This is NOT the log message!
>> This is an important demonstration file
>> .
done
$
```

You're allowed multiple comment lines. Terminate the prompting with a single period (.) on a line by itself, or by typing the end-of-file character, usually Ctrl+D.

After this command, rcs has created a new read-only file with a ,v extension:

```
$ ls -l
-rw-r--r--    1 neil      users        225 2007-07-09 07:52 important.c
-r--r--r--    1 neil      users        105 2007-07-09 07:52 important.c,v
$
```

If you prefer to keep your RCS files in a separate directory, simply create a subdirectory called RCS before you use rcs for the first time. All the rcs commands will automatically use the RCS subdirectory for RCS files.

The ci Command

You can now check in your file, using the ci command to store the current version:

```
$ ci important.c
important.c,v  <--  important.c
initial revision: 1.1
done
$
```

If you had forgotten to do rcs -i first, RCS would have asked for a description of the file. If you now look at the directory, you'll see that important.c has been deleted:

```
$ ls -l
-r--r--r--    1 neil      users        443 2007-07-07 07:54 important.c,v
$
```

The file contents and control information are all are stored in the RCS file: important.c,v.

The co Command

If you want to change the file, you must first "check out" the file. If you just want to read the file, you can use co to re-create the current version of the file and change the permissions to make it read-only. If you want to edit it, you must *lock* the file with co -l. The reason for this is that, in a team project, it's important to ensure that only one person at a time is modifying a given file, which is why only one copy of a given version of a file has write permission. When a file is checked out with write permission, the RCS file becomes locked. Lock a copy of the file

```
$ co -l important.c
important.c,v  -->  important.c
revision 1.1 (locked)
done
$
```

and look at the directory:

```
$ ls -l
-rw-r--r--    1 neil     users          225 2007-07-09 07:55 important.c
-r--r--r--    1 neil     users          453 2007-07-09 07:55 important.c,v
$
```

There's now a file for you to edit to put in your new changes. Now do some edits, store the new version, and use the ci command again to store the changes. The output section of important.c is now

```
        printf("Hello World\n");
        printf("This is an extra line added later\n");
```

You use ci like this:

```
$ ci important.c
important.c,v  <--  important.c
new revision: 1.2; previous revision: 1.1
enter log message, terminated with single '.' or end of file:
>> Added an extra line to be printed out.
>> .
done
$
```

To check in the file and retain the lock so that the user can continue to work on it, you should call ci *with its* -l *option. The file is automatically checked out again to the same user.*

You've now stored the revised version of the file. If you look at the directory, you see that important.c has again been removed:

```
$ ls -l
-r--r--r--    1 neil     users          635 2007-07-09 07:55 important.c,v
$
```

The rlog Command

It's often useful to look at a summary of changes to a file. You can do this with the rlog command:

```
$ rlog important.c

RCS file: important.c,v
Working file: important.c
head: 1.2
branch:
locks: strict
```

```
access list:
symbolic names:
keyword substitution: kv
total revisions: 2;     selected revisions: 2
description:
This is an important demonstration file
---------------------------
revision 1.2
date: 2007/07/09 06:57:33;  author: neil;  state: Exp;  lines: +1 -0
Added an extra line to be printed out.
---------------------------
revision 1.1
date: 2007/07/09 06:54:36;  author: neil;  state: Exp;
Initial revision
=============================================================================
$
```

The first part gives a description of the file and the options that `rcs` is using. The `rlog` command then lists the revisions of the file, most recent first, along with the text you entered when you checked in the revision. `lines: +1 -0` in revision 1.2 tells you that one line was added and none were deleted.

> Note that file modification times are stored without daylight savings adjustments to avoid any issues when the clocks change.

If you now want the first version of the file back, you can ask `co` for it by specifying the revision you require:

```
$ co -r1.1 important.c
important.c,v  -->  important.c
revision 1.1
done
$
```

`ci` also has a -r option, which forces the version number to a specified value. For example,

```
ci -r2 important.c
```

would check in `important.c` as version 2.1. Both RCS and SCCS default to using 1 as the first minor version number.

The rcsdiff Command

If you just want to know what was changed between two revisions, you can use the `rcsdiff` command:

```
$ rcsdiff -r1.1 -r1.2 important.c
===============================================================
RCS file: important.c,v
retrieving revision 1.1
retrieving revision 1.2
diff -r1.1 -r1.2
11a12
>     printf("This is an extra line added later\n");
$
```

The output tells you that a single line was inserted after the original line 11.

Identifying Revisions

The RCS system can use some special strings (macros) inside the source file to help track the changes. The most common two macros are $RCSfile$ and Id. The macro $RCSfile$ is expanded to the name of the file and Id expands to a string identifying the revision. Consult the manual pages for a full list of the special strings supported. The macros are expanded whenever a file revision is checked out and updated automatically when a revision is checked in.

Let's change the file for a third time and add some of these macros:

```
$ co -l important.c
important.c,v  -->  important.c
revision 1.2 (locked)
done
$
```

Edit the file so it now looks like this:

```c
#include <stdlib.h>
#include <stdio.h>

/*
  This is an important file for managing this project.
  It implements the canonical "Hello World" program.
  Filename: $RCSfile$
*/

static char *RCSinfo = "$Id$";

int main() {
    printf("Hello World\n");
    printf("This is an extra line added later\n");
    printf("This file is under RCS control. Its ID is\n%s\n", RCSinfo);
    exit(EXIT_SUCCESS);
}
```

Now check in this revision and see how RCS manages the special strings:

```
$ ci important.c
important.c,v  <--  important.c
new revision: 1.3; previous revision: 1.2
enter log message, terminated with single '.' or end of file:
>> Added $RCSfile$ and $Id$ strings
>> .
done
$
```

If you look in the directory, you find only the RCS file:

```
$ ls -l
-r--r--r--    1 neil     users        907 2007-07-09 08:07 important.c,v
$
```

If you check out (with the `co` command) and examine the current version of the source file, you can see the macros that have been expanded.

```
#include <stdlib.h>
#include <stdio.h>

/*
  This is an important file for managing this project.
  It implements the canonical "Hello World" program.
  Filename: $RCSfile: important.c,v $
*/

static char *RCSinfo = "$Id: important.c,v 1.3 2007/07/09 07:07:08 neil Exp $";

int main() {
    printf("Hello World\n");
    printf("This is an extra line added later\n");
    printf("This file is under RCS control. Its ID is\n%s\n", RCSinfo);
    exit(EXIT_SUCCESS);
}
```

Try It Out   GNU make with RCS

GNU `make` already has some built-in rules for managing RCS files. In this example you see how `make` deals with a missing source file.

```
$ rm -f important.c
$ make important
co  important.c,v important.c
important.c,v  -->  important.c
revision 1.3
done
cc    -c important.c -o important.o
cc    important.o   -o important
rm important.o important.c
$
```

How It Works

`make` has a default rule that to make a file with no extension you can compile a file of the same name but with a `.c` extension. A second default rule allows `make` to create `important.c` from `important.c,v` by using RCS. Because no file called `important.c` exists, `make` has created the `.c` file by checking out the latest revision with `co`. After compiling, it tidied up by deleting the file `important.c`.

The ident Command

You can use the `ident` command to find the version of a file that contains a `$Id$` string. Because you stored the string in a variable, it also appears in the resulting executable. You may find that if you include special strings but never access them in the code, some compilers will optimize them away. You can normally get around this problem by adding some dummy accesses to the string, although as compilers get better this is becoming more difficult!

Here is a simple example to show how you can use the ident command to double-check the RCS source version of a file used to build an executable.

Try It Out   ident

```
$ ./important
Hello World
This is an extra line added later
This file is under RCS control. Its ID is
$Id: important.c,v 1.3 2007/07/09 07:07:08 neil Exp $
$ ident important
important:
      $Id: important.c,v 1.3 2007/07/09 07 :07 :08 neil Exp $
$
```

How It Works

By executing the program, you show the string has been incorporated into the executable. Then you show how the ident command can extract Id strings from an executable file.

This technique of using RCS and Id strings that appear in executables can be a very powerful tool for checking which version of a file a customer is reporting a problem in. You can also use RCS (or SCCS) as part of a project-tracking facility to track problems being reported and how they are fixed. If you're selling software, or even giving it away, it's very important to know what was changed between different releases.

If you'd like more information, the rcsintro page in the manual gives a thorough introduction to the RCS system, in addition to the standard RCS pages. There are also manual pages for the individual commands ci, co, and so on.

SCCS

SCCS offers facilities very similar to RCS. The advantage of SCCS is that it's specified in X/Open, so all branded versions of UNIX should support it. On a more practical level, RCS is very portable and can be freely distributed. So if you have a UNIX-like system, whether it's X/Open-conformant or not, you should be able to obtain and install RCS for it. For this reason we don't describe SCCS further here, except to provide a brief command comparison for those moving between the two systems.

Comparing RCS and SCCS

It's difficult to provide a direct comparison of commands between the two systems, so the following table should only be considered as a quick pointer. The commands listed here don't take the same options to perform the same tasks. If you have to use SCCS, you'll need to find the appropriate options, but at least you'll know where to start looking.

RCS	SCCS
rcs	admin
ci	delta
co	get
rcsdiff	sccsdiff
ident	what

In addition to those listed previously, the SCCS sccs command has some crossover with the rcs and co commands in RCS. For example, sccs edit and sccs create are equivalent to co -l, and rcs -i, respectively.

CVS

An alternative to using RCS to manage changes to files is CVS, which stands for *Concurrent Versions System*. CVS has become extremely popular, probably because it has one distinct advantage over RCS: It's practical to use CVS over the Internet, not just on a shared local directory like RCS. CVS also allows for parallel development; that is, many programmers can work on the same file at once, whereas RCS allows only one user to work on one particular file at a time. CVS commands resemble RCS commands, because CVS was initially developed as a front end to RCS.

Because it can work across a network in a flexible way, CVS is suitable for use if the only network linking the developers is the Internet. Many Linux and GNU projects are using CVS to help the different developers coordinate their work. In general, the way that you use CVS on a remote set of files is almost identical to how you would use it on a local set.

In this chapter, we look briefly at the basics of CVS, so that you can get started with local repositories and understand how to get a copy of the latest sources of a project when the CVS server is on the Internet. More information is in the CVS manual, written by Per Cederqvist et al., available at http://ximbiot.com/cvs/manual/, where you will also find FAQ files and various other helpful files.

First you need to create a repository where CVS will store both its control files and the master copies of files that it is managing. A repository has a tree structure, so you can use a single repository to store not just a whole directory structure for a single project, but many projects in the same repository. However, you can use separate repositories for separate unrelated projects as well. In the following sections you'll see how to tell CVS which repository to use.

Using CVS Locally

Start by creating a repository. To keep it simple, this will be a local repository, and because you will be using only one, a convenient place to put it is somewhere in /usr/local. On most Linux distributions all normal users are members of the group users, so use this as the group of the repository so that all users can access it.

As superuser, create a directory for the repository:

```
# mkdir /usr/local/repository
# chgrp users /usr/local/repository
# chmod g+w /usr/local/repository
```

As a normal user again, initialize it as a CVS repository. You will need to have obtained write access to /usr/local/repository to do this, if you are not in the normal users group.

```
$ cvs -d /usr/local/repository init
```

The -d option tells CVS where you want the repository to be created.

Now that the repository has been created, you can store your initial versions of the project in CVS. However, at this point you can save yourself some typing. All cvs commands have two ways of looking for the CVS directory. First, they look for a -d <path> on the command line (as you used with the init command); if the -d option is not present, it looks for an environment variable CVSROOT. Rather than use the -d option all the time, you will set up this environment variable. This is the command to use if you use bash as your shell:

```
$ export CVSROOT=/usr/local/repository
```

First you change to the directory where the project is; then you tell CVS to import all the files in the directory. As far as CVS is concerned, a project is any collection of related files and directories. Typically this will include all the files necessary to create an application. The term *import* means to bring files under CVS control and copy them into the CVS repository. For this example you have a directory called cvs-sp (for CVS simple project) containing two files, hello.c and Makefile:

```
$ cd cvs-sp
$ ls -l
-rw-r--r--    1 neil      users           68 2003-02-15 11:07 Makefile
-rw-r--r--    1 neil      users          109 2003-02-15 11:04 hello.c
```

The CVS import command is cvs import and is used like this:

```
$ cvs import -m"Initial version of Simple Project" wrox/chap9-cvs wrox start
```

This bit of magic tells CVS to import all the files in the current directory (cvs-sp) and gives it a log message.

The wrox/chap9-cvs argument tells CVS where, relative to the root of the CVS tree, to store the new project. Remember that CVS can store multiple projects in the same repository if you want. The option wrox is a vendor tag used to identify the supplier of the initial version of files being imported, and start is a release tag. Release tags can be used to identify, as a group, sets of related files, such as those that make up a particular release of an application. CVS responds with

```
N wrox/chap9-cvs/hello.c
N wrox/chap9-cvs/Makefile

No conflicts created by this import
```

telling you that it imported two files correctly.

Now is a good time to check that you can retrieve your files from CVS. You can create a `junk` directory and check your files back out again to make sure all is well.

```
$ mkdir junk
$ cd junk
$ cvs checkout wrox/chap9-cvs
U wrox/chap9-cvs/Makefile
U wrox/chap9-cvs/hello.c
```

You give CVS the same path as when you checked the files in. CVS creates a directory `wrox/chap9-cvs` in the current directory and puts the files there.

Now you are ready to make some changes to your project. Edit `hello.c` in `wrox/chap9-cvs` and make a minor change by adding a line:

```
printf("Have a nice day\n");
```

Then recompile and run the program to check all is well.

```
$ make
cc hello.c -o hello
$ ./hello
Hello World
Have a nice day
$
```

You can ask CVS what has been changed in the project. You don't have to tell CVS which file you are interested in; it can work on a whole directory at a time:

```
$ cvs diff
```

CVS responds with

```
cvs diff: Diffing .
Index: hello.c
===================================================================
RCS file: /usr/local/repository/wrox/chap9-cvs/hello.c,v
retrieving revision 1.1.1.1
diff -r1.1.1.1 hello.c
6a7
>       printf("Have a nice day\n");
```

You are happy with the change, so you want to commit it to CVS.

When you commit a change with CVS, it will start an editor to allow you to enter a log message. You may want to set the environment variable CVSEDITOR to force a particular editor before you run the commit command.

```
$ cvs commit
```

CVS responds by telling you what it is checking in:

```
cvs commit: Examining .
Checking in hello.c;
/usr/local/repository/wrox/chap9-cvs/hello.c,v  <--  hello.c
new revision: 1.2; previous revision: 1.1
done
```

Now you can ask CVS about changes to the project since you first checked it in. Ask for a set of differences since revision 1.1 (the initial version) on project wrox/chap9-cvs.

```
$ cvs rdiff -r1.1 wrox/chap9-cvs
```

CVS tells you the details:

```
cvs rdiff: Diffing wrox/chap9-cvs
Index: wrox/chap9-cvs/hello.c
diff -c wrox/chap9-cvs/hello.c:1.1 wrox/chap9-cvs/hello.c:1.2
*** wrox/chap9-cvs/hello.c:1.1  Mon Jul  9 09:37:13 2007
--- wrox/chap9-cvs/hello.c      Mon Jul  9 09:44:36 2007
***************
*** 4,8 ****
--- 4,9 ----
  int main()
  {
      printf("Hello World\n");
+     printf("Have a nice day\n");
      exit (EXIT_SUCCESS);
  }
```

Suppose you have had a copy of code out of CVS for a while in a local directory and want to refresh files in your local directory that others have changed but that you have not edited. CVS can do this for you using the update command. Move to the top part of the path, in this case to the directory containing wrox, and execute the following command:

```
$ cvs update -Pd wrox/chap9-cvs
```

CVS will refresh files for you, extracting from the repository files that others have changed but that you have not and putting them in your local directory. Of course, some of the changes might be incompatible with your changes, but that is a problem you will have to work on. CVS is good, but it can't perform magic!

You can see by now that using CVS is very like using RCS. However, there is one very important difference that we haven't mentioned yet — the ability to operate over a network without using a mounted file system.

Accessing CVS over a Network

You told CVS where the repository was by either using a -d option to each command or setting the CVSROOT environment variable. If you want to operate over a network, you simply use a more advanced syntax for this parameter. For example, at the time of writing, the GNOME (GNU Network Object Model Environment, a popular open source graphical desktop system) development sources are all accessible on the Internet using CVS. You need only specify where the appropriate CVS repository is by pre-pending some network information to the front of the path specifier.

As another example, you can point CVS at the web standards body W3C CVS repository by setting CVS-ROOT to :pserver:anonymous@dev.w3.org:/sources/public. This tells CVS that the repository is using password authentication (pserver), and is on the server dev.w3.org.

Before you can access the sources, you need to do a login, like this:

```
$ export CVSROOT=:pserver:anonymous@dev.w3.org:/sources/public
$ cvs login
```

Enter anonymous when prompted for the password.

You are now ready to use cvs commands, much as though you were working on a local repository, with one minor exception — add the -z3 option to all cvs commands to force compression, saving network bandwidth.

If you want to fetch the W3C HTML validator sources, for example, the command is

```
$ cvs -z3 checkout validator
```

If you want to set your own repository to be accessible over the network, you need to start a CVS server on your machine. You can do this by starting it via either xinetd or inetd depending on your Linux system configuration. For xinetd, edit the file /etc/xinetd.d/cvs to reflect the CVS repository location and use the system configuration tool to enable and start the cvs service. For inetd, simply add a line to /etc/inetd.conf and restart inetd. The line you need is

```
2401 stream tcp nowait root /usr/bin/cvs cvs –b /usr/bin --allow-root =
/usr/local/repository pserver
```

This instructs inetd to automatically start a CVS session to clients connecting on port 2401, the standard CVS server port. For more information on starting network services via inetd, see the manual pages for inetd and inetd.conf.

To use CVS against your repository using network access you have to set your CVSROOT appropriately. For example,

```
$ export CVSROOT=:pserver:neil@localhost:/usr/local/repository
```

In this brief section, we have barely had room to scratch the surface of the facilities of CVS. If you want to use CVS seriously, we strongly urge you to set up a local repository to experiment on, get the extensive CVS documentation, and have fun! Remember, this is Open Source, so if you ever get seriously stuck about what the code is doing, or (unlikely, but possible!) think you have found a bug, you can always get the source code and have a look for yourself. The CVS home page is at http://ximbiot.com/cvs/cvshome/.

CVS Front Ends

Many graphical front ends are available for accessing CVS repositories. Probably the best collection for multiple operating systems is available from http://www.wincvs.org/. There are clients for Windows, Macintosh, and of course, Linux.

A CVS front end typically allows a repository to be created and managed, including remote access to network-based repositories.

Figure 9-1 shows the history of our simple application being displayed by WinCVS on a Windows network client.

```
wincvs - [C:\wrox\chap9-cvs\]
File  Edit  View  Admin  Remote  Modify  Query  Trace  Macros  Window  Help
```

Name	/	Ext	Rev.	Option	Encoding	State	Tag	Info	Modified
hello.c		c	1.2		Text				09/07/2007 09:44:26
Makefile			1.1.1.1		Text				09/07/2007 09:37:13

```
Rcs file : '/usr/local/repository/wrox/chap9-cvs/hello.c,v'
Working file : 'hello.c'
Head revision : 1.2
Branch revision :
Locks : strict
Access :
Symbolic names :
      1.1.1.1 : 'start'
      1.1.1 : 'wrox'
Keyword substitution : 'kv'
Total revisions : 3
Selected revisions : 3
Description :


------------------------------
Revision : 1.2
Date : 2007/7/9 8:44:26
Author : 'neil'
State : 'Exp'
Lines : +1 0
CommitID : '354c4691f54a4567'
Description :
*** empty log message ***

------------------------------
Revision : 1.1
Date : 2007/7/9 8:37:13
Author : 'neil'
State : 'Exp'
Lines : +0 0
```

Figure 9-1

Subversion

Subversion is intended to be a version control system that is a compelling replacement for CVS in the open source community. It is designed as a "better CVS" according to the Subversion home page at http://subversion.tigris.org/ and therefore has most of CVS's features, and the interface works in a similar way.

Subversion is certainly gaining in popularity, especially amongst community-developed projects where many developers work together to develop an application over the Internet. Most Subversion users connect to a network-based repository set up by the managers of the development project. It is not used as much to control individual or small group projects, where CVS is still the tool of choice.

The following table offers a comparison of equivalent important commands in CVS and Subversion.

CVS	Subversion
`cvs -d /usr/local/repository init`	`svnadmin create /usr/local/repository`
`cvs import wrox/chap9-cvs`	`svn import cvs-sp file:///usr/local/repository/trunk`
`cvs checkout wrox/chap9-cvs`	`svn checkout file:///usr/local/repository/trunk cvs-sp`
`cvs diff`	`svn diff`
`cvs rdiff`	`svn diff tag1 tag2`
`cvs update`	`svn status -u`
`cvs commit`	`svn commit`

For complete documentation on Subversion see the online book, "Version Control with Subversion" at `http://svnbook.red-bean.com/`.

Writing a Manual Page

If you're writing a new command as part of a task, you should create a manual page to go with it. As you've probably noticed, the layout of most manual pages follows a closely set pattern, which is of this form:

- ❑ Header
- ❑ Name
- ❑ Synopsis
- ❑ Description
- ❑ Options
- ❑ Files
- ❑ See also
- ❑ Bugs

You can leave out sections that aren't relevant. An "Author" section also often appears toward the bottom of Linux manual pages.

UNIX manual pages are formatted with a utility called `nroff`, or on most Linux systems the GNU project's equivalent, `groff`. Both of these are developments of an earlier `roff`, or run-off, command. The input to `nroff` or `groff` is plain text, except that at first glance the syntax looks impenetrably difficult.

Don't panic! As with UNIX programming, where the easiest way of writing a new program is to start with an existing program and adapt it, so it is with manual pages.

It's beyond the scope of this book to explain in detail the many options, commands, and macros that the `groff` (or `nroff`) command can use. Rather, we present a simple template that you can borrow and adapt for your own pages.

Here's the source of a simple manual page for the `myapp` application, in the file `myapp.1`:

```
.TH MYAPP 1
.SH NAME
Myapp \- A simple demonstration application that does very little.
.SH SYNOPSIS
.B myapp
[\-option ...]
.SH DESCRIPTION
.PP
\fImyapp\fP is a complete application that does nothing useful.
.PP
It was written for demonstration purposes.
.SH OPTIONS
.PP
It doesn't have any, but let's pretend, to make this template complete:
.TP
.BI \-option
If there was an option, it would not be -option.
.SH RESOURCES
.PP
myapp uses almost no resources.
.SH DIAGNOSTICS
The program shouldn't output anything, so if you find it doing so there's
probably something wrong. The return value is zero.
.SH SEE ALSO
The only other program we know with this little functionality is the
ubiquitous hello world application.
.SH COPYRIGHT
myapp is Copyright (c) 2007 Wiley Publishing, Inc.
This program is free software; you can redistribute it and/or modify
it under the terms of the GNU General Public License as published by
the Free Software Foundation; either version 2 of the License, or
(at your option) any later version.
This program is distributed in the hope that it will be useful,
but WITHOUT ANY WARRANTY; without even the implied warranty of
MERCHANTABILITY or FITNESS FOR A PARTICULAR PURPOSE.  See the
GNU General Public License for more details.
You should have received a copy of the GNU General Public License
along with this program; if not, write to the Free Software
Foundation, Inc., 59 Temple Place, Suite 330, Boston, MA  021111307  USA.
.SH BUGS
There probably are some, but we don't know what they are yet.
.SH AUTHORS
Neil Matthew and Rick Stones
```

As you can see, macros are introduced with a period (.) at the start of the line and tend to be abbreviated. The 1 at the end of the top line is the section of the manual in which the command appears. Because commands appear in section 1, that is where we place our new application.

You should be able to generate your own manual pages by modifying this one and inspecting the source for others. You might also take a look at the Linux Man Page mini-HowTo, written by Jens Schweikhardt as part of the Linux Documentation Project archives at http://www.tldp.org/.

Now that you have the source to the manual page, you can process it with groff. The groff command commonly produces ASCII text (-Tascii) or PostScript (-Tps) output. Tell groff it's a manual page using the -man option, which causes special manual page macro definitions to be loaded:

```
$ groff -Tascii -man myapp.1
```

This gives the output

```
MYAPP(1)                                                      MYAPP(1)
NAME
       Myapp  - A simple demonstration application that does very
       little.

SYNOPSIS
       myapp [-option ...]

DESCRIPTION
       myapp is a complete application that does nothing useful.

       It was written for demonstration purposes.

OPTIONS
       It doesn't have any, but let's pretend, to make this tem-
       plate complete:

       -option
              If there was an option, it would not be -option.

RESOURCES
       myapp uses almost no resources.

DIAGNOSTICS
       The program shouldn't output anything, so if you find  it
       doing so there's probably something wrong. The return
       value is zero.

SEE ALSO
       The only other program we know with this little func-
       tionality is the ubiquitous Hello World application.

COPYRIGHT
       myapp is Copyright (c) 2007 Wiley Publishing, Inc.
       This  program  is  free  software; you can redistribute it
       and/or modify it under the terms of the GNU General Public
       License  as  published  by  the Free Software Foundation;
```

```
either version 2 of the License, or (at your  option)  any
later version.
This  program  is  distributed in the hope that it will be
useful, but WITHOUT ANY WARRANTY; without even the implied
warranty  of  MERCHANTABILITY  or FITNESS FOR A PARTICULAR
PURPOSE.  See the GNU  General  Public  License  for  more
details.
```

1

MYAPP(1)   MYAPP(1)

```
You should have received a copy of the GNU General Public
License along with this program; if not, write to the Free
Software  Foundation,  Inc.,  59  Temple Place - Suite 330
Boston, MA 02111-1307, USA
```

BUGS
```
There probably are some, but we don't know what they  are
yet.
```

AUTHORS
```
Neil Matthew and Rick Stones
```

Now that you've tested the manual page, you need to install the source for it. The man command that shows manual pages uses the MANPATH environment variable to search for manual pages. You can either put the new page in a directory for local manual pages or store it directly in the system /usr/man/man1 directory.

The first time someone asks for this manual page, the man command will automatically format and display it. Some versions of man can automatically generate and store preformatted (and possibly compressed) ASCII text versions of manual pages to speed up subsequent requests for the same page.

Distributing Software

The main problem with program distribution is ensuring that all the files are included and are of exactly the right version. Fortunately, the Internet programming community has evolved a very robust set of methods that go a long way toward removing the problems. These methods include:

❑   Packaging all component files into a single package file using standard tools available on all Linux machines

❑   Controlled version numbering of packages

❑   A file-naming convention that includes the version number in the package file so that users can easily see which version they are dealing with

❑   Use of subdirectories in the package to ensure that, when files are extracted from the package file, they are placed in a separate directory so there's no confusion about what's included in the package and what isn't

The evolution of these methods has meant that programs can be easily and reliably distributed. The ease with which a program can be installed is another matter, because that depends on the program and the system on which it's being installed, but at least you can be sure that you have the right component files.

The patch Program

When programs are distributed, it's almost inevitable that users will discover bugs or that the author will want to issue enhancements and updates. When authors distribute programs as binaries, they often simply ship new binaries. Sometimes (all too often), vendors simply release a new version of the program, often with an obscure revision reference and little information about what has changed.

On the other hand, distributing your software as source code is an excellent idea because it allows people to see how you have implemented things and how you have used features. It also allows people to check exactly what programs are doing and to reuse parts of the source code (providing they comply with the licensing agreement).

However, with the source of the Linux kernel weighing in at tens of megabytes of compressed source code, shipping an updated set of kernel sources would involve considerable resources, when, in fact, probably only a small percentage of the source has changed between each release.

Fortunately, there is a utility program for solving this problem: patch. It was written by Larry Wall, who also wrote the Perl programming language. The patch command allows you to distribute just the differences between the two versions so that anyone with version 1 of a file and a difference file for version 1 to version 2 can use the patch command to generate version 2 for themselves.

If you start with version 1 of a file,

```
This is file one
line 2
line 3
there is no line 4, this is line 5
line 6
```

and then produce version 2,

```
This is file two
line 2
line 3
line 4
line 5
line 6
a new line 8
```

you can create a difference listing with the diff command:

```
$ diff file1.c file2.c > diffs
```

The diffs file contains

```
1c1
< This is file one
--
> This is file two
4c4,5
< there is no line 4, this is line 5
--
> line 4
```

```
> line 5
5a7
> a new line 8
```

This is actually a set of editor commands for changing one file into another. Suppose you have file1.c and the diffs file. You can update your file using patch as follows:

```
$ patch file1.c diffs
Hmm...  Looks like a normal diff to me...
Patching file file1.c using Plan A...
Hunk #1 succeeded at 1.
Hunk #2 succeeded at 4.
Hunk #3 succeeded at 7.
done
$
```

The patch command has now changed file1.c to be the same as file2.c.

patch has an extra trick: the ability to unpatch. Suppose you decide you don't like the changes and want your original file1.c back. No problem; just use patch again, using the -R (reverse patch) option:

```
$ patch -R file1.c diffs
Hmm...  Looks like a normal diff to me...
Patching file file1.c using Plan A...
Hunk #1 succeeded at 1.
Hunk #2 succeeded at 4.
Hunk #3 succeeded at 6.
done
$
```

file1.c is returned to its original state.

The patch command has several other options, but is generally very good at deciding from its input what you're trying to do and then simply "doing the right thing." If patch ever fails, it creates a file with the .rej extension containing the parts that couldn't be patched.

When you're dealing with software patches, it's a good idea to use the diff -c option, which produces a "context diff." This provides a number of lines before and after each change so that patch can verify that the context matches before applying the patch. The patch is also easier to read.

If you find and fix a bug in a program, it's easier, more precise, and more polite to send the author a patch rather than just a description of the fix.

Other Distribution Utilities

Linux programs and sources are commonly distributed in a file whose name contains the version number, with an extension of .tar.gz or .tgz. These are gzipped TAR (tape archive) files, also known as "tarballs." If you're using normal tar, you must process these files in two steps. The following code creates a gzipped TAR file of your application:

```
$ tar cvf myapp-1.0.tar main.c 2.c 3.c *.h myapp.1 Makefile5
main.c
```

411

```
2.c
3.c
a.h
b.h
c.h
myapp.1
Makefile5
$
```

You now have a TAR file:

```
$ ls -l *.tar
-rw-r--r--    1 neil     users        10240 2007-07-09 11:23 myapp-1.0.tar
$
```

You can make this smaller using the compression program `gzip`:

```
$ gzip myapp-1.0.tar
$ ls -l *.gz
-rw-r--r--    1 neil     users         1648 2007-07-09 11:23 myapp-1.0.tar.gz
$
```

As you can see, the result is a very impressive reduction in size. This .tar.gz may then be renamed to a simple .tgz extension:

```
$ mv myapp-1.0.tar.gz myapp_v1.tgz
```

This practice of renaming files to end with a dot and three characters seems to be a concession to Windows software, which, unlike Linux and UNIX, is heavily dependent on the correct extension being present. To get your files back, decompress and extract them from the tar file again:

```
$ mv myapp_v1.tgz myapp-1.0.tar.gz
$ gzip -d myapp-1.0.tar.gz
$ tar xvf myapp-1.0.tar
main.c
2.c
3.c
a.h
b.h
c.h
myapp.1
Makefile5
$
```

With GNU's version of `tar`, things are even easier — you can create the compressed archive in a single step:

```
$ tar zcvf myapp_v1.tgz main.c 2.c 3.c *.h myapp.1 Makefile5
main.c
2.c
3.c
a.h
b.h
c.h
```

```
myapp.1
Makefile5
$
```

You can also decompress it just as easily:

```
$ tar zxvf myapp_v1.tgz
main.c
2.c
3.c
a.h
b.h
c.h
myapp.1
Makefile5
$
```

If you want to list the contents of the archive without extracting them, you should call the `tar` program with the slightly different option `tar ztvf`.

We've been using `tar` for the preceding examples without describing the options any more than absolutely necessary. We'll now take a quick look at the command and a few of its more popular options. As you can see from the examples, the basic syntax is

```
tar [options] [list of files]
```

The first item in the list is the target, and although we've been dealing with files, it could just as well be a device. The other items in the list are added to a new or existing archive, depending on the options. The list can also include directories, in which case all subdirectories are included in the file by default. If you're extracting files, there's no need to specify names because full paths are preserved by `tar`.

In this section, we've used combinations of six different options:

- ❑   c: Creates a new archive.
- ❑   f: Specifies that the target is a file rather than a device.
- ❑   t: Lists the contents of an archive without actually extracting them.
- ❑   v (verbose): `tar` displays messages as it goes.
- ❑   x: Extracts file from an archive.
- ❑   z: Filters the archive through `gzip` from within GNU `tar`.

There are many more options to `tar` that allow finer control over the operation of the command and the archives it creates. Refer to the `tar` manual pages for more information.

RPM Packages

The RPM Package Manager, or RPM (don't you just love recursive abbreviations?), started life as the packaging format for Red Hat Linux (and was originally known as the Red Hat Package Manager). Since then, RPM has grown to be the accepted package format for many other Linux distributions, including SUSE Linux. RPM has also been adopted as the official package file format by the Linux Standards Base, or LSB, at www.linuxbase.org.

The main advantages of RPM include:

❑ It is widely used. Many Linux distributions can at least install RPM packages or use RPM as its native packaging format. RPM has been ported to a number of other operating systems as well.

❑ It allows you to install packages with a single command. You can also install packages automatically, because RPM was designed for unattended usage. You can remove a package or upgrade a package with a single command as well.

❑ You have only a single file to deal with. An RPM package is stored in a single file, making it much easier to transport a package from one system to another.

❑ RPM automatically handles dependency checks. The RPM system includes a database of all the packages you have installed, along with what each package provides to your system and information about each package's requirements.

❑ RPM packages are designed to be built from pristine sources, allowing you to reproduce a build. RPM supports Linux tools such as `patch` for applying changes to program source code during the build process.

Working with RPM Package Files

Each RPM package is stored in a file with an `rpm` extension. Package files usually follow a naming convention with the following structure:

```
name-version-release.architecture.rpm
```

With this structure, the *name* holds a generic name for the package, such as `mysql` for the MySQL database, or `make` for the make build tool. The *version* holds the version number of the software, such as version `5.0.41` of MySQL. The *release* holds a number that specifies which release of the RPM of that version of the software is contained in the file. This is important because RPM packages are built by a set of instructions (covered in the "Creating an RPM Spec File" section a bit later in this chapter). The release number allows you to track changes to the build instructions.

The *architecture* holds a specifier for the program architecture, such as `i386` for an Intel-based system. For compiled programs this is very important, because an executable created for a SPARC processor will likely not run on an Intel processor, for example. The architecture can be generic, such as `sparc` for a SPARC processor, or specific, such as `sparcv9` for a v9 SPARC or `athlon` for an AMD Athlon chip. Unless you override it, the RPM system will prevent you from installing packages built for a different architecture.

The architecture can also hold special values of `noarch` for packages that are not specific to a particular architecture, such as documentation files, Java programs, or Perl modules, and `src` for a source RPM. Source RPMs contain the files and build instructions to build a binary RPM package. Most RPM packages you will find for downloading are prebuilt for a particular architecture, which adds to the convenience. You can find thousands of Linux programs prebuilt and ready to install as RPM packages. This saves you the hassle of compiling.

In addition, some packages are so dependent on particular versions that it is far easier to download the prebuilt package than it is to test all the components by hand. For example, 802.11b wireless networking packages at one time came prebuilt for specific kernel patch levels for specific distributions of Linux, such as `kernel-wlan-ng-modules-rh9.18-0.2.0-7-athlon.rpm`, which contained kernel modules for Red Hat 9.0 with a 2.4.20-18 kernel on an AMD Athlon processor system.

Installing RPM Packages

To install an RPM package, run the `rpm` command. The format is simple:

```
rpm -Uhv name-version-release.architecture.rpm
```

For example,

```
$ rpm -Uhv MySQL-server-5.0.41-0.glibc23.i386.rpm
```

This command installs (or upgrades if needed) the MySQL database server package, for an Intel *x*86 architecture system.

The `rpm` command provides for most user interactions with the RPM system. You can query if a package is installed with a command such as the following:

```
$ rpm -qa xinetd
xinetd-2.3.14-40
```

Building RPM Packages

To build an RPM package, run the `rpmbuild` command. The process is relatively straightforward. You need to

- ❑ Gather the software you want to package.
- ❑ Create the spec file that describes how to build the package.
- ❑ Build the package with the `rpmbuild` command.

Because RPM creation can be very complex, we will stick to a simple example in this chapter, one that should be enough to distribute a reasonable application as source or binary. We will leave to the interested reader the more esoteric options and support for packages derived via patches. Check out the manual page for the `rpm` program, or the RPM HOWTO (usually found in `/usr/share/doc`) for more information. Also, check out the *Red Hat RPM Guide* by Eric Foster-Johnson (Red Hat Press/Wiley) also available online at `http://docs.fedoraproject.org/drafts/rpm-guide-en/`.

The following sections follow the preceding three steps for our trivial application, `myapp`.

Gathering the Software

The first step in building an RPM package is gathering the software you want to package. In most cases, you will have the application source code, a build file such as a *makefile*, and perhaps an online manual page.

The easiest way to gather this software together is to bundle these files into a *tarball*. Name the tarball with the application name and version number, such as myapp-1.0.tar.gz.

You can modify your earlier makefile, Makefile6, to add a new target to bundle the files into a tarball. The final version of the makefile, simply called Makefile, follows:

```
all: myapp

# Which compiler
CC = gcc

# Where are include files kept
INCLUDE = .

# Options for development
CFLAGS = -g -Wall -ansi

# Options for release
# CFLAGS = -O -Wall -ansi

# Local Libraries
MYLIB = mylib.a

myapp: main.o $(MYLIB)
    $(CC) -o myapp main.o $(MYLIB)

$(MYLIB): $(MYLIB)(2.o) $(MYLIB)(3.o)
main.o: main.c a.h
2.o: 2.c a.h b.h
3.o: 3.c b.h c.h

clean:
    -rm main.o 2.o 3.o $(MYLIB)

dist: myapp-1.0.tar.gz

myapp-1.0.tar.gz: myapp myapp.1
    -rm -rf myapp-1.0
    mkdir myapp-1.0
    cp *.c *.h *.1 Makefile myapp-1.0
    tar zcvf $@ myapp-1.0
```

The myapp-1.0.tar.gz target in the makefile builds a tarball of the sources for our trivial example application. This code added a dist target that calls the same commands for simplicity. Run the following command to make the bundle:

```
$ make dist
```

You then need to copy the file myapp-1.0.tar.gz to the RPM SOURCES directory, typically /usr/src/redhat/SOURCES on a Red Hat Linux system and /usr/src/packages/SOURCES on SUSE Linux. For example,

```
$ cp myapp-1.0.tar.gz /usr/src/redhat/SOURCES
```

The RPM system expects the sources to be located in the SOURCES directory as a tarball. (There are other options; this is the simplest.) SOURCES is just one of the directories expected by the RPM system.

The RPM system expects the five directories in the following table:

RPM Directory	Usage
BUILD	The rpmbuild command builds software in this directory.
RPMS	The rpmbuild command stores the binary RPMs it creates in this directory.
SOURCES	You should put the sources for the application in this directory.
SPECS	You should place the spec file for each RPM you plan to make in this directory, although this is not necessary.
SRPMS	The rpmbuild command places source RPMs in this directory.

The RPMS directory usually has a number of architecture-specific subdirectories, such as the following (on an Intel *x86* architecture system):

```
$ ls RPMS
athlon
i386
i486
i586
i686
noarch
```

By default, Red Hat Linux systems expect RPMs to be built in the /usr/src/redhat directory.

This directory is specific to Red Hat Linux. Other Linux distributions will use other directories, such as /usr/src/packages.

Once you have gathered the sources for your RPM package, the next step is to create a spec file, the file that describes to the rpmbuild command exactly how to build your package.

Creating an RPM Spec File

Creating a spec file can be daunting, given that the RPM system supports thousands of options. Luckily, the RPM system provides reasonable defaults for most options. You can follow the simple example in this section, which should suffice for most packages you will build. In addition, you can copy commands from other spec files.

Good sources for spec file examples are other RPM packages. Look at source RPMs, which are stored in files ending in .src.rpm. *Install these RPMs and look through the spec files. You should find more complicated examples than you will ever need. Interesting spec files include those for* anonftp, telnet, vnc, *and* sendmail.

In addition, the designers of the RPM system wisely decided not to try to replace common build tools such as `make` or `configure`. The RPM system contains many shorthand features to take advantage of makefiles and `configure` scripts.

In this example, you create a spec file for the simple `myapp` application. Name your spec file `myapp.spec`. Start the spec file with a set of definitions of the name, version number, and other information about your package. For example,

```
Vendor:          Wrox Press
Distribution:    Any
Name:            myapp
Version:         1.0
Release:         1
Packager:        neil@provider.com
License:         Copyright 2007 Wiley Publishing, Inc.
Group:           Applications/Media
```

This section of an RPM spec file is often called a *preamble*. In this preamble, the most important settings are the `Name`, `Version`, and `Release`. This example sets the name to `myapp`, the version number to `1.0`, and the release of the RPM package at `1`, your first attempt at making an RPM package.

The `Group` setting is used to help graphical installation programs sort the thousands of Linux applications by type. The `Distribution` is important if you build a package just for one Linux distribution, such as Red Hat or SUSE Linux.

Adding comments to your spec file is a good idea. Like shell scripts and *makefiles*, the `rpmbuild` command treats any line starting with a # character as a comment. For example,

```
# This line is a comment.
```

To help users decide whether to install your package, provide a `Summary` and a `%description` (note the inconsistency in the RPM syntax, with a percent sign before description). For example, you can describe your package as follows:

```
Summary:         Trivial application

%description
MyApp Trivial Application
A trivial application used to demonstrate development tools.
This version pretends it requires MySQL at or above 3.23.
Authors: Neil Matthew and Richard Stones
```

The `%description` section can take up multiple lines (and normally should).

The spec file can contain dependency information, both what your package provides and what your package depends on. (You can also define what the source package depends on, such as special header files necessary for compiling.)

The `Provides` setting defines what capabilities your system provides. For example,

```
Provides:        goodness
```

This example states that the package provides the imaginary capability called goodness. The RPM system will also automatically add a Provides entry for the name of the package, myapp in this case. The Provides settings are useful for multiple packages that may provide the same thing. For example, the Apache Web server package provides the capability webserver. Other packages, such as Thy, may also provide the same capability. (To help deal with conflicting packages, RPM allows you to specify Conflicts and Obsoletes information as well.)

The most important dependency information, though, is the Requires settings. You can state all the packages your package requires for operation. For example, a Web server requires networking and security packages. In the example, you define a requirement for the MySQL database, at version 3.23 or higher. The syntax for this follows:

```
Requires:          mysql >= 3.23
```

If you only want to require the MySQL database, at any version, you can use a setting like the following:

```
Requires:          mysql
```

RPM will prevent users from installing packages if the required packages are not also installed. (Users can override this behavior, though.)

The RPM system will automatically add dependencies such as /bin/sh for shell scripts, the Perl interpreter for Perl scripts, and any shared libraries (.so files) your application calls. Each release of the RPM system adds more smarts to the automatic dependency checks.

After you have defined the requirements, you need to define the sources that make up your application. For most applications, you can simply copy the following setting:

```
source:            %{name}-%{version}.tar.gz
```

The %{name} syntax refers to an RPM macro, in this case, the name of the package. Because you previously set the name to myapp, the rpmbuild command will expand %{name} to myapp, and similarly expand %{version} to 1.0, making for a file named myapp-1.0.tar.gz. The rpmbuild command will look for this file in the SOURCES directory described previously.

The example sets up a Buildroot, which defines a staging area to test the installation. You can copy the following for your packages:

```
Buildroot:         %{_tmppath}/%{name}-%{version}-root
```

Once a Buildroot is set up, install your applications to the Buildroot directory. You can use the handy variable $RPM_BUILD_ROOT, which is defined for all the shell scripts in the spec file.

After defining all these settings about the package, the next step is to define how to build the package. There are four main sections for building: %prep, %build, %install, and %clean.

As the name implies, the %prep section is for preparing to build. In most cases, you can run the %setup macro, shown here with a -q parameter to set it to quiet mode:

```
%prep
%setup -q
```

The `%build` section builds your application. In most cases, you can use a simple `make` command. For example,

```
%build
make
```

This is one way that the RPM system takes advantage of the work you've already done in creating your *makefile*.

The `%install` section installs your application, any manual pages, and any support files. You can often use the RPM macro `%makeinstall`, which calls the `install` target of the *makefile*. In this case, though, you can manually install the files to show more RPM macros:

```
%install
mkdir -p $RPM_BUILD_ROOT%{_bindir}
mkdir -p $RPM_BUILD_ROOT%{_mandir}
install -m755 myapp $RPM_BUILD_ROOT%{_bindir}/myapp
install -m755 myapp.1 $RPM_BUILD_ROOT%{_mandir}/myapp.1
```

This example creates the directories for the files, if needed, and then installs the `myapp` executable and `myapp.1` manual page. The `$RPM_BUILD_ROOT` environment variable holds the `Buildroot` location set previously. The `%{_bindir}` and `%{_mandir}` macros expand to the current binary directory and manual page directory, respectively.

If you use a `configure` script to create the makefile, all the various directories get set properly into your makefile. In most cases, you will not need to set up all the installation commands manually in the spec file as shown in the previous example.

The `%clean` target cleans up the files created by the `rpmbuild` command. For example,

```
%clean
rm -rf $RPM_BUILD_ROOT
```

After specifying how to build the package, you need to define all the files that will be installed. RPM is very rigid on this; it has to be rigid so that it can properly track every file from every package. The `%files` section names the files to include in the package. In this case, you have only two files to distribute in the binary package: the `myapp` executable and `myapp.1` manual page. For example,

```
%files
%{_bindir}/myapp
%{_mandir}/myapp.1
```

The RPM system can run scripts before and after your package is installed. For example, if your package is a demon process, you probably need to modify the system initialization scripts to start your demon. Do that with a `%post` script. A simple example that merely sends an e-mail message follows:

```
%post
mail root -s "myapp installed - please register" </dev/null
```

Look for examples in server RPM spec files.

The complete spec file for your trivial application follows:

```
#
# spec file for package myapp (Version 1.0)
#
Vendor:            Wrox Press
Distribution:      Any
Name:              myapp
Version:           1.0
Release:           1
Packager:          neil@provider.com
License:           Copyright 2007 Wiley Publishing, Inc.
Group:             Applications/Media

Provides:          goodness
Requires:          mysql >= 3.23

Buildroot:         %{_tmppath}/%{name}-%{version}-root
source:            %{name}-%{version}.tar.gz

Summary:           Trivial application

%description
MyApp Trivial Application
A trivial application used to demonstrate development tools.
This version pretends it requires MySQL at or above 3.23.
Authors: Neil Matthew and Richard Stones

%prep
%setup -q

%build
make

%install
mkdir -p $RPM_BUILD_ROOT%{_bindir}
mkdir -p $RPM_BUILD_ROOT%{_mandir}
install -m755 myapp $RPM_BUILD_ROOT%{_bindir}/myapp
install -m755 myapp.1 $RPM_BUILD_ROOT%{_mandir}/myapp.1

%clean
rm -rf $RPM_BUILD_ROOT

%post
mail root -s "myapp installed - please register" </dev/null

%files
%{_bindir}/myapp
%{_mandir}/myapp.1
```

You are now ready to build the RPM package.

Building an RPM Package with rpmbuild

Build packages with the rpmbuild command, which uses the following syntax:

```
rpmbuild -bBuildStage spec_file
```

The -b option tells rpmbuild to build an RPM. The extra BuildStage option is a special code that tells the rpmbuild command how far to go when building. We list the options in the following table.

Option	Usage
-ba	Build all, both a binary and source RPM.
-bb	Build a binary RPM.
-bc	Build (compile) the program but do not make the full RPM.
-bp	Prepare for building a binary RPM.
-bi	Create a binary RPM and install it.
-bl	Check the listing of files for the RPM.
-bs	Build a source RPM only.

To build both a binary and a source RPM, use the -ba option. The source RPM allows you to re-create the binary RPM.

Copy the RPM spec file to the correct SOURCES directory alongside the application source:

```
$ cp myapp.spec /usr/src/redhat/SOURCES
```

The following shows the output from building the package on a SUSE Linux installation where packages are built from /usr/src/packages/SOURCES:

```
$ rpmbuild -ba myapp.spec
Executing(%prep): /bin/sh -e /var/tmp/rpm-tmp.47290
+ umask 022
+ cd /usr/src/packages/BUILD
+ cd /usr/src/packages/BUILD
+ rm -rf myapp-1.0
+ /usr/bin/gzip -dc /usr/src/packages/SOURCES/myapp-1.0.tar.gz
+ tar -xf -
+ STATUS=0
+ '[' 0 -ne 0 ']'
+ cd myapp-1.0
++ /usr/bin/id -u
+ '[' 1000 = 0 ']'
++ /usr/bin/id -u
+ '[' 1000 = 0 ']'
+ /bin/chmod -Rf a+rX,u+w,g-w,o-w .
```

```
+ exit 0
Executing(%build): /bin/sh -e /var/tmp/rpm-tmp.99663
+ umask 022
+ cd /usr/src/packages/BUILD
+ /bin/rm -rf /var/tmp/myapp-1.0-root
++ dirname /var/tmp/myapp-1.0-root
+ /bin/mkdir -p /var/tmp
+ /bin/mkdir /var/tmp/myapp-1.0-root
+ cd myapp-1.0
+ make
gcc -g -Wall -ansi   -c -o main.o main.c
gcc -g -Wall -ansi   -c -o 2.o 2.c
ar rv mylib.a 2.o
ar: creating mylib.a
a - 2.o
gcc -g -Wall -ansi   -c -o 3.o 3.c
ar rv mylib.a 3.o
a - 3.o
gcc -o myapp main.o mylib.a
+ exit 0
Executing(%install): /bin/sh -e /var/tmp/rpm-tmp.47320
+ umask 022
+ cd /usr/src/packages/BUILD
+ cd myapp-1.0
+ mkdir -p /var/tmp/myapp-1.0-root/usr/bin
+ mkdir -p /var/tmp/myapp-1.0-root/usr/share/man
+ install -m755 myapp /var/tmp/myapp-1.0-root/usr/bin/myapp
+ install -m755 myapp.1 /var/tmp/myapp-1.0-root/usr/share/man/myapp.1
+ RPM_BUILD_ROOT=/var/tmp/myapp-1.0-root
+ export RPM_BUILD_ROOT
+ test -x /usr/sbin/Check -a 1000 = 0 -o
    -x /usr/sbin/Check -a '!' -z /var/tmp/myapp-1.0-root
+ echo 'I call /usr/sbin/Check...'
I call /usr/sbin/Check...
+ /usr/sbin/Check
-rwxr-xr-x 1 neil users 926 2007-07-09 13:35
    /var/tmp/myapp-1.0-root//usr/share/man/myapp.1.gz
Checking permissions and ownerships - using the permissions files
        /tmp/Check.perms.017506
setting /var/tmp/myapp-1.0-root/ to root:root 0755. (wrong owner/group neil:users)
setting /var/tmp/myapp-1.0-root/usr to root:root 0755. (wrong owner/group
 neil:users)
+ /usr/lib/rpm/brp-compress
+ /usr/lib/rpm/brp-symlink
Processing files: myapp-1.0-1
Finding  Provides: /usr/lib/rpm/find-provides myapp
Finding  Requires: /usr/lib/rpm/find-requires myapp
Finding  Supplements: /usr/lib/rpm/find-supplements myapp
Provides: goodness
Requires(interp): /bin/sh
Requires(rpmlib): rpmlib(PayloadFilesHavePrefix) <= 4.0-1
    rpmlib(CompressedFileNames) <= 3.0.4-1
Requires(post): /bin/sh
Requires: mysql >= 3.23 libc.so.6 libc.so.6(GLIBC_2.0)
```

```
Checking for unpackaged file(s): /usr/lib/rpm/check-files /var/tmp/myapp-1.0-root
Wrote: /usr/src/packages/SRPMS/myapp-1.0-1.src.rpm
Wrote: /usr/src/packages/RPMS/i586/myapp-1.0-1.i586.rpm
Executing(%clean): /bin/sh -e /var/tmp/rpm-tmp.10065
+ umask 022
+ cd /usr/src/packages/BUILD
+ cd myapp-1.0
+ rm -rf /var/tmp/myapp-1.0-root
+ exit 0
```

When the build is complete, you should see two packages: the binary RPM in the RPMS directory, under an architecture subdirectory such as RPMS/i586, and a source RPM in SRPMS.

The binary RPM filename will appear something like the following:

```
myapp-1.0-1.i586.rpm
```

The architecture on your system may be different.

The source RPM filename will appear as follows:

```
myapp-1.0-1.src.rpm
```

> **You need to install packages as the superuser. You do not have to build packages as root, so long as you have write access to the RPM directories, typically** /usr/src/ redhat. **Normally, you should not create RPM packages as root, because a spec file could have commands that may damage your system.**

Other Package Formats

Although RPM is a popular way of distributing applications in a way that allows users to control installing and uninstalling packages, there are competing packages out there. Some software is still distributed as gzipped tar files (tgz). Typically the installation steps consist of unpacking the archive into a temporary directory and running a script to perform the actual installation.

The Debian and Debian-based Linux distributions (and some others) support another package format, similar in functionality to RPM, called dpkg. The dpkg utility on Debian unpacks and installs package files that usually have a .deb extension. If you need to distribute an application using .deb file packages, it is possible to convert an RPM package to dpkg format using a utility called Alien. You can find more details on Alien at http://kitenet.net/programs/alien/.

Development Environments

Almost all of the tools we have looked at so far in this chapter are essentially command-line tools. Developers that have experience with Windows will no doubt have some experience with integrated development environments, or IDEs for short. IDEs are graphical environments that typically bring together some or all of the tools needed to create, debug, and run an application. Usually, they provide at least an editor, a file browser, and a method of running the application and capturing the output. More complete environments add support for generating source code files from templates for certain types of applications, integration with a source code control system, and automatic documentation.

In the following sections, we explore one such IDE, KDevelop, and mention a few of the other IDEs available for Linux today. These environments are under active development, with the most advanced of them beginning to rival the quality of commercial offerings.

KDevelop

KDevelop is an IDE for C and C++ programs. It includes particular support for the creation of applications to run under the K Desktop Environment (KDE), one of the two main graphical user interfaces on Linux today. It can also be used for other project types, including simple C programs.

KDevelop is free software released under the terms of the GNU General Public License (GPL) and is available with many Linux distributions. You can download the latest version from `http://www.kdevelop` `.org`. Projects created with KDevelop by default follow the standard for GNU projects. For example, they will use the `autoconf` utility to generate makefiles that are tailored to the environment for which they are being built. This means that the project is ready to be distributed as source code that stands a good chance of being able to be compiled on other systems.

KDevelop projects also contain templates for documentation, the GPL license text, and generic installation instructions. The number of files that are generated when making a new KDevelop project can be daunting, but should be familiar to anyone who has downloaded and compiled a typical GPL application.

There is support with KDevelop for CVS and Subversion source code control, and applications can be both edited and debugged without leaving the environment. Figures 9-2 and 9-3 show the default KDevelop C application (yet another Hello World! program) being edited and executed.

Other Environments

Many other editors and IDEs, both free and commercial, are available for Linux or under development. A few of the most interesting are listed in the following table.

Environment	Type	Product URL
Eclipse	Java-based tool platform and IDE	`http://www.eclipse.org`
Anjuta	An IDE for GNOME	`http://anjuta.sourceforge.net/`
QtEZ	An IDE for KDE	`http://projects.uid0.sk/qtez/`
SlickEdit	A commercial multi-language code editor	`http://www.slickedit.com/`

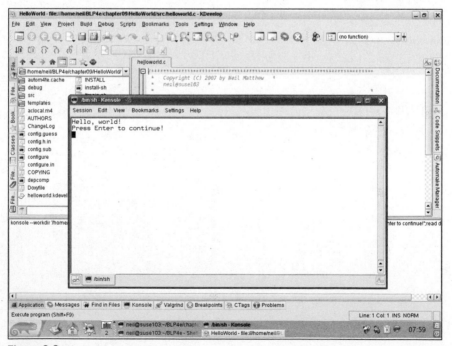

Figure 9-2

Figure 9-3

Summary

In this chapter, you've seen just a few of the Linux tools that make development and distribution of programs manageable. First, and perhaps most important, you used `make` and makefiles to manage multiple source files. You then looked at source code control with RCS and CVS, which lets you track changes as you develop your code. You then explored program distribution with `patch`, `tar` with `gzip`, and RPM packages. Finally, you took a look at one of the tools that make the edit-run-debug cycle of development a little easier, the KDevelop IDE.

10

Debugging

According to the Software Engineering Institute and the IEEE, every significant piece of software will initially contain defects, typically around two per 100 lines of code. These mistakes lead to programs and libraries that don't perform as required, often causing a program to behave differently than it's supposed to. Bug tracking, identification, and removal can consume a large amount of a programmer's time during software development.

In this chapter, we look at software defects and consider some tools and techniques for tracking down specific instances of erroneous behavior. This isn't the same as testing (the task of verifying the program's operation in all possible conditions), although testing and debugging are, of course, related, and many bugs are discovered during the testing process.

Topics we cover include

- ❑ Types of errors
- ❑ General debugging techniques
- ❑ Debugging with GDB and other tools
- ❑ Assertions
- ❑ Memory use debugging

Types of Errors

A bug usually arises from one of a small number of causes, each of which suggests a specific method of detection and removal:

- ❑ **Specification errors:** If a program is incorrectly specified, it will inevitably fail to perform as required. Even the best programmer in the world can sometimes write the wrong program. Before you start programming (or designing), make sure that you know and understand clearly what your program needs to do. You can detect and remove many (if not all) specification errors by reviewing the requirements and agreeing that they are correct with those who will use the program.

❑ **Design errors:** Programs of any size need to be designed before they're created. It's not usually enough to sit down at a computer keyboard, type source code directly, and expect the program to work the first time. Take time to think about how you will construct the program, what data structures you'll need, and how they will be used. Try to work out the details in advance, because it can save many rewrites later on.

❑ **Coding errors:** Of course, everyone makes typing errors. Creating the source code from your design is an imperfect process. This is where many bugs will creep in. When you're faced with a bug in a program, don't overlook the possibility of simply rereading the source code or asking someone else to. It's surprising just how many bugs you can detect and remove by talking through the implementation with someone else.

Languages with compilers, such as C, have an advantage here in that syntax errors can be caught at compile time, whereas interpreted languages such as the Linux shell might detect syntax errors only when you try to run the program. If the problem is with error-handling code, it might not be easy to spot in testing.

❑ Try executing the core of the program on paper, a process sometimes called *dry running*. For the most important routines, write down the values of inputs and calculate the outputs step by step. You don't always have to use a computer to debug, and sometimes it can be the computer causing the problems. Even the people who write libraries, compilers, and operating systems make mistakes! On the other hand, don't be too quick to blame the tools; it is more likely that there's a bug in a new program than in the compiler.

General Debugging Techniques

There are several distinct approaches to debugging and testing a typical Linux program. You generally run the program and see what happens. If it doesn't work, you need to decide what to do about it. You can change the program and try again (code inspection, trial and error), you can try to gain more information about what's happening inside the program (instrumentation), or you can inspect the program operation directly (controlled execution). The five stages of debugging are

❑ **Testing:** Finding out what defects or bugs exist

❑ **Stabilization:** Making the bugs reproducable

❑ **Localization:** Identifying the line(s) of code responsible

❑ **Correction:** Fixing the code

❑ **Verification:** Making sure the fix works

A Program with Bugs

Let's look at an example program that contains bugs. During the course of this chapter, you'll try to debug it. The program was written during the development of a larger software system. Its purpose is to test a single function, sort, which is intended to implement a bubble sort algorithm on an array of structures of type item. The items are sorted in ascending order of the member, key. The program calls sort on a sample array to test it. In the real world you would never seek to use this particular sort of algorithm, because it's far too inefficient. We have used it here because it is short, relatively simple to understand, and also easy to get wrong. In fact, the standard C library has a function that performs the desired task already called qsort.

Unfortunately, the code is not very readable, there are no comments, and the original programmer isn't available. You'll have to struggle with it on your own, starting from the basic routine debug1.c.

```
/*    1  */  typedef struct {
/*    2  */       char *data;
/*    3  */       int key;
/*    4  */  } item;
/*    5  */
/*    6  */  item array[] = {
/*    7  */       {"bill", 3},
/*    8  */       {"neil", 4},
/*    9  */       {"john", 2},
/*   10  */       {"rick", 5},
/*   11  */       {"alex", 1},
/*   12  */  };
/*   13  */
/*   14  */  sort(a,n)
/*   15  */  item *a;
/*   16  */  {
/*   17  */       int i = 0, j = 0;
/*   18  */       int s = 1;
/*   19  */
/*   20  */       for(; i < n && s != 0; i++) {
/*   21  */            s = 0;
/*   22  */            for(j = 0; j < n; j++) {
/*   23  */                 if(a[j].key > a[j+1].key) {
/*   24  */                      item t = a[j];
/*   25  */                      a[j] = a[j+1];
/*   26  */                      a[j+1] = t;
/*   27  */                      s++;
/*   28  */                 }
/*   29  */            }
/*   30  */            n--;
/*   31  */       }
/*   32  */  }
/*   33  */
/*   34  */  main()
/*   35  */  {
/*   36  */       sort(array,5);
/*   37  */  }
```

Now try to compile this program:

```
$ cc -o debug1 debug1.c
```

It compiles successfully, with no reported errors or warnings.

Before you run this program, add some code to print out the result. Otherwise, you won't know whether the program has worked. You will add some additional lines to display the array after it's been sorted. Call the new version debug2.c.

```
/*   33  */  #include <stdio.h>
/*   34  */  main()
/*   35  */  {
```

```
/*  36  */              int i;
/*  37  */              sort(array,5);
/*  38  */              for(i = 0; i < 5; i++)
/*  39  */                      printf("array[%d] = {%s, %d}\n",
/*  40  */                              i, array[i].data, array[i].key);
/*  41  */      }
```

This additional code isn't strictly part of the programmer's remit. We've had you put it in just for testing. You'll have to be very careful that you don't introduce further bugs in your test code. Now compile again and, this time, run the program.

```
$ cc -o debug2 debug2.c
$ ./debug2
```

What happens when you do this will depend on your flavor of Linux (or UNIX) and on how it's set up. On one of the authors' systems, we got

```
array[0] = {john, 2}
array[1] = {alex, 1}
array[2] = {(null), -1}
array[3] = {bill, 3}
array[4] = {neil, 4}
```

But on the other author's system (running a different Linux kernel), we got

```
Segmentation fault
```

On your Linux system, you may see either of these outputs or a different result entirely. We expected to see

```
array[0] = {alex, 1}
array[1] = {john, 2}
array[2] = {bill, 3}
array[3] = {neil, 4}
array[4] = {rick, 5}
```

Clearly there's a serious problem with this code. If it runs at all, it's failing to sort the array correctly, and if it's being terminated with a segmentation fault, the operating system is sending a signal to the program saying that it has detected an illegal memory access and is prematurely terminating the program to prevent memory from being corrupted.

The ability of the operating system to detect illegal memory access depends on its hardware configuration and some subtleties of its memory management implementation. On most systems, the memory allocated to the program by the operating system is larger than the memory actually being used. If the illegal memory access occurs in this region of memory, the hardware may not be able to detect the illegal access. This is why not all versions of Linux and UNIX will generate a segmentation violation.

> Some library functions, such as printf, will also prevent illegal accesses in some special circumstances, such as using a null pointer.

When you're tracking down array access problems, it's often a good idea to increase the size of array elements, because this increases the size of the error. If you read a single byte beyond the end of an array of bytes, you may get away with it, because the memory allocated to the program will be rounded up to an operating system–specific boundary, possibly as much as 8K.

If you increase the array element size, in this case by changing the item member data to be an array of 4,096 characters, any access to a nonexistent array element will probably be to a memory location beyond that allocated. Each element of the array is 4K in size, so the memory you use incorrectly will be 0–4K off the end.

If we do this, calling the result debug3.c, we get a segmentation fault on both the authors' flavors of Linux:

```
/*   2   */       char data[4096];
$ cc -o debug3 debug3.c
$ ./debug3
Segmentation fault
```

It's possible that some flavors of Linux or UNIX still won't produce a segmentation fault. When the ANSI C standard states that the behavior is undefined, it truly does allow the program to do anything. It certainly looks like we have written a non-conforming C program here, and a non-conforming C program may exhibit very strange behavior! As you will see, the fault does turn out to fall into the category of undefined behavior.

Code Inspection

As we mentioned earlier, it's often a good idea to reread your program when it fails to run as expected. For the purposes of this chapter, let's assume that the code has been reviewed and that obvious faults have been dealt with.

Code inspection is also a term for the more formal process of a group of developers tracing through a few hundred lines of code in detail, but the scale really doesn't matter; it's still code inspection and it's still a very useful technique.

There are tools that you can use to help with code reviews, the compiler being an obvious one. It will tell you if you have any syntax errors in your program.

Some compilers also have options to raise warnings on dubious practices, such as failing to initialize variables and using assignments in conditions. For example, the GNU compiler can be run with these options:

```
gcc -Wall -pedantic -ansi
```

They enable many warnings and additional checks for conformance to C standards. We recommend that you get into the habit of using these options, Wall especially. It can generate helpful information when tracking down program faults.

We'll mention other tools, lint and splint, a little later. Like the compiler, they analyze source code and report on code that might be incorrect.

Instrumentation

Instrumentation is the adding of code to a program for the purpose of collecting more information about the behavior of the program as it runs. It's very common to add `printf` calls, as in the example, to print out the values of variables at different stages in a program's execution. You could usefully add several `printf` calls, but you should be aware that the process entails an additional edit and compile whenever the program is changed, and of course, you will need to remove the code when the bugs are fixed.

There are two instrumentation techniques that can help here. The first uses the C preprocessor to selectively include instrumentation code so that you only need to recompile the program to include or exclude debugging code. You can do this quite simply with constructs such as

```
#ifdef DEBUG
    printf("variable x has value = %d\n", x);
#endif
```

You can compile the program with the compiler flag –DDEBUG to define the DEBUG symbol and include the extra code or without to exclude it. You can make more sophisticated use of a numeric debug macro, like this:

```
#define BASIC_DEBUG 1
#define EXTRA_DEBUG 2
#define SUPER_DEBUG 4

#if (DEBUG & EXTRA_DEBUG)
    printf...
#endif
```

In this case, you must always define the DEBUG macro, but you can set it to represent a set of debug information, or a level of detail. The compiler flag –DDEBUG=5 would, in this case, enable BASIC_DEBUG and SUPER_DEBUG, but not EXTRA_DEBUG. The flag –DDEBUG=0 would disable all debug information. Alternatively, including the following lines eliminates the need to specify DEBUG on the command line in the case where no debugging is required:

```
#ifndef DEBUG
#define DEBUG 0
#endif
```

Several macros defined by the C preprocessor can help with debug information. These are macros that expand to give information about the current compilation:

Macro	Description
__LINE__	A decimal constant representing the current line number
__FILE__	A string representing the current filename
__DATE__	A string of the form `"mmm dd yyyy"`, the current date
__TIME__	A string of the form `"hh:mm:ss"`, the current time

Note that these symbols are prefixed and suffixed by two underscores. This is common for standard preprocessor symbols, and you should take care to avoid choosing symbols that might clash. The term *current* in the preceding descriptions refers to the point at which the preprocessing is being performed, that is, the time and date the compiler was run and the file processed.

Try It Out   **Debug Information**

Here's a program, cinfo.c, that prints information about its compilation date and time if debugging is enabled:

```
#include <stdio.h>
#include <stdlib.h>

int main()
{
#ifdef DEBUG
    printf("Compiled: " __DATE__ " at " __TIME__ "\n");
    printf("This is line %d of file %s\n", __LINE__, __FILE__);
#endif
    printf("hello world\n");
    exit(0);
}
```

When you compile this program with debug enabled (using -DDEBUG), you see the compilation information:

```
$ cc -o cinfo -DDEBUG cinfo.c
$ ./cinfo
Compiled: Jun 30 2007 at 22:58:43
This is line 8 of file cinfo.c
hello world
$
```

How It Works

The C preprocessor part of the compiler keeps track of the current line and file when it's compiling. It substitutes the current (compile time) values of these variables whenever it encounters the symbols __LINE__ and __FILE__. The date and time of compilation are made available similarly. Because __DATE__ and __TIME__ are strings, you can concatenate them with format strings for printf because ANSI C specifies that adjacent strings be treated as one.

Debugging without Recompiling

Before we move on, it's worth mentioning that there's a way of using the printf function to help with debugging without using the #ifdef DEBUG technique, which requires a program to be recompiled before it can be used.

The method is to add a global variable as a debug flag, allow a -d option at the command line, which allows the user to switch debugging on even after the program has been released, and add a debug logging function. Now you can intersperse things like this in the program code:

```
if (debug) {
    sprintf(msg, ...)
    write_debug(msg)
}
```

You should write debug output to stderr, or, if this isn't practical because of the nature of the program, use the logging facilities provided by the syslog function.

If you add traces like this to solve problems during development, just leave the code in there. Provided you use a small amount of care, this can be quite safe. The benefit comes when the program has been released; if users encounter a problem, they can run it with debugging on and diagnose the errors for you. Instead of reporting that the program gave the message segmentation fault, they can also report exactly what the program was doing at the time, not just what the user was doing. The difference can be immense.

There is obviously a downside to this approach: the program is larger than it needs to be. In most cases, this is more an apparent problem than a real one. The program could be 20 percent or 30 percent larger, but in most cases this doesn't have any real impact on performance. Poor performance comes from increasing size by orders of magnitude, not by a small factor.

Controlled Execution

Let's get back to the example program. You have a bug. You can modify the program by adding additional code to print out the values of variables as the program runs, or you can use a debugger to control the program's execution and view its state as execution proceeds.

A number of debuggers are available on commercial UNIX systems, depending on the vendor. Common ones are adb, sdb, idebug, and dbx. The more sophisticated ones allow you to look at the state of the program in some detail at a source-code level. This is the case with the GNU debugger, gdb, which can be used with Linux and many UNIX variants. There also exist "front ends" to gdb, which make it more user-friendly; xxgdb, KDbg, and ddd are such programs. Some IDEs, such as the ones you saw in Chapter 9, also provide debugging facilities or a front end to gdb. The Emacs editor even has a facility (gdb-mode) that allows you to run gdb on your program, set breakpoints, and see which line in the source code is being executed.

To prepare a program for debugging, you need to compile it with one or more special compiler options. These options instruct the compiler to include extra debugging information into the program. This information includes symbols and line numbers — information the debugger can use to show the user where in the source code execution has reached.

The -g flag is the usual one used to compile a program for debugging. You must use it for compiling each source file that needs to be debugged and also for the linker, so that special versions of the standard C library can be used to provide debug support in library functions. The compiler program will pass the flag to the linker automatically. Debugging can be used with libraries that aren't compiled for the purpose, but with less flexibility.

Debug information can make the executable many (up to ten) times larger. Even though the executable may be larger (and take up more disk space) the amount of memory the program needs to run is effectively the same. It is usually a good idea to remove debug information before you release your programs, but only after they have been debugged.

You can remove debug information from an executable file without recompiling by running `strip <file>`.

Debugging with gdb

You'll use the GNU debugger, gdb, to debug this program. It's a very capable debugger that is freely available and can be used on many UNIX platforms. It's also the default debugger on Linux systems. gdb has been ported to many other platforms and can be used to debug embedded real-time systems.

Starting gdb

Recompile the example program for debugging and start gdb:

```
$ cc -g -o debug3 debug3.c
$ gdb debug3
GNU gdb 6.6
Copyright (C) 2006 Free Software Foundation, Inc.
GDB is free software, covered by the GNU General Public License, and you are
welcome to change it and/or distribute copies of it under certain conditions.
Type "show copying" to see the conditions.
There is absolutely no warranty for GDB.  Type "show warranty" for details.
This GDB was configured as "i586-suse-linux"...
Using host libthread_db library "/lib/libthread_db.so.1".
(gdb)
```

gdb has extensive online help and the complete manual is available as a set of files that can be viewed with the `info` program, or from within Emacs.

```
(gdb) help
List of classes of commands:

aliases -- Aliases of other commands
breakpoints -- Making program stop at certain points
data -- Examining data
files -- Specifying and examining files
internals -- Maintenance commands
obscure -- Obscure features
running -- Running the program
stack -- Examining the stack
status -- Status inquiries
support -- Support facilities
tracepoints -- Tracing of program execution without stopping the program
user-defined -- User-defined commands

Type "help" followed by a class name for a list of commands in that class.
Type "help all" for the list of all commands.
```

```
Type "help" followed by command name for full documentation.
Type "apropos word" to search for commands related to "word".
Command name abbreviations are allowed if unambiguous.
(gdb)
```

gdb is itself a text-based application, but it does provide a few shortcuts to help with repetitive tasks. Many versions have command-line editing with a history so that you can scroll back and execute the same command again (try using the cursor keys). All versions support an "empty command"; hitting Enter executes the last command again. This is especially useful when stepping through a program line by line with the step or next commands.

To exit gdb, use the quit command.

Running a Program

You can execute the program with the run command. Any arguments that you give to the run command are passed to the program as its arguments. In this case, you don't need any arguments.

We'll assume here that your system, like both the authors', is now generating a segmentation fault. If it isn't, read on. You'll find out what to do when one of your own programs does generate a segmentation violation. If you're not getting a segmentation violation, but want to work though this example as you read the book, you can pick up the program again at debug4.c, when the first of the memory access problems has been fixed.

```
(gdb) run
Starting program: /home/neil/BLP4e/chapter10/debug3

Program received signal SIGSEGV, Segmentation fault.
0x0804846f in sort (a=0x804a040, n=5) at debug3.c:23
23      /*  23  */                          if(a[j].key > a[j+1].key) {
(gdb)
```

The program runs incorrectly as before. When the program faults, gdb shows the reason and the location. You can now investigate the underlying cause of the problem.

Depending on your kernel, C library, and compiler version, you may see the program fault at a slightly different place, for example, on line 25, when array items are exchanged, rather than line 23, when array item keys are compared. If this is the case, you'll see something like

```
Program received signal SIGSEGV, Segmentation fault.
0x8000613 in sort (a=0x8001764, n=5) at debug3.c:25
25      /*  25  */                          a[j] = a[j+1];
```

You should still be able to follow the gdb sample session that follows.

Stack Trace

The program has been halted in the sort function at line 23 of the source file debug3.c. If you hadn't compiled the program with additional debug information (cc -g), you wouldn't be able to see where the program had failed, nor would you be able to use variable names to examine data.

You can see how you got to this position by using the backtrace command:

```
(gdb) backtrace
#0  0x0804846f in sort (a=0x804a040, n=5) at debug3.c:23
#1  0x08048583 in main () at debug3.c:37
 (gdb)
```

This is a very simple program, and the trace is short because you haven't called many functions from within other functions. You can see that sort was called from main at line 37 of the same file, debug3.c. Usually, the problem is much more complex and you use backtrace to discover the route you took to the error position. This can be very useful when debugging functions that are called from many different places.

The backtrace command may be abbreviated bt, and, for compatibility with other debuggers, the where command has the same function.

Examining Variables

The information printed by gdb when it stopped the program and in the stack trace shows you the values of function arguments.

The sort function was called with a parameter, a, that has the value 0x804a040. This is the address of the array. It will typically be different on different systems, depending on the compiler used and the operating system.

The offending line, 23, is a comparison of one array element with another:

```
/*  23  */                          if(a[j].key > a[j+1].key) {
```

You can use the debugger to examine the contents of function parameters, local variables, and global data. The print command shows the contents of variables and other expressions:

```
(gdb) print j
$1 = 4
```

Here you can see that the local variable j has the value 4. Any values reported by gdb commands like this are kept for future use in pseudo variables. Here the variable $1 is assigned the value 4 in case you need it later. Subsequent commands will store their results as $2, $3, and so on.

The fact that j has the value 4 means that the program has attempted to execute the statement

```
if(a[4].key > a[4+1].key)
```

The array that you have passed to sort, array, has only five elements, which will be indexed 0 through 4. So this statement reads from the nonexistent array[5]. The loop variable j has taken an incorrect value.

If your program faulted at line 25, your system detected a read past the end of the array only when it got to exchanging elements, executing

```
/*  25  */                          a[j] = a[j+1];
```

which, with j set to 4, results in

```
a[4] = a[4+1];
```

You can take a look at the elements of the passed array by using an expression with print. With gdb, you can use almost any legal C expression to print the value of variables, array elements, and pointers.

```
(gdb) print a[3]
$2 = {data = "alex", '\0' <repeats 4091 times>, key = 1}
(gdb)
```

gdb keeps the results of commands in pseudo variables, $<number>. The last result is always $, and the one before that is $$. This allows one result to be used in another command. For example,

```
(gdb) print j
$3 = 4
(gdb) print a[$-1].key
$4 = 1
```

Listing the Program

You can view the source code of the program from within gdb by using the list command. This prints out a portion of the code around the current position. Subsequent uses of list will print out more. You can also give list a function name as an argument and it will show the code at that position, or a pair of line numbers and it will list the code between those line numbers.

```
(gdb) list
18        /*  18  */      int s = 1;
19        /*  19  */
20        /*  20  */      for(; i < n && s != 0; i++) {
21        /*  21  */          s = 0;
22        /*  22  */          for(j = 0; j < n; j++) {
23        /*  23  */              if(a[j].key > a[j+1].key) {
24        /*  24  */                  item t = a[j];
25        /*  25  */                  a[j] = a[j+1];
26        /*  26  */                  a[j+1] = t;
27        /*  27  */                  s++;
(gdb)
```

You can see that on line 22 the loop is set to execute while the variable j is less than n. In this case, n is 5, so j will have the final value of 4, which is one too far. A value of 4 causes a comparison of a[4] with a[5] and possibly a swap. One solution to this particular problem is to correct the loop termination condition to be j < n-1.

Let's make that change, call the new program debug4.c, recompile, and try again:

```
/*  22  */              for(j = 0; j < n-1; j++) {
$ cc -g -o debug4 debug4.c
$ ./debug4
array[0] = {john, 2}
array[1] = {alex, 1}
```

```
array[2] = {bill, 3}
array[3] = {neil, 4}
array[4] = {rick, 5}
```

The program still doesn't work, because it has printed an incorrectly sorted list. Let's use gdb to step through the program as it runs.

Setting Breakpoints

To find out where the program is failing, you need to be able to see what it's doing as it runs. You can stop the program at any point by setting breakpoints. These cause the program to stop and return control to the debugger. You'll be able to inspect variables and then allow the program to continue.

There are two loops in the sort function. The outer loop, with loop variable i, is run once for each element in the array. The inner loop swaps the element with those further down the list. This has the effect of bubbling up the smaller elements to the top. After each run of the outer loop, the largest element should have made its way to the bottom. You can confirm this by stopping the program at the outer loop and examining the state of the array.

A number of commands are used for setting breakpoints. These are listed by gdb with help breakpoint:

```
(gdb) help breakpoint
Making program stop at certain points.

List of commands:

awatch -- Set a watchpoint for an expression
break -- Set breakpoint at specified line or function
catch -- Set catchpoints to catch events
clear -- Clear breakpoint at specified line or function
commands -- Set commands to be executed when a breakpoint is hit
condition -- Specify breakpoint number N to break only if COND is true
delete -- Delete some breakpoints or auto-display expressions
delete breakpoints -- Delete some breakpoints or auto-display expressions
delete checkpoint -- Delete a fork/checkpoint (experimental)
delete mem -- Delete memory region
delete tracepoints -- Delete specified tracepoints
disable -- Disable some breakpoints
disable breakpoints -- Disable some breakpoints
disable display -- Disable some expressions to be displayed when program stops
disable mem -- Disable memory region
disable tracepoints -- Disable specified tracepoints
enable -- Enable some breakpoints
enable delete -- Enable breakpoints and delete when hit
enable display -- Enable some expressions to be displayed when program stops
enable mem -- Enable memory region
enable once -- Enable breakpoints for one hit
enable tracepoints -- Enable specified tracepoints
hbreak -- Set a hardware assisted breakpoint
ignore -- Set ignore-count of breakpoint number N to COUNT
rbreak -- Set a breakpoint for all functions matching REGEXP
rwatch -- Set a read watchpoint for an expression
```

```
tbreak -- Set a temporary breakpoint
tcatch -- Set temporary catchpoints to catch events
thbreak -- Set a temporary hardware assisted breakpoint
watch -- Set a watchpoint for an expression

Type "help" followed by command name for full documentation.
Type "apropos word" to search for commands related to "word".
Command name abbreviations are allowed if unambiguous.
```

Set a breakpoint at line 21 and run the program:

```
$ gdb debug4
(gdb) break 21
Breakpoint 1 at 0x8048427: file debug4.c, line 21.
(gdb) run
Starting program: /home/neil/BLP4e/chapter10/debug4

Breakpoint 1, sort (a=0x804a040, n=5) at debug4.c:21
21      /*  21  */              s = 0;
```

You can print out the array value and then allow the program to continue with the cont command. This allows the program to run until it hits the next breakpoint, in this case, until it executes line 21 again. You can have many breakpoints active at any time.

```
(gdb) print array[0]
$1 = {data = "bill", '\0' <repeats 4091 times>, key = 3}
```

To print a number of consecutive items, you can use the construction @<number> to cause gdb to print a number of array elements. To print all five elements of array, you can use

```
(gdb) print array[0]@5
$2 = {{data = "bill", '\0' <repeats 4091 times>, key = 3}, {
    data = "neil", '\0' <repeats 4091 times>, key = 4}, {
    data = "john", '\0' <repeats 4091 times>, key = 2}, {
    data = "rick", '\0' <repeats 4091 times>, key = 5}, {
    data = "alex", '\0' <repeats 4091 times>, key = 1}}
```

Note that the output has been tidied up slightly to make it easier to read. Because this is the first time through the loop, the array is unchanged. When you allow the program to continue, you see successive alterations to array as execution proceeds:

```
(gdb) cont
Continuing.

Breakpoint 1, sort (a=0x8049580, n=4) at debug4.c:21
21      /*  21  */              s = 0;

(gdb) print array[0]@5
$3 = {{data = "bill", '\0' <repeats 4091 times>, key = 3}, {
    data = "john", '\0' <repeats 4091 times>, key = 2}, {
    data = "neil", '\0' <repeats 4091 times>, key = 4}, {
    data = "alex", '\0' <repeats 4091 times>, key = 1}, {
    data = "rick", '\0' <repeats 4091 times>, key = 5}}
(gdb)
```

You can use the `display` command to set gdb to display the array automatically whenever the program stops at a breakpoint:

```
(gdb) display array[0]@5
1: array[0] @ 5 = {{data = "bill", '\0' <repeats 4091 times>, key = 3}, {
    data = "john", '\0' <repeats 4091 times>, key = 2}, {
    data = "neil", '\0' <repeats 4091 times>, key = 4}, {
    data = "alex", '\0' <repeats 4091 times>, key = 1}, {
    data = "rick", '\0' <repeats 4091 times>, key = 5}}
```

Furthermore, you can change the breakpoint so that, instead of stopping the program, it simply displays the data you have requested and carries on. To do this, use the `commands` command. This allows you to specify what debugger commands to execute when a breakpoint is hit. Because you have already specified a display, you need only set the breakpoint command to continue execution.

```
(gdb) commands
Type commands for when breakpoint 1 is hit, one per line.
End with a line saying just "end".
> cont
> end
```

Now when you allow the program to continue, it runs to completion, printing the value of the array each time around the outer loop.

```
(gdb) cont
Continuing.

Breakpoint 1, sort (a=0x8049684, n=3) at debug4.c:21
21      /*  21  */              s = 0;
1: array[0] @ 5 = {{data = "john", '\000' <repeats 4091 times>, key = 2}, {
    data = "bill", '\000' <repeats 4091 times>, key = 3}, {
    data = "alex", '\000' <repeats 4091 times>, key = 1}, {
    data = "neil", '\000' <repeats 4091 times>, key = 4}, {
    data = "rick", '\000' <repeats 4091 times>, key = 5}}

array[0] = {john, 2}
array[1] = {alex, 1}
array[2] = {bill, 3}
array[3] = {neil, 4}
array[4] = {rick, 5}

Program exited with code 025.
(gdb)
```

gdb reports that the program exits with an unusual exit code. This is because the program itself doesn't call `exit` and doesn't return a value from `main`. The exit code is effectively meaningless in this case, and a meaningful one ought to be provided by a call to `exit`.

The program doesn't seem to execute the outer loop as many times as expected. You can see that the value of the parameter, n, used in the loop termination condition is reducing at each breakpoint. This means that the loop won't execute enough times. The culprit is the decrement of n on line 30:

```
/*  30  */              n--;
```

This is an attempt to optimize the program by taking advantage of the fact that at the end of each outer loop the largest element of array will be at the bottom, and so there is less left to sort. But, as you've seen, this interferes with the outer loop and causes problems. The simplest fix (though there are others) is to delete the offending line. Let's test whether this change will fix the problem by using the debugger to apply a patch.

Patching with the Debugger

You've already seen that you can use the debugger to set breakpoints and examine the value of variables. By using a breakpoint with actions, you can try out a fix, called a *patch*, before changing the source code and recompiling. In this case, you need to break the program on line 30 and increment the variable n. Then, when line 30 is executed, the value will be unchanged.

Let's restart the program from the beginning. First, you must delete your breakpoint and display. You can see what breakpoints and displays you have enabled using the info command:

```
(gdb) info display
Auto-display expressions now in effect:
Num Enb Expression
1:   y  array[0] @ 5
(gdb) info break
Num Type           Disp Enb Address    What
1   breakpoint     keep y   0x08048427 in sort at debug4.c:21
        breakpoint already hit 3 times
        cont
```

You can either disable these or delete them entirely. If you disable them, you retain the option to re-enable them at a later time if you need to:

```
(gdb) disable break 1
(gdb) disable display 1
(gdb) break 30
Breakpoint 2 at 0x8048545: file debug4.c, line 30.
(gdb) commands 2
Type commands for when breakpoint 2 is hit, one per line.
End with a line saying just "end".
>set variable n = n+1
>cont
>end
(gdb) run
Starting program: /home/neil/BLP4e/chapter10/debug4

Breakpoint 2, sort (a=0x804a040, n=5) at debug4.c:30
30      /*  30  */                 n--;

Breakpoint 2, sort (a=0x804a040, n=5) at debug4.c:30
30      /*  30  */                 n--;

Breakpoint 2, sort (a=0x804a040, n=5) at debug4.c:30
30      /*  30  */                 n--;

Breakpoint 2, sort (a=0x804a040, n=5) at debug4.c:30
```

```
30       /*  30  */                  n--;

Breakpoint 2, sort (a=0x804a040, n=5) at debug4.c:30
30       /*  30  */                  n--;
array[0] = {alex, 1}
array[1] = {john, 2}
array[2] = {bill, 3}
array[3] = {neil, 4}
array[4] = {rick, 5}

Program exited with code 025.
(gdb)
```

The program runs to completion and prints the correct result. You can now make the change and move on to test it with more data.

Learning More about gdb

The GNU debugger is an exceptionally powerful tool that can provide a lot of information about the internal state of executing programs. On systems that support a facility called *hardware breakpoints*, you can use gdb to monitor changes to variables in real time. Hardware breakpoints are a feature of some CPUs; these processors are able to stop automatically if certain conditions arise, typically a memory access in a given region. Alternatively, gdb can *watch* expressions. This means that, with a performance penalty, gdb can stop a program when an expression takes a particular value, regardless of where in the program the calculation took place.

Breakpoints can be set with counts and conditions so that they trigger only after a fixed number of times or when a condition is met.

gdb is also able to attach itself to programs that are already running. This can be very useful when you're debugging client/server systems, because you can debug a misbehaving server process as it runs without having to stop and restart it. You can compile programs with, for example, gcc -o -g to get the benefit of optimization and debug information. The downside is that optimization may reorder code a bit, so, as you single-step through code, you may find yourself jumping around to achieve the same effect as intended by the original source code.

You can also use gdb to debug programs that have crashed. Linux and UNIX will often produce a core dump in a file called core when a program fails. This is an image of the program's memory and will contain the values of global variables at the time of the failure. You can use gdb to work out where the program was when it crashed. Check out the gdb manual page for more details.

gdb is available under the terms of the GNU Public License and most UNIX systems can support it. We strongly recommend that you get to know it.

More Debugging Tools

Apart from out-and-out debuggers such as gdb, Linux systems typically provide a number of other tools that you can use to aid the debugging process. Some of these provide static information about a program; others provide a dynamic analysis.

Static analysis provides information from the program source code only. Programs such as ctags, cxref, and cflow work with the source files and provide useful information about function calling and location.

Dynamic analysis provides information about how a program behaves during execution. Programs such as prof and gprof provide information about which functions have been executed and for how long.

Let's take a look at some of these tools and their output. Not all of these tools will be available on all systems, although many of them have freely available versions.

Lint: Removing the Fluff from Your Programs

Original UNIX systems provided a utility called lint. It was essentially the front end of a C compiler with added tests designed to apply some common sense and produce warnings. It would detect cases where variables were used before being set and where function arguments were not used, among other things.

More modern C compilers can, at a cost to compile-time performance, produce similar warnings. lint itself has been overtaken by the standardization of C. Because the tool was based on an early C compiler, it doesn't cope at all well with ANSI syntax. There are some commercial versions of lint available for UNIX and at least one on the Internet for Linux, called splint. This used to be known as LClint, part of a project at MIT to produce tools for formal specifications. A lint-like tool, splint can provide useful code review comments. You can find splint at http://www.splint.org.

Here's an early version (debug0.c) of the example program that you debugged earlier:

```
/*   1  */  typedef struct {
/*   2  */      char *data;
/*   3  */      int key;
/*   4  */  } item;
/*   5  */
/*   6  */  item array[] = {
/*   7  */      {"bill", 3},
/*   8  */      {"neil", 4},
/*   9  */      {"john", 2},
/*  10  */      {"rick", 5},
/*  11  */      {"alex", 1},
/*  12  */  };
/*  13  */
/*  14  */  sort(a,n)
/*  15  */  item *a;
/*  16  */  {
/*  17  */      int i = 0, j = 0;
/*  18  */      int s;
/*  19  */
/*  20  */      for(; i < n & s != 0; i++) {
/*  21  */          s = 0;
/*  22  */          for(j = 0; j < n; j++) {
/*  23  */              if(a[j].key > a[j+1].key) {
/*  24  */                  item t = a[j];
/*  25  */                  a[j] = a[j+1];
/*  26  */                  a[j+1] = t;
```

```
/*  27  */                                      s++;
/*  28  */                            ·}
/*  29  */                      }
/*  30  */                  n--;
/*  31  */            }
/*  32  */  }
/*  33  */
/*  34  */  main()
/*  35  */  {
/*  36  */      sort(array,5);
/*  37  */  }
```

This version has an additional problem with line 20 where the & operator has been used in place of the intended &&. The following is an edited sample output from splint running on this version. Notice how it picks up the problems on line 20 — the fact that you have not initialized the variable s, and that you may have a problem with the test caused by the incorrect operator.

```
neil@suse103:~/BLP4e/chapter10> splint -strict debug0.c
Splint 3.1.1 --- 19 Mar 2005

debug0.c:7:18: Read-only string literal storage used as initial value for
               unqualified storage: array[0].data = "bill"
 A read-only string literal is assigned to a non-observer reference. (Use
 -readonlytrans to inhibit warning)
debug0.c:8:18: Read-only string literal storage used as initial value for
               unqualified storage: array[1].data = "neil"
debug0.c:9:18: Read-only string literal storage used as initial value for
               unqualified storage: array[2].data = "john"
debug0.c:10:18: Read-only string literal storage used as initial value for
               unqualified storage: array[3].data = "rick"
debug0.c:11:18: Read-only string literal storage used as initial value for
               unqualified storage: array[4].data = "alex"
debug0.c:14:22: Old style function declaration
  Function definition is in old style syntax. Standard prototype syntax is
  preferred. (Use -oldstyle to inhibit warning)
debug0.c: (in function sort)
debug0.c:20:31: Variable s used before definition
  An rvalue is used that may not be initialized to a value on some execution
  path. (Use -usedef to inhibit warning)
debug0.c:20:23: Left operand of & is not unsigned value (boolean):
                i < n & s != 0
  An operand to a bitwise operator is not an unsigned values.  This may have
  unexpected results depending on the signed representations. (Use
  -bitwisesigned to inhibit warning)
debug0.c:20:23: Test expression for for not boolean, type unsigned int:
                i < n & s != 0
  Test expression type is not boolean or int. (Use -predboolint to inhibit
  warning)
debug0.c:25:41: Undocumented modification of a[]: a[j] = a[j + 1]
  An externally-visible object is modified by a function with no /*@modifies@*/
  comment. The /*@modifies ... @*/ control comment can be used to give a
  modifies list for an unspecified function. (Use -modnomods to inhibit
  warning)
```

```
debug0.c:26:41: Undocumented modification of a[]: a[j + 1] = t
debug0.c:20:23: Operands of & are non-integer (boolean) (in post loop test):
                          i < n & s != 0
  A primitive operation does not type check strictly. (Use -strictops to
  inhibit warning)
debug0.c:32:14: Path with no return in function declared to return int
  There is a path through a function declared to return a value on which there
  is no return statement. This means the execution may fall through without
  returning a meaningful result to the caller. (Use -noret to inhibit warning)
debug0.c:34:13: Function main declared without parameter list
  A function declaration does not have a parameter list. (Use -noparams to
  inhibit warning)
debug0.c: (in function main)
debug0.c:36:22: Undocumented use of global array
  A checked global variable is used in the function, but not listed in its
  globals clause. By default, only globals specified in .lcl files are checked.
  To check all globals, use +allglobals. To check globals selectively use
  /*@checked@*/ in the global declaration. (Use -globs to inhibit warning)
debug0.c:36:17: Undetected modification possible from call to unconstrained
                      function sort: sort
  An unconstrained function is called in a function body where modifications
  are checked. Since the unconstrained function may modify anything, there may
  be undetected modifications in the checked function. (Use -modunconnomods to
  inhibit warning)
debug0.c:36:17: Return value (type int) ignored: sort(array, 5)
  Result returned by function call is not used. If this is intended, can cast
  result to (void) to eliminate message. (Use -retvalint to inhibit warning)
debug0.c:37:14: Path with no return in function declared to return int
debug0.c:6:18: Variable exported but not used outside debug0: array
  A declaration is exported, but not used outside this module. Declaration can
  use static qualifier. (Use -exportlocal to inhibit warning)
debug0.c:14:13: Function exported but not used outside debug0: sort
    debug0.c:15:17: Definition of sort
debug0.c:6:18: Variable array exported but not declared in header file
  A variable declaration is exported, but does not appear in a header file.
  (Used with exportheader.) (Use -exportheadervar to inhibit warning)
debug0.c:14:13: Function sort exported but not declared in header file
  A declaration is exported, but does not appear in a header file. (Use
  -exportheader to inhibit warning)
    debug0.c:15:17: Definition of sort

Finished checking --- 22 code warnings
$
```

The utility complains about old-style (non-ANSI) function declarations and inconsistencies between function return types and the values they do (or do not) return. These don't affect the operation of the program, but ought to be addressed.

It has also detected two real bugs in the following code fragment:

```
/*  18  */        int s;
/*  19  */
/*  20  */        for(; i < n & s != 0; i++) {
/*  21  */            s = 0;
```

The splint tool has determined (in the highlighted lines of the preceding output) that the variable s is used on line 20, but hasn't been initialized and that the operator & has been used in place of the more usual &&. In this case, the operator precedence alters the meaning of the test and is a problem for the program.

Both of these errors were fixed in a code review before debugging started. Although this example is a little contrived for the purposes of demonstration, these are errors that regularly crop up in real-world programs.

Function Call Tools

Three utilities — ctags, cxref, and cflow — form part of the X/Open specification and therefore must be present on UNIX-branded systems with software development capabilities.

> *These utilities and others mentioned in this chapter may not be present in your Linux distribution. If they are missing, you might like to search for implementations on the Internet. Good places to start (for Linux distributions that support the RPM package format) are* http://rpmfind.net *and* http://rpm.pbone.net. *There are also several distribution-specific repositories to try, including* http://ftp.gwdg.de/pub/opensuse/ *for openSUSE,* http://rpm.livna.org *for Fedora, and* http://packages.slackware.it/ *for Slackware.*

ctags

The ctags program creates an index of functions. For each function, you get a list of the places it's used, like the index of a book.

```
ctags [-a] [-f filename] sourcefile sourcefile ...
ctags -x sourcefile sourcefile ...
```

By default, ctags creates a file, called tags, in the current directory, which contains, for each function declared in any of the input source files, lines of the form

```
announce          app_ui.c          /^static void announce(void) /
```

Each line in the file consists of a function name, the file it's declared in, and a regular expression that can be used to find the function definition within the file. Some editors such as Emacs can use files of this kind to help navigate through source code.

Alternatively, by using the -x option to ctags (if available in your version), you can produce lines of a similar form on the standard output:

```
find_cat          403 app_ui.c          static cdc_entry find_cat(
```

You can redirect the output to a different file by using the option -f filename and append it to an existing file by specifying the -a option.

cxref

The cxref program analyzes C source code and produces a cross-reference. It shows where each symbol (variable, #define, and function) is mentioned in the program. It produces a sorted list with each symbol's definition location marked with an asterisk, as shown on next page.

SYMBOL	FILE	FUNCTION	LINE						
BASENID	prog.c	--	*12	*96	124	126	146	156	166
BINSIZE	prog.c	--	*30	197	198	199	206		
BUFMAX	prog.c	--	*44	45	90				
BUFSIZ	/usr/include/stdio.h	--	*4						
EOF	/usr/include/stdio.h	--	*27						
argc	prog.c	--	36						
	prog.c	main	*37	61	81				
argv	prog.c	--	36						
	prog.c	main	*38	61					
calldata	prog.c	--	*5						
	prog.c	main	64	188					
calls	prog.c	--	*19						
	prog.c	main	54						

On the author's machine, the preceding output was generated in the source directory of an application, with the command

```
$ cxref *.c *.h
```

but the exact syntax varies from version to version. Consult the documentation for your system or the man pages for more information on whether cxref is available and how to use it.

cflow

The cflow program prints a *function call tree*, a diagram that shows which function calls which others, and which functions are called by them, and so on. It can be useful to find out the structure of a program to understand how it operates and to see what impact changes to a function will have. Some versions of cflow can operate on object files as well as source code. Refer to the manual page for details of operation.

Here's some sample output taken from a version of cflow (cflow-2.0) that is available on the Internet and maintained by Marty Leisner:

```
1       file_ungetc {prcc.c 997}
2       main {prcc.c 70}
3               getopt {}
4               show_all_lists {prcc.c 1070}
5                       display_list {prcc.c 1056}
6                               printf {}
7                       exit {}
8               exit {}
9               usage {prcc.c 59}
10                      fprintf {}
11                      exit {}
```

This sample tells you that main calls (among others) show_all_lists and that show_all_lists in turn calls display_list, which itself calls printf.

One option to this version of cflow is -i, which produces an inverted flow graph. For each function, cflow lists the other functions that make a call to it. It sounds complicated, but it really isn't. Here's a sample.

```
19      display_list {prcc.c 1056}
20              show_all_lists {prcc.c 1070}
```

```
21      exit {}
22              main {prcc.c 70}
23              show_all_lists {prcc.c 1070}
24              usage {prcc.c 59}
...
74      printf {}
75              display_list {prcc.c 1056}
76              maketag {prcc.c 487}
77      show_all_lists {prcc.c 1070}
78              main {prcc.c 70}
...
99      usage {prcc.c 59}
100             main {prcc.c 70}
```

This shows that the functions that call `exit`, for example, are `main`, `show_all_lists`, and `usage`.

Execution Profiling with prof/gprof

A technique that is often useful when you're trying to track down performance problems with a program is *execution profiling*. Normally supported by special compiler options and ancillary programs, a profile of a program shows where it's spending its time.

The `prof` program (and its GNU equivalent, `gprof`) prints a report from an execution trace file that is produced when a profiled program is run. A profiled executable is created by specifying the –p flag (for `prof`) or –pg flag (for `gprof`) to the compiler:

```
$ cc -pg -o program program.c
```

The program is linked with a special version of the C library and is changed to include monitoring code. This may vary with specific systems, but is commonly achieved by arranging for the program to be interrupted frequently and the execution location to be recorded. The monitor data is written to a file in the current directory, `mon.out` (`gmon.out` for `gprof`).

```
$ ./program
$ ls -ls
  2 -rw-r--r--   1 neil     users        1294 Feb  4 11:48 gmon.out
```

The `prof`/`gprof` program reads this monitoring data and produces a report. Refer to the manual pages for details on program options. Here is some (abbreviated) `gprof` output as an example:

cumulative time	self seconds	self seconds	total calls	ms/call	ms/call	name
18.5	0.10	0.10	8664	0.01	0.03	_doscan [4]
18.5	0.20	0.10				mcount (60)
14.8	0.28	0.08	43320	0.00	0.00	_number [5]
9.3	0.33	0.05	8664	0.01	0.01	_format_arg [6]
7.4	0.37	0.04	112632	0.00	0.00	_ungetc [8]
7.4	0.41	0.04	8757	0.00	0.00	_memccpy [9]
7.4	0.45	0.04	1	40.00	390.02	_main [2]
3.7	0.47	0.02	53	0.38	0.38	_read [12]
3.7	0.49	0.02				w4str [10]
1.9	0.50	0.01	26034	0.00	0.00	_strlen [16]
1.9	0.51	0.01	8664	0.00	0.00	strncmp [17]

Assertions

Although it's common to introduce debug code such as `printf` calls, possibly by conditional compilation, during the development of a program, it's sometimes impractical to leave these messages in a delivered system. However, it's often the case that problems occur during the program operation that are related to incorrect assumptions rather than coding errors. These are events that "can't happen." For example, a function may be written with the understanding that its input parameters will be within a certain range. If it's passed incorrect data, it might invalidate the whole system.

For these cases, where the internal logic of the system needs to be confirmed, X/Open provides the `assert` macro that can be used to test that an assumption is correct and halt the program if not.

```
#include <assert.h>

void assert(int expression)
```

The `assert` macro evaluates the expression and, if it's nonzero, writes some diagnostic information to the standard error and calls `abort` to end the program.

The header file `assert.h` defines the macro depending on the definition of NDEBUG. If NDEBUG is defined when the header file is processed, `assert` is defined to be essentially nothing. This means that you can turn off assertions at compile time by compiling with -DNDEBUG or by including the line

```
#define NDEBUG
```

in each source file before including `assert.h`.

This method of use is one problem with `assert`. If you use `assert` during testing, but turn it off for production code, your production code could have less safety checking than when you are testing it. Leaving assertions enabled in production code is not normally an option — would you like your code to present a customer with the unfriendly error `assert failed` and a stopped program? You may consider it better to write your own error-trapping routine that still checks the assertion but doesn't need to be completely disabled in production code.

You must also be careful that there are no side effects in the `assert` expression. For example, if you use a function call with a side effect, the effect won't happen in the production code if assertions are removed.

Try It Out   assert

Here's a program, `assert.c`, that defines a function that must take a positive value. It protects against the possibility of a bad argument by using an assertion.

After including the `assert.h` header file and a "square root" function that checks that the parameter is positive, you can then write the `main` function:

```
#include <stdio.h>
#include <math.h>
#include <assert.h>
#include <stdlib.h>
```

```
double my_sqrt(double x)
{
    assert(x >= 0.0);
    return sqrt(x);
}

int main()
{
    printf("sqrt +2 = %g\n", my_sqrt(2.0));
    printf("sqrt -2 = %g\n", my_sqrt(-2.0));
    exit(0);
}
```

Now when you run the program, you see an assertion violation when you pass an illegal value. The exact format of the assertion failure message will vary from system to system.

```
$ cc -o assert assert.c -lm
$ ./assert
sqrt +2 = 1.41421
assert: assert.c:7: my_sqrt: Assertion `x >= 0.0' failed.
Aborted
$
```

How It Works

When you try to call the function my_sqrt with a negative number, the assertion fails. The assert macro provides the file and line number where the assertion violation occurred, as well as the condition that failed. The program terminates with an abort trap. This is the result of assert calling abort.

If you recompile the program with -DNDEBUG, the assertion is compiled out and you get a NaN (Not a Number) value indicating an invalid result when you call the sqrt function from my_sqrt.

```
$ cc -o assert -DNDEBUG assert.c -lm
$ ./assert
sqrt +2 = 1.41421
sqrt -2 = nan
$
```

Some older mathematics library versions will raise an exception on a mathematical error and your program will terminate with a message such as Floating point exception instead of returning a NaN.

Memory Debugging

One area that is a rich source of bugs that are difficult to track down is dynamic memory allocation. If you write a program that uses malloc and free to allocate memory, it's important that you keep good track of the blocks you allocate and make sure that you don't use a block that you've freed up.

Typically, memory blocks are allocated by `malloc` and assigned to pointer variables. If the pointer variable is changed and there are no other pointers pointing to the memory block, it will become inaccessible. This is a memory leak and it causes your program to grow in size. If you leak a lot of memory, your system will eventually slow down and run out of memory.

If you write beyond the end of an allocated block (or before the beginning of a block), you'll very likely corrupt the data structures used by the `malloc` library to keep track of allocations. In this case, at some future time, a call to `malloc`, or even `free`, will cause a segmentation violation and your program will crash. Tracking down the precise point at which the fault occurred can be very difficult, because it may have happened a long time before the event that caused the crash.

Unsurprisingly, there are tools, commercial and free, that can help with these two problem types. There are, for example, many different versions of `malloc` and `free`, some of which contain additional code to check on allocations and deallocations to try to cater for the cases where a block is freed twice and some other types of misuse.

ElectricFence

The ElectricFence library was developed by Bruce Perens. It is available as an optional component in some Linux distributions such as Red Hat (Enterprise and Fedora), SUSE and openSUSE, and can be readily found on the Internet. It attempts to use the virtual memory facilities of Linux to protect the memory used by `malloc` and `free` to halt the program at the point of memory corruption.

Try It Out   ElectricFence

Here's a program, `efence.c`, that allocates a memory block with `malloc` and then writes beyond the end of the block. Check it out and see what happens.

```
#include <stdio.h>
#include <stdlib.h>

int main()
{
    char *ptr = (char *) malloc(1024);
    ptr[0] = 0;

    /* Now write beyond the block */
    ptr[1024] = 0;
    exit(0);
}
```

When you compile and run the program, you see no untoward behavior. However, it's likely that the `malloc` memory area has sustained some corruption and you would eventually run into trouble.

```
$ cc -o efence efence.c
$ ./efence
$
```

However, if you take exactly the same program and link with the ElectricFence library, `libefence.a`, you get an immediate response.

```
$ cc -o efence efence.c -lefence
$ ./efence

  Electric Fence 2.2.0 Copyright (C) 1987-1999 Bruce Perens <bruce@perens.com>
Segmentation fault
$
```

Running under the debugger pinpoints the problem:

```
$ cc -g -o efence efence.c -lefence
$ gdb efence
 (gdb) run
Starting program: /home/neil/BLP4e/chapter10/efence

  Electric Fence 2.2.0 Copyright (C) 1987-1999 Bruce Perens <bruce@perens.com>

Program received signal SIGSEGV, Segmentation fault.
[Switching to Thread 1024 (LWP 1869)]
0x08048512 in main () at efence.c:10
10          ptr[1024] = 0;
(gdb)
```

How It Works

ElectricFence replaces `malloc` and associated functions with versions that use virtual memory features of the computer's processor to protect against illegal memory access. When such an access occurs, a segmentation violation signal is raised and the program halts.

---

valgrind

`valgrind` is a tool that is capable of detecting many of the problems that we have discussed. In particular, it can detect array access errors and memory leaks. It may not be included with your Linux distribution, but you can find it at `http://valgrind.org`.

Programs do not even need to be recompiled to use `valgrind`, and you can even debug the memory accesses of a running program. It is well worth a look; it has been used on major developments, including KDE version 3.

Try It Out   **valgrind**

Here's a program, `checker.c`, that allocates some memory, reads a location beyond the limit of that memory, writes beyond the end of it, and then makes it inaccessible:

```
#include <stdio.h>
#include <stdlib.h>
```

```
int main()
{
    char *ptr = (char *) malloc(1024);
    char ch;

    /* Uninitialized read */
    ch = ptr[1024];

    /* Write beyond the block */
    ptr[1024] = 0;

    /* Orphan the block */
    ptr = 0;
    exit(0);
}
```

To use valgrind, you simply have to run the valgrind command passing options that you would like to check, followed by the program to run with its arguments (if any).

When you run your program with valgrind, you see many problems diagnosed:

```
$ valgrind --leak-check=yes -v ./checker
==4780== Memcheck, a memory error detector.
==4780== Copyright (C) 2002-2007, and GNU GPL'd, by Julian Seward et al.
==4780== Using LibVEX rev 1732, a library for dynamic binary translation.
==4780== Copyright (C) 2004-2007, and GNU GPL'd, by OpenWorks LLP.
==4780== Using valgrind-3.2.3, a dynamic binary instrumentation framework.
==4780== Copyright (C) 2000-2007, and GNU GPL'd, by Julian Seward et al.
==4780==
--4780-- Command line
--4780--    ./checker
--4780-- Startup, with flags:
--4780--    --leak-check=yes
--4780--    -v
--4780-- Contents of /proc/version:
--4780--    Linux version 2.6.20.2-2-default (geeko@buildhost) (gcc version 4.1.3
 20070218 (prerelease) (SUSE Linux)) #1 SMP Fri Mar 9 21:54:10 UTC 2007
--4780-- Arch and hwcaps: X86, x86-sse1-sse2
--4780-- Page sizes: currently 4096, max supported 4096
--4780-- Valgrind library directory: /usr/lib/valgrind
--4780-- Reading syms from /lib/ld-2.5.so (0x4000000)
--4780-- Reading syms from /home/neil/BLP4e/chapter10/checker (0x8048000)
--4780-- Reading syms from /usr/lib/valgrind/x86-linux/memcheck (0x38000000)
--4780--    object doesn't have a symbol table
--4780--    object doesn't have a dynamic symbol table
--4780-- Reading suppressions file: /usr/lib/valgrind/default.supp
--4780-- REDIR: 0x40158B0 (index) redirected to 0x38027EDB (???)
--4780-- Reading syms from /usr/lib/valgrind/x86-linux/vgpreload_core.so
 (0x401E000)
--4780--    object doesn't have a symbol table
--4780-- Reading syms from /usr/lib/valgrind/x86-linux/vgpreload_memcheck.so
 (0x4021000)
--4780--    object doesn't have a symbol table
```

```
==4780== WARNING: new redirection conflicts with existing -- ignoring it
--4780--     new: 0x040158B0 (index      ) R-> 0x04024490 index
--4780-- REDIR: 0x4015A50 (strlen) redirected to 0x4024540 (strlen)
--4780-- Reading syms from /lib/libc-2.5.so (0x4043000)
--4780-- REDIR: 0x40ADFF0 (rindex) redirected to 0x4024370 (rindex)
--4780-- REDIR: 0x40AAF00 (malloc) redirected to 0x4023700 (malloc)
==4780== Invalid read of size 1
==4780==    at 0x804842C: main (checker.c:10)
==4780==  Address 0x4170428 is 0 bytes after a block of size 1,024 alloc'd
==4780==    at 0x4023785: malloc (in /usr/lib/valgrind/x86-
linux/vgpreload_memcheck.so)
==4780==    by 0x8048420: main (checker.c:6)
==4780==
==4780== Invalid write of size 1
==4780==    at 0x804843A: main (checker.c:13)
==4780==  Address 0x4170428 is 0 bytes after a block of size 1,024 alloc'd
==4780==    at 0x4023785: malloc (in /usr/lib/valgrind/x86-
linux/vgpreload_memcheck.so)
==4780==    by 0x8048420: main (checker.c:6)
--4780-- REDIR: 0x40A8BB0 (free) redirected to 0x402331A (free)
--4780-- REDIR: 0x40AEE70 (memset) redirected to 0x40248A0 (memset)
==4780==
==4780== ERROR SUMMARY: 2 errors from 2 contexts (suppressed: 3 from 1)
==4780==
==4780== 1 errors in context 1 of 2:
==4780== Invalid write of size 1
==4780==    at 0x804843A: main (checker.c:13)
==4780==  Address 0x4170428 is 0 bytes after a block of size 1,024 alloc'd
==4780==    at 0x4023785: malloc (in /usr/lib/valgrind/x86-
linux/vgpreload_memcheck.so)
==4780==    by 0x8048420: main (checker.c:6)
==4780==
==4780== 1 errors in context 2 of 2:
==4780== Invalid read of size 1
==4780==    at 0x804842C: main (checker.c:10)
==4780==  Address 0x4170428 is 0 bytes after a block of size 1,024 alloc'd
==4780==    at 0x4023785: malloc (in /usr/lib/valgrind/x86-
linux/vgpreload_memcheck.so)
==4780==    by 0x8048420: main (checker.c:6)
--4780--
--4780-- supp:    3 dl-hack3
==4780==
==4780== IN SUMMARY: 2 errors from 2 contexts (suppressed: 3 from 1)
==4780==
==4780== malloc/free: in use at exit: 1,024 bytes in 1 blocks.
==4780== malloc/free: 1 allocs, 0 frees, 1,024 bytes allocated.
==4780==
==4780== searching for pointers to 1 not-freed blocks.
==4780== checked 65,444 bytes.
==4780==
==4780==
==4780== 1,024 bytes in 1 blocks are definitely lost in loss record 1 of 1
==4780==    at 0x4023785: malloc (in /usr/lib/valgrind/x86-
linux/vgpreload_memcheck.so)
```

```
==4780==      by 0x8048420: main (checker.c:6)
==4780==
==4780== LEAK SUMMARY:
==4780==    definitely lost: 1,024 bytes in 1 blocks.
==4780==      possibly lost: 0 bytes in 0 blocks.
==4780==    still reachable: 0 bytes in 0 blocks.
==4780==         suppressed: 0 bytes in 0 blocks.
--4780--  memcheck: sanity checks: 0 cheap, 1 expensive
--4780--  memcheck: auxmaps: 0 auxmap entries (0k, 0M) in use
--4780--  memcheck: auxmaps: 0 searches, 0 comparisons
--4780--  memcheck: SMs: n_issued      = 9 (144k, 0M)
--4780--  memcheck: SMs: n_deissued    = 0 (0k, 0M)
--4780--  memcheck: SMs: max_noaccess  = 65535 (1048560k, 1023M)
--4780--  memcheck: SMs: max_undefined = 0 (0k, 0M)
--4780--  memcheck: SMs: max_defined   = 19 (304k, 0M)
--4780--  memcheck: SMs: max_non_DSM   = 9 (144k, 0M)
--4780--  memcheck: max sec V bit nodes:   0 (0k, 0M)
--4780--  memcheck: set_sec_vbits8 calls: 0 (new: 0, updates: 0)
--4780--  memcheck: max shadow mem size:   448k, 0M
--4780-- translate:          fast SP updates identified: 1,456 ( 90.3%)
--4780-- translate:   generic_known SP updates identified: 79 ( 4.9%)
--4780-- translate: generic_unknown SP updates identified: 76 ( 4.7%)
--4780--     tt/tc: 3,341 tt lookups requiring 3,360 probes
--4780--     tt/tc: 3,341 fast-cache updates, 3 flushes
--4780--   transtab: new        1,553 (33,037 -> 538,097; ratio 162:10) [0 scs]
--4780--   transtab: dumped     0 (0 -> ??)
--4780--   transtab: discarded  6 (143 -> ??)
--4780-- scheduler: 21,623 jumps (bb entries).
--4780-- scheduler: 0/1,828 major/minor sched events.
--4780--     sanity: 1 cheap, 1 expensive checks.
--4780--     exectx: 30,011 lists, 6 contexts (avg 0 per list)
--4780--     exectx: 6 searches, 0 full compares (0 per 1000)
--4780--     exectx: 0 cmp2, 4 cmp4, 0 cmpAll
  $
```

Here you can see that the bad reads and writes have been caught and the memory blocks concerned are given along with the place they were allocated. You can use the debugger to break the program at the point of the error.

There are many options to valgrind, including the suppression of certain types of error and memory-leak detection. To detect the example leak, you must use one of the options that are passed to valgrind. To check for memory leaks when the program ends, you need to specify --leak-check=yes. You can get a list of options with valgrind --help.

How It Works

The program is executed under the control of valgrind, which intercepts various actions your program takes and performs many checks — including memory accesses. If the access concerns an allocated memory block and is illegal, valgrind prints a message. At the end of the program, a garbage collection routine is run that determines if any memory blocks have been allocated but not freed. These orphaned blocks are reported.

Summary

In this chapter, you've looked at some debugging tools and techniques. Linux provides some powerful aids to help with removing defects from programs. You eliminated some bugs from a program using `gdb` and looked at some static analysis tools such as `cflow` and `splint`. Finally, you looked at problems that arise when you use dynamically allocated memory and some utilities that can help diagnose them, such as `ElectricFence` and `valgrind`.

The utility programs discussed in this chapter have mostly been made available on FTP servers on the Internet. The authors concerned may, in some cases, retain copyright. Information about many of the utilities is available from the Linux archive `http://www.ibiblio.org/pub/Linux` and we expect that new versions will be found there as they are released.

Processes and Signals

Processes and signals form a fundamental part of the Linux operating environment. They control almost all activities performed by Linux and all other UNIX-like computer systems. An understanding of how Linux and UNIX manage processes will hold any systems programmer, applications programmer, or system administrator in good stead.

In this chapter, you learn how processes are handled in the Linux environment and how to find out exactly what the computer is doing at any given time. You also see how to start and stop other processes from within your own programs, how to make processes send and receive messages, and how to avoid zombies. In particular, you learn about

- ❑ Process structure, type, and scheduling
- ❑ Starting new processes in different ways
- ❑ Parent, child, and zombie processes
- ❑ What signals are and how to use them

What Is a Process?

The UNIX standards, specifically IEEE Std 1003.1, 2004 Edition, defines a process as "an address space with one or more threads executing within that address space, and the required system resources for those threads." We look at threads in Chapter 12. For now, we will regard a process as just a program that is running.

A multitasking operating system such as Linux lets many programs run at once. Each instance of a running program constitutes a process. This is especially evident with a windowing system such as the X Window System (often simply called X). Like Windows, X provides a graphical user interface that allows many applications to be run at once. Each application can display one or more windows.

As a multiuser system, Linux allows many users to access the system at the same time. Each user can run many programs, or even many instances of the same program, at the same time. The system itself runs other programs to manage system resources and control user access.

As you saw in Chapter 4, a program — or process — that is running consists of program code, data, variables (occupying system memory), open files (file descriptors), and an environment. Typically, a Linux system will share code and system libraries among processes so that there's only one copy of the code in memory at any one time.

Process Structure

Let's have a look at how a couple of processes might be arranged within the operating system. If two users, neil and rick, both run the grep program at the same time to look for different strings in different files, the processes being used might look like Figure 11-1.

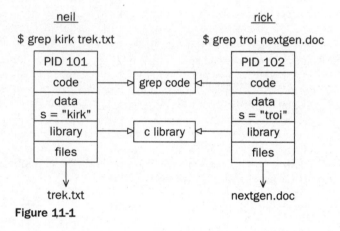

Figure 11-1

If you could run the ps command as in the following code quickly enough and before the searches had finished, the output might contain something like this:

```
$ ps -ef
UID     PID    PPID   C   STIME   TTY    TIME       CMD
rick    101    96     0   18:24   tty2   00:00:00   grep troi nextgen.doc
neil    102    92     0   18:24   tty4   00:00:00   grep kirk trek.txt
```

Each process is allocated a unique number, called a *process identifier* or *PID*. This is usually a positive integer between 2 and 32,768. When a process is started, the next unused number in sequence is chosen and the numbers restart at 2 so that they wrap around. The number 1 is typically reserved for the special init process, which manages other processes. We will come back to init shortly. Here you see that the two processes started by neil and rick have been allocated the identifiers 101 and 102.

The program code that will be executed by the grep command is stored in a disk file. Normally, a Linux process can't write to the memory area used to hold the program code, so the code is loaded into memory as read-only. You saw in Figure 11-1 that, although this area can't be written to, it can safely be shared.

The system libraries can also be shared. Thus, there need be only one copy of printf, for example, in memory, even if many running programs call it. This is a more sophisticated, but similar, scheme to the way dynamic link libraries (DLLs) work in Windows.

As you can see in the preceding diagram, an additional benefit is that the disk file containing the executable program `grep` is smaller because it doesn't contain shared library code. This might not seem like much saving for a single program, but extracting the common routines for (say) the standard C library saves a significant amount of space over a whole operating system.

Of course, not everything that a program needs to run can be shared. For example, the variables that it uses are distinct for each process. In this example, you see that the search string passed to the `grep` command appears as a variable, `s`, in the data space of each process. These are separate and usually can't be read by other processes. The files that are being used in the two `grep` commands are also different; the processes have their own set of file descriptors used for file access.

Additionally, a process has its own stack space, used for local variables in functions and for controlling function calls and returns. It also has its own environment space, containing environment variables that may be established solely for this process to use, as you saw with `putenv` and `getenv` in Chapter 4. A process must also maintain its own program counter, a record of where it has gotten to in its execution, which is the *execution thread*. In the next chapter you will see that when you use threads, processes can have more than one thread of execution.

On many Linux systems, and some UNIX systems, there is a special set of "files" in a directory called `/proc`. These are special in that rather than being true files they allow you to "look inside" processes while they are running as if they were files in directories. We took a brief look at the `/proc` file system back in Chapter 3.

Finally, because Linux, like UNIX, has a virtual memory system that pages code and data out to an area of the hard disk, many more processes can be managed than would fit into the physical memory.

The Process Table

The Linux *process table* is like a data structure describing all of the processes that are currently loaded with, for example, their PID, status, and command string, the sort of information output by `ps`. The operating system manages processes using their PIDs, and they are used as an index into the process table. The table is of limited size, so the number of processes a system will support is limited. Early UNIX systems were limited to 256 processes. More modern implementations have relaxed this restriction considerably and may be limited only by the memory available to construct a process table entry.

Viewing Processes

The `ps` command shows the processes you're running, the process another user is running, or all the processes on the system. Here is more sample output:

```
$ ps -ef
UID        PID  PPID  C STIME TTY          TIME CMD
root       433   425  0 18:12 tty1     00:00:00 [bash]
rick       445   426  0 18:12 tty2     00:00:00 -bash
rick       456   427  0 18:12 tty3     00:00:00 [bash]
root       467   433  0 18:12 tty1     00:00:00 sh /usr/X11R6/bin/startx
root       474   467  0 18:12 tty1     00:00:00 xinit /etc/X11/xinit/xinitrc --
root       478   474  0 18:12 tty1     00:00:00 /usr/bin/gnome-session
root       487     1  0 18:12 tty1     00:00:00 gnome-smproxy --sm-client-id def
root       493     1  0 18:12 tty1     00:00:01 [enlightenment]
root       506     1  0 18:12 tty1     00:00:03 panel --sm-client-id default8
```

```
root        508     1   0 18:12 tty1      00:00:00 xscreensaver -no-splash -timeout
root        510     1   0 18:12 tty1      00:00:01 gmc --sm-client-id default10
root        512     1   0 18:12 tty1      00:00:01 gnome-help-browser --sm-client-i
root        649   445   0 18:24 tty2      00:00:00 su
root        653   649   0 18:24 tty2      00:00:00 bash
neil        655   428   0 18:24 tty4      00:00:00 -bash
root        713     1   2 18:27 tty1      00:00:00 gnome-terminal
root        715   713   0 18:28 tty1      00:00:00 gnome-pty-helper
root        717   716  13 18:28 pts/0     00:00:01 emacs
root        718   653   0 18:28 tty2      00:00:00 ps -ef
```

This shows information about many processes, including the processes involved with the Emacs editor under X on a Linux system. For example, the TTY column shows which terminal the process was started from, TIME gives the CPU time used so far, and the CMD column shows the command used to start the process. Let's take a closer look at some of these.

```
neil        655   428   0 18:24 tty4      00:00:00 -bash
```

The initial login was performed on virtual console number 4. This is just the console on this machine. The shell program that is running is the Linux default, bash.

```
root        467   433   0 18:12 tty1      00:00:00 sh /usr/X11R6/bin/startx
```

The X Window System was started by the command startx. This is a shell script that starts the X server and runs some initial X programs.

```
root        717   716  13 18:28 pts/0     00:00:01 emacs
```

This process represents a window in X running Emacs. It was started by the window manager in response to a request for a new window. A new pseudo terminal, pts/0, has been assigned for the shell to read from and write to.

```
root        512     1   0 18:12 tty1      00:00:01 gnome-help-browser --sm-client-i
```

This is the GNOME help browser started by the window manager.

By default, the ps program shows only processes that maintain a connection with a terminal, a console, a serial line, or a pseudo terminal. Other processes run without needing to communicate with a user on a terminal. These are typically system processes that Linux uses to manage shared resources. You can use ps to see all such processes using the -e option and to get "full" information with -f.

The exact syntax for the ps command and the format of the output may vary slightly from system to system. The GNU version of ps used in Linux supports options taken from several previous implementations of ps, including those in BSD and AT&T variants of UNIX and adds more of its own. Refer to the manual for more details on the available options and output format of ps.

System Processes

Here are some of the processes running on another Linux system. The output has been abbreviated for clarity. In the following examples you will see how to view the status of a process. The STAT output from ps provides codes indicating the current status. Common codes are given in the following table. The meanings of some of these will become clearer later in this chapter. Others are beyond the scope of this book and can be safely ignored.

STAT Code	Description
S	Sleeping. Usually waiting for an event to occur, such as a signal or input to become available.
R	Running. Strictly speaking, "runnable," that is, on the run queue either executing or about to run.
D	Uninterruptible Sleep (Waiting). Usually waiting for input or output to complete.
T	Stopped. Usually stopped by shell job control or the process is under the control of a debugger.
Z	Defunct or "zombie" process.
N	Low priority task, "nice."
W	Paging. (Not for Linux kernel 2.6 onwards.)
s	Process is a session leader.
+	Process is in the foreground process group.
l	Process is multithreaded.
<	High priority task.

```
$ ps ax
  PID TTY      STAT    TIME COMMAND
    1 ?        Ss      0:03 init [5]
    2 ?        S       0:00 [migration/0]
    3 ?        SN      0:00 [ksoftirqd/0]
    4 ?        S<      0:05 [events/0]
    5 ?        S<      0:00 [khelper]
    6 ?        S<      0:00 [kthread]
  840 ?        S<      2:52 [kjournald]
  888 ?        S<s     0:03 /sbin/udevd --daemon
 3069 ?        Ss      0:00 /sbin/acpid
 3098 ?        Ss      0:11 /usr/sbin/hald --daemon=yes
 3099 ?        S       0:00 hald-runner
 8357 ?        Ss      0:03 /sbin/syslog-ng
 8677 ?        Ss      0:00 /opt/kde3/bin/kdm
 9119 ?        S       0:11 konsole [kdeinit]
 9120 pts/2    Ss      0:00 /bin/bash
 9151 ?        Ss      0:00 /usr/sbin/cupsd
 9457 ?        Ss      0:00 /usr/sbin/cron
 9479 ?        Ss      0:00 /usr/sbin/sshd -o PidFile=/var/run/sshd.init.pid
```

```
 9618 tty1    Ss+    0:00 /sbin/mingetty --noclear tty1
 9619 tty2    Ss+    0:00 /sbin/mingetty tty2
 9621 tty3    Ss+    0:00 /sbin/mingetty tty3
 9622 tty4    Ss+    0:00 /sbin/mingetty tty4
 9623 tty5    Ss+    0:00 /sbin/mingetty tty5
 9638 tty6    Ss+    0:00 /sbin/mingetty tty6
10359 tty7    Ss+   10:05 /usr/bin/Xorg -br -nolisten tcp :0 vt7 -auth
10360 ?       S      0:00 -:0
10381 ?       Ss     0:00 /bin/sh /usr/bin/kde
10438 ?       Ss     0:00 /usr/bin/ssh-agent /bin/bash /etc/X11/xinit/xinitrc
10478 ?       S      0:00 start_kdeinit --new-startup +kcminit_startup
10479 ?       Ss     0:00 kdeinit Running...
10500 ?       S      0:53 kdesktop [kdeinit]
10502 ?       S      1:54 kicker [kdeinit]
10524 ?       Sl     0:47 beagled /usr/lib/beagle/BeagleDaemon.exe --bg
10530 ?       S      0:02 opensuseupdater
10539 ?       S      0:02 kpowersave [kdeinit]
10541 ?       S      0:03 klipper [kdeinit]
10555 ?       S      0:01 kio_uiserver [kdeinit]
10688 ?       S      0:53 konsole [kdeinit]
10689 pts/1   Ss+    0:07 /bin/bash
10784 ?       S      0:00 /opt/kde3/bin/kdesud
11052 ?       S      0:01 [pdflush]
19996 ?       SN1    0:20 beagled-helper /usr/lib/beagle/IndexHelper.exe
20254 ?       S      0:00 qmgr -l -t fifo -u
21192 ?       Ss     0:00 /usr/sbin/ntpd -p /var/run/ntp/ntpd.pid -u ntp -i /v
21198 ?       S      0:00 pickup -l -t fifo -u
21475 pts/2   R+     0:00 ps ax
```

Here you can see one very important process indeed.

```
    1 ?   Ss     0:03 init [5]
```

In general, each process is started by another process known as its *parent process*. A process so started is known as a *child process*. When Linux starts, it runs a single program, the prime ancestor and process number 1, init. This is, if you like, the operating system process manager and the grandparent of all processes. Other system processes you'll meet soon are started by init or by other processes started by init.

One such example is the login procedure. init starts the getty program once for each serial terminal or dial-in modem that you can use to log in. These are shown in the ps output like this:

```
 9619 tty2    Ss+    0:00 /sbin/mingetty tty2
```

The getty processes wait for activity at the terminal, prompt the user with the familiar login prompt, and then pass control to the login program, which sets up the user environment and finally starts a shell. When the user shell exits, init starts another getty process.

You can see that the ability to start new processes and to wait for them to finish is fundamental to the system. You'll see later in this chapter how to perform the same tasks from within your own programs with the system calls fork, exec, and wait.

Process Scheduling

One further ps output example is the entry for the ps command itself:

```
21475 pts/2    R+     0:00 ps ax
```

This indicates that process 21475 is in a run state (R) and is executing the command ps ax. Thus the process is described in its own output! The status indicator shows only that the program is ready to run, not necessarily that it's actually running. On a single-processor computer, only one process can run at a time, while others wait their turn. These turns, known as time slices, are quite short and give the impression that programs are running at the same time. The R+ just shows that the program is a foreground task not waiting for other processes to finish or waiting for input or output to complete. That is why you may see two such processes listed in ps output. (Another commonly seen process marked as running is the X display server.)

The Linux kernel uses a process scheduler to decide which process will receive the next time slice. It does this using the process priority (we discussed priorities back in Chapter 4). Processes with a high priority get to run more often, whereas others, such as low-priority background tasks, run less frequently. With Linux, processes can't overrun their allocated time slice. They are preemptively multitasked so that they are suspended and resumed without their cooperation. Older systems, such as Windows 3.x, generally require processes to yield explicitly so that others may resume.

In a multitasking system such as Linux where several programs are likely to be competing for the same resource, programs that perform short bursts of work and pause for input are considered better behaved than those that hog the processor by continually calculating some value or continually querying the system to see if new input is available. Well-behaved programs are termed *nice* programs, and in a sense this "niceness" can be measured. The operating system determines the priority of a process based on a "nice" value, which defaults to 0, and on the behavior of the program. Programs that run for long periods without pausing generally get lower priorities. Programs that pause while, for example, waiting for input, get rewarded. This helps keep a program that interacts with the user responsive; while it is waiting for some input from the user, the system increases its priority, so that when it's ready to resume, it has a high priority. You can set the process nice value using nice and adjust it using renice. The nice command increases the nice value of a process by 10, giving it a lower priority. You can view the nice values of active processes using the -l or -f (for long output) option to ps. The value you are interested in is shown in the NI (nice) column.

```
$ ps -l
  F S   UID   PID  PPID  C PRI  NI ADDR SZ WCHAN  TTY          TIME CMD
000 S   500  1259  1254  0  75   0 -    710 wait4  pts/2    00:00:00 bash
000 S   500  1262  1251  0  75   0 -    714 wait4  pts/1    00:00:00 bash
000 S   500  1313  1262  0  75   0 -   2762 schedu pts/1    00:00:00 emacs
000 S   500  1362  1262  2  80   0 -    789 schedu pts/1    00:00:00 oclock
000 R   500  1363  1262  0  81   0 -    782 -      pts/1    00:00:00 ps
```

Here you can see that the oclock program is running (as process 1362) with a default nice value. If it had been started with the command

```
$ nice oclock &
```

it would have been allocated a nice value of +10. If you adjust this value with the command

```
$ renice 10 1362
1362: old priority 0, new priority 10
```

the clock program will run less often. You can see the modified nice value with ps again:

```
$ ps -l
  F S   UID   PID  PPID  C PRI  NI ADDR SZ WCHAN  TTY          TIME CMD
000 S   500  1259  1254  0  75   0 -    710 wait4  pts/2    00:00:00 bash
000 S   500  1262  1251  0  75   0 -    714 wait4  pts/1    00:00:00 bash
000 S   500  1313  1262  0  75   0 -   2762 schedu pts/1    00:00:00 emacs
000 S   500  1362  1262  0  90  10 -    789 schedu pts/1    00:00:00 oclock
000 R   500  1365  1262  0  81   0 -    782 -      pts/1    00:00:00 ps
```

The status column now also contains N to indicate that the nice value has changed from the default.

```
$ ps x
  PID TTY      STAT   TIME COMMAND
 1362 pts/1    SN     0:00 oclock
```

The PPID field of ps output indicates the parent process ID, the PID of either the process that caused this process to start or, if that process is no longer running, init (PID 1).

The Linux scheduler decides which process it will allow to run on the basis of priority. Exact implementations vary, of course, but higher-priority processes run more often. In some cases, low-priority processes don't run at all if higher-priority processes are ready to run.

Starting New Processes

You can cause a program to run from inside another program and thereby create a new process by using the system library function.

```
#include <stdlib.h>

int system (const char *string);
```

The system function runs the command passed to it as a string and waits for it to complete. The command is executed as if the command

```
$ sh -c string
```

has been given to a shell. system returns 127 if a shell can't be started to run the command and –1 if another error occurs. Otherwise, system returns the exit code of the command.

Try It Out   **system**

You can use `system` to write a program to run `ps`. Though this is not tremendously useful in and of itself, you'll see how to develop this technique in later examples. (We don't check that the system call actually worked for the sake of simplicity in the example.)

```
#include <stdlib.h>
#include <stdio.h>

int main()
{
    printf("Running ps with system\n");
    system("ps ax");
    printf("Done.\n");
    exit(0);
}
```

When you compile and run this program, `system1.c`, you get something like the following:

```
$ ./system1
Running ps with system
  PID TTY       STAT    TIME COMMAND
    1 ?         Ss      0:03 init [5]
...

 1262 pts/1     Ss      0:00 /bin/bash
 1273 pts/2     S       0:00 su -
 1274 pts/2     S+      0:00 -bash
 1463 pts/2     SN      0:00 oclock
 1465 pts/1     S       0:01 emacs Makefile
 1480 pts/1     S+      0:00 ./system1
 1481 pts/1     R+      0:00 ps ax
Done.
```

Because the `system` function uses a shell to start the desired program, you could put it in the background by changing the function call in `system1.c` to the following:

```
    system("ps ax &");
```

When you compile and run this version of the program, you get something like

```
$ ./system2
Running ps with system
  PID TTY       STAT    TIME COMMAND
    1 ?         S       0:03 init [5]
...
Done.
$   1274 pts/2     S+      0:00 -bash
 1463 pts/1     SN      0:00 oclock
 1465 pts/1     S       0:01 emacs Makefile
 1484 pts/1     R       0:00 ps ax
```

How It Works

In the first example, the program calls `system` with the string `"ps ax"`, which executes the `ps` program. The program returns from the call to `system` when the `ps` command has finished. The `system` function can be quite useful but is also limited. Because the program has to wait until the process started by the call to `system` finishes, you can't get on with other tasks.

In the second example, the call to `system` returns as soon as the shell command finishes. Because it's a request to run a program in the background, the shell returns as soon as the `ps` program is started, just as would happen if you had typed

```
$ ps ax &
```

at a shell prompt. The `system2` program then prints `Done.` and exits before the `ps` command has had a chance to finish all of its output. The `ps` output continues to produce output after `system2` exits and in this case does not include an entry for system2. This kind of process behavior can be quite confusing for users. To make good use of processes, you need finer control over their actions. Let's look at a lower-level interface to process creation, `exec`.

In general, using `system` *is a far from ideal way to start other processes, because it invokes the desired program using a shell. This is both inefficient, because a shell is started before the program is started, and also quite dependent on the installation for the shell and environment that are used. In the next section, you see a much better way of invoking programs, which should almost always be used in preference to the* `system` *call.*

Replacing a Process Image

There is a whole family of related functions grouped under the `exec` heading. They differ in the way that they start processes and present program arguments. An `exec` function replaces the current process with a new process specified by the `path` or `file` argument. You can use `exec` functions to "hand off" execution of your program to another. For example, you could check the user's credentials before starting another application that has a restricted usage policy. The `exec` functions are more efficient than `system` because the original program will no longer be running after the new one is started.

```
#include <unistd.h>

char **environ;

int execl(const char *path, const char *arg0, ...,  (char *)0);
int execlp(const char *file, const char *arg0, ...,  (char *)0);
int execle(const char *path, const char *arg0, ...,  (char *)0, char *const
envp[]);
int execv(const char *path, char *const argv[]);
int execvp(const char *file, char *const argv[]);
int execve(const char *path, char *const argv[], char *const envp[]);
```

These functions belong to two types. `execl`, `execlp`, and `execle` take a variable number of arguments ending with a null pointer. `execv` and `execvp` have as their second argument an array of strings. In both cases, the new program starts with the given arguments appearing in the `argv` array passed to `main`.

These functions are usually implemented using execve, though there is no requirement for it to be done this way.

The functions with names suffixed with a p differ in that they will search the PATH environment variable to find the new program executable file. If the executable isn't on the path, an absolute filename, including directories, will need to be passed to the function as a parameter.

The global variable environ is available to pass a value for the new program environment. Alternatively, an additional argument to the functions execle and execve is available for passing an array of strings to be used as the new program environment.

If you want to use an exec function to start the ps program, you can choose from among the six exec family functions, as shown in the calls in the code fragment that follows:

```c
#include <unistd.h>

/* Example of an argument list */
/* Note that we need a program name for argv[0] */
char *const ps_argv[] =
    {"ps", "ax", 0};

/* Example environment, not terribly useful */
char *const ps_envp[] =
    {"PATH=/bin:/usr/bin", "TERM=console", 0};

/* Possible calls to exec functions */
execl("/bin/ps", "ps", "ax", 0);            /* assumes ps is in /bin */
execlp("ps", "ps", "ax", 0);                /* assumes /bin is in PATH */
execle("/bin/ps", "ps", "ax", 0, ps_envp);  /* passes own environment */

execv("/bin/ps", ps_argv);
execvp("ps", ps_argv);
execve("/bin/ps", ps_argv, ps_envp);
```

Try It Out   execlp

Let's modify the example to use an execlp call:

```c
#include <unistd.h>
#include <stdio.h>
#include <stdlib.h>

int main()
{
    printf("Running ps with execlp\n");
    execlp("ps", "ps", "ax", 0);
    printf("Done.\n");
    exit(0);
}
```

When you run this program, pexec.c, you get the usual ps output, but no Done. message at all. Note also that there is no reference to a process called pexec in the output.

```
$ ./pexec
Running ps with execlp
  PID TTY      STAT    TIME COMMAND
    1 ?        S       0:03 init [5]
...
 1262 pts/1    Ss      0:00 /bin/bash
 1273 pts/2    S       0:00 su -
 1274 pts/2    S+      0:00 -bash
 1463 pts/1    SN      0:00 oclock
 1465 pts/1    S       0:01 emacs Makefile
 1514 pts/1    R+      0:00 ps ax
```

How It Works

The program prints its first message and then calls execlp, which searches the directories given by the PATH environment variable for a program called ps. It then executes this program in place of the pexec program, starting it as if you had given the shell command

```
$ ps ax
```

When ps finishes, you get a new shell prompt. You don't return to pexec, so the second message doesn't get printed. The PID of the new process is the same as the original, as are the parent PID and nice value. In effect, all that has happened is that the running program has started to execute new code from a new executable file specified in the call to exec.

There is a limit on the combined size of the argument list and environment for a process started by exec functions. This is given by ARG_MAX and on Linux systems is 128K bytes. Other systems may set a more reduced limit that can lead to problems. The POSIX specification indicates that ARG_MAX should be at least 4,096 bytes.

The exec functions generally don't return unless an error occurs, in which case the error variable errno is set and the exec function returns -1.

The new process started by exec inherits many features from the original. In particular, open file descriptors remain open in the new process unless their "close on exec flag" has been set (refer to the fcntl system call in Chapter 3 for more details). Any open directory streams in the original process are closed.

Duplicating a Process Image

To use processes to perform more than one function at a time, you can either use threads, covered in Chapter 12, or create an entirely separate process from within a program, as init does, rather than replace the current thread of execution, as in the exec case.

You can create a new process by calling fork. This system call duplicates the current process, creating a new entry in the process table with many of the same attributes as the current process. The new process is almost identical to the original, executing the same code but with its own data space, environment, and file descriptors. Combined with the exec functions, fork is all you need to create new processes.

```
#include <sys/types.h>
#include <unistd.h>

pid_t fork(void);
```

As you can see in Figure 11-2, the call to fork in the parent returns the PID of the new child process. The new process continues to execute just like the original, with the exception that in the child process the call to fork returns 0. This allows both the parent and child to determine which is which.

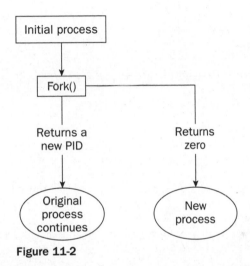

Figure 11-2

If fork fails, it returns -1. This is commonly due to a limit on the number of child processes that a parent may have (CHILD_MAX), in which case errno will be set to EAGAIN. If there is not enough space for an entry in the process table, or not enough virtual memory, the errno variable will be set to ENOMEM.

A typical code fragment using fork is

```
    pid_t new_pid;

    new_pid = fork();

    switch(new_pid) {
    case -1 :      /* Error */
        break;
    case 0 :       /* We are child */
        break;
    default :      /* We are parent */
        break;
    }
```

Try It Out   fork

Let's look at a simple example, `fork1.c`:

```c
#include <sys/types.h>
#include <unistd.h>
#include <stdio.h>
#include <stdlib.h>

int main()
{
    pid_t pid;
    char *message;
    int n;

    printf("fork program starting\n");
    pid = fork();
    switch(pid)
    {
    case -1:
        perror("fork failed");
        exit(1);
    case 0:
        message = "This is the child";
        n = 5;
        break;
    default:
        message = "This is the parent";
        n = 3;
        break;
    }

    for(; n > 0; n--) {
        puts(message);
        sleep(1);
    }
    exit(0);
}
```

This program runs as two processes. A child is created and prints a message five times. The original process (the parent) prints a message only three times. The parent process finishes before the child has printed all of its messages, so the next shell prompt appears mixed in with the output.

```
$ ./fork1
fork program starting
This is the child
This is the parent
This is the parent
This is the child
This is the parent
This is the child
$ This is the child
This is the child
```

How It Works

When `fork` is called, this program divides into two separate processes. The parent process is identified by a nonzero return from `fork` and is used to set a number of messages to print, each separated by one second.

Waiting for a Process

When you start a child process with `fork`, it takes on a life of its own and runs independently. Sometimes, you would like to find out when a child process has finished. For example, in the previous program, the parent finishes ahead of the child and you get some messy output as the child continues to run. You can arrange for the parent process to wait until the child finishes before continuing by calling `wait`.

```
#include <sys/types.h>
#include <sys/wait.h>

pid_t wait(int *stat_loc);
```

The `wait` system call causes a parent process to pause until one of its child processes is stopped. The call returns the PID of the child process. This will normally be a child process that has terminated. The status information allows the parent process to determine the exit status of the child process, that is, the value returned from `main` or passed to `exit`. If `stat_loc` is not a null pointer, the status information will be written to the location to which it points.

You can interpret the status information using macros defined in `sys/wait.h`, shown in the following table.

Macro	Definition
WIFEXITED(stat_val)	Nonzero if the child is terminated normally.
WEXITSTATUS(stat_val)	If WIFEXITED is nonzero, this returns child exit code.
WIFSIGNALED(stat_val)	Nonzero if the child is terminated on an uncaught signal.
WTERMSIG(stat_val)	If WIFSIGNALED is nonzero, this returns a signal number.
WIFSTOPPED(stat_val)	Nonzero if the child has stopped.
WSTOPSIG(stat_val)	If WIFSTOPPED is nonzero, this returns a signal number.

Try It Out   wait

In this Try It Out, you modify the program slightly so you can wait for and examine the child process exit status. Call the new program `wait.c`.

```
#include <sys/types.h>
#include <sys/wait.h>
#include <unistd.h>
#include <stdio.h>
```

```c
#include <stdlib.h>

int main()
{
    pid_t pid;
    char *message;
    int n;
    int exit_code;

    printf("fork program starting\n");
    pid = fork();
    switch(pid)
    {

    case -1:
        perror("fork failed");
        exit(1);
    case 0:
        message = "This is the child";
        n = 5;
        exit_code = 37;
        break;
    default:
        message = "This is the parent";
        n = 3;
        exit_code = 0;
        break;
    }

    for(; n > 0; n--) {
        puts(message);
        sleep(1);
    }
```

This section of the program waits for the child process to finish.

```c
    if (pid != 0) {
        int stat_val;
        pid_t child_pid;

        child_pid = wait(&stat_val);

        printf("Child has finished: PID = %d\n", child_pid);
        if(WIFEXITED(stat_val))
            printf("Child exited with code %d\n", WEXITSTATUS(stat_val));
        else
            printf("Child terminated abnormally\n");
    }
    exit(exit_code);
}
```

When you run this program, you see the parent wait for the child.

```
$ ./wait
fork program starting
```

```
This is the child
This is the parent
This is the parent
This is the child
This is the parent
This is the child
This is the child
This is the child
Child has finished: PID = 1582
Child exited with code 37
$
```

How It Works

The parent process, which got a nonzero return from the fork call, uses the wait system call to suspend its own execution until status information becomes available for a child process. This happens when the child calls exit; we gave it an exit code of 37. The parent then continues, determines that the child terminated normally by testing the return value of the wait call, and extracts the exit code from the status information.

Zombie Processes

Using fork to create processes can be very useful, but you must keep track of child processes. When a child process terminates, an association with its parent survives until the parent in turn either terminates normally or calls wait. The child process entry in the process table is therefore not freed up immediately. Although no longer active, the child process is still in the system because its exit code needs to be stored in case the parent subsequently calls wait. It becomes what is known as defunct, or a *zombie process*.

You can see a zombie process being created if you change the number of messages in the fork example program. If the child prints fewer messages than the parent, it will finish first and will exist as a zombie until the parent has finished.

Try It Out **Zombies**

fork2.c is the same as fork1.c, except that the number of messages printed by the child and parent processes is reversed. Here are the relevant lines of code:

```
switch(pid)
{
case -1:
    perror("fork failed");
    exit(1);
case 0:
    message = "This is the child";
    n = 3;
    break;
default:
    message = "This is the parent";
    n = 5;
    break;
}
```

How It Works

If you run the preceding program with `./fork2 &` and then call the `ps` program after the child has finished but before the parent has finished, you'll see a line such as this. (Some systems may say `<zombie>` rather than `<defunct>`.)

```
$ ps -al

  F S   UID   PID  PPID  C  PRI  NI ADDR SZ WCHAN  TTY         TIME CMD
004 S     0  1273  1259  0   75   0 -   589 wait4  pts/2   00:00:00 su
000 S     0  1274  1273  0   75   0 -   731 schedu pts/2   00:00:00 bash
000 S   500  1463  1262  0   75   0 -   788 schedu pts/1   00:00:00 oclock
000 S   500  1465  1262  0   75   0 -  2569 schedu pts/1   00:00:01 emacs
000 S   500  1603  1262  0   75   0 -   313 schedu pts/1   00:00:00 fork2
003 Z   500  1604  1603  0   75   0 -     0 do_exi pts/1   00:00:00 fork2 <defunct>
000 R   500  1605  1262  0   81   0 -   781 -      pts/1   00:00:00 ps
```

If the parent then terminates abnormally, the child process automatically gets the process with PID 1 (`init`) as parent. The child process is now a zombie that is no longer running but has been inherited by `init` because of the abnormal termination of the parent process. The zombie will remain in the process table until collected by the `init` process. The bigger the table, the slower this procedure. You need to avoid zombie processes, because they consume resources until `init` cleans them up.

There's another system call that you can use to wait for child processes. It's called `waitpid`, and you can use it to wait for a specific process to terminate.

```
#include <sys/types.h>
#include <sys/wait.h>

pid_t waitpid(pid_t pid, int *stat_loc, int options);
```

The `pid` argument specifies the PID of a particular child process to wait for. If it's –1, `waitpid` will return information for any child process. Like `wait`, it will write status information to the location pointed to by `stat_loc`, if that is not a null pointer. The `options` argument allows you to modify the behavior of `waitpid`. The most useful option is `WNOHANG`, which prevents the call to `waitpid` from suspending execution of the caller. You can use it to find out whether any child processes have terminated and, if not, to continue. Other options are the same as for `wait`.

So, if you wanted to have a parent process regularly check whether a specific child process has terminated, you could use the call

```
waitpid(child_pid, (int *) 0, WNOHANG);
```

This will return zero if the child has not terminated or stopped, or `child_pid` if it has. `waitpid` will return –1 on error and set `errno`. This can happen if there are no child processes (`errno` set to `ECHILD`), if the call is interrupted by a signal (`EINTR`), or if the option argument is invalid (`EINVAL`).

Input and Output Redirection

You can use your knowledge of processes to alter the behavior of programs by exploiting the fact that open file descriptors are preserved across calls to `fork` and `exec`. The next example involves a *filter program* — a program that reads from its standard input and writes to its standard output, performing some useful transformation as it does so.

Try It Out   **Redirection**

Here's a very simple filter program, `upper.c`, that reads input and converts it to uppercase:

```c
#include <stdio.h>
#include <ctype.h>
#include <stdlib.h>

int main()
{
    int ch;
    while((ch = getchar()) != EOF) {
        putchar(toupper(ch));
    }
    exit(0);
}
```

When you run the program, it does what you expect:

```
$ ./upper
hello THERE
HELLO THERE
^D
$
```

You can, of course, use it to convert a file to uppercase by using the shell redirection

```
$ cat file.txt
this is the file, file.txt, it is all lower case.
$ ./upper < file.txt
THIS IS THE FILE, FILE.TXT, IT IS ALL LOWER CASE.
```

What if you want to use this filter from within another program? This program, `useupper.c`, accepts a filename as an argument and will respond with an error if called incorrectly.

```c
#include <unistd.h>
#include <stdio.h>
#include <stdlib.h>

int main(int argc, char *argv[])
{
    char *filename;

    if (argc != 2) {
        fprintf(stderr, "usage: useupper file\n");
```

```
        exit(1);
    }

    filename = argv[1];
```

You reopen the standard input, again checking for any errors as you do so, and then use execl to call upper.

```
    if(!freopen(filename, "r", stdin)) {
        fprintf(stderr, "could not redirect stdin from file %s\n", filename);
        exit(2);
    }

    execl("./upper", "upper", 0);
```

Don't forget that execl replaces the current process; if there is no error, the remaining lines are not executed.

```
    perror("could not exec ./upper");
    exit(3);
}
```

How It Works

When you run this program, you can give it a file to convert to uppercase. The job is done by the program upper, which doesn't handle filename arguments. Note that you don't require the source code for upper; you can run any executable program in this way:

```
$ ./useupper file.txt
THIS IS THE FILE, FILE.TXT, IT IS ALL LOWER CASE.
```

The useupper program uses freopen to close the standard input and associate the file stream stdin with the file given as a program argument. It then calls execl to replace the running process code with that of the upper program. Because open file descriptors are preserved across the call to execl, the upper program runs exactly as it would have under the shell command:

```
$ ./upper < file.txt
```

Threads

Linux processes can cooperate, can send each other messages, and can interrupt one another. They can even arrange to share segments of memory between themselves, but they are essentially separate entities within the operating system. They do not readily share variables.

There is a class of process known as a *thread* that is available in many UNIX and Linux systems. Though threads can be difficult to program, they can be of great value in some applications, such as multithreaded database servers. Programming threads on Linux (and UNIX generally) is not as common as using multiple processes, because Linux processes are quite lightweight, and programming multiple cooperation processes is much easier than programming threads. Threads are covered in Chapter 12.

Signals

A *signal* is an event generated by the UNIX and Linux systems in response to some condition, upon receipt of which a process may in turn take some action. We use the term *raise* to indicate the generation of a signal, and the term *catch* to indicate the receipt of a signal. Signals are raised by some error conditions, such as memory segment violations, floating-point processor errors, or illegal instructions. They are generated by the shell and terminal handlers to cause interrupts and can also be explicitly sent from one process to another as a way of passing information or modifying behavior. In all these cases, the programming interface is the same. Signals can be raised, caught and acted upon, or (for some at least) ignored.

Signal names are defined by including the header file `signal.h`. They all begin with SIG and include those listed in the following table.

Signal Name	Description
SIGABORT	*Process abort
SIGALRM	Alarm clock
SIGFPE	*Floating-point exception
SIGHUP	Hangup
SIGILL	*Illegal instruction
SIGINT	Terminal interrupt
SIGKILL	Kill (can't be caught or ignored)
SIGPIPE	Write on a pipe with no reader
SIGQUIT	Terminal quit
SIGSEGV	*Invalid memory segment access
SIGTERM	Termination
SIGUSR1	User-defined signal 1
SIGUSR2	User-defined signal 2

*Implementation-dependent actions may also be taken.

If a process receives one of these signals without first arranging to catch it, the process will be terminated immediately. Usually, a core dump file is created. This file, called `core` and placed in the current directory, is an image of the process that can be useful in debugging.

Additional signals include those in the following table.

Signal Name	Description
SIGCHLD	Child process has stopped or exited.
SIGCONT	Continue executing, if stopped.
SIGSTOP	Stop executing. (Can't be caught or ignored.)
SIGTSTP	Terminal stop signal.
SIGTTIN	Background process trying to read.
SIGTTOU	Background process trying to write.

SIGCHLD can be useful for managing child processes. It's ignored by default. The remaining signals cause the process receiving them to stop, except for SIGCONT, which causes the process to resume. They are used by shell programs for job control and are rarely used by user programs.

We'll look at the first group of signals in a little more detail later. For now, it's enough to know that if the shell and terminal driver are configured normally, typing the interrupt character (usually Ctrl+C) at the keyboard will result in the SIGINT signal being sent to the foreground process, that is, the program currently running. This will cause the program to terminate unless it has arranged to catch the signal.

If you want to send a signal to a process other than the current foreground task, use the kill command. This takes an optional signal number or name, and the PID (usually found using the ps command) to send the signal to. For example, to send a "hangup" signal to a shell running on a different terminal with PID 512, you would use the command

```
$ kill -HUP 512
```

A useful variant of the kill command is killall, which allows you to send a signal to all processes running a specified command. Not all versions of UNIX support it, though Linux generally does. This is useful when you do not know the PID, or when you want to send a signal to several different processes executing the same command. A common use is to tell the inetd program to reread its configuration options. To do this you can use the command

```
$ killall -HUP inetd
```

Programs can handle signals using the signal library function.

```
#include <signal.h>

void (*signal(int sig, void (*func)(int)))(int);
```

This rather complex declaration says that signal is a function that takes two parameters, sig and func. The signal to be caught or ignored is given as argument sig. The function to be called when the specified signal is received is given as func. This function must be one that takes a single int argument (the signal received) and is of type void. The signal function itself returns a function of the same type, which is the previous value of the function set up to handle this signal, or one of these two special values:

SIG_IGN	Ignore the signal.
SIG_DFL	Restore default behavior.

An example should make things clear. In the following Try It Out, you write a program, ctrlc.c, that reacts to typing Ctrl+C by printing an appropriate message rather than terminating. Pressing Ctrl+C a second time will end the program.

Try It Out   Signal Handling

The function ouch reacts to the signal that is passed in the parameter sig. This function will be called when a signal occurs. It prints a message and then resets the signal handling for SIGINT (by default, generated by typing Ctrl+C) back to the default behavior.

```c
#include <signal.h>
#include <stdio.h>
#include <unistd.h>

void ouch(int sig)
{
    printf("OUCH! - I got signal %d\n", sig);
    (void) signal(SIGINT, SIG_DFL);
}
```

The main function has to intercept the SIGINT signal generated when you type Ctrl+C. For the rest of the time, it just sits in an infinite loop, printing a message once a second.

```c
int main()
{
    (void) signal(SIGINT, ouch);

    while(1) {
        printf("Hello World!\n");
        sleep(1);
    }
}
```

Typing Ctrl+C (shown as ^C in the following output) for the first time causes the program to react and then continue. When you type Ctrl+C again, the program ends because the behavior of SIGINT has returned to the default behavior of causing the program to exit.

```
$ ./ctrlc1
Hello World!
Hello World!
Hello World!
Hello World!
^C
OUCH! - I got signal 2
```

```
Hello World!
Hello World!
Hello World!
Hello World!
^C
$
```

As you can see from this example, the signal handling function takes a single integer parameter, the signal number that caused the function to be called. This can be useful if the same function is used to handle more than one signal. Here you print out the value of SIGINT, which on this system happens to have the value 2. You shouldn't rely on traditional numeric values for signals; always use signal names in new programs.

It is not safe to call all functions, such as printf, from within a signal handler. A useful technique is to use a signal handler to set a flag and then check that flag from the main program and print a message if required. Toward the end of the chapter, you will find a list of calls that can safely be made inside signal handlers.

How It Works

The program arranges for the function ouch to be called when you give the SIGINT signal by typing Ctrl+C. After the interrupt function ouch has completed, the program carries on, but the signal action is restored to the default. (Different versions of UNIX, particularly those derived from Berkeley UNIX, have historically had subtly different signal behaviors. If you want the default action to a signal restored after it has occurred, it's always best to code it that way specifically.) When it receives a second SIGINT signal, the program takes the default action, which is to terminate the program.

If you wanted to retain the signal handler and continue to react to Ctrl+C, you would need to re-establish it by calling signal again. This leads to a short time when the signal is not handled, from the start of the interrupt function to just before the signal handler is re-established. It's possible for a second signal to be received in this time and terminate the program against your wishes.

We don't recommend that you use the signal interface for catching signals. We include it here because you will find it in many older programs. You'll see sigaction, a more cleanly defined and reliable interface later, which you should use in all new programs.

The signal function returns the previous value of the signal handler for the specified signal if there is one, or SIG_ERR otherwise, in which case, errno will be set to a positive value. errno will be set to EINVAL if an invalid signal is specified or an attempt is made to handle a signal that may not be caught or ignored, such as SIGKILL.

Sending Signals

A process may send a signal to another process, including itself, by calling kill. The call will fail if the program doesn't have permission to send the signal, often because the target process is owned by another user. This is the program equivalent of the shell command of the same name.

```
#include <sys/types.h>
#include <signal.h>

int kill(pid_t pid, int sig);
```

The `kill` function sends the specified signal, `sig`, to the process whose identifier is given by `pid`. It returns 0 on success. To send a signal, the sending process must have permission to do so. Normally, this means that both processes must have the same user ID (that is, you can send a signal only to one of your own processes, although the superuser can send signals to any process).

`kill` will fail, return -1, and set `errno` if the signal given is not a valid one (`errno` set to `EINVAL`), if it doesn't have permission (`EPERM`), or if the specified process doesn't exist (`ESRCH`).

Signals provide you with a useful alarm clock facility. The alarm function call can be used by a process to schedule a `SIGALRM` signal at some time in the future.

```
#include <unistd.h>

unsigned int alarm(unsigned int seconds);
```

The alarm call schedules the delivery of a `SIGALRM` signal in seconds seconds. In fact, the alarm will be delivered shortly after that, due to processing delays and scheduling uncertainties. A value of 0 will cancel any outstanding alarm request. Calling `alarm` before the signal is received will cause the alarm to be rescheduled. Each process can have only one outstanding alarm. `alarm` returns the number of seconds left before any outstanding alarm call would be sent, or -1 if the call fails.

To see how `alarm` works, you can simulate its effect by using `fork`, `sleep`, and `signal`. A program could start a new process for the sole purpose of sending a signal at some time later.

Try It Out   An Alarm Clock

In `alarm.c`, the first function, `ding`, simulates an alarm clock.

```
#include <sys/types.h>
#include <signal.h>
#include <stdio.h>
#include <unistd.h>
#include <stdlib.h>

static int alarm_fired = 0;

void ding(int sig)
{
    alarm_fired = 1;
}
```

In `main`, you tell the child process to wait for five seconds before sending a `SIGALRM` signal to its parent.

```
int main()
{
    pid_t pid;

    printf("alarm application starting\n");

    pid = fork();
    switch(pid) {
    case -1:
```

```
      · /* Failure */
        perror("fork failed");
        exit(1);
    case 0:
        /* child */
        sleep(5);
        kill(getppid(), SIGALRM);
        exit(0);
    }
```

The parent process arranges to catch SIGALRM with a call to signal and then waits for the inevitable.

```
        /* if we get here we are the parent process */
        printf("waiting for alarm to go off\n");
        (void) signal(SIGALRM, ding);

        pause();
        if (alarm_fired)
            printf("Ding!\n");

        printf("done\n");
        exit(0);
    }
```

When you run this program, it pauses for five seconds while it waits for the simulated alarm clock.

```
$ ./alarm
alarm application starting
waiting for alarm to go off
<5 second pause>
Ding!
done
$
```

This program introduces a new function, pause, which simply causes the program to suspend execution until a signal occurs. When it receives a signal, any established handler is run and execution continues as normal. It's declared as

```
#include <unistd.h>

int pause(void);
```

and returns –1 (if the next received signal doesn't cause the program to terminate) with errno set to EINTR when interrupted by a signal. It is more common to use sigsuspend when waiting for signals, which we discuss a bit later in the chapter.

How It Works

The alarm clock simulation program starts a new process via fork. This child process sleeps for five seconds and then sends a SIGALRM to its parent. The parent arranges to catch SIGALRM and then pauses until a signal is received. You do not call printf in the signal handler directly; rather, you set a flag and then check the flag afterward.

Using signals and suspending execution is an important part of Linux programming. It means that a program need not necessarily run all the time. Rather than run in a loop continually checking whether an event has occurred, it can wait for an event to happen. This is especially important in a multiuser environment where processes share a single processor and this kind of busy wait has a large impact on system performance. A particular problem with signals is that you never know quite "What will happen if a signal occurs in the middle of a system call?" (The answer is a rather unsatisfactory "it depends.") In general, you need to worry only about "slow" system calls, such as reading from a terminal, where the system call will return with an error if a signal occurs while it is waiting. If you start using signals in your programs, you need to be aware that some system calls could fail if a signal causes an error condition that you may not have considered before signal handling was added.

You must program your signals carefully, because there are a number of "race conditions" that can occur in programs that use them. For example, if you intend to call pause to wait for a signal and that signal occurs before the call to pause, your program may wait indefinitely for an event that won't occur. These race conditions, critical timing problems, catch many a novice programmer. Always check signal code very carefully.

A Robust Signals Interface

We've covered raising and catching signals using signal and friends in some depth, because they are very common in older UNIX programs. However, the X/Open and UNIX specifications recommend a newer programming interface for signals that is more robust: sigaction.

```
#include <signal.h>

int sigaction(int sig, const struct sigaction *act, struct sigaction *oact);
```

The sigaction structure, used to define the actions to be taken on receipt of the signal specified by sig, is defined in signal.h and has at least the following members:

```
void (*) (int) sa_handler    /*  function, SIG_DFL or SIG_IGN
sigset_t sa_mask             /*  signals to block in sa_handler
int sa_flags                 /*  signal action modifiers
```

The sigaction function sets the action associated with the signal sig. If oact is not null, sigaction writes the previous signal action to the location it refers to. If act is null, this is all sigaction does. If act isn't null, the action for the specified signal is set.

As with signal, sigaction returns 0 if successful and –1 if not. The error variable errno will be set to EINVAL if the specified signal is invalid or if an attempt is made to catch or ignore a signal that can't be caught or ignored.

Within the sigaction structure pointed to by the argument act, sa_handler is a pointer to a function called when signal sig is received. This is much like the function func you saw earlier passed to signal. You can use the special values SIG_IGN and SIG_DFL in the sa_handler field to indicate that the signal is to be ignored or the action is to be restored to its default, respectively.

The sa_mask field specifies a set of signals to be added to the process's signal mask before the sa_handler function is called. These are the set of signals that are blocked and won't be delivered to the process. This prevents the case you saw earlier where a signal is received before its handler has run to completion. Using the sa_mask field can eliminate this race condition.

However, signals caught with handlers set by sigaction are by default not reset, and the sa_flags field must be set to contain the value SA_RESETHAND if you want to obtain the behavior you saw earlier with signal. Before we look in any more detail at sigaction, let's rewrite the program ctrlc.c, using sigaction instead of signal.

Try It Out   sigaction

Make the changes that follow so that SIGINT is intercepted by sigaction. Call the new program ctrlc2.c.

```c
#include <signal.h>
#include <stdio.h>
#include <unistd.h>

void ouch(int sig)
{
    printf("OUCH! - I got signal %d\n", sig);
}

int main()
{
    struct sigaction act;

    act.sa_handler = ouch;
    sigemptyset(&act.sa_mask);
    act.sa_flags = 0;

    sigaction(SIGINT, &act, 0);

    while(1) {
        printf("Hello World!\n");
        sleep(1);
    }
}
```

When you run this version of the program, you always get a message when you type Ctrl+C because SIGINT is handled repeatedly by sigaction. To terminate the program, you have to type Ctrl+\, which generates the SIGQUIT signal by default.

```
$ ./ctrlc2
Hello World!
Hello World!
Hello World!
^C
OUCH! - I got signal 2
Hello World!
Hello World!
^C
OUCH! - I got signal 2
```

```
Hello World!
Hello World!
^\
Quit
$
```

How It Works

The program calls `sigaction` instead of `signal` to set the signal handler for Ctrl+C (`SIGINT`) to the function `ouch`. It first has to set up a `sigaction` structure that contains the handler, a signal mask, and flags. In this case, you don't need any flags, and an empty signal mask is created with the new function, `sigemptyset`.

> *After running this program, you may find a core dump (in a file called* core*) has been created. You can safely delete it.*

Signal Sets

The header file `signal.h` defines the type `sigset_t` and functions used to manipulate sets of signals. These sets are used in `sigaction` and other functions to modify process behavior on receipt of signals.

```
#include <signal.h>

int sigaddset(sigset_t *set, int signo);
int sigemptyset(sigset_t *set);
int sigfillset(sigset_t *set);
int sigdelset(sigset_t *set, int signo);
```

These functions perform the operations suggested by their names. `sigemptyset` initializes a signal set to be empty. `sigfillset` initializes a signal set to contain all defined signals. `sigaddset` and `sigdelset` add and delete a specified signal (`signo`) from a signal set. They all return 0 if successful and –1 with `errno` set on error. The only error defined is `EINVAL` if the specified signal is invalid.

The function `sigismember` determines whether the given signal is a member of a signal set. It returns 1 if the signal is a member of the set, 0 if it isn't, and –1 with `errno` set to `EINVAL` if the signal is invalid.

```
#include <signal.h>

int sigismember(sigset_t *set, int signo);
```

The process signal mask is set or examined by calling the function `sigprocmask`. This signal mask is the set of signals that are currently blocked and will therefore not be received by the current process.

```
#include <signal.h>

int sigprocmask(int how, const sigset_t *set, sigset_t *oset);
```

`sigprocmask` can change the process signal mask in a number of ways according to the `how` argument. New values for the signal mask are passed in the argument `set` if it isn't null, and the previous signal mask will be written to the signal set `oset`.

The how argument can be one of the following:

SIG_BLOCK	The signals in set are added to the signal mask.
SIG_SETMASK	The signal mask is set from set.
SIG_UNBLOCK	The signals in set are removed from the signal mask.

If the set argument is a null pointer, the value of how is not used and the only purpose of the call is to fetch the value of the current signal mask into oset.

If it completes successfully, sigprocmask returns 0, or it returns −1 if the how parameter is invalid, in which case errno will be set to EINVAL.

If a signal is blocked by a process, it won't be delivered, but will remain pending. A program can determine which of its blocked signals are pending by calling the function sigpending.

```
#include <signal.h>

int sigpending(sigset_t *set);
```

This writes a set of signals that are blocked from delivery and are pending into the signal set pointed to by set. It returns 0 if successful, otherwise, −1 with errno set to indicate the error. This function can be useful when a program needs to handle signals and to control when the handling function is called.

A process can suspend execution until the delivery of one of a set of signals by calling sigsuspend. This is a more general form of the pause function you met earlier.

```
#include <signal.h>

int sigsuspend(const sigset_t *sigmask);
```

The sigsuspend function replaces the process signal mask with the signal set given by sigmask and then suspends execution. It will resume after the execution of a signal handling function. If the received signal terminates the program, sigsuspend will never return. If a received signal doesn't terminate the program, sigsuspend returns −1 with errno set to EINTR.

sigaction Flags

The sa_flags field of the sigaction structure used in sigaction may contain the values shown in the following table to modify signal behavior:

SA_NOCLDSTOP	Don't generate SIGCHLD when child processes stop.
SA_RESETHAND	Reset signal action to SIG_DFL on receipt.
SA_RESTART	Restart interruptible functions rather than error with EINTR.
SA_NODEFER	Don't add the signal to the signal mask when caught.

The SA_RESETHAND flag can be used to automatically clear a signal function when a signal is caught, as we saw before.

Many system calls that a program uses are interruptible; that is, when they receive a signal they will return with an error and errno will be set to EINTR to indicate that the function returned due to a signal. This behavior requires extra care by an application using signals. If SA_RESTART is set in the sa_flags field in a call to sigaction, a function that might otherwise be interrupted by a signal will instead be restarted once the signal handling function has been executed.

Ordinarily, when a signal handling function is being executed, the signal received is added to the process signal mask for the duration of the handling function. This prevents a subsequent occurrence of the same signal, causing the signal handling function to run again. If the function is not re-entrant, having it called by another occurrence of a signal before it finishes handling the first may cause problems. If, however, the SA_NODEFER flag is set, the signal mask is not altered when it receives this signal.

A signal handling function could be interrupted in the middle and called again by something else. When you come back to the first call, it's vital that it still operates correctly. It's not just recursive (calling itself), but re-entrant (can be entered and executed again without problems). Interrupt service routines in the kernel that deal with more than one device at a time need to be re-entrant, because a higher-priority interrupt might "get in" during the execution of the same code.

Functions that are safe to call inside a signal handler, those guaranteed by the X/Open specification either to be re-entrant or not to raise signals themselves, are listed in the following table.

All functions not listed in the following table should be considered unsafe with respect to signals.

access	alarm	cfgetispeed	cfgetospeed
cfsetispeed	cfsetospeed	chdir	chmod
chown	close	creat	dup2
dup	execle	execve	_exit
fcntl	fork	fstat	getegid
geteuid	getgid	getgroups	getpgrp
getpid	getppid	getuid	kill
link	lseek	mkdir	mkfifo
open	pathconf	pause	pipe
read	rename	rmdir	setgid
setpgid	setsid	setuid	sigaction
sigaddset	sigdelset	sigemptyset	sigfillset

Continued on next page

sigismember	signal	sigpending	sigprocmask
sigsuspend	sleep	stat	sysconf
tcdrain	tcflow	tcflush	tcgetattr
tcgetpgrp	tcsendbreak	tcsetattr	tcsetpgrp
time	times	umask	uname
unlink	utime	wait	waitpid
write			

Common Signal Reference

In this section, we list the signals that Linux and UNIX programs typically need with their default behaviors.

The default action for the signals in the following table is abnormal termination of the process with all the consequences of _exit (which is like exit but performs no cleanup before returning to the kernel). However, the status is made available to wait, and waitpid indicates abnormal termination by the specified signal.

Signal Name	Description
SIGALRM	Generated by the timer set by the alarm function.
SIGHUP	Sent to the controlling process by a disconnecting terminal, or by the controlling process on termination to each foreground process.
SIGINT	Typically raised from the terminal by typing Ctrl+C or the configured interrupt character.
SIGKILL	Typically used from the shell to forcibly terminate an errant process, because this signal can't be caught or ignored.
SIGPIPE	Generated by an attempt to write to a pipe with no associated reader.
SIGTERM	Sent as a request for a process to finish. Used by UNIX when shutting down to request that system services stop. This is the default signal sent from the kill command.
SIGUSR1, SIGUSR2	May be used by processes to communicate with each other, possibly to cause them to report status information.

By default, the signals in the next table also cause abnormal termination. Additionally, implementation-dependent actions, such as creation of a core file, may occur.

Signal Name	Description
SIGFPE	Generated by a floating-point arithmetic exception.
SIGILL	An illegal instruction has been executed by the processor. Usually caused by a corrupt program or invalid shared memory module.
SIGQUIT	Typically raised from the terminal by typing Ctrl+\ or the configured quit character.
SIGSEGV	A segmentation violation, usually caused by reading or writing at an illegal location in memory either by exceeding array bounds or dereferencing an invalid pointer. Overwriting a local array variable and corrupting the stack can cause a SIGSEGV to be raised when a function returns to an illegal address.

A process is suspended by default on receipt of one of the signals in the following table.

Signal Name	Description
SIGSTOP	Stop executing (can't be caught or ignored).
SIGTSTP	Terminal stop signal, often raised by typing Ctrl+Z.
SIGTTIN, SIGTTOU	Used by the shell to indicate that background jobs have stopped because they need to read from the terminal or produce output.

SIGCONT restarts a stopped process and is ignored if received by a process that is not stopped. The SIGCHLD signal is ignored by default.

Signal Name	Description
SIGCONT	Continue executing, if stopped.
SIGCHLD	Raised when a child process stops or exits.

Summary

In this chapter, you have seen how processes are a fundamental part of the Linux operating system. You have learned how they can be started, terminated, and viewed, and how you can use them to solve programming problems. You've also taken a look at signals, events that can be used to control the actions of running programs. You have seen that all Linux processes, down to and including init, use the same set of system calls available to any programmer.

12

POSIX Threads

In Chapter 11, you saw how processes are handled in Linux (and indeed in UNIX). These multi-processing features have long been a feature of UNIX-like operating systems. Sometimes it may be very useful to make a single program do two things at once, or at least to appear to do so, or you might want two or more things to happen at the same time in a closely coupled way but consider the overhead of creating a new process with `fork` too great. For these occasions you can use threads, which allow a single process to multitask.

In this chapter, you look at

- ❑ Creating new threads within a process
- ❑ Synchronizing data access between threads in a single process
- ❑ Modifying the attributes of a thread
- ❑ Controlling one thread from another in the same process

What Is a Thread?

Multiple strands of execution in a single program are called *threads*. A more precise definition is that a thread is a sequence of control within a process. All the programs you have seen so far have executed as a single process, although, like many other operating systems, Linux is quite capable of running multiple processes simultaneously. Indeed, all processes have at least one thread of execution. All the processes that you have seen so far in this book have had just one thread of execution.

It's important to be clear about the difference between the `fork` system call and the creation of new threads. When a process executes a `fork` call, a new copy of the process is created with its own variables and its own PID. This new process is scheduled independently, and (in general) executes almost independently of the process that created it. When we create a new thread in a process, in contrast, the new thread of execution gets its own stack (and hence local variables) but shares global variables, file descriptors, signal handlers, and its current directory state with the process that created it.

The concept of threads has been around for some time, but until the IEEE POSIX committee published some standards, they had not been widely available in UNIX-like operating systems, and the implementations that did exist tended to vary between different vendors. With the advent of the POSIX 1003.1c specification, all that changed; threads are not only better standardized, but are also available on most Linux distributions. Now that multi-core processors have also become common even in desktop machines, most machines also have underlying hardware support that allows them to physically execute multiple threads simultaneously. Previously, with single-core CPUs, the simultaneous execution of threads was just a clever, though very efficient, illusion.

Linux first acquired thread support around 1996, with a library often referred to as "LinuxThreads." This was very close to the POSIX standard (indeed, for many purposes the differences are not noticeable) and it was a significant step forward that enabled Linux programmers to use threads for the first time. However, there where slight discrepancies between the Linux implementation and the POSIX standard, most notably with regard to signal handling. These limitations were imposed not so much by the library implementation, but more by the limitations of the underlying support from the Linux kernel.

Various projects looked at how the thread support on Linux might be improved, not just to clear up the slight discrepancies between the POSIX standard and the Linux implementation, but also to improve performance and remove any unnecessary restrictions. Much work centered on how user-level threads should map to kernel-level threads. The two principal projects were New Generation POSIX Threads (NGPT) and Native POSIX Thread Library (NPTL). Both projects had to make changes to the Linux kernel to support the new libraries, and both offered significant performance improvements over the older Linux threads.

In 2002, the NGPT team announced that they did not wish to split the community and would cease adding new features to NGPT, but would continue to work on thread support in Linux, effectively throwing their weight behind the NPTL effort. NPTL became the new standard for threads on Linux, with its first mainstream release in Red Hat Linux 9. You can find some interesting background information on NPTL in a paper titled "The Native POSIX Thread Library for Linux" by Ulrich Drepper and Ingo Molnar, which, at the time of this book's writing, is at `http://people.redhat.com/drepper/nptl-design.pdf`.

Most of the code in this chapter should work with any of the thread libraries, because it is based on the POSIX standard that is common across all the thread libraries. However, you may see some slight differences if you are using an older Linux distribution, particularly if you use ps to look at the examples while they are running.

Advantages and Drawbacks of Threads

Creating a new thread has some distinct advantages over creating a new process in certain circumstances. The overhead cost of creating a new thread is significantly less than that of creating a new process (though Linux is particularly efficient at creating new processes compared with many other operating systems).

Following are some advantages of using threads:

❑ Sometimes it is very useful to make a program appear to do two things at once. The classic example is to perform a real-time word count on a document while still editing the text. One thread can manage the user's input and perform editing. The other, which can see the same document content, can continuously update a word count variable. The first thread (or even a third one) can use this shared variable to keep the user informed. Another example is a multithreaded database server where an apparent single process serves multiple clients, improving the overall data throughput by servicing some requests while blocking others, waiting for disk activity. For a database server, this apparent multitasking is quite hard to do efficiently in different processes, because the requirements for locking and data consistency cause the different processes to be very tightly coupled. This can be done much more easily with multiple threads than with multiple processes.

❏ The performance of an application that mixes input, calculation, and output may be improved by running these as three separate threads. While the input or output thread is waiting for a connection, one of the other threads can continue with calculations. A server application processing multiple network connects may also be a natural fit for a multithreaded program.

❏ Now that multi-cored CPUs are common even in desktop and laptop machines, using multiple threads inside a process can, if the application is suitable, enable a single process to better utilize the hardware resources available.

❏ In general, switching between threads requires the operating system to do much less work than switching between processes. Thus, multiple threads are much less demanding on resources than multiple processes, and it is more practical to run programs that logically require many threads of execution on single-processor systems. That said, the design difficulties of writing a multithreaded program are significant and should not be taken lightly.

Threads also have drawbacks:

❏ Writing multithreaded programs requires very careful design. The potential for introducing subtle timing faults, or faults caused by the unintentional sharing of variables in a multithreaded program is considerable. Alan Cox (the well respected Linux guru) has commented that threads are also known as "how to shoot yourself in both feet at once."

❏ Debugging a multithreaded program is much, much harder than debugging a single-threaded one, because the interactions between the threads are very hard to control.

❏ A program that splits a large calculation into two and runs the two parts as different threads will not necessarily run more quickly on a single processor machine, unless the calculation truly allows multiple parts to be calculated simultaneously and the machine it is executing on has multiple processor cores to support true multiprocessing.

A First Threads Program

There is a whole set of library calls associated with threads, most of whose names start with pthread. To use these library calls, you must define the macro _REENTRANT, include the file pthread.h, and link with the threads library using -lpthread.

When the original UNIX and POSIX library routines were designed, it was assumed that there would be only a single thread of execution in any process. An obvious example is errno, the variable used for retrieving error information after a call fails. In a multithreaded program there would, by default, be only one errno variable shared between all the threads. The variable could easily be updated by a call in one thread before a different thread has been able to retrieve a previous error code. Similar problems exist with functions, such as tputs, that normally use a single global area for buffering output.

You need routines known as *re-entrant* routines. Re-entrant code can be called more than once, whether by different threads or by nested invocations in some way, and still function correctly. Thus, the re-entrant section of code usually must use local variables only in such a way that each and every call to the code gets its own unique copy of the data.

In multithreaded programs, you tell the compiler that you need this feature by defining the _REENTRANT macro before any #include lines in your program. This does three things, and does them so elegantly that usually you don't even need to know what was done:

❑ Some functions get prototypes for a re-entrant safe equivalent. These are normally the same function name, but with _r appended so that, for example, gethostbyname is changed to gethostbyname_r.

❑ Some stdio.h functions that are normally implemented as macros become proper re-entrant safe functions.

❑ The variable errno, from errno.h, is changed to call a function, which can determine the real errno value in a multithread safe way.

Including the file pthread.h provides you with other definitions and prototypes that you will need in your code, much like stdio.h for standard input and output routines. Finally, you need to ensure that you include the appropriate thread header file and link with the appropriate threads library that implements the pthread functions. The Try It Out example later in this section offers more detail about compiling your program, but first let's look at the new functions you need for managing threads. pthread_create creates a new thread, much as fork creates a new process.

```
#include <pthread.h>

int pthread_create(pthread_t *thread, pthread_attr_t *attr, void
*(*start_routine)(void *), void *arg);
```

This may look imposing, but it is actually quite easy to use. The first argument is a pointer to pthread_t. When a thread is created, an identifier is written to the memory location to which this variable points. This identifier enables you to refer to the thread. The next argument sets the thread attributes. You do not usually need any special attributes, and you can simply pass NULL as this argument. Later in the chapter you will see how to use these attributes. The final two arguments tell the thread the function that it is to start executing and the arguments that are to be passed to this function.

```
void *(*start_routine)(void *)
```

The preceding line simply says that you must pass the address of a function taking a pointer to void as a parameter and the function will return a pointer to void. Thus, you can pass any type of single argument and return a pointer to any type. Using fork causes execution to continue in the same location with a different return code, whereas using a new thread explicitly provides a pointer to a function where the new thread should start executing.

The return value is 0 for success or an error number if anything goes wrong. The manual pages have details of error conditions for this and other functions used in this chapter.

pthread_create, *like most* pthread_*functions, is among the few Linux functions that do not follow the convention of using a return value of 1 for errors. Unless you are very sure, it's always safest to double-check the manual before checking the return code.*

When a thread terminates, it calls the `pthread_exit` function, much as a process calls `exit` when it terminates. This function terminates the calling thread, returning a pointer to an object. Never use it to return a pointer to a local variable, because the variable will cease to exist when the thread does so, causing a serious bug. `pthread_exit` is declared as follows:

```
#include <pthread.h>

void pthread_exit(void *retval);
```

`pthread_join` is the thread equivalent of `wait` that processes use to collect child processes. This function is declared as follows:

```
#include <pthread.h>

int pthread_join(pthread_t th, void **thread_return);
```

The first parameter is the thread for which to wait, the identifier that `pthread_create` filled in for you. The second argument is a pointer to a pointer that itself points to the return value from the thread. Like `pthread_create`, this function returns zero for success and an error code on failure.

Try It Out   A Simple Threaded Program

This program creates a single extra thread, shows that it is sharing variables with the original thread, and gets the new thread to return a result to the original thread. Multithreaded programs don't get much simpler than this! Here is `thread1.c`:

```c
#include <stdio.h>
#include <unistd.h>
#include <stdlib.h>
#include <string.h>
#include <pthread.h>

void *thread_function(void *arg);

char message[] = "Hello World";

int main() {
    int res;
    pthread_t a_thread;
    void *thread_result;

    res = pthread_create(&a_thread, NULL, thread_function, (void *)message);
    if (res != 0) {
        perror("Thread creation failed");
        exit(EXIT_FAILURE);
    }
    printf("Waiting for thread to finish...\n");
    res = pthread_join(a_thread, &thread_result);
    if (res != 0) {
        perror("Thread join failed");
        exit(EXIT_FAILURE);
    }
```

```
        printf("Thread joined, it returned %s\n", (char *)thread_result);
        printf("Message is now %s\n", message);
        exit(EXIT_SUCCESS);
}

void *thread_function(void *arg) {
        printf("thread_function is running. Argument was %s\n", (char *)arg);
        sleep(3);
        strcpy(message, "Bye!");
        pthread_exit("Thank you for the CPU time");
}
```

1. To compile this, first you need to ensure that _REENTRANT is defined. On a few systems, you may also need to define _POSIX_C_SOURCE, but normally this will not be necessary.

2. Next you must ensure that the appropriate thread library is linked. In the unlikely event that you are using an older Linux distribution where NPTL is not the default thread library, you may want to consider an upgrade, although most code in this chapter is compatible with the older Linux threads implementation. An easy way to check is to look in /usr/include/pthread.h. If this file shows a copyright date of 2003 or later, it's almost certainly the NPTL implementation. If the date is earlier, it's probably time to get a more recent Linux installation.

3. Having identified and installed the appropriate files, you can now compile and link your program like this:

```
$ cc -D_REENTRANT -I/usr/include/nptl thread1.c
-o thread1 -L/usr/lib/nptl -lpthread
```

If NPTL is the default on your system (which is quite likely), you almost certainly don't need the –I and –L options, and can use the simpler:

```
$ cc -D_REENTRANT thread1.c -o thread1 -lpthread
```

We will use the simpler version of the compile line throughout this chapter.

4. When you run this program, you should see the following:

```
$ ./thread1
Waiting for thread to finish...
thread_function is running. Argument was Hello World
Thread joined, it returned Thank you for the CPU time
Message is now Bye!
```

It's worth spending a little time on understanding this program, because we will be using it as the basis for most of the examples in this chapter.

How It Works

You declare a prototype for the function that the thread will call when you create it:

```
void *thread_function(void *arg);
```

As required by `pthread_create`, it takes a pointer to `void` as its only argument and returns a pointer to `void`. (We will come to the implementation of `thread_function` in a moment.)

In `main`, you declare some variables and then call `pthread_create` to start running your new thread.

```
pthread_t a_thread;
void *thread_result;

res = pthread_create(&a_thread, NULL, thread_function, (void *)message);
```

You pass the address of a `pthread_t` object that you can use to refer to the thread afterward. You don't want to modify the default thread attributes, so you pass `NULL` as the second parameter. The final two parameters are the function to call and a parameter to pass to it.

If the call succeeds, two threads will now be running. The original thread (`main`) continues and executes the code after `pthread_create`, and a new thread starts executing in the imaginatively named `thread_function`.

The original thread checks that the new thread has started and then calls `pthread_join`.

```
res = pthread_join(a_thread, &thread_result);
```

Here you pass the identifier of the thread that you are waiting to join and a pointer to a result. This function will wait until the other thread terminates before it returns. It then prints the return value from the thread and the contents of a variable, and exits.

The new thread starts executing at the start of `thread_function`, which prints out its arguments, sleeps for a short period, updates global variables, and then exits, returning a string to the main thread. The new thread writes to the same array, `message`, to which the original thread has access. If you had called `fork` rather than `pthread_create`, the array would have been a copy of the original `message`, rather than the same array.

Simultaneous Execution

The next example shows you how to write a program that checks that the execution of two threads occurs simultaneously. (Of course, if you are using a single-processor system, the CPU would be cleverly switched between the threads, rather than having the hardware simultaneously execute both threads using separate processor cores). Because you haven't yet met any of the thread synchronization functions, this will be a very inefficient program that does what is known as a *polling* between the two threads. Again, you will make use of the fact that everything except local function variables are shared between the different threads in a process.

Try It Out   **Simultaneous Execution of Two Threads**

The program you create in this section, `thread2.c`, is created by slightly modifying `thread1.c`. You add an extra file scope variable to test which thread is running:

The full code files for the examples are provided in the downloads from the book's website.

```
int run_now = 1;
```

Set run_now to 1 when the main function is executing and to 2 when your new thread is executing.

In the main function, after the creation of the new thread, add the following code:

```
int print_count1 = 0;

while(print_count1++ < 20) {
    if (run_now == 1) {
        printf("1");
        run_now = 2;
    }
    else {
        sleep(1);
    }
}
```

If run_now is 1, print "1" and set it to 2. Otherwise, you sleep briefly and check the value again. You are waiting for the value to change to 1 by checking over and over again. This is called a *busy wait*, although here it is slowed down by sleeping for a second between checks. You'll see a better way to do this later in the chapter.

In thread_function, where your new thread is executing, you do much the same but with the values reversed:

```
int print_count2 = 0;

while(print_count2++ < 20) {
    if (run_now == 2) {
        printf("2");
        run_now = 1;
    }
    else {
        sleep(1);
    }
}
```

You remove the parameter passing and return value passing because you are no longer interested in them.

When you run the program, you see the following output. (You may find that it takes a few seconds for the program to produce output, particularly on a single-core CPU machine.)

```
$ cc -D_REENTRANT thread2.c -o thread2 -lpthread
$ ./thread2
12121212121212121212
Waiting for thread to finish...
Thread joined
```

How It Works

Each thread tells the other one to run by setting the run_now variable and then waits till the other thread has changed its value before running again. This shows that execution passes between the two threads automatically and again illustrates the point that both threads are sharing the run_now variable.

Synchronization

In the previous section, you saw that both threads execute together, but the method of switching between them was clumsy and very inefficient. Fortunately, there is a set functions specifically designed to provide better ways to control the execution of threads and access to critical sections of code.

We look at two basic methods here: *semaphores*, which act as gatekeepers around a piece of code, and *mutexes*, which act as a mutual exclusion (hence the name mutex) device to protect sections of code. These methods are similar; indeed, one can be implemented in terms of the other. However, there are some cases where the semantics of the problem suggest that one is more expressive than the other. For example, controlling access to some shared memory, which only one thread can access at a time, would most naturally involve a mutex. However, controlling access to a set of identical objects as a whole, such as giving one telephone line out of a set of five available lines to a thread, suits a counting semaphore better. Which one you choose depends on personal preference and the most appropriate mechanism for your program.

Synchronization with Semaphores

There are two sets of interface functions for semaphores: One is taken from POSIX Realtime Extensions and used for threads, and the other is known as System V semaphores, which are commonly used for process synchronization. (We discuss the second type in Chapter 14.) The two are not guaranteed to be interchangeable and, although very similar, use different function calls.

Dijkstra, a Dutch computer scientist, first conceived the concept of semaphores. A semaphore is a special type of variable that can be incremented or decremented, but crucial access to the variable is guaranteed to be atomic, even in a multithreaded program. This means that if two (or more) threads in a program attempt to change the value of a semaphore, the system guarantees that all the operations will in fact take place in sequence. With normal variables the result of conflicting operations from different threads within the same program is undefined.

In this section we look at the simplest type of semaphore, a *binary* semaphore that takes only values 0 or 1. There is also a more general semaphore, a *counting* semaphore that takes a wider range of values. Normally, semaphores are used to protect a piece of code so that only one thread of execution can run it at any one time. For this job a binary semaphore is needed. Occasionally, you want to permit a limited number of threads to execute a given piece of code; for this you would use a counting semaphore. Because counting semaphores are much less common, we won't consider them further here except to say that they are just a logical extension of a binary semaphore and that the actual function calls needed are identical.

The semaphore functions do not start with pthread_, as most thread-specific functions do, but with sem_. Four basic semaphore functions are used in threads. They are all quite simple.

A semaphore is created with the sem_init function, which is declared as follows:

```
#include <semaphore.h>

int sem_init(sem_t *sem, int pshared, unsigned int value);
```

This function initializes a semaphore object pointed to by sem, sets its sharing option (which we discuss more in a moment), and gives it an initial integer value. The pshared parameter controls the type of semaphore. If the value of pshared is 0, the semaphore is local to the current process. Otherwise, the semaphore may be shared between processes. Here we are interested only in semaphores that are not shared between processes. At the time of writing, Linux doesn't support this sharing, and passing a nonzero value for pshared will cause the call to fail.

The next pair of functions controls the value of the semaphore and is declared as follows:

```
#include <semaphore.h>

int sem_wait(sem_t * sem);

int sem_post(sem_t * sem);
```

These both take a pointer to the semaphore object initialized by a call to sem_init.

The sem_post function atomically increases the value of the semaphore by 1. *Atomically* here means that if two threads simultaneously try to increase the value of a single semaphore by 1, they do not interfere with each other, as might happen if two programs read, increment, and write a value to a file at the same time. If both programs try to increase the value by 1, the semaphore will always be correctly increased in value by 2.

The sem_wait function atomically decreases the value of the semaphore by one, but always waits until the semaphore has a nonzero count first. Thus, if you call sem_wait on a semaphore with a value of 2, the thread will continue executing but the semaphore will be decreased to 1. If sem_wait is called on a semaphore with a value of 0, the function will wait until some other thread has incremented the value so that it is no longer 0. If two threads are both waiting in sem_wait for the same semaphore to become nonzero and it is incremented once by a third process, only one of the two waiting processes will get to decrement the semaphore and continue; the other will remain waiting. This atomic "test and set" ability in a single function is what makes semaphores so valuable.

> *There is another semaphore function, sem_trywait, that is the nonblocking partner of sem_wait. We don't discuss it further here; you can find more details in the manual pages.*

The last semaphore function is sem_destroy. This function tidies up the semaphore when you have finished with it. It is declared as follows:

```
#include <semaphore.h>

int sem_destroy(sem_t * sem);
```

Again, this function takes a pointer to a semaphore and tidies up any resources that it may have. If you attempt to destroy a semaphore for which some thread is waiting, you will get an error.

Like most Linux functions, these functions all return 0 on success.

Try It Out   A Thread Semaphore

This code, `thread3.c`, is also based on `thread1.c`. Because a lot has changed, we present it in full.

```c
#include <stdio.h>
#include <unistd.h>
#include <stdlib.h>
#include <string.h>
#include <pthread.h>
#include <semaphore.h>

void *thread_function(void *arg);
sem_t bin_sem;

#define WORK_SIZE 1024
char work_area[WORK_SIZE];

int main() {
    int res;
    pthread_t a_thread;
    void *thread_result;

    res = sem_init(&bin_sem, 0, 0);
    if (res != 0) {
        perror("Semaphore initialization failed");
        exit(EXIT_FAILURE);
    }
    res = pthread_create(&a_thread, NULL, thread_function, NULL);
    if (res != 0) {
        perror("Thread creation failed");
        exit(EXIT_FAILURE);
    }
    printf("Input some text. Enter 'end' to finish\n");
    while(strncmp("end", work_area, 3) != 0) {
        fgets(work_area, WORK_SIZE, stdin);
        sem_post(&bin_sem);
    }
    printf("\nWaiting for thread to finish...\n");
    res = pthread_join(a_thread, &thread_result);
    if (res != 0) {
        perror("Thread join failed");
        exit(EXIT_FAILURE);
    }
    printf("Thread joined\n");
    sem_destroy(&bin_sem);
    exit(EXIT_SUCCESS);
}

void *thread_function(void *arg) {
    sem_wait(&bin_sem);
    while(strncmp("end", work_area, 3) != 0) {
        printf("You input %d characters\n", strlen(work_area) -1);
        sem_wait(&bin_sem);
```

```
        }
        pthread_exit(NULL);
}
```

The first important change is the inclusion of `semaphore.h` to provide access to the semaphore functions. Then you declare a semaphore and some variables and initialize the semaphore *before* you create your new thread.

```
sem_t bin_sem;

#define WORK_SIZE 1024
char work_area[WORK_SIZE];

int main() {
    int res;
    pthread_t a_thread;
    void *thread_result;
    res = sem_init(&bin_sem, 0, 0);
    if (res != 0) {
        perror("Semaphore initialization failed");
        exit(EXIT_FAILURE);
    }
```

Note that the initial value of the semaphore is set to 0.

In the function `main`, after you have started the new thread, you read some text from the keyboard, load your work area, and then increment the semaphore with `sem_post`.

```
    printf("Input some text. Enter 'end' to finish\n");
    while(strncmp("end", work_area, 3) != 0) {
        fgets(work_area, WORK_SIZE, stdin);
        sem_post(&bin_sem);
    }
```

In the new thread, you wait for the semaphore and then count the characters from the input.

```
    sem_wait(&bin_sem);
    while(strncmp("end", work_area, 3) != 0) {
      printf("You input %d characters\n", strlen(work_area) -1);
      sem_wait(&bin_sem);
    }
```

While the semaphore is set, you are waiting for keyboard input. When you have some input, you release the semaphore, allowing the second thread to count the characters before the first thread reads the keyboard again.

Again both threads share the same `work_area` array. Again, we have omitted some error checking, such as the returns from `sem_wait` to make the code samples more succinct and easier to follow. However, in production code you should always check for error returns unless there is a very good reason to omit this check.

Give the program a run:

```
$ cc -D_REENTRANT thread3.c -o thread3 -lpthread
$ ./thread3
Input some text. Enter 'end' to finish
The Wasp Factory
You input 16 characters
Iain Banks
You input 10 characters
end

Waiting for thread to finish...
Thread joined
```

In threaded programs, timing faults are always hard to find, but the program seems resilient to both quick input of text and more leisurely pauses.

How It Works

When you initialize the semaphore, you set its value to 0. Thus, when the thread's function starts, the call to sem_wait blocks and waits for the semaphore to become nonzero.

In the main thread, you wait until you have some text and then increment the semaphore with sem_post, which immediately allows the other thread to return from its sem_wait and start executing. Once it has counted the characters, it again calls sem_wait and is blocked until the main thread again calls sem_post to increment the semaphore.

It is easy to overlook subtle design errors that result in subtle errors. Let's modify the program slightly to thread3a.c to pretend that text input from the keyboard is sometimes replaced with automatically available text. Modify the reading loop in the main to this:

```
printf("Input some text. Enter 'end' to finish\n");
while(strncmp("end", work_area, 3) != 0) {
  if (strncmp(work_area, "FAST", 4) == 0) {
    sem_post(&bin_sem);
    strcpy(work_area, "Wheeee...");
  } else {
    fgets(work_area, WORK_SIZE, stdin);
  }
  sem_post(&bin_sem);
}
```

Now if you type **FAST**, the program calls sem_post to allow the character counter to run, but immediately updates work_area with something different.

```
$ cc -D_REENTRANT thread3a.c -o thread3a -lpthread
$ ./thread3a
Input some text. Enter 'end' to finish
Excession
You input 9 characters
```

```
FAST
You input 7 characters
You input 7 characters
You input 7 characters
end

Waiting for thread to finish...
Thread joined
```

The problem is that the program was relying on text input from the program taking so long that there was time for the other thread to count the words before the main thread was ever ready to give it more words to count. When you tried to give it two different sets of words to count in quick succession (**FAST** from the keyboard and then **Wheeee...** automatically), there was no time for the second thread to execute. However, the semaphore had been incremented more than once, so the counter thread just kept counting the words and decreasing the semaphore until it became zero again.

This shows just how careful you need to be with timing considerations in multithreaded programs. It's possible to fix the program by using an extra semaphore to make the main thread wait until the counter thread has had the chance to finish its counting, but an easier way is to use a *mutex*, which we look at next.

Synchronization with Mutexes

The other way of synchronizing access in multithreaded programs is with *mutexes* (short for *mutual exclusions*), which act by allowing the programmer to "lock" an object so that only one thread can access it. To control access to a critical section of code you lock a mutex before entering the code section and then unlock it when you have finished.

The basic functions required to use mutexes are very similar to those needed for semaphores. They are declared as follows:

```
#include <pthread.h>

int pthread_mutex_init(pthread_mutex_t *mutex, const pthread_mutexattr_t
*mutexattr);

int pthread_mutex_lock(pthread_mutex_t *mutex));

int pthread_mutex_unlock(pthread_mutex_t *mutex);

int pthread_mutex_destroy(pthread_mutex_t *mutex);
```

As usual, 0 is returned for success, and on failure an error code is returned, but errno is not set; you must use the return code.

As with semaphores, they all take a pointer to a previously declared object, in this case a pthread_mutex_t. The extra attribute parameter pthread_mutex_init allows you to provide attributes for the mutex, which control its behavior. The attribute type by default is "fast." This has the slight drawback that, if your program tries to call pthread_mutex_lock on a mutex that it has already locked, the program will block. Because the thread that holds the lock is the one that is now blocked, the mutex can never be unlocked and the program is deadlocked. It is possible to alter the attributes of the mutex so that it either checks for this and returns an error or acts recursively and allows multiple locks by the same thread if there are the same number of unlocks afterward.

Setting the attribute of a mutex is beyond the scope of this book, so we will pass NULL for the attribute pointer and use the default behavior. You can find more about changing the attributes by reading the manual page for pthread_mutex_init.

A Thread Mutex

Again, this is a modification of the original thread1.c but heavily modified. This time, you will be extra careful about access to your critical variables and use a mutex to ensure they are ever accessed by only one thread at any one time. To keep the example code easy to read, we have omitted some error checking on the returns from mutex lock and unlock. In production code, we would check these return values. Here is the new program, thread4.c:

```c
#include <stdio.h>
#include <unistd.h>
#include <stdlib.h>
#include <string.h>
#include <pthread.h>
#include <semaphore.h>

void *thread_function(void *arg);
pthread_mutex_t work_mutex; /* protects both work_area and time_to_exit */

#define WORK_SIZE 1024
char work_area[WORK_SIZE];
int time_to_exit = 0;

int main() {
    int res;
    pthread_t a_thread;
    void *thread_result;
    res = pthread_mutex_init(&work_mutex, NULL);
    if (res != 0) {
        perror("Mutex initialization failed");
        exit(EXIT_FAILURE);
    }
    res = pthread_create(&a_thread, NULL, thread_function, NULL);
    if (res != 0) {
        perror("Thread creation failed");
        exit(EXIT_FAILURE);
    }
    pthread_mutex_lock(&work_mutex);
    printf("Input some text. Enter 'end' to finish\n");
    while(!time_to_exit) {
        fgets(work_area, WORK_SIZE, stdin);
        pthread_mutex_unlock(&work_mutex);
        while(1) {
            pthread_mutex_lock(&work_mutex);
            if (work_area[0] != '\0') {
                pthread_mutex_unlock(&work_mutex);
                sleep(1);
            }
            else {
                break;
            }
```

```
            }
        }
        pthread_mutex_unlock(&work_mutex);
        printf("\nWaiting for thread to finish...\n");
        res = pthread_join(a_thread, &thread_result);
        if (res != 0) {
            perror("Thread join failed");
            exit(EXIT_FAILURE);
        }
        printf("Thread joined\n");
        pthread_mutex_destroy(&work_mutex);
        exit(EXIT_SUCCESS);
}

void *thread_function(void *arg) {
    sleep(1);
    pthread_mutex_lock(&work_mutex);
    while(strncmp("end", work_area, 3) != 0) {
        printf("You input %d characters\n", strlen(work_area) -1);
        work_area[0] = '\0';
        pthread_mutex_unlock(&work_mutex);
        sleep(1);
        pthread_mutex_lock(&work_mutex);
        while (work_area[0] == '\0' ) {
            pthread_mutex_unlock(&work_mutex);
            sleep(1);
            pthread_mutex_lock(&work_mutex);
        }
    }
    time_to_exit = 1;
    work_area[0] = '\0';
    pthread_mutex_unlock(&work_mutex);
    pthread_exit(0);
}
```

```
$ cc -D_REENTRANT thread4.c -o thread4 -lpthread
$ ./thread4
Input some text. Enter 'end' to finish
Whit
You input 4 characters
The Crow Road
You input 13 characters
end

Waiting for thread to finish...
Thread joined
```

How It Works

You start by declaring a mutex, your work area, and this time, an additional variable: time_to_exit.

```
pthread_mutex_t work_mutex; /* protects both work_area and time_to_exit */

#define WORK_SIZE 1024
char work_area[WORK_SIZE];
int time_to_exit = 0;
```

Then initialize the mutex:

```
res = pthread_mutex_init(&work_mutex, NULL);
if (res != 0) {
    perror("Mutex initialization failed");
    exit(EXIT_FAILURE);
}
```

Next start the new thread. Here is the code that executes in the thread function:

```
pthread_mutex_lock(&work_mutex);
while(strncmp("end", work_area, 3) != 0) {
    printf("You input %d characters\n", strlen(work_area) -1);
    work_area[0] = '\0';
    pthread_mutex_unlock(&work_mutex);
    sleep(1);
    pthread_mutex_lock(&work_mutex);
    while (work_area[0] == '\0' ) {
        pthread_mutex_unlock(&work_mutex);
        sleep(1);
        pthread_mutex_lock(&work_mutex);
    }
}
time_to_exit = 1;
work_area[0] = '\0';
pthread_mutex_unlock(&work_mutex);
```

First, the new thread tries to lock the mutex. If it's already locked, the call will block until it is released. Once you have access, you check to see whether you are being requested to exit. If you are requested to exit, simply set `time_to_exit`, zap the first character of the work area, and exit.

If you don't want to exit, count the characters and then zap the first character to a null. You use the first character being null as a way of telling the reader program that you have finished the counting. You then unlock the mutex and wait for the main thread to run. Periodically, you attempt to lock the mutex and, when you succeed, check whether the main thread has given you any more work to do. If it hasn't, you unlock the mutex and wait some more. If it has, you count the characters and go around the loop again.

Here is the main thread:

```
pthread_mutex_lock(&work_mutex);
printf("Input some text. Enter 'end' to finish\n");
while(!time_to_exit) {
    fgets(work_area, WORK_SIZE, stdin);
    pthread_mutex_unlock(&work_mutex);
    while(1) {
        pthread_mutex_lock(&work_mutex);
        if (work_area[0] != '\0') {
            pthread_mutex_unlock(&work_mutex);
            sleep(1);
        }
        else {
            break;
        }
```

```
        }
    }
    pthread_mutex_unlock(&work_mutex);
```

This is quite similar. You lock the work area so that you can read text into it and then unlock it to allow the other thread access to count the words. Periodically, you relock the mutex, check whether the words have been counted (`work_area[0]` set to a null), and release the mutex if you need to wait longer. As we noted earlier, this kind of polling for an answer is generally not good programming practice, and in the real world you would probably have used a semaphore to avoid this. However, the code served its purpose as an example of using a mutex.

Thread Attributes

When we first looked at threads, we did not discuss the more advanced topic of thread attributes. Now that we have covered the key topic of synchronizing threads, we can come back and look at these more advanced features of threads themselves. There are quite a few attributes of threads that you can control; here we are only going to look at those that you are most likely to need. You can find details of the others in the manual pages.

In all of the previous examples, you had to resynchronize your threads using `pthread_join` before allowing the program to exit. You needed to do this if you wanted to allow one thread to return data to the thread that created it. Sometimes you neither need the second thread to return information to the main thread nor want the main thread to wait for it.

Suppose that you create a second thread to spool a backup copy of a data file that is being edited while the main thread continues to service the user. When the backup has finished, the second thread can just terminate. There is no need for it to rejoin the main thread.

You can create threads that behave like this. They are called *detached threads*, and you create them by modifying the thread attributes or by calling `pthread_detach`. Because we want to demonstrate attributes, we use the former method here.

The most important function that you need is `pthread_attr_init`, which initializes a thread attribute object.

```
#include <pthread.h>

int pthread_attr_init(pthread_attr_t *attr);
```

Once again, 0 is returned for success and an error code is returned on failure.

There is also a destroy function: `pthread_attr_destroy`. Its purpose is to allow clean destruction of the attribute object. Once the object has been destroyed, it cannot be used again until it has been reinitialized.

When you have a thread attribute object initialized, there are many additional functions that you can call to set different attribute behaviors. We list the main ones here (you can find the complete list in the man pages, usually under the pthread.h entry), but look closely at only two, detachedstate and schedpolicy:

```
#include <pthread.h>

int pthread_attr_setdetachstate(pthread_attr_t *attr, int detachstate);

int pthread_attr_getdetachstate(const pthread_attr_t *attr, int *detachstate);

int pthread_attr_setschedpolicy(pthread_attr_t *attr, int policy);

int pthread_attr_getschedpolicy(const pthread_attr_t *attr, int *policy);

int pthread_attr_setschedparam(pthread_attr_t *attr, const struct sched_param
*param);

int pthread_attr_getschedparam(const pthread_attr_t *attr, struct sched_param
*param);

int pthread_attr_setinheritsched(pthread_attr_t *attr, int inherit);

int pthread_attr_getinheritsched(const pthread_attr_t *attr, int *inherit);

int pthread_attr_setscope(pthread_attr_t *attr, int scope);

int pthread_attr_getscope(const pthread_attr_t *attr, int *scope);

int pthread_attr_setstacksize(pthread_attr_t *attr, int scope);

int pthread_attr_getstacksize(const pthread_attr_t *attr, int *scope);
```

As you can see, there are quite a few attributes you can use, but fortunately you will generally get by without ever having to use most of these.

❑   detachedstate: This attribute allows you to avoid the need for threads to rejoin. As with most of these _set functions, it takes a pointer to the attribute and a flag to determine the state required. The two possible flag values for pthread_attr_setdetachstate are PTHREAD_CREATE_JOINABLE and PTHREAD_CREATE_DETACHED. By default, the attribute will have the value PTHREAD_CREATE_JOINABLE so that you can allow the two threads to join. If the state is set to PTHREAD_CREATE_DETACHED, you cannot call pthread_join to recover the exit state of another thread.

❑   schedpolicy: This controls how threads are scheduled. The options are SCHED_OTHER, SCHED_RP, and SCHED_FIFO. By default, the attribute is SCHED_OTHER. The other two types of scheduling are available only to processes running with superuser permissions, because they both have real-time scheduling but with slightly different behavior. SCHED_RR uses a round-robin scheduling scheme, and SCHED_FIFO uses a "first in, first out" policy. Discussion of these is beyond the scope of this book.

❑   schedparam: This is a partner to schedpolicy and allows control over the scheduling of threads running with schedule policy SCHED_OTHER. We take a look at an example of this a bit later in the chapter.

❑   inheritsched: This attribute takes two possible values: PTHREAD_EXPLICIT_SCHED and PTHREAD_INHERIT_SCHED. By default, the value is PTHREAD_EXPLICIT_SCHED, which means scheduling is explicitly set by the attributes. By setting it to PTHREAD_INHERIT_SCHED, a new thread will instead use the parameters that its creator thread was using.

❑   scope: This attribute controls how the scheduling of a thread is calculated. Because Linux currently supports only the value PTHREAD_SCOPE_SYSTEM, we will not look at this further here.

❑   stacksize: This attribute controls the thread creation stack size, set in bytes. This is part of the "optional" section of the specification and is supported only on implementations where _POSIX_THREAD_ATTR_STACKSIZE is defined. Linux implements threads with a large amount of stack by default, so the feature is generally redundant on Linux.

Try It Out   Setting the Detached State Attribute

For the detached thread example, thread5.c, you create a thread attribute, set it to be detached, and then create a thread using the attribute. Now when the child thread has finished, it calls pthread_exit in the normal way. This time, however, the originating thread no longer waits for the thread that it created to rejoin. In this example, you use a simple thread_finished flag to allow the main thread to detect whether the child has finished and to show that the threads are still sharing variables.

```c
#include <stdio.h>
#include <unistd.h>
#include <stdlib.h>
#include <pthread.h>

void *thread_function(void *arg);

char message[] = "Hello World";
int thread_finished = 0;

int main() {
    int res;
    pthread_t a_thread;

    pthread_attr_t thread_attr;

    res = pthread_attr_init(&thread_attr);
    if (res != 0) {
        perror("Attribute creation failed");
        exit(EXIT_FAILURE);
    }
    res = pthread_attr_setdetachstate(&thread_attr, PTHREAD_CREATE_DETACHED);
    if (res != 0) {
        perror("Setting detached attribute failed");
        exit(EXIT_FAILURE);
    }
    res = pthread_create(&a_thread, &thread_attr,
thread_function, (void *)message);
    if (res != 0) {
        perror("Thread creation failed");
        exit(EXIT_FAILURE);
    }
```

```
        (void)pthread_attr_destroy(&thread_attr);
        while(!thread_finished) {
            printf("Waiting for thread to say it's finished...\n");
            sleep(1);
        }
        printf("Other thread finished, bye!\n");
        exit(EXIT_SUCCESS);
    }

    void *thread_function(void *arg) {
        printf("thread_function is running. Argument was %s\n", (char *)arg);
        sleep(4);
        printf("Second thread setting finished flag, and exiting now\n");
        thread_finished = 1;
        pthread_exit(NULL);
    }
```

There are no surprises in the output:

```
$ ./thread5
Waiting for thread to say it's finished...
thread_function is running. Argument was Hello World
Waiting for thread to say it's finished...
Waiting for thread to say it's finished...
Waiting for thread to say it's finished...
Second thread setting finished flag, and exiting now
Other thread finished, bye!
```

As you can see, setting the detached state allowed the secondary thread to complete independently, without the originating thread needing to wait for it.

How It Works

The two important sections of code are

```
        pthread_attr_t thread_attr;

        res = pthread_attr_init(&thread_attr);
        if (res != 0) {
            perror("Attribute creation failed");
            exit(EXIT_FAILURE);
        }
```

which declares a thread attribute and initializes it, and

```
        res = pthread_attr_setdetachstate(&thread_attr, PTHREAD_CREATE_DETACHED);
        if (res != 0) {
            perror("Setting detached attribute failed");
            exit(EXIT_FAILURE);
        }
```

which sets the attribute values to have the detached state.

The other slight differences are creating the thread, passing the address of the attributes,

```
res = pthread_create(&a_thread, &thread_attr, thread_function, (void
*)message);
```

and, for completeness, destroying the attributes when you have used them:

```
pthread_attr_destroy(&thread_attr);
```

Thread Attributes Scheduling

Let's take a look at a second thread attribute you might want to change: scheduling. Changing the scheduling attribute is very similar to setting the detached state, but there are two more functions that you can use to find the available priority levels, sched_get_priority_max and sched_get_priority_min.

Try It Out   Scheduling

Because this thread6.c is very similar to the previous example, we'll just look at the differences.

1. First, you need some additional variables:

```
int max_priority;
int min_priority;
struct sched_param scheduling_value;
```

2. After you have set the detached attribute, you set the scheduling policy:

```
res = pthread_attr_setschedpolicy(&thread_attr, SCHED_OTHER);
if (res != 0) {
    perror("Setting scheduling policy failed");
    exit(EXIT_FAILURE);
}
```

3. Next find the range of priorities that are allowed:

```
max_priority = sched_get_priority_max(SCHED_OTHER);
min_priority = sched_get_priority_min(SCHED_OTHER);
```

4. and set one:

```
scheduling_value.sched_priority = min_priority;
res = pthread_attr_setschedparam(&thread_attr, &scheduling_value);
if (res != 0) {
    perror("Setting scheduling priority failed");
    exit(EXIT_FAILURE);
}
```

When you run it, the output you get is:

```
$ ./thread6
Waiting for thread to say it's finished...
```

```
thread_function is running. Argument was Hello World
Waiting for thread to say it's finished...
Waiting for thread to say it's finished...
Waiting for thread to say it's finished...
Second thread setting finished flag, and exiting now
Other thread finished, bye!
```

How It Works

This is very similar to setting a detached state attribute, except that you set the scheduling policy instead.

Canceling a Thread

Sometimes, you want one thread to be able to ask another thread to terminate, rather like sending it a signal. There is a way to do this with threads, and, in parallel with signal handling, threads get a way of modifying how they behave when they are asked to terminate.

Let's look first at the function to request a thread to terminate:

```
#include <pthread.h>

int pthread_cancel(pthread_t thread);
```

This is pretty straightforward: Given a thread identifier, you can request that it be canceled. On the receiving end of the cancel request, things are slightly more complicated, but not much. A thread can set its cancel state using pthread_setcancelstate.

```
#include <pthread.h>

int pthread_setcancelstate(int state, int *oldstate);
```

The first parameter is either PTHREAD_CANCEL_ENABLE, which allows it to receive cancel requests, or PTHREAD_CANCEL_DISABLE, which causes them to be ignored. The oldstate pointer allows the previous state to be retrieved. If you are not interested, you can simply pass NULL. If cancel requests are accepted, there is a second level of control the thread can take, the cancel type, which is set with pthread_setcanceltype.

```
#include <pthread.h>

int pthread_setcanceltype(int type, int *oldtype);
```

The type can take one of two values, PTHREAD_CANCEL_ASYNCHRONOUS, which causes cancellation requests to be acted upon immediately, and PTHREAD_CANCEL_DEFERRED, which makes cancellation requests wait until the thread executes one of these functions: pthread_join, pthread_cond_wait, pthread_cond_timedwait, pthread_testcancel, sem_wait, or sigwait.

We have not covered all of these calls in this chapter, because not all are generally needed. As ever, you can find more details in the manual pages.

According to the POSIX standard, other system calls that may block, such as read, wait, *and so on, should also be cancellation points. At the time of this writing, support for this in Linux seems to be incomplete. Some experimentation does, however, suggest that some blocked calls, such as* sleep, *do allow cancellation to take place. To be on the safe side, you may want to add some* pthread_testcancel *calls in code that you expect to be canceled.*

Again, the oldtype allows the previous state to be retrieved, or a NULL can be passed if you are not interested in knowing the previous state. By default, threads start with the cancellation state PTHREAD_CANCEL_ENABLE and the cancellation type PTHREAD_CANCEL_DEFERRED.

Try It Out   Canceling a Thread

The program thread7.c is derived, yet again, from thread1.c. This time, the main thread sends a cancel request to the thread that it has created.

```
#include <stdio.h>
#include <unistd.h>
#include <stdlib.h>
#include <pthread.h>

void *thread_function(void *arg);

int main() {
    int res;
    pthread_t a_thread;
    void *thread_result;

    res = pthread_create(&a_thread, NULL, thread_function, NULL);
    if (res != 0) {
        perror("Thread creation failed");
        exit(EXIT_FAILURE);
    }

    sleep(3);
    printf("Canceling thread...\n");
    res = pthread_cancel(a_thread);
    if (res != 0) {
        perror("Thread cancelation failed");
        exit(EXIT_FAILURE);
    }
    printf("Waiting for thread to finish...\n");
    res = pthread_join(a_thread, &thread_result);
    if (res != 0) {
        perror("Thread join failed");
        exit(EXIT_FAILURE);
    }
    exit(EXIT_SUCCESS);
}
```

```
void *thread_function(void *arg) {
    int i, res;
    res = pthread_setcancelstate(PTHREAD_CANCEL_ENABLE, NULL);
    if (res != 0) {
        perror("Thread pthread_setcancelstate failed");
        exit(EXIT_FAILURE);
    }
    res = pthread_setcanceltype(PTHREAD_CANCEL_DEFERRED, NULL);
    if (res != 0) {
        perror("Thread pthread_setcanceltype failed");
        exit(EXIT_FAILURE);
    }
    printf("thread_function is running\n");
    for(i = 0; i < 10; i++) {
        printf("Thread is still running (%d)...\n", i);
        sleep(1);
    }
    pthread_exit(0);
}
```

When you run this, you get the following output, showing that the thread is canceled:

```
$ ./thread7
thread_function is running
Thread is still running (0)...
Thread is still running (1)...
Thread is still running (2)...
Canceling thread...
Waiting for thread to finish...
$
```

How It Works

After the new thread has been created in the usual way, the main thread sleeps (to allow the new thread some time to get started) and then issues a cancel request:

```
sleep(3);
printf("Cancelling thread...\n");
res = pthread_cancel(a_thread);
if (res != 0) {
    perror("Thread cancelation failed");
    exit(EXIT_FAILURE);
}
```

In the created thread, you first set the cancel state to allow canceling:

```
res = pthread_setcancelstate(PTHREAD_CANCEL_ENABLE, NULL);
if (res != 0) {
    perror("Thread pthread_setcancelstate failed");
    exit(EXIT_FAILURE);
}
```

Then you set the cancel type to be deferred:

```
res = pthread_setcanceltype(PTHREAD_CANCEL_DEFERRED, NULL);
if (res != 0) {
    perror("Thread pthread_setcanceltype failed");
    exit(EXIT_FAILURE);
}
```

Finally, the thread waits around to be canceled:

```
for(i = 0; i < 10; i++) {
    printf("Thread is still running (%d)...\n", i);
    sleep(1);
}
```

Threads in Abundance

Up until now, we have always had the normal thread of execution of a program create just one other thread. However, we don't want you to think that you can create only one extra thread.

Try It Out   **Many Threads**

For the final example in this chapter, `thread8.c`, we show how to create several threads in the same program and then collect them again in an order different from that in which they were started.

```
#include <stdio.h>
#include <unistd.h>
#include <stdlib.h>
#include <pthread.h>

#define NUM_THREADS 6

void *thread_function(void *arg);

int main() {
    int res;
    pthread_t a_thread[NUM_THREADS];
    void *thread_result;
    int lots_of_threads;

    for(lots_of_threads = 0; lots_of_threads < NUM_THREADS; lots_of_threads++) {
        res = pthread_create(&(a_thread[lots_of_threads]),
NULL, thread_function, (void *)&lots_of_threads);
        if (res != 0) {
            perror("Thread creation failed");
            exit(EXIT_FAILURE);
        }
        sleep(1);
    }
    printf("Waiting for threads to finish...\n");
```

```
    for(lots_of_threads = NUM_THREADS - 1; lots_of_threads >= 0;
lots_of_threads--) {
        res = pthread_join(a_thread[lots_of_threads], &thread_result);
        if (res == 0) {
            printf("Picked up a thread\n");
        }
        else {
            perror("pthread_join failed");
        }
    }
    printf("All done\n");
    exit(EXIT_SUCCESS);
}

void *thread_function(void *arg) {
    int my_number = *(int *)arg;
    int rand_num;

    printf("thread_function is running. Argument was %d\n", my_number);
    rand_num=1+(int)(9.0*rand()/(RAND_MAX+1.0));
    sleep(rand_num);
    printf("Bye from %d\n", my_number);
    pthread_exit(NULL);
}
```

When you run this program, you get the following output:

```
$ ./thread8
thread_function is running. Argument was 0
thread_function is running. Argument was 1
thread_function is running. Argument was 2
thread_function is running. Argument was 3
thread_function is running. Argument was 4
Bye from 1
thread_function is running. Argument was 5
Waiting for threads to finish...
Bye from 5
Picked up a thread
Bye from 0
Bye from 2
Bye from 3
Bye from 4
Picked up a thread
Picked up a thread
Picked up a thread
Picked up a thread
Picked up a thread
All done
```

As you can see, you created many threads and allowed them to finish out of sequence. There is a subtle bug in this program that makes itself evident if you remove the call to sleep from the loop that starts the threads. We have included it to show you just how careful you need to be when writing programs that use threads. Can you spot it? We explain in the following "How It Works" section.

How It Works

This time you create an array of thread IDs:

```
pthread_t a_thread[NUM_THREADS];
```

and loop around creating several threads:

```
for(lots_of_threads = 0; lots_of_threads < NUM_THREADS; lots_of_threads++) {
    res = pthread_create(&(a_thread[lots_of_threads]), NULL,
                            thread_function, (void *)&lots_of_threads);
    if (res != 0) {
        perror("Thread creation failed");
        exit(EXIT_FAILURE);
    }
    sleep(1);
}
```

The threads themselves then wait for a random time before exiting:

```
void *thread_function(void *arg) {
    int my_number = *(int *)arg;
    int rand_num;

    printf("thread_function is running. Argument was %d\n", my_number);
    rand_num=1+(int)(9.0*rand()/(RAND_MAX+1.0));
    sleep(rand_num);
    printf("Bye from %d\n", my_number);
    pthread_exit(NULL);
}
```

While in the main (original) thread, you wait to pick them up, but not in the order in which you created them:

```
for(lots_of_threads = NUM_THREADS - 1; lots_of_threads >= 0; lots_of_threads--)
{
        res = pthread_join(a_thread[lots_of_threads], &thread_result);
        if (res == 0) {
            printf("Picked up a thread\n");
        }
        else {
            perror("pthread_join failed");
        }
    }
```

If you try to run the program with no sleep, you might see some strange effects, including some threads being started with the same argument; for example, you might see output similar to this:

```
thread_function is running. Argument was 0
thread_function is running. Argument was 2
thread_function is running. Argument was 2
thread_function is running. Argument was 4
thread_function is running. Argument was 4
thread_function is running. Argument was 5
Waiting for threads to finish...
```

```
Bye from 5
Picked up a thread
Bye from 2
Bye from 0
Bye from 2
Bye from 4
Bye from 4
Picked up a thread
Picked up a thread
Picked up a thread
Picked up a thread
Picked up a thread
All done
```

Did you spot why this could happen? The threads are being started using a local variable for the argument to the thread function. This variable is updated in the loop. The offending lines are

```
for(lots_of_threads = 0; lots_of_threads < NUM_THREADS; lots_of_threads++) {
    res = pthread_create(&(a_thread[lots_of_threads]), NULL,
                         thread_function, (void *)&lots_of_threads);
```

If the main thread runs fast enough, it might alter the argument (lots_of_threads) for some of the threads. Behavior like this arises when not enough care is taken with shared variables and multiple execution paths. We did warn you that programming threads required careful attention to design! To correct the problem, you need to pass the value directly like this:

```
res = pthread_create(&(a_thread[lots_of_threads]), NULL, thread_function, (void
*)lots_of_threads);
```

and of course change thread_function:

```
void *thread_function(void *arg) {
    int my_number = (int)arg;
```

This is shown in the program thread8a.c, with the changes highlighted:

```
#include <stdio.h>
#include <unistd.h>
#include <stdlib.h>
#include <string.h>
#include <pthread.h>

#define NUM_THREADS 6

void *thread_function(void *arg);

int main() {

    int res;
    pthread_t a_thread[NUM_THREADS];
    void *thread_result;
    int lots_of_threads;
```

```
    for(lots_of_threads = 0; lots_of_threads < NUM_THREADS; lots_of_threads++) {

        res = pthread_create(&(a_thread[lots_of_threads]), NULL,
    thread_function, (void *)lots_of_threads);
        if (res != 0) {
            perror("Thread creation failed");
            exit(EXIT_FAILURE);
        }
    }

    printf("Waiting for threads to finish...\n");
    for(lots_of_threads = NUM_THREADS - 1; lots_of_threads >= 0; lots_of_threads--) {
        res = pthread_join(a_thread[lots_of_threads], &thread_result);
        if (res == 0) {
            printf("Picked up a thread\n");
        } else {
            perror("pthread_join failed");
        }
    }

    printf("All done\n");

    exit(EXIT_SUCCESS);
}

void *thread_function(void *arg) {
    int my_number = (int)arg;
    int rand_num;

    printf("thread_function is running. Argument was %d\n", my_number);
    rand_num=1+(int)(9.0*rand()/(RAND_MAX+1.0));
    sleep(rand_num);
    printf("Bye from %d\n", my_number);

    pthread_exit(NULL);
}
```

Summary

In this chapter, you learned how to create several threads of execution inside a process, where each thread shares file scope variables. You looked at the two ways that threads can control access to critical code and data, using both semaphores and mutexes. Next, you saw how to control the attributes of threads and, in particular, how you could separate them from the main thread so that it no longer had to wait for threads that it had created to complete. After a quick look at how one thread can request another to finish and at how the receiving thread can manage such requests, we presented an example of a program with many simultaneous threads executing.

We haven't had the space to cover every last function call and nuance associated with threads, but you should now have sufficient understanding to start writing your own programs with threads and to investigate the more esoteric aspects of threads by reading the manual pages.

Inter-Process Communication: Pipes

In Chapter 11, you saw a very simple way of sending messages between two processes using signals. You created notification events that could be used to provoke a response, but the information transferred was limited to a signal number.

In this chapter, you take a look at pipes, which allow more useful data to be exchanged between processes. By the end of the chapter, you'll be using your newfound knowledge to re-implement the CD database program as a very simple client/server application.

We cover the following topics in this chapter:

❑   The definition of a pipe

❑   Process pipes

❑   Pipe calls

❑   Parent and child processes

❑   Named pipes: FIFOs

❑   Client/server considerations

What Is a Pipe?

We use the term *pipe* to mean connecting a data flow from one process to another. Generally you attach, or pipe, the output of one process to the input of another.

Most Linux users will already be familiar with the idea of a pipeline, linking shell commands together so that the output of one process is fed straight to the input of another. For shell commands, this is done using the pipe character to join the commands, such as

```
cmd1 | cmd2
```

The shell arranges the standard input and output of the two commands, so that

❑   The standard input to cmd1 comes from the terminal keyboard.

❑   The standard output from cmd1 is fed to cmd2 as its standard input.

❑   The standard output from cmd2 is connected to the terminal screen.

What the shell has done, in effect, is reconnect the standard input and output streams so that data flows from the keyboard input through the two commands and is then output to the screen. See Figure 13-1 for a visual representation of this process.

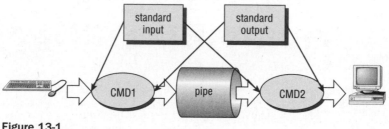

Figure 13-1

In this chapter, you see how to achieve this effect within a program and how you can use pipes to connect multiple processes to allow you to implement a simple client/server system.

Process Pipes

Perhaps the simplest way of passing data between two programs is with the popen and pclose functions. These have the following prototypes:

```
#include <stdio.h>

FILE *popen(const char *command, const char *open_mode);
int pclose(FILE *stream_to_close);
```

popen

The popen function allows a program to invoke another program as a new process and either pass data to it or receive data from it. The command string is the name of the program to run, together with any parameters. open_mode must be either "r" or "w".

If the open_mode is "r", output from the invoked program is made available to the invoking program and can be read from the file stream FILE * returned by popen, using the usual stdio library functions for reading (for example, fread). However, if open_mode is "w", the program can send data to the invoked command with calls to fwrite. The invoked program can then read the data on its standard input. Normally, the program being invoked won't be aware that it's reading data from another process; it simply reads its standard input stream and acts on it.

A call to popen must specify either "r" or "w"; no other option is supported in a standard implementation of popen. This means that you can't invoke another program and both read from and write to it. On failure, popen returns a null pointer. If you want bidirectional communication using pipes, the normal solution is to use two pipes, one for data flow in each direction.

pclose

When the process started with popen has finished, you can close the file stream associated with it using pclose. The pclose call will return only when the process started with popen finishes. If it's still running when pclose is called, the pclose call will wait for the process to finish.

The pclose call normally returns the exit code of the process whose file stream it is closing. If the invoking process has already executed a wait statement before calling pclose, the exit status will be lost because the invoked process has finished and pclose will return –1, with errno set to ECHILD.

Try It Out   Reading Output from an External Program

Let's try a simple popen and pclose example, popen1.c. You'll use popen in a program to access information from uname. The uname a command prints system information, including the machine type, the OS name, version and release, and the machine's network name.

Having initialized the program, you open the pipe to uname, making it readable and setting read_fp to point to the output. At the end, the pipe pointed to by read_fp is closed.

```
#include <unistd.h>
#include <stdlib.h>
#include <stdio.h>
#include <string.h>

int main()
{
    FILE *read_fp;
    char buffer[BUFSIZ + 1];
    int chars_read;
    memset(buffer, '\0', sizeof(buffer));
    read_fp = popen("uname -a", "r");
    if (read_fp != NULL) {
        chars_read = fread(buffer, sizeof(char), BUFSIZ, read_fp);
        if (chars_read > 0) {
            printf("Output was:-\n%s\n", buffer);
        }
        pclose(read_fp);
        exit(EXIT_SUCCESS);
    }
    exit(EXIT_FAILURE);
}
```

When you run this program, you should get output like the following (from one of the authors' machines):

```
$ ./popen1
Output was:-
Linux suse103 2.6.20.2-2-default #1 SMP Fri Mar 9 21:54:10 UTC 2007 i686 i686 i386
GNU/Linux
```

527

How It Works

The program uses the popen call to invoke the uname command with the -a parameter. It then uses the returned file stream to read data up to BUFSIZ characters (as this is a #define from stdio.h) and then prints it out so it appears on the screen. Because you've captured the output of uname inside a program, it's available for processing.

Sending Output to popen

Now that you've seen an example of capturing output from an external program, let's look at sending output to an external program. Here's a program, popen2.c, that pipes data to another. Here, you'll use od (octal dump).

Try It Out   Sending Output to an External Program

Have a look at the following code; you can see that it is very similar to the preceding example, except you are writing down a pipe instead of reading from it. This is popen2.c.

```
#include <unistd.h>
#include <stdlib.h>
#include <stdio.h>
#include <string.h>

int main()
{
    FILE *write_fp;
    char buffer[BUFSIZ + 1];

    sprintf(buffer, "Once upon a time, there was...\n");
    write_fp = popen("od -c", "w");
    if (write_fp != NULL) {
        fwrite(buffer, sizeof(char), strlen(buffer), write_fp);
        pclose(write_fp);
        exit(EXIT_SUCCESS);
    }
    exit(EXIT_FAILURE);
}
```

When you run this program, you should get the following output:

```
$ ./popen2
0000000   O   n   c   e       u   p   o   n       a       t   i   m   e
0000020   ,       t   h   e   r   e       w   a   s   .   .   .  \n
0000037
```

How It Works

The program uses popen with the parameter "w" to start the od -c command, so that it can send data to that command. It then sends a string that the od -c command receives and processes; the od -c command then prints the result of the processing on its standard output.

From the command line, you can get the same output with the command

```
$ echo "Once upon a time, there was..." | od -c
```

Passing More Data

The mechanism that you've used so far simply sends or receives all the data in a single `fread` or `fwrite`. Sometimes you may want to send the data in smaller pieces, or perhaps you may not know the size of the output. To avoid having to declare a very large buffer, you can just use multiple `fread` or `fwrite` calls and process the data in parts.

Here's a program, `popen3.c`, that reads all of the data from a pipe.

Try It Out   Reading Larger Amounts of Data from a Pipe

In this program, you read data from an invoked `ps ax` process. There's no way to know in advance how much output there will be, so you must allow for multiple reads of the pipe.

```c
#include <unistd.h>
#include <stdlib.h>
#include <stdio.h>
#include <string.h>

int main()
{
    FILE *read_fp;
    char buffer[BUFSIZ + 1];
    int chars_read;

    memset(buffer, '\0', sizeof(buffer));
    read_fp = popen("ps ax", "r");
    if (read_fp != NULL) {
        chars_read = fread(buffer, sizeof(char), BUFSIZ, read_fp);
        while (chars_read > 0) {
            buffer[chars_read - 1] = '\0';
            printf("Reading %d:-\n %s\n", BUFSIZ, buffer);
            chars_read = fread(buffer, sizeof(char), BUFSIZ, read_fp);
        }
        pclose(read_fp);
        exit(EXIT_SUCCESS);
    }
    exit(EXIT_FAILURE);
}
```

The output, edited for brevity, is similar to this:

```
$ ./popen3
Reading 1024:-
    PID TTY STAT  TIME COMMAND
      1 ?  Ss    0:03 init [5]
```

```
   2  ?  SW     0:00 [kflushd]
   3  ?  SW     0:00 [kpiod]
   4  ?  SW     0:00 [kswapd]
   5  ?  SW<    0:00 [mdrecoveryd]
...
 240 tty2 S     0:02 emacs draft1.txt
Reading 1024:-
 368 tty1 S     0:00 ./popen3
 369 tty1 R     0:00 ps -ax
...
```

How It Works

The program uses popen with an "r" parameter in a similar fashion to popen1.c. This time, it continues reading from the file stream until there is no more data available. Notice that, although the ps command takes some time to execute, Linux arranges the process scheduling so that both programs run when they can. If the reader process, popen3, has no input data, it's suspended until some becomes available. If the writer process, ps, produces more output than can be buffered, it's suspended until the reader has consumed some of the data.

In this example, you may not see Reading:- output a second time. This will be the case if BUFSIZ is greater than the length of the ps command output. Some (mostly more recent) Linux systems set BUFSIZ as high as 8,192 or even higher. To test that the program works correctly when reading several chunks of output, try reading less than BUFSIZ, maybe BUFSIZE/10, characters at a time.

How popen Is Implemented

The popen call runs the program you requested by first invoking the shell, sh, passing it the command string as an argument. This has two effects, one good and the other not so good.

In Linux (as in all UNIX-like systems), all parameter expansion is done by the shell, so invoking the shell to parse the command string before the program is invoked allows any shell expansion, such as determining what files *.c actually refers to, to be done before the program starts. This is often quite useful, and it allows complex shell commands to be started with popen. Other process creation functions, such as execl, can be much more complex to invoke, because the calling process has to perform its own shell expansion.

The unfortunate effect of using the shell is that for every call to popen, a shell is invoked along with the requested program. Each call to popen then results in two extra processes being started, which makes the popen function a little expensive in terms of system resources and invocation of the target command is slower than it might otherwise have been.

Here's a program, popen4.c, that you can use to demonstrate the behavior of popen. You can count the lines in all the popen example source files by cating the files and then piping the output to wc -1, which counts the number of lines. On the command line, the equivalent command is

```
$ cat popen*.c | wc -1
```

Actually, wc -1 popen.c is easier to type and much more efficient, but the example serves to illustrate the principle.*

Try It Out   **popen Starts a Shell**

This program uses exactly the preceding command, but through popen so that it can read the result:

```
#include <unistd.h>
#include <stdlib.h>
#include <stdio.h>
#include <string.h>

int main()
{
    FILE *read_fp;
    char buffer[BUFSIZ + 1];
    int chars_read;


    memset(buffer, '\0', sizeof(buffer));
    read_fp = popen("cat popen*.c | wc -l", "r");
    if (read_fp != NULL) {
        chars_read = fread(buffer, sizeof(char), BUFSIZ, read_fp);
        while (chars_read > 0) {
            buffer[chars_read - 1] = '\0';
            printf("Reading:-\n %s\n", buffer);
            chars_read = fread(buffer, sizeof(char), BUFSIZ, read_fp);
        }
        pclose(read_fp);
        exit(EXIT_SUCCESS);
    }
    exit(EXIT_FAILURE);
}
```

When you run this program, the output is

```
$ ./popen4
Reading:-
     94
```

How It Works

The program shows that the shell is being invoked to expand popen*.c to the list of all files starting popen and ending in .c and also to process the pipe (|) symbol and feed the output from cat into wc. You invoke the shell, the cat program, and wc and cause an output redirection, all in a single popen call. The program that invokes the command sees only the final output.

The Pipe Call

You've seen the high-level popen function, but now let's move on to look at the lower-level pipe function. This function provides a means of passing data between two programs, without the overhead of invoking a shell to interpret the requested command. It also gives you more control over the reading and writing of data.

The `pipe` function has the following prototype:

```
#include <unistd.h>

int pipe(int file_descriptor[2]);
```

`pipe` is passed (a pointer to) an array of two integer file descriptors. It fills the array with two new file descriptors and returns a zero. On failure, it returns –1 and sets `errno` to indicate the reason for failure. Errors defined in the Linux manual page for `pipe` (in section 2 of the manual) are

❑ EMFILE: Too many file descriptors are in use by the process.

❑ ENFILE: The system file table is full.

❑ EFAULT: The file descriptor is not valid.

The two file descriptors returned are connected in a special way. Any data written to `file_descriptor[1]` can be read back from `file_descriptor[0]`. The data is processed in a *first in, first out* basis, usually abbreviated to *FIFO*. This means that if you write the bytes 1, 2, 3 to `file_descriptor[1]`, reading from `file_descriptor[0]` will produce 1, 2, 3. This is different from a stack, which operates on a *last in, first out* basis, usually abbreviated to *LIFO*.

> *It's important to realize that these are file descriptors, not file streams, so you must use the lower-level* read *and* write *system calls to access the data, rather than the stream library functions* fread *and* fwrite.

Here's a program, `pipe1.c`, that uses `pipe` to create a pipe.

Try It Out   The pipe Function

The following example is `pipe1.c`. Note the `file_pipes` array, the address of which is passed to the `pipe` function as a parameter.

```c
#include <unistd.h>
#include <stdlib.h>
#include <stdio.h>
#include <string.h>

int main()
{
    int data_processed;
    int file_pipes[2];
    const char some_data[] = "123";
    char buffer[BUFSIZ + 1];

    memset(buffer, '\0', sizeof(buffer));

    if (pipe(file_pipes) == 0) {
        data_processed = write(file_pipes[1], some_data, strlen(some_data));
        printf("Wrote %d bytes\n", data_processed);
        data_processed = read(file_pipes[0], buffer, BUFSIZ);
        printf("Read %d bytes: %s\n", data_processed, buffer);
```

```
            exit(EXIT_SUCCESS);
    }
    exit(EXIT_FAILURE);
}
```

When you run this program, the output is

```
$ ./pipe1
Wrote 3 bytes
Read 3 bytes: 123
```

How It Works

The program creates a `pipe` using the two file descriptors in the array `file_pipes[]`. It then writes data into the pipe using the file descriptor `file_pipes[1]` and reads it back from `file_pipes[0]`. Notice that the pipe has some internal buffering that stores the data in between the calls to `write` and `read`.

You should be aware that the effect of trying to write using `file_descriptor[0]`, or read using `file_descriptor[1]`, is undefined, so the behavior could be very strange and may change without warning. On the authors' systems, such calls fail with a −1 return value, which at least ensures that it's easy to catch this mistake.

At first glance, this example of a pipe doesn't seem to offer us anything that we couldn't have done with a simple file. The real advantage of pipes comes when you want to pass data between two processes. As you saw in Chapter 12, when a program creates a new process using the `fork` call, file descriptors that were previously open remain open. By creating a pipe in the original process and then `fork`ing to create a new process, you can pass data from one process to the other down the pipe.

Try It Out   Pipes across a fork

1.   This is `pipe2.c`. It starts rather like the first example, up until you make the call to `fork`.

```c
#include <unistd.h>
#include <stdlib.h>
#include <stdio.h>
#include <string.h>

int main()
{
    int data_processed;
    int file_pipes[2];
    const char some_data[] = "123";
    char buffer[BUFSIZ + 1];
    pid_t fork_result;

    memset(buffer, '\0', sizeof(buffer));

    if (pipe(file_pipes) == 0) {
        fork_result = fork();
        if (fork_result == -1) {
```

```
        fprintf(stderr, "Fork failure");
        exit(EXIT_FAILURE);
    }
```

2. You've made sure the `fork` worked, so if `fork_result` equals zero, you're in the child process:

```
    if (fork_result == 0) {
        data_processed = read(file_pipes[0], buffer, BUFSIZ);
        printf("Read %d bytes: %s\n", data_processed, buffer);
        exit(EXIT_SUCCESS);
    }
```

3. Otherwise, you must be in the parent process:

```
    else {
        data_processed = write(file_pipes[1], some_data,
                            strlen(some_data));
        printf("Wrote %d bytes\n", data_processed);
    }
  }
  exit(EXIT_SUCCESS);
}
```

When you run this program, the output is, as before,

```
$ ./pipe2
Wrote 3 bytes
Read 3 bytes: 123
```

You may find that in practice the command prompt reappears before the last part of the output because the parent will finish before the child, so we have tidied the output here to make it easier to read.

How It Works

First, the program creates a pipe with the `pipe` call. It then uses the `fork` call to create a new process. If the `fork` was successful, the parent writes data into the pipe, while the child reads data from the pipe. Both parent and child exit after a single `write` and `read`. If the parent exits before the child, you might see the shell prompt between the two outputs.

Although the program is superficially very similar to the first `pipe` example, we've taken a big step forward by being able to use separate processes for the reading and writing, as illustrated in Figure 13-2.

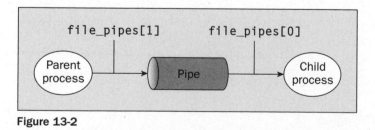

Figure 13-2

Parent and Child Processes

The next logical step in our investigation of the `pipe` call is to allow the child process to be a different program from its parent, rather than just a different process running the same program. You do this using the `exec` call. One difficulty is that the new `exec`ed process needs to know which file descriptor to access. In the previous example, this wasn't a problem because the child had access to its copy of the `file_pipes` data. After an `exec` call, this will no longer be the case, because the old process has been replaced by the new child process. You can get around this by passing the file descriptor (which is, after all, just a number) as a parameter to the newly `exec`ed program.

To show how this works, you need two programs. The first is the *data producer*. It creates the pipe and then invokes the child, the *data consumer*.

Try It Out   **Pipes and exec**

1. For the first program, you adapt `pipe2.c` to `pipe3.c`. The changed lines are shown shaded:

```c
#include <unistd.h>
#include <stdlib.h>
#include <stdio.h>
#include <string.h>

int main()
{

    int data_processed;
    int file_pipes[2];
    const char some_data[] = "123";
    char buffer[BUFSIZ + 1];
    pid_t fork_result;

    memset(buffer, '\0', sizeof(buffer));

    if (pipe(file_pipes) == 0) {
        fork_result = fork();
        if (fork_result == (pid_t)-1) {
            fprintf(stderr, "Fork failure");
            exit(EXIT_FAILURE);
        }

        if (fork_result == 0) {
            sprintf(buffer, "%d", file_pipes[0]);
            (void)execl("pipe4", "pipe4", buffer, (char *)0);
            exit(EXIT_FAILURE);
        }
        else {
            data_processed = write(file_pipes[1], some_data,
                                   strlen(some_data));
            printf("%d - wrote %d bytes\n", getpid(), data_processed);
        }
    }
    exit(EXIT_SUCCESS);
}
```

2. The consumer program, `pipe4.c`, which reads the data, is much simpler:

```
#include <unistd.h>
#include <stdlib.h>
#include <stdio.h>
#include <string.h>

int main(int argc, char *argv[])
{
    int data_processed;
    char buffer[BUFSIZ + 1];
    int file_descriptor;

    memset(buffer, '\0', sizeof(buffer));
    sscanf(argv[1], "%d", &file_descriptor);
    data_processed = read(file_descriptor, buffer, BUFSIZ);

    printf("%d - read %d bytes: %s\n", getpid(), data_processed, buffer);
    exit(EXIT_SUCCESS);
}
```

Remembering that `pipe3` invokes the `pipe4` program, you get something similar to the following output when you run `pipe3`:

```
$ ./pipe3
22460 - wrote 3 bytes
22461 - read 3 bytes: 123
```

How It Works

The `pipe3` program starts like the previous example, using the `pipe` call to create a pipe and then using the `fork` call to create a new process. It then uses `sprintf` to store the "read" file descriptor number of the pipe in a buffer that will form an argument of `pipe4`.

A call to `execl` is used to invoke the `pipe4` program. The arguments to `execl` are

❑   The program to invoke

❑   `argv[0]`, which takes the program name

❑   `argv[1]`, which contains the file descriptor number you want the program to read from

❑   `(char *)0`, which terminates the parameters

The `pipe4` program extracts the file descriptor number from the argument string and then reads from that file descriptor to obtain the data.

Reading Closed Pipes

Before we move on, we need to look a little more carefully at the file descriptors that are open. Up to this point you have allowed the reading process simply to read some data and then exit, assuming that Linux will clean up the files as part of the process termination.

Most programs that read data from the standard input do so differently than the examples you've seen so far. They don't usually know how much data they have to read, so they will normally loop — reading data, processing it, and then reading more data until there's no more data to read.

A read call will normally block; that is, it will cause the process to wait until data becomes available. If the other end of the pipe has been closed, then no process has the pipe open for writing, and the read blocks. Because this isn't very helpful, a read on a pipe that isn't open for writing returns zero rather than blocking. This allows the reading process to detect the pipe equivalent of end of file and act appropriately. Notice that this isn't the same as reading an invalid file descriptor, which read considers an error and indicates by returning –1.

If you use a pipe across a fork call, there are two different file descriptors that you can use to write to the pipe: one in the parent and one in the child. You must close the write file descriptors of the pipe in both parent and child processes before the pipe is considered closed and a read call on the pipe will fail. You'll see an example of this later when we return to this subject in more detail to look at the O_NON-BLOCK flag and FIFOs.

Pipes Used as Standard Input and Output

Now that you know how to make a read on an empty pipe fail, you can look at a much cleaner method of connecting two processes with a pipe. You arrange for one of the pipe file descriptors to have a known value, usually the standard input, 0, or the standard output, 1. This is slightly more complex to set up in the parent, but it allows the child program to be much simpler.

The one big advantage is that you can invoke standard programs, ones that don't expect a file descriptor as a parameter. In order to do this, you need to use the dup function, which you met in Chapter 3. There are two closely related versions of dup that have the following prototypes:

```
#include <unistd.h>

int dup(int file_descriptor);
int dup2(int file_descriptor_one, int file_descriptor_two);
```

The purpose of the dup call is to open a new file descriptor, a little like the open call. The difference is that the new file descriptor created by dup refers to the same file (or pipe) as an existing file descriptor. In the case of dup, the new file descriptor is always the lowest number available, and in the case of dup2 it's the same as, or the first available descriptor greater than, the parameter file_descriptor_two.

You can get the same effect as dup and dup2 by using the more general fcntl call, with a command F_DUPFD. Having said that, the dup call is easier to use because it's tailored specifically to the needs of creating duplicate file descriptors. It's also very commonly used, so you'll find it more frequently in existing programs than fcntl and F_DUPFD.

So how does dup help in passing data between processes? The trick is knowing that the standard input file descriptor is always 0 and that dup always returns a new file descriptor using the lowest available number. By first closing file descriptor 0 and then calling dup, the new file descriptor will have the number 0. Because the new descriptor is a duplicate of an existing one, standard input will have been changed to access the file or pipe whose file descriptor you passed to dup. You will have created two file descriptors that refer to the same file or pipe, and one of them will be the standard input.

File Descriptor Manipulation by close and dup

The easiest way to understand what happens when you close file descriptor 0, and then call dup, is to look at how the state of the first four file descriptors changes during the sequence. This is shown in the following table.

File Descriptor Number	Initially	After close of File Descriptor 0	After dup
0	Standard input	{closed}	Pipe file descriptor
1	Standard output	Standard output	Standard output
2	Standard error	Standard error	Standard error
3	Pipe file descriptor	Pipe file descriptor	Pipe file descriptor

Try It Out   Pipes and dup

Let's return to the previous example, but this time you'll arrange for the child program to have its stdin file descriptor replaced with the read end of the pipe you create. You'll also do some tidying up of file descriptors so the child program can correctly detect the end of the data in the pipe. As usual, we'll omit some error checking for the sake of brevity.

Modify pipe3.c to pipe5.c using the following code:

```c
#include <unistd.h>
#include <stdlib.h>
#include <stdio.h>
#include <string.h>

int main()
{
    int data_processed;
    int file_pipes[2];
    const char some_data[] = "123";
    pid_t fork_result;

    if (pipe(file_pipes) == 0) {
        fork_result = fork();
        if (fork_result == (pid_t)-1) {
            fprintf(stderr, "Fork failure");
            exit(EXIT_FAILURE);
        }

        if (fork_result == (pid_t)0) {
            close(0);
            dup(file_pipes[0]);
            close(file_pipes[0]);
            close(file_pipes[1]);
```

```
            execlp("od", "od", "-c", (char *)0);
            exit(EXIT_FAILURE);
        }
        else {
            close(file_pipes[0]);
            data_processed = write(file_pipes[1], some_data,
                                    strlen(some_data));
            close(file_pipes[1]);
            printf("%d - wrote %d bytes\n", (int)getpid(), data_processed);
        }
    }
    exit(EXIT_SUCCESS);
}
```

The output from this program is

```
$ ./pipe5
22495 - wrote 3 bytes
0000000   1   2   3
0000003
```

How It Works

As before, the program creates a pipe and then forks, creating a child process. At this point, both the parent and child have file descriptors that access the pipe, one each for reading and writing, so there are four open file descriptors in total.

Let's look at the child process first. The child closes its standard input with close(0) and then calls dup(file_pipes[0]). This duplicates the file descriptor associated with the read end of the pipe as file descriptor 0, the standard input. The child then closes the original file descriptor for reading from the pipe, file_pipes[0]. Because the child will never write to the pipe, it also closes the write file descriptor associated with the pipe, file_pipes[1]. It now has a single file descriptor associated with the pipe: file descriptor 0, its standard input.

The child can then use exec to invoke any program that reads standard input. In this case, you use the od command. The od command will wait for data to be available to it as if it were waiting for input from a user terminal. In fact, without some special code to explicitly detect the difference, it won't know that the input is from a pipe rather than a terminal.

The parent starts by closing the read end of the pipe file_pipes[0], because it will never read the pipe. It then writes data to the pipe. When all the data has been written, the parent closes the write end of the pipe and exits. Because there are now no file descriptors open that could write to the pipe, the od program will be able to read the three bytes written to the pipe, but subsequent reads will then return 0 bytes, indicating an end of file. When the read returns 0, the od program exits. This is analogous to running the od command on a terminal, then pressing Ctrl+D to send end of file to the od command.

Figure 13-3 shows the sequence after the call to the pipe, Figure 13-4 shows the sequence after the call to fork, and Figure 13-5 represents the program when it's ready to transfer data.

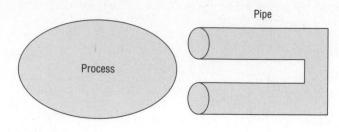

Figure 13-3

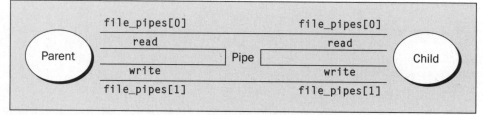

Figure 13-4

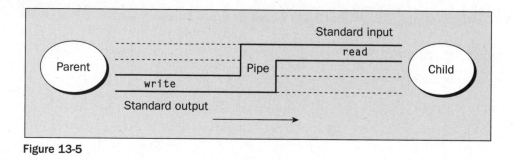

Figure 13-5

Named Pipes: FIFOs

So far, you have only been able to pass data between related programs, that is, programs that have been started from a common ancestor process. Often this isn't very convenient, because you would like unrelated processes to be able to exchange data.

You do this with *FIFOs*, often referred to as *named pipes*. A named pipe is a special type of file (remember that everything in Linux is a file!) that exists as a name in the file system but behaves like the unnamed pipes that you've met already.

You can create named pipes from the command line and from within a program. Historically, the command-line program for creating them was mknod:

```
$ mknod filename p
```

However, the mknod command is not in the X/Open command list, so it may not be available on all UNIX-like systems. The preferred command-line method is to use

```
$ mkfifo filename
```

Some older versions of UNIX only had the mknod *command. X/Open Issue 4 Version 2 has the* mknod *function call, but not the command-line program. Linux, friendly as ever, supplies both* mknod *and* mkfifo.

From inside a program, you can use two different calls:

```
#include <sys/types.h>
#include <sys/stat.h>

int mkfifo(const char *filename, mode_t mode);
int mknod(const char *filename, mode_t mode | S_IFIFO, (dev_t) 0);
```

Like the mknod command, you can use the mknod function for making many special types of files. Using a dev_t value of 0 and ORing the file access mode with S_IFIFO is the only portable use of this function that creates a named pipe. We'll use the simpler mkfifo function in the examples.

Try It Out   Creating a Named Pipe

The following example is fifo1.c:

```
#include <unistd.h>
#include <stdlib.h>
#include <stdio.h>
#include <sys/types.h>
#include <sys/stat.h>

int main()
{
    int res = mkfifo("/tmp/my_fifo", 0777);
    if (res == 0) printf("FIFO created\n");
    exit(EXIT_SUCCESS);
}
```

You can create and look for the pipe with

```
$ ./fifo1
FIFO created
$ ls -lF /tmp/my_fifo
prwxr-xr-x   1 rick      users              0 2007-06-16 17:18 /tmp/my_fifo|
```

Notice that the first character of output is a p, indicating a pipe. The | symbol at the end is added by the ls command's -F option and also indicates a pipe.

How It Works

The program uses the mkfifo function to create a special file. Although you ask for a mode of 0777, this is altered by the user mask (umask) setting (in this case 022), just as in normal file creation, so the resulting file has mode 755. If your umask is set differently, for example to 0002, you will see different permissions on the created file.

You can remove the FIFO just like a conventional file by using the rm command, or from within a program by using the unlink system call.

Accessing a FIFO

One very useful feature of named pipes is that, because they appear in the file system, you can use them in commands where you would normally use a filename. Before you do more programming using the FIFO file you created, let's investigate the behavior of the FIFO file using normal file commands.

Try It Out   Accessing a FIFO File

1. First, try reading the (empty) FIFO:

```
$ cat < /tmp/my_fifo
```

2. Now try writing to the FIFO. You will have to use a different terminal because the first command will now be hanging, waiting for some data to appear in the FIFO.

```
$ echo "Hello World" > /tmp/my_fifo
```

You will see the output appear from the cat command. If you don't send any data down the FIFO, the cat command will hang until you interrupt it, conventionally with Ctrl+C.

3. You can do both at once by putting the first command in the background:

```
$ cat < /tmp/my_fifo &
[1] 1316
$ echo "Hello World" > /tmp/my_fifo
Hello World

[1]+  Done                    cat </tmp/my_fifo
$
```

How It Works

Because there was no data in the FIFO, the cat and echo programs both block, waiting for some data to arrive and some other process to read the data, respectively.

Looking at the third stage, the cat process is initially blocked in the background. When echo makes some data available, the cat command reads the data and prints it to the standard output. Notice that the `cat` program then exits without waiting for more data. It doesn't block because the pipe will have been closed when the second command putting data in the FIFO completed, so calls to `read` in the `cat` program will return 0 bytes, indicating the end of file.

Now that you've seen how the FIFO behaves when you access it using command-line programs, let's look in more detail at the program interface, which allows you more control over how `reads` and `writes` behave when you're accessing a FIFO.

> *Unlike a pipe created with the `pipe` call, a FIFO exists as a named file, not as an open file descriptor, and it must be opened before it can be read from or written to. You open and close a FIFO using the same `open` and `close` functions that you saw used earlier for files, with some additional functionality. The `open` call is passed the path name of the FIFO, rather than that of a regular file.*

Opening a FIFO with open

The main restriction on opening FIFOs is that a program may not open a FIFO for reading and writing with the mode `O_RDWR`. If a program violates this restriction, the result is undefined. This is quite a sensible restriction because, normally, you use a FIFO only for passing data in a single direction, so there is no need for an `O_RDWR` mode. A process would read its own output back from a pipe if it were opened read/write.

If you do want to pass data in both directions between programs, it's much better to use either a pair of FIFOs or pipes, one for each direction, or (unusually) explicitly change the direction of the data flow by closing and reopening the FIFO. We return to bidirectional data exchange using FIFOs later in the chapter.

The other difference between opening a FIFO and a regular file is the use of the `open_flag` (the second parameter to `open`) with the option `O_NONBLOCK`. Using this `open` mode not only changes how the `open` call is processed, but also changes how `read` and `write` requests are processed on the returned file descriptor.

There are four legal combinations of `O_RDONLY`, `O_WRONLY`, and the `O_NONBLOCK` flag. We'll consider each in turn.

```
open(const char *path, O_RDONLY);
```

In this case, the `open` call will block; it will not return until a process opens the same FIFO for writing. This is like the first `cat` example.

```
open(const char *path, O_RDONLY | O_NONBLOCK);
```

The `open` call will now succeed and return immediately, even if the FIFO has not been opened for writing by any process.

```
open(const char *path, O_WRONLY);
```

In this case, the `open` call will block until a process opens the same FIFO for reading.

```
open(const char *path, O_WRONLY | O_NONBLOCK);
```

This will always return immediately, but if no process has the FIFO open for reading, open will return an error, –1, and the FIFO won't be opened. If a process does have the FIFO open for reading, the file descriptor returned can be used for writing to the FIFO.

Notice the asymmetry between the use of O_NONBLOCK *with* O_RDONLY *and* O_WRONLY, *in that a non-blocking* open *for writing fails if no process has the pipe open for reading, but a nonblocking* read *doesn't fail. The behavior of the* close *call isn't affected by the* O_NONBLOCK *flag.*

Try It Out   Opening FIFO Files

Now look at how you can use the behavior of open with the O_NONBLOCK flag to synchronize two processes. Rather than use a number of example programs, you'll write a single test program, fifo2.c, which allows you to investigate the behavior of FIFOs by passing in different parameters.

1. Start with the header files, a #define, and the check that the correct number of command-line arguments has been supplied:

```
#include <unistd.h>
#include <stdlib.h>
#include <stdio.h>
#include <string.h>
#include <fcntl.h>
#include <sys/types.h>
#include <sys/stat.h>

#define FIFO_NAME "/tmp/my_fifo"

int main(int argc, char *argv[])
{
    int res;
    int open_mode = 0;
    int i;

    if (argc < 2) {
        fprintf(stderr, "Usage: %s <some combination of\
                O_RDONLY O_WRONLY O_NONBLOCK>\n", *argv);
        exit(EXIT_FAILURE);
    }
```

2. Assuming that the program passed the test, you now set the value of open_mode from those arguments:

```
    for(i = 1; i <argc; i++) {
        if (strncmp(*++argv, "O_RDONLY", 8) == 0)
            open_mode |= O_RDONLY;
        if (strncmp(*argv, "O_WRONLY", 8) == 0)
            open_mode |= O_WRONLY;
        if (strncmp(*argv, "O_NONBLOCK", 10) == 0)
            open_mode |= O_NONBLOCK;
    }
```

3. Next check whether the FIFO exists, and create it if necessary. Then the FIFO is opened and output given to that effect while the program catches forty winks. Last of all, the FIFO is closed.

```
if (access(FIFO_NAME, F_OK) == -1) {
    res = mkfifo(FIFO_NAME, 0777);
    if (res != 0) {
        fprintf(stderr, "Could not create fifo %s\n", FIFO_NAME);
        exit(EXIT_FAILURE);
    }
}

printf("Process %d opening FIFO\n", getpid());
res = open(FIFO_NAME, open_mode);
printf("Process %d result %d\n", getpid(), res);
sleep(5);
if (res != -1) (void)close(res);
printf("Process %d finished\n", getpid());
exit(EXIT_SUCCESS);
}
```

How It Works

This program allows you to specify on the command line the combinations of O_RDONLY, O_WRONLY, and O_NONBLOCK that you want to use. It does this by comparing known strings with command-line parameters and setting (with |=) the appropriate flag if the string matches. The program uses the access function to check whether the FIFO file already exists and will create it if required.

You never destroy the FIFO, because you have no way of telling if another program already has the FIFO in use.

O_RDONLY and O_WRONLY without O_NONBLOCK

You now have your test program, so you can try out a couple of combinations. Notice that the first program, the reader, has been put in the background:

```
$ ./fifo2 O_RDONLY &
[1] 152
Process 152 opening FIFO
$ ./fifo2 O_WRONLY
Process 153 opening FIFO
Process 152 result 3
Process 153 result 3
Process 152 finished
Process 153 finished
```

This is probably the most common use of named pipes. It allows the reader process to start and wait in the open call and then allows both programs to continue when the second program opens the FIFO. Notice that both the reader and writer processes have synchronized at the open call.

When a Linux process is blocked, it doesn't consume CPU resources, so this method of process synchronization is very CPU-efficient.

O_RDONLY with O_NONBLOCK and O_WRONLY

In the following example, the reader process executes the open call and continues immediately, even though no writer process is present. The writer also immediately continues past the open call, because the FIFO is already open for reading.

```
$ ./fifo2 O_RDONLY O_NONBLOCK &
[1] 160
Process 160 opening FIFO
$ ./fifo2 O_WRONLY
Process 161 opening FIFO
Process 160 result 3
Process 161 result 3
Process 160 finished
Process 161 finished
[1]+  Done                    ./fifo2 O_RDONLY O_NONBLOCK
```

These two examples are probably the most common combinations of open modes. Feel free to use the example program to experiment with some other combinations.

Reading and Writing FIFOs

Using the O_NONBLOCK mode affects how read and write calls behave on FIFOs.

A read on an empty blocking FIFO (that is, one not opened with O_NONBLOCK) will wait until some data can be read. Conversely, a read on a nonblocking FIFO with no data will return 0 bytes.

A write on a full blocking FIFO will wait until the data can be written. A write on a FIFO that can't accept all of the bytes being written will either:

❑   Fail, if the request is for PIPE_BUF bytes or less and the data can't be written.

❑   Write part of the data, if the request is for more than PIPE_BUF bytes, returning the number of bytes actually written, which could be 0.

The size of a FIFO is an important consideration. There is a system-imposed limit on how much data can be "in" a FIFO at any one time. This is the #define PIPE_BUF, usually found in limits.h. On Linux and many other UNIX-like systems, this is commonly 4,096 bytes, but it could be as low as 512 bytes on some systems. The system guarantees that writes of PIPE_BUF or fewer bytes on a FIFO that has been opened O_WRONLY (that is, blocking) will either write all or none of the bytes.

Although this limit is not very important in the simple case of a single FIFO writer and a single FIFO reader, it's quite common to use a single FIFO to allow many different programs to send requests to a single FIFO reader. If several different programs try to write to the FIFO at the same time, it's usually vital that the blocks of data from different programs don't get interleaved — that is, each write must be "atomic." How do you do this?

Well, if you ensure that all your write requests are to a blocking FIFO and are less than PIPE_BUF bytes in size, the system will ensure that data never gets interleaved. In general, it's a good idea to restrict the data transferred via a FIFO to blocks of PIPE_BUF bytes, unless you're using only a single-writer and a single-reader process.

| Try It Out | **Inter-Process Communication with FIFOs** |

To show how unrelated processes can communicate using named pipes, you need two separate programs, `fifo3.c` and `fifo4.c`.

1. The first program is the producer program. It creates the pipe if required, and then writes data to it as quickly as possible.

Note that, for illustration purposes, we don't mind what the data is, so we don't bother to initialize a buffer. In both listings, shaded lines show the changes from `fifo2.c`, *with all the command-line argument code removed.*

```c
#include <unistd.h>
#include <stdlib.h>
#include <stdio.h>
#include <string.h>
#include <fcntl.h>
#include <limits.h>
#include <sys/types.h>
#include <sys/stat.h>

#define FIFO_NAME "/tmp/my_fifo"
#define BUFFER_SIZE PIPE_BUF
#define TEN_MEG (1024 * 1024 * 10)

int main()
{
    int pipe_fd;
    int res;
    int open_mode = O_WRONLY;
    int bytes_sent = 0;
    char buffer[BUFFER_SIZE + 1];

    if (access(FIFO_NAME, F_OK) == -1) {
        res = mkfifo(FIFO_NAME, 0777);
        if (res != 0) {
            fprintf(stderr, "Could not create fifo %s\n", FIFO_NAME);
            exit(EXIT_FAILURE);
        }
    }

    printf("Process %d opening FIFO O_WRONLY\n", getpid());
    pipe_fd = open(FIFO_NAME, open_mode);
    printf("Process %d result %d\n", getpid(), pipe_fd);

    if (pipe_fd != -1) {
        while(bytes_sent < TEN_MEG) {
            res = write(pipe_fd, buffer, BUFFER_SIZE);
            if (res == -1) {
                fprintf(stderr, "Write error on pipe\n");
                exit(EXIT_FAILURE);
            }
```

```
            bytes_sent += res;
        }
        (void)close(pipe_fd);
    }
    else {
        exit(EXIT_FAILURE);
    }

    printf("Process %d finished\n", getpid());
    exit(EXIT_SUCCESS);
}
```

2. The second program, the consumer, is much simpler. It reads and discards data from the FIFO.

```
#include <unistd.h>
#include <stdlib.h>
#include <stdio.h>
#include <string.h>
#include <fcntl.h>
#include <limits.h>
#include <sys/types.h>
#include <sys/stat.h>


#define FIFO_NAME "/tmp/my_fifo"
#define BUFFER_SIZE PIPE_BUF

int main()
{
    int pipe_fd;
    int res;
    int open_mode = O_RDONLY;
    char buffer[BUFFER_SIZE + 1];
    int bytes_read = 0;

    memset(buffer, '\0', sizeof(buffer));

    printf("Process %d opening FIFO O_RDONLY\n", getpid());
    pipe_fd = open(FIFO_NAME, open_mode);
    printf("Process %d result %d\n", getpid(), pipe_fd);

    if (pipe_fd != -1) {
        do {
            res = read(pipe_fd, buffer, BUFFER_SIZE);
            bytes_read += res;
        } while (res > 0);
        (void)close(pipe_fd);
    }
    else {
        exit(EXIT_FAILURE);
    }

    printf("Process %d finished, %d bytes read\n", getpid(), bytes_read);
    exit(EXIT_SUCCESS);
}
```

When you run these programs at the same time, using the `time` command to time the reader, the output you get (with some tidying for clarity) is

```
$ ./fifo3 &
[1] 375
Process 375 opening FIFO O_WRONLY
$ time ./fifo4
Process 377 opening FIFO O_RDONLY
Process 375 result 3
Process 377 result 3
Process 375 finished
Process 377 finished, 10485760 bytes read

real    0m0.053s
user    0m0.020s
sys     0m0.040s

[1]+  Done                    ./fifo3
```

How It Works

Both programs use the FIFO in blocking mode. You start `fifo3` (the writer/producer) first, which blocks, waiting for a reader to open the FIFO. When `fifo4` (the consumer) is started, the writer is then unblocked and starts writing data to the pipe. At the same time, the reader starts reading data from the pipe.

Linux arranges the scheduling of the two processes so that they both run when they can and are blocked when they can't. Thus, the writer is blocked when the pipe is full, and the reader is blocked when the pipe is empty.

The output from the `time` command shows that it took the reader well under one-tenth of a second to run, reading 10 megabytes of data in the process. This shows that pipes, at least as implemented in modern versions of Linux, can be an efficient way of transferring data between programs.

Advanced Topic: Client/Server Using FIFOs

For your final look at FIFOs, let's consider how you might build a very simple client/server application using named pipes. You want to have a single-server process that accepts requests, processes them, and returns the resulting data to the requesting party: the client.

You want to allow multiple client processes to send data to the server. In the interests of simplicity, we'll assume that the data to be processed can be broken into blocks, each smaller than `PIPE_BUF` bytes. Of course, you could implement this system in many ways, but we'll consider only one method as an illustration of how named pipes can be used.

Because the server will process only one block of information at a time, it seems logical to have a single FIFO that is read by the server and written to by each of the clients. By opening the FIFO in blocking mode, the server and the clients will be automatically blocked as required.

Returning the processed data to the clients is slightly more difficult. You need to arrange a second pipe, one per client, for the returned data. By passing the process identifier (PID) of the client in the original data sent to the server, both parties can use this to generate the unique name for the return pipe.

Try It Out   **An Example Client/Server Application**

1.   First, you need a header file, client.h, that defines the data common to both client and server programs. It also includes the required system headers, for convenience.

```
#include <unistd.h>
#include <stdlib.h>
#include <stdio.h>
#include <string.h>
#include <fcntl.h>
#include <limits.h>
#include <sys/types.h>
#include <sys/stat.h>

#define SERVER_FIFO_NAME "/tmp/serv_fifo"
#define CLIENT_FIFO_NAME "/tmp/cli_%d_fifo"

#define BUFFER_SIZE 20

struct data_to_pass_st {
    pid_t  client_pid;
    char   some_data[BUFFER_SIZE - 1];
};
```

2.   Now for the server program, server.c. In this section, you create and then open the server pipe. It's set to be read-only, with blocking. After sleeping (for demonstration purposes), the server reads in any data from the client, which has the data_to_pass_st structure.

```
#include "client.h"
#include <ctype.h>

int main()
{
    int server_fifo_fd, client_fifo_fd;
    struct data_to_pass_st my_data;
    int read_res;
    char client_fifo[256];
    char *tmp_char_ptr;

    mkfifo(SERVER_FIFO_NAME, 0777);
    server_fifo_fd = open(SERVER_FIFO_NAME, O_RDONLY);
    if (server_fifo_fd == -1) {
        fprintf(stderr, "Server fifo failure\n");
        exit(EXIT_FAILURE);
    }

    sleep(10); /* lets clients queue for demo purposes */

    do {
        read_res = read(server_fifo_fd, &my_data, sizeof(my_data));
        if (read_res > 0) {
```

3. In this next stage, you perform some processing on the data just read from the client: Convert all the characters in `some_data` to uppercase and combine the CLIENT_FIFO_NAME with the received `client_pid`.

```
            tmp_char_ptr = my_data.some_data;
            while (*tmp_char_ptr) {
                *tmp_char_ptr = toupper(*tmp_char_ptr);
                tmp_char_ptr++;
            }
            sprintf(client_fifo, CLIENT_FIFO_NAME, my_data.client_pid);
```

4. Then send the processed data back, opening the client pipe in write-only, blocking mode. Finally, shut down the server FIFO by closing the file and then `unlinking` the FIFO.

```
            client_fifo_fd = open(client_fifo, O_WRONLY);
            if (client_fifo_fd != -1) {
                write(client_fifo_fd, &my_data, sizeof(my_data));
                close(client_fifo_fd);
            }
        }
    } while (read_res > 0);
    close(server_fifo_fd);
    unlink(SERVER_FIFO_NAME);
    exit(EXIT_SUCCESS);
}
```

5. Here's the client, `client.c`. The first part of this program opens the server FIFO, if it already exists, as a file. It then gets its own process ID, which forms some of the data that will be sent to the server. The client FIFO is created, ready for the next section.

```
#include "client.h"
#include <ctype.h>

int main()
{
    int server_fifo_fd, client_fifo_fd;
    struct data_to_pass_st my_data;
    int times_to_send;
    char client_fifo[256];

    server_fifo_fd = open(SERVER_FIFO_NAME, O_WRONLY);
    if (server_fifo_fd == -1) {
        fprintf(stderr, "Sorry, no server\n");
        exit(EXIT_FAILURE);
    }

    my_data.client_pid = getpid();
    sprintf(client_fifo, CLIENT_FIFO_NAME, my_data.client_pid);
    if (mkfifo(client_fifo, 0777) == -1) {
        fprintf(stderr, "Sorry, can't make %s\n", client_fifo);
        exit(EXIT_FAILURE);
    }
```

6. For each of the five loops, the client data is sent to the server. Then the client FIFO is opened (read-only, blocking mode) and the data read back. Finally, the server FIFO is closed and the client FIFO removed from the file system.

```
for (times_to_send = 0; times_to_send < 5; times_to_send++) {
    sprintf(my_data.some_data, "Hello from %d", my_data.client_pid);
    printf("%d sent %s, ", my_data.client_pid, my_data.some_data);
    write(server_fifo_fd, &my_data, sizeof(my_data));
    client_fifo_fd = open(client_fifo, O_RDONLY);
    if (client_fifo_fd != -1) {
        if (read(client_fifo_fd, &my_data, sizeof(my_data)) > 0) {
            printf("received: %s\n", my_data.some_data);
        }
        close(client_fifo_fd);
    }
}
close(server_fifo_fd);
unlink(client_fifo);
exit(EXIT_SUCCESS);
}
```

To test this application, you need to run a single copy of the server and several clients. To get them all started at close to the same time, use the following shell commands:

```
$ ./server &
$ for i in 1 2 3 4 5
do
./client &
done
$
```

This starts one server process and five client processes. The output from the clients, edited for brevity, looks like this:

```
531 sent Hello from 531, received: HELLO FROM 531
532 sent Hello from 532, received: HELLO FROM 532
529 sent Hello from 529, received: HELLO FROM 529
530 sent Hello from 530, received: HELLO FROM 530
531 sent Hello from 531, received: HELLO FROM 531
532 sent Hello from 532, received: HELLO FROM 532
```

As you can see in this output, different client requests are being interleaved, but each client is getting the suitably processed data returned to it. Note that you may or may not see this interleaving; the order in which client requests are received may vary between machines and possibly between runs on the same machine.

How It Works

Now we'll cover the sequence of client and server operations as they interact, something that we haven't covered so far.

The server creates its FIFO in read-only mode and blocks. It does this until the first client connects by opening the same FIFO for writing. At that point, the server process is unblocked and the `sleep` is executed, so the `writes` from the clients queue up. (In a real application, the `sleep` would be removed; we're only using it to demonstrate the correct operation of the program with multiple simultaneous clients.)

In the meantime, after the client has opened the server FIFO, it creates its own uniquely named FIFO for reading data back from the server. Only then does the client write data to the server (blocking if the pipe is full or the server's still sleeping) and then blocks on a `read` of its own FIFO, waiting for the reply.

On receiving the data from the client, the server processes it, opens the client pipe for writing, and writes the data back, which unblocks the client. When the client is unblocked, it can read from its pipe the data written to it by the server.

The whole process repeats until the last client closes the server pipe, causing the server's `read` to fail (returning 0) because no process has the server pipe open for writing. If this were a real server process that needed to wait for further clients, you would need to modify it to either

❑   Open a file descriptor to its own server pipe, so `read` always blocks rather than returning 0.

❑   Close and reopen the server pipe when `read` returns 0 bytes, so the server process blocks in the `open` waiting for a client, just as it did when it first started.

Both of these techniques are illustrated in the rewrite of the CD database application to use named pipes.

The CD Database Application

Now that you've seen how you can use named pipes to implement a simple client/server system, you can revisit the CD database application and convert it accordingly. You'll also incorporate some signal handling to allow you to perform some tidy-up actions when the process is interrupted. You will use the earlier dbm version of the application that had a command-line interface to see the code as straightforwardly as possible.

Before you get to look in detail at this new version, you must compile the application. If you have the source code from the website, use the `makefile` to compile it into the `server` and `client` programs.

> As you saw early in Chapter 7, different distributions name and install the dbm files in slightly different ways. If the provided files do not compile on your distribution, check back to Chapter 7 for further advice on the naming and location of the dbm files.

Running `server -i` allows the program to initialize a new CD database.

Needless to say, the client won't run unless the server is up and running. Here's the `makefile` to show how the programs fit together:

```
all:    server client
```

```
CC=cc
CFLAGS= -pedantic -Wall

# For debugging un-comment the next line
# DFLAGS=-DDEBUG_TRACE=1 -g

# Where, and which version, of dbm are we using.
# This assumes gdbm is pre-installed in a standard place, but we are
# going to use the gdbm compatibility routines, that make it emulate ndbm.
# We do this because ndbm is the 'most standard' of the dbm versions.
# Depending on your distribution, these may need changing.
DBM_INC_PATH=/usr/include/gdbm
DBM_LIB_PATH=/usr/lib
DBM_LIB_FILE=-lgdbm
# On some distributions you may need to change the above line to include
# the compatibility library, as shown below.
# DBM_LIB_FILE=-lgdbm_compat -lgdbm

.c.o:
    $(CC) $(CFLAGS) -I$(DBM_INC_PATH) $(DFLAGS) -c $<

app_ui.o: app_ui.c cd_data.h
cd_dbm.o: cd_dbm.c cd_data.h
client_f.o: clientif.c cd_data.h cliserv.h
pipe_imp.o: pipe_imp.c cd_data.h cliserv.h
server.o: server.c cd_data.h cliserv.h

client: app_ui.o clientif.o pipe_imp.o
    $(CC) -o client $(DFLAGS) app_ui.o clientif.o pipe_imp.o

server:  server.o cd_dbm.o pipe_imp.o
    $(CC) -o server -L$(DBM_LIB_PATH) $(DFLAGS) server.o cd_dbm.o pipe_imp.o -
l$(DBM_LIB_FILE)

clean:
    rm -f server client_app *.o *~
```

Aims

The aim is to split the part of the application that deals with the database away from the user inter-face part of the application. You also want to run a single-server process, but allow many simultane-ous clients, and to minimize changes to the existing code. Wherever possible, you will leave existing code unchanged.

To keep things simple, you also want to be able to create (and delete) pipes within the application, so there's no need for a system administrator to create named pipes before you can use them.

It's also important to ensure that you never "busy wait," wasting CPU time, for an event. As you've seen, Linux allows you to block, waiting for events without using significant resources. You should use the blocking nature of pipes to ensure that you use the CPU efficiently. After all, the server could, in the-ory, wait for many hours for a request to arrive.

Implementation

The earlier, single-process version of the application that you saw in Chapter 7 used a set of data access routines for manipulating the data. These were

```
int database_initialize(const int new_database);
void database_close(void);
cdc_entry get_cdc_entry(const char *cd_catalog_ptr);
cdt_entry get_cdt_entry(const char *cd_catalog_ptr, const int track_no);
int add_cdc_entry(const cdc_entry entry_to_add);
int add_cdt_entry(const cdt_entry entry_to_add);
int del_cdc_entry(const char *cd_catalog_ptr);
int del_cdt_entry(const char *cd_catalog_ptr, const int track_no);
cdc_entry search_cdc_entry(const char *cd_catalog_ptr,
                           int *first_call_ptr);
```

These functions provide a convenient place to make a clean separation between client and server.

In the single-process implementation, you can view the application as having two parts, even though it was compiled as a single program, as shown in Figure 13-6.

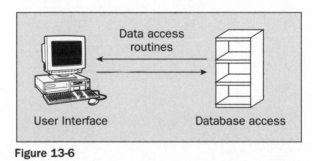

Figure 13-6

In the client-server implementation, you want to insert some named pipes and supporting code between the two major parts of the application. Figure 13-7 shows the structure you need.

In the implementation, both the client and server interface routines are put in the same file, `pipe_imp.c`. This keeps all the code that depends on the use of named pipes for the client/server implementation in a single file. The formatting and packaging of the data being passed is kept separate from the routines that implement the named pipes. You end up with more source files, but a better logical division between them. The calling structure in the application is illustrated in Figure 13-8.

The files `app_ui.c`, `client_if.c`, and `pipe_imp.c` are compiled and linked together to give a client program. The files `cd_dbm.c`, `server.c`, and `pipe_imp.c` are compiled and linked together to give a server program. A header file, `cliserv.h`, acts as a common definitions header file to tie the two together.

The files `app_ui.c` and `cd_dbm.c` have only very minor changes, principally to allow for the split into two programs. Because the application is now quite large and a significant proportion of the code is unchanged from that previously seen, we show here only the files `cliserv.h`, `client_if.c`, and `pipe_imp.c`.

Some parts of this file are dependent on the specific client/server implementation, in this case named pipes. We'll be changing to a different client/server model at the end of Chapter 14.

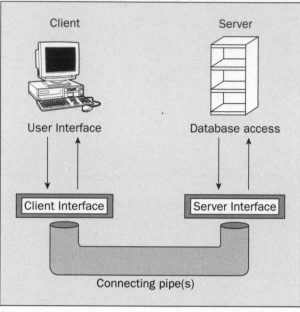

Figure 13-7

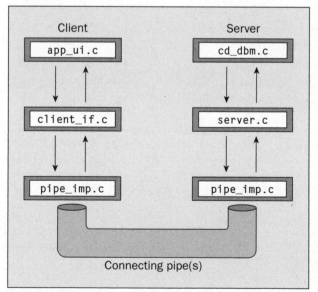

Figure 13-8

The Header File, cliserv.h

First look at `cliserv.h`. This file defines the client/server interface. It's required by both client and server implementations.

1. Following are the required `#include` headers:

```
#include <unistd.h>
#include <stdlib.h>
#include <stdio.h>
#include <fcntl.h>
#include <limits.h>
#include <sys/types.h>
#include <sys/stat.h>
```

2. You then define the named pipes. Use one pipe for the server and one pipe for each client. Because there may be multiple clients, the client incorporates a process ID into the name to ensure that its pipe is unique:

```
#define SERVER_PIPE "/tmp/server_pipe"
#define CLIENT_PIPE "/tmp/client_%d_pipe"

#define ERR_TEXT_LEN 80
```

3. Implement the commands as enumerated types, rather than `#defines`.

This is a good way of allowing the compiler to do more type checking and also helps in debugging the application, because many debuggers are able to show the name of enumerated constants, but not the name defined by a `#define` directive.

The first `typedef` gives the type of request being sent to the server; the second gives the server response to the client:

```
typedef enum {
    s_create_new_database = 0,
    s_get_cdc_entry,
    s_get_cdt_entry,
    s_add_cdc_entry,
    s_add_cdt_entry,
    s_del_cdc_entry,
    s_del_cdt_entry,
    s_find_cdc_entry
} client_request_e;

typedef enum {
    r_success = 0,
    r_failure,
    r_find_no_more
} server_response_e;
```

4. Next, declare a structure that will form the message passed in both directions between the two processes.

Because you don't actually need to return both a cdc_entry *and* cdt_entry *in the same response, you could have combined them in a union. However, for simplicity you can keep them separate. This also makes the code easier to maintain.*

```
typedef struct {
    pid_t               client_pid;
    client_request_e    request;
    server_response_e   response;
    cdc_entry           cdc_entry_data;
    cdt_entry           cdt_entry_data;
    char                error_text[ERR_TEXT_LEN + 1];
} message_db_t;
```

5. Finally, here are the pipe interface functions that perform data transfer, implemented in pipe_imp.c. These divide into server- and client-side functions, in the first and second blocks, respectively:

```
int server_starting(void);
void server_ending(void);
int read_request_from_client(message_db_t *rec_ptr);
int start_resp_to_client(const message_db_t mess_to_send);
int send_resp_to_client(const message_db_t mess_to_send);
void end_resp_to_client(void);

int client_starting(void);
void client_ending(void);
int send_mess_to_server(message_db_t mess_to_send);
int start_resp_from_server(void);
int read_resp_from_server(message_db_t *rec_ptr);
void end_resp_from_server(void);
```

We split the rest of the discussion into the client interface functions and details of the server- and client-side functions found in pipe_imp.c, and we look at the source code as necessary.

Client Interface Functions

Now look at clientif.c. This provides "fake" versions of the database access routines. These encode the request in a message_db_t structure and then use the routines in pipe_imp.c to transfer the request to the server. This allows you to make minimal changes to the original app_ui.c.

The Client's Interpreter

1. This file implements the nine database functions prototyped in cd_data.h. It does so by passing requests to the server and then returning the server response from the function, acting as an intermediary. The file starts with #include files and constants:

```
#define _POSIX_SOURCE
```

```
#include <unistd.h>
#include <stdlib.h>
#include <stdio.h>
#include <fcntl.h>
#include <limits.h>
#include <sys/types.h>
#include <sys/stat.h>

#include "cd_data.h"
#include "cliserv.h"
```

2. The static variable `mypid` reduces the number of calls to `getpid` that would otherwise be required. We use a local function, `read_one_response`, to eliminate duplicated code:

```
static pid_t mypid;

static int read_one_response(message_db_t *rec_ptr);
```

3. The `database_initialize` and `close` routines are still called, but are now used, respectively, for initializing the client side of the pipes interface and for removing redundant named pipes when the client exits:

```
int database_initialize(const int new_database)
{
    if (!client_starting()) return(0);
    mypid = getpid();
    return(1);

} /* database_initialize */

void database_close(void) {
    client_ending();
}
```

4. The `get_cdc_entry` routine is called to get a catalog entry from the database, given a CD catalog title. Here you encode the request in a `message_db_t` structure and pass it to the server. You then read the response back into a different `message_db_t` structure. If an entry is found, it's included inside the `message_db_t` structure as a `cdc_entry` structure, so you pass back the appropriate part of the structure:

```
cdc_entry get_cdc_entry(const char *cd_catalog_ptr)
{
    cdc_entry ret_val;
    message_db_t mess_send;
    message_db_t mess_ret;

    ret_val.catalog[0] = '\0';
    mess_send.client_pid = mypid;
    mess_send.request = s_get_cdc_entry;
    strcpy(mess_send.cdc_entry_data.catalog, cd_catalog_ptr);

    if (send_mess_to_server(mess_send)) {
```

```
            if (read_one_response(&mess_ret)) {
                if (mess_ret.response == r_success) {
                    ret_val = mess_ret.cdc_entry_data;
                } else {
                    fprintf(stderr, "%s", mess_ret.error_text);
                }
            } else {
                fprintf(stderr, "Server failed to respond\n");
            }
        } else {
            fprintf(stderr, "Server not accepting requests\n");
        }
        return(ret_val);
    }
```

5. Here's the source for the function `read_one_response` that you use to avoid duplicating code:

```
static int read_one_response(message_db_t *rec_ptr) {

    int return_code = 0;
    if (!rec_ptr) return(0);

    if (start_resp_from_server()) {
        if (read_resp_from_server(rec_ptr)) {
            return_code = 1;
        }
        end_resp_from_server();
    }
    return(return_code);
}
```

6. The other `get_xxx`, `del_xxx`, and `add_xxx` routines are implemented in a similar way to the `get_cdc_entry` function and are reproduced here for completeness. First, the function for retrieving CD tracks:

```
cdt_entry get_cdt_entry(const char *cd_catalog_ptr, const int track_no)
{
    cdt_entry ret_val;
    message_db_t mess_send;
    message_db_t mess_ret;

    ret_val.catalog[0] = '\0';
    mess_send.client_pid = mypid;
    mess_send.request = s_get_cdt_entry;
    strcpy(mess_send.cdt_entry_data.catalog, cd_catalog_ptr);
    mess_send.cdt_entry_data.track_no = track_no;

    if (send_mess_to_server(mess_send)) {
        if (read_one_response(&mess_ret)) {
            if (mess_ret.response == r_success) {
                ret_val = mess_ret.cdt_entry_data;
            } else {
                fprintf(stderr, "%s", mess_ret.error_text);
```

```
            }
        } else {
            fprintf(stderr, "Server failed to respond\n");
        }
    } else {
        fprintf(stderr, "Server not accepting requests\n");
    }
    return(ret_val);
}
```

7. Next, two functions for adding data, first to the catalog and then to the tracks database:

```
int add_cdc_entry(const cdc_entry entry_to_add)
{
    message_db_t mess_send;
    message_db_t mess_ret;

    mess_send.client_pid = mypid;
    mess_send.request = s_add_cdc_entry;
    mess_send.cdc_entry_data = entry_to_add;

    if (send_mess_to_server(mess_send)) {
        if (read_one_response(&mess_ret)) {
            if (mess_ret.response == r_success) {
                return(1);
            } else {
                fprintf(stderr, "%s", mess_ret.error_text);
            }
        } else {
            fprintf(stderr, "Server failed to respond\n");
        }
    } else {
        fprintf(stderr, "Server not accepting requests\n");
    }
    return(0);
}

int add_cdt_entry(const cdt_entry entry_to_add)
{
    message_db_t mess_send;
    message_db_t mess_ret;

    mess_send.client_pid = mypid;
    mess_send.request = s_add_cdt_entry;
    mess_send.cdt_entry_data = entry_to_add;

    if (send_mess_to_server(mess_send)) {
        if (read_one_response(&mess_ret)) {
            if (mess_ret.response == r_success) {
                return(1);
            } else {
                fprintf(stderr, "%s", mess_ret.error_text);
            }
        } else {
```

```
            fprintf(stderr, "Server failed to respond\n");
        }
    } else {
        fprintf(stderr, "Server not accepting requests\n");
    }
    return(0);
}
```

8. Last, two functions for data deletion:

```
int del_cdc_entry(const char *cd_catalog_ptr)
{
    message_db_t mess_send;
    message_db_t mess_ret;

    mess_send.client_pid = mypid;
    mess_send.request = s_del_cdc_entry;
    strcpy(mess_send.cdc_entry_data.catalog, cd_catalog_ptr);

    if (send_mess_to_server(mess_send)) {
        if (read_one_response(&mess_ret)) {
            if (mess_ret.response == r_success) {
                return(1);
            } else {
                fprintf(stderr, "%s", mess_ret.error_text);
            }
        } else {
            fprintf(stderr, "Server failed to respond\n");
        }
    } else {
        fprintf(stderr, "Server not accepting requests\n");
    }
    return(0);
}

int del_cdt_entry(const char *cd_catalog_ptr, const int track_no)
{
    message_db_t mess_send;
    message_db_t mess_ret;

    mess_send.client_pid = mypid;
    mess_send.request = s_del_cdt_entry;
    strcpy(mess_send.cdt_entry_data.catalog, cd_catalog_ptr);
    mess_send.cdt_entry_data.track_no = track_no;

    if (send_mess_to_server(mess_send)) {
        if (read_one_response(&mess_ret)) {
            if (mess_ret.response == r_success) {
                return(1);
            } else {
                fprintf(stderr, "%s", mess_ret.error_text);
            }
        } else {
            fprintf(stderr, "Server failed to respond\n");
        }
```

```
    } else {
        fprintf(stderr, "Server not accepting requests\n");
    }
    return(0);
}
```

Searching the Database

The function for the search on the CD key is more complex. The user of this function expects to call it once to start a search. We catered to this expectation in Chapter 7 by setting *first_call_ptr to true on this first call and the function then to return the first match. On subsequent calls to the search function, *first_call_ptr is false and further matches are returned, one per call.

Now that you've split the application across two processes, you can no longer allow the search to proceed one entry at a time in the server, because a different client may request a different search from the server while your search is in progress. You can't make the server side store the context (how far the search has gotten) for each client search separately, because the client side can simply stop searching part of the way through a search, when a user finds the CD he is looking for or if the client "falls over."

You can either change the way the search is performed or, as in the following code, hide the complexity in the interface routine. This code arranges for the server to return all the possible matches to a search and then store them in a temporary file until the client requests them.

1. This function looks more complicated than it is because it calls three pipe functions that you'll be looking at in the next section: send_mess_to_server, start_resp_from_server, and read_resp_from_server.

```
cdc_entry search_cdc_entry(const char *cd_catalog_ptr, int *first_call_ptr)
{
    message_db_t mess_send;
    message_db_t mess_ret;

    static FILE *work_file = (FILE *)0;
    static int entries_matching = 0;
    cdc_entry ret_val;

    ret_val.catalog[0] = '\0';

    if (!work_file && (*first_call_ptr == 0)) return(ret_val);
```

2. Here's the first call to search, that is, with *first_call_ptr set to true. It's set to false immediately, in case you forget. A work_file is created and the client message structure initialized.

```
    if (*first_call_ptr) {
        *first_call_ptr = 0;
        if (work_file) fclose(work_file);
        work_file = tmpfile();
        if (!work_file) return(ret_val);

        mess_send.client_pid = mypid;
        mess_send.request = s_find_cdc_entry;
        strcpy(mess_send.cdc_entry_data.catalog, cd_catalog_ptr);
```

3. Next, there's this three-deep condition test, which makes calls to functions in `pipe_imp.c`. If the message is successfully sent to the server, the client waits for the server's response. While `read`s from the server are successful, the search matches are returned to the client's `work_file` and the `entries_matching` counter is incremented.

```
if (send_mess_to_server(mess_send)) {
    if (start_resp_from_server()) {
        while (read_resp_from_server(&mess_ret)) {
            if (mess_ret.response == r_success) {
                fwrite(&mess_ret.cdc_entry_data, sizeof(cdc_entry), 1, work_file);
                entries_matching++;
            } else {
                break;
            }
        } /* while */
    } else {
        fprintf(stderr, "Server not responding\n");
    }
} else {
    fprintf(stderr, "Server not accepting requests\n");
}
```

4. The next test checks whether the search had any luck. Then the `fseek` call sets the `work_file` to the next place for data to be written.

```
if (entries_matching == 0) {
    fclose(work_file);
    work_file = (FILE *)0;
    return(ret_val);
}
(void)fseek(work_file, 0L, SEEK_SET);
```

5. If this is not the first call to the search function with this particular search term, the code checks whether there are any matches left. Finally, the next matching entry is read to the `ret_val` structure. The previous checks guarantee that a matching entry exists.

```
} else {
            /* not *first_call_ptr */
    if (entries_matching == 0) {
        fclose(work_file);
        work_file = (FILE *)0;
        return(ret_val);
    }
}

fread(&ret_val, sizeof(cdc_entry), 1, work_file);
entries_matching--;

return(ret_val);
}
```

The Server Interface, server.c

Just as the client side has an interface to the app_ui.c program, so the server side needs a program to control the (renamed) cd_access.c, now cd_dbm.c. The server's main function is listed here.

1. Start by declaring some global variables, a prototype for the process_command function, and a signal-catcher function to ensure a clean exit:

```c
#include <unistd.h>
#include <stdlib.h>
#include <stdio.h>
#include <fcntl.h>
#include <limits.h>
#include <signal.h>
#include <string.h>
#include <errno.h>
#include <sys/types.h>
#include <sys/stat.h>

#include "cd_data.h"
#include "cliserv.h"

int save_errno;
static int server_running = 1;

static void process_command(const message_db_t mess_command);

void catch_signals()
{
    server_running = 0;
}
```

2. Now you come to the main function. After checking that the signal-catching routines are all right, the program checks to see whether you passed -i on the command line. If you did, it will create a new database. If the call to the database_initialize routine in cd_dbm.c fails, an error message is shown. If all is well and the server is running, any requests from the client are fed to the process_command function, which you'll see in a moment.

```c
int main(int argc, char *argv[]) {
    struct sigaction new_action, old_action;
    message_db_t mess_command;
    int database_init_type = 0;

    new_action.sa_handler = catch_signals;
    sigemptyset(&new_action.sa_mask);
    new_action.sa_flags = 0;
    if ((sigaction(SIGINT, &new_action, &old_action) != 0) ||
        (sigaction(SIGHUP, &new_action, &old_action) != 0) ||
        (sigaction(SIGTERM, &new_action, &old_action) != 0)) {
        fprintf(stderr, "Server startup error, signal catching failed\n");
        exit(EXIT_FAILURE);
    }
```

```
        if (argc > 1) {
            argv++;
            if (strncmp("-i", *argv, 2) == 0) database_init_type = 1;
        }
        if (!database_initialize(database_init_type)) {
                fprintf(stderr, "Server error:-\
                        could not initialize database\n");
                exit(EXIT_FAILURE);
        }

        if (!server_starting()) exit(EXIT_FAILURE);

        while(server_running) {
            if (read_request_from_client(&mess_command)) {
                process_command(mess_command);
            } else {
                if(server_running) fprintf(stderr, "Server ended - can not \
                                            read pipe\n");
                server_running = 0;
            }
        } /* while */
        server_ending();
        exit(EXIT_SUCCESS);
}
```

3. Any client messages are fed to the `process_command` function, where they are fed into a `case` statement that makes the appropriate calls to `cd_dbm.c`:

```
static void process_command(const message_db_t comm)
{
    message_db_t resp;
    int first_time = 1;

    resp = comm; /* copy command back, then change resp as required */

    if (!start_resp_to_client(resp)) {
        fprintf(stderr, "Server Warning:-\
                start_resp_to_client %d failed\n", resp.client_pid);
        return;
    }

    resp.response = r_success;
    memset(resp.error_text, '\0', sizeof(resp.error_text));
    save_errno = 0;

    switch(resp.request) {
        case s_create_new_database:
            if (!database_initialize(1)) resp.response = r_failure;
            break;
        case s_get_cdc_entry:
            resp.cdc_entry_data =
                            get_cdc_entry(comm.cdc_entry_data.catalog);
            break;
        case s_get_cdt_entry:
```

```
            resp.cdt_entry_data =
                        get_cdt_entry(comm.cdt_entry_data.catalog,
                                     comm.cdt_entry_data.track_no);
            break;
        case s_add_cdc_entry:
            if (!add_cdc_entry(comm.cdc_entry_data)) resp.response =
                        r_failure;
            break;
        case s_add_cdt_entry:
            if (!add_cdt_entry(comm.cdt_entry_data)) resp.response =
                        r_failure;
            break;
        case s_del_cdc_entry:
            if (!del_cdc_entry(comm.cdc_entry_data.catalog)) resp.response
                       = r_failure;
            break;
        case s_del_cdt_entry:
            if (!del_cdt_entry(comm.cdt_entry_data.catalog,
                 comm.cdt_entry_data.track_no)) resp.response = r_failure;
            break;
        case s_find_cdc_entry:
            do {
                resp.cdc_entry_data =
                           search_cdc_entry(comm.cdc_entry_data.catalog,
                                            &first_time);
                if (resp.cdc_entry_data.catalog[0] != 0) {
                    resp.response = r_success;
                    if (!send_resp_to_client(resp)) {
                        fprintf(stderr, "Server Warning:-\
                            failed to respond to %d\n", resp.client_pid);
                        break;
                    }
                } else {
                    resp.response = r_find_no_more;
                }
            } while (resp.response == r_success);
        break;
        default:
            resp.response = r_failure;
            break;
    } /* switch */

    sprintf(resp.error_text, "Command failed:\n\t%s\n",
            strerror(save_errno));

    if (!send_resp_to_client(resp)) {
        fprintf(stderr, "Server Warning:-\
                failed to respond to %d\n", resp.client_pid);
    }

    end_resp_to_client();
    return;
}
```

Before you look at the actual pipe implementation, let's discuss the sequence of events that needs to occur to pass data between the client and server processes. Figure 13-9 shows both client and server processes starting and how both parties loop while processing commands and responses.

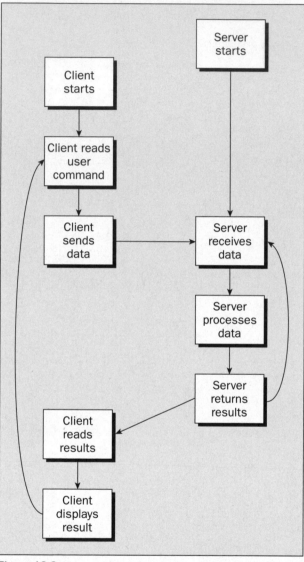

Figure 13-9

In this implementation, the situation is slightly more difficult, because, for a search request, the client passes a single command to the server and then expects to receive one or more responses from the server. This leads to some additional complexity, mainly in the client.

The Pipe

Here's the pipes implementation file, `pipe_imp.c`, which has both the client- and server-side functions.

As you saw in Chapter 10, the symbol DEBUG_TRACE *can be defined to show the sequence of calls as the client and server processes pass messages to each other.*

Pipes Implementation Header

1. First the #includes:

```
#include "cd_data.h"
#include "cliserv.h"
```

2. You also define some values that you need in different functions within the file:

```
static int server_fd = -1;
static pid_t mypid = 0;
static char client_pipe_name[PATH_MAX + 1] = {'\0'};
static int client_fd = -1;
static int client_write_fd = -1;
```

Server-Side Functions

Next, you need to look at the server-side functions. The next section shows the functions that open and close the named pipe and read messages from the clients. The following section shows the code that opens, sends, and closes the client pipes based on the process ID the client includes in its message.

Server Functions

1. The `server_starting` routine creates the named pipe from which the server will read commands. It then opens that pipe for reading. This open will block until a client opens the pipe for writing. Use a blocking mode so that the server can perform blocking reads on the pipe while waiting for commands to be sent to it.

```
int server_starting(void)
{
    #if DEBUG_TRACE
        printf("%d :- server_starting()\n",  getpid());
    #endif

        unlink(SERVER_PIPE);
    if (mkfifo(SERVER_PIPE, 0777) == -1) {
        fprintf(stderr, "Server startup error, no FIFO created\n");
        return(0);
    }

    if ((server_fd = open(SERVER_PIPE, O_RDONLY)) == -1) {
        if (errno == EINTR) return(0);
        fprintf(stderr, "Server startup error, no FIFO opened\n");
        return(0);
    }
    return(1);
}
```

2. When the server ends, it removes the named pipe so that clients can detect that no server is running:

```
void server_ending(void)
{
    #if DEBUG_TRACE
        printf("%d :- server_ending()\n", getpid());
    #endif

    (void)close(server_fd);
    (void)unlink(SERVER_PIPE);
}
```

3. The `read_request_from_client` function shown in the following example will block reading in the server pipe until a client writes a message into it:

```
int read_request_from_client(message_db_t *rec_ptr)
{
    int return_code = 0;
    int read_bytes;

    #if DEBUG_TRACE
        printf("%d :- read_request_from_client()\n", getpid());
    #endif

    if (server_fd != -1) {
        read_bytes = read(server_fd, rec_ptr, sizeof(*rec_ptr));
```

```
...
```

```
    }
    return(return_code);
}
```

4. In the special case where no clients have the pipe open for writing, the `read` will return 0; that is, it detects an EOF. Then the server closes the pipe and opens it again, so that it blocks until a client also opens the pipe. This is just the same as when the server first starts; you have reinitialized the server. Insert this code into the preceding function:

```
        if (read_bytes == 0) {
            (void)close(server_fd);
            if ((server_fd = open(SERVER_PIPE, O_RDONLY)) == -1) {
                if (errno != EINTR) {
                    fprintf(stderr, "Server error, FIFO open failed\n");
                }
                return(0);
            }
            read_bytes = read(server_fd, rec_ptr, sizeof(*rec_ptr));
        }
        if (read_bytes == sizeof(*rec_ptr)) return_code = 1;
```

The server is a single process that may be serving many clients simultaneously. Because each client uses a different pipe to receive its responses, the server needs to write to a different pipe to send responses to different clients. Because file descriptors are a limited resource, the server opens a client pipe for writing only when it has data to send.

The code splits the opening, writing, and closing of the client pipe into three separate functions. You need to do this when you're returning multiple results to a search, so you can open the pipe once, write many responses, and close it again.

Plumbing the Pipes

1.   First open the client pipe:

```
int start_resp_to_client(const message_db_t mess_to_send)
{
    #if DEBUG_TRACE
        printf("%d :- start_resp_to_client()\n", getpid());
    #endif

    (void)sprintf(client_pipe_name, CLIENT_PIPE, mess_to_send.client_pid);
    if ((client_fd = open(client_pipe_name, O_WRONLY)) == -1) return(0);
    return(1);
}
```

2.   The messages are all sent using calls to this function. You'll see the corresponding client-side functions that field the message later.

```
int send_resp_to_client(const message_db_t mess_to_send)
{
    int write_bytes;

    #if DEBUG_TRACE
        printf("%d :- send_resp_to_client()\n", getpid());
    #endif

    if (client_fd == -1) return(0);
    write_bytes = write(client_fd, &mess_to_send, sizeof(mess_to_send));
    if (write_bytes != sizeof(mess_to_send)) return(0);
    return(1);
}
```

3.   Finally, close the client pipe:

```
void end_resp_to_client(void)
{
    #if DEBUG_TRACE
        printf("%d :- end_resp_to_client()\n", getpid());
    #endif

    if (client_fd != -1) {
        (void)close(client_fd);
```

```
                     client_fd = -1;
          }
     }
```

Client-Side Functions

Complementing the server are the client functions in `pipe_imp.c`. They are very similar to the server-side functions, except for the worryingly named `send_mess_to_server` function.

Client Functions

1. After checking that a server is accessible, the `client_starting` function initializes the client-side pipe:

```
int client_starting(void)
{
    #if DEBUG_TRACE
        printf("%d :- client_starting\n",  getpid());
    #endif

    mypid = getpid();
    if ((server_fd = open(SERVER_PIPE, O_WRONLY)) == -1) {
        fprintf(stderr, "Server not running\n");
        return(0);
    }

    (void)sprintf(client_pipe_name, CLIENT_PIPE, mypid);
    (void)unlink(client_pipe_name);
    if (mkfifo(client_pipe_name, 0777) == -1) {
        fprintf(stderr, "Unable to create client pipe %s\n",
                    client_pipe_name);
        return(0);
    }
    return(1);
}
```

2. The `client_ending` function closes file descriptors and deletes the now-redundant named pipe:

```
void client_ending(void)
{
    #if DEBUG_TRACE
        printf("%d :- client_ending()\n",  getpid());
    #endif

    if (client_write_fd != -1) (void)close(client_write_fd);
    if (client_fd != -1) (void)close(client_fd);
    if (server_fd != -1) (void)close(server_fd);
    (void)unlink(client_pipe_name);
}
```

3. The `send_mess_to_server` function passes the request through the server pipe:

```
int send_mess_to_server(message_db_t mess_to_send)
{
```

```
    int write_bytes;

#if DEBUG_TRACE
    printf("%d :- send_mess_to_server()\n",  getpid());
#endif

    if (server_fd == -1) return(0);
    mess_to_send.client_pid = mypid;
    write_bytes = write(server_fd, &mess_to_send, sizeof(mess_to_send));
    if (write_bytes != sizeof(mess_to_send)) return(0);
    return(1);
}
```

As with the server-side functions you saw earlier, the client gets results back from the server using three functions, to cater to multiple search results.

Getting Server Results

1. This client function starts to listen for the server response. It opens a client pipe as read-only and then reopens this pipe's file as write-only. You'll see why a bit later in the section.

```
int start_resp_from_server(void)
{
#if DEBUG_TRACE
    printf("%d :- start resp_from_server()\n",  getpid());
#endif

    if (client_pipe_name[0] == '\0') return(0);
    if (client_fd != -1) return(1);

    client_fd = open(client_pipe_name, O_RDONLY);
    if (client_fd != -1) {
        client_write_fd = open(client_pipe_name, O_WRONLY);
        if (client_write_fd != -1) return(1);
        (void)close(client_fd);
        client_fd = -1;
    }
    return(0);
}
```

2. Here's the main `read` from the server that gets the matching database entries:

```
int read_resp_from_server(message_db_t *rec_ptr)
{
    int read_bytes;
    int return_code = 0;

#if DEBUG_TRACE
    printf("%d :- read_resp_from_server()\n",  getpid());
#endif

    if (!rec_ptr) return(0);
    if (client_fd == -1) return(0);

    read_bytes = read(client_fd, rec_ptr, sizeof(*rec_ptr));
```

```
        if (read_bytes == sizeof(*rec_ptr)) return_code = 1;
        return(return_code);
}
```

3.   And finally, here's the client function that marks the end of the server response:

```
void end_resp_from_server(void)
{
    #if DEBUG_TRACE
        printf("%d :- end_resp_from_server()\n", getpid());
    #endif

    /* This function is empty in the pipe implementation */
}
```

The second, additional open of the client pipe for writing in start_resp_from_server,

```
    client_write_fd = open(client_pipe_name, O_WRONLY);
```

is used to prevent a race condition when the server needs to respond to several requests from the client in quick succession.

To explain this a little more, consider the following sequence of events:

1.   The client writes a request to the server.

2.   The server reads the request, opens the client pipe, and sends the response back, but is suspended before it gets as far as closing the client pipe.

3.   The client opens its pipe for reading, reads the first response, and closes its pipe.

4.   The client then sends a new command and opens the client pipe for reading.

5.   The server then resumes running, closing its end of the client pipe.

Unfortunately, at this point the client is trying to read the pipe, looking for a response to its next request, but the read will return with 0 bytes because no process has the client pipe open for writing.

By allowing the client to open its pipe for both reading and writing, thus removing the need for repeatedly reopening the pipe, you avoid this race condition. Note that the client never writes to the pipe, so there's no danger of reading erroneous data.

Application Summary

You've now separated the CD database application into a client and a server, enabling you to develop the user interface and the underlying database technology independently. You can see that a well-defined database interface allows each major element of the application to make the best use of computer resources. If you took things a little further, you could change the pipes implementation to a networked one and use a dedicated database server machine. You learn more about networking in Chapter 15.

Summary

In this chapter, you looked at passing data between processes using pipes. First, you looked at unnamed pipes, created with the popen or the pipe call, and saw how, using a pipe and the dup call, you can pass data from one program to the standard input of another. You then looked at named pipes and showed how you can pass data between unrelated programs. Finally, you implemented a simple client/server example, using FIFOs to provide not only for process synchronization, but also bidirectional data flow.

Semaphores, Shared Memory, and Message Queues

In this chapter, we discuss a set of inter-process communication facilities that were originally introduced in the AT&T System V.2 release of UNIX. Because all these facilities appeared in the same release and have a similar programmatic interface, they are often referred to as the IPC (Inter-Process Communication) facilities, or more commonly System V IPC. As you've already seen, they are by no means the only way of communicating between processes, but the expression System V IPC is usually used to refer to these specific facilities.

We cover the following topics in this chapter:

❑ Semaphores, for managing access to resources

❑ Shared memory, for highly efficient data sharing between programs

❑ Messaging, for an easy way of passing data between programs

Semaphores

When you write programs that use threads operating in multiuser systems, multiprocessing systems, or a combination of the two, you may often discover that you have *critical sections* of code, where you need to ensure that a single process (or a single thread of execution) has exclusive access to a resource.

Semaphores have a complex programming interface. Fortunately, you can easily provide a much-simplified interface that is sufficient for most semaphore-programming problems.

In the first example application in Chapter 7 — using dbm to access a database — the data could be corrupted if multiple programs tried to update the database at exactly the same time. There's no trouble with two different programs asking different users to enter data for the database; the only potential problem is in the parts of the code that update the database. These sections of code, which actually perform data updates and need to execute exclusively, are called *critical sections*. Frequently they are just a few lines of code from much larger programs.

To prevent problems caused by more than one program simultaneously accessing a shared resource, you need a way of generating and using a token that grants access to only one thread of execution in a critical section at a time. You saw briefly in Chapter 12 some thread-specific ways you could use a mutex or semaphores to control access to critical sections in a threaded program. In this chapter, we return to the topic of semaphores, but look more generally at how they are used between different processes.

The semaphore functions used with threads that you saw in Chapter 12 are not the more general ones we discuss in this chapter, so be careful not to confuse the two types.

It's surprisingly difficult to write general-purpose code that ensures that one program has exclusive access to a particular resource, although there's a solution known as Dekker's Algorithm. Unfortunately, this algorithm relies on a "busy wait," or "spin lock," where a process runs continuously, waiting for a memory location to be changed. In a multitasking environment such as Linux, this is an undesirable waste of CPU resources. The situation is much easier if hardware support, generally in the form of specific CPU instructions, is available to support exclusive access. An example of hardware support would be an instruction to access and increment a register in an atomic way, such that no other instruction (not even an interrupt) could occur between the read/increment/write operations.

One possible solution that you've already seen is to create files using the O_EXCL flag with the open function, which provides atomic file creation. This allows a single process to succeed in obtaining a token: the newly created file. This method is fine for simple problems, but rather messy and very inefficient for more complex examples.

An important step forward in this area of concurrent programming occurred when Edsger Dijkstra, a Dutch computer scientist, introduced the concept of the semaphore. As briefly mentioned in Chapter 12, a semaphore is a special variable that takes only whole positive numbers and upon which programs can only act atomically. In this chapter we expand on that earlier simplified definition. We show in more detail how semaphores function, and how the more general-purpose functions can be used between separate processes, rather than the special case of multi-threaded programs you saw in Chapter 12.

A more formal definition of a semaphore is a special variable on which only two operations are allowed; these operations are officially termed *wait* and *signal*. Because "wait" and "signal" already have special meanings in Linux programming, we'll use the original notation:

❑   P(semaphore variable) for wait

❑.   V(semaphore variable) for signal

These letters come from the Dutch words for wait (*passeren*: to pass, as in a checkpoint before the critical section) and signal (*vrijgeven*: to give or release, as in giving up control of the critical section). You may also come across the terms "up" and "down" used in relation to semaphores, taken from the use of signaling flags.

Semaphore Definition

The simplest semaphore is a variable that can take only the values 0 and 1, a *binary semaphore*. This is the most common form. Semaphores that can take many positive values are called *general semaphores*. For the remainder of this chapter, we concentrate on binary semaphores.

The definitions of P and V are surprisingly simple. Suppose you have a semaphore variable sv. The two operations are then defined as follows:

P(sv)	If sv is greater than zero, decrement sv. If sv is zero, suspend execution of this process.
V(sv)	If some other process has been suspended waiting for sv, make it resume execution. If no process is suspended waiting for sv, increment sv.

Another way of thinking about semaphores is that the semaphore variable, sv, is true when the critical section is available, is decremented by P(sv) so it's false when the critical section is busy, and is incremented by V(sv) when the critical section is again available. Be aware that simply having a normal variable that you decrement and increment is not good enough, because you can't express in C, C++, C#, or almost any conventional programming language the need to make a single, atomic operation of the test to see whether the variable is true, and if so change the variable to make it false. This is what makes the semaphore operations special.

A Theoretical Example

You can see how this works with a simple theoretical example. Suppose you have two processes proc1 and proc2, both of which need exclusive access to a database at some point in their execution. You define a single binary semaphore, sv, which starts with the value 1 and can be accessed by both processes. Both processes then need to perform the same processing to access the critical section of code; indeed, the two processes could simply be different invocations of the same program.

The two processes share the sv semaphore variable. Once one process has executed P(sv), it has obtained the semaphore and can enter the critical section. The second process is prevented from entering the critical section because when it attempts to execute P(sv), it's made to wait until the first process has left the critical section and executed V(sv) to release the semaphore.

The required pseudocode is identical for both processes:

```
semaphore sv = 1;

loop forever {
    P(sv);
    critical code section;
    V(sv);
    noncritical code section;
}
```

The code is surprisingly simple because the definition of the P and V operations is very powerful.
Figure 14-1 shows a diagram showing how the P and V operations act as a gate into critical sections of code.

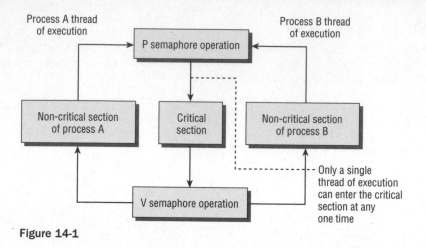

Figure 14-1

Linux Semaphore Facilities

Now that you've seen what semaphores are and how they work in theory, you can look at how the features are implemented in Linux. The interface is rather elaborate and offers far more facilities than are generally required. All the Linux semaphore functions operate on arrays of general semaphores rather than a single binary semaphore. At first sight, this just seems to make things more complicated, but in complex cases where a process needs to lock multiple resources, the ability to operate on an array of semaphores is a big advantage. In this chapter, we concentrate on using single semaphores, because in most cases that's all you will need to use.

The semaphore function definitions are

```
#include <sys/sem.h>

int semctl(int sem_id, int sem_num, int command, ...);
int semget(key_t key, int num_sems, int sem_flags);
int semop(int sem_id, struct sembuf *sem_ops, size_t num_sem_ops);
```

The header file sys/sem.h *usually relies on two other header files,* sys/types.h *and* sys/ipc.h. *Normally they are automatically included by* sys/sem.h *and you do not need to explicitly add a* #include *for them.*

As you work through each function in turn, remember that these functions were designed to work for arrays of semaphore values, which makes their operation significantly more complex than would have been required for a single semaphore.

Notice that key acts very much like a filename in that it represents a resource that programs may use and cooperate in using if they agree on a common name. Similarly, the identifier returned by semget and used by the other shared memory functions is very much like the FILE * file stream returned by fopen in that it's a value used by the process to access the shared file. Just as with files different processes will have different semaphore identifiers, though they refer to the same semaphore. This use of a key and identifiers is common to all of the IPC facilities discussed here, although each facility uses independent keys and identifiers.

semget

The `semget` function creates a new semaphore or obtains the semaphore key of an existing semaphore:

```
int semget(key_t key, int num_sems, int sem_flags);
```

The first parameter, `key`, is an integral value used to allow unrelated processes to access the same semaphore. All semaphores are accessed indirectly by the program supplying a key, for which the system then generates a semaphore identifier. The semaphore key is used only with `semget`. All other semaphore functions use the semaphore identifier returned from `semget`.

There is a special semaphore `key` value, `IPC_PRIVATE`, that is intended to create a semaphore that only the creating process could access, but this rarely has any useful purpose. You should provide a unique, non-zero integer value for `key` when you want to create a new semaphore.

The `num_sems` parameter is the number of semaphores required. This is almost always 1.

The `sem_flags` parameter is a set of flags, very much like the flags to the `open` function. The lower nine bits are the permissions for the semaphore, which behave like file permissions. In addition, these can be bitwise ORed with the value `IPC_CREAT` to create a new semaphore. It's not an error to have the `IPC_CREAT` flag set and give the key of an existing semaphore. The `IPC_CREAT` flag is silently ignored if it is not required. You can use `IPC_CREAT` and `IPC_EXCL` together to ensure that you obtain a new, unique semaphore. It will return an error if the semaphore already exists.

The `semget` function returns a positive (nonzero) value on success; this is the semaphore identifier used in the other semaphore functions. On error, it returns −1.

semop

The function `semop` is used for changing the value of the semaphore:

```
int semop(int sem_id, struct sembuf *sem_ops, size_t num_sem_ops);
```

The first parameter, `sem_id`, is the semaphore identifier, as returned from `semget`. The second parameter, `sem_ops`, is a pointer to an array of structures, each of which will have at least the following members:

```
struct sembuf {
    short sem_num;
    short sem_op;
    short sem_flg;
}
```

The first member, `sem_num`, is the semaphore number, usually 0 unless you're working with an array of semaphores. The `sem_op` member is the value by which the semaphore should be changed. (You can change a semaphore by amounts other than 1.) In general, only two values are used, −1, which is your P operation to wait for a semaphore to become available, and +1, which is your V operation to signal that a semaphore is now available.

The final member, `sem_flg`, is usually set to `SEM_UNDO`. This causes the operating system to track the changes made to the semaphore by the current process and, if the process terminates without releasing the semaphore, allows the operating system to automatically release the semaphore if it was held by this process. It's good practice to set sem_flg to SEM_UNDO, unless you specifically require different behavior. If you do decide you need a value other than SEM_UNDO, it's important to be consistent, or you can get very confused as to whether the kernel is attempting to "tidy up" your semaphores when your process exits.

All actions called for by semop are taken together to avoid a race condition implied by the use of multiple semaphores. You can find full details of the processing of semop in the manual pages.

semctl

The semctl function allows direct control of semaphore information:

```
int semctl(int sem_id, int sem_num, int command, ...);
```

The first parameter, sem_id, is a semaphore identifier, obtained from semget. The sem_num parameter is the semaphore number. You use this when you're working with arrays of semaphores. Usually, this is 0, the first and only semaphore. The command parameter is the action to take, and a fourth parameter, if present, is a union semun, which according to the X/OPEN specification must have at least the following members:

```
union semun {
    int val;
    struct semid_ds *buf;
    unsigned short *array;
}
```

Most versions of Linux have a definition of the semun union in a header file (usually sem.h), though X/Open does say that you have to declare your own. If you do find that you need to declare your own, check the manual pages for semctl to see if there is a definition given. If there is, we suggest you use exactly the definition given in your manual, even if it differs from that given here.

There are many different possible values of command allowed for semctl. Only the two that we describe here are commonly used. For full details of the semctl function, you should consult the manual page.

The two common values of command are:

❑   SETVAL: Used for initializing a semaphore to a known value. The value required is passed as the val member of the union semun. This is required to set the semaphore up before it's used for the first time.

❑   IPC_RMID: Used for deleting a semaphore identifier when it's no longer required.

The semctl function returns different values depending on the command parameter. For SETVAL and IPC_RMID it returns 0 for success and –1 on error.

Using Semaphores

As you can see from the previous section's descriptions, semaphore operations can be rather complex. This is most unfortunate, because programming multiple processes or threads with critical sections is quite a difficult problem on its own and having a complex programming interface simply adds to the intellectual burden.

Fortunately you can solve most problems that require semaphores using only a single binary semaphore, the simplest type. In the following example, you use the full programming interface to create a much simpler P and V type interface for a binary semaphore. You then use this much simpler interface to demonstrate how semaphores function.

To experiment with semaphores, you use a single program, sem1.c, that you can invoke several times. You use an optional parameter to specify whether the program is responsible for creating and destroying the semaphore.

You use the output of two different characters to indicate entering and leaving the critical section. The program invoked with a parameter prints an X on entering and exiting its critical section. Other invocations of the program print an O on entering and exiting their critical sections. Because only one process should be able to enter its critical section at any given time, all X and O characters should appear in pairs.

Try It Out   Semaphores

1.   After the system #includes, you include a file semun.h. This defines the union semun, as required by X/OPEN, if the system include sys/sem.h doesn't already define it. Then come the function prototypes, and the global variable, before you come to the main function. There the semaphore is created with a call to semget, which returns the semaphore ID. If the program is the first to be called (that is, it's called with a parameter and argc > 1), a call is made to set_semvalue to initialize the semaphore and op_char is set to X:

```
#include <unistd.h>
#include <stdlib.h>
#include <stdio.h>


#include <sys/sem.h>

#include "semun.h"


static int set_semvalue(void);
static void del_semvalue(void);
static int semaphore_p(void);
static int semaphore_v(void);

static int sem_id;


int main(int argc, char *argv[])
{
    int i;
    int pause_time;
    char op_char = 'O';

    srand((unsigned int)getpid());

    sem_id = semget((key_t)1234, 1, 0666 | IPC_CREAT);

    if (argc > 1) {
```

```
        if (!set_semvalue()) {
            fprintf(stderr, "Failed to initialize semaphore\n");
            exit(EXIT_FAILURE);
        }
        op_char = 'X';
        sleep(2);
    }
```

2. Then you have a loop that enters and leaves the critical section 10 times. There you first make a
    call to `semaphore_p`, which sets the semaphore to wait as this program is about to enter the
    critical section:

```
    for(i = 0; i < 10; i++) {

        if (!semaphore_p()) exit(EXIT_FAILURE);
        printf("%c", op_char);fflush(stdout);
        pause_time = rand() % 3;
        sleep(pause_time);
        printf("%c", op_char);fflush(stdout);
```

3. After the critical section, you call `semaphore_v`, setting the semaphore as available, before
    going through the `for` loop again after a random wait. After the loop, the call to `del_semvalue`
    is made to clean up the code:

```
        if (!semaphore_v()) exit(EXIT_FAILURE);

        pause_time = rand() % 2;
        sleep(pause_time);
    }

    printf("\n%d - finished\n", getpid());

    if (argc > 1) {
        sleep(10);
        del_semvalue();
    }

    exit(EXIT_SUCCESS);
}
```

4. The function `set_semvalue` initializes the semaphore using the `SETVAL` command in a `semctl`
    call. You need to do this before you can use the semaphore:

```
static int set_semvalue(void)
{
    union semun sem_union;

    sem_union.val = 1;
    if (semctl(sem_id, 0, SETVAL, sem_union) == -1) return(0);
    return(1);
}
```

5. The `del_semvalue` function has almost the same form, except that the call to `semctl` uses the command `IPC_RMID` to remove the semaphore's ID:

```
static void del_semvalue(void)
{
    union semun sem_union;

    if (semctl(sem_id, 0, IPC_RMID, sem_union) == -1)
        fprintf(stderr, "Failed to delete semaphore\n");
}
```

6. `semaphore_p` changes the semaphore by –1. This is the "wait" operation:

```
static int semaphore_p(void)
{
    struct sembuf sem_b;

    sem_b.sem_num = 0;
    sem_b.sem_op = -1; /* P() */
    sem_b.sem_flg = SEM_UNDO;
    if (semop(sem_id, &sem_b, 1) == -1) {
        fprintf(stderr, "semaphore_p failed\n");
        return(0);
    }
    return(1);
}
```

7. `semaphore_v` is similar except for setting the `sem_op` part of the `sembuf` structure to 1. This is the "release" operation, so that the semaphore becomes available:

```
static int semaphore_v(void)
{
    struct sembuf sem_b;

    sem_b.sem_num = 0;
    sem_b.sem_op = 1; /* V() */
    sem_b.sem_flg = SEM_UNDO;
    if (semop(sem_id, &sem_b, 1) == -1) {
        fprintf(stderr, "semaphore_v failed\n");
        return(0);
    }
    return(1);
}
```

Notice that this simple program allows only a single binary semaphore per program, although you could extend it to pass the semaphore variable if you need more semaphores. Normally, a single binary semaphore is sufficient.

You can test your program by invoking it several times. The first time, you pass a parameter to tell the program that it's responsible for creating and deleting the semaphore. The other invocations have no parameter.

Here's some sample output, with two invocations of the program.

```
$ cc sem1.c -o sem1
$ ./sem1 1 &
[1] 1082
$ ./sem1
OOXXOOXXOOXXOOXXOOXXOOOOXXOOXXOOXXOOXXXX
1083 - finished
1082 - finished
$
```

Remember that "O" represents the first invocation of the program, and "X" the second invocation of the program. Because each program prints a character as it enters and again as it leaves the critical section, each character should only appear as part of a pair. As you can see, the Os and Xs are indeed properly paired, indicating that the critical section is being correctly processed. If this doesn't work on your particular system, you may have to use the command stty -tostop before invoking the program to ensure that the background program generating tty output does not cause a signal to be generated.

How It Works

The program starts by obtaining a semaphore identity from the (arbitrary) key that you've chosen using the semget function. The IPC_CREAT flag causes the semaphore to be created if one is required.

If the program has a parameter, it's responsible for initializing the semaphore, which it does with the function set_semvalue, a simplified interface to the more general semctl function. It also uses the presence of the parameter to determine which character it should print out. The sleep simply allows you some time to invoke other copies of the program before this copy gets to execute too many times around its loop. You use srand and rand to introduce some pseudo-random timing into the program.

The program then loops 10 times, with pseudo-random waits in its critical and noncritical sections. The critical section is guarded by calls to your semaphore_p and semaphore_v functions, which are simplified interfaces to the more general semop function.

Before it deletes the semaphore, the program that was invoked with a parameter then waits to allow other invocations to complete. If the semaphore isn't deleted, it will continue to exist in the system even though no programs are using it. In real programs, it's very important to ensure you don't unintentionally leave semaphores around after execution. It may cause problems next time you run the program, and semaphores are a limited resource that you must conserve.

Shared Memory

Shared memory is the second of the three IPC facilities. It allows two unrelated processes to access the same logical memory. Shared memory is a very efficient way of transferring data between two running processes. Although the X/Open standard doesn't require it, it's probable that most implementations of shared memory arrange for the memory being shared between different processes to be the same physical memory.

Shared memory is a special range of addresses that is created by IPC for one process and appears in the address space of that process. Other processes can then "attach" the same shared memory segment into their own address space. All processes can access the memory locations just as if the memory had been allocated by `malloc`. If one process writes to the shared memory, the changes immediately become visible to any other process that has access to the same shared memory.

Shared memory provides an efficient way of sharing and passing data between multiple processes. By itself, shared memory doesn't provide any synchronization facilities. Because it provides no synchronization facilities, you usually need to use some other mechanism to synchronize access to the shared memory. Typically, you might use shared memory to provide efficient access to large areas of memory and pass small messages to synchronize access to that memory.

There are no automatic facilities to prevent a second process from starting to read the shared memory before the first process has finished writing to it. It's the responsibility of the programmer to synchronize access. Figure 14-2 shows an illustration of how shared memory works.

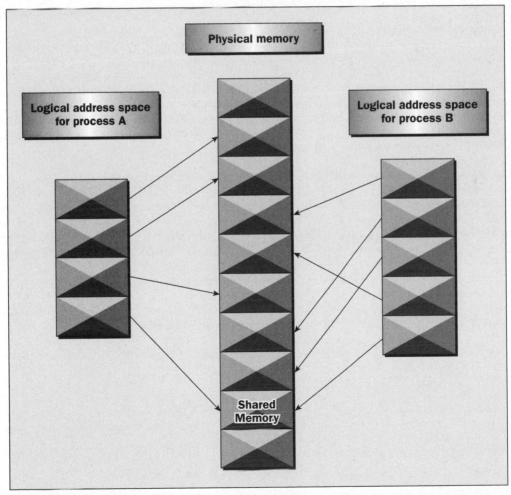

Figure 14-2

The arrows show the mapping of the logical address space of each process to the physical memory available. In practice, the situation is more complex because the available memory actually consists of a mix of physical memory and memory pages that have been swapped out to disk.

The functions for shared memory resemble those for semaphores:

```
#include <sys/shm.h>

void *shmat(int shm_id, const void *shm_addr, int shmflg);
int shmctl(int shm_id, int cmd, struct shmid_ds *buf);
int shmdt(const void *shm_addr);
int shmget(key_t key, size_t size, int shmflg);
```

As with semaphores, the include files sys/types.h and sys/ipc.h are normally automatically included by shm.h.

shmget

You create shared memory using the shmget function:

```
int shmget(key_t key, size_t size, int shmflg);
```

As with semaphores, the program provides key, which effectively names the shared memory segment, and the shmget function returns a shared memory identifier that is used in subsequent shared memory functions. There's a special key value, IPC_PRIVATE, that creates shared memory private to the process. You wouldn't normally use this value, and you may find the private shared memory is not actually private on some Linux systems.

The second parameter, size, specifies the amount of memory required in bytes.

The third parameter, shmflg, consists of nine permission flags that are used in the same way as the mode flags for creating files. A special bit defined by IPC_CREAT must be bitwise ORed with the permissions to create a new shared memory segment. It's not an error to have the IPC_CREAT flag set and pass the key of an existing shared memory segment. The IPC_CREAT flag is silently ignored if it is not required.

The permission flags are very useful with shared memory because they allow a process to create shared memory that can be written by processes owned by the creator of the shared memory, but only read by processes that other users have created. You can use this to provide efficient read-only access to data by placing it in shared memory without the risk of its being changed by other users.

If the shared memory is successfully created, shmget returns a nonnegative integer, the shared memory identifier. On failure, it returns –1.

shmat

When you first create a shared memory segment, it's not accessible by any process. To enable access to the shared memory, you must attach it to the address space of a process. You do this with the shmat function:

```
void *shmat(int shm_id, const void *shm_addr, int shmflg);
```

The first parameter, `shm_id`, is the shared memory identifier returned from `shmget`.

The second parameter, `shm_addr`, is the address at which the shared memory is to be attached to the current process. This should almost always be a null pointer, which allows the system to choose the address at which the memory appears.

The third parameter, `shmflg`, is a set of bitwise flags. The two possible values are SHM_RND, which, in conjunction with `shm_addr`, controls the address at which the shared memory is attached, and SHM_RDONLY, which makes the attached memory read-only. It's very rare to need to control the address at which shared memory is attached; you should normally allow the system to choose an address for you, because doing otherwise will make the application highly hardware-dependent.

If the `shmat` call is successful, it returns a pointer to the first byte of shared memory. On failure –1 is returned.

The shared memory will have read or write access depending on the owner (the creator of the shared memory), the permissions, and the owner of the current process. Permissions on shared memory are similar to the permissions on files.

An exception to this rule arises if `shmflg & SHM_RDONLY` is `true`. Then the shared memory won't be writable, even if permissions would have allowed write access.

shmdt

The `shmdt` function detaches the shared memory from the current process. It takes a pointer to the address returned by `shmat`. On success, it returns 0, on error –1. Note that detaching the shared memory doesn't delete it; it just makes that memory unavailable to the current process.

shmctl

The control functions for shared memory are (thankfully) somewhat simpler than the more complex ones for semaphores:

```
int shmctl(int shm_id, int command, struct shmid_ds *buf);
```

The `shmid_ds` structure has at least the following members:

```
struct shmid_ds {
    uid_t shm_perm.uid;
    uid_t shm_perm.gid;
    mode_t shm_perm.mode;
}
```

The first parameter, `shm_id`, is the identifier returned from `shmget`.

The second parameter, `command`, is the action to take. It can take three values, shown in the following table.

Command	Description
IPC_STAT	Sets the data in the shmid_ds structure to reflect the values associated with the shared memory.
IPC_SET	Sets the values associated with the shared memory to those provided in the shmid_ds data structure, if the process has permission to do so.
IPC_RMID	Deletes the shared memory segment.

The third parameter, buf, is a pointer to the structure containing the modes and permissions for the shared memory.

On success, it returns 0, on failure, –1. X/Open doesn't specify what happens if you attempt to delete a shared memory segment while it's attached. Generally, a shared memory segment that is attached but deleted continues to function until it has been detached from the last process. However, because this behavior isn't specified, it's best not to rely on it.

Try It Out   Shared Memory

Now that you've seen the shared memory functions, you can write some code to use them. In this Try It Out, you write a pair of programs, shm1.c and shm2.c. The first (the consumer) will create a shared memory segment and then display any data that is written into it. The second (the producer) will attach to an existing shared memory segment and allow you to enter data into that segment.

1. First create a common header file to describe the shared memory you want to pass around. Call this shm_com.h:

```
#define TEXT_SZ 2048

struct shared_use_st {
    int written_by_you;
    char some_text[TEXT_SZ];
};
```

This defines a structure to use in both the consumer and producer programs. You use an int flag written_by_you to tell the consumer when data has been written to the rest of the structure and arbitrarily decide that you need to transfer up to 2k of text.

2. The first program, shm1.c, is the consumer. After the headers, the shared memory segment (the size of your shared memory structure) is created with a call to shmget, with the IPC_CREAT bit specified:

```
#include <unistd.h>
#include <stdlib.h>
#include <stdio.h>
#include <string.h>


#include <sys/shm.h>
```

```
#include "shm_com.h"

int main()
{
    int running = 1;
    void *shared_memory = (void *)0;
    struct shared_use_st *shared_stuff;
    int shmid;

    srand((unsigned int)getpid());

    shmid = shmget((key_t)1234, sizeof(struct shared_use_st), 0666 | IPC_CREAT);

    if (shmid == -1) {
        fprintf(stderr, "shmget failed\n");
        exit(EXIT_FAILURE);
    }
```

3. You now make the shared memory accessible to the program:

```
    shared_memory = shmat(shmid, (void *)0, 0);
    if (shared_memory == (void *)-1) {
        fprintf(stderr, "shmat failed\n");
        exit(EXIT_FAILURE);
    }

    printf("Memory attached at %X\n", (int)shared_memory);
```

4. The next portion of the program assigns the shared_memory segment to shared_stuff, which then prints out any text in written_by_you. The loop continues until end is found in written_by_you. The call to sleep forces the consumer to sit in its critical section, which makes the producer wait:

```
    shared_stuff = (struct shared_use_st *)shared_memory;
    shared_stuff->written_by_you = 0;
    while(running) {
        if (shared_stuff->written_by_you) {
            printf("You wrote: %s", shared_stuff->some_text);
            sleep( rand() % 4 ); /* make the other process wait for us ! */
            shared_stuff->written_by_you = 0;
            if (strncmp(shared_stuff->some_text, "end", 3) == 0) {
                running = 0;
            }
        }
    }
```

5. Finally, the shared memory is detached and then deleted:

```
    if (shmdt(shared_memory) == -1) {
        fprintf(stderr, "shmdt failed\n");
        exit(EXIT_FAILURE);
    }

    if (shmctl(shmid, IPC_RMID, 0) == -1) {
```

```
        fprintf(stderr, "shmctl(IPC_RMID) failed\n");
        exit(EXIT_FAILURE);
    }

    exit(EXIT_SUCCESS);
}
```

6.   The second program, shm2.c, is the producer; it allows you to enter data for consumers. It's very similar to shm1.c and looks like this:

```c
#include <unistd.h>
#include <stdlib.h>
#include <stdio.h>
#include <string.h>


#include <sys/shm.h>

#include "shm_com.h"

int main()
{
    int running = 1;
    void *shared_memory = (void *)0;
    struct shared_use_st *shared_stuff;
    char buffer[BUFSIZ];
    int shmid;

    shmid = shmget((key_t)1234, sizeof(struct shared_use_st), 0666 | IPC_CREAT);

    if (shmid == -1) {
        fprintf(stderr, "shmget failed\n");
        exit(EXIT_FAILURE);
    }
    shared_memory = shmat(shmid, (void *)0, 0);
    if (shared_memory == (void *)-1) {
        fprintf(stderr, "shmat failed\n");
        exit(EXIT_FAILURE);
    }

    printf("Memory attached at %X\n", (int)shared_memory);

    shared_stuff = (struct shared_use_st *)shared_memory;
    while(running) {
        while(shared_stuff->written_by_you == 1) {
            sleep(1);
            printf("waiting for client...\n");
        }
        printf("Enter some text: ");
        fgets(buffer, BUFSIZ, stdin);

        strncpy(shared_stuff->some_text, buffer, TEXT_SZ);
        shared_stuff->written_by_you = 1;
```

```
        if (strncmp(buffer, "end", 3) == 0) {
                running = 0;
        }
    }

    if (shmdt(shared_memory) == -1) {
        fprintf(stderr, "shmdt failed\n");
        exit(EXIT_FAILURE);
    }
    exit(EXIT_SUCCESS);
}
```

When you run these programs, you get sample output such as this:

```
$ ./shm1 &
[1] 294
Memory attached at 40017000
$ ./shm2
Memory attached at 40017000
Enter some text: hello
You wrote: hello
waiting for client...
waiting for client...
Enter some text: Linux!
You wrote: Linux!
waiting for client...
waiting for client...
waiting for client...
Enter some text: end
You wrote: end
$
```

How It Works

The first program, shm1, creates the shared memory segment and then attaches it to its address space. You impose a structure, shared_use_st on the first part of the shared memory. This has a flag, written_by_you, which is set when data is available. When this flag is set, the program reads the text, prints it out, and clears the flag to show it has read the data. Use the special string, end, to allow a clean exit from the loop. The program then detaches the shared memory segment and deletes it.

The second program, shm2, gets and attaches the same shared memory segment, because it uses the same key, 1234. It then prompts the user to enter some text. If the flag written_by_you is set, shm2 knows that the client process hasn't yet read the previous data and waits for it. When the other process clears this flag, shm2 writes the new data and sets the flag. It also uses the magic string end to terminate and detach the shared memory segment.

Notice that you had to provide your own, rather crude synchronization flag, written_by_you, which involves a very inefficient busy wait (by continuously looping). This keeps the example simple, however in real programs you would have used a semaphore, or perhaps passed a message, either using a pipe or IPC messages (which we discuss in the next section), or generated a signal (as shown in Chapter 11) to provide a more efficient synchronization mechanism between the reading and writing parts of the application.

Message Queues

We'll now take a look at the third and final System V IPC facility: *message queues*. In many ways, message queues are like named pipes, but without the complexity associated with opening and closing the pipe. However, using messages doesn't get you away from the problems that you have with named pipes, such as blocking on full pipes.

Message queues provide a reasonably easy and efficient way of passing data between two unrelated processes. They have the advantage over named pipes that the message queue exists independently of both the sending and receiving processes, which removes some of the difficulties that occur in synchronizing the opening and closing of named pipes.

Message queues provide a way of sending a block of data from one process to another. Additionally, each block of data is considered to have a type, and a receiving process may receive blocks of data having different type values independently. The good news is that you can almost totally avoid the synchronization and blocking problems of named pipes by sending messages. Even better, you can "look ahead" for messages that are urgent in some way. The bad news is that, just like pipes, there's a maximum size limit imposed on each block of data and also a limit on the maximum total size of all blocks on all queues throughout the system.

While stating that these limits are imposed, the X/Open specification offers no way of discovering what the limits are, except that exceeding them is a valid reason for some message queue functions to fail. Linux does have two `defines`, `MSGMAX` and `MSGMNB`, which define the maximum size in bytes of an individual message and the maximum size of a queue, respectively. These macros may be different or, for that matter, not even present on other systems.

The message queue function definitions are:

```
#include <sys/msg.h>

int msgctl(int msqid, int cmd, struct msqid_ds *buf);
int msgget(key_t key, int msgflg);
int msgrcv(int msqid, void *msg_ptr, size_t msg_sz, long int msgtype, int msgflg);
int msgsnd(int msqid, const void *msg_ptr, size_t msg_sz, int msgflg);
```

As with semaphores and shared memory, the include files `sys/types.h` and `sys/ipc.h` are normally automatically included by `msg.h`.

msgget

You create and access a message queue using the `msgget` function:

```
int msgget(key_t key, int msgflg);
```

The program must provide a `key` value that, as with other IPC facilities, names a particular message queue. The special value `IPC_PRIVATE` creates a private queue, which in theory is accessible only by the current process. As with semaphores and messages, on some Linux systems the message queue may not actually be private. Because a private queue has very little purpose, that's not a significant problem. As before, the second parameter, `msgflg`, consists of nine permission flags. A special bit defined by `IPC_CREAT` must be bitwise ORed with the permissions to create a new message queue. It's not an error to set the `IPC_CREAT` flag and give the key of an existing message queue. The IPC_CREAT flag is silently ignored if the message queue already exists.

The msgget function returns a positive number, the queue identifier, on success or –1 on failure.

msgsnd

The msgsnd function allows you to add a message to a message queue:

```
int msgsnd(int msqid, const void *msg_ptr, size_t msg_sz, int msgflg);
```

The structure of the message is constrained in two ways. First, it must be smaller than the system limit, and second, it must start with a long int, which will be used as a message type in the receive function. When you're using messages, it's best to define your message structure something like this:

```
struct my_message {
    long int message_type;
    /* The data you wish to transfer */
}
```

Because the message_type is used in message reception, you can't simply ignore it. You must declare your data structure to include it, and it's also wise to initialize it so that it contains a known value.

The first parameter, msqid, is the message queue identifier returned from a msgget function.

The second parameter, msg_ptr, is a pointer to the message to be sent, which must start with a long int type as described previously.

The third parameter, msg_sz, is the size of the message pointed to by msg_ptr. This size must not include the long int message type.

The fourth parameter, msgflg, controls what happens if either the current message queue is full or the systemwide limit on queued messages has been reached. If msgflg has the IPC_NOWAIT flag set, the function will return immediately without sending the message and the return value will be –1. If the msgflg has the IPC_NOWAIT flag clear, the sending process will be suspended, waiting for space to become available in the queue.

On success, the function returns 0, on failure –1. If the call is successful, a copy of the message data has been taken and placed on the message queue.

msgrcv

The msgrcv function retrieves messages from a message queue:

```
int msgrcv(int msqid, void *msg_ptr, size_t msg_sz, long int msgtype, int msgflg);
```

The first parameter, msqid, is the message queue identifier returned from a msgget function.

The second parameter, msg_ptr, is a pointer to the message to be received, which must start with a long int type as described previously in the msgsnd function.

The third parameter, msg_sz, is the size of the message pointed to by msg_ptr, not including the long int message type.

The fourth parameter, msgtype, is a long int, which allows a simple form of reception priority to be implemented. If msgtype has the value 0, the first available message in the queue is retrieved. If it's greater than zero, the first message with the same message type is retrieved. If it's less than zero, the first message that has a type the same as or less than the absolute value of msgtype is retrieved.

This sounds more complicated than it actually is in practice. If you simply want to retrieve messages in the order in which they were sent, set msgtype to 0. If you want to retrieve only messages with a specific message type, set msgtype equal to that value. If you want to receive messages with a type of n or smaller, set msgtype to -n.

The fifth parameter, msgflg, controls what happens when no message of the appropriate type is waiting to be received. If the IPC_NOWAIT flag in msgflg is set, the call will return immediately with a return value of –1. If the IPC_NOWAIT flag of msgflg is clear, the process will be suspended, waiting for an appropriate type of message to arrive.

On success, msgrcv returns the number of bytes placed in the receive buffer, the message is copied into the user-allocated buffer pointed to by msg_ptr, and the data is deleted from the message queue. It returns –1 on error.

msgctl

The final message queue function is msgctl, which is very similar to that of the control function for shared memory:

```
int msgctl(int msqid, int command, struct msqid_ds *buf);
```

The msqid_ds structure has at least the following members:

```
struct msqid_ds {
    uid_t   msg_perm.uid;
    uid_t   msg_perm.gid
    mode_t  msg_perm.mode;
}
```

The first parameter, msqid, is the identifier returned from msgget.

The second parameter, command, is the action to take. It can take three values, described in the following table:

Command	Description
IPC_STAT	Sets the data in the msqid_ds structure to reflect the values associated with the message queue.
IPC_SET	If the process has permission to do so, this sets the values associated with the message queue to those provided in the msqid_ds data structure.
IPC_RMID	Deletes the message queue.

0 is returned on success, –1 on failure. If a message queue is deleted while a process is waiting in a `msgsnd` or `msgrcv` function, the send or receive function will fail.

Try It Out   **Message Queues**

Now that you've seen the definitions for message queues, you can see how they work in practice. As before, you'll write two programs: `msg1.c` to receive and `msg2.c` to send. You'll allow either program to create the message queue, but use the receiver to delete it after it receives the last message.

1.   Here's the receiver program, `msg1.c`:

```
#include <stdlib.h>
#include <stdio.h>
#include <string.h>
#include <errno.h>
#include <unistd.h>


#include <sys/msg.h>


struct my_msg_st {
    long int my_msg_type;
    char some_text[BUFSIZ];
};

int main()
{
    int running = 1;
    int msgid;
    struct my_msg_st some_data;
    long int msg_to_receive = 0;
```

2.   First, set up the message queue:

```
    msgid = msgget((key_t)1234, 0666 | IPC_CREAT);

    if (msgid == -1) {
        fprintf(stderr, "msgget failed with error: %d\n", errno);
        exit(EXIT_FAILURE);
    }
```

3.   Then the messages are retrieved from the queue until an `end` message is encountered. Finally, the message queue is deleted:

```
    while(running) {
        if (msgrcv(msgid, (void *)&some_data, BUFSIZ,
                msg_to_receive, 0) == -1) {
            fprintf(stderr, "msgrcv failed with error: %d\n", errno);
            exit(EXIT_FAILURE);
        }
        printf("You wrote: %s", some_data.some_text);
        if (strncmp(some_data.some_text, "end", 3) == 0) {
            running = 0;
```

```
        }
    }

    if (msgctl(msgid, IPC_RMID, 0) == -1) {
        fprintf(stderr, "msgctl(IPC_RMID) failed\n");
        exit(EXIT_FAILURE);
    }

    exit(EXIT_SUCCESS);
}
```

4.   The sender program, msg2.c, is very similar to msg1.c. In the main setup, delete the msg_to_receive declaration, and replace it with buffer[BUFSIZ]. Remove the message queue delete, and make the following changes to the running loop. You now have a call to msgsnd to send the entered text to the queue. The program msg2.c is shown here with the differences from msg1.c highlighted:

```
#include <stdlib.h>
#include <stdio.h>
#include <string.h>
#include <errno.h>
#include <unistd.h>


#include <sys/msg.h>

#define MAX_TEXT 512

struct my_msg_st {
    long int my_msg_type;
    char some_text[MAX_TEXT];
};

int main()
{
    int running = 1;
    struct my_msg_st some_data;
    int msgid;
    char buffer[BUFSIZ];

msgid = msgget((key_t)1234, 0666 | IPC_CREAT);

    if (msgid == -1) {
        fprintf(stderr, "msgget failed with error: %d\n", errno);
        exit(EXIT_FAILURE);
    }

    while(running) {
        printf("Enter some text: ");
        fgets(buffer, BUFSIZ, stdin);
        some_data.my_msg_type = 1;
        strcpy(some_data.some_text, buffer);
```

```
            if (msgsnd(msgid, (void *)&some_data, MAX_TEXT, 0) == -1) {
                fprintf(stderr, "msgsnd failed\n");
                exit(EXIT_FAILURE);
            }
            if (strncmp(buffer, "end", 3) == 0) {
                running = 0;
            }
        }

        exit(EXIT_SUCCESS);
    }
```

Unlike in the pipes example, there's no need for the processes to provide their own synchronization method. This is a significant advantage of messages over pipes.

Providing there's room in the message queue, the sender can create the queue, put some data into the queue, and then exit before the receiver even starts. You'll run the sender, msg2, first. Here's some sample output:

```
$ ./msg2
Enter some text: hello
Enter some text: How are you today?
Enter some text: end
$ ./msg1
You wrote: hello
You wrote: How are you today?
You wrote: end
$
```

How It Works

The sender program creates a message queue with msgget; then it adds messages to the queue with msgsnd. The receiver obtains the message queue identifier with msgget and then receives messages until the special text end is received. It then tidies up by deleting the message queue with msgctl.

The CD Database Application

You're now in a position to modify your CD database application to use the IPC facilities that you've seen in this chapter.

You could use many different combinations of the three IPC facilities, but because the information you need to pass is quite small, it's sensible to implement the passing of requests and responses directly using message queues.

If the amounts of data that you needed to pass were large, you could have considered passing the actual data in shared memory and using either semaphores or messages to pass a "token" to inform the other process that data was available in shared memory.

The message queue interface removes the problem that you had in Chapter 11, where you needed both processes to have the pipe open while data was passed. Using message queues allows one process to put messages in the queue, even if that process is currently the only user of the queue.

The only significant decision you need to make is how to return answers to clients. A simple choice would be to have one queue for the server and one queue for each client. If there were a large number of simultaneous clients, this could cause problems by requiring a large number of message queues. By using the message ID field in the message, you can allow all the clients to use a single queue and "address" response messages to particular client processes by using the client process ID in the message. Each client can then retrieve messages addressed only to itself, leaving messages for other clients in the queue.

To convert your CD application to use IPC facilities, you need to replace only the file `pipe_imp.c` from the code accompanying Chapter 13. In the following pages, we describe the principal sections of the replacement file, `ipc_imp.c`.

Revising the Server Functions

First you need to update the server functions.

1. First, include the appropriate headers, declare some message queue keys, and define a structure to hold your message data:

```
#include "cd_data.h"
#include "cliserv.h"


#include <sys/msg.h>

#define SERVER_MQUEUE 1234
#define CLIENT_MQUEUE 4321

struct msg_passed {
    long int msg_key; /* used for client pid */
    message_db_t real_message;
};
```

2. Two variables with file scope hold the two queue identifiers returned from the `msgget` function:

```
static int serv_qid = -1;
static int cli_qid = -1;
```

3. Make the server responsible for creating both message queues:

```
int server_starting()
{
    #if DEBUG_TRACE
        printf("%d :- server_starting()\n",  getpid());
    #endif

    serv_qid = msgget((key_t)SERVER_MQUEUE, 0666 | IPC_CREAT);
    if (serv_qid == -1) return(0);
```

```
        cli_qid = msgget((key_t)CLIENT_MQUEUE, 0666 | IPC_CREAT);
        if (cli_qid == -1) return(0);

        return(1);
}
```

4. The server is also responsible for tidying up if it ever exits. When the server ends, you set your
    file-scope variables to illegal values. This will catch any bugs if the server attempts to send mes-
    sages after it has called `server_ending`.

```
void server_ending()
{
    #if DEBUG_TRACE
        printf("%d :- server_ending()\n",  getpid());
    #endif

    (void)msgctl(serv_qid, IPC_RMID, 0);
    (void)msgctl(cli_qid, IPC_RMID, 0);

    serv_qid = -1;
    cli_qid - -1;
}
```

5. The server `read` function reads a message of any type (that is, from any client) from the queue,
    and it returns the data part (ignoring the type) of the message:

```
int read_request_from_client(message_db_t *rec_ptr)
{
    struct msg_passed my_msg;
    #if DEBUG_TRACE
        printf("%d :- read_request_from_client()\n",  getpid());
    #endif

    if (msgrcv(serv_qid, (void *)&my_msg, sizeof(*rec_ptr), 0, 0) == -1) {
        return(0);
    }
    *rec_ptr = my_msg.real_message;
    return(1);
}
```

6. Sending a response uses the client process ID that was stored in the request to address the message:

```
int send_resp_to_client(const message_db_t mess_to_send)
{
    struct msg_passed my_msg;
    #if DEBUG_TRACE
        printf("%d :- send_resp_to_client()\n",  getpid());
    #endif

    my_msg.real_message = mess_to_send;
    my_msg.msg_key = mess_to_send.client_pid;

    if (msgsnd(cli_qid, (void *)&my_msg, sizeof(mess_to_send), 0) == -1) {
        return(0);
```

```
        }
        return(1);
}
```

Revising the Client Functions

Next, you perform the changes to the client functions.

1. When the client starts, it needs to find the server and client queue identifiers. The client doesn't create the queues. This function will fail if the server isn't running, because the message queues won't exist.

```
int client_starting()
{
    #if DEBUG_TRACE
        printf("%d :- client_starting\n", getpid());
    #endif

    serv_qid = msgget((key_t)SERVER_MQUEUE, 0666);
    if (serv_qid == -1) return(0);

    cli_qid = msgget((key_t)CLIENT_MQUEUE, 0666);
    if (cli_qid == -1) return(0);
    return(1);
}
```

2. As with the server, when the client ends, you set your file-scope variables to illegal values. This will catch any bugs where the client attempts to send messages after it has called client_ending.

```
void client_ending()
{
    #if DEBUG_TRACE
        printf("%d :- client_ending()\n", getpid());
    #endif

    serv_qid = -1;
    cli_qid = -1;
}
```

3. To send a message to the server, store the data inside your structure. Notice that you must set the message key. Because 0 is an illegal value for the key, leaving the key undefined would mean that it takes an (apparently) random value, so this function could occasionally fail if the value happens to be 0.

```
int send_mess_to_server(message_db_t mess_to_send)
{
    struct msg_passed my_msg;
    #if DEBUG_TRACE
        printf("%d :- send_mess_to_server()\n", getpid());
    #endif

    my_msg.real_message = mess_to_send;
    my_msg.msg_key = mess_to_send.client_pid;
```

```
    if (msgsnd(serv_qid, (void *)&my_msg, sizeof(mess_to_send), 0) == -1) {
        perror("Message send failed");
        return(0);
    }
    return(1);
}
```

4.   When the client retrieves a message from the server, it uses its process ID to receive only messages addressed to itself, ignoring any messages for other clients.

```
int read_resp_from_server(message_db_t *rec_ptr)
{
    struct msg_passed my_msg;
#if DEBUG_TRACE
        printf("%d :- read_resp_from_server()\n",  getpid());
#endif

    if (msgrcv(cli_qid, (void *)&my_msg, sizeof(*rec_ptr), getpid(), 0) == -1) {
        return(0);
    }
    *rec_ptr = my_msg.real_message;
    return(1);
}
```

5.   To retain complete compatibility with `pipe_imp.c`, you need to define four extra functions. In your new program, however, the functions are empty. The operations they implemented when using pipes are simply not needed anymore.

```
int start_resp_to_client(const message_db_t mess_to_send)
{
    return(1);
}

void end_resp_to_client(void)
{
}

int start_resp_from_server(void)
{
    return(1);
}

void end_resp_from_server(void)
{
}
```

You can now simply start the server, which does the actual data storage and retrieval, in the background, and then run the client application to connect to it using messages.

All you have had to do here is replace the interface functions from Chapter 11 with a different implementation using message queues. The conversion of the application to message queues illustrates the power of IPC message queues, because you require fewer functions than the pipes application, and even those functions that you do need are much simpler than they were in the earlier implementation.

IPC Status Commands

Although they're not required for X/Open compliance, most Linux systems provide a set of commands that allow command-line access to IPC information, and to tidy up stray IPC facilities. These are the `ipcs` and `ipcrm` commands, which are very useful when you're developing programs.

One of the irritations of the IPC facilities is that a poorly written program, or a program that fails for some reason, can leave its IPC resources (such as data in a message queue) loitering on the system long after the program completes. This can cause a new invocation of the program to fail, because the program expects to start with a clean system, but actually finds some leftover resource. The status (`ipcs`) and remove (`ipcrm`) commands provide a way of checking and tidying up IPC facilities.

Displaying Semaphore Status

To examine the state of semaphores on the system, use the `ipcs -s` command. If any semaphores are present, the output will have this form:

```
$ ./ipcs -s

------ Semaphore Arrays --------
key          semid       owner       perms       nsems
0x4d00df1a 768           rick        666         1
```

You can use the `ipcrm` command to remove any semaphores accidentally left by programs. To delete the preceding semaphore, the command (on Linux) is

```
$ ./ipcrm -s 768
```

Some much older Linux systems used to use a slightly different syntax:

```
$ ./ipcrm sem 768
```

but that style is now rare. Check the manual pages for your system to see which format is valid on your particular system.

Displaying Shared Memory Status

Like semaphores, many systems provide command-line programs for accessing the details of shared memory. These are `ipcs -m` and `ipcrm -m <id>` (or `ipcrm shm <id>`).

Here's some sample output from `ipcs -m`:

```
$ ipcs -m

------ Shared Memory Segments --------
key          shmid       owner       perms       bytes       nattch      status
0x00000000 384           rick        666         4096        2           dest
```

This shows a single shared memory segment of 4 KB attached by two processes.

The ipcrm -m <id> command allows shared memory to be removed. This is sometimes useful when a program has failed to tidy up shared memory.

Displaying Message Queue Status

For message queues the commands are ipcs -q and ipcrm -q <id> (or ipcrm msg <id>).

Here's some sample output from ipcs -q:

```
$ ipcs -q

------ Message Queues --------
key        msqid    owner    perms    used-bytes    messages
0x000004d2 3384     rick     666      2048          2
```

This shows two messages, with a total size of 2,048 bytes in a message queue.

The ipcrm -q <id> command allows a message queue to be removed.

Summary

In this chapter, you looked at the three inter-process communication facilities that first became widely available in UNIX System V.2 and have been available in Linux from the early distributions. These facilities are semaphores, shared memory, and message queues. You've seen the sophisticated functionality that they offer and how, once these functions are understood, they offer a powerful solution to many inter-process communication requirements.

Sockets

In this chapter, you look at yet another method of process communication, but one with a crucial difference from those we've discussed in Chapters 13 and 14. Until now, all the facilities we've discussed have relied on shared resources on a single computer system. The resource varies; it can be file system space, shared physical memory, or message queues, but only processes running on a single machine can use them.

The Berkeley versions of UNIX introduced a new communication tool, the *socket interface*, which is an extension of the concept of a pipe, covered in Chapter 13. Socket interfaces are available on Linux. You can use sockets in much the same way as pipes, but they include communication across a network of computers. A process on one machine can use sockets to communicate with a process on another, which allows for client/server systems that are distributed across a network. Sockets may also be used between processes on the same machine.

Also, the sockets interface has been made available for Windows via a publicly available specification called *Windows Sockets*, or *WinSock*. Windows socket services are provided by a `Winsock.dll` system file. So, Windows programs can communicate across a network to Linux and UNIX computers and vice versa, thus implementing client/server systems. Although the programming interface for WinSock isn't quite the same as UNIX sockets, it still has sockets as its basis.

We can't cover the extensive Linux networking capabilities in a single chapter, so you'll find here a description of the principal programmatic networking interfaces. These should allow you to write your own network programs. Specifically, we look at the following:

- ❑ How a socket connection operates
- ❑ Socket attributes, addresses, and communications
- ❑ Network information and the Internet daemon (`inetd`/`xinetd`)
- ❑ Clients and servers

What Is a Socket?

A *socket* is a communication mechanism that allows client/server systems to be developed either locally, on a single machine, or across networks. Linux functions such as printing, connecting to databases, and serving web pages as well as network utilities such as `rlogin` for remote login and `ftp` for file transfer usually use sockets to communicate.

Sockets are created and used differently from pipes because they make a clear distinction between client and server. The socket mechanism can implement multiple clients attached to a single server.

Socket Connections

You can think of socket connections as telephone calls into a busy building. A call comes into an organization and is answered by a receptionist who puts the call through to the correct department (the server process) and from there to the right person (the server socket). Each incoming call (client) is routed to an appropriate end point and the intervening operators are free to deal with further calls. Before you look at the way socket connections are established in Linux systems, you need to understand how they operate for socket applications that maintain a connection.

First, a server application creates a socket, which like a file descriptor is a resource assigned to the server process and that process alone. The server creates it using the system call `socket`, and it can't be shared with other processes.

Next, the server process gives the socket a name. Local sockets are given a filename in the Linux file system, often to be found in `/tmp` or `/usr/tmp`. For network sockets, the filename will be a service identifier (port number/access point) relevant to the particular network to which the clients can connect. This identifier allows Linux to route incoming connections specifying a particular port number to the correct server process. For example, a web server typically creates a socket on port 80, an identifier reserved for the purpose. Web browsers know to use port 80 for their HTTP connections to web sites the user wants to read. A socket is named using the system call `bind`. The server process then waits for a client to connect to the named socket. The system call, `listen`, creates a queue for incoming connections. The server can accept them using the system call `accept`.

When the server calls `accept`, a new socket is created that is distinct from the named socket. This new socket is used solely for communication with this particular client. The named socket remains for further connections from other clients. If the server is written appropriately, it can take advantage of multiple connections. A web server will do this so that it can serve pages to many clients at once. For a simple server, further clients wait on the listen queue until the server is ready again.

The client side of a socket-based system is more straightforward. The client creates an unnamed socket by calling `socket`. It then calls `connect` to establish a connection with the server by using the server's named socket as an address.

Once established, sockets can be used like low-level file descriptors, providing two-way data communications.

Try It Out   A Simple Local Client

Here's an example of a very simple socket client program, client1.c. It creates an unnamed socket and connects it to a server socket called server_socket. We cover the details of the socket system call a little later, after we've discussed some addressing issues.

1. Make the necessary includes and set up the variables:

```
#include <sys/types.h>
#include <sys/socket.h>
#include <stdio.h>
#include <sys/un.h>
#include <unistd.h>
#include <stdlib.h>

int main()
{
    int sockfd;
    int len;
    struct sockaddr_un address;
    int result;
    char ch = 'A';
```

2. Create a socket for the client:

```
    sockfd = socket(AF_UNIX, SOCK_STREAM, 0);
```

3. Name the socket as agreed with the server:

```
    address.sun_family = AF_UNIX;
    strcpy(address.sun_path, "server_socket");
    len = sizeof(address);
```

4. Connect your socket to the server's socket:

```
    result = connect(sockfd, (struct sockaddr *)&address, len);

    if(result == -1) {
        perror("oops: client1");
        exit(1);
    }
```

5. You can now read and write via sockfd:

```
    write(sockfd, &ch, 1);
    read(sockfd, &ch, 1);
    printf("char from server = %c\n", ch);
    close(sockfd);
    exit(0);
}
```

This program fails when you run it because you haven't yet created the server-side named socket. (The exact error message may differ from system to system.)

```
$ ./client1
oops: client1: No such file or directory
$
```

Try It Out   A Simple Local Server

Here's a very simple server program, server1.c, that accepts connections from the client. It creates the server socket, binds it to a name, creates a listen queue, and accepts connections.

1. Make the necessary includes and set up the variables:

```
#include <sys/types.h>
#include <sys/socket.h>
#include <stdio.h>
#include <sys/un.h>
#include <unistd.h>
#include <stdlib.h>

int main()
{
    int server_sockfd, client_sockfd;
    int server_len, client_len;
    struct sockaddr_un server_address;
    struct sockaddr_un client_address;
```

2. Remove any old sockets and create an unnamed socket for the server:

```
    unlink("server_socket");
    server_sockfd = socket(AF_UNIX, SOCK_STREAM, 0);
```

3. Name the socket:

```
    server_address.sun_family = AF_UNIX;
    strcpy(server_address.sun_path, "server_socket");
    server_len = sizeof(server_address);
    bind(server_sockfd, (struct sockaddr *)&server_address, server_len);
```

4. Create a connection queue and wait for clients:

```
    listen(server_sockfd, 5);
    while(1) {
        char ch;

        printf("server waiting\n");
```

5. Accept a connection:

```
        client_len = sizeof(client_address);
        client_sockfd = accept(server_sockfd,
            (struct sockaddr *)&client_address, &client_len);
```

6. Read and write to client on `client_sockfd`:

```
        read(client_sockfd, &ch, 1);
        ch++;
        write(client_sockfd, &ch, 1);
        close(client_sockfd);
    }
}
```

How It Works

The server program in this example can serve only one client at a time. It just reads a character from the client, increments it, and writes it back. In more sophisticated systems, where the server has to perform more work on the client's behalf, this wouldn't be acceptable, because other clients would be unable to connect until the server had finished. You'll see a couple of ways to allow multiple connections later.

When you run the server program, it creates a socket and waits for connections. If you start it in the background so that it runs independently, you can then start clients in the foreground.

```
$ ./server1 &
[1] 1094
$ server waiting
```

As it waits for connections, the server prints a message. In the preceding example, the server waits for a file system socket and you can see it with the normal `ls` command.

Remember that it's good practice to remove a socket when you've finished with it, even if the program terminates abnormally via a signal. This keeps the file system from getting cluttered with unused files.

```
$ ls -lF server_socket
srwxr-xr-x    1 neil     users          0 2007-06-23 11:41 server_socket=
```

The device type is "socket," shown by the s at the front of the permissions and the = at the end of the name. The socket has been created just as an ordinary file would be, with permissions modified by the current `umask`. If you use the `ps` command, you can see the server running in the background. It's shown sleeping (`STAT` is `S`) and is therefore not consuming CPU resources.

```
$ ps lx
F   UID   PID  PPID PRI  NI   VSZ  RSS WCHAN  STAT TTY        TIME COMMAND
0  1000 23385 10689  17   0  1424  312 361800 S    pts/1      0:00 ./server1
```

Now, when you run the client program, you are successful in connecting to the server. Because the server socket exists, you can connect to it and communicate with the server.

```
$ ./client1
server waiting
char from server = B
$
```

The output from the server and the client get mixed on the terminal, but you can see that the server has received a character from the client, incremented it, and returned it. The server then continues and waits for the next client. If you run several clients together, they will be served in sequence, although the output you see may be more mixed up.

```
$ ./client1 & ./client1 & ./client1 &
[2] 23412
[3] 23413
[4] 23414
server waiting
char from server = B
server waiting
char from server = B
server waiting
char from server = B
server waiting
[2]    Done                client1
[3]-   Done                client1
[4]+   Done                client1
$
```

Socket Attributes

To fully understand the system calls used in this example, you need to learn a little about UNIX networking.

Sockets are characterized by three attributes: *domain*, *type*, and *protocol*. They also have an address used as their name. The formats of the addresses vary depending on the domain, also known as the *protocol family*. Each protocol family can use one or more address families to define the address format.

Socket Domains

Domains specify the network medium that the socket communication will use. The most common socket domain is AF_INET, which refers to Internet networking that's used on many Linux local area networks and, of course, the Internet itself. The underlying protocol, *Internet Protocol* (IP), which only has one address family, imposes a particular way of specifying computers on a network. This is called the *IP address*.

The "next generation" Internet Protocol, IPv6, has been designed to overcome some of the problems with the standard IP, notably the limited number of addresses that are available. IPv6 uses a different socket domain, AF_INET6, and a different address format. It is expected to eventually replace IP, but this process will take many years. Although there are implementations of IPv6 for Linux, it is beyond the scope of this book.

Although names almost always refer to networked machines on the Internet, these are translated into lower-level IP addresses. An example IP address is 192.168.1.99. All IP addresses are represented by four numbers, each less than 256, a so-called *dotted quad*. When a client connects across a network via sockets, it needs the IP address of the server computer.

There may be several services available at the server computer. A client can address a particular service on a networked machine by using an IP port. A port is identified within the system by assigning a unique 16-bit integer and externally by the combination of IP address and port number. The sockets are communication end points that must be bound to ports before communication is possible.

Servers wait for connections on particular ports. Well-known services have allocated port numbers that are used by all Linux and UNIX machines. These are usually, but not always, numbers less than 1024. Examples are the printer spooler (515), `rlogin` (513), `ftp` (21), and `httpd` (80). The last of these is the standard port for web servers. Usually, port numbers less than 1024 are reserved for system services and may only be served by processes with superuser privileges. X/Open defines a constant in `netdb.h`, `IPPORT_RESERVED`, to stand for the highest reserved port number.

Because there is a standard set of port numbers for standard services, computers can easily connect to each other without having to figure out the correct port. Local services may use nonstandard port addresses.

The domain in the first example is the UNIX file system domain, `AF_UNIX`, which can be used by sockets based on a single computer that perhaps isn't networked. When this is so, the underlying protocol is file input/output and the addresses are filenames. The address that you used for the server socket was `server_socket`, which you saw appear in the current directory when you ran the server application.

Other domains that might be used include `AF_ISO` for networks based on ISO standard protocols and `AF_XNS` for the Xerox Network System. We won't cover these here.

Socket Types

A socket domain may have a number of different ways of communicating, each of which might have different characteristics. This isn't an issue with `AF_UNIX` domain sockets, which provide a reliable two-way communication path. In networked domains, however, you need to be aware of the characteristics of the underlying network and how different communication mechanisms are affected by them.

Internet protocols provide two communication mechanisms with distinct levels of service: *streams* and *datagrams*.

Stream Sockets

Stream sockets (in some ways similar to standard input/output streams) provide a connection that is a sequenced and reliable two-way byte stream. Thus, data sent is guaranteed not to be lost, duplicated, or reordered without an indication that an error has occurred. Large messages are fragmented, transmitted, and reassembled. This is similar to a file stream, which also accepts large amounts of data and splits it up for writing to the low-level disk in smaller blocks. Stream sockets have predictable behavior.

Stream sockets, specified by the type `SOCK_STREAM`, are implemented in the `AF_INET` domain by TCP/IP connections. They are also the usual type in the `AF_UNIX` domain. We concentrate on `SOCK_STREAM` sockets in this chapter because they are more commonly used in programming network applications.

TCP/IP stands for Transmission Control Protocol/Internet Protocol. IP is the low-level protocol for packets that provides routing through the network from one computer to another. TCP provides sequencing, flow control, and retransmission to ensure that large data transfers arrive with all of the data present and correct or with an appropriate error condition reported.

Datagram Sockets

In contrast, a datagram socket, specified by the type SOCK_DGRAM, doesn't establish and maintain a connection. There is also a limit on the size of a datagram that can be sent. It's transmitted as a single network message that may get lost, duplicated, or arrive out of sequence — ahead of datagrams sent after it.

Datagram sockets are implemented in the AF_INET domain by UDP/IP connections and provide an unsequenced, unreliable service. (UDP stands for User Datagram Protocol.) However, they are relatively inexpensive in terms of resources, because network connections need not be maintained. They're fast because there is no associated connection setup time.

Datagrams are useful for "single-shot" inquiries to information services, for providing regular status information, or for performing low-priority logging. They have the advantage that the death of a server doesn't unduly inconvenience a client and would not require a client restart. Because datagram-based servers usually retain no connection information, they can be stopped and restarted without disturbing their clients.

For now, we leave the topic of datagrams; see the "Datagrams" section near the end of this chapter for more information.

Socket Protocols

Where the underlying transport mechanism allows for more than one protocol to provide the requested socket type, you can select a specific protocol for a socket. In this chapter, we concentrate on UNIX network and file system sockets, which don't require you to choose a protocol other than the default.

Creating a Socket

The socket system call creates a socket and returns a descriptor that can be used for accessing the socket.

```
#include <sys/types.h>
#include <sys/socket.h>

int socket(int domain, int type, int protocol);
```

The socket created is one end point of a communication channel. The domain parameter specifies the address family, the type parameter specifies the type of communication to be used with this socket, and protocol specifies the protocol to be employed.

Domains include those in the following table:

Domain	Description
AF_UNIX	UNIX internal (file system sockets)
AF_INET	ARPA Internet protocols (UNIX network sockets)

Domain	Description
AF_ISO	ISO standard protocols
AF_NS	Xerox Network Systems protocols
AF_IPX	Novell IPX protocol
AF_APPLETALK	Appletalk DDS

The most common socket domains are AF_UNIX, which is used for local sockets implemented via the UNIX and Linux file systems, and AF_INET, which is used for UNIX network sockets. The AF_INET sockets may be used by programs communicating across a TCP/IP network including the Internet. The Windows Winsock interface also provides access to this socket domain.

The socket parameter type specifies the communication characteristics to be used for the new socket. Possible values include SOCK_STREAM and SOCK_DGRAM.

SOCK_STREAM is a sequenced, reliable, connection-based two-way byte stream. For an AF_INET domain socket, this is provided by default by a TCP connection that is established between the two end points of the stream socket when it's connected. Data may be passed in both directions along the socket connection. The TCP protocols include facilities to fragment and reassemble long messages and to retransmit any parts that may be lost in the network.

SOCK_DGRAM is a datagram service. You can use this socket to send messages of a fixed (usually small) maximum size, but there's no guarantee that the message will be delivered or that messages won't be reordered in the network. For AF_INET sockets, this type of communication is provided by UDP datagrams.

The protocol used for communication is usually determined by the socket type and domain. There is normally no choice. The protocol parameter is used where there is a choice. 0 selects the default protocol, which is used in all the examples in this chapter.

The socket system call returns a descriptor that is in many ways similar to a low-level file descriptor. When the socket has been connected to another end-point socket, you can use the read and write system calls with the descriptor to send and receive data on the socket. The close system call is used to end a socket connection.

Socket Addresses

Each socket domain requires its own address format. For an AF_UNIX socket, the address is described by a structure, sockaddr_un, defined in the sys/un.h include file.

```
struct sockaddr_un {
    sa_family_t    sun_family;    /* AF_UNIX */
    char           sun_path[];    /* pathname */
};
```

So that addresses of different types may be passed to the socket-handling system calls, each address format is described by a similar structure that begins with a field (in this case, `sun_family`) that specifies the address type (the socket domain). In the `AF_UNIX` domain, the address is specified by a filename in the `sun_path` field of the structure.

On current Linux systems, the type `sa_family_t`, defined by X/Open as being declared in `sys/un.h`, is taken to be a `short`. Also, the `pathname` specified in `sun_path` is limited in size (Linux specifies 108 characters; others may use a manifest constant such as `UNIX_MAX_PATH`). Because address structures may vary in size, many socket calls require or provide as an output a length to be used for copying the particular address structure.

In the `AF_INET` domain, the address is specified using a structure called `sockaddr_in`, defined in `netinet/in.h`, which contains at least these members:

```
struct sockaddr_in {
    short int            sin_family;   /* AF_INET */
    unsigned short int   sin_port;     /* Port number */
    struct in_addr       sin_addr;     /* Internet address */
};
```

The IP address structure, `in_addr`, is defined as follows:

```
struct in_addr {
    unsigned long int    s_addr;
};
```

The four bytes of an IP address constitute a single 32-bit value. An `AF_INET` socket is fully described by its domain, IP address, and port number. From an application's point of view, all sockets act like file descriptors and are addressed by a unique integer value.

Naming a Socket

To make a socket (as created by a call to `socket`) available for use by other processes, a server program needs to give the socket a name. Thus, `AF_UNIX` sockets are associated with a file system pathname, as you saw in the `server1` example. `AF_INET` sockets are associated with an IP port number.

```
#include <sys/socket.h>

int bind(int socket, const struct sockaddr *address, size_t address_len);
```

The `bind` system call assigns the address specified in the parameter, `address`, to the unnamed socket associated with the file descriptor `socket`. The length of the address structure is passed as `address_len`.

The length and format of the address depend on the address family. A particular address structure pointer will need to be cast to the generic address type (`struct sockaddr *`) in the call to `bind`.

On successful completion, `bind` returns 0. If it fails, it returns –1 and sets `errno` to one of the following values:

Errno Value	Description
EBADF	The file descriptor is invalid.
ENOTSOCK	The file descriptor doesn't refer to a socket.
EINVAL	The file descriptor refers to an already-named socket.
EADDRNOTAVAIL	The address is unavailable.
EADDRINUSE	The address has a socket bound to it already.

There are some more values for AF_UNIX sockets:

Errno value	Description
EACCESS	Can't create the file system name due to permissions.
ENOTDIR, ENAMETOOLONG	Indicates a poor choice of filename.

Creating a Socket Queue

To accept incoming connections on a socket, a server program must create a queue to store pending requests. It does this using the listen system call.

```
#include <sys/socket.h>

int listen(int socket, int backlog);
```

A Linux system may limit the maximum number of pending connections that may be held in a queue. Subject to this maximum, listen sets the queue length to backlog. Incoming connections up to this queue length are held pending on the socket; further connections will be refused and the client's connection will fail. This mechanism is provided by listen to allow incoming connections to be held pending while a server program is busy dealing with a previous client. A value of 5 for backlog is very common.

The listen function will return 0 on success or -1 on error. Errors include EBADF, EINVAL, and ENOT-SOCK, as for the bind system call.

Accepting Connections

Once a server program has created and named a socket, it can wait for connections to be made to the socket by using the accept system call.

```
#include <sys/socket.h>

int accept(int socket, struct sockaddr *address, size_t *address_len);
```

The accept system call returns when a client program attempts to connect to the socket specified by the parameter socket. The client is the first pending connection from that socket's queue. The accept function creates a new socket to communicate with the client and returns its descriptor. The new socket will have the same type as the server listen socket.

The socket must have previously been named by a call to bind and had a connection queue allocated by listen. The address of the calling client will be placed in the sockaddr structure pointed to by address. A null pointer may be used here if the client address isn't of interest.

The address_len parameter specifies the length of the client structure. If the client address is longer than this value, it will be truncated. Before calling accept, address_len must be set to the expected address length. On return, address_len will be set to the actual length of the calling client's address structure.

If there are no connections pending on the socket's queue, accept will block (so that the program won't continue) until a client does make connection. You can change this behavior by using the O_NONBLOCK flag on the socket file descriptor, using the fcntl function in your code like this:

```
int flags = fcntl(socket, F_GETFL, 0);

fcntl(socket, F_SETFL, O_NONBLOCK|flags);
```

The accept function returns a new socket file descriptor when there is a client connection pending or –1 on error. Possible errors are similar to those for bind and listen, with the addition of EWOULDBLOCK, where O_NONBLOCK has been specified and there are no pending connections. The error EINTR will occur if the process is interrupted while blocked in accept.

Requesting Connections

Client programs connect to servers by establishing a connection between an unnamed socket and the server listen socket. They do this by calling connect.

```
#include <sys/socket.h>

int connect(int socket, const struct sockaddr *address, size_t address_len);
```

The socket specified by the parameter socket is connected to the server socket specified by the parameter address, which is of length address_len. The socket must be a valid file descriptor obtained by a call to socket.

If it succeeds, connect returns 0, and –1 is returned on error. Possible errors this time include the following:

Errno Value	Description
EBADF	An invalid file descriptor was passed in socket.
EALREADY	A connection is already in progress for this socket.
ETIMEDOUT	A connection timeout has occurred.
ECONNREFUSED	The requested connection was refused by the server.

If the connection can't be set up immediately, connect will block for an unspecified timeout period. Once this timeout has expired, the connection will be aborted and connect will fail. However, if the call to connect is interrupted by a signal that is handled, the connect call will fail (with errno set to EINTR), but the connection attempt won't be aborted — it will be set up asynchronously, and the program will have to check later to see if the connection was successful.

As with accept, the blocking nature of connect can be altered by setting the O_NONBLOCK flag on the file descriptor. In this case, if the connection can't be made immediately, connect will fail with errno set to EINPROGRESS and the connection will be made asynchronously.

Though asynchronous connections can be tricky to handle, you can use a call to select on the socket file descriptor to check that the socket is ready for writing. We cover select later in this chapter.

Closing a Socket

You can terminate a socket connection at the server and client by calling close, just as you would for low-level file descriptors. You should always close the socket at both ends. For the server, you should do this when read returns zero. Note that the close call may block if the socket has untransmitted data, is of a connection-oriented type, and has the SOCK_LINGER option set. You learn about setting socket options later in this chapter.

Socket Communications

Now that we have covered the basic system calls associated with sockets, let's take a closer look at the example programs. You'll try to convert them to use a network socket rather than a file system socket. The file system socket has the disadvantage that, unless the author uses an absolute pathname, it's created in the server program's current directory. To make it more generally useful, you need to create it in a globally accessible directory (such as /tmp) that is agreed between the server and its clients. For network sockets, you need only choose an unused port number.

For the example, select port number 9734. This is an arbitrary choice that avoids the standard services (you can't use port numbers below 1024 because they are reserved for system use). Other port numbers are often listed, with the services provided on them, in the system file /etc/services. When you're writing socket-based applications, always choose a port number not listed in this configuration file.

> **Be aware that there is a deliberate error in the programs** client2.c **and** server2.c **that you will fix in** client3.c **and** server3.c. **Please do not use the code from** client2.c **and** server2.c **in your own programs.**

You'll run your client and server across a local network, but network sockets are not only useful on a local area network; any machine with an Internet connection (even a modem dial-up) can use network sockets to communicate with others. You can even use a network-based program on a stand-alone UNIX computer because a UNIX computer is usually configured to use a loopback network that contains only itself. For illustration purposes, this example uses this loopback network, which can also be useful for debugging network applications because it eliminates any external network problems.

The loopback network consists of a single computer, conventionally called localhost, with a standard IP address of 127.0.0.1. This is the local machine. You'll find its address listed in the network hosts file, /etc/hosts, with the names and addresses of other hosts on shared networks.

Each network with which a computer communicates has a hardware interface associated with it. A computer may have different network names on each network and certainly will have different IP addresses. For example, Neil's machine tilde has three network interfaces and therefore three addresses. These are recorded in /etc/hosts as follows:

```
127.0.0.1      localhost          # Loopback
192.168.1.1    tilde.localnet     # Local, private Ethernet
158.152.X.X    tilde.demon.co.uk  # Modem dial-up
```

The first is the simple loopback network, the second is a local area network accessed via an Ethernet adapter, and the third is the modem link to an Internet service provider. You can write a network socket-based program to communicate with servers accessed via any of these interfaces without alteration.

Try It Out   Network Client

Here's a modified client program, client2.c, to connect to a network socket via the loopback network. It contains a subtle bug concerned with hardware dependency, but we'll discuss that later in this chapter.

1. Make the necessary includes and set up the variables:

```
#include <sys/types.h>
#include <sys/socket.h>
#include <stdio.h>
#include <netinet/in.h>
#include <arpa/inet.h>
#include <unistd.h>
#include <stdlib.h>

int main()
{
    int sockfd;
    int len;
    struct sockaddr_in address;
    int result;
    char ch = 'A';
```

2. Create a socket for the client:

```
    sockfd = socket(AF_INET, SOCK_STREAM, 0);
```

3. Name the socket, as agreed with the server:

```
    address.sin_family = AF_INET;
    address.sin_addr.s_addr = inet_addr("127.0.0.1");
    address.sin_port = 9734;
    len = sizeof(address);
```

The rest of this program is the same as client1.c from earlier in this chapter. When you run this version, it fails to connect because there isn't a server running on port 9734 on this machine.

```
$ ./client2
oops: client2: Connection refused
$
```

How It Works

The client program used the sockaddr_in structure from the include file netinet/in.h to specify an AF_INET address. It tries to connect to a server on the host with IP address 127.0.0.1. It uses a function, inet_addr, to convert the text representation of an IP address into a form suitable for socket addressing. The manual page for inet has more information on other address translation functions.

Try It Out   **Network Server**

You also need to modify the server program to wait for connections on your chosen port number. Here's a modified server: server2.c.

1.   Make the necessary includes and set up the variables:

```
#include <sys/types.h>
#include <sys/socket.h>
#include <stdio.h>
#include <netinet/in.h>
#include <arpa/inet.h>
#include <unistd.h>
#include <stdlib.h>

int main()
{
    int server_sockfd, client_sockfd;
    int server_len, client_len;
    struct sockaddr_in server_address;
    struct sockaddr_in client_address;
```

2.   Create an unnamed socket for the server:

```
    server_sockfd = socket(AF_INET, SOCK_STREAM, 0);
```

3.   Name the socket:

```
    server_address.sin_family = AF_INET;
    server_address.sin_addr.s_addr = inet_addr("127.0.0.1");
    server_address.sin_port = 9734;
    server_len = sizeof(server_address);
    bind(server_sockfd, (struct sockaddr *)&server_address, server_len);
```

From here on, the listing follows server1.c exactly. Running client2 and server2 will show the same behavior you saw earlier with client1 and server1.

How It Works

The server program creates an AF_INET domain socket and arranges to accept connections on it. The socket is bound to your chosen port. The address specified determines which computers are allowed to connect. By specifying the loopback address, as in the client program, you are restricting communications to the local machine.

If you want to allow the server to communicate with remote clients, you must specify a set of IP addresses that you are willing to allow. You can use the special value, INADDR_ANY, to specify that you'll accept connections from all of the interfaces your computer may have. If you chose to, you could distinguish between different network interfaces to separate, for example, internal Local Area Network and external Wide Area Network connections. INADDR_ANY is a 32-bit integer value that you can use in the sin_addr.s_addr field of the address structure. However, you have a problem to resolve first.

Host and Network Byte Ordering

When we run these versions of the server and client programs on an Intel processor–based Linux machine, we can see the network connections by using the netstat command. This command will also be available on most UNIX systems configured for networking. It shows the client/server connection waiting to close down. The connection closes down after a small timeout. (Again, the exact output may vary among different versions of Linux.)

```
$ ./server2 & ./client2
[3] 23770
server waiting
server waiting
char from server = B
$ netstat -A inet
Active Internet connections (w/o servers)
Proto Recv-Q Send-Q Local Address    Foreign Address   (State)       User
tcp        1      0 localhost:1574    localhost:1174    TIME_WAIT     root
```

> **Before you try out further examples in this book, be sure to terminate running example server programs, because they will compete to accept connections from clients and you'll see confusing results. You can kill them all (including ones covered later in the chapter) with the following command:**
>
> `killall server1 server2 server3 server4 server5`

You can see the port numbers that have been assigned to the connection between the server and the client. The local address shows the server, and the foreign address is the remote client. (Even though it's on the same machine, it's still connected over a network.) To ensure that all sockets are distinct, these client ports are typically different from the server listen socket and unique to the computer.

However, the local address (the server socket) is given as 1574 (or you may see mvel-1m as a service name), but the port chosen in the example is 9734. Why are they different? The answer is that port numbers and addresses are communicated over socket interfaces as binary numbers. Different computers use different byte ordering for integers. For example, an Intel processor stores the 32-bit integer as four consecutive bytes in memory in the order 1-2-3-4, where 1 is the most significant byte. IBM PowerPC processors would store the integer in the byte order 4-3-2-1. If the memory used for integers were simply copied byte-by-byte, the two different computers would not be able to agree on integer values.

To enable computers of different types to agree on values for multibyte integers transmitted over a network, you need to define a network ordering. Client and server programs must convert their internal integer representation to the network ordering before transmission. They do this by using functions defined in netinet/in.h. These are

```
#include <netinet/in.h>

unsigned long int htonl(unsigned long int hostlong);
unsigned short int htons(unsigned short int hostshort);
unsigned long int ntohl(unsigned long int netlong);
unsigned short int ntohs(unsigned short int netshort);
```

These functions convert 16-bit and 32-bit integers between native host format and the standard network ordering. Their names are abbreviations for conversions — for example, "host to network, long" (htonl) and "host to network, short" (htons). For computers where the native ordering is the same as network ordering, these represent null operations.

To ensure correct byte ordering of the 16-bit port number, your server and client need to apply these functions to the port address. The change to server3.c is

```
server_address.sin_addr.s_addr = htonl(INADDR_ANY);
server_address.sin_port = htons(9734);
```

You don't need to convert the function call, inet_addr("127.0.0.1"), because inet_addr is defined to produce a result in network order. The change to client3.c is

```
address.sin_port = htons(9734);
```

The server has also been changed to allow connections from any IP address by using INADDR_ANY.

Now, when you run server3 and client3, you see the correct port being used for the local connection.

```
$ netstat
Active Internet connections
Proto Recv-Q Send-Q Local Address    Foreign Address    (State)      User
tcp        1      0 localhost:9734  localhost:1175     TIME_WAIT    root
```

Remember that if you're using a computer that has the same native and network byte ordering, you won't see any difference. It's still important always to use the conversion functions to allow correct operation with clients and servers on computers with a different architecture.

Network Information

So far, your client and server programs have had addresses and port numbers compiled into them. For a more general server and client program, you can use network information functions to determine addresses and ports to use.

If you have permission to do so, you can add your server to the list of known services in /etc/services, which assigns a name to port numbers so that clients can use symbolic services rather than numbers.

Similarly, given a computer's name, you can determine the IP address by calling host database functions that resolve addresses for you. They do this by consulting network configuration files, such as /etc/hosts, or network information services, such as NIS (Network Information Services, formerly known as Yellow Pages) and DNS (Domain Name Service).

Host database functions are declared in the interface header file netdb.h.

```
#include <netdb.h>

struct hostent *gethostbyaddr(const void *addr, size_t len, int type);
struct hostent *gethostbyname(const char *name);
```

The structure returned by these functions must contain at least these members:

```
struct hostent {
    char *h_name;          /* name of the host */
    char **h_aliases;      /* list of aliases (nicknames) */
    int h_addrtype;        /* address type */
    int h_length;          /* length in bytes of the address */
    char **h_addr_list     /* list of address (network order) */
};
```

If there is no database entry for the specified host or address, the information functions return a null pointer.

Similarly, information concerning services and associated port numbers is available through some service information functions.

```
#include <netdb.h>

struct servent *getservbyname(const char *name, const char *proto);
struct servent *getservbyport(int port, const char *proto);
```

The proto parameter specifies the protocol to be used to connect to the service, either "tcp" for SOCK_STREAM TCP connections or "udp" for SOCK_DGRAM UDP datagrams.

The structure servent contains at least these members:

```
struct servent {
    char *s_name;          /* name of the service */
    char **s_aliases;      /* list of aliases (alternative names) */
    int s_port;            /* The IP port number */
    char *s_proto;         /* The service type, usually "tcp" or "udp" */
};
```

You can gather host database information about a computer by calling gethostbyname and printing the results. Note that the address list needs to be cast to the appropriate address type and converted from network ordering to a printable string using the inet_ntoa conversion, which has the following definition:

```
#include <arpa/inet.h>

char *inet_ntoa(struct in_addr in)
```

The function converts an Internet host address to a string in dotted quad format. It returns –1 on error, but POSIX doesn't define any specific errors. The other new function you use is gethostname.

```
#include <unistd.h>

int gethostname(char *name, int namelength);
```

This function writes the name of the current host into the string given by name. The hostname will be null-terminated. The argument namelength indicates the length of the string name, and the returned hostname will be truncated if it's too long to fit. gethostname returns 0 on success and –1 on error, but again no errors are defined in POSIX.

Try It Out   Network Information

This program, getname.c, gets information about a host computer.

1. As usual, make the appropriate includes and declare the variables:

```
#include <netinet/in.h>
#include <arpa/inet.h>
#include <unistd.h>
#include <netdb.h>
#include <stdio.h>
#include <stdlib.h>

int main(int argc, char *argv[])
{
    char *host, **names, **addrs;
    struct hostent *hostinfo;
```

2. Set the host to the argument supplied with the getname call, or by default to the user's machine:

```
    if(argc == 1) {
        char myname[256];
        gethostname(myname, 255);
        host = myname;
    }
    else
        host = argv[1];
```

3. Call gethostbyname and report an error if no information is found:

```
    hostinfo = gethostbyname(host);
    if(!hostinfo) {
```

```
        fprintf(stderr, "cannot get info for host: %s\n", host);
        exit(1);
    }
```

4. Display the hostname and any aliases that it may have:

```
    printf("results for host %s:\n", host);
    printf("Name: %s\n", hostinfo -> h_name);
    printf("Aliases:");
    names = hostinfo -> h_aliases;
    while(*names) {
        printf(" %s", *names);
        names++;
    }
    printf("\n");
```

5. Warn and exit if the host in question isn't an IP host:

```
    if(hostinfo -> h_addrtype != AF_INET) {
        fprintf(stderr, "not an IP host!\n");
        exit(1);
    }
```

6. Otherwise, display the IP address(es):

```
    addrs = hostinfo -> h_addr_list;
    while(*addrs) {
        printf(" %s", inet_ntoa(*(struct in_addr *)*addrs));
        addrs++;
    }
    printf("\n");
    exit(0);
}
```

Alternatively, you could use the function gethostbyaddr to determine which host has a given IP address. You might use this in a server to find out where the client is calling from.

How It Works

The getname program calls gethostbyname to extract the host information from the host database. It prints out the hostname, its aliases (other names the computer is known by), and the IP addresses that the host uses on its network interfaces. On one of the authors' systems, running the example and specifying tilde gave the two interfaces: Ethernet and modem.

```
$ ./getname tilde
results for host tilde:
Name: tilde.localnet
Aliases: tilde
 192.168.1.1 158.152.x.x
```

When you use the hostname, localhost, the loopback network is given.

```
$ ./getname localhost
results for host localhost:
Name: localhost
Aliases:
 127.0.0.1
```

You can now modify your client to connect to any named host. Instead of connecting to your example server, you'll connect to a standard service so that you can extract the port number.

Most UNIX and some Linux systems make their system time and date available as a standard service called daytime. Clients may connect to this service to discover the server's idea of the current time and date. Here's a client program, getdate.c, that does just that.

Try It Out   Connecting to a Standard Service

1.   Start with the usual includes and declarations:

```
#include <sys/socket.h>
#include <netinet/in.h>
#include <netdb.h>
#include <stdio.h>
#include <unistd.h>
#include <stdlib.h>

int main(int argc, char *argv[])
{
    char *host;
    int sockfd;
    int len, result;
    struct sockaddr_in address;
    struct hostent *hostinfo;
    struct servent *servinfo;
    char buffer[128];

    if(argc == 1)
        host = "localhost";
    else
        host = argv[1];
```

2.   Find the host address and report an error if none is found:

```
    hostinfo = gethostbyname(host);
    if(!hostinfo) {
        fprintf(stderr, "no host: %s\n", host);
        exit(1);
    }
```

3. Check that the `daytime` service exists on the host:

```
servinfo = getservbyname("daytime", "tcp");
if(!servinfo) {
    fprintf(stderr,"no daytime service\n");
    exit(1);
}
printf("daytime port is %d\n", ntohs(servinfo -> s_port));
```

4. Create a socket:

```
sockfd = socket(AF_INET, SOCK_STREAM, 0);
```

5. Construct the address for use with `connect`:

```
address.sin_family = AF_INET;
address.sin_port = servinfo -> s_port;
address.sin_addr = *(struct in_addr *)*hostinfo -> h_addr_list;
len = sizeof(address);
```

6. Then connect and get the information:

```
result = connect(sockfd, (struct sockaddr *)&address, len);
if(result == -1) {
    perror("oops: getdate");
    exit(1);
}

result = read(sockfd, buffer, sizeof(buffer));
buffer[result] = '\0';
printf("read %d bytes: %s", result, buffer);

close(sockfd);
exit(0);
}
```

You can use `getdate` to get the time of day from any known host.

```
$ ./getdate localhost
daytime port is 13
read 26 bytes: 24 JUN 2007 06:03:03 BST
$
```

If you receive an error message such as

```
oops: getdate: Connection refused
```

or

```
oops: getdate: No such file or directory
```

it may be because the computer you are connecting to has not enabled the daytime service. This has become the default behavior in more recent Linux systems. In the next section, you see how to enable this and other services.

How It Works

When you run this program, you can specify a host to connect to. The daytime service port number is determined from the network database function getservbyname, which returns information about network services in a similar way to host information. The program getdate tries to connect to the address given first in the list of alternate addresses for the specified host. If successful, it reads the information returned by the daytime service, a character string representing the UNIX time and date.

The Internet Daemon (xinetd/inetd)

UNIX systems providing a number of network services often do so by way of a super-server. This program (the Internet daemon, xinetd or inetd) listens for connections on many port addresses at once. When a client connects to a service, the daemon program runs the appropriate server. This cuts down on the need for servers to be running all the time; they can be started as required.

> *The Internet daemon is implemented in modern Linux systems by* xinetd. *This implementation has replaced the original UNIX program,* inetd, *although you will still see* inetd *in older Linux systems and on other UNIX-like systems.*

xinetd is usually configured through a graphical user interface for managing network services, but it is also possible to modify its configuration files directly. These are typically /etc/xinetd.conf and files in the /etc/xinetd.d directory.

Each service that is to be provided via xinetd has a configuration file in /etc/xinetd.d. xinetd will read all of these configuration files when it starts up, and again if instructed to do so.

Here are a couple of example xinetd configuration files, first for the daytime service:

```
#default: off
# description: A daytime server. This is the tcp version.
service daytime
{
        socket_type     = stream
        protocol        = tcp
        wait            = no
        user            = root
        type            = INTERNAL
        id              = daytime-stream
        FLAGS           = IPv6 IPv4
}
```

The following configuration is for the file transfer service:

```
# default: off
# description:
#   The vsftpd FTP server serves FTP connections. It uses
#   normal, unencrypted usernames and passwords for authentication.
# vsftpd is designed to be secure.
#
```

```
# NOTE: This file contains the configuration for xinetd to start vsftpd.
#       the configuration file for vsftp itself is in /etc/vsftpd.conf
service ftp
{
#       server_args             =
#       log_on_success          += DURATION USERID
#       log_on_failure          += USERID
#       nice                    = 10
 socket_type        = stream
 protocol           = tcp
 wait               = no
 user               = root
 server             = /usr/sbin/vsftpd
}
```

The `daytime` service that the `getdate` program connects to is actually handled by `xinetd` itself (it is marked as internal) and can be made available using both SOCK_STREAM (`tcp`) and SOCK_DGRAM (`udp`) sockets.

The `ftp` file transfer service is available only via SOCK_STREAM sockets and is provided by an external program, in this case `vsftpd`. The daemon will start these external programs when a client connects to the `ftp` port.

To activate service configuration changes, you can edit the `xinetd` configuration and send a hang-up signal to the daemon process, but we recommend that you use a more friendly way of configuring services. To allow your time-of-day client to connect, enable the `daytime` service using the tools provided on your Linux system. On SUSE and openSUSE the services may be configured from the SUSE Control Center as shown in Figure 15-1. Red Hat versions (both Enterprise Linux and Fedora) have a similar configuration interface. Here, the `daytime` service is being enabled for both TCP and UDP queries.

For systems that use `inetd` rather than `xinetd`, here's the equivalent extract from the `inetd` configuration file, `/etc/inetd.conf`, which is used by `inetd` to decide which servers to run:

```
#
# <service_name> <sock_type> <proto> <flags> <user> <server_path> <args>
#
# Echo, discard, daytime, and chargen are used primarily for testing.
#
daytime    stream    tcp    nowait    root    internal
daytime    dgram     udp    wait      root    internal
#
# These are standard services.
#
ftp        stream    tcp    nowait    root    /usr/sbin/tcpd    /usr/sbin/wu.ftpd
telnet     stream    tcp    nowait    root    /usr/sbin/tcpd    /usr/sbin/in.telnetd
#
# End of inetd.conf.
```

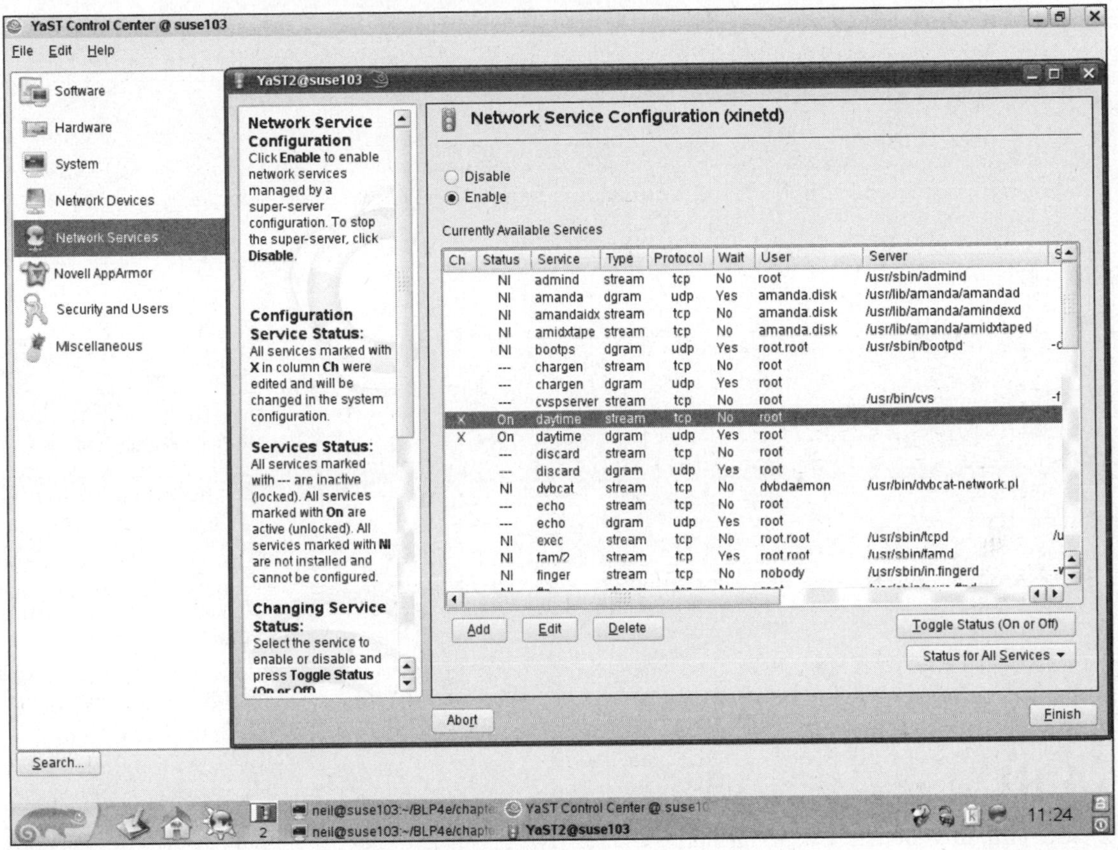

Figure 15-1

Note that in this example the ftp service is provided by the external program wu.ftpd. If your system is running inetd, you can change the services provided by editing /etc/inetd.conf (a # at the start of a line indicates that the line is a comment) and restarting the inetd process. This can be done by sending it a hang-up signal using kill. To make this easier, some systems are configured so that inetd writes its process ID to a file. Alternatively, killall can be used:

```
# killall -HUP inetd
```

Socket Options

There are many options that you can use to control the behavior of socket connections — too many to detail here. The setsockopt function is used to manipulate options.

```
#include <sys/socket.h>

int setsockopt(int socket, int level, int option_name,
        const void *option_value, size_t option_len);
```

You can set options at various levels in the protocol hierarchy. To set options at the socket level, you must set `level` to `SOL_SOCKET`. To set options at the underlying protocol level (TCP, UDP, and so on), set `level` to the number of the protocol (from either the header file `netinet/in.h` or as obtained by the function `getprotobyname`).

The `option_name` parameter selects an option to set; the `option_value` parameter is an arbitrary value of length `option_len` bytes passed unchanged to the underlying protocol handler.

Socket level options defined in `sys/socket.h` include the following.

OPTION	DESCRIPTION
SO_DEBUG	Turn on debugging information.
SO_KEEPALIVE	Keep connections active with periodic transmissions.
SO_LINGER	Complete transmission before close.

`SO_DEBUG` and `SO_KEEPALIVE` take an integer `option_value` used to turn the option on (1) or off (0). `SO_LINGER` requires a `linger` structure defined in `sys/socket.h` to define the state of the option and the linger interval.

`setsockopt` returns 0 if successful, -1 otherwise. The manual pages describe further options and errors.

Multiple Clients

So far in this chapter, you've seen how you can use sockets to implement client/server systems both locally and across networks. Once established, socket connections behave like low-level open file descriptors and in many ways like bi-directional pipes.

You might need to consider the case of multiple, simultaneous clients connecting to a server. You've seen that when a server program accepts a new connection from a client, a new socket is created and the original listen socket remains available for further connections. If the server doesn't immediately accept further connections, they will be held pending in a queue.

The fact that the original socket is still available and that sockets behave as file descriptors gives you a method of serving multiple clients at the same time. If the server calls `fork` to create a second copy of itself, the open socket will be inherited by the new child process. It can then communicate with the connecting client while the main server continues to accept further client connections. This is, in fact, a fairly easy change to make to your server program, which is shown in the following Try It Out section.

Because you're creating child processes but not waiting for them to complete, you must arrange for the server to ignore `SIGCHLD` signals to prevent zombie processes.

Try It Out   **A Server for Multiple Clients**

1. This program, `server4.c`, begins in a similar vein to the last server, with the notable addition of an `include` for the `signal.h` header file. The variables and the procedure of creating and naming a socket are the same:

```
#include <sys/types.h>
#include <sys/socket.h>
#include <stdio.h>
#include <netinet/in.h>
#include <signal.h>
#include <unistd.h>
#include <stdlib.h>

int main()
{
    int server_sockfd, client_sockfd;
    int server_len, client_len;
    struct sockaddr_in server_address;
    struct sockaddr_in client_address;

    server_sockfd = socket(AF_INET, SOCK_STREAM, 0);

    server_address.sin_family = AF_INET;
    server_address.sin_addr.s_addr = htonl(INADDR_ANY);
    server_address.sin_port = htons(9734);
    server_len = sizeof(server_address);
    bind(server_sockfd, (struct sockaddr *)&server_address, server_len);
```

2. Create a connection queue, ignore child exit details, and wait for clients:

```
listen(server_sockfd, 5);

signal(SIGCHLD, SIG_IGN);

while(1) {
    char ch;

    printf("server waiting\n");
```

3. Accept the connection:

```
    client_len = sizeof(client_address);
    client_sockfd = accept(server_sockfd,
        (struct sockaddr *)&client_address, &client_len);
```

4. Fork to create a process for this client and perform a test to see whether you're the parent or the child:

```
    if(fork() == 0) {
```

5. If you're the child, you can now read/write to the client on `client_sockfd`. The five-second delay is just for this demonstration:

```
        read(client_sockfd, &ch, 1);
        sleep(5);
        ch++;
        write(client_sockfd, &ch, 1);
        close(client_sockfd);
        exit(0);
    }
```

6. Otherwise, you must be the parent and your work for this client is finished:

```
        else {
            close(client_sockfd);
        }
    }
}
```

The code inserts a five-second delay in the processing of the client's request to simulate server calcula-tion or database access. If you had done this with the previous server, each run of client3 would have taken five seconds. With the new server, you can handle multiple client3 programs concurrently, with an overall elapsed time of just over five seconds.

```
$ ./server4 &
[1] 26566
server waiting
$ ./client3 & ./client3 & ./client3 & ps x
[2] 26581
[3] 26582
[4] 26583
server waiting
server waiting
server waiting
  PID TTY        STAT    TIME COMMAND
26566 pts/1      S       0:00 ./server4
26581 pts/1      S       0:00 ./client3
26582 pts/1      S       0:00 ./client3
26583 pts/1      S       0:00 ./client3
26584 pts/1      R+      0:00 ps x
26585 pts/1      S       0:00 ./server4
26586 pts/1      S       0:00 ./server4
26587 pts/1      S       0:00 ./server4
$ char from server = B
char from server = B
char from server = B
ps x
  PID TTY        STAT    TIME COMMAND
26566 pts/1      S       0:00 ./server4
26590 pts/1      R+      0:00 ps x
[2]   Done                     ./client3
[3]-  Done                     ./client3
[4]+  Done                     ./client3
$
```

How It Works

The server program now creates a new child process to handle each client, so you see several server waiting messages as the main program continues to wait for new connections. The ps output (edited here) shows the main server4 process, PID 26566, waiting for new clients while the three client3 processes are being served by three children of the server. After a five-second pause, all of the clients get their results and finish. The child server processes exit to leave just the main server alone again.

The server program uses `fork` to handle multiple clients. In a database application, this may not be the best solution, because the server program may be quite large and there is still the problem of coordinating database accesses from multiple server copies. In fact, what you really need is a way for a single server to handle multiple clients without blocking and waiting on client requests to arrive. The solution to this problem involves handling multiple open file descriptors at once and isn't limited to socket applications. Enter `select`.

---

select

Quite often when you're writing Linux applications, you may need to examine the state of a number of inputs to determine the next action to take. For example, a communication program such as a terminal emulator needs to read the keyboard and the serial port effectively at the same time. In a single-user system, it might be acceptable to run in a "busy wait" loop, repeatedly scanning the input for data and reading it if it arrives. This behavior is expensive in terms of CPU time.

The `select` system call allows a program to wait for input to arrive (or output to complete) on a number of low-level file descriptors at once. This means that the terminal emulator program can block until there is something to do. Similarly, a server can deal with multiple clients by waiting for a request on many open sockets at the same time.

The `select` function operates on data structures, `fd_set`, that are sets of open file descriptors. A number of macros are defined for manipulating these sets:

```
#include <sys/types.h>
#include <sys/time.h>

void FD_ZERO(fd_set *fdset);
void FD_CLR(int fd, fd_set *fdset);
void FD_SET(int fd, fd_set *fdset);
int FD_ISSET(int fd, fd_set *fdset);
```

As suggested by their names, `FD_ZERO` initializes an `fd_set` to the empty set, `FD_SET` and `FD_CLR` set and clear elements of the set corresponding to the file descriptor passed as `fd`, and `FD_ISSET` returns nonzero if the file descriptor referred to by `fd` is an element of the `fd_set` pointed to by `fdset`. The maximum number of file descriptors in an `fd_set` structure is given by the constant `FD_SETSIZE`.

The `select` function can also use a timeout value to prevent indefinite blocking. The timeout value is given using a `struct timeval`. This structure, defined in `sys/time.h`, has the following members:

```
struct timeval {
    time_t    tv_sec;     /* seconds */
    long      tv_usec;    /* microseconds */
}
```

The `time_t` type is defined in `sys/types.h` as an integral type.

The `select` system call has the following prototype:

```
#include <sys/types.h>
#include <sys/time.h>

int select(int nfds, fd_set *readfds, fd_set *writefds,
           fd_set *errorfds, struct timeval *timeout);
```

A call to `select` is used to test whether any one of a set of file descriptors is ready for reading or writing or has an error condition pending and will optionally block until one is ready.

The `nfds` argument specifies the number of file descriptors to be tested, and descriptors from 0 to `nfds-1` are considered. Each of the three descriptor sets may be a null pointer, in which case the associated test isn't carried out.

The `select` function will return if any of the descriptors in the `readfds` set are ready for reading, if any in the `writefds` set are ready for writing, or if any in `errorfds` have an error condition. If none of these conditions apply, `select` will return after an interval specified by `timeout`. If the `timeout` parameter is a null pointer and there is no activity on the sockets, the call will block forever.

When `select` returns, the descriptor sets will have been modified to indicate which descriptors are ready for reading or writing or have errors. You should use `FD_ISSET` to test them, to determine the descriptor(s) needing attention. You can modify the `timeout` value to indicate the time remaining until the next timeout, but this behavior isn't specified by X/Open. In the case of a timeout occurring, all descriptor sets will be empty.

The `select` call returns the total number of descriptors in the modified sets. It returns –1 on failure, setting `errno` to describe the error. Possible errors are `EBADF` for invalid descriptors, `EINTR` for return due to interrupt, and `EINVAL` for bad values for `nfds` or `timeout`.

Although Linux modifies the structure pointed to by `timeout` *to indicate the time remaining, most versions of UNIX do not. Much existing code that uses the* `select` *function initializes a* `timeval` *structure and then continues to use it without ever reinitializing the contents. On Linux, this code may operate incorrectly because Linux is modifying the* `timeval` *structure every time a timeout occurs. If you're writing or porting code that uses the* `select` *function, you should watch out for this difference and always reinitialize the timeout. Note that both behaviors are correct; they're just different!*

Try It Out   select

Here is a program, `select.c`, to illustrate the use of `select`. You'll see a more complete example a little later. This program reads the keyboard (standard input — file descriptor 0) with a timeout of 2.5 seconds. It reads the keyboard only when input is ready. It's quite straightforward to extend it to include other descriptors, such as serial lines or pipes and sockets, depending on the application.

1. Begin as usual with the `includes` and declarations and then initialize `inputs` to handle input from the keyboard:

```
#include <sys/types.h>
#include <sys/time.h>
#include <stdio.h>
#include <fcntl.h>
```

```
#include <sys/ioctl.h>
#include <unistd.h>
#include <stdlib.h>

int main()
{
    char buffer[128];
    int result, nread;

    fd_set inputs, testfds;
    struct timeval timeout;

    FD_ZERO(&inputs);
    FD_SET(0,&inputs);
```

2. Wait for input on `stdin` for a maximum of 2.5 seconds:

```
while(1) {
    testfds = inputs;
    timeout.tv_sec = 2;
    timeout.tv_usec = 500000;

    result = select(FD_SETSIZE, &testfds, (fd_set *)NULL, (fd_set *)NULL,
                    &timeout);
```

3. After this time, test `result`. If there has been no input, the program loops again. If there has been an error, the program exits:

```
switch(result) {
case 0:
    printf("timeout\n");
    break;
case -1:
    perror("select");
    exit(1);
```

4. If, during the wait, you have some action on the file descriptor, read the input on `stdin` and echo it whenever an <end of line> character is received, until that input is Ctrl+D:

```
default:
    if(FD_ISSET(0,&testfds)) {
        ioctl(0,FIONREAD,&nread);
        if(nread == 0) {
            printf("keyboard done\n");
            exit(0);
        }
        nread = read(0,buffer,nread);
        buffer[nread] = 0;
        printf("read %d from keyboard: %s", nread, buffer);
    }
    break;
    }
  }
}
```

When you run this program, it prints `timeout` every two and a half seconds. If you type at the keyboard, it reads the standard input and reports what was typed. With most shells, the input will be sent to the program when the user presses the Enter (or Return) key or keys in a control sequence, so your program will print the input whenever you press Enter. Note that the Enter key itself is read and processed like any other character (try this by not pressing Enter, but a number of characters followed by Ctrl+D).

```
$ ./select
timeout
hello
read 6 from keyboard: hello
fred
read 5 from keyboard: fred
timeout
^D
keyboard done
$
```

How It Works

The program uses the `select` call to examine the state of the standard input. By arranging a timeout value, the program resumes every 2.5 seconds to print a timeout message. This is indicated by `select` returning zero. On end of file, the standard input descriptor is flagged as ready for input, but there are no characters to be read.

Multiple Clients

Your simple server program can benefit by using `select` to handle multiple clients simultaneously, without resorting to child processes. For real applications using this technique, you must take care that you do not make other clients wait too long while you deal with the first to connect.

The server can use `select` on both the listen socket and the clients' connection sockets at the same time. Once activity has been indicated, you can use `FD_ISSET` to cycle through all the possible file descriptors to discover which one the activity is on.

If the listen socket is ready for input, this will mean that a client is attempting to connect and you can call `accept` without risk of blocking. If a client descriptor is indicated ready, this means that there's a client request pending that you can read and deal with. A read of zero bytes will indicate that a client process has ended and you can close the socket and remove it from your descriptor set.

Try It Out   **An Improved Multiple Client/Server**

1.   For the final example, `server5.c`, you'll include the `sys/time.h` and `sys/ioctl.h` headers instead of `signal.h` as in the last program, and declare some extra variables to deal with `select`:

```
#include <sys/types.h>
#include <sys/socket.h>
#include <stdio.h>
```

```
#include <netinet/in.h>
#include <sys/time.h>
#include <sys/ioctl.h>
#include <unistd.h>
#include <stdlib.h>

int main()
{
    int server_sockfd, client_sockfd;
    int server_len, client_len;
    struct sockaddr_in server_address;
    struct sockaddr_in client_address;
    int result;
    fd_set readfds, testfds;
```

2. Create and name a socket for the server:

```
    server_sockfd = socket(AF_INET, SOCK_STREAM, 0);

    server_address.sin_family = AF_INET;
    server_address.sin_addr.s_addr = htonl(INADDR_ANY);
    server_address.sin_port = htons(9734);
    server_len = sizeof(server_address);

    bind(server_sockfd, (struct sockaddr *)&server_address, server_len);
```

3. Create a connection queue and initialize `readfds` to handle input from `server_sockfd`:

```
    listen(server_sockfd, 5);

    FD_ZERO(&readfds);
    FD_SET(server_sockfd, &readfds);
```

4. Now wait for clients and requests. Because you have passed a null pointer as the `timeout` parameter, no timeout will occur. The program will exit and report an error if `select` returns a value less than 1:

```
while(1) {
        char ch;
        int fd;
        int nread;

        testfds = readfds;

        printf("server waiting\n");
        result = select(FD_SETSIZE, &testfds, (fd_set *)0,
            (fd_set *)0, (struct timeval *) 0);

        if(result < 1) {
            perror("server5");
            exit(1);
        }
```

5. Once you know you've got activity, you can find which descriptor it's on by checking each in turn using `FD_ISSET`:

```
for(fd = 0; fd < FD_SETSIZE; fd++) {
    if(FD_ISSET(fd,&testfds)) {
```

6. If the activity is on `server_sockfd`, it must be a request for a new connection, and you add the associated `client_sockfd` to the descriptor set:

```
if(fd == server_sockfd) {
    client_len = sizeof(client_address);
    client_sockfd = accept(server_sockfd,
        (struct sockaddr *)&client_address, &client_len);
    FD_SET(client_sockfd, &readfds);
    printf("adding client on fd %d\n", client_sockfd);
}
```

7. If it isn't the server, it must be client activity. If `close` is received, the client has gone away, and you remove it from the descriptor set. Otherwise, you "serve" the client as in the previous examples.

```
else {
    ioctl(fd, FIONREAD, &nread);

    if(nread == 0) {
        close(fd);
        FD_CLR(fd, &readfds);
        printf("removing client on fd %d\n", fd);
    }

    else {
        read(fd, &ch, 1);
        sleep(5);
        printf("serving client on fd %d\n", fd);
        ch++;
        write(fd, &ch, 1);
    }
}
}
}
}
}
```

In a real-world program, it would be advisable to include a variable holding the largest fd number con-nected (not necessarily the most recent fd number connected). This would prevent looping through potentially thousands of fds that aren't even connected and couldn't possibly be ready for reading. We've omitted it here simply for brevity's sake and to make the code simpler.

When you run this version of the server, it deals with multiple clients sequentially in a single process.

```
$ ./server5 &
[1] 26686
server waiting
$ ./client3 & ./client3 & ./client3 & ps x
[2] 26689
[3] 26690
adding client on fd 4
server waiting
[4] 26691
   PID TTY       STAT    TIME COMMAND
26686 pts/1      S       0:00 ./server5
26689 pts/1      S       0:00 ./client3
26690 pts/1      S       0:00 ./client3
26691 pts/1      S       0:00 ./client3
26692 pts/1      R+      0:00 ps x
$ serving client on fd 4
server waiting
adding client on fd 5
server waiting
adding client on fd 6
char from server = B
serving client on fd 5
server waiting
removing client on fd 4
char from server = B
serving client on fd 6
server waiting
removing client on fd 5
server waiting
char from server = B
removing client on fd 6
server waiting

[2]    Done                    ./client3
[3]-   Done                    ./client3
[4]+   Done                    ./client3
$
```

To complete the analogy at the start of the chapter, the following table shows the parallels between socket connections and a telephone exchange.

Telephone	Network Sockets
Call company on 555-0828	Connect to IP address 127.0.0.1.
Call answered by reception	Connection established to remote host.
Ask for finance department	Route using specified port (9734).

Continued on next page

Telephone	Network Sockets
Call answered by finance administration	Server returns from `select`.
Call put through to free account manager	Server calls `accept`, creating new socket on extension 456.

Datagrams

In this chapter, we have concentrated on programming applications that maintain connections to their clients, using connection-oriented TCP socket connections. There are cases where the overhead of establishing and maintaining a socket connection is unnecessary.

The `daytime` service used in `getdate.c` earlier provides a good example. You create a socket, make a connection, read a single response, and close the connection. That's a lot of operations just to get the date.

The `daytime` service is also available by UDP using datagrams. To use it, you send a single datagram to the service and get a single datagram containing the date and time in response. It's simple.

Services provided by UDP are typically used where a client needs to make a short query of a server and expects a single short response. If the cost in terms of processing time is low enough, the server is able to provide this service by dealing with requests from clients one at a time, allowing the operating system to hold incoming requests in a queue. This simplifies the coding of the server.

Because UDP is not a guaranteed service, however, you may find that your datagram or your response goes missing. So if the data is important to you, you would need to code your UDP clients carefully to check for errors and retry if necessary. In practice, on a local area network, UDP datagrams are very reliable.

To access a service provided by UDP, you need to use the `socket` and `close` system calls as before, but rather than using `read` and `write` on the socket, you use two datagram-specific system calls, `sendto` and `recvfrom`.

Here's a modified version of `getdate.c` that gets the date via a UDP datagram service. Changes from the earlier version are highlighted.

```
/*  Start with the usual includes and declarations.  */

#include <sys/socket.h>
#include <netinet/in.h>
#include <netdb.h>
#include <stdio.h>
#include <unistd.h>
#include <stdlib.h>

int main(int argc, char *argv[])
{
    char *host;
    int sockfd;
```

```
        int len, result;
        struct sockaddr_in address;
        struct hostent *hostinfo;
        struct servent *servinfo;
        char buffer[128];

        if(argc == 1)
            host = "localhost";
        else
            host = argv[1];

/*  Find the host address and report an error if none is found.  */

        hostinfo = gethostbyname(host);
        if(!hostinfo) {
            fprintf(stderr, "no host: %s\n", host);
            exit(1);
        }

/*  Check that the daytime service exists on the host.  */

        servinfo = getservbyname("daytime", "udp");
        if(!servinfo) {
            fprintf(stderr,"no daytime service\n");
            exit(1);
        }
        printf("daytime port is %d\n", ntohs(servinfo -> s_port));

/*  Create a UDP socket.  */

        sockfd = socket(AF_INET, SOCK_DGRAM, 0);

/*  Construct the address for use with sendto/recvfrom...  */

        address.sin_family = AF_INET;
        address.sin_port = servinfo -> s_port;
        address.sin_addr = *(struct in_addr *)*hostinfo -> h_addr_list;
        len = sizeof(address);

        result = sendto(sockfd, buffer, 1, 0, (struct sockaddr *)&address, len);
        result = recvfrom(sockfd, buffer, sizeof(buffer), 0,
                        (struct sockaddr *)&address, &len);
        buffer[result] = '\0';
        printf("read %d bytes: %s", result, buffer);

        close(sockfd);
        exit(0);
}
```

As you can see, the changes required are very small. You find the daytime service with `getservbyname` as before, but you specify the datagram service by requesting the UDP protocol. You create a datagram socket using socket with a `SOCK_DGRAM` parameter. You set up the destination address as before, but now you have to send a datagram rather than just read from the socket.

Because you are not making an explicit connection to services provided by UDP, you have to have some way of letting the server know that you want to receive a response. In this case, you send a datagram (here you send a single byte from the buffer you are going to receive the response into) to the service, and it responds with the date and time.

The `sendto` system call sends a datagram from a buffer on a socket using a socket address and address length. Its prototype is essentially

```
int sendto(int sockfd, void *buffer, size_t len, int flags,
           struct sockaddr *to, socklen_t tolen);
```

In normal use, the `flags` parameter can be kept zero.

The `recvfrom` system call waits on a socket for a datagram from a specified address and receives it into a buffer. Its prototype is essentially

```
int recvfrom(int sockfd, void *buffer, size_t len, int flags,
             struct sockaddr *from, socklen_t *fromlen);
```

Again, in normal use, the `flags` parameter can be kept zero.

To keep the example short, we have omitted error handling. Both sendto and recvfrom will return |1 if an error occurs and will set errno appropriately. Possible errors include the following:

To keep the example short we have omitted error

Errno Value	Description
EBADF	An invalid file descriptor was passed.
EINTR	A signal occurred.

Unless the socket is set nonblocking using `fcntl` (as you saw for accepting TCP connections earlier), the `recvfrom` call will block indefinitely. The socket can, however, be used with `select` and a timeout to determine whether any data has arrived in the same way that you have seen with the connection-based servers earlier. Alternatively, an alarm clock signal can be used to interrupt a receive operation (see Chapter 11).

Summary

In this chapter, we've covered another method of inter-process communication: sockets. These allow you to develop true distributed client/server applications to run across networks. We briefly covered some of the host database information functions and how Linux handles standard system services with the Internet daemon. You worked through a number of client/server example programs that demonstrate networking and handling multiple clients.

Finally, you learned about the `select` system call that allows a program to be advised of input and output activity on several open file descriptors and sockets at once.

Programming GNOME Using GTK+

So far in this book, we've covered the major topics in Linux programming that deal with complex, under-the-hood stuff. Now it's time to breathe some life into your applications and look at how to add a Graphical User Interface (GUI) to them. In this chapter and Chapter 17, we're going to look at the two most popular GUI libraries for Linux: GTK+ and KDE/Qt. These libraries correspond to the two most popular Linux desktop environments: GNOME (GTK+) and KDE.

All GUI libraries in Linux sit on top of the underlying windowing system called the *X Window System* (or more commonly *X11* or just *X*), so before we delve into GNOME/GTK+ details we provide an overview of how X operates and help you understand how the various layers of the windowing system fit together to create what we call the *desktop*.

In this chapter, we cover

- ❑ The X Window System
- ❑ An introduction to GNOME/GTK+
- ❑ GTK+ widgets
- ❑ GNOME widgets and menus
- ❑ Dialogs
- ❑ CD Database GUI using GNOME/GTK+

Introducing X

If you've ever used a desktop windowing system on Linux, then you've most likely used X, an open source graphics system. One of the most innovative, and ultimately frustrating, features of X is the rigid adherence to the mantra of *mechanism, not policy*. That means X defines no user interface, but provides the means to make one. This means you're free to create your own entire desktop environment, experimenting and innovating at will. But, it also hindered user interfaces on Linux and UNIX for a long time. Into this relative void, two desktop projects emerged as the favorites of Linux users: GNOME and KDE. The Linux desktop does not begin and end with X, however. In truth, the desktop in Linux is a rather nebulous thing, with no single project or group releasing a definitive version. A modern installation contains a myriad of libraries, utilities, and applications that collectively are called "the desktop."

X has a long and illustrious history, having been originally developed at MIT in the early 1980s. X was developed to provide a unified windowing system for the high-end scientific workstations of the day, which were hugely expensive, number-crunching beasts.

As the 1990s came and hardware prices dropped, X was ported by enthusiasts to run on inexpensive home PCs, a project that became known as XFree86 (PC processors made by Intel and other companies are known as x86 processors), and it is the descendants of XFree86 that are distributed today with Linux, with most Linux distributions using an X variant called X.Org.

The X Window System is separated into hardware-level and application-level components known as the X server and the X client. These components communicate using the aptly named X Protocol. The following sections look at each of these in turn.

X Server

The X server runs on the user's local machine and is the part that performs the low-level operation of drawing the graphics onscreen. The *server* part of the name often confuses: the X server runs on your desktop PC. X clients may run on your desktop PC, or X clients can actually run on other systems on your network — including servers. The reversed terminology actually makes sense when you think about it, but it often seems backwards.

Because the X server talks directly to the graphics card, you must use an X server specific to your graphics card, and it must be configured with appropriate resolution, refresh rate, color depth, and so on. The configuration file is named xorg.conf or Xfree86Config. In the past, you usually had to manually edit the configuration file to get X working properly. Thankfully, modern Linux distributions autodetect the correct settings, saving users time and a great deal of head scratching!

The X server listens for user input via the mouse and keyboard and relays keyboard presses and mouse clicks to X client applications. These messages are called *events*; they form a key element of GUI programming. We look at events and their logical GTK+ extension, *signals*, in detail later in this chapter.

X Client

An X client is any program that uses the X Window System as a GUI. Examples are xterm, xcalc, and more advanced applications, like Abiword. An X client typically waits for user events sent by the X server and responds by sending redraw messages back to the server.

The X client need not be on the same machine as the X server.

X Protocol

The X client and X server communicate using the X Protocol, which enables the client and server to be separated over a network. For instance, you can run an X client application from a remote computer on the Internet or over an encrypted Virtual Private Network (VPN). For the vast majority of personal Linux systems, X clients and the X server run on the same system.

Xlib

Xlib is the library used indirectly by an X client to generate the X Protocol messages. It provides a very low-level API to allow the client to draw very basic elements on the X server and to respond to the simplest of inputs. We must emphasize that Xlib is *very* low level — to create something even as simple as a menu using Xlib is an incredibly laborious process that needs hundreds of lines of code.

A GUI programmer cannot sensibly program directly with Xlib. You need an API that makes GUI elements such as menus, buttons, and drop-down lists easy and simple to create. In a nutshell, this is the role of the *toolkit*.

Toolkits

A toolkit is a GUI library that X clients utilize to greatly simplify the creation of windows, menus, buttons, and so on. Using a toolkit, you can create buttons, menus, frames, and the like with single function calls. The generic term for GUI elements such as these is *widgets*, a universal term you'll find in all modern GUI libraries.

There are dozens of toolkits for X to choose from, each with their defining strengths and weaknesses. Which one you choose is an important design decision for your application, and some of the factors you should consider are

❑   Who are you targeting with your application?

❑   Will your users have the toolkit libraries installed?

❑   Does the toolkit have a port for other popular operating systems?

❑   What software license does the toolkit use, and is it compatible with your intended use?

❑   Does the toolkit support your programming language?

❑   Does the toolkit have a modern look and feel?

Historically, the most popular toolkits were Motif, OpenLook, and Xt, but these have been largely superceded by the technically superior GTK+ and Qt toolkits that form the basis of the GNOME and KDE desktops, respectively.

Window Managers

The final piece in the X puzzle is the window manager, which is responsible for positioning windows onscreen. Window managers often support separate "workspaces" that divide the desktop, increasing the area with which you can interact. The window manager is also responsible for adding decoration around each window, which usually consists of a frame and title bar with maximize, minimize, and close icons. Window managers provide part of the look and feel of the desktop, such as the window title bars.

Common window managers include:

❑   Metacity, the default window manager for the GNOME desktop.

❑   KWin, the default window manager for the KDE desktop.

❑   Openbox, designed to conserve resources and run on older, slower systems.

❑   Enlightenment, a window manager that displays awesome graphics and effects.

As with everything in X, you can switch window managers. Most users, though, run the window manager that comes with their desktop environment.

Other Ways to Create a GUI — Platform-Independent Windowing APIs

It's worth mentioning other ways to create GUIs that are not specific to Linux — there are languages that have native GUI support that function under Linux:

❑   **The Java Language** supports programming GUIs using the Swing and older AWT APIs. The look and feel of Java GUIs isn't to everybody's taste, and on older machines the interface can feel clunky and unresponsive. A great advantage of Java is that once you've compiled your Java code, it runs unchanged on any platform with a Java Virtual Machine, which includes Linux, Windows, Mac OS, and mobile devices. See http://java.sun.com for more information.

❑   **C#** is a programming language very similar to Java. On Linux, the C# Common Language Runtime, or CLR, platform comes from the Mono project at http://www.mono-project.com. C# on the Mono platform supports both Windows. Forms, also used on Windows, and a special binding to the GTK+ toolkit, called Gtk#.

❑   **Tcl/Tk** is a scripting language that is excellent for rapid development of GUIs and works with X, Windows, and Mac OS. It's great for rapid prototyping or for small utilities where you want the simplicity and maintainability of a script. You can find all the details at http://tcl.tk.

❑   **Python** is also a scripting language. You can use the Tk part of Tcl/Tk from Python, or you can program to the Python GTK+ binding, writing GTK+ programs in Python. You can find more about Python at http://www.python.org.

❑   **Perl** is another common Linux scripting language. You can use the Tk part of Tcl/Tk from Perl, as Perl/Tk. You can find more about Perl at http://www.perl.org/.

With the platform independence that these languages bring there is a price to pay. Sharing information with native applications — for instance, using "drag and drop" — is difficult, and saving configuration usually has to be done in a proprietary rather than the desktop standard way. Sometimes vendors of Java software cheat by shipping with platform-specific extensions to get around these sorts of problems.

Introducing GTK+

Now that you've looked at the X Window System, it's time to look at the GTK+ Toolkit. GTK+ started out life as part of the popular GNU Image Manipulation Program, The GIMP, which is how GTK derives its name (The *Gimp ToolKit*). The GIMP programmers clearly had great foresight in making GTK+ a project in its own right because it has grown and developed into one of the most powerful and popular toolkits around. The homepage of the GTK+ project is http://www.gtk.org.

> *To recap, GTK+ is a library that greatly simplifies the creation of Graphical User Interfaces (GUIs) by providing a set of ready-made components called widgets that you bolt together with easy-to-use function calls to your application logic.*

Although GTK+ is a GNU project like The GIMP, it is released under the terms of the more liberal LGPL (Lesser General Public License) that permits software (including closed source proprietary software) to be written using GTK+ without payment of fees, royalties, or other restrictions. The freedom offered by the GTK+ license is in contrast to its competitor Qt (the subject of the next chapter), whose GPL license prohibits commercial software from being developed using Qt (you must instead purchase a commercial Qt license in that case).

GTK+ is written entirely in C, and the majority of GTK+ software is also written in C. Fortunately there are a number of language bindings that allow you to use GTK+ in your preferred language, be it C++, Python, PHP, Ruby, Perl, C#, or Java.

GTK+ itself is built on top of a number of other libraries. These include:

❑ GLib — provides low-level data structures, types, thread support, the event loop, and dynamic loading.

❑ GObject — implements an object-oriented system in C without requiring C++.

❑ Pango — supports text rendering and layout.

❑ ATK — helps you create accessible applications and allows users to run your applications with screen readers and other accessibility tools.

❑ GDK, the GIMP Drawing Kit — handles low-level graphics rendering on top of the Xlib.

❑ GdkPixbuf — helps manipulate images within GTK+ programs.

❑ Xlib — provides the low-level graphics on Linux and UNIX systems.

GLib Type System

If you've ever browsed through GTK+ code, you may have wondered why you saw a lot of C data types prefixed with the letter g, such as gint, gchar, gshort, as well as unfamiliar types such as gint32 and gpointer. This is because GTK+ is based on C portability libraries called *GLib* and *GObject* that define these types to aid in cross-platform development.

GLib and GObject aid cross-platform development by providing a standard set of replacement data types, functions, and macros to handle memory management and common tasks. These types, functions, and macros mean that as GTK+ programmers we can be confident that our code will port reliably to other platforms and architectures.

GLib also defines some convenient constants:

```
#include <glib/gmacros.h>

#define FALSE  0
#define TRUE   !FALSE
```

The additional data types are essentially those that are replacements for the standard C types (for consistency and readability) and those that guarantee byte length across all platforms:

❑ gint, guint, gchar, guchar, glong, gulong, gfloat, and gdouble are simple replacements for the standard C types for consistency.

❑ gpointer is synonymous with (void *).

❑ gboolean is useful for representing boolean values and is a wrapper for int.

❑ gint8, guint8, gint16, guint16, gint32, and guint32 are signed and unsigned types with a guaranteed byte length.

Usefully, using GLib and GObject is almost transparent. GLib is used extensively in GTK+, so if you have a working GTK+ setup, you'll find GLib installed. When programming with GTK+ you don't even need to explicitly include the glib.h header file, as you'll see later in the chapter.

GTK+ Object System

Anybody who has experimented with GUI programming before will probably understand when we write that GUI libraries strongly lend themselves to the paradigm of object-oriented (OO) programming; so much so that all modern toolkits are written in an object-oriented fashion, including GTK+.

Despite GTK+ being written purely in C, it supports objects and OO programming through the GObject library. This library supports object inheritance and polymorphism using macros.

Let's look at an example of inheritance and polymorphism by looking at the GtkWindow object hierarchy taken from the GTK+ API documentation:

```
GObject
    +----GInitiallyUnowned
    +----GtkObject
            +----GtkWidget
                    +----GtkContainer
                            +----GtkBin
                                    +----GtkWindow
```

This list of objects tells you that GtkWindow is a child of GtkBin, and therefore any function you can call with a GtkBin can be called with GtkWindow. Similarly, GtkWindow inherits from GtkContainer, which inherits from GtkWidget.

As a matter of convenience, all widget creation functions return a GtkWidget type. For example:

```
GtkWidget*  gtk_window_new (GtkWindowType type);
```

Suppose you create a GtkWindow, and want to pass the returned value to a function that expects a GtkContainer such as gtk_container_add:

```
void gtk_container_add (GtkContainer *container, GtkWidget *widget);
```

You use the GTK_CONTAINER macro to cast between a GtkWidget and GtkContainer:

```
GtkWidget * window = gtk_window_new(GTK GTK_WINDOW_TOPLEVEL);
gtk_container_add(GTK_CONTAINER(window), awidget);
```

You'll see the meaning of these functions later; for now, notice that macros are frequently used. Macros exist for every conceivable cast.

Don't worry if all this is a little unclear; you don't need to understand OO programming in any detail to come to grips with GNOME/GTK+. In fact, it's a painless way to learn the ideas and benefits behind OO programming while still in the comfort zone of C.

Introducing GNOME

GNOME is the name given to a project started in 1997 by programmers working on the GNU Image Manipulation Program (The GIMP) to create a unified desktop for Linux. There was a general consensus that adoption of Linux as a desktop platform was being held back by the lack of a coherent strategy. At that time, the Linux desktop resembled the Wild West, with no overall standards or agreed-upon practices and an "anything goes" programmer mentality. With no overarching group controlling things such as desktop menus, a consistent look and feel, documentation, translation, and so on, the newbie experience on the desktop was at best confusing and at worst unusable.

The GNOME team set out to create a desktop for Linux licensed entirely under the GPL, developing utilities and configuration programs in a uniform and consistent style while promoting standards for inter-application communication, printing, session-management, and best-practices in GUI application programming.

The results of their efforts are clear for all to see — GNOME is the basis of the default Linux desktop for the Fedora, Red Hat, Ubuntu, and openSUSE distributions, among others (see Figure 16-1).

Figure 16-1

GNOME originally stood for the GNU Network Object Model Environment — this reflects one of the early goals, which was to introduce an object framework to Linux like the Microsoft OLE, so that you could embed, for example, a spreadsheet in a word processor document. Now the design goals have moved on, and what we know as GNOME refers to the complete desktop environment, which consists of a panel for launching apps, a suite of programs and utilities, programming libraries, and developer support features.

Before you start programming, you need to make sure you've got all the libraries installed.

Installing the GNOME/GTK+ Development Libraries

The complete GNOME desktop with its standard applications and the GNOME/GTK+ development libraries stretches over more than 60 packages; as a result, installing GNOME from scratch either manually or from source code is a daunting prospect. Thankfully, modern Linux distributions have excellent package management utilities that make installing GNOME/GTK+ and the development libraries a breeze.

In Red Hat and Fedora Linux you open the Package Management tool by clicking the Applications menu button (in the top left) and choosing Add/Remove Software. When the Package Management tool appears (see Figure 16-2), make sure that the GNOME Software Development checkbox is checked. Look in the Development area for this setting.

> **In this chapter, you will be working with GNOME/GTK+ 2, so make sure your installation contains the version 2.x libraries.**

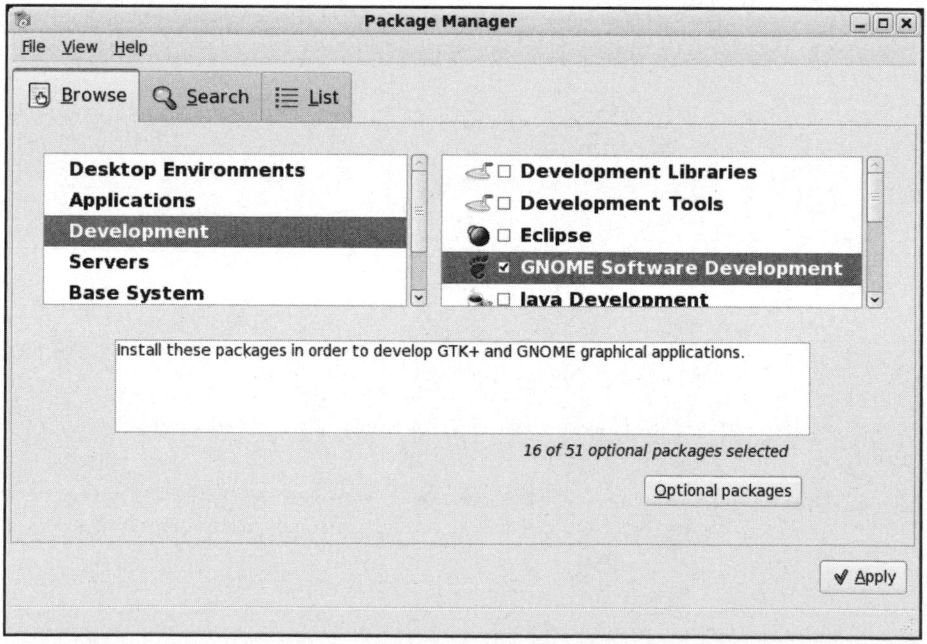

Figure 16-2

For distributions that use RPM packages, you should have at least the following RPM packages installed:

```
gtk2-2.10.11-7.fc7.rpm
gtk2-devel-2.10.11-7.fc7.rpm
gtk2-engines-2.10.0-3.fc7.rpm
libgnome-2.18.0-4.fc7.rpm
libgnomeui-2.18.1-2.fc7.rpm
libgnome-devel-2.18.0-4.fc7.rpm
libgnomeui-devel-2.18.1-2.fc7.rpm
```

In this example, the fc7 *in the file names references the Fedora 7 Linux distribution. On your system, you may see slightly different names.*

In Debian or Debian-based systems like Ubuntu, you can use apt-get to install the GNOME/GTK+ packages from various mirrors — follow the links from http://www.gnome.org for details.

Also try out the GTK+ demo application that shows off all the widgets in their finery (see Figure 16-3):

```
$ gtk-demo
```

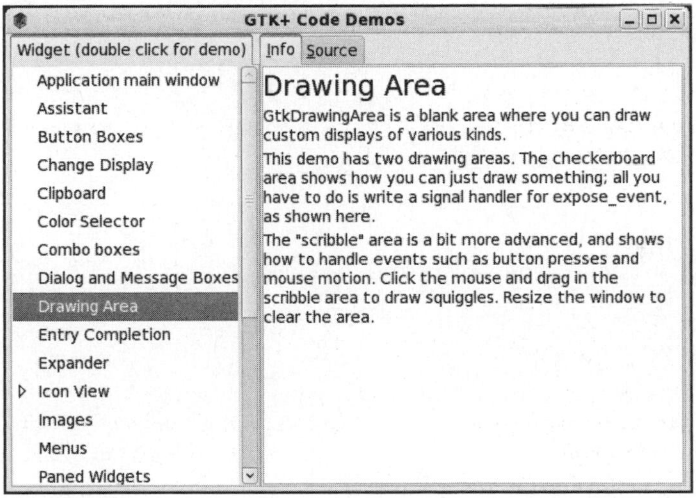

Figure 16-3

With each widget, you can see both an Info tab and a Source tab. The Source tab shows actual C source code for using the given widget. This can provide a great set of examples.

Try It Out   A Plain GtkWindow

Let's start programming GTK+ with the simplest of GUI programs: displaying a window. You'll see the GTK+ libraries in action, and see how much functionality you get from surprisingly little code.

1.   Type this program and call it gtk1.c:

```c
#include <gtk/gtk.h>

int main (int argc, char *argv[])
```

```
{
    GtkWidget *window;

    gtk_init(&argc, &argv);
    window = gtk_window_new(GTK_WINDOW_TOPLEVEL);
    gtk_widget_show(window);
    gtk_main ();

    return 0;
}
```

2.   To compile gtk1.c type:

$ gcc gtk1.c -o gtk1 `pkg-config --cflags --libs gtk+-2.0`

Take care to type backticks, not apostrophes — remember that backticks are instructions to the shell to execute and append the output of the enclosed command.

When you run this program with the following command, your window should pop up (see Figure 16-4):

$ ./gtk1

Figure 16-4

Note that you can move, resize, minimize, and maximize the window.

How It Works

You include the necessary GTK+ and related library headers (including GLib) with a single #include <gtk/gtk.h> statement. Next, you declare the window to be a pointer to a GtkWidget.

Next, to initialize the GTK+ libraries, you must make a call to gtk_init, passing in the command-line arguments argc and argv. This gives GTK+ a chance to parse any command-line parameters it needs to know about. Note that you must always initialize GTK+ in this way before calling any GTK+ functions.

The core of the example is the call you make to gtk_window_new. The prototype is

GtkWidget* gtk_window_new (GtkWindowType type);

type can take one of two values depending on the purpose of the window:

❑   GTK_WINDOW_TOPLEVEL: A standard framed window

❑   GTK_WINDOW_POPUP: A frameless window suitable for dialog boxes

You'll almost always use GTK_WINDOW_TOPLEVEL, because there are far more convenient ways of creating dialogs, as you'll see later.

The call to gtk_window_new sets up the window in memory, so you have a chance to populate it with widgets, resize it, change the window title, and so forth, before actually displaying it onscreen. To make the window actually appear onscreen, call gtk_widget_show:

```
gtk_widget_show(window);
```

Conveniently, this takes a GtkWidget pointer, so you simply pass in the reference to your window.

The final call you make is to gtk_main. This key function starts up the interactivity process by passing control to GTK+ and doesn't return until a call to gtk_main_quit is made. As you can see, in gtk1.c this never happens, so the application doesn't end even after the window is closed. Try this out by clicking the close icon and seeing that the command prompt doesn't return. You'll rectify this after you've learned about signals and callbacks in the next section. For now, quit the application by typing Ctrl+C in the shell window you used to launch the gtk1 program.

Events, Signals, and Callbacks

All GUI libraries have one thing in common: Some mechanism must exist to execute code in response to a user action. A command-line program has the luxury of halting execution to wait for input and can then use something like a switch statement to branch execution based on the input. This approach is impractical with a GUI application because the application must continually respond to user input; for example, it needs to continually update areas of the window.

Modern windowing systems have systems of events and event listeners that address this problem. The idea is that each user input, usually from the mouse or keyboard, triggers an event. A keyboard press would trigger a "keyboard event," for example. Code is then written to listen for these events and to execute when such an event is triggered.

As you saw earlier, the X Window System emits these events, but they aren't much help to you as a GTK+ programmer, because they're very low level. When a mouse button is clicked, X emits an event that contains the coordinates of the pointer — what you really need to know is when a user activates a widget.

Accordingly, GTK+ has its own system of events and event listeners, known as signals and callbacks. They're very easy to use because you can use a very useful feature of C, a pointer to a function, to set the signal handler.

First some definitions: A GTK+ *signal* is emitted by a GtkObject when something such as user input occurs. A function that is connected to a signal, and therefore called whenever that signal is emitted, is known as a *callback function*.

Note that a GTK+ signal is quite separate from a UNIX signal, discussed in Chapter 11.

As a GTK+ programmer, all you need to worry about is writing and connecting callback functions, because the signal-emitting code is internal to the particular widget.

The callback function prototype is typically like this:

```
void a_callback_function ( GtkWidget *widget, gpointer user_data);
```

You are passed two parameters, the first a pointer to the widget that emitted the signal and the second an arbitrary pointer that you pick yourself when you connect the callback. You can use this pointer for any purpose.

Connecting the callback is just as simple. You simply call g_signal_connect and pass in the widget, a signal name as a string, a callback function pointer, and your arbitrary pointer:

```
gulong g_signal_connect(gpointer *object, const gchar *name, GCallback func,
                        gpointer  user_data );
```

One point worthy of noting — there are no restrictions in connecting callbacks. You can have multiple signals to a single callback function, and multiple callback functions connected to a single signal. You can see in detail the signals that each widget emits by reading the GTK+ API documentation.

> Prior to GTK+ 2, the function to connect callback functions was gtk_signal_connect. This function has been replaced by g_signal_connect and should not be used in new code.

You try out g_signal_connect in your next example.

Try It Out   A Callback Function

In gtk2.c, add a button to your window and attach the button's "clicked" signal to your callback function to print a short message:

```c
#include <gtk/gtk.h>
#include <stdio.h>

static int count = 0;

void button_clicked(GtkWidget *button, gpointer data)
{
  printf("%s pressed %d time(s) \n", (char *) data, ++count);
}

int main (int argc, char *argv[])
{
  GtkWidget *window;
  GtkWidget *button;

  gtk_init(&argc, &argv);
  window = gtk_window_new(GTK_WINDOW_TOPLEVEL);
```

```
    button = gtk_button_new_with_label("Hello World!");
    gtk_container_add(GTK_CONTAINER(window), button);


    g_signal_connect(GTK_OBJECT (button), "clicked",
                    GTK_SIGNAL_FUNC (button_clicked),
                    "Button 1");
    gtk_widget_show(button);
    gtk_widget_show(window);

    gtk_main ();

    return 0;
}
```

Enter the program source code and save the file under the name gtk2.c. Compile and link the program similarly to the previous gtk1.c example. When running this program, you'll get a window with a button. Each time you click the button, it prints out a short message (see Figure 16-5).

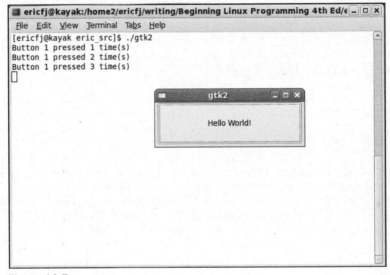

Figure 16-5

How It Works

You've introduced two new features in gtk2.c: a GtkButton and a callback function. A GtkButton is a simple button widget that can contain text, in this case "Hello World," and emits a signal called "clicked" whenever the button is pressed with the mouse.

The callback function button_clicked is connected to the "clicked" signal of the button widget using the g_signal_connect function:

```
    g_signal_connect(GTK_OBJECT (app), "clicked",
                    GTK_SIGNAL_FUNC (button_clicked),
                    "Button 1");
```

Note that the name of the button — `"Button 1"` — is passed as user data to the callback function.

The rest of the additional code deals with the button widget, which is created in the same way as the window — a call to a `gtk_button_new_with_label` function — and `gtk_widget_show` makes it visible.

To place the button on the window, you call `gtk_container_add`. This simple function places a `GtkWidget` inside a `GtkContainer` and takes the container and widget as arguments:

```
void gtk_container_add (GtkContainer *container, GtkWidget *widget);
```

As you saw before, `GtkWindow` is a child of `GtkContainer`, so you can cast your *window* object to a `GtkContainer` type using the `GTK_CONTAINER` macro:

```
gtk_container_add(GTK_CONTAINER(window), button);
```

`gtk_container_add` is great for placing a single widget inside a container, but more often you'll need to arrange several widgets in various positions in a window to create a decent interface. GTK+ has special widgets just for this purpose, called *box* or *container* widgets.

Packing Box Widgets

The layout of a GUI is of key importance to its usability and one of the hardest things to get right. The real difficulty with arranging widgets is that you can't rely on all users to have the same screen resolution, or to have the same window size, theme, font, or color scheme. What might be a pleasing interface on one system might be impossible to read on another.

To create a GUI that appears uniform on all systems, you need to avoid placing widgets using absolute coordinates and instead use a more flexible system of layout. GTK+ has container widgets for this purpose. Container widgets allow you to control the layout of widgets within your application windows. Box widgets provide a very useful type of container widget. GTK+ offers many other types of container widgets, covered in the GTK+ online documentation discussed previously.

Box widgets are invisible widgets whose job it is to contain other widgets and control their layout. To control the size of the individual widgets contained inside the box widget, you specify rules instead of coordinates. Because box widgets contain any `GtkWidget`, and a `GtkBox` is itself a `GtkWidget`, you can nest box widgets inside one another to create complex layouts.

There are two main subclasses of `GtkBox`:

❑ `GtkHBox` is a single row horizontal packing box widget.

❑ `GtkVBox` is a single column vertical packing box widget.

When the packing boxes are created, you should specify two parameters, `homogeneous` and `spacing`:

```
GtkWidget*   gtk_hbox_new (gboolean homogeneous, gint spacing);
GtkWidget*   gtk_vbox_new (gboolean homogeneous, gint spacing);
```

These parameters control layout for all of the widgets in that particular packing box. homogeneous is a boolean that, when set to TRUE, forces contained widgets to occupy equal space, regardless of individual size. spacing sets the gap between widgets in pixels.

Once you've created the packing box, add widgets using gtk_box_pack_start and gtk_box_pack_end functions:

```
void gtk_box_pack_start (GtkBox *box, GtkWidget *child,
                         gboolean expand, gboolean fill,
                         guint padding);

void gtk_box_pack_end (GtkBox *box, GtkWidget *child,
                       gboolean expand, gboolean fill,
                       guint padding);
```

gtk_box_pack_start adds widgets to the left side of a GtkHBox and to the bottom of a GtkVBox; conversely gtk_box_pack_end from the right and top. Their parameters control the spacing and format of each widget within the packing box.

The following table describes the parameters you can pass to gtk_box_pack_start or gtk_box_pack_end.

Parameter	Description
GtkBox *box	The packing box to be filled.
GtkWidget *child	The widget to be placed in the packing box.
gboolean expand	If TRUE, this widget fills all available space shared between the other widgets with this flag also set to TRUE.
gboolean fill	If TRUE, this widget will fill the space allocated to it, rather than use it as padding around the edges. Only valid when expand is TRUE.
guint padding	Padding size in pixels around widget.

Let's take a look at these packing box widgets now and create a more complex user interface, showing off nested packing boxes.

Try It Out   Widget Container Layout

In this example, you lay out some simple GtkLabel widgets using GtkHBox and GtkVBox. Label widgets are simple widgets that are useful for displaying short amounts of text. Call this program container.c.

```
#include <gtk/gtk.h>

void closeApp ( GtkWidget *window, gpointer data)
{
  gtk_main_quit();
}
```

```
/* Callback allows the application to cancel

a close/destroy event. (Return TRUE to cancel.) */

gboolean delete_event(GtkWidget *widget, GdkEvent *event, gpointer data)

{

  printf("In delete_event\n");

  return FALSE;

}

int main (int argc, char *argv[])
{
  GtkWidget *window;
  GtkWidget *label1, *label2, *label3;
  GtkWidget *hbox;
  GtkWidget *vbox;

  gtk_init(&argc, &argv);
  window = gtk_window_new(GTK_WINDOW_TOPLEVEL);

  gtk_window_set_title(GTK_WINDOW(window), "The Window Title");
  gtk_window_set_position(GTK_WINDOW(window), GTK_WIN_POS_CENTER);
  gtk_window_set_default_size(GTK_WINDOW(window), 300, 200);

  g_signal_connect ( GTK_OBJECT (window), "destroy",
                     GTK_SIGNAL_FUNC ( closeApp), NULL);

  g_signal_connect ( GTK_OBJECT (window), "delete_event",

                     GTK_SIGNAL_FUNC ( delete_event), NULL);

  label1 = gtk_label_new("Label 1");
  label2 = gtk_label_new("Label 2");
  label3 = gtk_label_new("Label 3");

  hbox = gtk_hbox_new ( TRUE, 5 );
  vbox = gtk_vbox_new ( FALSE, 10);

  gtk_box_pack_start(GTK_BOX(vbox), label1, TRUE, FALSE, 5);
  gtk_box_pack_start(GTK_BOX(vbox), label2, TRUE, FALSE, 5);

  gtk_box_pack_start(GTK_BOX(hbox), vbox, FALSE, FALSE, 5);
  gtk_box_pack_start(GTK_BOX(hbox), label3, FALSE, FALSE, 5);

  gtk_container_add(GTK_CONTAINER(window), hbox);
  gtk_widget_show_all(window);
  gtk_main ();

  return 0;
}
```

When you run this program, you see the layout of label widgets in your window (see Figure 16-6).

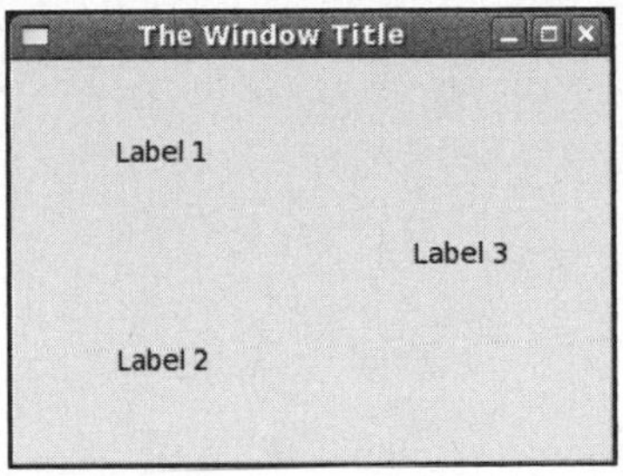

The Window Title

Label 1

Label 3

Label 2

Figure 16-6

How It Works

You create two packing box widgets, hbox and vbox. You fill vbox with label1 and label2 using gtk_box_pack_start, so label2 appears at the bottom because it is added after label1. Next vbox itself is added to hbox along with label3.

hbox is finally added to the window and is shown onscreen using gtk_widget_show_all.

The packing box layout is understood best with a diagram, as shown in Figure 16-7.

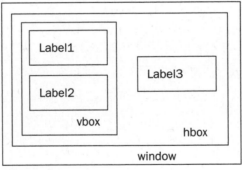

Figure 16-7

Now that you've looked at widgets, signals, callbacks, and container widgets, you've seen the essentials of GTK+. Becoming a knowledgeable GTK+ programmer involves understanding how best to use the available widgets.

GTK+ Widgets

In this section, we look at the API of the common GTK+ widgets you'll use most often in your applications.

GtkWindow

GtkWindow is the basic element of all GTK+ applications. You've used it so far to hold your widgets:

```
GtkWidget
    +----GtkContainer
              +----GtkBin
                        +----GtkWindow
```

There are dozens of GtkWindow API calls, but here are the functions worthy of special attention:

```
GtkWidget* gtk_window_new (GtkWindowType type);
void gtk_window_set_title (GtkWindow *window, const gchar *title);
void gtk_window_set_position (GtkWindow *window, GtkWindowPosition position);
void gtk_window_set_default_size (GtkWindow *window, gint width, gint height);
void gtk_window_resize (GtkWindow *window, gint width, gint height);
void gtk_window_set_resizable (GtkWindow *window, gboolean resizable);
void gtk_window_present (GtkWindow *window);
void gtk_window_maximize (GtkWindow *window);
void gtk_window_unmaximize (GtkWindow *window);
```

As you've just seen, gtk_window_new creates a new, empty window in memory. The window title is unset, and the size and screen position of the window are undefined. You will normally populate the window with widgets and set up a menu and toolbar before making the window visible onscreen with a call to gtk_widget_show.

The gtk_window_set_title function changes the text of the title bar by informing the window manager of the request.

Note that because it is the window manager, not GTK+, that is responsible for painting the window surround, the font, color, and size of the text are dependent on your choice of window manager.

gtk_window_set_position controls the position of the initial placement onscreen. The position parameter can take five values, described in the following table.

Position Parameter	Description
GTK_WIN_POS_NONE	The window is placed at the discretion of the window manager.
GTK_WIN_POS_CENTER	The window is positioned centrally onscreen.
GTK_WIN_POS_MOUSE	The window is positioned at the mouse pointer.
GTK_WIN_POS_CENTER_ALWAYS	Keeps the window centered regardless of size.
GTK_WIN_POS_CENTER_ON_PARENT	Sets the window centrally on its parent (useful for dialog boxes).

`gtk_window_set_default_size` sets the size of the window onscreen in GTK+ drawing units. Explicitly setting the size of the window ensures that the contents of the window aren't obscured or hidden. To force a resize of the window once it's onscreen, you can use `gtk_window_resize`. By default, the user is able to resize the window by dragging the frame in the usual way. To prevent this, you can call `gtk_window_set_resizeable` set to FALSE.

To ensure that your window is onscreen and visible to the user — that is, not minimized or hidden — `gtk_window_present` fits the bill. `gtk_window_present` is useful for dialog boxes to make sure they're not minimized when you need some user input. Alternatively, to force maximizing and minimizing you have `gtk_window_maximize` and `gtk_window_minimize`.

GtkEntry

The `GtkEntry` widget is a single-line text entry widget that is commonly used to enter simple textual information, for example an e-mail address, a username, or a hostname. There are API calls that enable you to set as well as read the entered text, set the maximum number of allowed characters, and set other things to control the positioning and selection of the text:

```
GtkWidget
    +----GtkEntry
```

`GtkEntry` can be set to display asterisks (or any other user-definable character) in place of the literal typed characters, which can be very useful for entering passwords when you don't want anybody to lean over your shoulder and read the text.

We'll describe the most useful `GtkEntry` functions:

```
GtkWidget*  gtk_entry_new (void);
GtkWidget*  gtk_entry_new_with_max_length (gint max);
void  gtk_entry_set_max_length (GtkEntry *entry, gint max);
G_CONST_RETURN gchar* gtk_entry_get_text (GtkEntry *entry);
void  gtk_entry_set_text (GtkEntry *entry, const gchar *text);
void  gtk_entry_append_text (GtkEntry *entry, const gchar *text);
void  gtk_entry_prepend_text (GtkEntry *entry, const gchar *text);
void  gtk_entry_set_visibility (GtkEntry *entry, gboolean visible);
void  gtk_entry_set_invisible_char (GtkEntry *entry, gchar invch);
void  gtk_entry_set_editable (GtkEntry *entry, gboolean editable);
```

You can create a `GtkEntry` with either `gtk_entry_new`, or with a fixed maximum length of input text with `gtk_entry_new_with_max_length`. Restricting the input to a certain length saves you the effort of validating the input length and possibly having to inform the user that the text is too long.

To get the contents of the `GtkEntry`, you call `gtk_entry_get_text`, which returns a `const char` pointer internal to the `GtkEntry` (`G_CONST_RETURN` is a GLib-defined macro). If you want to modify the text, or pass it to a function that might modify it, you must copy the string using, for example, `strcpy`.

You can manually set and modify the contents of the `GtkEntry` using the `_set_text`, `_append_text`, and `_modify_text` functions. Note that these take `const` pointers.

To use `GtkEntry` as a password entry box that displays asterisks in place of characters, use `gtk_entry_set_visibilility` passing FALSE as the visible parameter. The invisible character can be changed using `gtk_entry_set_invisible_char` to suit your requirements.

Try It Out   Username and Password Entry

Now that you've seen the `GtkEntry` functions, let's look at them in action with a short program. `entry.c` will create a username and password entry window and compare the entered password with a secret password.

1. First define the secret password, cunningly chosen to be `secret`:

```
#include <gtk/gtk.h>
#include <stdio.h>
#include <string.h>

const char * password = "secret";
```

2. You have two callback functions that are called when the window is destroyed and the OK button is clicked:

```
void closeApp ( GtkWidget *window, gpointer data)
{
  gtk_main_quit();
}

void button_clicked (GtkWidget *button, gpointer data)
{
  const char *password_text = gtk_entry_get_text(GTK_ENTRY((GtkWidget *) data));

  if (strcmp(password_text, password) == 0)
    printf("Access granted!\n");
  else
    printf("Access denied!\n");
}
```

3. In `main`, the interface is created and laid out, and the callbacks connected. Use `hbox` and `vbox` container widgets to lay out the label and entry widgets.

```
int main (int argc, char *argv[])
{
  GtkWidget *window;
  GtkWidget *username_label, *password_label;
  GtkWidget *username_entry, *password_entry;
  GtkWidget *ok_button;
  GtkWidget *hbox1, *hbox2;
  GtkWidget *vbox;

  gtk_init(&argc, &argv);

  window = gtk_window_new(GTK_WINDOW_TOPLEVEL);
  gtk_window_set_title(GTK_WINDOW(window), "GtkEntryBox");
```

```
    gtk_window_set_position(GTK_WINDOW(window), GTK_WIN_POS_CENTER);
    gtk_window_set_default_size(GTK_WINDOW(window), 200, 200);

    g_signal_connect ( GTK_OBJECT (window), "destroy",
                       GTK_SIGNAL_FUNC ( closeApp), NULL);

    username_label = gtk_label_new("Login:");
    password_label = gtk_label_new("Password:");

    username_entry = gtk_entry_new();
    password_entry = gtk_entry_new();
    gtk_entry_set_visibility(GTK_ENTRY (password_entry), FALSE);

    ok_button = gtk_button_new_with_label("Ok");

    g_signal_connect (GTK_OBJECT (ok_button), "clicked",
                      GTK_SIGNAL_FUNC(button_clicked), password_entry);

    hbox1 = gtk_hbox_new ( TRUE, 5 );
    hbox2 = gtk_hbox_new ( TRUE, 5 );

    vbox = gtk_vbox_new ( FALSE, 10);

    gtk_box_pack_start(GTK_BOX(hbox1), username_label, TRUE, FALSE, 5);
    gtk_box_pack_start(GTK_BOX(hbox1), username_entry, TRUE, FALSE, 5);

    gtk_box_pack_start(GTK_BOX(hbox2), password_label, TRUE, FALSE, 5);
    gtk_box_pack_start(GTK_BOX(hbox2), password_entry, TRUE, FALSE, 5);

    gtk_box_pack_start(GTK_BOX(vbox), hbox1, FALSE, FALSE, 5);
    gtk_box_pack_start(GTK_BOX(vbox), hbox2, FALSE, FALSE, 5);
    gtk_box_pack_start(GTK_BOX(vbox), ok_button, FALSE, FALSE, 5);

    gtk_container_add(GTK_CONTAINER(window), vbox);

    gtk_widget_show_all(window);
    gtk_main ();

    return 0;
}
```

When you run this program, you get a window that appears as in Figure 16-8.

How It Works

The program creates two GtkEntry widgets, username_entry and password_entry, and sets password_entry with a visibility of FALSE to hide the entered password. It then creates a GtkButton with which you connect the "clicked" signal to the button_clicked callback function.

Once in the callback function, the program retrieves the entered password and compares it to the secret password, printing the appropriate message.

Notice that you have repeated gtk_box_pack_start statements to add the widgets to their containers. To reduce this repeated code, you'll define a helper function in later examples.

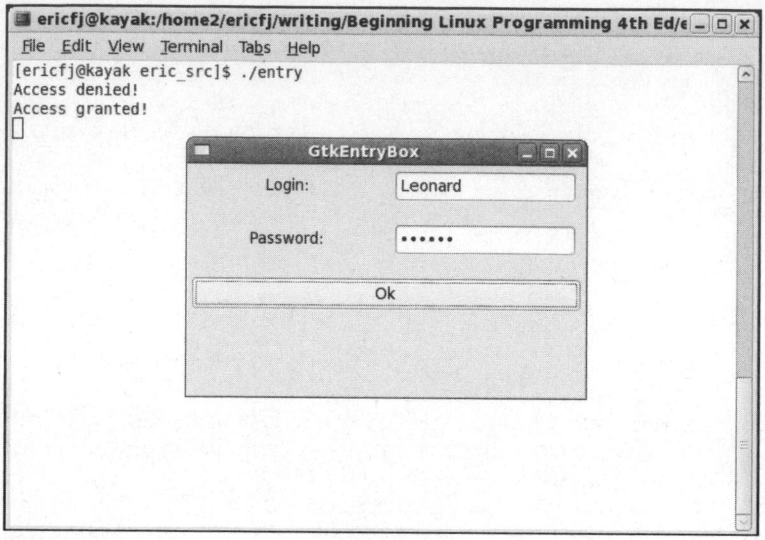

Figure 16-8

GtkSpinButton

Sometimes you'll want the user to enter a numeric value such as a maximum speed or length of device, and in these situations, a GtkSpinButton is ideal. GtkSpinButton restricts a user to entering numeric characters only, and you can set the range for allowed values between a lower and upper bound. The widget also provides up and down arrows so the user can "spin" the value using only the mouse for convenience:

```
GtkWidget
    +--,--GtkEntry
            +----GtkSpinButton
```

Again, the API is straightforward, and we'll list the most commonly used calls:

```
GtkWidget* gtk_spin_button_new (GtkAdjustment *adjustment, gdouble climb_rate,
                                guint digits);
GtkWidget* gtk_spin_button_new_with_range (gdouble min, gdouble max, gdouble step);
void gtk_spin_button_set_digits (GtkSpinButton *spin_button, guint digits);
void gtk_spin_button_set_increments (GtkSpinButton *spin_button, gdouble step,
                                     gdouble page);
void gtk_spin_button_set_range (GtkSpinButton *spin_button, gdouble min,
                                gdouble max);
gdouble gtk_spin_button_get_value (GtkSpinButton *spin_button);
gint gtk_spin_button_get_value_as_int (GtkSpinButton *spin_button);
void gtk_spin_button_set_value (GtkSpinButton *spin_button, gdouble value);
```

To create a GtkSpinButton using gtk_spin_button_new, you first need to create a GtkAdjustment object. A GtkAdjustment widget is an abstract object that contains logic to deal with controlling bounded values. GtdAdjustment is also used in other widgets, such as GtkHScale and GtkVScale.

To create a GtkAdjustment, pass in an initial value, lower and upper bounds, and increment sizes:

```
GtkObject* gtk_adjustment_new (gdouble value, gdouble lower, gdouble upper,
                               gdouble step_increment, gdouble page_increment,
                               gdouble page_size);
```

The values of step_increment and page_increment set the size of minor and major size increments. In the case of GtkSpinButton, the step_increment sets how much the value changes when the arrows are clicked. page_increment and page_size are not important when used with GtkSpinButton widgets.

climb_rate, the second parameter of gtk_spin_button_new, controls how quickly the values "spin" when you press and hold the arrow buttons. Finally, digits sets the precision of the widget, so a digit of 3 would set the spin button to display 0.00.

gtk_spin_button_new_with_range is a convenience method that creates a GtkAdjustment for you. Simply pass in the lower bound, upper bound, and step rate.

Reading the current value is easy with gtk_spin_button_get_value, and if you want an integer value, you can use gtk_spin_button_get_value_as_int.

Try It Out   GtkSpinButton

You'll now see a GtkSpinButton in action with a short example. Name this file spin.c.

```c
#include <gtk/gtk.h>

void closeApp ( GtkWidget *window, gpointer data)
{
  gtk_main_quit();
}

int main (int argc, char *argv[])
{
  GtkWidget *window;
  GtkWidget *spinbutton;
  GtkObject *adjustment;

  gtk_init (&argc, &argv);
  window = gtk_window_new(GTK_WINDOW_TOPLEVEL);
  gtk_window_set_default_size ( GTK_WINDOW(window), 300, 200);
  g_signal_connect ( GTK_OBJECT (window), "destroy",
                     GTK_SIGNAL_FUNC ( closeApp), NULL);

  adjustment = gtk_adjustment_new(100.0, 50.0, 150.0, 0.5, 0.05, 0.05);
  spinbutton = gtk_spin_button_new(GTK_ADJUSTMENT(adjustment), 0.01, 2);
```

```
gtk_container_add(GTK_CONTAINER(window), spinbutton);
gtk_widget_show_all(window);
gtk_main ();

return 0;
}
```

When you run this program, you get a spin button bounded between 50 and 150 (see Figure 16-9).

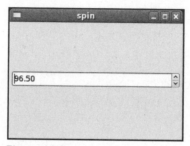

Figure 16-9

GtkButton

You've already seen GtkButton in action, but there are more button widgets descended from GtkButton that have slightly more functionality and deserve a mention:

```
GtkButton
    +----GtkToggleButton
            +----GtkCheckButton
                    +----GtkRadioButton
```

As you can see from the widget hierarchy, GtkToggleButton is descended directly from GtkButton, GtkCheckButton from GtkToggleButton and similarly with GtkRadioButton, each child widget specializing in purpose.

GtkToggleButton

GtkToggleButton is identical to a GtkButton except in one important regard: GtkToggleButton possesses *state*. That is, it can be on or off. When the user clicks a GtkToggleButton, it emits the "clicked" signal in the usual manner and changes (or "toggles") its state.

The API for GtkToggleButton is very straightforward:

```
GtkWidget* gtk_toggle_button_new (void);
GtkWidget* gtk_toggle_button_new_with_label (const gchar *label);
gboolean gtk_toggle_button_get_active (GtkToggleButton *toggle_button);
void gtk_toggle_button_set_active (GtkToggleButton *toggle_button,
                                   gboolean is_active);
```

The interesting functions are `gtk_toggle_button_get_active` and `gtk_toggle_button_set_active`, which you call to read and set the state of the toggle button. An activity of TRUE indicates the `GtkToggleButton` is "on."

GtkCheckButton

`GtkCheckButton` is a `GtkToggleButton` in disguise. Instead of the boring, rectangular blob of `GtkToggleButton`, `GtkCheckButton` appears as an exciting checkbox with text at the side. There are no functional differences.

```
GtkWidget* gtk_check_button_new (void);
GtkWidget* gtk_check_button_new_with_label (const gchar *label);
```

GtkRadioButton

This next button is rather different, because it can be grouped with other buttons of the same type. `GtkRadioButton` is one of those buttons that allows you to select only one option at a time from a group of options. The name comes from old-style radios that have mechanical buttons that pop back out when you press in another button.

```
GtkWidget* gtk_radio_button_new (GSList *group);
GtkWidget* gtk_radio_button_new_from_widget (GtkRadioButton *group);
GtkWidget* gtk_radio_button_new_with_label (GSList *group, const gchar *label);
void gtk_radio_button_set_group (GtkRadioButton *radio_button, GSList *group);
GSList* gtk_radio_button_get_group (GtkRadioButton *radio_button);
```

The `RadioButton` group is represented in a GLib list object, called a `GSList`. To place radio buttons in a group, you can create a `GSList` and pass it to each button using `gtk_radio_button_new` and `gtk_radio_button_get_group`. There's an easier way, however, in the shape of `gtk_radio_button_new_with_widget`, which grabs the `GSList` out of an existing button for you. You'll see this in action in the next example, where you try out different `GtkButtons`.

Try It Out GtkCheckButton, GtkToggleButton, and GtkRadioButton

Enter the following under the file name `buttons.c`.

1. First, declare the button pointers as global variables:

```
#include <gtk/gtk.h>
#include <stdio.h>

GtkWidget *togglebutton;
GtkWidget *checkbutton;
GtkWidget *radiobutton1, *radiobutton2;

void closeApp ( GtkWidget *window, gpointer data)
{
  gtk_main_quit();
}
```

2. Here you define a helper function that packs a GtkWidget and GtkLabel into a GtkHbox and then adds this GtkHbox into a given container widget. This helps cut down on repeated code.

```
void add_widget_with_label(GtkContainer * box, gchar * caption, GtkWidget * widget)
{
  GtkWidget *label = gtk_label_new (caption);
  GtkWidget *hbox = gtk_hbox_new (TRUE, 4);

  gtk_container_add(GTK_CONTAINER (hbox), label);
  gtk_container_add(GTK_CONTAINER (hbox), widget);

  gtk_container_add(box, hbox);
}
```

3. print_active is another helper function that prints out the current state of the given GtkToggleButton with a describing string. It is called from button_clicked, which is a callback function attached to the clicked signal of the OK button. Every time this button is clicked, you get a printout of the state of the buttons.

```
void print_active(char * button_name, GtkToggleButton *button)
{
  gboolean active = gtk_toggle_button_get_active(button);

  printf("%s is %s\n", button_name, active?"active":"not active");
}

void button_clicked(GtkWidget *button, gpointer data)
{
  print_active("Checkbutton", GTK_TOGGLE_BUTTON(checkbutton));
  print_active("Togglebutton", GTK_TOGGLE_BUTTON(togglebutton));
  print_active("Radiobutton1", GTK_TOGGLE_BUTTON(radiobutton1));
  print_active("Radiobutton2", GTK_TOGGLE_BUTTON(radiobutton2));
  printf("\n");
}
```

4. In main, you create the button widgets, stack them up in a GtkVBox adding descriptive labels, and connect the callback signal to the OK button:

```
gint main (gint argc, gchar *argv[])
{
  GtkWidget *window;
  GtkWidget *button;
  GtkWidget *vbox;

  gtk_init (&argc, &argv);
  window = gtk_window_new(GTK_WINDOW_TOPLEVEL);
  gtk_window_set_default_size(GTK_WINDOW(window), 200, 200);
  g_signal_connect ( GTK_OBJECT (window), "destroy",
                     GTK_SIGNAL_FUNC (closeApp), NULL);

  button = gtk_button_new_with_label("Ok");
  togglebutton = gtk_toggle_button_new_with_label("Toggle");
```

```
    checkbutton = gtk_check_button_new();
    radiobutton1 = gtk_radio_button_new(NULL);
    radiobutton2 = gtk_radio_button_new_from_widget(GTK_RADIO_BUTTON(radiobutton1));

    vbox = gtk_vbox_new (TRUE, 4);
    add_widget_with_label (GTK_CONTAINER(vbox), "ToggleButton:", togglebutton);
    add_widget_with_label (GTK_CONTAINER(vbox), "CheckButton:", checkbutton);
    add_widget_with_label (GTK_CONTAINER(vbox), "Radio 1:", radiobutton1);
    add_widget_with_label (GTK_CONTAINER(vbox), "Radio 2:", radiobutton2);
    add_widget_with_label (GTK_CONTAINER(vbox), "Button:", button);

    g_signal_connect(GTK_OBJECT(button), "clicked",
                     GTK_SIGNAL_FUNC(button_clicked), NULL);

    gtk_container_add(GTK_CONTAINER(window), vbox);
    gtk_widget_show_all(window);
    gtk_main ();

    return 0;
}
```

Figure 16-10 shows `buttons.c` in action, with the four common types of `GtkButton`.

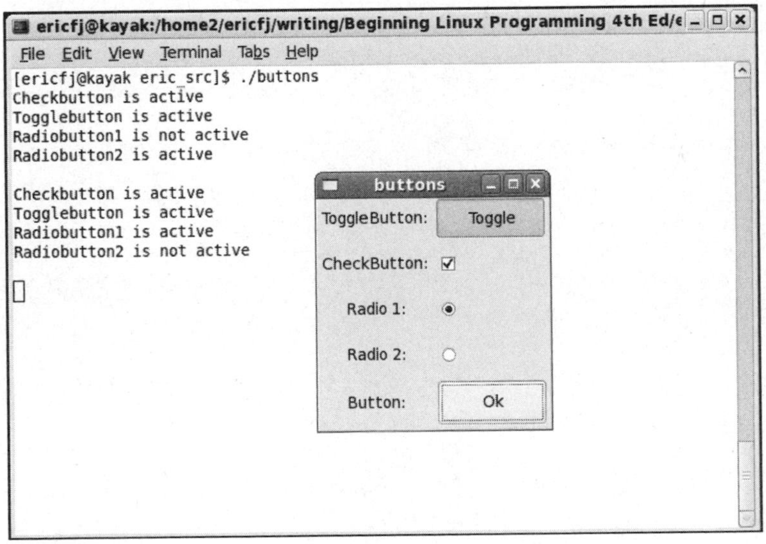

Figure 16-10

Click OK to see the state of the various buttons.

This program is a simple example of using the four types of `GtkButton` and shows how you can read the state of the `GtkToggleButton`, `GtkCheckButton`, and `GtkRadioButton` using the single `gtk_toggle_button_get_active`. This is one of the great benefits of an object-oriented approach — because you don't need separate `get_active` functions for each type of button, you can cut down the amount of code you need.

GtkTreeView

Up until now, we've looked at some of the simple GTK+ widgets, but not all widgets are single-line input or display devices. There are, of course, no limits to the complexity of a GtkWidget, and GtkTreeView is a great example of a widget that encapsulates a vast amount of functionality:

```
GtkWidget
    +----GtkContainer
              +----GtkTreeView
```

GtkTreeView is part of a family of widgets new to GTK+ 2 that creates list and tree views of data of the sort you find in a spreadsheet or file manager. Using GtkTreeView, you can create complex views of data, mix text, and bitmap graphics, and even input data using GtkEntry widgets, and so forth.

The quickest way of taking GtkTreeView for a test drive is to fire up the gtk-demo application that ships with GTK+. The demo application shows off the capability of each GTK+ widget including GtkTreeView, which is shown in Figure 16-11.

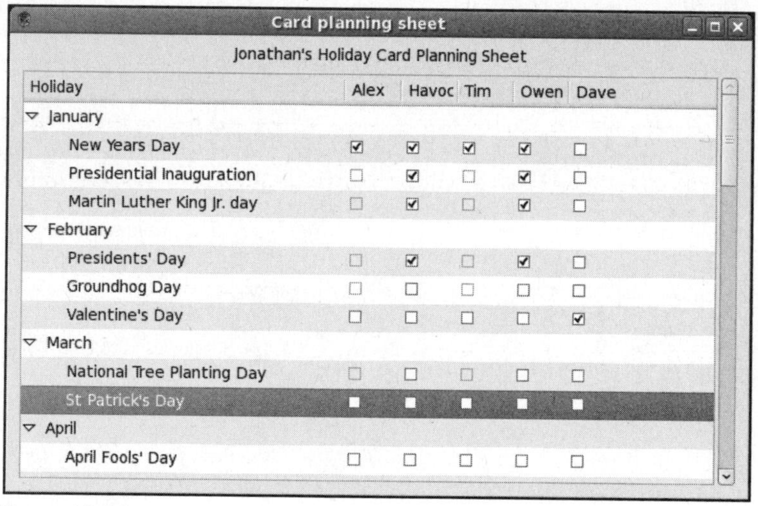

Figure 16-11

The GtkTreeView family is made up of four components:

- ❑ GtkTreeView: The Tree and List View
- ❑ GtkTreeViewColumn: Represents a list or tree column
- ❑ GtkCellRenderer: Controls drawing cells
- ❑ GtkTreeModel: Represents Tree and List data

The first three make up what is known as the *View*, and the last is the *Model*. The concept of separating the View from the Model (often called the Model/View/Controller design pattern, or MVC for short) is not particular to GTK+, but a design increasingly favored in all programming circles.

The key advantage of the MVC design pattern is that data can be rendered simultaneously by different views without unnecessary duplication. For example, text editors can have split panes and edit different parts of the document without two copies of the document in memory.

The MVC pattern is also very popular in Web programming because it makes it easy to create a website that renders differently in mobile or WAP browsers than it does in desktop browsers, simply by having separate View components optimized for each browser type. You can also separate the logic of acquiring the data, such as querying a database, from the logic for the user interface.

We'll start by looking at the Model component, of which GTK+ has two. GtkTreeStore holds multilevel data such as a directory hierarchy, and GtkListStore is for flat data.

To create a GtkTreeStore, pass in the number of columns followed by the type of each column:

```
Gtkwidget *store = gtk_tree_store_new (3, G_TYPE_STRING, G_TYPE_INT,
G_TYPE_BOOLEAN);
```

Reading, adding, editing, and removing data from the store are done with the aid of GtkTreeIter structures. These iterator structures point to nodes in the tree (or rows in a list) and aid in locating and manipulating parts of the potentially very large data structure. There are several API calls to get the iterator object at various points in a tree, but we'll look at the simplest, gtk_tree_store_append.

Before you can add any data to the tree store, you need an iterator to point to a new row. gtk_tree_store_append fills in a GtkTreeIter object that represents a new row in the tree, as either a top-level row (if you pass NULL to the third argument) or as a child row (if you pass the iterator of the parent row).

```
GtkTreeIter   iter;
gtk_tree_store_append (store, &iter, NULL);
```

Once you have an iterator, you can populate the row using gtk_tree_store_set:

```
gtk_tree_store_set (store, &iter,
                    0, "Def Leppard",
                    1, 1987,
                    2, TRUE,
                    -1);
```

You pass the column number and data in pairs, terminated by −1. You'll use an enum later to make the column numbers descriptive.

To add a branch to this row (a child row), you just need an iterator for the child row that you get by calling gtk_tree_store_append again, passing in the top-level row this time:

```
GtkTreeIter   child;
gtk_tree_store_append (store, &child, &iter);
```

You can read more about GtkTreeStore and GtkListStore functions in the API documentation, so let's move on and look at the GtkTreeView View component.

Creating a GtkTreeView is simplicity itself; just pass in the GtkTreeStore or GtkListStore model to the constructor:

```
GtkWidget *view = gtk_tree_view_new_with_model (GTK_TREE_MODEL (store));
```

It's now a case of configuring the widget to display the data exactly as you want it. For each column you must define a GtkCellRenderer and set the data source. You can choose to display only certain data columns, for example, or swap the display order of columns.

GtkCellRenderer is the object that deals with drawing each cell onscreen, and there are three subclasses that deal with text cells, pixmap graphic cells, and togglebutton cells:

- ❑ GtkCellRendererText

- ❑ GtkCellRendererPixBuf

- ❑ GtkCellRendererToggle

You'll use the text renderer in your View, GtkCellRendererText:

```
GtkCellRenderer *renderer = gtk_cell_renderer_text_new ();
gtk_tree_view_insert_column_with_attributes (GTK_TREE_VIEW(view),
                                             0,
                                             "This is the column title",
                                             renderer,
                                             "text", 0,
                                             NULL);
```

Here you create the renderer and pass it to the column insert function. This function enables you to set the GtkCellRendererText properties in one go, passed as NULL-terminated key/value pairs. The parameters are the tree view, the column number, column title, renderer, and renderer properties. You're setting the "text" attribute here, passing in the column number of the data source. GtkCellRendererText defines several other attributes, including underlining, font, size, and so forth.

You'll see how this works in practice in the next example, where you put a GtkTreeView through its paces.

Try It Out   GtkTreeView

Enter the following code and name the file tree.c.

1. Use an enum to label the columns so you can refer to them by name. N_COLUMNS conveniently is the total number of columns.

```
#include <gtk/gtk.h>

enum {
  COLUMN_TITLE,
  COLUMN_ARTIST,
  COLUMN_CATALOGUE,
  N_COLUMNS
};
```

```
void closeApp ( GtkWidget *window, gpointer data)
{
  gtk_main_quit();
}

int main (int argc, char *argv[])
{
  GtkWidget *window;
  GtkTreeStore *store;
  GtkWidget *view;
  GtkTreeIter parent_iter, child_iter;
  GtkCellRenderer *renderer;

  gtk_init(&argc, &argv);
  window = gtk_window_new(GTK_WINDOW_TOPLEVEL);
  gtk_window_set_default_size ( GTK_WINDOW(window), 300, 200);
  g_signal_connect ( GTK_OBJECT (window), "destroy",
                     GTK_SIGNAL_FUNC ( closeApp), NULL);
```

2.   Here you create the tree store, passing in the number and type of each column:

```
store = gtk_tree_store_new (N_COLUMNS, G_TYPE_STRING,  G_TYPE_STRING,
                            G_TYPE_STRING);
```

3.   The next part adds a parent and child row to the tree:

```
gtk_tree_store_append (store, &parent_iter, NULL);

gtk_tree_store_set (store, &parent_iter, COLUMN_TITLE, "Dark Side of the Moon",
                           COLUMN_ARTIST, "Pink Floyd",
                           COLUMN_CATALOGUE, "B000024D4P",
                           -1);

gtk_tree_store_append (store, &child_iter, &parent_iter);

gtk_tree_store_set (store, &child_iter, COLUMN_TITLE, "Speak to Me",
                    -1);


view = gtk_tree_view_new_with_model (GTK_TREE_MODEL (store));
```

4.   Finally, add columns to the view, setting their data source and titles:

```
renderer = gtk_cell_renderer_text_new ();
gtk_tree_view_insert_column_with_attributes (GTK_TREE_VIEW(view),
                                             COLUMN_TITLE,
                                             "Title", renderer,
                                             "text", COLUMN_TITLE,
                                             NULL);
gtk_tree_view_insert_column_with_attributes (GTK_TREE_VIEW(view),
                                             COLUMN_ARTIST,
                                             "Artist", renderer,
                                             "text", COLUMN_ARTIST,
```

```
                                                        NULL);
    gtk_tree_view_insert_column_with_attributes (GTK_TREE_VIEW(view),
                                                 COLUMN_CATALOGUE,
                                                 "Catalogue", renderer,
                                                 "text", COLUMN_CATALOGUE,
                                                 NULL);



    gtk_container_add(GTK_CONTAINER(window), view);

    gtk_widget_show_all(window);
    gtk_main ();

    return 0;
}
```

You'll use a `GtkTreeView` as the core of your CD application, where you'll modify the contents of the `GtkTreeView` as you query the CD database.

We've finished our tour of GTK+ widgets, and now we'll turn our attention to the other half of the story: GNOME. You'll see how to add menus to your application using the GNOME libraries and how the GNOME widgets make programming for the GNOME desktop even easier.

GNOME Widgets

GTK+ is designed to be desktop neutral; that is, GTK+ doesn't make any assumptions that it's running in GNOME, or even that it's running on Linux. The reason behind this is that GTK+ can be ported to run on Windows or any other windowing system with relative ease. The upshot of this is that GTK+ lacks the means to tie the program into the desktop, such as a means of saving program configuration, displaying help files, or programming applets (applets are small utilities that run on the edge panels).

The GNOME libraries include GNOME widgets that extend GTK+ and replace parts of GTK+ with easier-to-use widgets. In this section we look at how to program using GNOME widgets.

Before you use the GNOME libraries, you must initialize them at the start of your programs in the same way you did GTK+. You call `gnome_program_init` just as you do `gtk_init` for purely GTK+ programs.

This function takes an `app_id` and `app_version` that you use to describe your program to GNOME, a `module_info` that tells GNOME which library module to initialize, command-line parameters, and application properties set as a `NULL`-terminated list of name/value pairs.

```
GnomeProgram* gnome_program_init (const char *app_id, const char *app_version,
                                  const GnomeModuleInfo *module_info,
                                  int argc, char **argv,
                                  const char *first_property_name,
                                  ...);
```

The optional property list allows you to set things such as the directory to look for bitmap graphics.

Try It Out   **A GNOME Window**

Let's look at a GNOME program now, by looking at the GNOME replacement to GtkWindow, a GnomeApp widget.

Type in this program and call it gnome1.c:

```
#include <gnome.h>

int main (int argc, char *argv[])
{
  GtkWidget *app;

  gnome_program_init ("gnome1", "1.0", MODULE, argc, argv, NULL);
  app = gnome_app_new ("gnome1", "The Window Title");
  gtk_widget_show(app);
  gtk_main ();

  return 0;
}
```

To compile, you need to include the GNOME headers, so pass libgnomeui and libgnome to pkg-config:

```
$ gcc gnome1.c -o gnome1 `pkg-config --cflags --libs libgnome-2.0 libgnomeui-2.0`
```

A GnomeApp widget extends GtkWindow and makes it easy to add menus, toolbars, and a status bar along the bottom. Because it inherits from GtkWindow, you can use any GtkWindow function with a GnomeApp widget. Next you'll look at creating menus, and you'll add a status bar in your final example.

You can use GTK+ to create menus, but GNOME provides helpful structures and macros that make the job much easier. The online GTK+ documentation describes how to create menus in GTK+.

GNOME Menus

Creating a drop-down menu bar in GNOME is pleasantly simple. Each menu in the menu bar is represented by an array of GNOMEUIInfo structs with each element in the array corresponding to a single menu item. For example, if you have File, Edit, and View menus, you will have three arrays describing the contents of each menu.

Once you've defined each individual menu, you create the menu bar itself by referencing these arrays in another array of GNOMEUIInfo structs.

The GNOMEUIInfo struct is a little complicated and needs to be explained:

```
typedef struct {
```

```
        GnomeUIInfoType type;
        gchar const *label;
        gchar const *hint;
        gpointer moreinfo;
        gpointer user_data;
        gpointer unused_data;
        GnomeUIPixmapType pixmap_type;
        gconstpointer pixmap_info;
        guint accelerator_key;
        GdkModifierType ac_mods;
        GtkWidget *widget;
} GnomeUIInfo;
```

The first item in the struct, type, defines the type of the menu element that follows. It can be one of 10 GnomeUIInfoTypes defined by GNOME, described in the following table.

GnomeUIInfoType	Description
GNOME_APP_UI_ENDOFINFO	Denotes that this is last menu item in the array.
GNOME_APP_UI_ITEM	A normal menu item or a radio button if preceded by a GNOME_APP_UI_RADIOITEMS entry.
GNOME_APP_UI_TOGGLEITEM	A toggle button or check button menu item.
GNOME_APP_UI_RADIOITEMS	A radio button group.
GNOME_APP_UI_SUBTREE	Denotes this element is a submenu. Set moreinfo to point to the submenu array.
GNOME_APP_UI_SEPARATOR	Inserts a separator line in the menu.
GNOME_APP_UI_HELP	Creates a help topic list for use in a Help menu.
GNOME_APP_UI_BUILDER_DATA	Specifies builder data for the following entries.
GNOME_APP_UI_ITEM_CONFIGURABLE	A configurable menu item.
GNOME_APP_UI_SUBTREE_STOCK	Same as GNOME_APP_UI_SUBTREE except that the label text should be looked up in the gnome-libs catalog.
GNOME_APP_UI_INCLUDE	Same as GNOME_APP_UI_SUBTREE except that the items are included in the current menu and not as a submenu.

The second and third members of the struct define the text of the menu item and the pop-up hint. (The hint is shown in the status bar at the bottom of the window.)

The purpose of moreinfo depends on type. For ITEM and TOGGLEITEM, it points to the callback function to be called when the menu item is activated. For RADIOITEMS it points to an array of GnomeUIInfo structs that are grouped radio buttons.

user_data is an arbitrary pointer passed to the callback function. `pixmap_type` and `pixmap_info` allow you to add a bitmap icon to the menu item, and `accelerator_key` and `ac_mods` help you define a keyboard shortcut.

Finally, `widget` is used to internally hold the menu item widget pointer by the menu creation function.

| Try It Out | **GNOME Menus** |

You can try out menus with this short program. Call it menu1.c.

```
#include <gnome.h>

void closeApp ( GtkWidget *window, gpointer data)
{
  gtk_main_quit();
}
```

1. Define a callback function for the menu items called `item_clicked`:

```
void item_clicked(GtkWidget *widget, gpointer user_data)
{
  printf("Item Clicked!\n");
}
```

2. Next are the menu definitions. You have a submenu, top-level menu, and a menu bar array:

```
static GnomeUIInfo submenu[] = {
  {GNOME_APP_UI_ITEM, "SubMenu", "SubMenu Hint",
   GTK_SIGNAL_FUNC(item_clicked), NULL, NULL, 0, NULL, 0, 0, NULL},
  {GNOME_APP_UI_ENDOFINFO, NULL, NULL, NULL, NULL, NULL, 0, NULL, 0, 0, NULL}
};

static GnomeUIInfo menu[] = {
  {GNOME_APP_UI_ITEM, "Menu Item 1", "Menu Hint",
   NULL, NULL, NULL, 0, NULL, 0, 0, NULL},
  {GNOME_APP_UI_SUBTREE, "Menu Item 2", "Menu Hint", submenu,
   NULL, NULL, 0, NULL, 0, 0, NULL},
  {GNOME_APP_UI_ENDOFINFO, NULL, NULL, NULL, NULL, NULL, 0, NULL, 0, 0, NULL}
};

static GnomeUIInfo menubar[] = {
  {GNOME_APP_UI_SUBTREE, "Toplevel Item", NULL, menu, NULL,
   NULL, 0, NULL, 0, 0, NULL},
  {GNOME_APP_UI_ENDOFINFO, NULL, NULL, NULL, NULL, NULL, 0, NULL, 0, 0, NULL}
};
```

3. In `main`, you deal with the usual initialization and then create your `GnomeApp` widget and set the menus:

```
int main (int argc, char *argv[])
{
```

```
    GtkWidget *app;

    gnome_program_init ("gnome1", "0.1", LIBGNOMEUI_MODULE,
                        argc, argv,
                        GNOME_PARAM_NONE);
    app = gnome_app_new("gnome1", "Menus, menus, menus");

    gtk_window_set_default_size ( GTK_WINDOW(app), 300, 200);
    g_signal_connect ( GTK_OBJECT (app), "destroy",
                       GTK_SIGNAL_FUNC ( closeApp), NULL);

    gnome_app_create_menus ( GNOME_APP(app), menubar);

    gtk_widget_show(app);

    gtk_main();
    return 0;

}
```

Try running `menu1` and see the menu bar, submenu, and callback GNOME menu in action, as shown in Figure 16-12.

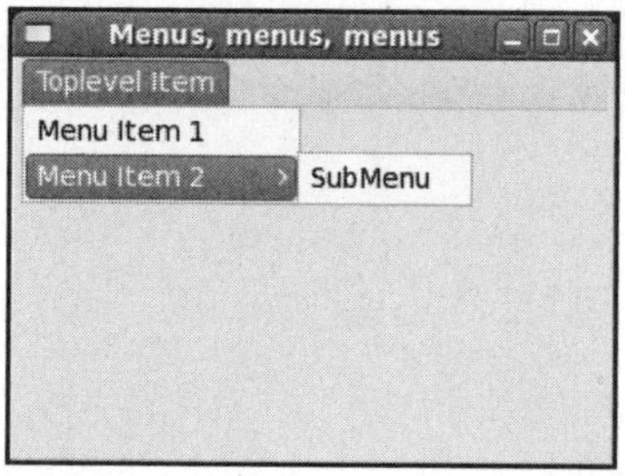

Figure 16-12

The `GnomeUIInfo` struct is hardly programmer-friendly, given that it consists of 11 entries, most of which are normally NULL or zero valued. It's quite easy to make a mistake typing them in, and it's difficult to tell one field from another in a long array of items. To improve the situation, GNOME defines macros to take out the hard work of writing the structs by hand. These macros also add icons and keyboard accelerators for you, all for no cost. In fact, there's rarely any reason to use anything but these macros.

There are two sets of macros, the first of which defines individual menu items. They take two parameters, the callback function pointer and user data.

```
#include <libgnomeui/libgnomeui.h>

#define      GNOMEUIINFO_MENU_OPEN_ITEM           (cb, data)
#define      GNOMEUIINFO_MENU_SAVE_ITEM           (cb, data)
#define      GNOMEUIINFO_MENU_SAVE_AS_ITEM        (cb, data)
#define      GNOMEUIINFO_MENU_PRINT_ITEM          (cb, data)
#define      GNOMEUIINFO_MENU_PRINT_SETUP_ITEM(cb, data)
```

```
#define     GNOMEUIINFO_MENU_CLOSE_ITEM      (cb, data)
#define     GNOMEUIINFO_MENU_EXIT_ITEM       (cb, data)
#define     GNOMEUIINFO_MENU_QUIT_ITEM       (cb, data)
#define     GNOMEUIINFO_MENU_CUT_ITEM        (cb, data)
#define     GNOMEUIINFO_MENU_COPY_ITEM       (cb, data)
#define     GNOMEUIINFO_MENU_PASTE_ITEM      (cb, data)
#define     GNOMEUIINFO_MENU_SELECT_ALL_ITEM(cb, data)
... etc
```

And the second set is for top-level definitions to which you simply pass the array:

```
#define     GNOMEUIINFO_MENU_FILE_TREE       (tree)
#define     GNOMEUIINFO_MENU_EDIT_TREE       (tree)
#define     GNOMEUIINFO_MENU_VIEW_TREE       (tree)
#define     GNOMEUIINFO_MENU_SETTINGS_TREE   (tree)
#define     GNOMEUIINFO_MENU_FILES_TREE      (tree)
#define     GNOMEUIINFO_MENU_WINDOWS_TREE    (tree)
#define     GNOMEUIINFO_MENU_HELP_TREE       (tree)
#define     GNOMEUIINFO_MENU_GAME_TREE       (tree)
```

Try It Out   Menus with GNOME Macros

In this example, you make use of these menus and see how the macros work. Make the following changes to menu1.c, and call this menu2.c. (For simplicity, the menu choices in this example do not define callback functions. The purpose here is just to show the convenience of the GNOME menu macros.)

```
#include <gnome.h>

static GnomeUIInfo filemenu[] = {
  GNOMEUIINFO_MENU_NEW_ITEM ("New", "Menu Hint", NULL, NULL ),
  GNOMEUIINFO_MENU_OPEN_ITEM (NULL, NULL),
  GNOMEUIINFO_MENU_SAVE_AS_ITEM (NULL, NULL),
  GNOMEUIINFO_SEPARATOR,
  GNOMEUIINFO_MENU_EXIT_ITEM (NULL, NULL),
  GNOMEUIINFO_END
};

static GnomeUIInfo editmenu[] = {
  GNOMEUIINFO_MENU_FIND_ITEM (NULL, NULL),
  GNOMEUIINFO_END
};

static GnomeUIInfo menubar[] = {
  GNOMEUIINFO_MENU_FILE_TREE (filemenu),
  GNOMEUIINFO_MENU_EDIT_TREE (editmenu),
  GNOMEUIINFO_END
};

int main (int argc, char *argv[])
{
  GtkWidget *app, *toolbar;

  gnome_program_init ("gnome1", "0.1", LIBGNOMEUI_MODULE,
```

```
                            argc, argv,
                            GNOME_PARAM_NONE);
        app = gnome_app_new("gnome1", "Menus, menus, menus");
        gtk_window_set_default_size ( GTK_WINDOW(app), 300, 200);
        gnome_app_create_menus ( GNOME_APP(app), menubar);

        gtk_widget_show(app);

        gtk_main();
        return 0;
}
```

By using the `libgnomeui` macros in `menu2.c`, you've significantly reduced the code you need to type and made the menu code much more readable. The macros save you time and effort when creating menus and make the wording, keyboard shortcuts, and icons consistent with other GNOME applications. Try to use them in your applications whenever you can.

Figure 16-13 shows `menu3.c` in action with the now standardized GNOME menu items.

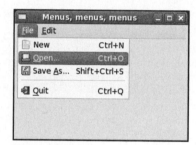

Figure 16-13

Dialogs

An important part of any GUI application is interacting with and informing users of important events. Usually, you'll create a temporary window with OK and Cancel buttons for this, and if the information is important enough to require an immediate response, such as deleting a file, you'll want to block access to all other windows until the user has made a choice (such windows are called *modal dialogs*).

What we've described here is a *dialog*, and GTK+ provides special dialog widgets that are descended from `GtkWindow` to make your programming job that much easier.

GtkDialog

As you can see, `GtkDialog` is a child of `GtkWindow` and therefore inherits all its functions and properties:

```
GtkWindow
    +----GtkDialog
```

GtkDialog divides the window into two areas, one for widget content and one for buttons that run along the bottom. You can specify the buttons you want as well as other dialog settings when you create the dialog box.

```
GtkWidget* gtk_dialog_new_with_buttons (const gchar *title,
                                        GtkWindow *parent,
                                        GtkDialogFlags flags,
                                        const gchar *first_button_text,
                                        ...);
```

This function creates a dialog window complete with a title and buttons. The second parameter, parent, should point to the main window of your application so that GTK+ can make sure the dialog stays attached to the window and is minimized when the main window is minimized.

flags determines the combination of properties the dialog can take:

❑ GTK_DIALOG_MODAL

❑ GTK_DIALOG_DESTROY_WITH_PARENT

❑ GTK_DIALOG_NO_SEPARATOR

You can combine the flags using the bitwise OR operator; for example,
(GTK_DIALOG_MODAL|GTK_DIALOG_NO_SEPARATOR) is both a modal dialog *and* one with no separator line between the main window area and the button area.

The remaining parameters are a NULL-terminated list of buttons and corresponding response code. You'll see exactly what this response code means when you see gtk_dialog_run. Normally you'll pick buttons from the long list of stock buttons that GTK+ defines as you get ready-made icons in the buttons.

Here's how you would create a dialog with OK and Cancel buttons that return GTK_RESPONSE_ACCEPT and GTK_RESPONSE_REJECT when those respective buttons are clicked:

```
GtkWidget *dialog = gtk_dialog_new_with_buttons ("Important question",
                                    parent_window,
                                    GTK_DIALOG_DESTROY_WITH_PARENT,
                                    GTK_STOCK_OK, GTK_RESPONSE_ACCEPT,
                                    GTK_STOCK_CANCEL, GTK_RESPONSE_REJECT,
                                    NULL);
```

We've chosen to have two buttons here, but there's no limit to the number of buttons you can have in the dialog. Furthermore, you can select from a number of response type flags. The accept and reject flags are not used by standard GNOME and are therefore available for you to use in your applications as you wish. (Keep in mind that accept ought to mean accept in your application.) Other possibilities here include the OK and CANCEL responses shown the GtkResponseType enum in the following section.

Naturally, you'll need to add content to your dialog, and for this GtkDialog contains a ready-made GtkVBox to populate with widgets. You get a pointer directly from the object:

```
GtkWidget *vbox  = GTK_DIALOG(dialog)->vbox;
```

You use this GtkVBox in the usual way, with gtk_box_pack_start or something similar.

Once you've created a dialog box, the next step is to present it to the user and wait for a response. This can be done in one of two ways: in a modal fashion, which blocks all input except to the dialog box, or a nonmodal way, which treats the dialog the same as any other window. Let's look at running a modal dialog first.

Modal Dialog Box

A modal dialog box forces the user to respond before any other action can take place. It's useful in situations where the user is about to do something with serious repercussions or to report errors and warning messages.

You can make a dialog box modal by setting the GTK_DIALOG_MODAL flag and calling gtk_widget_show, but there's a better way. gtk_dialog_run does the hard work for you by stopping further program execution until a button is pressed.

When the user presses a button (or the dialog is destroyed), gtk_dialog_run returns with an int result that indicates which button the user pressed. GTK+ usefully defines an enum to describe the possible values:

```
typedef enum
{
    GTK_RESPONSE_NONE = -1,
    GTK_RESPONSE_REJECT = -2,
    GTK_RESPONSE_ACCEPT = -3,
    GTK_RESPONSE_DELETE_EVENT = -4
    GTK_RESPONSE_OK       = -5,
    GTK_RESPONSE_CANCEL = -6,
    GTK_RESPONSE_CLOSE   = -7,
    GTK_RESPONSE_YES     = -8,
    GTK_RESPONSE_NO      = -9,
    GTK_RESPONSE_APPLY   = -10,
    GTK_RESPONSE_HELP    = -11
} GtkResponseType;
```

Now we can explain the result code passed in gtk_dialog_new_with_buttons — the result code is a GtkResponseType that gtk_dialog_run returns when that button is pressed. You get a result of GTK_RESPONSE_NONE if the dialog is destroyed (this happens if the user clicks the close icon, for example).

The switch construction is ideal for calling the appropriate logic:

```
GtkWidget *dialog = create_dialog();
int result = gtk_dialog_run(GTK_DIALOG(dialog));

switch (result)
{
    case GTK_RESPONSE_ACCEPT:
        delete_file();
        break;
    case GTK_RESPONSE_REJECT:
        do_nothing();
        break;
    default:
```

```
        dialog_was_cancelled ();
        break;
    }
gtk_widget_destroy (dialog);
```

That's all there is to simple modal dialogs in GTK+. As you can see, there's very little code involved or effort expended. All you do at the end is tidy up with a gtk_widget_destroy.

Things aren't so straightforward, however, when you want a nonmodal dialog box. You can't use gtk_dialog_run — instead you must connect callback functions to the dialog buttons.

Nonmodal Dialogs

You've seen how to use gtk_dialog_run to create a modal (blocking) dialog. Nonmodal dialogs work slightly differently, although you create them in the same way. Instead of calling gtk_dialog_run, you connect a callback function to the GtkDialog "response" signal that is emitted when a button is clicked or the window is destroyed.

Connecting the callback signal is done in the usual way, with the difference being that the callback function has an extra response argument that plays the same role as the return value of gtk_dialog_run. This code snippet shows the basic use of a nonmodal dialog:

```
void dialog_button_clicked (GtkWidget *dialog, gint response, gpointer user_data)
{
  switch (response)
  {

    case GTK_RESPONSE_ACCEPT:
        do_stuff();
        break;
    case GTK_RESPONSE_REJECT:
        do_nothing();
        break;
    default:
        dialog_was_cancelled ();
        break;

  }
gtk_widget_destroy(dialog);
}

int main()
{
  ...
  GtkWidget *dialog = create_dialog();

  g_signal_connect ( GTK_OBJECT (dialog), "response",
                     GTK_SIGNAL_FUNC (dialog_button_clicked), user_data );

  gtk_widget_show(dialog);
  ...
}
```

With nonmodal dialogs, complications can arise because the user isn't compelled to respond instantly and can minimize and forget about the dialog. You need to consider what to do if the user tries to open the dialog a second time before closing the first instance. What you need to do is check if the dialog pointer is NULL, and if not to reshow the existing dialog by calling gtk_window_present. You can see this in action in the "CD Database Application" section near the end of this chapter.

GtkMessageDialog

For very simple dialog boxes, even GtkDialog is unnecessarily complicated:

```
GtkDialog
    +----GtkMessageDialog
```

With GtkMessageDialog, you can create a message dialog box in a single line of code.

```
GtkWidget* gtk_message_dialog_new (GtkWindow *parent, GtkDialogFlags flags,
                                   GtkMessageType type,
                                   GtkButtonsType buttons,
                                   const gchar *message_format,
                                   ...);
```

This function creates a dialog complete with icons, a title, and configurable buttons. The parameter type sets the stock icon and title of the dialog according to its intended purpose; for instance, the warning type has a warning triangle icon. There are four possible values to cover the simple dialog types you most often come across:

- ❏ GTK_MESSAGE_INFO
- ❏ GTK_MESSAGE_WARNING
- ❏ GTK_MESSAGE_QUESTION
- ❏ GTK_MESSAGE_ERROR

(You can also select a GTK_MESSAGE_OTHER value, used in cases where the preceding dialog types don't apply.) With a GtkMessageDialog, you can pass a GtkButtonsType rather than list each button individually, as described in the following table.

GtkButtonsType	Description
GTK_BUTTONS_OK	An OK button
GTK_BUTTONS_CLOSE	A Close button
GTK_BUTTONS_CANCEL	A Cancel button
GTK_BUTTONS_YES_NO	Yes and No buttons
GTK_BUTTONS_OK_CANCEL	OK and Cancel buttons
GTK_BUTTONS_NONE	No buttons

All that remains is the text of the dialog, which you can make up from a substituted string in the same way you do with `printf`. In this example, you ask the user if she is sure she wants to delete a file:

```
GtkWidget *dialog = gtk_message_dialog_new (main_window,
                        GTK_DIALOG_DESTROY_WITH_PARENT,
                        GTK_MESSAGE_QUESTION,
                        GTK_BUTTONS_YES_NO,
                        "Are you sure you wish to delete %s?",
                        filename);
result = gtk_dialog_run (GTK_DIALOG (dialog));
gtk_widget_destroy (dialog);
```

This dialog appears like that in Figure 16-14.

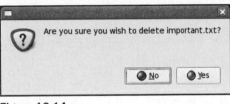

Figure 16-14

`GtkMessageDialog` is the simplest way of communicating information or asking yes/no type questions. You'll make use of them in the following section, when you put your knowledge to use by creating a GUI for your CD application.

CD Database Application

In the previous chapters you've developed a CD database with MySQL and a C interface. You'll now see how easy it is to put a GUI front end using GNOME/GTK+, and how quickly you can develop a rich user interface.

You must have the MySQL database and the MySQL developer's libraries installed to try out the example CD database application, the same requirement as the CD database application in Chapter 8.

For the sake of brevity and clarity you'll develop a basic, bare-bones interface that implements only a subset of the features — you won't allow adding of track information to CDs or deleting of CDs, for example. You'll see the widgets that were covered in this chapter in action in your application so that you can see how they are used in a real-life situation.

The key features you'll code are

❑   Logging on to the database from the GUI

❑   Searching for a CD

❑   Displaying CD and track information

❑   Adding a CD to the database

❑   Creating an About window

❑   Confirming when the user wishes to quit

You'll divide your code into three source files that share a common header file, cdapp_gnome.h. The source files will separate the functions that create windows and dialogs — interface generating functions — from callback functions.

Try It Out   cdapp_gnome.h

First look at cdapp_gnome.h and see the functions that you'll be implementing.

1.   Include the GNOME headers and the header file for the interface functions you developed in Chapter 8. This example program uses the app_mysql.h and app_mysql.c files from Chapter 8, along with the same database created in that chapter.

```
#include <gnome.h>
#include "app_mysql.h"
```

2.   The enum labels the columns of the GtkTreeView widget that you'll use to display the CDs and tracks:

```
enum {
  COLUMN_TITLE,
  COLUMN_ARTIST,
  COLUMN_CATALOGUE,
  N_COLUMNS
};
```

3.   You have three window-creation functions in interface.c:

```
GtkWidget *create_main_window();

GtkWidget *create_login_dialog();

GtkWidget *create_addcd_dialog();
```

4.   Callback functions for the menu items, toolbar, dialog buttons, and search button are in callbacks.c:

```
/* Callback to quit application */
void quit_app( GtkWidget * window, gpointer data);

/* Callback useful for confirming exit before quitting */
gboolean delete_event_handler ( GtkWidget *window, GdkEvent *event, gpointer data);

/* Callback connected to 'response' signal of addcd dialog */
void addcd_dialog_button_clicked (GtkDialog * dialog, gint response,
                                  gpointer userdata);

/* Callback for menu and toolbar 'Add CD' button */
```

```
void on_addcd_activate (GtkWidget *widget, gpointer user_data);

/* Callback for menu 'About' button */
void on_about_activate (GtkWidget  *widget, gpointer user_data);

/* Callback for search button */
void on_search_button_clicked (GtkWidget *widget, gpointer userdata);
```

Try It Out   **interface.c**

Next, take a look first at `interface.c`, where you define the windows and dialogs you use in the application.

1. First, some widget pointers that you refer to in `callbacks.c` and `main.c`:

```
#include "app_gnome.h"

GtkWidget *treeview;
GtkWidget *appbar;
GtkWidget *artist_entry;
GtkWidget *title_entry;
GtkWidget *catalogue_entry;
GtkWidget *username_entry;
GtkWidget *password_entry;
```

2. `app` is the main window pointer that has file scope:

```
static GtkWidget *app;
```

3. Define a helper function that adds a widget with given label text to a container:

```
void add_widget_with_label ( GtkContainer *box, gchar *caption, GtkWidget *widget)
{
  GtkWidget *label = gtk_label_new (caption);
  GtkWidget *hbox = gtk_hbox_new (TRUE, 4);

  gtk_container_add(GTK_CONTAINER (hbox), label);
  gtk_container_add(GTK_CONTAINER (hbox), widget);

  gtk_container_add(box, hbox);
}
```

4. The menubar definitions use GNOMEUIINFO macros for convenience:

```
static GnomeUIInfo filemenu[] =
{
  GNOMEUIINFO_MENU_NEW_ITEM ("_New CD", NULL, on_addcd_activate, NULL),
  GNOMEUIINFO_SEPARATOR,
  GNOMEUIINFO_MENU_EXIT_ITEM (close_app, NULL),
  GNOMEUIINFO_END
};
```

```
static GnomeUIInfo helpmenu[] =
{
  GNOMEUIINFO_MENU_ABOUT_ITEM (on_about_activate, NULL),
  GNOMEUIINFO_END
};

static GnomeUIInfo menubar[] =
{
  GNOMEUIINFO_MENU_FILE_TREE (filemenu),
  GNOMEUIINFO_MENU_HELP_TREE (helpmenu),
  GNOMEUIINFO_END
};
```

5. Here you create the main window, add menu and toolbar, set its size, center onscreen, and assemble the widgets that make up the interface. Note that the function doesn't show the window onscreen, but returns a pointer to the window instead.

```
GtkWidget * create_main_window()
{
  GtkWidget *toolbar;
  GtkWidget *vbox;
  GtkWidget *hbox;
  GtkWidget *label;
  GtkWidget *entry;
  GtkWidget *search_button;
  GtkWidget *scrolledwindow;
  GtkCellRenderer *renderer;

  app = gnome_app_new ("GnomeCD", "CD Database");

  gtk_window_set_position ( GTK_WINDOW( app), GTK_WIN_POS_CENTER);
  gtk_window_set_default_size ( GTK_WINDOW( app ), 540, 480);

  gnome_app_create_menus (GNOME_APP (app), menubar);
```

6. Create the toolbar using GTK+ stock icons and connect the callback functions:

```
toolbar = gtk_toolbar_new ();
gnome_app_add_toolbar (GNOME_APP (app), GTK_TOOLBAR (toolbar), "toolbar",
                       BONOBO_DOCK_ITEM_BEH_EXCLUSIVE,
                       BONOBO_DOCK_TOP, 1, 0, 0);
gtk_container_set_border_width (GTK_CONTAINER (toolbar), 1);
gtk_toolbar_insert_stock (GTK_TOOLBAR (toolbar),
                          "gtk-add",
                          "Add new CD",
                          NULL, GTK_SIGNAL_FUNC (on_addcd_activate),
                                NULL, -1);
gtk_toolbar_insert_space (GTK_TOOLBAR (toolbar), 1);
gtk_toolbar_insert_stock (GTK_TOOLBAR (toolbar),
                          "gtk-quit",
                          "Quit the Application",
                          NULL, GTK_SIGNAL_FUNC (on_quit_activate),
                                NULL, -1);
```

7. Here you create widgets that you'll use to search for a CD:

```
label = gtk_label_new("Search String:");
entry = gtk_entry_new ();
search_button = gtk_button_new_with_label("Search");
```

8. `gtk_scrolled_window` provides scrollbars to allow a widget (in this case a `GtkTreeView`) to expand beyond the window size:

```
scrolledwindow = gtk_scrolled_window_new (NULL, NULL);
gtk_scrolled_window_set_policy (GTK_SCROLLED_WINDOW (scrolledwindow),
                                GTK_POLICY_AUTOMATIC,
                                GTK_POLICY_AUTOMATIC);
```

9. Next, arrange the interface using container widgets in the usual way:

```
vbox = gtk_vbox_new (FALSE, 0);
hbox = gtk_hbox_new (FALSE, 0);
gtk_box_pack_start (GTK_BOX (vbox), hbox, FALSE, FALSE, 5);
gtk_box_pack_start (GTK_BOX (hbox), label, FALSE, FALSE, 5);
gtk_box_pack_start (GTK_BOX (hbox), entry, TRUE, TRUE, 6);
gtk_box_pack_start (GTK_BOX (hbox), search_button, FALSE, FALSE, 5);
gtk_box_pack_start (GTK_BOX (vbox), scrolledwindow, TRUE, TRUE, 0);
```

10. Then create the `GtkTreeView` widget, add three columns, and place it in the `GtkScrolledWindow`:

```
treeview = gtk_tree_view_new();
renderer = gtk_cell_renderer_text_new ();
gtk_tree_view_insert_column_with_attributes (GTK_TREE_VIEW(treeview),
                                             COLUMN_TITLE,
                                             "Title", renderer,
                                             "text", COLUMN_TITLE,
                                             NULL);
gtk_tree_view_insert_column_with_attributes (GTK_TREE_VIEW(treeview),
                                             COLUMN_ARTIST,
                                             "Artist", renderer,
                                             "text", COLUMN_ARTIST,
                                             NULL);
gtk_tree_view_insert_column_with_attributes (GTK_TREE_VIEW(treeview),
                                             COLUMN_CATALOGUE,
                                             "Catalogue", renderer,
                                             "text", COLUMN_CATALOGUE,
                                             NULL);

gtk_tree_view_set_search_column (GTK_TREE_VIEW (treeview),
                                 COLUMN_TITLE);

gtk_container_add (GTK_CONTAINER (scrolledwindow), treeview);
```

11. Finally, set the contents of the main window, add a `GnomeAppbar`, and connect the necessary callbacks:

```
gnome_app_set_contents (GNOME_APP (app), vbox);
```

```
      appbar = gnome_appbar_new (FALSE, TRUE, GNOME_PREFERENCES_NEVER);
      gnome_app_set_statusbar (GNOME_APP (app), appbar);

      gnome_app_install_menu_hints (GNOME_APP (app), menubar);

      g_signal_connect (GTK_OBJECT (search_button), "clicked",
                        GTK_SIGNAL_FUNC (on_search_button_clicked),
                        entry);

      g_signal_connect (GTK_OBJECT(app), "delete_event",
                        GTK_SIGNAL_FUNC ( delete_event_handler ),
                        NULL);

      g_signal_connect (GTK_OBJECT(app), "destroy",
                        GTK_SIGNAL_FUNC ( quit_app ), NULL);

      return app;
}
```

12. The next function creates a simple dialog box that enables you to add a new CD to the database. It consists of entry boxes for the artist, title, and catalogue fields, as well as OK and Cancel buttons:

```
GtkWidget *create_addcd_dialog()
{
  artist_entry = gtk_entry_new();
  title_entry = gtk_entry_new();
  catalogue_entry = gtk_entry_new();

  GtkWidget *dialog =  gtk_dialog_new_with_buttons ("Add CD",
                                                    app,
                                                    GTK_DIALOG_DESTROY_WITH_PARENT,
                                                    GTK_STOCK_OK,
                                                    GTK_RESPONSE_ACCEPT,
                                                    GTK_STOCK_CANCEL,
                                                    GTK_RESPONSE_REJECT,
                                                    NULL);

  add_widget_with_label ( GTK_CONTAINER (GTK_DIALOG (dialog)->vbox),
                          "Artist", artist_entry);
  add_widget_with_label ( GTK_CONTAINER (GTK_DIALOG (dialog)->vbox),
                          "Title", title_entry);
  add_widget_with_label ( GTK_CONTAINER (GTK_DIALOG (dialog)->vbox),
                          "Catalogue", catalogue_entry);

  g_signal_connect ( GTK_OBJECT (dialog), "response",
                     GTK_SIGNAL_FUNC (addcd_dialog_button_clicked), NULL);

  return dialog;
}
```

13. The database requires the user to log in before she can query it, so this function creates a dialog to enter the username and password:

```
GtkWidget *create_login_dialog()
{
```

```
        GtkWidget *dialog = gtk_dialog_new_with_buttons ("Database Login",
                                              app,
                                              GTK_DIALOG_MODAL,
                                              GTK_STOCK_OK,
                                              GTK_RESPONSE_ACCEPT,
                                              GTK_STOCK_CANCEL,
                                              GTK_RESPONSE_REJECT,
                                              NULL);

    username_entry = gtk_entry_new();
    password_entry = gtk_entry_new();

    gtk_entry_set_visibility(GTK_ENTRY (password_entry), FALSE);

    add_widget_with_label ( GTK_CONTAINER (GTK_DIALOG (dialog)->vbox) , "Username",
                        username_entry);
    add_widget_with_label ( GTK_CONTAINER (GTK_DIALOG (dialog)->vbox) , "Password",
                        password_entry);

    gtk_widget_show_all(GTK_WIDGET (GTK_DIALOG (dialog)->vbox));

    return dialog;
}
```

Try It Out   callbacks.c

The file callbacks.c contains the functions set up as callbacks for the UI widgets.

1. First, you need to include the header file and reference some global variables defined in interface.c so that you can read and update certain widget properties:

```
#include "app_gnome.h"

extern GtkWidget *treeview;
extern GtkWidget *app;
extern GtkWidget *appbar;
extern GtkWidget *artist_entry;
extern GtkWidget *title_entry;
extern GtkWidget *catalogue_entry;

static GtkWidget *addcd_dialog;
```

2. In quit_app you call database_end to tidy up and close the database before quitting:

```
void quit_app( GtkWidget *window, gpointer data)
{
  database_end();
  gtk_main_quit();
}
```

3. The next function pops up a simple dialog box to confirm that you want to exit the application, returning the response as a gboolean:

```
gboolean confirm_exit()
{
  gint result;
  GtkWidget *dialog = gtk_message_dialog_new (NULL,
                                  GTK_DIALOG_MODAL,
                                  GTK_MESSAGE_QUESTION,
                                  GTK_BUTTONS_YES_NO,
                                  "Are you sure you want to quit?");

  result = gtk_dialog_run (GTK_DIALOG (dialog));
  gtk_widget_destroy (dialog);

  return (result == GTK_RESPONSE_YES);
}
```

4. delete_event_handler is a callback function that you connect to the Gdk delete event of the main window. The event is emitted when you attempt to close a window, but critically before the GTK+ destroy signal is sent.

```
gboolean delete_event_handler ( GtkWidget *window, GdkEvent *event, gpointer data)
{
  return !confirm_exit();
}
```

5. The next function is called when a button is clicked on the add CD dialog. If you click OK, the program copies the strings into a non–const char array and passes the data in it to the MySQL interface function add_cd:

```
void addcd_dialog_button_clicked (GtkDialog * dialog, gint response,
    gpointer userdata)
{
  const gchar *artist_const;
  const gchar *title_const;
  const gchar *catalogue_const;
  gchar artist[200];
  gchar title[200];
  gchar catalogue[200];
  gint *cd_id;

  if (response == GTK_RESPONSE_ACCEPT)
  {
    artist_const = gtk_entry_get_text(GTK_ENTRY (artist_entry));
    title_const =  gtk_entry_get_text(GTK_ENTRY (title_entry));
    catalogue_const = gtk_entry_get_text(GTK_ENTRY (catalogue_entry));

    strcpy(artist, artist_const);
    strcpy(title, title_const);
    strcpy(catalogue, catalogue_const);

    add_cd(artist, title, catalogue, cd_id);
  }
```

```
   addcd_dialog = NULL;
   gtk_widget_destroy(GTK_WIDGET(dialog));
}
```

6. This is the heart of the application: retrieving the search results and populating the GtkTreeView.

```
void on_search_button_clicked (GtkButton *button, gpointer userdata)
{
  struct cd_search_st cd_res;
  struct current_cd_st cd;
  struct current_tracks_st ct;
  gint res1, res2, res3;
  gchar track_title[110];
  const gchar *search_string_const;
  gchar search_string[200];
  gchar search_text[200];
  gint i = 0, j = 0;

  GtkTreeStore *tree_store;
  GtkTreeIter parent_iter, child_iter;

  memset(&track_title, 0, sizeof(track_title));
```

7. Here you get the search string from the entry widget, copy into a non-const variable, and fetch the matching CD IDs:

```
search_string_const = gtk_entry_get_text(GTK_ENTRY (userdata));
strcpy (search_string, search_string_const);
res1 = find_cds(search_string, &cd_res);
```

8. Next you update the appbar to display a message informing the user of the result of the search:

```
sprintf(search_text, " Displaying %d result(s) for search string ' %s '",
        MIN(res1, MAX_CD_RESULT), search_string);
gnome_appbar_push (GNOME_APPBAR( appbar), search_text);
```

9. Now you have the search results and can populate the GtkTreeStore with the results. For each CD ID you need to fetch the corresponding current_cd_st struct that contains the title and author of the CD and then fetch the list of its tracks. Limit the number of entries to MAX_CD_RESULT defined in app_mysql.h to ensure you don't overfill the GtkTreeStore.

```
tree_store = gtk_tree_store_new (N_COLUMNS,
                                 G_TYPE_STRING,
                                 G_TYPE_STRING,
                                 G_TYPE_STRING);

while (i < res1 && i < MAX_CD_RESULT)
{
   res2 = get_cd(cd_res.cd_id[i], &cd);

    /* Add a new row to the model */
    gtk_tree_store_append (tree_store, &parent_iter, NULL);
```

```
            gtk_tree_store_set (tree_store, &parent_iter,
                                COLUMN_TITLE, cd.title,
                                COLUMN_ARTIST, cd.artist_name,
                                COLUMN_CATALOGUE, cd.catalogue, -1
                                );

        res3 = get_cd_tracks(cd_res.cd_id[i++], &ct);
        j = 0;
        /* Populate the tree with the current cd's tracks */
        while (j < res3)
        {

          sprintf(track_title, " Track %d. ", j+1);
          strcat(track_title, ct.track[j++]);

          gtk_tree_store_append (tree_store, &child_iter, &parent_iter);
          gtk_tree_store_set (tree_store, &child_iter,
                              COLUMN_TITLE, track_title, -1);
        }
    }

    gtk_tree_view_set_model (GTK_TREE_VIEW (treeview), GTK_TREE_MODEL(tree_store));

}
```

10.   The `addcd` dialog is nonmodal. Therefore, you check to see if it's already active before creating and showing it:

```
void on_addcd_activate (GtkMenuItem * menuitem, gpointer user_data)
{
  if (addcd_dialog != NULL)
      return;

  addcd_dialog = create_addcd_dialog();
  gtk_widget_show_all (addcd_dialog);

}

gboolean close_app ( GtkWidget * window, gpointer data)
{
  gboolean exit;

  if ((exit = confirm_exit()))
  {
    quit_app(NULL, NULL);
  }
  return exit;
}
```

11.   When you click the About button, a standard GNOME about box pops up:

```
void on_about_activate (GtkMenuItem  * menuitem, gpointer user_data)
{
  const char * authors[] = {"Wrox Press", NULL};
```

```
GtkWidget *about = gnome_about_new ("CD Database", "1.0",
                                    "(c) Wrox Press",
                                    "Beginning Linux Programming",
                                    (const char ** ) authors, NULL,
                                    "Translators", NULL);

    gtk_widget_show(about);
}
```

Try It Out   **main.c**

Enter the following code as `main.c`, which contains the `main` function for the program.

1. After the `include` statements, you reference username and password entry boxes from `interface.c`:

```
#include <stdio.h>
#include <stdlib.h>

#include "app_gnome.h"

extern GtkWidget *username_entry;
extern GtkWidget *password_entry;

gint main(gint argc, gchar *argv[])
{
  GtkWidget *main_window;
  GtkWidget *login_dialog;
  const char *user_const;
  const char *pass_const;
  gchar username[100];
  gchar password[100];
  gint result;
```

2. Initialize the GNOME libraries as usual, and then create and display the main window and your login dialog:

```
gnome_program_init ("CdDatabase", "0.1", LIBGNOMEUI_MODULE,
                    argc, argv,
                    GNOME_PARAM_APP_DATADIR, "",
                    NULL);
main_window = create_main_window();
gtk_widget_show_all(main_window);

login_dialog = create_login_dialog();
```

3. You loop until the user enters a correct username-password combination. The user can quit by clicking Cancel, in which case she is then asked to confirm the action.

```
while (1)
{
  result = gtk_dialog_run (GTK_DIALOG (login_dialog));
```

```
    if (result != GTK_RESPONSE_ACCEPT)
    {
      if (confirm_exit())
        return 0;
      else
        continue;
    }
    user_const = gtk_entry_get_text(GTK_ENTRY (username_entry));
    pass_const = gtk_entry_get_text(GTK_ENTRY (password_entry));
    strcpy(username, user_const);
    strcpy(password, pass_const);

    if (database_start(username, password) == TRUE)
      break;
```

4. If `database_start` fails, you display an error message and the login dialog is shown again:

```
    GtkWidget * error_dialog = gtk_message_dialog_new (GTK_WINDOW(main_window),
                GTK_DIALOG_DESTROY_WITH_PARENT,
                GTK_MESSAGE_ERROR,
                GTK_BUTTONS_CLOSE,
                "Could not log on! - Check Username and Password");
    gtk_dialog_run (GTK_DIALOG (error_dialog));
    gtk_widget_destroy (error_dialog);
  }

  gtk_widget_destroy (login_dialog);
  gtk_main();

  return 0;
}
```

5. You'll write a makefile to compile this application. As in Chapter 8, you may need to add the location of the mysqlclient library with something like the following:

```
-L/usr/lib/mysql
```

Place the directory where your system has the MySQL libraries after the `-L`.

```
all:  app

app: app_mysql.c callbacks.c interface.c main.c app_gnome.h app_mysql.h
     gcc -o app -I/usr/include/mysql app_mysql.c callbacks.c interface.c main.c -
lmysqlclient `pkg-config --cflags --libs libgnome-2.0 libgnomeui-2.0`

clean:
     rm -f app
```

6. Now just use the `make` command to compile the CD application:

make -f Makefile

When you run `app`, you should get your CD application — GNOME style (see Figure 16-15)!

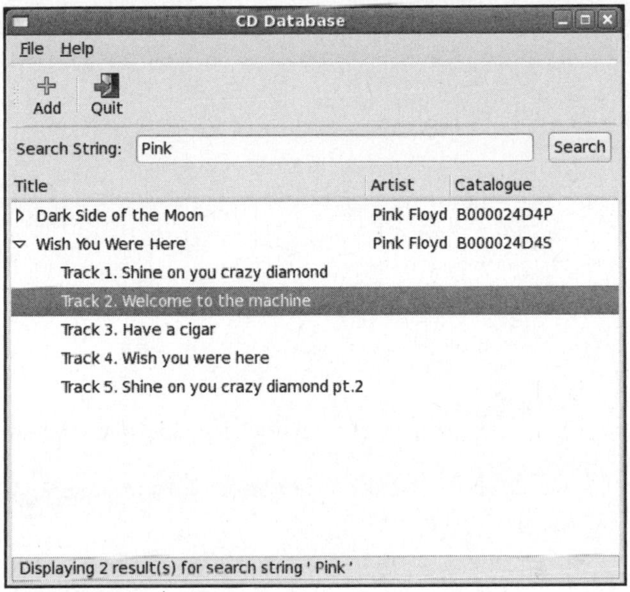

Figure 16-15

Summary

In this chapter, you've learned about programming with the GTK+/GNOME libraries to produce professional-looking GUI applications. First, you looked at the X Window System and how toolkits fit into the picture and then saw briefly how GTK+ works under the hood with its object system and signal/callback mechanism.

You then moved on to look at the API of GTK+ widgets, showing simple and more advanced examples in action in several program listings. In looking at the GnomeApp widget, you learned how to easily create menus using helper macros. Finally, you saw how to create modal and nonmodal dialog boxes to interact with the user.

Last, you created a GNOME/GTK+ GUI for your CD database, enabling you to log on to the database, search for CDs, and add CDs to the database.

In Chapter 17, you look at the rival toolkit to GTK+ and learn how to program KDE using Qt.

17

Programming KDE Using Qt

In Chapter 16, you looked at the GNOME/GTK+ GUI libraries for creating graphical user interfaces under X. These libraries are only half of the story; the other big player on the GUI scene in Linux is KDE/Qt, and in this chapter you look at these libraries and see how they shape up against the competition.

Qt is written in C++, the standard language in which to write Qt/KDE applications, so in this chapter you'll be obliged to take a diversion from the usual C and get your hands dirty with C++. You might like to take this opportunity to refresh your memory on C++, especially reminding yourself of the principles of derivation, encapsulation, method overloading, and virtual functions.

In this chapter, we cover

- ❑ An introduction to Qt
- ❑ Installing Qt
- ❑ Getting started
- ❑ Signal/slot mechanism
- ❑ Qt widgets
- ❑ Dialogs
- ❑ Menus and toolbars with KDE
- ❑ Building your CD database application with KDE/Qt

Introducing KDE and Qt

KDE (K Desktop Environment) is an open source desktop environment based on the Qt GUI library. A host of applications and utilities are part of KDE, including a complete office suite, a Web browser, and even a fully featured IDE for programming KDE/Qt applications (KDevelop, covered in Chapter 9). Industry recognition of how advanced KDE's applications are came when Apple chose to use KDE's Web browser as the core of the primary Web browser for Mac OS X, called Safari, known as a very fast browser.

The KDE project's homepage is at http://www.kde.org, where you can find detailed information, download KDE and KDE applications, find documentation, join mailing lists, and get other developer information.

> *The latest version of KDE at the time of writing is 3.5.7, and because this is the version that ships with current Linux distributions, we'll assume you have KDE 3.5 or higher installed. Work progresses on a major upgrade called KDE 4.0. You can also download pre-release versions of KDE 4.0. Similarly, the latest version of Qt is 4.3 but most Linux distributions have set up a version of Qt 3, such as 3.3, as the default Qt version. This chapter covers Qt 3.3, because it is most commonly available.*

From a programmer's perspective, KDE offers dozens of KDE widgets, usually derived from their Qt counterparts to provide enhancements and greater ease of use. KDE widgets offer greater integration with the KDE desktop than you get with Qt alone; for example, you get session management.

Qt is a mature, cross-platform GUI toolkit written in C++. Qt is the brainchild of Trolltech, a Norwegian company that develops, markets, and supports Qt and Qt-related software for the commercial market. Trolltech loudly touts the cross-platform capabilities of Qt, which is undeniably impressive; Qt has native support on Linux and UNIX derivatives, Windows, Mac OS X, and even embedded platforms, which gives Qt a great competitive advantage over its rivals.

> *A specialized version of Qt runs on cell phones. Another version runs on the Sharp Zaurus PDA and similar platform. Qt Jambi provides a Java version of the toolkit.*

Trolltech currently sells the commercial versions of Qt at a prohibitively high price for the casual user or hobbyist. Fortunately, Trolltech realizes the value in offering a zero-price version to the free software community, and therefore it offers a free version, Qt Open Source Edition for Linux, Windows, and Mac OS X. In return for a free version of Qt, Trolltech gets a large user install base, a large programmer community, and a high profile for its product.

Qt Open Source Edition is licensed under the GPL, which means you can program using the Qt libraries and distribute your own GPL software free of charge. As far as we can tell, the two main differences between the Open Source and the professional versions are the lack of support and the fact that you can't use Qt software in commercial applications. Trolltech's website at http://www.trolltech.com has all the API documentation that you need.

Installing Qt

Unless you have a particular reason to compile from source, it's easiest to find a binary package or RPM for your distribution. Fedora Linux 7 ships with qt-3.3.8-4.i386.rpm, which you can install using the following command:

```
$ rpm -Uvh qt-3.3.8-4.i386.rpm
```

You can also install Qt and the KDE programming libraries with the Package Manager application (see Figure 17-1).

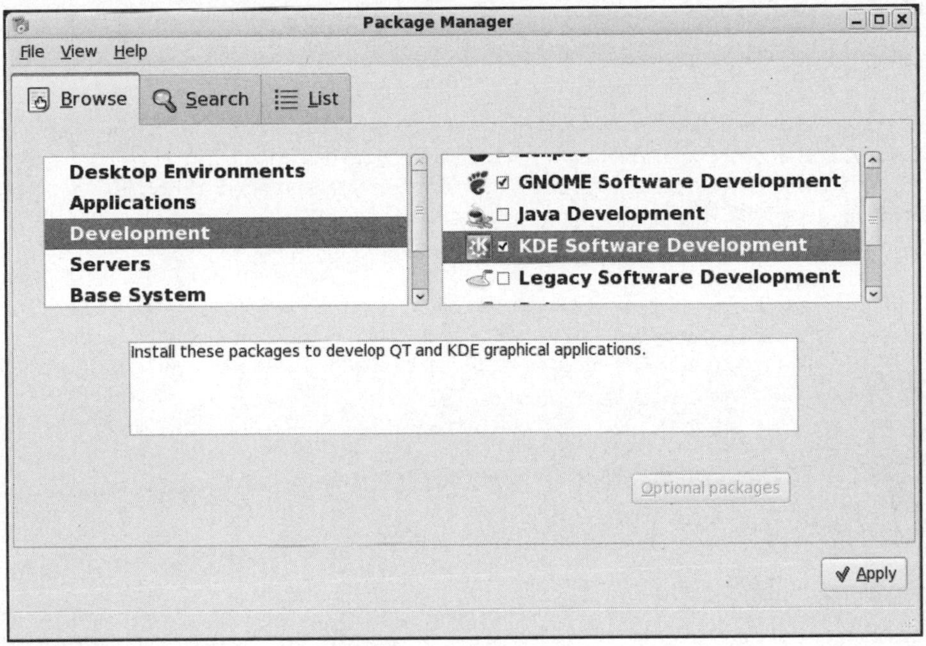

Figure 17-1

If you do want to download the source code and build Qt yourself, you can get the latest source from the Trolltech FTP site at `ftp://ftp.trolltech.com/qt/source/`. The source package comes with extensive instructions on how to compile and install Qt in the INSTALL file in the tarred package:

```
$ cd /usr/local
$ tar -xvzf qt-x11-free-3.3.8.tar.gz
$ ./configure
$ make
```

You'll also need to add a line to `/etc/ld.so.conf`:

```
/usr/lib/qt-3.3/lib
```

You can add this line anywhere in the file.

> *On Fedora and Red Hat Linux systems, the line should be stored in* `/etc/ld.so.conf.d/`
> `qt-i386.conf`*. If you have installed Qt as shown in Figure 17-1, this step will already be done.*

When Qt is properly installed, the QTDIR environment variable should be set to the Qt installation directory. You can check that this is the case as follows:

```
$ echo $QTDIR
/usr/lib/qt-3.3
```

Also make sure the lib directory is added to `/etc/ld.so.conf`.

Then run the following command as superuser:

```
# ldconfig
```

Try out the simplest Qt program and make sure your installation is working properly.

Type (or copy and paste from the code downloads) this program and call it qt1.cpp:

```
#include <qapplication.h>
#include <qmainwindow.h>

int main(int argc, char **argv)
{
  QApplication app(argc, argv);
  QMainWindow *window = new QMainWindow();

  app.setMainWidget(window);

  window->show();

  return app.exec();
}
```

To compile, you'll need to include the Qt include and lib directories:

```
$ g++ -o qt1 qt1.cpp -I$QTDIR/include -L$QTDIR/lib -lqui
```

On some platforms, the library at the end will be -lqt. *With Qt 3.3, though, use* -lqui.

When you run the application, you should get a Qt window (see Figure 17-2).

```
$ ./qt1
```

Figure 17-2

How It Works

Unlike GTK+, there's no all-encompassing qt.h header file, so you must explicitly include header files for each object you use.

The first object you encounter is QApplication. This is the main Qt object you must construct, passing in the command-line arguments before you begin. Each Qt application must have one and only one

QApplication object that you must create before doing anything else. QApplication deals with under-the-hood Qt operations such as event handling, string localization, and controlling the look and feel.

There are two QApplication methods you'll use: setMainWidget, which sets the main widget of your application, and exec, which starts the event loop running. exec doesn't return until either QApplication::quit() is called or the main widget is closed.

QMainWindow is the Qt base window widget that has support for menus, a toolbar, and a status bar. It's featured a great deal in this chapter as you learn how to extend it and add widgets to create an interface.

Next we introduce the mechanism of event-driven programming, and you'll add a PushButton widget to the application.

Signals and Slots

As you saw in Chapter 16, signals and signal handling are the primary mechanisms a GUI application uses to respond to user input and are central features of all GUI libraries. Qt's signal-handling mechanism consists of *signals* and *slots*, which are Qt's names for signals and callback functions in GTK+ or Java events and event handlers.

> *Note that a Qt signal is quite separate from a UNIX signal, as discussed in Chapter 11.*

Here's a reminder of how event-driven programming works: A GUI consists of menus, toolbars, buttons, entry boxes, and many other GUI elements that are collectively known as widgets. When the user interacts with a widget, for example activating a menu item or entering some text in an entry box, the widget will emit a named signal such as clicked, text_changed, or key_pressed. You'll usually want to do something in response to the user's action, such as save a document or quit the application, and you do this by connecting a signal to a callback function or, in Qt parlance, a *slot*.

Using signals and slots in Qt is rather special — Qt defines two new aptly named pseudo-keywords, signals and slots, to identify in your code the signals and slots of the class. This is great for readability and code maintenance, but it means you must pass your code through a separate pre-preprocessing stage to search and replace these pseudo-keywords with additional C++ code.

> *Qt code, therefore, is not true C++ code. This has sometimes been an issue for some developers. See* http://doc.trolltech.com/ *for Qt documentation, including reasons for these new pseudo C++ keywords. Furthermore, the use of signals and slots does not differ all that much from the Microsoft Foundation Classes, or MFC, on Windows, which also uses a modified definition of the C++ language.*

There are some restrictions to how signals and slots can be used in Qt, but these are not significantly limiting:

❑   Signals and slots must be member functions of a class derived from QObject.

❑   If using multiple inheritance, QObject must appear first in the class list.

❑   A Q_OBJECT statement must appear in the class declaration.

❑   Signals cannot be used in templates.

❑   Function pointers cannot be used as arguments to signals and slots.

❑   Signals and slots cannot be overridden and upgraded to public status.

Because you need to write your signals and slots in a descendant of QObject, it is logical to create your interface by extending and customizing a widget, since QWidget, the base Qt widget, is derived from QObject. In Qt, you'll nearly always create interfaces by extending widgets such as QMainWindow.

A typical class definition MyWindow.h for your GUI will look something like this:

```
class MyWindow : public QMainWindow
{
  Q_OBJECT
  public:
    MyWindow();
    virtual ~MyWindow();

  signals:
    void aSignal();

  private slots:
    void doSomething();
}
```

Your class derives from QMainWindow, which provides functionality for the main window in the application. Similarly, you'll subclass QDialog when you want a dialog box. First is the Q_OBJECT statement that acts as a marker for the preprocessor, followed by the usual constructor and destructor prototypes. Next are the signal and slot definitions.

You have one signal and one slot, both with no arguments. To emit aSignal(), all you need to do is call emit somewhere in your code:

```
emit aSignal();
```

That's it — everything else is handled by Qt. You don't even need an aSignal() implementation.

To use slots, you must connect them to a signal. You do this with the appropriately named static connect method in the QObject class:

```
bool QObject::connect (const QObject * sender, const char * signal,
                       const QObject * receiver, const char * member)
```

Simply pass in the object that owns the signal (the sender), the signal function, the object that owns the slot (the receiver), and finally the name of the slot.

In the MyWindow example, if you wanted to connect the clicked signal of a QPushButton widget to your doSomething slot, you'd write

```
connect (button, SIGNAL(clicked()), this, SLOT(doSomething()));
```

Note that you must use SIGNAL and SLOT macros to surround the signal and slot functions. Just as in GTK+, you can connect any number of slots to a given signal and also connect a slot to any number of signals by multiple connect calls. If connect fails for any reason, it returns FALSE.

All that remains is to implement your slot, and this takes the form of an ordinary member function:

```
void MyWindow::doSomething()
{
  // Slot code
}
```

Try It Out   Signals and Slots

Now that you've seen the principles of signals and slots, let's put this to use with an example. Extend QMainWindow and add a button, and connect the button's clicked signal to a slot.

1. Enter this class declaration, and call it ButtonWindow.h:

```
#include <qmainwindow.h>


class ButtonWindow : public QMainWindow
{
  Q_OBJECT

  public:
    ButtonWindow(QWidget *parent = 0, const char *name = 0);
    virtual ~ButtonWindow();

  private slots:
    void Clicked();

};
```

2. Next is the class implementation, ButtonWindow.cpp:

```
#include "ButtonWindow.moc"
#include <qpushbutton.h>
#include <qapplication.h>
#include <iostream>
```

3. In the constructor, you set the window title, create the button, and connect the button's clicked signal to your slot. setCaption is a QMainWindow method that unsurprisingly sets the window title.

```
ButtonWindow::ButtonWindow(QWidget *parent, const char *name)
             : QMainWindow(parent, name)
{
  this->setCaption("This is the window Title");
  QPushButton *button = new QPushButton("Click Me!", this, "Button1");
  button->setGeometry(50,30,70,20);
  connect (button, SIGNAL(clicked()), this, SLOT(Clicked()));
}
```

4. Qt manages the destruction of widgets automatically, so your destructor is empty:

```
ButtonWindow::~ButtonWindow()
{
}
```

5. Next, the slot implementation:

```
void ButtonWindow::Clicked(void)
{
    std::cout << "clicked!\n";
}
```

6. Finally, in main you just create an instance of ButtonWindow, set it as your application's main window, and show the window onscreen:

```
int main(int argc, char **argv)
{
    QApplication app(argc,argv);
    ButtonWindow *window = new ButtonWindow();

    app.setMainWidget(window);
    window->show();

    return app.exec();
}
```

7. Before you can compile this example, you need to run the preprocessor on the header file. This preprocessor program is called the Meta Object Compiler (moc) and should be present in the Qt package. Run moc on ButtonWindow.h, saving the output as ButtonWindow.moc:

```
$ moc ButtonWindow.h -o ButtonWindow.moc
```

Now you can compile as usual, linking in the moc output:

```
$ g++ -o button ButtonWindow.cpp -I$QTDIR/include -L$QTDIR/lib -lqui
```

When you run the program, you get the example shown in Figure 17-3.

How It Works

We've introduced a new widget and some new functions here, so let's take a look at these. QPushButton is a simple button widget that can hold a label and bitmap graphic and can be activated by the user clicking with the mouse or using the keyboard.

The constructor of QPushButton used is quite simple:

```
QPushButton::QPushButton(const QString &text, QWidget *parent, const char* name=0 )
```

The first argument is the text of the button label, then the parent widget, and last the name of the button used internally by Qt.

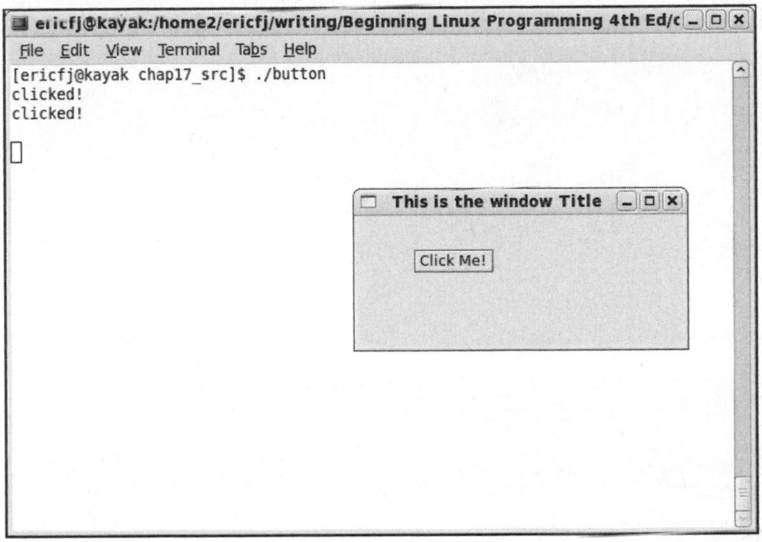

Figure 17-3

The parent parameter is common to all QWidgets, and the parent widget controls when it is displayed and destroyed, and various other characteristics. Passing NULL as the parent argument denotes that the widget is top-level and creates a blank window to contain it. In the example you pass the current ButtonWindow object using this, which adds the button to the ButtonWindow main area.

The name argument sets the name of the widget for use internally by Qt. If Qt encounters an error, the widget name will be printed in the error message, so it's a good idea to choose the appropriate widget name, because it's a great timesaver when debugging.

You might have noticed that the code rather crudely added the QPushButton to the ButtonWindow by using the parent parameter of the QPushButton constructor, without specifying the positioning, size, border, or anything like that. If you want precise control over widget layout, which is critical in creating an attractive interface, you must use Qt's layout objects. Let's take a look at these now.

There are a number of ways to arrange the positioning and layout of widgets in Qt. You've already seen using absolute coordinates by calling setGeometry, but this is rarely used, because the widgets don't scale and adjust to fit the window if it is resized.

The preferred method of arranging widgets is by using the QLayout classes or box widgets, which intelligently resize, after you've given them hints on margins and spacing between widgets.

The key difference between the QLayout classes and box widgets is that layout objects are *not* widgets.

The layout classes derive from QObject and not QWidget, so you are constrained in how you can use them. You cannot, for instance, make a QVBoxLayout a central widget of a QMainWindow.

Box widgets (such as QHBox and QVBox), by contrast, *are* derived from QWidget, and therefore you can treat them as ordinary widgets. You might well wonder why Qt has both QLayouts and QBox widgets with duplicate functionality. Actually QBox widgets are just for convenience, and in essence wrap a

QLayout within a QWidget. QLayouts have the advantage of automatically resizing, whereas widgets must be manually resized by calling QWidget::resizeEvent().

The QLayout subclasses QVBoxLayout and QHBoxLayout are the most popular way of creating an interface, and the ones you will most often see in Qt code.

QVBoxLayout and QHBoxLayout are invisible container objects that hold other widgets and layouts in a vertical and a horizontal orientation, respectively. You can create arbitrarily complex arrangements of widgets because you can nest layouts by placing a horizontal layout as an element inside a vertical layout, for example.

There are three QVBoxLayout constructors of interest (QHBoxLayout has an identical API):

```
QVBoxLayout::QVBoxLayout (QWidget *parent, int margin, int spacing, const char
                          *name)
QVBoxLayout::QVBoxLayout (QLayout *parentLayout, int spacing, const char * name)
QVBoxLayout::QVBoxLayout (int spacing, const char *name)
```

The parent of the QLayout can be either a widget or another QLayout. If you specify no parent, you can only add the layout to another QLayout later, using the addLayout method.

margin and spacing set the empty space in pixels placed around the outside of the QLayout and in between individual widgets.

Once you've created your QLayout, you add child widgets or layouts using a couple of methods:

```
QBoxLayout::addWidget (QWidget *widget, int stretch = 0, int alignment = 0 )
QBoxLayout::addLayout (QLayout *layout, int stretch = 0)
```

Try It Out   Using QBoxLayout Classes

In this example, you see the QBoxLayout classes in action by arranging QLabel widgets in a QMainWindow.

1. First, enter the header file, LayoutWindow.h:

```
#include <qmainwindow.h>

class LayoutWindow : public QMainWindow
{
  Q_OBJECT

  public:
    LayoutWindow(QWidget *parent = 0, const char *name = 0);
    virtual ~LayoutWindow();

};
```

2. Now enter the implementation, `LayoutWindow.cpp`:

```cpp
#include <qapplication.h>
#include <qlabel.h>
#include <qlayout.h>

#include "LayoutWindow.moc"

LayoutWindow::LayoutWindow(QWidget *parent, const char *name) : QMainWindow(parent, name)
{
  this->setCaption("Layouts");
```

3. You need to create a dummy `QWidget` to hold your `QHBoxLayout` because you cannot add a `QLayout` directly to a `QMainWindow`:

```cpp
  QWidget *widget = new QWidget(this);
  setCentralWidget(widget);

  QHBoxLayout *horizontal = new QHBoxLayout(widget, 5, 10, "horizontal");
  QVBoxLayout *vertical = new QVBoxLayout();

  QLabel* label1 = new QLabel("Top", widget, "textLabel1" );
  QLabel* label2 = new QLabel("Bottom", widget, "textLabel2");
  QLabel* label3 = new QLabel("Right", widget, "textLabel3");

  vertical->addWidget(label1);
  vertical->addWidget(label2);
  horizontal->addLayout(vertical);
  horizontal->addWidget(label3);
  resize( 150, 100 );
}

LayoutWindow::~LayoutWindow()
{
}

int main(int argc, char **argv)
{
  QApplication app(argc,argv);
  LayoutWindow *window = new LayoutWindow();

  app.setMainWidget(window);
  window->show();

  return app.exec();
}
```

As before, you need to run moc on the header file before compiling:

```
$ moc LayoutWindow.h -o LayoutWindow.moc
$ g++ -o layout LayoutWindow.cpp -I$QTDIR/include -L$QTDIR/lib -lqui
```

When you run this program, you get your arrangement of `QLabel`s (see Figure 17-4). Try resizing the window and see how the labels expand and shrink to fit the available space.

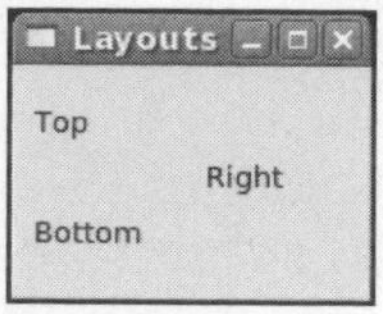

Figure 17-4

How It Works

The `LayoutWindow.cpp` code creates two box layout widgets for laying out widgets, both a horizontal and a vertical box layout. The vertical layout gets two labels, described appropriately enough, as `Top` and `Bottom`. The horizontal box layout also holds two widgets, a label shown as `Right`, as well as the vertical box layout. You can freely place layout widgets inside of layout widgets as shown in this example.

Try changing the code in `LayoutWindow.cpp` to experiment and better see how the box layouts work.

We've covered the basic principles of using Qt — signals and slots, `moc`, and layouts — so it's time to investigate the widgets more closely.

Qt Widgets

There are widgets for every occasion in Qt, and looking at them all would take up the rest of the book. In this section you take a look at the common Qt widgets, including data entry widgets, buttons, combo box, and list widgets.

QLineEdit

`QLineEdit` is Qt's single-line text entry widget. Use it for inputting brief amounts of text, such as a user's first name. With a `QLineEdit` widget, you can limit text input using an input mask to fit a template or, for the ultimate control, you can apply a validator function, for example, to ensure the user enters a proper date, phone number, or other similar value. `QLineEdit` has editing features, enabling you to select parts of the text, cut and paste, undo, redo, and the like from both a user's perspective and using the API.

The constructors and most useful methods are

```
#include <qlineedit.h>

QLineEdit::QlineEdit (QWidget *parent, const char* name = 0 )
QLineEdit::QlineEdit (const QString &contents, QWidget *parent,
                      const char *name = 0 )
QLineEdit::QlineEdit (const QString &contents, const QString &inputMask,
                      QWidget *parent, const char *name = 0 )

void    setInputMask (const QString &inputMask)
void    insert (const QString &newText )
bool    isModified (void)
void    setMaxLength (int length)
void    setReadOnly (bool read)
```

```
void      setText (const QString &text)
QString text (void)
void      setEchoMode(EchoMode mode)
```

In the constructors, you set the parent widget and widget name as usual with `parent` and `name`.

An interesting property is `EchoMode`, which determines how the text appears in the widget.

It can take one of three values:

- ❏ `QLineEdit::Normal`: Display inputted characters (default)
- ❏ `QLineEdit::Password`: Display asterisks in place of characters
- ❏ `QLineEdit::NoEcho`: Display nothing

Set the mode using the `setEchoMode`:

```
lineEdit->setEchoMode(QLineEdit::Password);
```

An enhancement introduced in Qt 3.2 is `inputMask`, which restricts input according to the mask rule.

`inputMask` is a string made up of characters, each of which corresponds to a rule that accepts a certain range of characters. If you're familiar with regular expressions, `inputMask` uses much the same principle.

There are two sorts of `inputMask` characters: those that denote a certain character must be present, and those that, if a character is present, restrict it to fall under the rule. The following table shows examples of these characters and their meanings.

Required Character	Characters That Are Permitted But Not Required	Meaning
A	a	ASCII A–Z, a–z
N	n	ASCII A–Z, a–z, 0–9
X	x	Any character
9	0	Numeric 0–9
D	d	Numeric 1–9

Our `inputMask` is a string made up from a combination of these characters, optionally terminated by a semicolon. There are further special characters that also have meaning as shown in the following table.

Character	Meaning
#	Plus/minus permitted but not required.
>	Converts following input to uppercase.

Continued on next page

Character	Meaning
<	Converts following input to lowercase.
!	Stops converting case.
\	Escape character to use special characters as separators.

All other characters in the `inputMask` act as separators in the `QLineEdit`.

The following table shows some examples of masks and their allowed input.

Example	Allowed Input
"AAAAAA-999D"	Allows Athens-2004 but not Sydney-2000 or Atlanta-1996.
"AAAAnn-99-99;"	Allows March-03-12 but not May-03-12 or September-03-12.
"000.000.000.000"	Allows IP address, for example, 192.168.0.1.

Try It Out   QLineEdit

Now see `QLineEdit` in action.

1.   First, the header file, `LineEdit.h`:

```
#include <qmainwindow.h>
#include <qlineedit.h>
#include <qstring.h>

class LineEdit : public QMainWindow
{
  Q_OBJECT

  public:
    LineEdit(QWidget *parent = 0, const char *name = 0);
    QLineEdit *password_entry;

  private slots:
    void Clicked();
};
```

2.   `LineEdit.cpp` is the now-familiar class implementation file:

```
#include "LineEdit.moc"
#include <qpushbutton.h>
#include <qapplication.h>
#include <qlabel.h>
#include <qlayout.h>
```

```
#include <iostream>

LineEdit::LineEdit(QWidget *parent, const char *name) : QMainWindow(parent, name)
{
  QWidget *widget = new QWidget(this);
  setCentralWidget(widget);
```

3. Use a QGridLayout to arrange the widgets. Specify the number of rows and columns, the margin settings, and the spacing:

```
  QGridLayout *grid = new QGridLayout(widget,3,2,10, 10,"grid");

  QLineEdit *username_entry = new QLineEdit( widget, "username_entry");
  password_entry = new QLineEdit( widget, "password_entry");
  password_entry->setEchoMode(QLineEdit::Password);

  grid->addWidget(new QLabel("Username", widget, "userlabel"), 0, 0, 0);
  grid->addWidget(new QLabel("Password", widget, "passwordlabel"), 1, 0, 0);

  grid->addWidget(username_entry, 0,1, 0);
  grid->addWidget(password_entry, 1,1, 0);

  QPushButton *button = new QPushButton ("Ok", widget, "button");
  grid->addWidget(button, 2,1,Qt::AlignRight);

  resize( 350, 200 );

  connect (button, SIGNAL(clicked()), this, SLOT(Clicked()));
}

void LineEdit::Clicked(void)
{
  std::cout << password_entry->text() << "\n";
}

int main(int argc, char **argv)
{
  QApplication app(argc,argv);
  LineEdit *window = new LineEdit();

  app.setMainWidget(window);
  window->show();

  return app.exec();
}
```

When you run this program, you should get the example shown in Figure 17-5.

How It Works

You've created two QLineEdit widgets, made one a password entry by setting the EchoMode, and set it to print its contents when you click the PushButton. Note the introduction of the QGridLayout widget, which is very useful for laying out widgets in a grid pattern. When you add a widget to the grid, you pass the row and column number, starting at 0, 0 for the top-left cell.

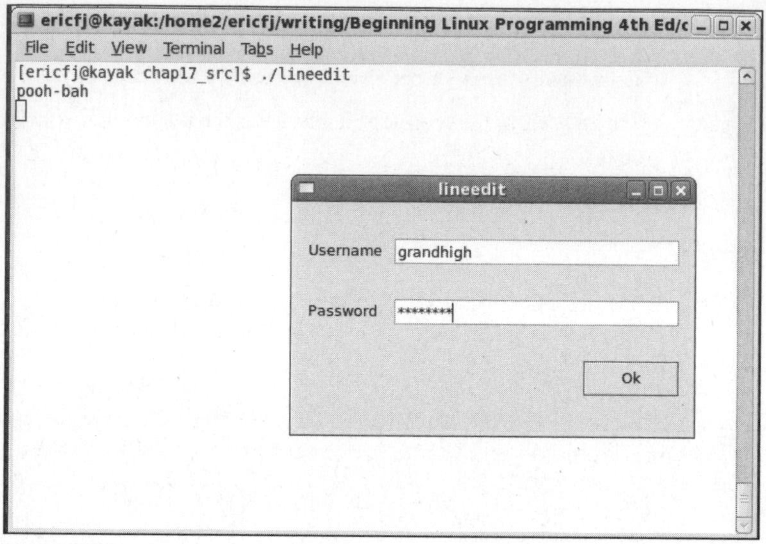

Figure 17-5

Qt Buttons

Button widgets are ubiquitous widgets, and they vary little in appearance, usage, and API from toolkit to toolkit. It's no surprise that Qt offers standard PushButton, CheckBox, and RadioButton variants.

QButton: The Button Base Class

Button widgets in Qt all derive from the abstract QButton class. This class has methods to query and toggle the on/off state of the button and to set the button's text or pixmap.

You should never need to instantiate a QButton widget itself (don't get confused between a QButton and QPushButton!), so you needn't show the constructors; however, here are the useful member functions:

```
#include <qbutton.h>

virtual void QButton::setText ( const QString & )
virtual void QButton::setPixmap ( const QPixmap & )
bool QButton::isToggleButton () const
virtual void QButton::setDown ( bool )
bool QButton::isDown () const
bool QButton::isOn () const
enum QButton::ToggleState { Off, NoChange, On }
ToggleState QButton::state () const
```

The isDown and isOn functions are identical in meaning. They both return TRUE if the button is pressed or activated.

Often, you'll want to disable or gray out an option if it isn't currently available. You can disable any widget including QButtons by calling QWidget::setEnable(FALSE).

There are three subclasses of QButton of interest here:

❑   QPushButton: A simple button widget that performs some action when clicked

❑   QCheckBox: A button widget that can toggle between on and off states to indicate some option

❑   QRadioButton: A button widget normally used in groups where only one button can be active in a group at a time

QPushButton

QPushButton is the standard generic button that contains text such as "OK" or "Cancel" and/or a pixmap icon. Like all QButtons, it emits the clicked signal when it's activated, and is usually used to connect a slot and perform some action.

You've already used QPushButton in your examples, and there's really only one other thing of interest to say about this simplest of Qt widgets. QPushButton can be switched from a stateless button into a toggle button (that is, can be turned on or off) by calling setToggleButton. (If you recall from the preceding chapter, GTK+ has separate widgets for the purpose.)

For completeness, here are the constructors and useful methods:

```
#include <qpushbutton.h>

QPushButton (QWidget *parent, const char *name = 0)
QPushButton (const QString &text, QWidget *parent, const char *name = 0)
QPushButton (const QIconSet &icon, const QString &text,
             QWidget *parent, const char * name = 0 )

void QPushButton::setToggleButton (bool);
```

QCheckBox

QCheckBox is a button that has state; that is, it can be turned on or off. The appearance of QCheckBox depends on the current windowing style (Motif, Windows, and so on) but is usually drawn as a ticked box with text to the right.

You can also set QCheckBox to be a third, in-between state that indicates "no change." This is useful on the rare occasions when you can't read the state of the option the QCheckBox represents (and therefore set the QCheckBox on or off yourself), but still want to give the user a chance to leave it unchanged as well as actively set it on or off.

```
#include <qcheckbox.h>

QCheckBox (QWidget *parent, const char *name = 0 )
QCheckBox (const QString &text, QWidget *parent, const char *name = 0 )

bool QCheckBox::isChecked ()
void QCheckBox::setTristate ( bool y = TRUE )
bool QCheckBox::isTristate ()
```

QRadioButton

Radio buttons are toggle buttons used to represent exclusive choices when you can select only one option out of a group of options presented (think back to those old car radios, where only one station button could be pressed in at a time). QRadioButtons themselves are hardly any different from QCheckBoxes, because the grouping and exclusivity are all handled by the QButtonGroup class, the main difference being that radio buttons appear as round buttons rather than ticked boxes.

QButtonGroup is a widget that makes handling groups of buttons easier by providing convenience methods:

```
#include <qbuttongroup.h>

QButtonGroup (QWidget *parent = 0, const char * name = 0 )
QButtonGroup (const QString & title, QWidget * parent = 0, const char * name = 0 )

int    insert (QButton *button, int id = -1)
void   remove (QButton *button)
int    id (QButton *button) const
int    count () const
int    selectedId () const
```

Using a QButtonGroup couldn't be simpler; it even offers an optional frame around the buttons if you use the title constructor.

You can add a button to a QButtonGroup using either insert or by specifying the QButtonGroup as the parent widget of the button. You can specify an id with insert to uniquely identify each button in the group. This is especially useful when querying which button is selected, because selectedId returns the id of the selected button.

All QRadioButtons you add to the group are automatically set to be exclusive.

The QRadioButton constructors and one unique method shouldn't be too surprising:

```
#include <qradiobutton.h>

QRadioButton (QWidget *parent, const char *name = 0 )
QRadioButton (const QString &text, QWidget *parent, const char *name = 0 )

bool   QRadioButton::isChecked ()
```

Try It Out   **QButtons**

Now put this knowledge to some use, with a Qt buttons example. The following program creates different types of buttons (radio, checkbox, and pushbuttons) to show how to use these widgets in your applications.

1. Enter Buttons.h:

```
#include <qmainwindow.h>
#include <qcheckbox.h>
#include <qbutton.h>
```

```
#include <qradiobutton.h>

class Buttons : public QMainWindow
{
  Q_OBJECT

  public:
    Buttons(QWidget *parent = 0, const char *name = 0);
```

2. You'll query the state of your buttons later in the slot function, so declare the button pointers as private in the class definition, as well as a helper function `PrintActive`:

```
  private:
    void PrintActive(QButton *button);
    QCheckBox *checkbox;
    QRadioButton *radiobutton1, *radiobutton2;

  private slots:
    void Clicked();

};
```

3. Here's `Buttons.cpp`:

```
#include "Buttons.moc"
#include <qbuttongroup.h>

#include <qpushbutton.h>

#include <qapplication.h>
#include <qlabel.h>
#include <qlayout.h>

#include <iostream>

Buttons::Buttons(QWidget *parent, const char *name) : QMainWindow(parent, name)
{
  QWidget *widget = new QWidget(this);
  setCentralWidget(widget);

  QVBoxLayout *vbox = new QVBoxLayout(widget,5, 10,"vbox");

  checkbox = new QCheckBox("CheckButton", widget, "check");
  vbox->addWidget(checkbox);
```

4. Here you create a `QButtonGroup` for your two radio buttons:

```
  QButtonGroup *buttongroup = new QButtonGroup(0);

  radiobutton1 = new QRadioButton("RadioButton1", widget, "radio1");
  buttongroup->insert(radiobutton1);
  vbox->addWidget(radiobutton1);
```

```
    radiobutton2 = new QRadioButton("RadioButton2", widget, "radio2");
    buttongroup->insert(radiobutton2);
    vbox->addWidget(radiobutton2);

    QPushButton *button = new QPushButton ("Ok", widget, "button");
    vbox->addWidget(button);

    resize( 350, 200 );

    connect (button, SIGNAL(clicked()), this, SLOT(Clicked()));
}
```

5.   Next is a convenience method for printing the state of the given `QButton`:

```
void Buttons::PrintActive(QButton *button)
{
  if (button->isOn())
    std::cout << button->name() << " is checked\n";
  else
    std::cout << button->name() << " is not checked\n";
}

void Buttons::Clicked(void)
{
    PrintActive(checkbox);
    PrintActive(radiobutton1);
    PrintActive(radiobutton2);
    std::cout << "\n";
}

int main(int argc, char **argv)
{
  QApplication app(argc,argv);
  Buttons *window = new Buttons();

  app.setMainWidget(window);
  window->show();

  return app.exec();
}
```

How It Works

This simple example shows how to query various Qt button widget types. As you can see, these widgets all work the same once created, for the most part. For example, the `PrintActive` function shows how to get the state of a button, `on` or `off`. Notice how this works for all the state-maintaining button types, such as the checkbox and radio buttons. For the most part, just the calls to create a button widget differ. And, radio buttons, being the most complex (because only one in a group can be on), require the most work to create. For radio buttons, you need to create a `QButtonGroup` to ensure that only one radio button in the group can be active at any time.

QComboBox

Radio buttons are an excellent way of enabling the user to select from a small number of options, say six or fewer. When you have more than six, things start to get out of hand and it becomes increasingly so as the number of options increases to keep the window to a sensible size. A perfect solution is to use an entry box with drop-down menu, also known as a combo box. The options appear when you click and reveal the menu, and the number of options is limited only by how practical it becomes to search through the list.

QComboBox combines the functionality of a QLineEdit, QPushButton, and drop-down menus, enabling the user to pick a single option from an unlimited choice of options.

A QComboBox can be either read/write or read-only. If it is read/write the user can type an alternative to the options offered; otherwise the user is limited to selecting from the drop-down list.

When you create a QComboBox, you can specify whether it's read/write or read-only as a boolean in the constructor:

```
QComboBox *combo = new QComboBox(TRUE, parent, "widgetname");
```

Passing TRUE sets the QComboBox to Read/Write mode. The other parameters are the usual parent widget pointer and widget name.

Like all Qt widgets, QComboBox is flexible in the way you can use it and it offers a good deal of functionality. You can add options individually or as a set, either as QStrings or using the traditional char* format.

To insert a single item, call insertItem:

```
combo->insertItem(QString("An Item"), 1);
```

This takes a QString object and a position index. Here, the value of 1 sets the item to be first in the list. To add it to the end, just pass any negative integer.

More commonly you'll add several items at a time, and for this you can use the QStrList class, or, as here, a char* array:

```
char* weather[] = {"Thunder", "Lightning", "Rain", 0};
combo->insertStrList(weather, 3);
```

Again, you can specify an index for the inserted items in the list.

If the QComboBox is read/write, values that the user types in can be automatically added to the list of options. This is a useful time-saving feature that saves the user from repeated typing if he or she wants to select the same typed-in value more than once.

InsertionPolicy controls where the new entry is added in the option list. You can pick from one of the options shown in the following table.

Options	What It Does
QComboBox::AtTop	Inserts the new entry as the first option in the list.
QComboBox::AtBottom	Inserts the new entry as the last option.
QComboBox::AtCurrent	Replaces the previously selected option.
QComboBox::BeforeCurrent	Inserts the entry before the previously selected option.
QComboBox::AfterCurrent	Inserts the entry after the previously selected option.
QComboBox::NoInsertion	New entry is not inserted into option list.

To set the policy, call the setInsertionPolicy method on the QComboBox:

```
combo->setInsertionPolicy(QComboBox::AtTop);
```

Let's take a peek at the constructors and a selection of the QComboBox methods:

```
#include <qcombobox.h>

QComboBox (QWidget *parent = 0, const char *name = 0)
QComboBox (bool readwrite, QWidget *parent = 0, const char *name = 0)

int      count ()
void     insertStringList (const QStringList &list, int index = -1)
void     insertStrList (const QStrList &list, int index = -1)
void     insertStrList (const QStrList *list, int index = -1)
void     insertStrList (const char **strings, int numStrings = -1, int index = -1)
void     insertItem (const QString &t, int index = -1)
void     removeItem (int index)
virtual void setCurrentItem (int index)
QString  currentText ()
virtual void setCurrentText (const QString &)
void     setEditable (bool)
```

The function count returns the number of options in the list. QStringList and QStrList are Qt string collection classes you can use to add options. You can remove options using removeItem, get and set the current option using currentText and setCurrentText, and toggle the editable state using setEditable.

QComboBox emits the textChanged(QString&) signal whenever a new option is selected, passing the newly selected option as an argument.

Try It Out   QComboBox

In this example you have a go at using QComboBox, and see how signals and slots with parameters work in action. You'll create a ComboBox class that inherits QMainWindow. It'll have two QComboBoxes, one read/write and one read-only, and you'll connect to the textChanged signal to get the currently selected value each time it changes.

1. Enter the following and name the file ComboBox.h:

```
#include <qmainwindow.h>
#include <qcombobox.h>

class ComboBox : public QMainWindow
{
  Q_OBJECT

  public:
    ComboBox(QWidget *parent = 0, const char *name = 0);

  private slots:
    void Changed(const QString& s);
};
```

2. The interface consists of two QComboBox widgets, one editable and the other read-only. You populate both widgets with the same list of items:

```
#include "ComboBox.moc"

#include <qlayout.h>
#include <iostream>

ComboBox::ComboBox(QWidget *parent, const char *name) : QMainWindow(parent, name)
{
  QWidget *widget = new QWidget(this);
  setCentralWidget(widget);

  QVBoxLayout *vbox = new QVBoxLayout(widget, 5, 10,"vbox");

  QComboBox *editablecombo = new QComboBox(TRUE, widget, "editable");
  vbox->addWidget(editablecombo);
  QComboBox *readonlycombo = new QComboBox(FALSE, widget, "readonly");
  vbox->addWidget(readonlycombo);

  static const char* items[] = { "Macbeth", "Twelfth Night", "Othello", 0 };
  editablecombo->insertStrList (items);
  readonlycombo->insertStrList (items);

  connect (editablecombo, SIGNAL(textChanged(const QString&)),
           this, SLOT(Changed(const QString&)));
  resize( 350, 200 );

}
```

3. This is the slot function. Note the QString parameter s that's passed by the signal:

```
void ComboBox::Changed(const QString& s)
{
  std::cout << s << "\n";
}
```

```
int main(int argc, char **argv)
{
  QApplication app(argc,argv);
  ComboBox *window = new ComboBox();

  app.setMainWidget(window);
  window->show();

  return app.exec();
}
```

You can see the newly selected options from the editable QComboBox printed out on the command line in Figure 17-6.

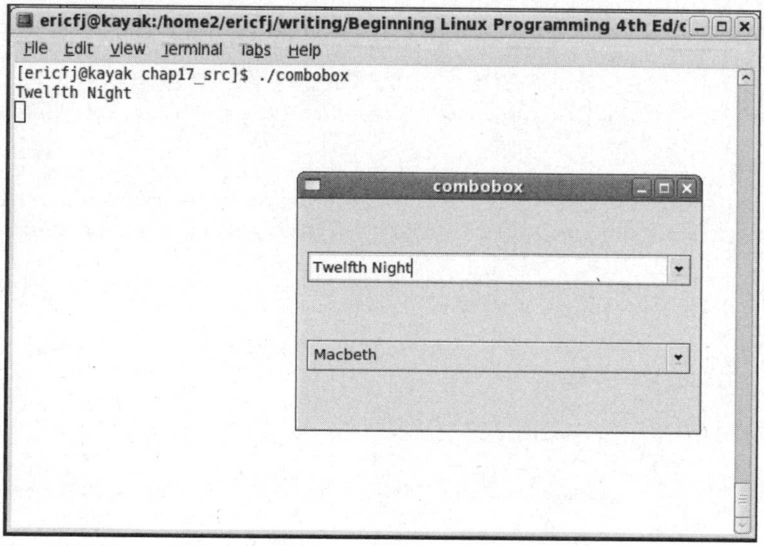

Figure 17-6

How It Works

Create combo box widgets much like you create any other widget. The key new element lies in calling the insertStrList function to store the list of combo box choices.

Like other text-holding widgets, you can set up a function to get called whenever the value, or more generically, the text, of the combo box changes.

QListView

Lists and trees in Qt are provided by the QListView widget. QListView displays both plain lists and hierarchical data divided into rows and columns. It's perfect for displaying things like directory structures, because the child elements can be expanded and contracted by clicking the plus and minus boxes, just like a file viewer.

Unlike the GTK+ `ListView` widget, `QListView` handles both the data and the view, which makes for ease of use if not outstanding flexibility.

With `QListView`, you can select rows or individual cells; then cut and paste the data, sort by column, and you'll have `QCheckBox` widgets rendered in cells. There's a great amount of functionality built in — all you need to do as a programmer is add data and set up some formatting rules.

Creating a `QListView` is done in the usual fashion, specifying the parent and widget name:

```
QListView *view = new QListView(parent, "name");
```

To set column headings, use the aptly named `addColumn` method:

```
view->addColumn("Left Column", width1 ); // Fixed width
view->addColumn("Right Column"); // Width autosizes
```

The column's width is set in pixels or, if omitted, defaults to the width of the widest element in the column. The column will then autosize as elements are added and removed.

Data is added to the `QListView` using a `QListViewItem` object to represent a row of data. All you need do is pass the `QListView` and row elements to the constructor, and it's appended to the view for you:

```
QListViewItem *toplevel = new QListViewItem(view, "Left Data", "Right Data");
```

The first parameter is either a `QListView`, as in this case, or another `QListViewItem`. If you pass a `QListViewItem`, the row appears as the child of that `QListViewItem`. The tree structure is therefore formed by passing the `QListView` for top-level nodes and then successive `QListViewItems` for the child nodes.

The remaining parameters are the data for each column that default to `NULL` if not specified.

Adding a child node is then just a case of passing in the top-level pointer. If you aren't adding further child nodes to a `QListViewItem`, you needn't store the returned pointer:

```
new QListViewItem(toplevel, "Left Data", "Right Data"); // A Child of toplevel
```

If you look at the `QListViewItem` API, you can see the methods to traverse the tree, should you wish to modify particular rows:

```
#include <qlistview.h>

virtual void    insertItem ( QListViewItem * newChild )
virtual void    setText ( int column, const QString & text )
virtual QString text ( int column ) const
QListViewItem   *firstChild () const
QListViewItem   *nextSibling () const
QListViewItem   *parent () const
QListViewItem   *itemAbove ()
QListViewItem   *itemBelow ()
```

You can get the first row in the tree by calling `firstChild` on the `QListView` itself. You can then repeatedly call `firstChild` and `nextSibling` to return parts or the entire tree.

This code snippet prints out the first column of all the top-level nodes:

```
QListViewItem *child = view->firstChild();
while(child)
{
  cout << myChild->text(1) << "\n";
  myChild = myChild->nextSibling();
}
```

You can find all the details about `QListView`, `QListViewItem`, and `QCheckListView` in the Qt API documentation.

Try It Out   QListView

In this Try It Out, you put everything together and write a short example of a `QListView` widget.

Let's skip the header file for brevity and see the class implementation, `ListView.cpp`:

```
#include "ListView.moc"

ListView::ListView(QWidget *parent, const char *name) : QMainWindow(parent, name)
{
  listview = new QListView(this, "listview1");

  listview->addColumn("Artist");
  listview->addColumn("Title");
  listview->addColumn("Catalogue");

  listview->setRootIsDecorated(TRUE);

  QListViewItem *toplevel = new QListViewItem(listview, "Avril Lavigne",
                                          "Let Go", "AVCD01");

  new QListViewItem(toplevel, "Complicated");
  new QListViewItem(toplevel, "Sk8er Boi");

  setCentralWidget(listview);
}

int main(int argc, char **argv)
{
  QApplication app(argc,argv);
  ListView *window = new ListView();

  app.setMainWidget(window);
  window->show();

  return app.exec();
}
```

How It Works

The QListView widget seems complicated in that it acts as both a list of items as well as a tree of items. Your code needs to create QListViewItem instances for each item you want in the list. Each of these QListViewItem instances has a parent. Those items with the widget itself as the parent appear as top-level items. Items with another QListViewItem as a parent appear as child items. This example shows QListViewItem instances just one level deep, but you can create far deeper trees of items.

After compiling and running the ListView example, you see the QListView widget in action as shown in Figure 17-7.

Figure 17-7

Note how the child rows are indented with respect to their parent. The plus and minus boxes indicating there are hidden or collapsible rows are not present by default; here you set them with setRootIsDecorated.

Dialogs

Up until now, you've been subclassing QMainWindow to create your interfaces. QMainWindow is appropriate for the primary window in your application, but for short-lived dialogs, you should look at using the QDialog widget.

Dialogs are useful whenever you want the user to input specific information for a particular task, or impart small amounts of information to the user, such as a warning or error message. It's preferable to subclass QDialog for these tasks because you get convenient methods for running the dialog and purpose-designed signals and slots to handle the user response.

As well as the usual modal and nonmodal (or modeless in Qt-speak) dialogs, Qt also offers a semimodal dialog box. The following list is a reminder of the differences between modal and nonmodal, and includes semimodal as well:

❑ **Modal dialog box:** Blocks input to all other windows to force the user to respond to the dialog. Modal dialogs are useful for grabbing an immediate response from the user and displaying critical error messages.

❑ **Nonmodal dialog box:** Nonblocking window that operates normally with other windows in the application. Nonmodal dialog boxes are useful for search or input windows where you might want to copy and paste values to and from the main window, for instance.

❑ **Semimodal dialog box:** A modal dialog that does not have its own event loop. This enables control to be returned to the application, but to still have input blocked to anything other than the dialog box. A semimodal dialog is useful in the rare occasions when you have a progress meter indicate the progress of time-consuming critical operation that you want to give the user the opportunity to cancel. Because it doesn't have its own event loop, you must call `QApplication::processEvents` periodically to update the dialog.

QDialog

QDialog is the base dialog class in Qt that provides `exec` and `show` methods for handling modal and nonmodal dialogs, has an integral `QLayout` you can use, and has several signals and slots useful for responding to button presses.

You'll normally create a class for your dialog, inherit from `QDialog`, and add widgets to create the dialog interface:

```
#include <qdialog.h>

MyDialog::MyDialog(QWidget *parent, const char *name) : QDialog(parent, name)
{
    QHBoxLayout *hbox = new QHBoxLayout(this);

    hbox->addWidget(new Qlabel("Enter your name"));
    hbox->addWidget(new QLineEdit());
    hbox->addWidget(ok_pushbutton);
    hbox->addWidget(cancel_pushbutton);

    connect (ok_pushbutton, SIGNAL(clicked()), this, SLOT(accept()));
    connect (cancel_pushbutton, SIGNAL(clicked()), this, SLOT(reject()));
}
```

Unlike with the `QMainWindow`, you can directly specify `MyDialog` as the parent of your `QLayout` object without creating a dummy `QWidget` and using that as the parent.

Note that this example omits the code to create the `ok_pushbutton` *and* `cancel_pushbutton` *widgets.*

QDialog has two slots — `accept` and `reject` — that are used to indicate the dialog result. This result is returned by the `exec` method. Normally, you'll connect OK and Cancel buttons to the slots, as in `MyDialog`.

Modal Dialogs

To use your dialog as a modal dialog, you call `exec`, which brings up the dialog and returns either `QDialog::Accepted` or `QDialog::Rejected` according to which slot was activated:

```
MyDialog *dialog = new MyDialog(this, "mydialog");
if (dialog->exec() == QDialog::Accepted)
{
    // User clicked 'Ok'
```

```
    doSomething();
}
else
{
    // user clicked 'Cancel' or dialog killed
    doSomethingElse();
}
delete dialog;
```

The dialog is automatically hidden when the exec returns, but you still delete the object from memory.

Note that all processing is blocked when exec is called, so if there is any time-critical code in your application, a nonmodal or semimodal dialog is more appropriate.

Nonmodal Dialogs

Nonmodal dialogs are little different from ordinary main windows, the key difference being that they position themselves over their parent window, share their taskbar entry, and hide automatically when the accept or reject slot is called.

To display a nonmodal dialog, call show as you would a QMainWindow:

```
MyDialog *dialog = new MyDialog(this, "mydialog");
dialog->show();
```

The show function displays the dialog and immediately returns to continue the processing loop. To handle button presses you need to write and connect to slots:

```
MyDialog::MyDialog(QWidget *parent, const char *name) : QDialog(parent, name)
{
    ...
    connect (ok_pushbutton, SIGNAL(clicked()), this, SLOT(OkClicked()));
    connect (cancel_pushbutton, SIGNAL(clicked()), this, SLOT(CancelClicked()));
}

MyDialog::OkClicked()
{
    //Do some processing
}
MyDialog::CancelClicked()
{
    //Do some other processing
}
```

The dialog is again automatically hidden when a button is pressed, as with a modal dialog.

Semimodal Dialog

To create a semimodal dialog you must set the modal flag in the QDialog constructor and use the show method:

```
QDialog (QWidget *parent=0, const char *name=0, bool modal=FALSE, WFlags f=0)
```

The reason you didn't set modal to TRUE with the modal dialog is that calling exec forces the dialog to be modal regardless of this flag.

Your dialog constructor will look something like this:

```
MySMDialog::MySMDialog(QWidget *parent, const char *name):QDialog(parent, name, TRUE)
{
  ...
}
```

Once you've got your dialog defined, you call show as normal and then progress with your processing, periodically calling QApplication::processEvents to keep the dialog updated:

```
MySMDialog *dialog = MySMDialog(this, "semimodal");
dialog->show();
while (processing)
{
  doSomeProcessing();
  app->processEvents();
  if (dialog->wasCancelled())
    break;
}
```

Check that the dialog hasn't been canceled before continuing processing. Note that wasCancelled isn't part of QDialog — you have to provide that yourself.

Qt provides ready-made subclasses of QDialog, specialized for particular tasks such as a file selection, text entry, progress meter, and message box. Using these widgets whenever you can saves you a lot of trouble.

QMessageBox

A QMessageBox is a modal dialog that displays a simple message with an icon and buttons. The icon depends on the severity of the message, which can be regular information or warnings and other critical information.

The QMessageBox class has static methods to create and show each of these three types:

```
#include <qmessagebox.h>

int information (QWidget *parent, const QString &caption, const QString &text,
                int button0, int button1=0, int button2=0)
int warning    (QWidget *parent, const QString &caption, const QString &text,
                int button0, int button1, int button2=0)
int critical   (QWidget *parent, const QString &caption, const QString &text,
                int button0, int button1, int button2=0)
```

You can choose buttons from a list of stock QMessageBox buttons, which match up with the returned value of the static methods:

❑   QMessageBox::Ok

❑   QMessageBox::Cancel

- ❑   QMessageBox::Yes

- ❑   QMessageBox::No

- ❑   QMessageBox::Abort

- ❑   QMessageBox::Retry

- ❑   QMessageBox::Ignore

A typical use of QMessageBox will look something like this:

```
int result = QMessageBox::information(this,
             "Engine Room Query", "Do you wish to engage the HyperDrive?",
             QMessageBox::Yes | QMessageBox::Default,
             QMessageBox::No  | QMessageBox::Escape);

switch (result) {
  case QMessageBox::Yes:
    hyperdrive->engage();
    break;
  case QMessageBox::No:
    // do something else
    break;
}
```

You OR the button codes with Default and Escape to set the default actions when the Enter (or Return) and Escape buttons are pressed on the keyboard. Figure 17-8 shows the resulting dialog.

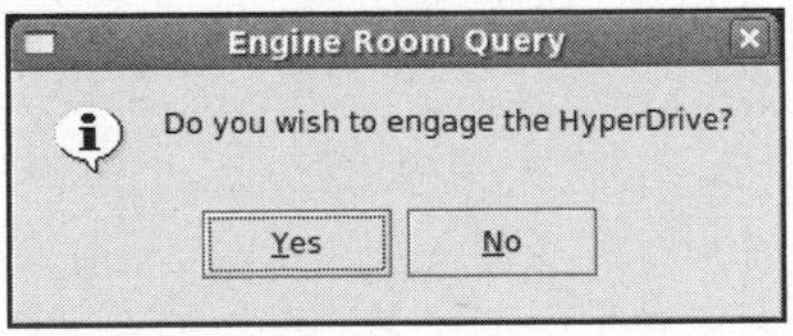

Figure 17-8

QInputDialog

QInputDialog is useful for inputting single values from the user, which can either be text, an option from a drop-down list, an integer, or a floating-point value. The QInputDialog class has static methods like QMessageBox that are a bit of a handful because they have many parameters, but fortunately most have default values.

```
#include <qinputdialog.h>

QString getText  (const QString &caption, const QString &label,
                 QLineEdit::EchoMode mode=QLineEdit::Normal,
                 const QString &text=QString::null, bool * ok = 0,
                 QWidget * parent = 0, const char * name = 0)

QString getItem  (const QString &caption, const QString &label,
```

```
                       const QStringList &list, int current=0, bool editable=TRUE,
                       bool * ok=0, QWidget *parent = 0, const char *name=0)

    int getInteger  (const QString &caption, const QString &label, int num=0,
                       int from = -2147483647, int to = 2147483647, int step = 1,
                       bool * ok = 0, QWidget * parent = 0, const char * name = 0)

    double getDouble (const QString &caption, const QString &label, double num = 0,
                       double from = -2147483647, double to = 2147483647,
                       int decimals = 1, bool * ok = 0, QWidget * parent = 0,
                       const char * name = 0 )
```

To input a line of text, you can write this:

```
bool result;
QString text = QInputDialog::getText("Question", "What is your Quest?:",
                                      QLineEdit::Normal,
                                      QString::null, &result, this, "input" );

if (result) {
  doSomething(text);
} else {
// user pressed cancel
}
```

`QInputDialog` is made up of a `QLineEdit` widget and OK and Cancel buttons, as you see in Figure 17-9.

Figure 17-9

The dialog created by `QInputDialog::getText` uses a `QLineEdit` widget. The edit mode parameter you pass to the `getText` function controls how the text will be echoed back to the user, exactly like the same mode for the `QLineEdit` widget. You can also specify default text or set it to empty as shown here. Every `QInputDialog` has OK and Cancel buttons, and passes a `bool` pointer to the method to indicate which button was pressed — `result` is TRUE if the user clicks OK.

`getItem` offers the user a list of options through a `QComboBox`:

```
bool result;
QStringList options;
options << "London" << "New York" << "Paris";
QString city = QInputDialog::getItem("Holiday", "Please select a destination:",
                                      options, 1, TRUE, &result, this, "combo");
if (result)
  selectDestination(city);
```

The resulting dialog is shown in Figure 17-10.

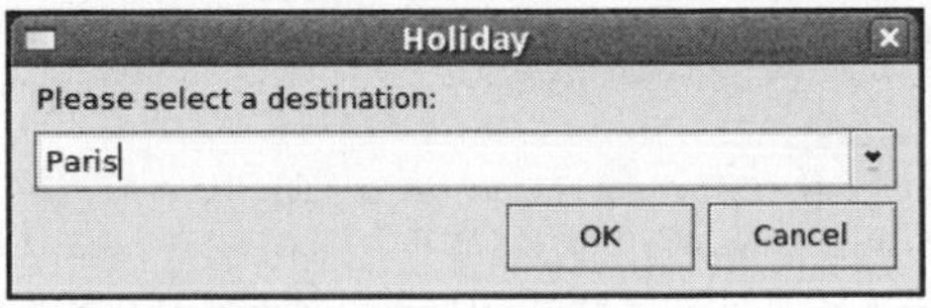

Figure 17-10

`getInteger` and `getDouble` work in much the same way, so we won't expand on them here.

Using qmake to Simplify Writing Makefiles

Compiling applications with both the KDE and Qt libraries becomes quite a chore because your makefile gets ever more complicated with the need to use `moc` and having libraries here, there, and everywhere. Fortunately, Qt comes with a utility called `qmake` to create makefiles for you.

If you've used Qt before, you may be familiar with `tmake` *— an earlier (and now deprecated) incarnation of* `qmake` *that shipped with previous versions of Qt.*

`qmake` takes a `.pro` file as input. This file contains the very basic information that the compilation requires, such as the sources, headers, target binary, and KDE/Qt library locations.

A typical KDE `.pro` file looks like this:

```
TARGET = app
MOC_DIR = moc
OBJECTS_DIR = obj
INCLUDEPATH = /usr/include/kde
QMAKE_LIBDIR_X11 += /usr/lib
QMAKE_LIBS_X11 += -lkdeui -lkdecore
SOURCES = main.cpp window.cpp
HEADERS = window.h
```

You specify the target binary, temporary `moc` and object directories, the KDE library path, and the sources and headers to build from. Note that the location of the KDE header and library files depends on your distribution. SUSE users should set `INCLUDEPATH` to `/opt/kde3/include` and `QMAKE_LIBS_X11` to `/opt/kde3/lib`.

```
$ qmake file.pro -o Makefile
```

Then you can run `make` as normal; it's that straightforward. For a KDE/Qt program of any complexity, you should use `qmake` to simplify the build routine.

Menus and Toolbars with KDE

As a demonstration of the power of KDE widgets, we've saved menus and toolbars to describe last, because they're a pretty good example of how the KDE libraries save time and effort compared to using plain Qt or other graphical user interface toolkits.

Usually in GUI libraries, menu items and toolbar items are distinct elements, each with their own item widgets. You have to create separate objects for each entry and keep track of changes; for example, disabling certain options individually.

The KDE programmers came up with a better solution. Instead of this detached approach, KDE defines a KAction widget to represent an action that the application can perform. This action could be opening a new document, saving a file, or showing a help box.

The KAction is given text, a keyboard accelerator, an icon, and a slot that's called when the KAction is activated:

```
KAction *new_file = new KAction("New", "filenew",
                        KstdAccel::shortcut(KstdAccel::New),
                        this, SLOT(newFile()), this, "newaction");
```

The KAction can then be plugged into a menu and toolbar without any further description:

```
new_file->plug(a_menu);
new_file->plug(a_toolbar);
```

You've now created a New menu and toolbar entry that calls newFile when clicked.

Now if you need to disable the KAction — say if you don't want the user to be able to create a new file — the call is centralized:

```
new_file->setEnabled(FALSE);
```

That's all there is to menus and toolbars with KDE — it's very easy indeed. Take a look at the KAction constructor:

```
#include <kde/kaction.h>

KAction (const QString &text, const KShortcut &cut, const QObject *receiver,
        const char *slot, QObject *parent, const char *name = 0)
```

KDE provides you with standard KAction objects to make sure text, icons, and keyboard accelerators are standard between KDE applications:

```
#include <kde/kaction.h>

KAction * openNew (const QObject *recvr, const char *slot,
        KActionCollection* parent,
        const char *name = 0 )
KAction * save ...
KAction * saveAs ...
KAction * revert ...
KAction * close ...
KAction * print ...
etc...
```

Each standard action takes the same parameters: the slot receiver and function, a KActionCollection, and the KAction name. The KActionCollection object manages the KActions in a window, and you can get the current object using the actionCollection method of KMainWindow:

```
KAction *saveas = KStdAction::saveAs(this, SLOT(saveAs()), actionCollection(),
                                     "saveas");
```

Try It Out   A KDE Application with Menus and Toolbars

You try using KActions in a KDE application with this next example.

1. Start with the header file KDEMenu.h. KDEMenu is a subclass of KMainWindow, itself a subclass of QMainWindow. KMainWindow handles session management within KDE and has an integral toolbar and status bar.

```
#include <kde/kmainwindow.h>

class KDEMenu : public KMainWindow
{
  Q_OBJECT

  public:
    KDEMenu(const char * name = 0);

  private slots:
    void newFile();
    void aboutApp();
};
```

2. In KDEMenu.cpp, start with #include directives for the widgets you'll be using:

```
#include "KDEMenu.h"

#include <kde/kapp.h>
#include <kde/kaction.h>
#include <kde/kstdaccel.h>
#include <kde/kmenubar.h>
#include <kde/kaboutdialog.h>
```

3. In the constructor, create three KAction widgets. new_file is created using a manual definition and quit_action and help_action use standard KAction definitions:

```
KDEMenu::KDEMenu(const char *name = 0) : KMainWindow (0L, name )
{
  KAction *new_file = new KAction("New", "filenew",
                          KstdAccel::shortcut(KstdAccel::New),
                          this, SLOT(newFile()), this, "newaction");

  KAction *quit_action = KStdAction::quit(KApplication::kApplication(),
                                      SLOT(quit()), actionCollection());

  KAction *help_action = KStdAction::aboutApp(this, SLOT(aboutApp()),
                                      actionCollection());
```

4. Create two top-level menus and insert them into the KApplication menuBar:

```
QPopupMenu *file_menu = new QPopupMenu;
QPopupMenu *help_menu = new QPopupMenu;

menuBar()->insertItem("&File", file_menu);
menuBar()->insertItem("&Help", help_menu);
```

5. Now plug the actions in the menus and toolbar, inserting a separator line between new_file and quit_action:

```
new_file->plug(file_menu);
file_menu->insertSeparator();
quit_action->plug(file_menu);
help_action->plug(help_menu);

new_file->plug(toolBar());
quit_action->plug(toolBar());
}
```

6. Finally some slot definitions: aboutApp creates a KAbout dialog to display information about the program. Note that the quit slot is defined as part of KApplication:

```
void KDEMenu::newFile()
{
  // Create new File
}

void KDEMenu::aboutApp()
{
  KAboutDialog *about = new KAboutDialog(this, "dialog");
  about->setAuthor(QString("A. N. Author"), QString("an@email.net"),
                   QString("http://url.com"), QString("work"));
  about->setVersion("1.0");
  about->show();
}

int main(int argc, char **argv)
{
  KApplication app( argc, argv, "cdapp" );;
  KDEMenu *window = new KDEMenu("kdemenu");

  app.setMainWidget(window);
  window->show();

  return app.exec();
}
```

7. Next you need a menu.pro file for qmake:

```
TARGET  = kdemenu
MOC_DIR = moc
OBJECTS_DIR = obj
```

```
INCLUDEPATH = /usr/include/kde
QMAKE_LIBDIR_X11 += -L$KDEDIR/lib
QMAKE_LIBS_X11 += -lkdeui -lkdecore
SOURCES = KDEMenu.cpp
HEADERS = KDEMenu.h
```

8. Now run qmake to create your Makefile, compile, and run.

```
$ qmake menu.pro -o Makefile
$ make
$ ./kdemenu
```

How It Works

Though this example appears longer than the other examples, the code is relatively terse for all the work it does creating a menu bar and menus. The best part of the KAction widgets is that you can use each one in multiple places, such as on the toolbar and in a menu on the menu bar, both shown in this example.

Building KDE applications requires more work than building most programs, at least at first glance. In reality, the menu.pro file and the qmake command hide a large number of settings you would otherwise have to place manually in your makefile.

Figures 17-11 and 17-12 show how the menus and toolbar buttons appear in the window.

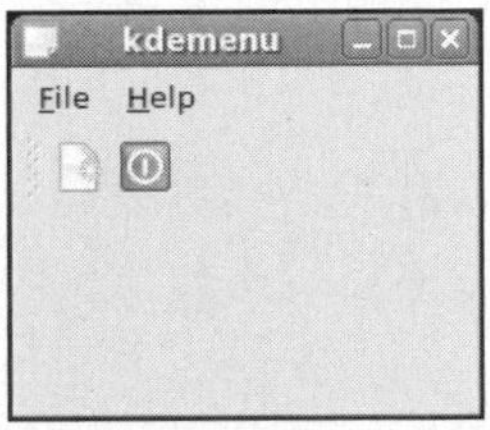

Figure 17-11

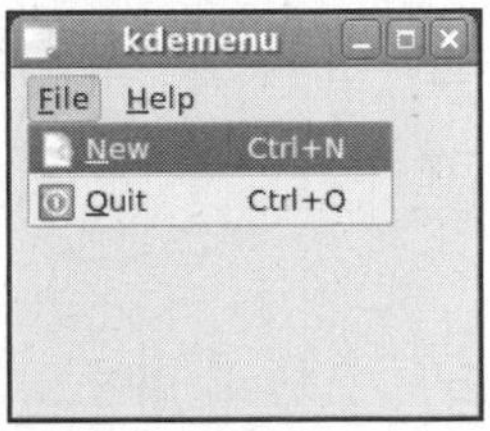

Figure 17-12

And that's it! We've finished the tour of Qt and KDE, looking at the basic elements of all GUI applications, windows, layouts, buttons, dialogs, and menus. There are countless Qt and KDE widgets we haven't covered, from QColorDialog — a color-choosing dialog — to KHTML — a Web browser widget — all fully documented on the Trolltech and KDE websites.

CD Database Application Using KDE/Qt

It's time to turn your attention to the CD application once again, now that you can use the power of KDE/Qt to bring it to life. You'll follow the same layout as in Chapter 16 and code similar functionality.

Remember what you want your CD database application to do:

❑ Log on to the database from the GUI

❑ Search for a CD

❑ Display CD and track information

❑ Add a CD to the database

❑ Display an About window

MainWindow

Start off with coding the main window of your application, which contains the search entry widget and search result list.

1. Start by typing in the code for `MainWindow.h` (or downloading it from the book's website). Because the window contains a `QLineEdit` widget for searching for CDs and a `QListView` to display the results, you need to include the `qlistview.h` and `qlineedit.h` header files:

```
#include <kde/kmainwindow.h>
#include <qlistview.h>
#include <qlineedit.h>

class MainWindow : public KMainWindow
{
  Q_OBJECT

  public:
    MainWindow (const char *name);

  public slots:
    void doSearch();
    void AddCd();

  private:
    QListView *list;
    QLineEdit *search_entry;

};
```

2. `MainWindow.cpp` is the most complicated part of the program. In the constructor, you create the main window interface and connect the necessary signals to your slots. As usual, start off with the `#include` files:

```
#include "MainWindow.h"
#include "AddCdDialog.h"
#include "app_mysql.h"
```

```
#include <qvbox.h>
#include <qlineedit.h>
#include <qpushbutton.h>
#include <qlabel.h>
#include <qlistview.h>
#include <kde/kapp.h>
#include <kde/kmenubar.h>
#include <kde/klocale.h>
#include <kde/kpopupmenu.h>
#include <kde/kstatusbar.h>
#include <kde/kaction.h>
#include <kde/kstdaccel.h>

#include <string.h>


MainWindow::MainWindow ( const char * name ) : KMainWindow ( OL, name )
{
  setCaption("CD Database");
```

3. Now create your menu and toolbar entries using the KAction widget:

```
KAction *addcd_action = new KAction("&Add CD", "filenew",
                         KStdAccel::shortcut(KStdAccel::New),
                         this,
                         SLOT(AddCd()),
                         this);

KAction *quit_action = KStdAction::quit(KApplication::kApplication(),
                         SLOT(quit()), actionCollection());

QPopupMenu * filemenu = new QPopupMenu;
QString about = ("CD App\n\n"
                "(C) 2007 Wrox Press\n"
                "email@email.com\n");

QPopupMenu *helpmenu = helpMenu(about);
menuBar()->insertItem( "&File", filemenu);
menuBar()->insertItem(i18n("&Help"), helpmenu);

addcd_action->plug(filemenu);
filemenu->insertSeparator();
quit_action->plug(filemenu);

addcd_action->plug(toolBar());
quit_action->plug(toolBar());
```

4. In the interest of variety, you'll use QBox layout widgets instead of the usual QLayout classes:

```
QVBox *vbox = new QVBox (this);
QHBox *hbox = new QHBox (vbox);
```

```
    QLabel *label = new QLabel(hbox);
    label->setText( "Search Text:" );

    search_entry = new QLineEdit ( hbox );
    QPushButton *button = new QPushButton( "Search", hbox);
```

5. Next up is the `QListView` widget, which occupies the majority of the window area. Then you connect the requisite signals to your `doSearch` slot to perform the CD database search. The `KMainWindow` status bar is made visible by adding an empty message:

```
    list = new QListView( vbox, "name", OL);
    list->setRootIsDecorated(TRUE);
    list->addColumn("Title");
    list->addColumn("Artist");
    list->addColumn("Catalogue");

    connect(button, SIGNAL (clicked()), this, SLOT (doSearch()));
    connect(search_entry , SIGNAL(returnPressed()), this, SLOT(doSearch()));

    statusBar()->message("");
    setCentralWidget(vbox);
    resize (300,400);
}
```

6. The `doSearch` slot is the business end of the application. It reads the search string and fetches all matching CDs and their tracks. The logic is identical to the GNOME/GTK+ `doSearch` function in Chapter 16.

```
void MainWindow::doSearch()
{
    cd_search_st *cd_res = new cd_search_st;
    current_cd_st *cd = new current_cd_st;
    struct current_tracks_st ct;
    int res1, i, j, res2, res3;
    char track_title[110];
    char search_text[100];
    char statusBar_text[200];
    QListViewItem *cd_item;

    strcpy(search_text, search_entry->text());
```

7. Fetch the matching CD `ids` and update the status bar to display the search results:

```
    res1 = find_cds(search_text, cd_res);
    sprintf(statusBar_text, " Displaying %d result(s) for search string ' %s '",
            res1, search_text);
    statusBar()->message(statusBar_text);

    i = 0;
    list->clear();
```

8. For each `id`, get the CD information, insert into the `QListView`, and get all tracks for this CD:

```
while (i < res1) {

  res2 = get_cd(cd_res->cd_id[i], cd);

  cd_item = new QListViewItem(list, cd->title, cd->artist_name, cd->catalogue);

  res3 = get_cd_tracks(cd_res->cd_id[i++], &ct);
  j = 0;
   /* Populate the tree with the current cd's tracks */
  while (j < res3) {

    sprintf(track_title, " Track %d. ", j+1);
    strcat(track_title, ct.track[j++]);

    new QListViewItem(cd_item, track_title);
    }
  }
}
```

9. The `AddCd` slot is called when the `addcd_action` menu item or toolbar button is activated:

```
void MainWindow::AddCd()
{
  AddCdDialog *dialog = new AddCdDialog(this);
  dialog->show();
}
```

The result is shown in Figure 17-13.

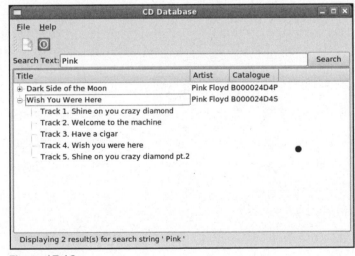

Figure 17-13

AddCdDialog

To add a CD to the database, you'll need to code a dialog with the necessary fields you need to input.

1. Enter the following code and call it AddCdDialog.h. Note that AddCdDialog inherits from KDialogBase, the KDE dialog widget.

```
#include <kde/kdialogbase.h>
#include <qlineedit.h>

class AddCdDialog : public KDialogBase
{
  Q_OBJECT

  public:
    AddCdDialog (QWidget *parent);

  private:
    QLineEdit *artist_entry, *title_entry, *catalogue_entry;

  public slots:
    void okClicked();
};
```

2. Next is AddCdDialog.cpp, which calls the add_cd function from the MySQL interface code in the okClicked slot:

```
#include "AddCdDialog.h"
#include "app_mysql.h"

#include <qlayout.h>
#include <qlabel.h>

AddCdDialog::AddCdDialog( QWidget *parent)
    : KDialogBase( parent, "AddCD", false, "Add CD",
      KDialogBase::Ok|KDialogBase::Cancel, KDialogBase::Ok, true )
{

  QWidget *widget = new QWidget(this);
  setMainWidget(widget);

  QGridLayout *grid = new QGridLayout(widget,3,2,10, 5,"grid");

  grid->addWidget(new QLabel("Artist", widget, "artistlabel"), 0, 0, 0);
  grid->addWidget(new QLabel("Title", widget, "titlelabel"), 1, 0, 0);
  grid->addWidget(new QLabel("Catalogue", widget, "cataloguelabel"), 2, 0, 0);

  artist_entry = new QLineEdit( widget, "artist_entry");
  title_entry = new QLineEdit( widget, "title_entry");
  catalogue_entry = new QLineEdit( widget, "catalogue_entry");

  grid->addWidget(artist_entry, 0,1, 0);
  grid->addWidget(title_entry, 1,1, 0);
```

```
    grid->addWidget(catalogue_entry, 2,1, 0);

    connect (this, SIGNAL(okClicked()), this, SLOT(okClicked()));
}

void AddCdDialog::okClicked()
{
    char artist[200];
    char title[200];
    char catalogue[200];
    int cd_id = 0;

    strcpy(artist, artist_entry->text());
    strcpy(title, title_entry->text());
    strcpy(catalogue, catalogue_entry->text());
    add_cd(artist, title, catalogue, &cd_id);

}
```

Figure 17-14 shows the AddCdDialog in action.

Figure 17-14

LogonDialog

Of course, you can't query the database without first logging on, so you need a simple dialog to enter your credentials. Call this class LogonDialog. (Yes, another subtle and imaginative title!)

1. First, the header file. Enter this, calling it LogonDialog.h. Note that for variety this time you inherit from QDialog rather than KDialogBase.

```
#include <qdialog.h>
#include <qlineedit.h>

class LogonDialog : public QDialog
{
    Q_OBJECT

    public:
        LogonDialog (QWidget *parent = 0, const char *name = 0);
        QString getUsername();
        QString getPassword();
```

```
    private:
      QLineEdit *username_entry, *password_entry;

};
```

2. Rather than encapsulating the database_start call in LogonDialog.cpp, you have better methods for the username and password. Here's LogonDialog.cpp:

```
#include "LogonDialog.h"
#include "app_mysql.h"

#include <qpushbutton.h>
#include <qlayout.h>
#include <qlabel.h>

LogonDialog::LogonDialog( QWidget *parent, const char *name): QDialog(parent, name)
{
  QGridLayout *grid = new QGridLayout(this, 3, 2, 10, 5,"grid");

  grid->addWidget(new QLabel("Username", this, "usernamelabel"), 0, 0, 0);
  grid->addWidget(new QLabel("Password", this, "passwordlabel"), 1, 0, 0);

  username_entry = new QLineEdit( this, "username_entry");
  password_entry = new QLineEdit( this, "password_entry");
  password_entry->setEchoMode(QLineEdit::Password);

  grid->addWidget(username_entry, 0, 1, 0);
  grid->addWidget(password_entry, 1, 1, 0);

  QPushButton *button = new QPushButton ("Ok", this, "button");
  grid->addWidget(button, 2, 1,Qt::AlignRight);

  connect (button, SIGNAL(clicked()), this, SLOT(accept()));

}

QString LogonDialog::getUsername()
{
  if (username_entry == NULL)
    return NULL;

  return username_entry->text();
}

QString LogonDialog::getPassword()
{
  if (password_entry == NULL)
    return NULL;

  return password_entry->text();
}
```

Figure 17-15 shows how the dialog will look.

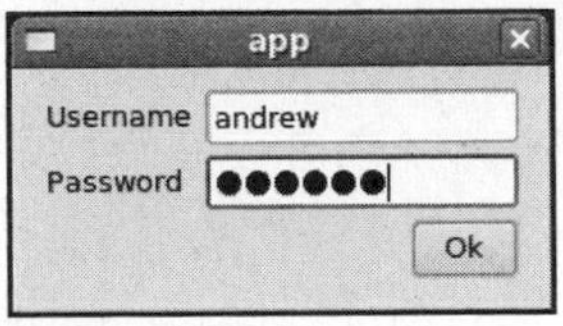

Figure 17-15

main.cpp

The only remaining code is the main function that you place in a separate source file, main.cpp.

1. In main.cpp, you open a LogonDialog and get a successful logon from database_start. If logging on isn't successful, you display a QMessageBox, or if you try to exit the LogonDialog, ask the users to confirm that they want to quit.

```cpp
#include "MainWindow.h"
#include "app_mysql.h"
#include "LogonDialog.h"

#include <kde/kapp.h>
#include <qmessagebox.h>


int main( int argc, char **argv )
{
  char username[100];
  char password[100];

  KApplication a( argc, argv, "cdapp" );

  LogonDialog *dialog = new LogonDialog();

  while (1)
  {
    if (dialog->exec() == QDialog::Accepted)
    {
      strcpy(username, dialog->getUsername());
      strcpy(password, dialog->getPassword());

      if (database_start(username, password))
        break;

      QMessageBox::information(0, "Title",
                        "Could not Logon: Check username and/or password",
                        QMessageBox::Ok);
      continue;
    }
    else
    {
      if (QMessageBox::information(0, "Title",
                    "Are you sure you want to quit?",
                    QMessageBox::Yes, QMessageBox::No)
```

```
            == QMessageBox::Yes)
    {
      return 0;
    }
  }
}
delete dialog;

MainWindow *window = new MainWindow( "Cd App" );
window->resize( 600, 400 );

a.setMainWidget( window );
window->show();

return a.exec();
}
```

2.   All that remains is to write a `.pro` file to pass to `qmake`. Call this `cdapp.pro`:

```
TARGET = app
MOC_DIR = moc
OBJECTS_DIR = obj
INCLUDEPATH = /usr/include/kde /usr/include/mysql
QMAKE_LIBDIR_X11 += -/usr/lib
QMAKE_LIBDIR_X11 += /usr/lib/mysql
QMAKE_LIBS_X11 += -lkdeui -lkdecore -lmysqlclient
SOURCES = MainWindow.cpp main.cpp app_mysql.cpp AddCdDialog.cpp LogonDialog.cpp
HEADERS = MainWindow.h app_mysql.h AddCdDialog.h LogonDialog.h
```

Note that the code lets you cheat slightly by simply renaming `app_mysql.c` *to* `app_mysql.cpp`; *therefore, you can treat it like an ordinary C++ source file. This avoids the (minor) complication of having to link a C object file to C++.*

```
$ qmake cdapp.pro -o Makefile
$ make
$ ./app
```

If all is well, you should have a working CD database!

You might like to try implementing the other functions in the MySQL interface, such as adding tracks to CDs or deleting CDs, to get a closer understanding of KDE/Qt. You'll need to create dialog boxes, new menu entries, and toolbar entries, and you'll have to write the underlying logic. Give it a shot!

Summary

In this chapter, you've learned about using the Qt GUI library and seen KDE widgets in action. You've seen that Qt is a C++ library that uses a signal/slot mechanism to implement event-driven programming. You took a tour of the basic Qt widgets and wrote several example programs to demonstrate how to use them in practice. Finally, you implemented a GUI front end to your CD application using KDE/Qt.

18

Standards for Linux

Linux started as just a kernel. Unfortunately, a kernel on its own is not very useful; programs are needed for logging in, managing files, compiling new programs, and so forth. To make a useful system, tools were added from the GNU project. These were clones of familiar programs available on the UNIX and UNIX-like systems around at the time. Making Linux look and feel like UNIX set the first standards for Linux, providing a familiar environment for C programmers.

Different UNIX (and later Linux) vendors added proprietary extensions to the commands and utilities they made available, and the layout of the file systems they used varied slightly. It became difficult to create applications that would work on more than one system. Even worse, a programmer could not even rely on system facilities being provided in the same way or configuration files being maintained in the same place.

It was clear that some standardization was needed to prevent the UNIX systems from fragmenting, and some excellent UNIX standardization work is now in place.

Over time not only have these standards moved forward, but Linux itself has been enhanced at an impressive speed by the community, often supported by commercial organizations like Red Hat and Canonical, and even non-Linux vendors such as IBM. As Linux has progressed, it, along with the gcc compiler collection, has not only tracked the relevant standards rather well, but has also defined new standards as existing standards have been found to be insufficient. Indeed, as Linux and its associated tools and utilities have become ever more popular, the UNIX vendors have started making changes to their UNIX offerings to make them more compatible with Linux.

In this final chapter, we are going to look at these standards, pointing out areas that you should be aware of if you want not only to write applications that work on your Linux systems through upgrades, but also to create code that will be portable to other Linux distributions, and maybe even other UNIX-style systems, so that you can share your programs with others.

In particular, we look at

❏   The C programming language standard

❏ The UNIX standards, particularly the POSIX standard developed by the IEEE and The Single UNIX Specification developed by the Open Group

❏ Work by the Free Standards Group, particularly the Linux Standard Base, which defines a standard Linux file system layout

A good starting place for standards relating to Linux is the Linux Standard Base (LSB), which you can find from the Linux Foundation web site at http://www.linux-foundation.org/.

We are not going to look in detail at the contents of the standards; many of them are as long as this book. We are going to point out the key standards you should know about, give you a little historic background on how those standards arose, and help you decide which standards you might find helpful when writing your own programs.

The C Programming Language

The programming language C is the de facto language for programming Linux, so in order to write portable C programs for Linux, it's worth understanding a little of its origins, how it has changed, and, most important, how to check that your program is conforming correctly to standards.

A Brief History Lesson

For those not enamored of history, don't worry; because this book is about programming, not history, we will keep this discussion very brief.

The C programming language dates from around 1970 and was based, in part, on the earlier programming language BCPL and extensions to the language B. Dennis M. Ritchie wrote a reference manual for the language in 1974, and C was used as the basis for a rewrite of the UNIX kernel on a PDP-11 around the same time. In 1978 Brian W. Kernighan and Ritchie wrote the classic reference book for the language, *The C Programming Language*.

The language became very popular very quickly, influenced no doubt in part by the rapid growth in the popularity of UNIX, but also by its own power and clean syntax. The C language syntax continued to evolve by consensus, but as it diverged further and further from the language described in the original book, it became clear that a standard that was both consistent with current usage, and more precise, was needed.

In 1983 ANSI established the X3J11 standards committee to develop a clean and concise definition of the language. Along the way they made some minor additions to the language, particularly giving it the very welcome ability to declare the type of parameters, but in general the committee simply clarified and rationalized the existing definition of what constituted common usage of the language. The standard was finally published in 1989 as the ANSI standard Programming Language C, X3.159-1989, or more briefly C89, or sometimes C90. (This later became an ISO standard, ISO/IEC 9899:1990, Programming Languages — C. The two standards are technically identical.)

As with most standards, publication did not end the work of the committee, which continued work on clarifying minor discrepancies found in the specification, and in 1993 started work on the next version of the standard, dubbed C9X. The committee also published minor corrections and updates to the current standard in 1994, 1995, and 1996.

The new edition of the standard just made it into the 1990s, and officially become the C99 standard; it was adopted by ISO as ISO/IEC 9899:1999. There is still a working committee, J11, looking at standardization of the C language and its libraries, but it is now working under the InterNational Committee for Information Technology Standards group. You can find more details on the current standards work for C at http://j11.incits.org/.

The GNU Compiler Collection

After developing the Emacs editor (yes, we love Emacs), the GNU project's next major accomplishment, as discussed in Chapter 1, was a completely free C compiler, gcc, with the first official version released in 1987.

Originally, gcc was the GNU C Compiler, but because the same basic compiler framework now supports many other languages, such as C++, Objective-C, FORTRAN, Java and Ada, as well as libraries for these languages, the definition has been adjusted to the more appropriate GNU Compiler Collection.

gcc has always been, and looks set to remain, the standard compiler for Linux, and C or C++ the primary language for writing programs on Linux. You can find the gcc home page at http://gcc.gnu.org/.

The GNU C Compiler has always been good at accurately tracking the developing C standard, although it does allow some extensions, and there are inevitably slight delays, as with almost all compilers, between the standard's becoming available and compilers that exactly implement that specification. Occasionally the opposite happens, and gcc anticipates that a standard will change slightly, which can also be quite confusing. gcc has a number of command-line and other options that allow you to specify the version of C standard you want gcc to conform to, as well as other options to control just how persnickety you would like the compiler to be.

gcc Options

Now that you know a little of the background of the C standard, let's look at the options the gcc compiler offers for ensuring that the C you write conforms accurately to the language standard. There are three ways to ensure your C code is both in conformity with standards and clean: options that control the version of the standard you intend to be compatible with; defines to control header files; and warning options that invoke more stringent checking of the code.

gcc has a huge range of options, and we look here only at the options we consider most important. You can find the full list of options on the gcc manual pages. We also look briefly at some additional #define options that can be used; these must normally be set in your source code before any #include lines or defined on the gcc command line. You might wonder why so many options are required for selecting the standard to use, rather than simply a flag that says to enforce the current standard. The reason is that many older programs rely on the historic behavior of the compiler and would require significant reworking to update them to the latest standards. Rarely, if ever, do we want a compiler update to start breaking working code. As the standards change, it's important to be able to work against a defined standard, even if that is not always the very latest version of the standard.

Even if you are just writing a small program for personal use, when maybe conforming to standards doesn't seem that important, it can often be worth turning on more of gcc's warnings to let the compiler find a mistake in your code before you even run the program. This is always more efficient than stepping through code in the debugger wondering where the problem might be. The compiler has many options that go well beyond simple checking for conformance to standards, such as the ability to spot code that does conform to the standard but may have dubious semantics. For example, there may be an order of execution that will allow a variable to be accessed before it is initialized.

If you do need to write code for other people to use, then — having selected the level of standards compliance and compiler warning you think appropriate — it's very important to put in that extra bit of effort to ensure that your code compiles with no warnings at all. If you allow some warnings to appear and make it a habit just to ignore them, then one day a more serious warning will appear that you may miss. If your code always compiles completely clean, a new warning will be obvious. Compiling clean code is a good habit to get into.

Compiler Options for Standards Tracking

These options are passed to gcc on the command line; we show only the most important options here:

❑   **-ansi:** This is the most important standards option, and tells the compiler to work to the ISO C90 standard of the language. It turns off certain gcc extensions that are incompatible with the standard, disables C++ (//) style comments in C programs, and enables the ANSI trigraph features. It also defines the macro __STRICT_ANSI__, which turns off some gcc extensions in header files that are incompatible with the standard. Later versions of the compiler may change the language standard targeted.

❑   **-std=:** This option allows more fine-grained control of the standard in use by supplying a parameter that sets the exact standard required. The main options are

  ❑   c89 supports the c89 standard.

  ❑   iso9899:1999 supports the latest ISO C90 standard.

  ❑   gnu89 supports the C89 standard, but allows GNU extensions and some C99 features as well. As of version 4.2 of gcc this is the default behavior.

Define Options for Standard Tracking

These are constants (#defines) that can either be set by options on the compiler command line or, alternatively, as definitions in the source code. We generally suggest using the compiler command line for these options.

❑   **__STRICT_ANSI__:** Force the use of ISO standard C. Defined when -ansi is given as a compile line option.

❑   **_POSIX_C_SOURCE=2:** Turn on features defined by the IEEE Std 1003.1 and 1003.2 standards. We mention these standards again later in this chapter.

❑   **_BSD_SOURCE:** This enables BSD-type features. If those features conflict with POSIX definitions, the BSD definitions take precedence.

❑   **_GNU_SOURCE:** Allows a wide range of features, including GNU extensions. If those features conflict with POSIX definitions, the POSIX definitions take precedence.

Compiler Options for Warnings

These options are passed to the compiler on the command line. Again we just list the main options; you can find a full list in the gcc manual pages.

- ❑ **-pedantic:** This is the most powerful compiler option for checking clean C code. Apart from turning on the option to check for standard conformant C, it also turns off some traditional C constructs that are not permitted by the standard, and disables all the GNU extensions to the standard. This is the option to use if you want your C code to be as portable as possible. The downside is that the compiler is very fussy indeed about your code being clean, and sometimes it can require you to think very carefully in order to get rid of the last few warnings.

- ❑ **-Wformat:** Checks that the argument types to the printf family of functions are correct.

- ❑ **-Wparentheses:** Checks that parentheses are always provided, even in some circumstances where they are not needed. This is quite a useful option for checking that initialization of complex structures is as intended.

- ❑ **-Wswitch-default:** Checks that all switch statements have a default case, which is generally good coding practice.

- ❑ **-Wunused:** Checks a variety of cases such as static functions declared but never defined, unused parameters, and discarded results.

- ❑ **-Wall:** Turns on most of gcc's warnings, including all of the preceding -W options (it does not select -pedantic) and is a good way to keep your code clean.

There are many, many more warning options; see the gcc web pages for the full details. In general we suggest you use -Wall; it's a good compromise between checking for good quality code and having the compiler generate so many trivial warnings it becomes a serious impediment to keeping the number of warnings from the compiler to zero.

Interfaces and the Linux Standards Base

We are now going to move up a level from the raw C code and look at the interfaces (system functions) provided by the operating system. This level of standardization has various components: the functions provided by libraries and the system calls provided by the underlying operating system. In both of these there are two levels of detail: which interfaces are present and the definition of what an interface does.

The definitive document in this area for Linux is The Linux Standards Base (LSB), which you can find at http://www.linuxbase.org or http://www.linux-foundation.org/en/LSB. Several versions of the standard have been issued, and work is ongoing.

You can find a list of distributions that have passed the certification at http://www.linux-foundation .org/en/Products. Various versions of Red Hat, SUSE, and Ubuntu are certified, but do remember it takes a while after a distribution is released for certification to be checked. The site also has a list of distributions that are undergoing testing, or only require some updates to pass the certification tests.

The Linux Standards Base defines (as of version 3.1) three areas for compliance:

- ❑ **Core:** The main libraries, utilities and some key file system locations.
- ❑ **C++:** The C++ libraries.
- ❑ **Desktop:** Additional files for desktop installs, principally various graphic libraries.

The main area we are interested in is the Core part of the specification.

The LSB specification covers a number of areas as part of its own documentation, but also refers to some external standards for particular interface definitions. The areas covered are

- ❑ Object formats for binary compatibility
- ❑ Dynamic linking standards
- ❑ Standard libraries, both base libraries and the X Window System libraries
- ❑ The shell and other command-line programs
- ❑ The execution environment, including users and groups
- ❑ System initialization and run levels

In this chapter, we are really only interested in the standard libraries, users, and system initialization, so those are the areas we look at here.

LSB Standard Libraries

The Linux Standard Base defines the interfaces that must be present in two ways. For some functions, primarily those that are implemented by the GNU C library or tend to be Linux-only standards, it defines the interface and its behavior. For other interfaces, mostly those that come from Linux being UNIX-like, the specification simply states that a particular interface must be present and must behave as defined by another standard, usually that of the Common Application Environment (CAE) or more commonly The Single UNIX Specification, which is available from The Open Group, http://www.opengroup.org. Some parts are available (currently registration is required) on the web at http://www.unix.org/online.html.

Unfortunately, the underlying standards for Linux, the UNIX standards, have a rather complex past, and rather too many standards to choose from, although mostly the various versions of the standards are closely compatible.

A Brief History Lesson

UNIX started in the late 1960s at AT&T Bell Laboratories, when Ken Thompson and Dennis Ritchie wrote an operating system, originally intended only for their personal use, that they called Unics. The name somehow changed into UNIX. AT&T allowed universities to have the source code for their own research, and UNIX quickly became extremely popular because of its very clean design and powerful concepts. The fact that the source code was available must also have been a significant incentive because it allowed people to make changes and experiment.

The BSD operating system was a variant that came out of work done at the University of California at Berkeley, where a lot of work was being done on networking.

When AT&T started to make UNIX commercial, which occurred mostly around the mid 1980s, it termed its releases UNIX System, and the most popular was UNIX System V.

Many other variants also appeared, far too numerous to list here, all of which had slight differences from and additions to the base standards, as companies have tried to add value by making proprietary extensions.

Things started to get really complicated when AT&T sold its UNIX business to Novell, which, in 1994, decided to exit the UNIX business, and the ownership of the rights and trademarks became somewhat confused and the subject of various court cases.

In 1988 the IEEE (http://www.ieee.org) issued the first of a set of standards: the POSIX, or IEEE 1003, standards, which were intended to be a definitive portable interface specification for computer environments. Although it's a good and well-defined standard, POSIX is also very much a core specification and is quite limited in scope.

In 1994 the X/OPEN Company, a vendor-neutral organization, produced a much larger set of specifications, the X/OPEN CAE, or Common Applications Environment, which is a superset of the IEEE POSIX standards and is technically identical to it in many areas. The X/OPEN company later merged with the OSF to found The Open Group; its home page is at http://www.opengroup.org/. The CAE standard was updated and released in 2002 as The Single UNIX Specification, Version 3, available from The Open Group.

It is this specification to which the Linux standards base most frequently refers.

> It should be noted that "Linux" is a trademark, owned by Linus Torvalds (see http://www
> .linuxmark.org/).

Using the LSB Standard for Libraries

That's enough about history of the standards. What does this mean for people writing C (or C++) programs that they want to be portable?

First, you should check that the library function you are using is listed in the LSB specification. If it isn't there, you may well be doing something that is not going to port easily, and you should look for a standard way of performing whatever you are trying to achieve. You might like to try the apropos Linux command, which searches the online manual pages for appropriate references.

Second, and more difficult, is to check that the function behavior you are using is part of the specification, and you are not relying on behavior that is not specified. You may have to refer to The Single UNIX Specification to do this if the function usage is not defined by the LSB.

A particularly good place to check for undefined or possibly erroneous behavior is the online Linux manuals. Many of the pages have a BUGS section, which is an invaluable source of information about where a particular call in Linux may not perfectly implement the standards or where there are known defects or oddities in behavior.

LSB Users and Groups

This section of the specification is nice and brief, and very easy to understand. Following are a few of the specifications:

❑ The specification tells us never to read files like /etc/passwd directly, but to always use the standard library calls such as getpwent, or standard utilities like passwd for accessing user details.

❑ It tells us that there must be a user called root in the root group, and that root is an administrative user with full privileges. We also discover that there are a number of optional user and group names that should never be used by standard applications; they are intended for use by distributions.

❑ It also tells us that user IDs below 100 are system accounts, 100–499 are allocated by system administrators and post-install scripts, and 500 and higher are for normal user accounts.

Generally, that is about all most Linux programmers need to know about the standards for users.

LSB System Initialization

The area of system initialization has always, at least to us, been an annoyance because of subtle differences between distributions.

Linux has inherited from UNIX-like operating systems the idea of run levels that define the services that are running at any time. For Linux, the usual definitions are given in the following table.

Run Level	Used for
0	Halt. Used as a logical state to change to when the system is shut down.
1	Single user mode, directories other than / may not be mounted, and networking will not be enabled. It is normally used for system maintenance.
2	Multiuser mode; however, networking is not enabled.
3	Normal multiuser mode with networking, using a text mode login screen.
4	Reserved.
5	Normal multiuser mode with networking and a graphical login screen.
6	A pseudo-level used for rebooting.

The LSB lists these levels but doesn't require them to be used, although they are very common.

Accompanying these run levels is a set of initialization scripts used to start, stop, and restart services. Previously these have lived in various locations under /etc, often /etc/init.d or /etc/rc.d/init.d. This variation was often a source of confusion, because people who changed distributions could no longer find the initialization scripts where they expected to find them, and install programs failed while trying to put initialization scripts in the wrong directory.

The LSB 3.1 defines the location of these initialization scripts as `/etc/init.d`, though it does allow this to be a link to a different location.

Each script in `/etc/init.d` has a name that relates to the service it provides. Because this is a common namespace that all services on Linux must share, it's important that names are unique. For example, life would get difficult if both MySQL and PostgreSQL decided to call their scripts "database." To avoid this conflict there is another set of standards. This is The Linux Assigned Names And Numbers Authority (LANANA), which you can find at `http://www.lanana.org/`. Fortunately, you need to know very little about it except that they keep a list of registered names for scripts and packages, and thereby make life easier for users of Linux systems.

An initialization script must take a parameter that controls what it should do. The defined parameters are as follows:

Parameter	Meaning
start	Start (or restart) the service.
stop	Stop the service.
restart	Restart the service; this is commonly implemented as simply a stop followed by a start of the service.
reload	This should reset the service, reloading any parameters, without actually stopping the service. Not all services can support this option, so this parameter may not be accepted by all scripts, or may be accepted but have no effect.
force-reload	This attempts to cause a reload if the service supports it, but if not, it does a restart.
status	This prints a textual message about the status of the service and returns a status code that can be used to determine the status of the service.

All commands return 0 on success, or an error code indicating the reason for failure. In the case of `status`, 0 is returned if the service is running; all other codes indicate the service is not running for some reason.

The Filesystem Hierarchy Standard

The last of the standards we are going to look at in this chapter is the Filesystem Hierarchy Standard (FHS), which you can find at `http://www.pathname.com/fhs/`.

The purpose of this standard is to define standard places in the Linux file system, so that developers and users alike can have reasonable expectations of where to find things. Long-time users of the various UNIX-like operating systems have long bemoaned the subtle differences between the way file systems are laid out, and the FHS provides a way for Linux distributions to avoid going down the same fragmented path.

The arrangement of files in a Linux system may seem at first to be a semi-arbitrary arrangement of files and directories, based on historic practice. To an extent that's true, but over the years the layout has evolved for good reasons into the hierarchy we see today. The general idea is to separate files and directories into three groups:

❑ Files and directories that are unique to a particular system running Linux, such as start-up scripts and configuration files

❑ Files and directories that are read-only and may be shared between systems running Linux, such as application executables

❑ Directories that are read/write, but may be shared between systems running Linux or other operating systems, such as user home directories

In this book, we are not overly interested in sharing files among different versions of Linux, although, where a network of Linux machines is in use, it can be an excellent way of ensuring that only a single copy of the key program directories exists, and of sharing that among many machines. This is particularly useful for diskless workstations.

The top-level structure is defined by FHS to have several mandatory subdirectories and a small number of optional directories; the main ones are shown in the following table.

Directory	Required?	Use
/bin	Y	Important system binary files.
/boot	Y	Files required to boot the system.
/dev	Y	Devices.
/etc	Y	System configuration files.
/home	N	Directories for user files.
/lib	Y	Standard libraries.
/media	Y	A place for removable media to be mounted, with separate subdirectories for each media type supported by the system.
/mnt	Y	A convenient point to temporarily mount devices, such as CD-ROMs and flash memory sticks.
/opt	Y	Additional application software.
/root	N	Files for the root user.
/sbin	Y	Important system binary files that are required during system startup.
/srv	Y	Read-only data for services provided by this system.
/tmp	Y	Temporary files.

Directory	Required?	Use
/usr	Y	A secondary hierarchy. Traditionally user files were also stored here, but that is now considered bad practice, and /usr should not be writable by ordinary users.
/var	Y	Variable data, such as log files.

In addition, there can be other directories starting with lib, although this is not common. You will also usually see a /lost+found directory (for file system recovery by fsck) and a /proc directory, which is a pseudo file system, providing a mapping into the current running system. The /proc file system is strongly encouraged by the current version of FHS standard, but is not required to be present. Details of the /proc system are generally beyond the scope of this book, though we took a brief tour in Chapter 4.

Here we look briefly at the purposes of each of the standard subdirectories of the / (root) directory:

❑ /bin — This contains binary files that can be used both by the root user and ordinary users, but are essential to operation in single-user mode, when some other directory structures may not be mounted. For example, core commands such as cat and ls would normally be found in here, as will sh.

❑ /boot — This directory is used for files required during booting of the Linux system. It is frequently quite small, less than 100 MB, and often a separate partition. This is handy on PC-based systems, where there are frequently BIOS limitations on the active partition, requiring it to be in the first 2 G or 4 G of the disk. Having this as a separate partition allows more flexibility when deciding how to lay out the rest of the disk partitions.

❑ /dev — This contains the special device files that map to hardware. For example, /dev/hda will be mapped to the first IDE disk.

❑ /etc — This contains configuration files. Historically some binaries could also be found in here, but that is no longer true on most Linux systems. The best known file in the /etc directory is probably passwd, which contains information on users. Other useful files are fstab, listing mount options; hosts, listing IP to host name mappings, and the httpd directory, which contains configuration for the Apache server.

❑ /home — This is a directory for user files. Normally each user will have a single directory under this directory with the same name as their login, and this will be their default login directory. For example, after logging in, the user rick will almost certainly find himself in the /home/rick directory.

❑ /lib — This contains essential shared libraries and kernel modules, specifically those that will be required while the system is booting or in single-user mode.

❑ /media — This is intended as a top-level directory to contain other directory mount points for removable media. The intention is to remove unnecessary top-level directories, such as /cdrom and /floppy.

❑ /mnt — This is simply a convenient place for mounting additional file systems temporarily. Historically some distributions have added subdirectories for the different devices, such as /cdrom and /floppy under /mnt, but the preferred location for these is now under /media, returning /mnt to its original purpose, as a single top-level temporary mount location.

❑   `/opt` — This is a directory for software vendors to use when adding additional software applications to the base distribution. Distributions should not use it for software they distribute as part of the standard distribution, but leave it free for third-party vendors to use. Generally, vendors will create a subdirectory with their name, and then further subdirectories such as `/bin` and `/lib` for files specific to their application.

By convention, many Open Source Linux packages use `/usr/local` for installation.

❑   `/root` — This is for files used by the root user. It is not in the `/home` directory part of the tree, because that may not be mounted in single-user mode.

❑   `/sbin` — This is used for commands normally used only by the system administrator, and required while the system is booting or in single-user mode. Commands such as `fsck`, `halt`, and `swapon` live here.

❑   `/srv` — This is intended as a location for site-specific read-only configuration data, however it is currently not in common use.

❑   `/tmp` — This is used for temporary files. It is usually, but not always, cleared when the system is booted.

❑   `/usr` — This is a rather complex secondary file system, generally containing all the system-type commands and libraries not required during system booting or in single-user mode. It has many subdirectories, such as `/bin`, `/lib`, `/X11R6`, and `/local`.

In the early days of UNIX and Linux, `/usr` also had subdirectories for logs, mail spooling, and the like. These have all now been removed from the `usr` directory and placed in the `var` directory. This has the advantage that `/usr` can now be a mountable file system, and in particular can be mounted read-only most of the time. When `/usr` is mounted read-only, it can be shared to other systems across a network and is less vulnerable to corruption should the system stop in an uncontrolled manner, perhaps because the power failed.

❑   `/var` — This contains data that changes frequently, such as spool files for printing, application log files, and mail-spooling directories.

Further Reading about Standards

There are, of course, many more things to consider if you want to write, and deploy, a fully portable Linux application.

Do you want to localize your application so that it works with different languages and locales? Even if you stick to English, there are still the issues of currency, number separators, date formats, and many other considerations. There are, you guessed it, people working on those standards; you can see their work at `http://www.openi18n.org/`.

Another consideration is what options, library versions, and so forth the target system has installed. Fortunately, this problem is getting less acute, largely thanks to the standardization work we have looked at in this chapter, but it can still be a difficult problem. There are a pair of GNU tools which help considerably with this problem: `autoconf` and `automake`. Although you may not have used them directly, you have almost certainly seen the benefits of them when installing software from source, when you typed `./configure; make`.

The use of these tools is beyond the scope of this book, but you can find more about them on the GNU web pages `http://www.gnu.org/software/autoconf/` and `http://www.gnu.org/software/automake`.

Summary

In this final chapter, we have looked briefly at some of the many standards that are helping to make Linux an easier platform to program for, and that ensure that the many different distributions of Linux conform to some basic standards. Conforming to standards helps to make life easier for us, its programmers and users, and we urge you use the standards and to encourage others to do so.

Index

D

Q